Java 1.1 Developer's Handbook

Java™ 1.1 Developer's Handbook™

Philip Heller and

Simon Roberts

with Peter Seymour and

Tom McGinn

SYBEX®

San Francisco • Paris • Düsseldorf • Soest

Associate Publisher: Amy Romanoff
Acquisitions Manager: Kristine Plachy
Acquisitions & Developmental Editor: Suzanne Rotondo
Editors: Steve Gilmartin, Maureen Adams, Laura Arendal,
        Krista Reid-McLaughlin
Technical Editor: John Zukowski
Graphic Illustrator: Inbar Berman
Electronic Publishing Specialist: Franz Baumhackl
Production Coordinator: Robin Kibby
Indexer: Ted Laux
Cover Designer: Design Site
Cover Illustrator: Gregory MacNicol

Screen reproductions produced with Collage Complete.

Collage Complete is a trademark of Inner Media Inc.

SYBEX is a registered trademark of SYBEX Inc.
Developer's Handbook is a trademark of SYBEX Inc.

TRADEMARKS: SYBEX has attempted throughout this book to
distinguish proprietary trademarks from descriptive terms by
following the capitalization style used by the manufacturer.

Netscape Communications, the Netscape Communications logo,
Netscape, and Netscape Navigator are trademarks of Netscape
Communications Corporation.

The author and publisher have made their best efforts to prepare
this book, and the content is based upon final release software
whenever possible. Portions of the manuscript may be based
upon pre-release versions supplied by software manufacturer(s).
The author and the publisher make no representation or warranties of any kind with regard to the completeness or accuracy of
the contents herein and accept no liability of any kind including
but not limited to performance, merchantability, fitness for any
particular purpose, or any losses or damages of any kind caused
or alleged to be caused directly or indirectly from this book.

Library of Congress Card Number: 96-72107
ISBN: 0-7821-1919-0

Manufactured in the United States of America

10 9 8 7 6 5 4 3 2

To Patricia, who reminds me what words are for.
Stories are the first important things.
—Philip Heller

For Ruth, Emily, Ma, and Pop.
—Simon Roberts

For my two boys, Patrick and Peter.
—Tom McGinn

To my parents, Dr. and Mrs. John C. Seymour.
They have always been there to provide me
with the opportunity to do
whatever I desire.
—Peter Seymour

ACKNOWLEDGMENTS

We would like to thank Ally Bailey, Cindy Lewis, Carol Stille, Georgianna Meagher, Mike Bridwell, Ray Moore, and Dr. Heather Young for their support. Tim Russell, Russel Taylor, Devon Tuck, Tim Lindholm, and Urs Eberle were generous with their knowledge and explanations. Jennifer Sullivan Volpe brought all of us together and helped edit some of our chapters, for which she deserves and receives many thanks.

We'd also like to thank Suzanne Rotondo, acquisitions & developmental editor; Krista Reid-McLaughlin, associate editorial supervisor; Laura Arendal, editorial supervisor; and Maureen Adams and Steve Gilmartin, editors at Sybex, for their infinite patience with our narrative voices and their fine editing. Big thanks to John Zukowski, technical editor, for sending our manuscript through the technical wringer. Thanks also to Robin Kibby, production coordinator, for her proofreading and organizational skills and to Franz Baumhackl, electronic publishing specialist, for his expert and speedy book layout.

Special thanks to Emily Roberts for striking the perfect pose with that enormous pastry (see `javadevhdbk\ch06\Emily.gif` on the CD-ROM).

CONTENTS AT A GLANCE

TABLE OF CONTENTS

5   Portability Issues   183

Appendices

INTRODUCTION

Because this is an introduction, let us take a moment and all introduce ourselves. Here we are together: the authors, the readers, and the book.

First the authors. One of us lives on the West coast, two on the East coast, and one in England. We bring a broad perspective, and not just because of geography. We are Java instructors by trade. Among us, we have taught Sun's Java classes to more than one thousand students.

We have not simply lectured. We have asked our students, "What will you be doing with Java?"; time after time the answer has surprised us. We have said, "Welcome to class, please turn to page one of your tutorial," and time after time someone in the back of the room has said, "Yes, yes, we all know this already. How do I connect an applet to a database via TCP/IP?" During lab exercises we have said, "Please do the lab on page thirty-three," and time after time someone has said, "I did that one last time. Now I'm writing my own layout manager, and it isn't working. What have I done wrong?"

In other words, we have been exposed to real-world uses of Java. Vicariously we have accompanied one thousand Java students through their learning processes and experiences. Where they got stuck, we were asked about it. Where the classroom theory broke down, we were told about it—in no uncertain terms.

We have explored the dark and dusty corners of Java, armed only with flashlights, feather dusters, the API pages, and the source code. We are here to tell you what we found.

That is who we are. Who are you? That is, who did we write this book for? What assumptions have we made about you?

We assume you have already digested your first Java book or your first Java class. You understand the theory. You know the syntax of the language. You know about objects. You know most of the basics of most of the packages. You are comfortable with looking up class and method descriptions in the API documentation. You have written applets and applications. You are moving beyond the well-lit regions of Java, into the dark and the dusty. You need a flashlight and a feather duster. That is what we're here for.

This is the book for you; this is the book that plunges right in. No introductory chapters on the history of the Internet. No discourse on object polymorphism. The name James Gosling is not mentioned even once in this book. Oops—well, once; but only once.

We kept a number of principles in mind when we wrote this book. Foremost, every chapter begins with a review of the relevant background material, then gets into the meat of the topic. If you're confident about the basics, you can skip right to the second or third section.

We have strong feelings about sample code. We have tried our best to keep it relevant. In the chapter on Threads, the sample code is intended to teach about Threads, not to impress you with how clever we are. Reading lengthy source code is difficult, and we have kept the samples as small as possible. However, in the real world it sometimes takes a lot of lines to make a program robust. The code in this book is as terse as possible but as long as necessary.

All the source code and class files can be found on the CD-ROM. Wherever we could, we implemented our sample code as applets and included simple Web pages so you can run them as is. Sometimes this strategy is not possible; some operations, especially those relating to the network and the file system, may only be executed by applications. These can still be invoked right off the CD-ROM.

We are introducing a new kind of sample program; we call them *labs*. The source for the labs is not discussed in the book (though it is provided for interest's sake on the CD-ROM). With these labs, learning happens not from reading the sources but from executing the applets. For example, there is a lab for Chapter 4, *Layout Managers*, called `GridBagLab`. The only way to develop an intuitive grasp of how to use the `GridBag` layout manager is to create a lot of layouts that mix and match the myriad possible combinations of values of the grid bag constraints. One way to create all these combinations is to write a lot of code. But with `GridBagLab`, you need only use the user interface to select constraint values, click on a button, and see the result. Experience and intuition are developed in much less time. The labs are educational toys.

So much for introductions. We are delighted to make your acquaintance. Now that we all know one another a bit better, we would like to make you aware of a few background details concerning this book.

The CD-ROM

The code in this book and on the CD-ROM has been compiled under the beta 2 of the Java Developer's Kit version 1.1. The CD-ROM has a directory called `javadevhdbk`; this directory has one subdirectory for each chapter of the book that contains code. The applications therein can be run by command-line invocation. The applets, of course, require a browser. Each applet has a simple `html` file whose name closely resembles the name of the applet subclass. Because commercial browser technology does not yet support JDK 1.1, we recommend using appletviewer to browse the applets. The applications and applets will run on any platform that supports JDK 1.1.

The Organization of the Book

This book is divided into four parts. The first part, *The Basics* (Chapters 1-5), discusses such issues as the Java environment, applets and applications, components, layout managers, and portability issues. Although the topics are basic, the discussions are broad and deep. The second part, *Advanced Topics* (Chapters 6-14), discusses images, threads, animation, files and streams, networking, database access, distributed objects, and content/protocol handlers. The third part, *The New APIs* (Chapters 15-17), examines functionality that is new to release 1.1 of the Java Developer's Kit. Sun Microsystems has organized these new features into application programming interfaces; the APIs covered in this book are Java Beans, Electronic Commerce, and Servlets. The last part of this book consists of three appendices: the first appendix is a lightweight API listing for all the core Java classes, the second is a discussion of Javadoc, the third is a collection of answers to frequently asked questions.

Conventions

This book uses various conventions to present information in as readable a manner as possible. Tips, Notes, and Warnings, shown here, appear throughout the text in order to call attention to specific highlights.

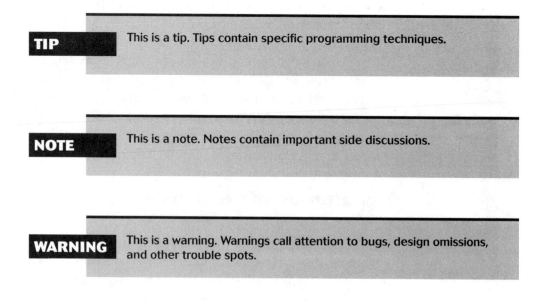

TIP This is a tip. Tips contain specific programming techniques.

NOTE This is a note. Notes contain important side discussions.

WARNING This is a warning. Warnings call attention to bugs, design omissions, and other trouble spots.

This book takes advantage of several font styles. **Bold font** in text indicates something that the user types. A `monospaced font` is used for program code, URLs, and file and directory names.

All these style conventions are intended to facilitate your learning experience with this book. We, the authors, are pleased and excited with how the book has turned out. We wish you a fruitful and pleasant learning experience.

PART 1

The Basics

These chapters present in-depth discussions of topics and techniques that are basic to the Java programming environment. You probably have had some degree of exposure to these topics already, but you may not have been exposed to the details provided here. For example, you have, without a doubt, used components and layout managers, but you may not have created your own.

CHAPTER
ONE

Java Ecology

- Networking

- Classes

- Security

- The file system

- Properties

- Threads

- Appearance

Java programs run on an imaginary machine which is implemented on a real platform. A Java program runs with considerable support from its environment. We begin this book with an examination of Java's environmental issues: Networking, Classes, Security, the File System, Properties, Threads, and Appearance. A programmer who has a clear understanding of this material will have an easier time developing code, and will understand how the *Java Developer's Kit* (JDK) works.

Networking

The most obvious component of Java's environment is the network. Applets exist on the Internet or on Intranets. There are classes that enable applets and applications to communicate across the network using the UDP or TCP/IP protocols. Java's class loader is designed to facilitate network operation. Java's security mechanisms are designed to protect against attack from across the network. Many of the functional restrictions imposed on applets are intended to prevent them from exhibiting inappropriate network behavior. In order to create robust networking applets and applications, it is important to understand the functionality provided by Java's networking classes, as well as the limitations imposed by Java's security model. Chapter 10, *Networking*, explores Java's networking capabilities.

Classes

Every line of executable Java code belongs to one class definition or another. Java uses classes to represent everything, such as: buttons, applets, URLs, files, and even classes themselves. This section discusses how classes are loaded and the role that class loading plays in Java's security mechanism.

Class Loading

Consider the simplest applet imaginable:

```
public class SimplestApplet extends java.applet.Applet
{
}
```

This code clearly does absolutely nothing, but it is valuable to study the process by which it comes to do absolutely nothing. First, being an applet, it must be mentioned in an HTML page so that a browser can download and execute it:

```
. . .
<APPLET CODE=SimplestApplet.class WIDTH=200 HEIGHT=150>
</APPLET>
. . .
```

Eventually a user will browse to this page, which will be parsed by the browser's HTML interpreter. The APPLET tag tells the browser that a Java class must be loaded.

By default (since there is no CODEBASE tag) the browser looks for the applet in the same directory where it found the HTML page. What the browser is looking for is a file named SimplestApplet.class. If this is found, it is loaded into the browser.

Now the applet definition file undergoes a thorough security check. A theorem prover, known as the bytecode verifier, decides whether or not the class definition meets its safety criteria. For example, every opcode must be valid and must be followed by the proper number of valid arguments. Access restrictions must be honored. There can not be any operand stack overflows or underflows.

NOTE The Java compiler converts Java source code to platform-independent *bytecode*, which can be thought of as machine language for the Java Virtual Machine (JVM). Just like machine language for actual hardware, bytecode is a series of instructions. Each instruction consists of an operation code or *opcode*, followed by some number of operands.

Once the bytecode verifier has given its approval, the Java runtime environment within the browser must build an internal representation of the SimplestApplet class. Since every Java class (except Object) is an extension of some other class, building this internal representation requires two steps:

- A representation of the superclass must be created, if one does not already exist. Unless the superclass is Object, this process is recursive.

- The new data and functionality contributed by the subclass must be represented.

The second step is easy: the class loader simply loads the Simplest-Applet class from the network. Before this can be accomplished, the first step is to represent the superclass, which is Applet. Assuming the browser's Java runtime does not yet have a representation for class Applet, that class must be loaded. But Applet extends Panel, which extends Container, which extends Component; so every one of those classes must be loaded as well. This raises the question of where Java looks for classes to load. Java uses the following search strategy for finding class definitions:

- The Java runtime system's own set of class definitions is searched.

- If the class is not found, other locations on the local file system are searched, as specified by the classpath.

- If the class is still not found, the remote Web server is searched.

More attention is given to each of these steps in the following material.

The Core Java API

Every Java runtime environment has its own copy of the standard JDK classes. Some vendors keep these files in plain sight while others obscure them. Typically the files are zipped together, although not compressed. Wherever and however they may appear, every runtime knows how to find its own system classes.

This strategy ensures that frequently used class files are close at hand. For example, every Java program needs the definition of `Object`, and every Java program with a GUI needs the definition of `Component`. While the more obscure classes (`LineNumberInputStream`, for instance) are rarely required, when they are needed it is important that what gets loaded is the correct standard version of the class.

The Classpath Classes

If a desired class file is not found in the system repository, the runtime next searches elsewhere on the local machine. If the environment variable `CLASSPATH` is set, all the directories listed there are searched in order of appearance. `CLASSPATH` is a list of pathnames, separated by semicolons on DOS platforms and colons on other machines. If `CLASSPATH` is not set, only the current working directory is searched.

The following command sets `CLASSPATH` on a Unix machine:

```
setenv CLASSPATH /w/x/java/classes:/y/z/morejava/classes
```

The following command does the same on a DOS machine:

```
SET CLASSPATH=C:\w\x\java\classes;C:\y\z\morejava\classes
```

Remote Classes

If a class required by an applet is not found on the local machine, the next place to search is the Web server. (If a class required by an application is not found locally however, there is no Web server, and the search fails.)

By default, the class file is expected to reside in the same directory where the browser found the Web page. This can be overridden by the optional CODEBASE tag. For details on CODEBASE and on the location of packages, please refer to Chapter 5. Java utilizes this three part search strategy as a method of security and time efficiency.

This three-part search strategy ensures that remote classes, which are less trustworthy and take longer to load than local classes, are only used when no local version is available.

Static Initialization

After a class is loaded and has passed the bytecode verifier's checks, storage is allocated for any static variables the class may declare. If a static declaration includes any initialization statements, the initialization is also performed at this time. For example, if a class had the declaration static int rev = 6;, then space would be allocated for the int, and initialized to 6.

The Java compiler permits blocks of code in a class to be static. The code has no method name, no parameters, and no return value; it is simply a block of static code within a class. For example, a class definition might begin like this:

```
class MyClass extends MyOtherClass
{
    int             i, j;
    static double   d = 123.456;

    static
    {
        System.out.println("MyClass was just loaded.");
        d = d * 2.1;
    }

        . . .

}
```

There may be more than one static code block within a class definition. After static variable initialization, the static code blocks are executed in their order of appearance in the class definition. Like static methods, static code blocks may only refer to static instance variables within their own class.

Static code blocks look strange, they are hard to read, and many programmers are unfamiliar with them. They always execute, whether or not the execution is ever needed. This adds up to a maintenance risk, so static blocks should only be used when there is a compelling reason to use them. Their benefit is that they run early—as early as possible. The most common use of static blocks is in classes that contain native methods. Native methods make calls to dynamically loaded libraries, and there is a great performance advantage to having the library fully loaded by the time any native call is made. To ensure this, classes with native methods have static blocks, which invoke the `System.loadLibrary()` call.

Security

Java has a number of mechanisms to protect clients from attacks by rogue applets. We have already mentioned the bytecode verifier. This protects Java runtime environments against loading disreputable class files. A good Java compiler is not capable of generating opcodes that violate the bytecode verifier's criteria, but bytecode can also be generated by an attacker.

Java applets have less access to resources on the client machine than do applications. This is not an inherent trait of applets, but rather a browser imposition. Every browser constructs an instance of the `SecurityManager` class. Before attempting certain operations, such as file or socket access, the various JDK classes that encapsulate the operations must get permission from the security manager. The security manager grants or denies access to a wide range of functionality. File system and network access are the two major categories of functionality that it controls.

It has often been said that "applets may not read or write from the local or the remote file system." This is not strictly accurate. The truth is that nearly all Java-enabled browsers have security managers, which do not allow applets to read or write locally or remotely. The limitation is a business decision on the part of the browser vendor, not a limitation inherent in the nature of applets. There is general consensus, however, as to what applets should and should not be allowed to do. Most browsers, including all Netscape Navigator products so far, implement security managers. These security managers do not let applets read or write locally or remotely, do not let applets be TCP/IP servers, and only let applets be TCP/IP clients if the server is the machine that served the applet itself.

In addition to the bytecode verifier and the security manager, the class-loading mechanism described above is an additional line of defense; it protects against a kind of attack known as *spoofing*. Spoofing involves creating a class of the same name as a standard class, in the hope that the counterfeit class will be loaded instead of the genuine one. Classes which control access to sensitive resources are candidates for spoofing. In Java, the `SecurityManager` class is a prime target for spoofing. As we shall see, the class-loading algorithm makes `SecurityManager` (and every other standard JDK class) spoof-proof.

The attacker creates an applet as bait, and includes it in an enticing Web page on a server. The attacker also creates a spoofing `Security-Manager.class` file, which grants permission to read and write anywhere. The applet, the counterfeit `SecurityManager.class` file, and the Web page are all placed in the same directory on a server. The attacker hopes that his own version of `SecurityManager` will be downloaded, and used in the place of the authentic version.

The attack fails because the counterfeit class never gets loaded. When the browser realizes that it needs to load the `SecurityManager` class, it looks first in its own repository of classes. It finds `SecurityManager` there, so no further searching is required. The counterfeit version is ignored.

There is much more to say about Java security and Appendix C answers many of the frequently asked questions.

The File System

Applets are not allowed to access the local file system, but applications may do so. The variety of pathname and permission conventions presents problems that single-platform programs do not have to deal with. UNIX uses a forward slash as a path separator, and supports a moderate variety of permissions. Windows 95 uses a backslash, requires a drive letter and a colon for absolute path names, and supports limited permissions.

The `java.io.File` class encapsulates access to the local conventions, enabling Java applications to use the file system in a platform-independent manner. In particular, path separator and permission issues are hidden from the programmer. The `FileDialog` class presents users with a platform-independent file selection dialog. Chapter 9, *File I/O and Streams*, goes into more detail about Java and file systems.

Properties

Java programs have no way to read environment variables from the local machine. This is to be expected, since not all platforms support environment variables. Java offers an alternative means of specifying environmental information, called *properties*.

Java properties resemble X resources. Applets read properties and property values from a table provided by the browser, while applications may get them from a file or from the command line. Due to security issues, applets have restricted access to properties on the local machine. Chapter 5, *Portability Issues*, goes into more detail about the uses and limitations of properties.

Threads

Since the Java environment is multi-threaded, programmers are offered access to Java's threads to create multi-threaded applications and applets.

Some implementations of Java use the thread support mechanisms of the underlying machine, while others build their own thread support from scratch. Different platforms have a variety of thread support. The result is that thread behavior varies noticeably from one platform to another. The major difference is that some implementations are preemptive and others are not. Writing successful portable Java thread programs requires an understanding of the different models and an ability to create code which is robust in all cases. Chapter 7, *Threads*, addresses these issues.

Appearance

Java runs on an ever-widening variety of platforms. Applets and applications do not have a consistent look and feel across these platforms. In fact, the intention of Java is quite the opposite: programs running on a Motif platform should have a Motif look and feel; while programs running on a Windows platform should have a Windows look and feel, and so on.

The classes of the `java.awt` package encapsulate this chameleon approach to platform independence. Writing a successful graphical user interface often requires a certain amount of knowledge as to how the whole mechanism is implemented. Chapter 3, *Creating Custom Components*, Chapter 4, *Layout Managers*, and Chapter 6, *Images*, explore various aspects of Java's platform independence from the point of view of developing robust code. For now, there are a few details to point out.

Color

Java's color model supports 24-bit color with eight bits for alpha (opacity). That is the model; very few machines running Java today have hardware capable of supporting that many colors. The runtime system must convert requested colors to possible colors.

There are three ways to map colors. The first way is to have a very expensive computer and actually support all the colors. The second way is to map requested colors to the closest available color. Under this scheme, many distinct combinations of red, green, and blue intensities map to the same color on the underlying platform. The third way is to create dither patterns to fool the eye.

The applet TrueColors on the CD-ROM shows how Java colors are rendered on the reader's machine. The applet displays three squares, each 256 x 256 pixels. The square on the left contains every color that can be created by mixing various intensities of red and green, leaving out blue. Red intensity varies from zero at the top to full on at the bottom, while green varies from zero at the left to full on at the right. The middle square mixes green with blue, and the square on the right mixes blue with red. The source code for this applet is also on the CD-ROM, although it uses classes which are not explained until Chapter 6, *Images*. Readers are invited to run the applet and see how colors are rendered on their own machine.

Fonts

Like colors, fonts vary from platform to platform. Java ports are supposed to support Helvetica, Times-Roman, Courier, and Dialog fonts, but they are free to map them to whatever actual font they please.

Java uses the `java.awt.Font` class to encapsulate font behavior and mapping. The constructor for `Font` builds an instance of the object, and also requests the underlying window system to build the font itself. By and large, fonts tend to stay cached within their window system for as long as possible, so there is not much penalty for multiple constructions of identical fonts. For example, consider an applet which calls the following constructor many times:

```
Font bigfont = new Font(Helvetica", Font.ITALIC, 55);
```

The first time this is called, an instance of `Font` is built, which takes practically no time all. Additionally, the window system is requested to make a 55-point italic Helvetica, which could be time-consuming, especially on X platforms. The next time the constructor is called, a new object is built, and the request to the window system returns almost immediately, since a 55-point italic Helvetica is already present.

The `Font` class has methods to retrieve an instance's family, style, and size, but they are not generally useful. What is returned is not the true family, style, or size as implemented in the window system, but only the requested values which were passed into the `Font` constructor.

Chapter 5, *Portability Issues*, examines font issues in more detail.

Component Layout

Even more than colors and fonts, GUI components show great variety from platform to platform. This creates a component layout problem. An OK button might be 50 pixels wide on one platform and 56 pixels wide on another. A program would have to take into account every possible button size (and scrollbar size, and textfield size, and so on) to create an aesthetic layout. In the worst case, components or vital screen regions could be obscured by components which turned out bigger than anticipated.

Java solves this problem by taking advantage of a platform's look and feel, rather than creating its own. Java encapsulates the task of precise layout into various layout manager classes. Instead of telling components precisely where to go, the programmer decides on a layout policy, and constructs combinations of layout managers to implement that policy. Chapter 4, *Layout Managers*, discusses these complexities in detail.

Components and Peers

A Java component—a button, for example—is no more than an object, an instance of some class. The `java.awt` package conceals a complicated mechanism for enabling a component to represent itself on the window system of the local computer. The `java.awt.Toolkit` class is the intermediary between the component subclasses such as `Button` and the underlying window system. The class is abstract. Part of the job of porting Java to a new platform is to create a subclass of `Toolkit` which is appropriate for the target machine.

When a toolkit is created, Java checks the value of the property `awt.toolkit`. This value is the name of the subclass of `Toolkit` for the local machine. Subsequently all activity that requires the creation of something (components, images, fonts, and so on) on the local window system works by making calls to the toolkit.

Consider the example of a button. At the moment when the button is added to its container, the toolkit is asked to construct an instance of some class that implements the `ButtonPeer` interface. A `ButtonPeer` is not much more than a bundle of native calls to a platform-specific library called `awt`, which interacts with the local window system. Every Java platform has its own local version of `ButtonPeer`. On a Motif system: the Motif subclass of `Toolkit` creates a Motif implementer of `ButtonPeer`, which interacts with the Motif version of the `awt` library, which in turn interacts with the X server on the local machine. Similarly, on a Windows platform: the Windows subclass of `Toolkit` creates a Windows implementor of `ButtonPeer`, which interacts with the Windows version of the `awt` library, which in turn interacts with Windows 95 on the local machine.

It is certainly not necessary to understand all the details of the peer mechanism to write good Java code, but it is instructive. Knowing a bit about peers helps in understanding why Java operates the way it does. It is important to understand that modifying or subclassing at the level of peers is, by and large, the job of those who port Java to new platforms. Applet and application programmers work one level higher, with the various subclasses of java.awt.Component. Even at that level, references to peers are commonly seen in the API documentation and in the Java source code.

Chapter 3, *Creating Custom Components*, discusses how to create custom components which behave like standard components, without coding on the peer level.

Summary

Modern computer programs run in a rich environment that includes graphical user interface, heterogeneous networks, the World Wide Web, security threats, and many other features. These environmental features are so much a part of today's computing landscape that we take them for granted. Java has been designed with today's environment in mind. Successful Java programming requires an understanding of how to use the tools that Java provides for communicating with the modern computing environment.

Every Java runtime environment has its own copy of the standard JDK classes. Some vendors keep these files in plain sight while others obscure them. Typically the files are zipped together, although not compressed. Wherever and however they may appear, every runtime knows how to find its own system classes.

CHAPTER

TWO

Applets and Applications Basics

- ■ Applets

- ■ Applications

- ■ The `repaint()`, `update()`, and `paint()` cycle

This is not an introductory book, and it is assumed that the reader already knows what applets and applications are. In this chapter the basics of these two kinds of Java programs will be reviewed, and some advanced information that will set the tone for the rest of this book will be introduced.

Applets

Every applet is a subclass of the `java.applet.Applet` class. Thus every applet inherits a large amount of functionality from `Applet`, and also from the superclasses of `Applet`: `java.awt.Component`, `java.awt.Container`, and `java.awt.Panel`. Figure 2.1 shows the applet inheritance hierarchy.

FIGURE 2.1

 class hierarchy

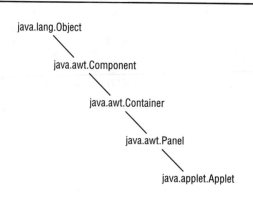

This section on applets is much longer than the subsequent section on applications, because applets have such a rich inheritance. There is simply more to say about applets than there is to say about applications.

Applets and HTML

Applets are displayed in browsers; that is what makes them different from applications. A browser constructs and manages an applet when, in the course of parsing an HTML file, it encounters the <APPLET> tag.

The format for the <APPLET> tag is:

```
<APPLET CODE=AppletClass.class WIDTH=width HEIGHT=height
[optional tags] >
[ <PARAM NAME=ParamName VALUE=ParamValue> ]
[ alternate HTML ]
</APPLET>
```

Everything within square brackets is optional. There may be any number of <PARAM> tags.

The optional tags are listed below. If used, they must appear within the first set of angle brackets.

ALIGN=*alignment*   Specifies the alignment for the applet on its HTML page. Possible values for *alignment* are left, right, top, texttop, middle, absmiddle, baseline, bottom, and absbottom. These values function the same as those used by the <IMG> tag.

ALT=*alternateMessage*   Specifies that *alternateMessage* should be displayed on the HTML page. This tag is for browsers that can parse the <APPLET> tag but are not Java-enabled and choose to ignore the alternate HTML.

ARCHIVE=*archive*   Specifies an archive directory of Java classes.

CODEBASE=*URL*   Specifies that the applet bytecode file is to be found in the directory specified by *URL*. This directory does not necessarily have to be on the same machine where the HTML file resides. It this tag is missing, the codebase directory is assumed to be the directory where the HTML file resides.

NAME=*appletName*   Specifies a name for the applet. Other applets on the same page may use this name for communicating with this applet. This technique is described below.

HSPACE=*spacing*   Specifies the number of empty pixels to the left and right of the applet.

VSPACE=*spacing*   Specifies the number of empty pixels above and below the applet.

MAYSCRIPT=*boolean*   Specifies whether the applet may interact with Javascript code. This tag is only recognized by Netscape Navigator browsers. The `boolean` parameter should be either `true` or `false`.

Arbitrary parameter/value pairs may be passed to an applet with the ⟨PARAM⟩ tag. This data appears within its own set of angle brackets. The format of the tag is:

```
<PARAM NAME=ParamName VALUE=ParamValue>
```

An applet may read the value of any parameter by calling the following method:

```
String getParameter(String paramName);
```

If `paramName` appears in a ⟨PARAM⟩ tag on the applet's page, then this method returns the parameter's value as a string. If `paramName` does not appear on the applet's page, the return value is `null`.

NOTE   `<param>` tags are especially useful for Web pages that change periodically. For example, consider an applet that draws a weather map with geographical regions color-coded by mean temperature over the past 24 hours. This applet could receive the raw temperature data via `<param>` tags. Every day a script could read the raw data from a file and emit an up-to-date HTML page with the current date. When the script writes the `<param>` tag portion of the HTML page, it inserts the raw temperature data. The result is a changing Web page with a stable applet.

Applet Life Cycle

An applet's life cycle begins when a browser visits the applet's Web page. The first part of this process is described in the previous chapter, in the section called *Class Loading*. In this section the story picks up at the point where the applet's class has been loaded.

Having loaded the class, the browser creates an instance of the applet class. It does this simply be calling the applet's constructor. From this moment on the applet instance is passive. In other words, it does nothing spontaneously. It simply reacts to method calls made by the browser.

After constructing the applet, the browser allocates space for the applet within its viewing area on the screen. At this point a very important thing happens: the applet is given a *peer*. Peers are discussed in detail in Chapter 6, *Images*. For now, suffice it to say that a peer is a component's connection to the local, platform-specific, underlying windows system. Java components receive much of their functionality by recruiting the facilities of the local windows system.

In the next step in the life cycle, the browser sends several start-up method calls to the applet. Each of these methods is inherited from the `java.applet.Applet` superclass. The inherited versions do nothing; programmers may override any of them to give the applet its desired character. It is important to note that by the time these methods are called, the applet has been completely constructed and has been given its peer.

init()

The first call that the browser makes to the applet is `init()`. This is the only start-up method that is only called once, so this is where the applet should perform one-time initialization. Functionality performed in `init()` commonly includes:

- Creating the applet's GUI
- Reading values from `<param>` tags
- Loading off-screen images from external files
- Loading audio clips from external files

Instance variables may be initialized in `init()`, or they may be initialized on their declaration lines. From the standpoint of maintenance, it is generally better to initialize them in the `init()` method so that everything gets initialized in one place.

NOTE The compiler guarantees that numeric instance variables are initialized to `zero`, chars to "`\u0000`", booleans to `false`, and object and array references to `null`. Thus any instance variables for which these are the correct start-up values need not be initialized explicitly. This initialization does *not* happen for automatic (method-scope) variables.

start() and *stop()*

The next method called by the browser is `start()`. The name is a bit ambiguous, as it does not make clear what it is that should be started. The `start()` method works in partnership with the `stop()` method. After the initial `start()` call, the browser calls `stop()` whenever the user browses away from the applet and calls `start()` again when the user browses back to the applet. This terminology is vague, and different browsers make the calls under different circumstances. As a general rule, `stop()` is called when the browser displays a new Web page or when it becomes iconified; `start()` is called when the browser returns to the applet's page or when it becomes de-iconified.

It may come as a surprise to some readers that an applet's code is not de-allocated when its page is left behind. The rationale is that the page may be visited again in the future and it would be a shame to have to reload the applet in this case. Moreover, in this situation the user would reasonably expect the applet to be in the same state it was left in, and not initialized. Thus browsers cache applets.

In general, there are three activities that an applet should suspend in the `stop()` method and resume in the `start()` method:

Animation   There is no benefit in wasting cycles on an animation that cannot be seen.

Sound   It would confuse the user to play sound for a different page than the one being viewed. Iconified programs of any kind should not play sounds.

General background thread processing   The thread would be doing work for a page other than the one currently being viewed. This would steal resources that should be available to the current page.

paint(Graphics g)

This method, like `start()`, is called both at start-up time and subsequently at the browser's discretion. The `paint()` method is passed an instance of the `Graphics` class. Every instance of `Graphics` is dedicated to drawing on a component's region of the screen or on an off-screen image. The instance passed into `paint()` draws on the applet's pixels.

After the initial call, the browser calls `paint()` whenever it needs the applet to render itself. The circumstances that cause this to happen are browser-specific. Most often the cause is damage repair. When the applet's portion of the browser is covered by another window and then becomes exposed again, something somewhere has to render the applet's exposed pixels in order to maintain the illusion that the screen is a three-dimensional desktop.

Some browsers, including Netscape Navigator, use a *backing store* strategy for damage repair; these browsers always cache their current appearance in an off-screen image. When part or all of the browser becomes exposed, the damage is repaired by rendering the backing store cache onto the screen. With this strategy it is never necessary to repair damage by asking the applet to paint() itself. Browsers that use a backing store pay a memory penalty but are able to repair damage very quickly.

Other browsers, including the appletviewer, require the applet to repair its own damage. When this happens, paint() is called, but the Graphics parameter is a bit different from the one passed into the initial paint() call. Every instance of Graphics has a clip rectangle; this defines the portion of the drawable area within which drawing operations have an effect. Methods such as Graphics.drawLine() or Graphics.fillRect() do not modify pixels outside this clip rectangle. When the appletviewer calls paint() in order to repair damage, it sets the clip rectangle of the Graphics parameter to be the smallest rectangle that encompasses all of the damaged area. This setting minimizes the number of screen pixels that must be updated.

NOTE The clip rectangle can be modified programmatically. Chapter 8, *Animation*, shows an example of when and how to do this.

destroy()

The browser calls destroy() when it no longer needs the applet. Because the browser caches the applet even when the applet's page is no longer displayed, destroy() is rarely called. In fact, the call only happens when the applet's page is reloaded (so that the old version is no longer needed) or when the browser itself terminates.

The destroy() method is the applet's opportunity to release any nonmemory resources it might have, such as threads and network connections.

The Applet Context

The applet method `getAppletContext()` returns an object that implements the `AppletContext` interface. This object has methods that give details about the applet's environment. The methods of the `AppletContext` interface are:

`Applet getApplet(String name)` Returns a handle to the named applet. An applet receives its name via the NAME=*applet-Name* tag.

`Enumeration getApplets()` Returns an enumeration of applets that were loaded by the same class loader as the current applet.

`AudioClip getAudioClip(URL soundFileUrl)` Returns an audio clip object. The `soundFileUrl` parameter should specify a sound file in the `.au` format.

`Image getImage(URL imageFileUrl)` Returns an image. The `imageFileUrl` parameter should specify a sound file in the `.gif`, `.jpg`, or `.xbm` format.

`void showDocument(URL documentUrl)` Requests the browser to display the HTML page specified by the `documentUrl` parameter.

`void showDocument(URL documentUrl, String where)` Same as above, but the `where` parameter specifies where in the browser the new page should be displayed relative to the current page's frame. The options for `where` are listed below. If any string is used other than the following ones, the new document is shown in a new top-level window whose name is the `where` string.

`"_self"` Uses the current page's frame.

`"_parent"` Uses the parent frame of the current page's frame.

"_top"   Uses the top-level frame.

"_blank"   Uses a new unnamed top-level window.

void showStatus(String message)   Displays message on the browser's status line. This method should not be relied on for communicating important information to the user because other subsystems of the browser may overwrite the status line at any time.

Inter-Applet Communication

The getApplet() and getApplets() methods of AppletContext are used for inter-applet communication. The returned values are references to applet objects, and they may be sent method calls just like any other object.

Browsers impose restrictions on applet communication. For example, 2.x versions of Netscape Navigator require that communicating applets reside on the same page. Netscape Navigator 3.0 is more restrictive: in order for two applets to communicate, they must share the same codebase, and their ARCHIVE and MAYSCRIPT tags, if present, must be identical.

As an example, consider two applets that meet their browser's communication requirements. The first applet's name (as specified by the NAME=appletName tag) is victim. The second applet could use the following code to draw a red diagonal line across the first applet:

```
Applet otherApplet = getAppletContext().getApplet();
if (otherApplet != null)
{
    int x = otherApplet.size().width;
    int y = otherApplet.size().height;
    Graphics g = otherApplet.getGraphics();
    g.setColor(Color.red);
    g.drawLine(0, 0, x, y);
}
```

Applet Restrictions

There are many restrictions on an applet's behavior. This is to be expected, as an applet is, in a sense, a stranger borrowing the host machine's CPU and display. Some of these restrictions are inherent in the implementation of Java, and some are imposed by the browser, through its instance of the `SecurityManager` class. (Some security FAQs are presented in Appendix C.) I will briefly mention four general categories of applet restriction.

First, an applet's access to both the local and the remote file system is restricted. Netscape Navigator and Internet Explorer browsers simply forbid all such access.

Second, an applet class (or any other class) that was loaded from the network may not make native calls. Remote classes also may not execute local commands via the `exec()` method of the `java.lang.Runtime` class. There is no restriction on classes that are used by the applet but loaded locally, such as `Object` or `Component`.

Third, an applet may not be a network socket server and may only be a socket client if the server machine is one that served the applet's Web page. Servers, clients, and sockets are discussed in detail in Chapter 10, *Networking*.

Fourth, although an applet may display a frame, the frame displays a warning message. The text and coloring of this message varies from browser to browser.

The Future of Applets

We can expect that as applets are called on to perform more tasks, the support for interactions among applets, browsers, and network resources will become more refined. Recent refinements include signed applets, which provide a basis for secure electronic commerce. (Java's commerce support is discussed in Chapter 16, *The Java Electronic*

Commerce Framework.) As new uses for the Internet emerge, new applet functionality will keep pace.

Applications

An application is a program that happens to have been written in Java. It runs without a browser, without a security manager, without an applet context. Compared to an applet, there is so little going on in an application's environment that there is not much to say on the general topic of applications. This section will just touch on a few of the relevant issues.

public, static, void

An application is invoked from the command line by typing **java** *Classname*.

The `.class` extension should not be typed. The command starts up a Java runtime environment and tells its class loader to load the named class from somewhere in the `CLASSPATH`. Once the class is loaded, a call is made to the class' `main()` method, whose signature must be:

```
public static void main(String[])
```

Clearly, `main()` must be public so that the runtime will have permission to call it. The `void` return type just means that a Java program, unlike a C or C++ program, does not return a value to the command line from which it was invoked. (A value still can be returned by calling `System.exit()`.)

The `static` designation requires some explanation. In Java, a static instance variable is associated with its class rather than with an individual instance of the class; thus a static instance variable may be read or written before any instances of the class are constructed. A method may be designated as static if it only accesses static methods and instance variables within its own class. Thus a static method also is associated with the class rather than with any instance of the class, and may be called before any instances of the class have been constructed.

Often applications have GUIs, which means that a frame must be constructed. It is common practice to subclass `java.awt.Frame` and to put the `main()` method in the `Frame` subclass. The result is code similar to the following:

```
public class MyApplication extends Frame
{
    // (Instance variable declarations here.)

    public static void main(String args[])
    {
        MyApplication that;
        that = new MyApplication();
        that.show();
    }

    // (Constructor and many other methods follow.)
}
```

The idea here is that on entry into `main()`, there is no instance of the `MyApplication` class. In programs with this structure, the first job of the `main()` method is to construct an instance of the class.

An alternate structure would be something like the following:

```
public class Launcher
{
    public static void main(String args[])
    {
        MyApplication that;
        that = new MyApplication();
        that.show();
    }
}


public class MyApplication extends Frame
{
    // (Data and code omitted.)
}
```

There is very little difference between these two approaches. The second way is cleaner, but requires one extra class definition.

Testing

A large application is likely to require the development of many classes. A good way to promote quality is to give every important class its own `main()` method. These methods are never invoked during normal execution of the program. They are only used for testing. Each of the various `main()` methods constructs an instance of the class and invokes methods on the instance, checking return values and instance variable values. All methods and instance variables are accessible to the `main()`, even those that are declared private.

This test strategy can be used with applets as well as with applications. If a class both extends `java.awt.Applet` and has its own `main()` method, then it is both an applet (when invoked by a browser) and an application (when invoked from a command line).

Peers

Applications generally have an easier life than applets. They have access to the file system and the network, and may invoke native methods. There is, however, a drawback to being an application.

An applet resides in a browser. The browser will not invoke the applet's `init()` method until the applet has a peer. As long as an applet performs all of its initialization in its `init()` method, there is no danger that operations relying on the peer will fail.

An application has no such luxury. Most initialization activities do not require a peer, but a very important one does. Empty off-screen images are created by the `createImage(int width, int height)` method of the `Component` class. If the component has a peer, an empty image is returned; if the component has no peer, the call returns `null`. The code below, which appears reasonable, will fail.

```java
import java.awt.*;
public class ImageNoPeer extends Frame
{
    Image    im;

    public static void main(String args[])
    {
        ImageNoPeer that = new ImageNoPeer();
        that.show();
    }

    public ImageNoPeer()
    {
        resize(500, 300);
        im = createImage(500, 300);
        Graphics g = im.getGraphics();          // Crash!  im is null
        // Various operations involving g
    }
}
```

Until the instance of the `Frame` subclass `ImageNoPeer` has a peer, the `createImage()` call will fail. The time to make the call is after the peer is created. This happens during the course of the `show()` call, when the `addNotify()` method is invoked. An easy way to create images safely is to override `addNotify()` and call `createImage()` after calling the superclass' `addNotify()`, as shown below:

```java
import java.awt.*;
public class ImageWithPeer extends Frame
{
    Image    im;

    public static void main(String args[])
    {
        ImageWithPeer that = new ImageWithPeer();
        that.show();
    }

    public ImageWithPeer()
```

```
    {
        resize(500, 300);
    }

    public void addNotify()
    {
        super.addNotify();
        im = createImage(500, 300);
        Graphics g = im.getGraphics();                // No problem
        // Various operations involving g
    }
}
```

The *repaint()*, *update()*, and *paint()* Cycle

The Component methods repaint(), update(), and paint() are the heart of Java's drawing mechanism. Understanding how these methods interact is essential to creating robust maintainable code.

Figure 2.2 shows the calling structure of these three methods.

FIGURE 2.2

Calling structure of repaint(), update(), and paint()

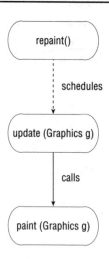

Every component has a background and a foreground color. The `update()` method clears the component to its background color, then sets the graphic object's drawing color to be the foreground color, and lastly calls `paint()`.

The important point about Figure 2.2 is that `repaint()` does not call `update()`. It schedules `update()`, which is very different. The first time a call is made to a component's `repaint()`, a request is made for a thread to call `update()` in the near future (in 100 milliseconds, by default; see Chapter 5, *Portability Issues*, for information on how to modify the default). Subsequently, `repaint()` checks to see whether an update is pending (that is, whether `repaint()` has previously been called, and called within the 100 milliseconds, so that the call to `update()` has not yet been made). If indeed there is an update pending, `repaint()` just returns. If no update is pending, then one is scheduled.

The result is that `update()` is never called more than 10 times per second, no matter how many calls are made to `repaint()`. Consider a large application or applet that handles a large number of events. Every event (mouse click, mouse movement, component action, and so on) could result in a screen change. By calling `repaint()` rather than `paint()`, the program does not need to worry about falling behind in its painting duties.

There are three design choices for a program that frequently modifies its display in response to user events:

1. The event handlers can call `getGraphics()` to obtain a `Graphics` object that is dedicated to the screen; the handlers can then make their own graphics calls to draw directly.

2. The event handlers can set instance variables to reflect the current state of the program; the handlers can then call `paint()`, which reads the values of those instance variables and modifies the screen appropriately.

3. Same as 2 above, but the event handlers call `repaint()` rather than `paint()`.

As mentioned, choice 2 is slower than choice 3, which eliminates intermediate `paint()` calls. But unlike choice 1, where event handlers draw directly to the screen, choice 3 imposes an intermediate step: the program's state must be encoded in instance variables, which are interpreted by the `paint()` method. For a small applet or application, this can be a burden. However, for a program that is of any significant size or that must be maintained over time, the discipline is well worth the effort. It is significantly easier to fix a display bug or to add a display feature if the display code is centralized rather than scattered. The instance variables always dictate what the screen is supposed to look like, so if the screen is wrong, either the instance variables are getting set to the wrong values (in the event handlers) or they are getting interpreted incorrectly (in `paint()`).

This design pattern has two other advantages. First, we have observed that some browsers may call `paint()` at any moment; should this happen, any drawing that was performed by methods other than `paint()` will be lost. Second, revision 1.1 of the Java Developer's Kit (JDK) includes support for printing components. This functionality is described in detail in Chapter 14, *The 1.1 AWT*; for now it is enough to say that any graphics to be printed must be drawn in a centralized `paint()` method.

This design pattern can be called the "always call `repaint()`" rule. For most programming tasks, the extra effort required pays off handsomely in terms of performance and maintainability.

Summary

This chapter has introduced some of the issues related to Java applets and applications, and the differences between them. The remainder of this book presents detailed information and techniques for developing fully functional, robust, maintainable applets and applications.

CHAPTER
THREE

3

Creating Custom Components

- Strategies for designing custom components

- Life cycle of an event

- Design considerations

- Subclassing canvas: the polar component

- Aggregation: the three-way component

- Subclassing a standard component: validating textfields

Java's Abstract Windowing Toolkit (AWT) provides a small but reasonable set of user interface components. In most cases these components provide enough functionality so that a good interface can be built. This chapter is concerned with what to do in those cases when the AWT is not enough. Three alternative strategies for creating custom components will be presented, along with criteria for selecting the most appropriate one. A set of design considerations will then be developed and applied to several detailed examples.

A major consideration in the development of custom components is the handling of events. This entire chapter is based on the pre-1.1 AWT event propagation model. Release 1.1 continues to support this model, and adds a new one. The new model is presented in Chapter 14, *The 1.1 AWT*, where one of the detailed examples from this chapter is reworked to use the new event model.

Event handling is only one of a large number of design considerations. Readers who will be creating custom components under the 1.1 event model are encouraged to become familiar with the non-event issues by reading this chapter before reading Chapter 14.

Strategies for Designing Custom Components

The Abstract Windowing Toolkit package necessarily provides a limited set of components. All of the fundamental Java components have a corresponding control on every underlying platform. Peers provide the connection. For example, in an applet running on a Solaris/Motif platform, adding a scrollbar causes a call to the constructor for the `MScrollBarPeer` class. This class contains a number of native calls that create and communicate with a Motif scrollbar. When Java is ported to a platform, a peer class and corresponding native methods for that platform must be created for every AWT component. Thus the designers of the AWT package chose to restrict the suite of Java components to those whose peers and native methods can be implemented easily on current windows systems. The result, generally speaking, is the set of user interface components that are common to Motif and Windows platforms.

This restriction provides a powerful benefit: as a Java programmer, if you only use the standard AWT components in your GUIs, your users will always be interacting with familiar devices. This is so valuable that, all other things being equal, it is better to use the existing components than to create your own. When choosing between existing and custom components, the most important consideration is how to make life as easy as possible for users. Once you have decided to create a custom component class, you have three options:

1. You can subclass `Canvas`, and have the subclass take care of all painting and event handling. The result is a completely new look and feel.

2. You can subclass `Panel` or some other container, and populate the subclass with standard components. These will interact with each other to provide higher-level behavior. The result is an aggregation of preexisting components.

3. You can subclass one of the standard AWT noncontainer components (`Button`, `Checkbox`, `Choice`, `Scrollbar`, `Scroll-Pane`, `Textfield`, or `Textarea`). The subclass will enhance the inherited behavior.

Each of these approaches has its pros and cons. When judging an approach, the primary consideration is ease of mastery. Users should be able to quickly figure out how to use a new component, and the component should assist users in doing productive work. Any feature of a component that is difficult to understand or difficult to use should be considered a serious liability.

In general, components designed with the first strategy (subclassing canvas) will be the most difficult to master. This is because the look and the feel are completely new; the user has no experience with similar components to suggest how to interact with the new one. To the extent that the new component is not intuitive, the user will have to be educated. Thus it is vital that the component match as closely as possible the user's mental image of the data to be entered. All in all, subclassing `Canvas` works best when the user's job is to enter a new kind of data, a kind that is not well represented as text, as a checkbox state, or as a scrollbar position. In the section *Subclassing Canvas: The Polar Component*, an example for entering a value in polar coordinates will be developed.

The second strategy is most likely to result in an easily learned class, because everything the panel contains is already well known. Only the interactions among the subcomponents within the panel are new. An example follows in which checkboxes, a textfield, and a scrollbar are available for inputting a value; when one of these is used its new value is reflected by the other two. Since users already know how to use checkboxes, textfields, and scrollbars, there is little for them to learn. In following this strategy, you get to take advantage of all the expensive usability research that has been done over the years to refine the subcomponents. Commonly this aggregation strategy is useful when a component must combine both input and output functionality, or when multiple input paradigms are to be offered. An example that offers three options for entering a numeric value will be examined in the section *Aggregation: The Three-Way Component*.

The third strategy provides a familiar look with a new feel. When you subclass a component, the user sees something familiar, and approaches it with the expectation that it will behave like its standard superclass. Some education will be required to overcome this expectation. This strategy works best when the set of valid inputs to a component must be restricted. The later section *Subclassing a Standard Component: Validating Textfields* contains an example of a textfield that only accepts numeric entries.

Life Cycle of an Event

One responsibility of any component is to participate in Java's event-handling structure. It is important to understand how events are handled, and to design the new component accordingly.

Consider what happens when a user clicks on a button in an applet running in a Netscape browser on a SparcStation. The first entity to notice the click is the Solaris operating system, which informs the X server. (On other platforms a different operating system informs a different windows system; otherwise there is little difference.) The X server allocates a struct called an Xevent, and fills in its fields to describe what happened (a mouse click), where it happened (x and y pixel coordinates, relative to the desktop's upper left corner), and when it happened. The X server then determines which of its client programs owns the pixel in which the click occurred. The event struct's x and y fields are translated to the client's coordinate system, and the client is notified. Note that "client" here means a client program of the windows server, not a client in the networking sense.

The client determines whether the click happened within one of its *widgets* (in X parlance, components are "widgets" or "gadgets"). In our example this is indeed the case: the click happened inside a Motif PushButton widget. The event is passed to the Motif library code that supports pushbuttons. The library code uses the event struct's event- type information as input to its internal state machine: some events merely modify internal state variables, while others require that the client program be notified. A Motif pushbutton only *notifies*—that is, it only considers that something of interest to the client has happened—if the mouse button goes up, *having previously gone down inside the same pushbutton widget.* Thus the user may click down inside the pushbutton's region of the screen, drag the mouse pointer around in an absentminded way, eventually return to the pushbutton's region, and finally release the mouse button. All this activity results in just a single notification to the client. In our Motif example, the notification takes the form of a *callback*: the Motif library code for the pushbutton makes a call to a callback function in the client code. The client code associates the callback function with the pushbutton widget at the time the widget is created.

All widgets, and their corresponding relatives on other platforms, do much the same: depending on internal state, some events are consumed by the component while others require that the client be notified.

In the example, the client program is the Netscape browser. The browser's pushbutton callback function realizes that the pushbutton resides inside a Java applet. The browser constructs an instance of Java's `Event` class, initializing its fields from the information in the `Xevent` struct. The Java `Event` class uses the following fields to describe what happened:

`int id`	Nature of the event
`long when`	A timestamp
`int x, y`	Pixel coordinates of the event
`int clickCount`	Number of consecutive mouse-down clicks
`int key`	The key, provided this was a keyboard event
`int modifiers`	Modifier key states (Shift, Ctrl, etc.)
`int target`	Innermost component in which the event happened
`Object arg`	Target-specific additional information

The value of `id` is a constant (actually a public static final int defined in the `Event` class) such as `Event.MOUSE_DOWN`, `Event.KEY_PRESS`, and so on. One possible value is `Event.ACTION_EVENT`, which indicates that a button, checkbox, choice, scrolled list, menu item, or textfield has been activated. From Java's point of view, a component action is just one more kind of event.

The `arg` field is declared to be of type `Object`. In other words, `arg` can be of any nonprimitive type, including an array. The `true` class of `arg` depends on the component that initiated the action. The intention is to provide a useful piece of information to describe what happened. (This is similar to the `client_data` mechanism used by X widgets.) The standard AWT components are simple enough so that generally nothing more needs be said about an action beyond the fact that it has happened; so in most cases `arg` is a string that tells the component's label. (The only exceptions are `TextField`, which sends a `String`, and `Checkbox`/`CheckboxMenuItem`, which send `Boolean`.)

Now, at last, it is time for the applet itself to become aware that something has happened. A call is made to the `deliverEvent()` method of the component—in this case the button. From this point on, it is Java objects that process the event. `deliverEvent()` calls `postEvent()`, which sets off an elegant recursive ripple that moves out through the button's containment hierarchy. The intention is to find some component that will handle the event. The button inherits `postEvent()` from the `Component` superclass; `postEvent()` simply makes a call to `handleEvent()`, which returns a boolean. A return value of `true` indicates that the event has been handled; in this case `postEvent()` is finished. A return value of `false` from `handleEvent()` tells `postEvent()` that the component is not willing to process the event; `postEvent()` must look elsewhere. Now `postEvent()` determines the component's immediate next-largest container (some kind of panel, applet, or frame), and calls *its* `postEvent()`, after first translating the event's x and y to the coordinate system of the new larger container. In this manner the search continues: increasingly larger containing components are requested to handle the event, until one of them does so, indicating this by returning `true`. If no component will handle the event, it is ignored.

The default behavior of `handleEvent()`, inherited from the `Component` superclass, is to execute a switch on the event's `id` instance variable, calling the appropriate specific event handler. If, for example, the id is `Event.MOUSE_DOWN`, `handleEvent()` will call mouseDown(), returning the boolean returned by mouseDown(). If the id is Event.KEY_RELEASE, then handleEvent() will call keyUp(), and so on. In the example, the event's id is Event.ACTION_EVENT, so a call is made to action(). In all cases where there is a specific handler for the event's id, handleEvent() returns whatever boolean is returned to it by the specific handler.

Figure 3.1 shows the calling structure of deliverEvent() and its subordinates.

FIGURE 3.1

Calling structure for
deliverEvent()

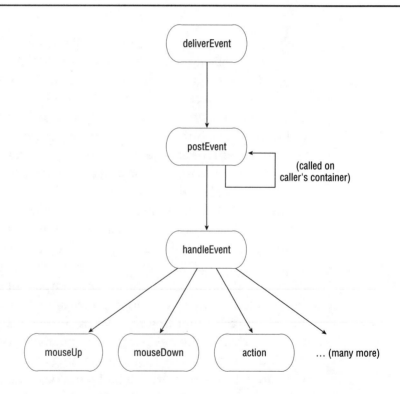

Some event types have specific handling routines and some do not. Those that do are listed in Table 3.1, along with the corresponding handlers and their parameters. The handlers are all inherited from the Component superclass. It is assumed that the event is referenced by the variable evt.

TABLE 3.1   Specific Event Handlers

evt.id	Handler called by handleEvent(evt)
Event.MOUSE_ENTER	mouseEnter(evt, evt.x evt.y)
Event.MOUSE_EXIT	mouseExit(evt, evt.x, evt.y)
Event.MOUSE_MOVE	mouseMove(evt, evt.x, evt.y)
Event.MOUSE_DOWN	mouseDown(evt, evt.x, evt.y)
Event.MOUSE_DRAG	mouseDrag(evt, evt.x, evt.y)
Event.MOUSE_UP	mouseUp(evt, evt.x, evt.y)
Event.KEY_PRESS	keyDown(evt, evt.key)
Event.KEY_ACTION	keyDown(evt, evt.key)
Event.KEY_RELEASE	keyUp(evt, evt.key)
Event.KEY_ACTION_RELEASE	keyUp(evt, evt.key)
Event.ACTION_EVENT	action(evt, evt.arg)
Event.GOT_FOCUS	gotFocus(evt, evt.arg)
Event.LOST_FOCUS	lostFocus(evt, evt.arg)

All of the handlers listed in Table 3.1 do nothing except return `false`, indicating that `postEvent()` must look elsewhere for a component that will process the event. Thus, if a user clicks on a button in an applet, for example, the button will be the first component to be notified; the button's `action()` method will return `false` to `handleEvent()`, so the event will next be posted to the applet. Typically an applet with a simple GUI will catch all action events from its several components, checking the event's target to determine which component was used. For more complicated interfaces, it is appropriate to subclass `Button`, one subclass for each (or nearly each) button in the GUI. These subclasses provide their own `action()` methods that return `true`, so that the applet is not required to handle them. Such subclassed components are sometimes called "self-contained," because they are responsible not only for look and feel, but also for behavior. This is very much in the spirit of object-oriented design and tends to improve the maintainability of code.

Primitive components are not the only ones that can be self-contained. Consider a panel that contains an Apply button and a Cancel button; one way to implement this structure would be to have the buttons themselves be ordinary (that is, not subclasses) but to subclass `Panel`. The subclass' constructor would construct and add the two buttons, and there would be an `action()` method that would determine which button was clicked and then do the appropriate thing. Here we have buttons inside a subclassed panel that is inside an applet. When a button is clicked, its `action()` returns `false`, so `action()` is sent to the panel. This returns `true`, so `action()` is not sent to the applet.

The following values for `id` have no corresponding specific handlers, and `handleEvent()` returns `false` when it attempts to deal with them:

```
Event.WINDOW_DESTROY
Event.WINDOW_EXPOSE
Event.WINDOW_ICONIFY
Event.WINDOW_DEICONIFY
Event.WINDOW_MOVED
Event.SCROLL_LINE_UP
Event.SCROLL_LINE_DOWN
Event.SCROLL_PAGE_UP
Event.SCROLL_PAGE_DOWN
Event.SCROLL_ABSOLUTE
Event.LIST_SELECT
Event.LIST_DESELECT
Event.LOAD_FILE
Event.SAVE_FILE
```

NOTE   In the 1.0 model, an event must be handled by the component where the event orignated, or by one of that component's containers. The 1.1 model, which is more complicated but more flexible, allows event processing by any object.

Design Considerations

Before deciding on a design strategy (subclassing Canvas, aggregation in a panel, or subclassing a primitive component), there are two questions that need to be considered:

- How should the component display its value?

- How should the user specify new values?

Once these look-and-feel issues are decided, the best subclassing strategy will generally be obvious. At this point, the following list of issues can help you to organize your thoughts and make well-founded design decisions:

- How can the programmer modify the component's appearance?

- What limits should be set on the component's possible values?

- How should the value be stored, set, and retrieved?

- When should the new component post an `ACTION_EVENT`?

- When `ACTION_EVENT` is posted, what component-specific data should be placed in the event's `arg` field?

- Should the component post other events?

- How should events be posted?

- How do we support subclassing to make the component self-contained?

- What happens when the component resizes?

Three detailed examples will be developed, each beginning with a consideration of these issues. It will become clear that the answers to these questions provide the basis for a sound design plan.

Subclassing Canvas:
The *Polar* Component

The first example is a component called `Polar`, used for inputting a point in polar coordinates. Polar coordinates describe a point in terms of its distance from the origin (usually called ρ, or rho for radius) and the angle it makes with the right-pointing horizontal (usually called θ, or theta).

> **NOTE**
>
> Polar coordinates are just an alternative way of using two numbers to describe a point in a two-dimensional space. It is easy to translate between the polar (ρ, θ) coordinates and the familiar (x,y) coordinates of rectangular Cartesian space: x = ρ cos θ; y = sin θ.

Look and Feel

The first consideration is appearance: How should the component display its value? Because the component is to represent a point in 2-D space, the only reasonable choice is a square region or a squarish rectangle. It is not necessary to force the component to be perfectly square, but neither dimension should be particularly narrow; the component will declare its minimum size to be 50 x 50 pixels (minimum and preferred size are of concern to layout managers and are the subject of the next chapter). As for what is to be drawn in this region, the appearance should match as closely as possible the picture in the user's mind's eye. Probably the user's mental picture is a textbook illustration: a pair of axes with a dot superimposed, possibly with an arrow from the origin to the dot, as shown in Figure 3.2.

FIGURE 3.2

Mental picture of polar
coordinates

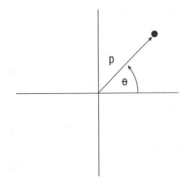

The intent is to create a component that will support copying this mental picture from the user's imagination to the computer. The `Polar` component should resemble Figure 3.2 as closely as possible; in practice, ease-of-use considerations will suggest some modifications and compromises. The current point should certainly be represented by a circular dot. In practice, rendering an arrowhead at the tip of the line produces visual clutter and obscures the dot, so there will not be an arrowhead. The user should be cued that this device operates in the polar domain and not the Cartesian, so that drawing a circle would be preferable to drawing a rectangle. If there is to be a circle, where should it go? By drawing a ring that passes through the current point, the user will receive additional feedback about the distance from the center. The result is shown in Figure 3.3, which is a screenshot of the finished product. Note how the ring cues the value of rho, while the line cues the value of theta.

FIGURE 3.3

The Polar component

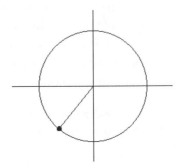

How should the user specify new values? The `Polar` component clearly wants to be clicked on. The simplest interface lets the user "grab the ring" by clicking down anywhere inside the component: the current point and the ring will jump to the mouse cursor location. Subsequently, as long as the mouse button is down, the value will track the mouse. When the mouse button goes up, the value ceases tracking. As long as the user is mouse-dragging, the dot, the line, and the ring will be rendered in blue, so the component can tell the user, "I'm listening." At times when the component is not responding to the mouse (which is almost always), it will be rendered in black. Because the axes never change and do not communicate information about the current value, they will be rendered in their own constant color. Proliferation of colors is dangerous, as a GUI with too many colors is confusing; it is best to take a conservative approach and draw the axes in gray.

This process gives satisfactory graphical feedback. Because numerical feedback is also required, the values of rho and theta will be displayed in the upper-left corner of the component.

Now that we have defined a look and a feel, it is time to choose a subclassing strategy. Clearly there are no standard components that render a ring or an arrow, so aggregation and simple subclassing are out of the question. Canvas will be subclassed and all the rendering and event-handling code will be written from scratch:

```
public class Polar extends Canvas
```

How can the programmer modify the component's appearance? Those aspects of the appearance that are susceptible to change need to be considered. The numeric value display comes to mind: programmers may want to disable it or modify its font. It is also possible to change the drawing colors and the component's background color. For the most part, the programmer can be given control over these aspects with no extra effort.

Every component has a background color, a foreground color, and a font. When the polar component is told to `repaint()`, a thread is scheduled that will eventually call update(), which clears the canvas using its background color, sets the current color to the foreground color, and calls paint(). So if the paint() method assumes that the canvas has been cleared using some appropriate background color, programmers can change a polar's background by calling its setBackground() method; because this method is inherited from the Component class, programmers have nothing extra to learn. Similarly, it is reasonable for programmers to expect that the ring, dot, and ray will be rendered using the foreground color. With this arrangement, programmers can simply call setForeground() to change the rendering color. As for the font used to render the textual value, if the code does not explicitly set one, the value will default to the component's own font. Thus this font can be controlled by calling setFont() on the component.

The only conditions that cannot be modified by using the component's inherited methods are the color of the display during dragging and the presence or absence of the textual feedback. For such modification, two public methods are needed: setDragColor() and enableText().

Next, the component's ability to put limits on its value needs to be considered. Theta is inherently constrained; there are no issues of scale. Rho, on the other hand, needs limits. There needs to be a maximum value for rho, represented by a ring that fills the component; this dictates a scale for translating distance in pixels into values for rho. This maximum is to be provided as an argument to Polar's constructor, and is stored in an instance variable called maxRho. In theory, maxRho value should correspond to a ring whose diameter (in pixels) is the lesser of the component's width and its height. In practice, a ring that grazes the boundary of the component is unsightly, so maxRho actually corresponds to a ring that is 10 percent smaller than the smaller dimension of the component.

There are many regions within the polar canvas—especially near the corners—that represent illegal values, because rho would be greater than maxRho. When the user drags through these regions, the ring should refuse to follow; instead it should remain at its maximum legal size. This is especially important because of the way event targets are determined. If the mouse goes down inside a canvas, all subsequent mouse events, until and including the next mouse up, are posted to the canvas, even if the mouse was dragged outside the canvas, and even if the mouse up occurred outside the canvas. Without a limitation on the ring size in the polar component, it would be possible to define a rho so large that no part of the ring would be visible.

Note that a limit is required to be passed to the constructor, and this limit dictates a scale. The alternative would be to have the programmer pass a scale to the constructor, but this has two disadvantages. First, without a limit the ring could grow until it was too large to be seen, as described above. Second, because of layout managers, clients do not have full control over the size of the component. If a scale is forced on a small component, it may be difficult or impossible to input large values. This suggests a good general principle: numerical components should not provide a means for specifying scale; instead, they should require limits that, along with the component's size, dictate scale.

The next issue is how the value should be stored, set, and retrieved. Rho and theta should be represented by floats or doubles, and doubles are more convenient because trig methods will be called in the `Math` class. Programmers who use the `Polar` class will also be likely to do trig operations on the results and will also prefer doubles. An auxiliary class called `PolarPoint` will be defined to encapsulate doubles for rho and theta.

NOTE   Readers who wish to use the `Polar` class are reminded that all of Java's trigonometric functions deal in radians. For conversion to and from degrees, the `Math` class defines a static final double called `PI`.

The source for the `PolarPoint` class appears on the accompanying CD-ROM in the file `javadevhdbk\ch03\PolarPoint.java`. The bytefile, `PolarPoint.class`, can be found in the same directory. The code looks like this:

PolarPoint.java

```
public class PolarPoint implements Cloneable
{
    public double           rho;
    public double           theta;


    public PolarPoint(double rho, double theta)
    {
        this.rho = rho;
        this.theta = theta;
    }


    public Object clone()
    {
        try
        {
            return(super.clone());
        }
        catch (CloneNotSupportedException e)
        {
            return(null);
        }
    }
}
```

Polar needs to return a copy of its value when requested. If it returns the value itself (or more correctly, a *reference* to the value), the caller and the polar will both have references to the same instance of `PolarPoint`, and if either one modifies the `PolarPoint`, the other one will suddenly have the wrong values. Therefore Polar will return a (reference to a) clone of its value, rather than (a reference to) the value itself.

> **NOTE**
>
> The `clone()` method is inherited from `Object`, where it is declared to be protected. This means that the inherited version may only be called from instances of `PolarPoint` or its subclasses. This system is of no use to class `Polar`, so `PolarPoint` must override `clone()`. Java classes are permitted to make overridden methods more public (but not less), and this version makes it public. Because the superclass' implementation throws `Clone-NotSupportedException`, this version must catch it.

Now the `Polar` class can be given a private instance variable called `value`, of type `PolarPoint`, and public methods to get and set the value. Setting the value should force a repaint, so that the component's appearance will reflect its new value.

```java
import (?)
import java.awt.*;
public class Polar extends Canvas
{
    private PolarPoint              value;

    public void setValue(PolarPoint newValue)
    {
        value = newValue;
        repaint();
    }



    public void setValue(double newRho, double newTheta)
    {
        setValue(new PolarPoint(newRho, newTheta));
    }



    public PolarPoint getValue()
    {
        return((PolarPoint)(value.clone()));
    }
```

Event Posting

Next, the question of when the new component should post an action event needs to be considered. Because the polar's value will change continuously as long as the mouse is dragged, `Event.ACTION_EVENT` can either be posted continuously or once when the mouse goes up. Continuous posting can be dangerous, because clients may implement lengthy `action()` methods. So it is better to post only when the mouse goes up. (Note that the `Scrollbar` class, which also continuously modifies a numerical value, likewise elects not to post continuous actions. In fact, it does not post actions at all.)

When `handleEvent()` handles `Event.ACTION_EVENT`, it calls `action()`, passing the `arg` of the `Event` into `action()`'s second argument. When the `Polar` class posts, it is free to place anything in `arg`. The obvious best choice is a copy of the current value. This way the client's `action()` method will not need to retrieve the `Polar`'s value.

At this point it is appropriate to wonder if `Polar` should post any event types besides `Event.ACTION_EVENT`. The only possible circumstances would be mouse drags and, for some clients, continuous updating. To support this, some event type other than `Event.ACTION_EVENT` should be posted. Certainly `Event.MOUSE_DRAG` is one possibility, but we should consider all of the possibilities.

If a scrollbar sends continuous events when the user drags its slider, it would be reasonable for `Polar` to post events of the same type. This is easily ascertained by experiment. `Scrollbar` can be subclassed so that its `handleEvent()` prints out the event's ID; then you put an instance of this subclass in an applet, run the applet, drag the slider, and see what gets printed out. When the experiment is run, continuous events are posted with ID = 605. This value in the source for the `Event` class is defined as `Event.SCROLL_ABSOLUTE`, which is therefore the event type that should be posted. Clients with an interest in continuous updates can override `handleEvent()` to check for Event.SCROLL_ABSOLUTE, and clients with no such interest only need to override action().

After it has been decided what events to post and when to post them, several issues concerning how to deliver them need to be looked at. Because mouseDown(), mouseDrag(), and mouseUp() all receive events as inputs, it is tempting to modify those events and pass them on. A cursory look at Java source code suggests that modifying the existing event is probably safe. This is not good enough. The fact that the current version of the system seems to have no further use for the event is no guarantee that future versions will not need it. If, however, the event is cloned, it is certain that there will be no problems with the original. In practice, Event cannot actually be cloned, because it does not implement its own clone() method, and the version inherited from Object is, unfortunately, protected. It is necessary to provide a method in Polar that constructs a new instance of Event and sets the appropriate fields. Because the target, id, and arg fields of the copy will be modified, the method permits the caller to specify the new values for them. The method is called copyEvent(), and it looks like this:

```
private Event copyEvent(Event eIn, int id, Object arg)
{
    Event eOut = new Event(this, id, arg);      // 1st arg is target
    eOut.x = eIn.x;
    eOut.y = eIn.y;
    eOut.when = eIn.when;
    return(eOut);
}
```

As the code above shows, the original event's x, y, and when instance variables should be copied into the clone without modification. The target should be this—that is, the instance of Polar that is posting the event; this reveals this polar as the one in which the event happened. id should be either Event.ACTION_EVENT or Event.SCROLL_ABSOLUTE. It has already been decided that arg should be a clone of the polar's value, which is an instance of PolarPoint.

Now that the event can be built, the question is where to deliver it. To be in keeping with Java's philosophy of event handling, it needs to be delivered to the polar itself. One could object that we might as well post to the polar's parent container. After all, implementation of the class has no action() method and no event handler for either Event.ACTION_EVENT or Event.SCROLL_ABSOLUTE, so events that the polar posts will end up posted to the parent container anyway. This is true as far as it goes: implementation does not catch Event.ACTION_EVENT or Event.SCROLL_ABSOLUTE; however, programmers may want to subclass Polar to make it self-contained, and to support this possibility any custom component must post all events to itself.

It is now known that the mouseDrag() and mouseUp() methods will have to modify the polar's value based on the mouse position, call repaint() to schedule a screen refresh, clone the triggering event with the modifications discussed above, and post the new event. The final issue is what value they should return. Ironically, there are three choices to consider, even though the return type is boolean. If true is returned, processing of the triggering event will terminate. If false is returned, processing of the triggering event will proceed. If super.handleEvent() is returned, processing of the triggering event may terminate and it may proceed, depending on what the superclass (Canvas) does. For both mouseDrag() and mouseUp(), processing needs to terminate, so both of these event handlers should return true. The mouseDrag() and mouseUp() methods appear below; they are quite similar. Note the setting or clearing of the boolean instance variable dragging, which paint() consults to determine what color to use. Note also the use of value, which is the instance variable (of type PolarPoint) that contains the current value of the component.

```
public boolean mouseDrag(Event e, int x, int y)
{
    dragging = true;
    xyToPolarPoint(x, y, value); repaint();
    Event el = copyEvent(e, Event.SCROLL_ABSOLUTE,
```

```
                        value.clone());
                        deliverEvent(el);
                        return(true);
                }

                public boolean mouseUp(Event e, int x, int y)
                {
                        dragging = false;
                        xyToPolarPoint(x, y, value);
                        repaint();
                        Event el = copyEvent(e, Event.ACTION_EVENT, value.clone());
                        deliverEvent(el);
                        return(true);
                }
```

Now it is important to verify that `Polar` can be subclassed to be self-contained. We have already taken certain precautions, but we should think this case through just to make sure. Would the following subclass ever report that it had received an action event?

```
public class SubPolar extends Polar
{
        public boolean action(Event e, Object ob)
        {
                System.out.println("Action!");
                return(true);
        }
}
```

When the mouse goes up in the component, `mouseUp()` is sent to the `SubPolar` instance and handled by the method inherited from the superclass. `Polar`'s `mouseUp()` repaints, delivers an event, and returns `true`. The delivered event's ID is `Event.ACTION_EVENT`. The event is first posted to the component itself; the component's `deliverEvent()` calls `postEvent()`, which in turn calls `handleEvent()`; the `Polar` superclass has not overridden either of these methods. So `handleEvent()` calls `action()`, and all is well. The only possible problems would arise if the `SubPolar` subclass overrode `mouseDown()`, `mouseDrag()`, or `mouseUp()`. The documentation should warn that this should be done with caution.

The final question is what to do when the component resizes. It has already been decided that the constructor should specify a maximum value for rho, which will define a scale conversion factor from rho's units to pixels. This conversion factor will be consulted whenever the value changes, so it should be stored as an instance variable. Appropriate variable naming is always important, but this is a case where it is doubly so. If the conversion factor is called `conversionFactor`, future developers who maintain this code will have to work out for themselves whether converting from pixels to units requires multiplying or dividing by `conversionFactor`. A mistake here could introduce a very subtle bug. It is much better to eliminate all possible confusion by calling the instance variable either `pixelsPerUnit` or `unitsPerPixel`. Here `unitsPerPixel` is used because the example converts from pixels to units, and this entails multiplication rather than division. Multiplication is commutative, so there is no possibility that in the future somebody will introduce a maintenance bug by getting the operands in the wrong order.

When the component resizes, `unitsPerPixel` is recomputed, as shown below:

```
private void adjustScale(int w, int h)
{
    unitsPerPixel = 2.0 * maxRho / Math.min(w, h);
    unitsPerPixel *= 1.1;
}
```

Multiplying by 1.1 ensures that when the component represents the maximum allowable rho, the ring occupies about 90 percent of the entire component and will never get so close to the edges that the component is difficult to read.

Although both resizing and reshaping must be considered, it turns out that only `reshape()` needs to be overridden because `resize()` just calls `reshape()` with the component's current x and y values. The `reshape()` method first recomputes `unitsPerPixel` and then calls the superclass' `reshape()`, so that the scale factor is adjusted before `paint()` is called:

```
public void reshape(int x, int y, int w, int h)
{
    adjustScale(w, h);
    super.reshape(x, y, w, h);
}
```

The full listings for `PolarPoint` (on the CD-ROM in `javadevhdbk\ ch03\PolarPoint.java`) and `Polar` (in `javadevhdbk\ch03\ Polar.java`) appear below:

PolarPoint.java

```
/*
 * The PolarPoint class describes a point in polar coordinates.  Used
 * by the Polar component class for storing its value.  Also placed in
 * the arg field of posted events; clients see this as the 2nd
 * param of action().
 */

public class PolarPoint implements Cloneable
{
    public double           rho;
    public double           theta;

    public PolarPoint(double rho, double theta)
    {
        this.rho = rho;
        this.theta = theta;
    }

    public Object clone()
    {
        try
        {
            return(super.clone());
        }
        catch (CloneNotSupportedException e)
```

```
        {
            return(null);
        }
    }
}
```

Polar.java

```java
import        java.awt.*;

public class Polar extends Canvas
{
    private PolarPoint              value;
    private double                  maxRho;
    private double                  unitsPerPixel;
    private boolean                 dragging = false;
    private Color                   dragColor = Color.blue;
    private boolean                 showTextValue = true;

    public Polar()
    {
        this(100.0, 0.0, 100.0);
    }

    public Polar(double initRho, double initTheta, double maxRho)
    {
        value = new PolarPoint(initRho, initTheta);
        this.maxRho = maxRho;
        setBackground(Color.white);
    }

    public void setDragColor(Color c)
    {
        dragColor = c;
    }

    public void enableText(boolean b)
    {
        showTextValue = b;
    }
```

```
public void setValue(PolarPoint newValue)
{
    value = newValue;
    repaint();
}

public void setValue(double newRho, double newTheta)
{
    setValue(new PolarPoint(newRho, newTheta));
}

public PolarPoint getValue()
{
    return((PolarPoint)(value.clone()));
}

/*
 * Adjust scale so that the largest permissible value takes up
 * not quite the entire component.
 */
private void adjustScale(int w, int h)
{
    unitsPerPixel = 2.0 * maxRho / Math.min(w, h);
    unitsPerPixel *= 1.1;
}

/*
 * When the component resizes, the scale needs to be adjusted.
 * Note that resize() does not need to be overridden, because
 * resize() calls reshape().
 */
public void reshape(int x, int y, int w, int h)
{
    adjustScale(w, h);
    super.reshape(x, y, w, h);
}

public void paint(Graphics g)
{
    int     radiusPix;
    int     centerX;
    int     centerY;
```

```java
        radiusPix = (int)(value.rho / unitsPerPixel);
        centerX = size().width / 2;
        centerY = size().height / 2;
        int ulx = centerX - radiusPix;
        int uly = centerY - radiusPix;

        // Draw axes in light gray.
        g.setColor(Color.lightGray);
        g.drawLine(centerX, 0, centerX, size().height);
        g.drawLine(0, centerY, size().width, centerY);

        // Draw label string in upper-left corner.
        g.setColor(getForeground());
        if (showTextValue)
        {
            g.drawString((value.rho + ", " + value.theta),
                         5, size().height-5);
        }

        // If dragging, subsequent drawing will use the drag color.
        if (dragging)
        {
            g.setColor(dragColor);
        }

        // Draw ring.
        g.drawOval(ulx, uly, 2*radiusPix, 2*radiusPix);

        // Draw dot.
        int arrowTipX = centerX +
                        (int)(radiusPix * Math.cos(value.theta));
        int arrowTipY = centerY -
                        (int)(radiusPix * Math.sin(value.theta));
        g.fillOval(arrowTipX-3, arrowTipY-3, 7, 7);

        // Draw line from center to dot, space permitting.
        if (radiusPix > 5)
        {
            g.drawLine(centerX, centerY, arrowTipX, arrowTipY);
        }
    }
```

```
/*
 *  Converts pixel coordinates x and y to polar coordinates,
 *  storing the result in dest,
 */
private void xyToPolarPoint(int x, int y, PolarPoint dest)
{
    int deltaX = x - size().width/2;
    int deltaY = size().height/2 - y;
    double deltaLen = Math.sqrt(deltaX*deltaX + deltaY*deltaY);
    dest.rho = unitsPerPixel * deltaLen;
    dest.rho = Math.min(dest.rho, maxRho);
    dest.theta = Math.atan2(deltaY, deltaX);
    while (dest.theta < 0.0)
        dest.theta += 2*Math.PI;
}


public boolean mouseDown(Event e, int x, int y)
{
    xyToPolarPoint(x, y, value);
    repaint();
    return(true);
}


/*
 *  Refreshes the screen.  Imitates a ScrollBar by posting a
 *  SCROLL_ABSOLUTE event.
 */
public boolean mouseDrag(Event e, int x, int y)
{
    dragging = true;
    xyToPolarPoint(x, y, value);
    repaint();
    Event e1 = copyEvent(e, Event.SCROLL_ABSOLUTE, value.clone());
    deliverEvent(e1);
    return(true);
}


/*
 *  Refreshes the screen and posts an ACTION_EVENT.
 */
```

```
public boolean mouseUp(Event e, int x, int y)
{
    dragging = false;
    xyToPolarPoint(x, y, value);
    repaint();
    Event el = copyEvent(e, Event.ACTION_EVENT, value.clone());
    deliverEvent(el);
    return(true);
}


/*
 *  Returns a duplicate of the specified event.  Required because
 *  Event's clone() method is protected.  Modifies the clone's id
 *  and arg fields as specified by the caller.  Sets the target to
 *  be this component.
 */
private Event copyEvent(Event eIn, int id, Object arg)
{
    Event eOut = new Event(this, id, arg);    // 1st arg is target
    eOut.x = eIn.x;
    eOut.y = eIn.y;
    eOut.when = eIn.when;
    return(eOut);
}


public Dimension minimumSize()
{
    return(new Dimension(50, 50));
}


public Dimension preferredSize()
{
    return(new Dimension(50, 50));
}
}
```

The `Polar` component class may now be used like any other component. Figure 3.4 shows a simple applet that contains a polar and a textfield.

FIGURE 3.4

Polar test program

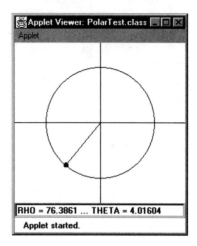

The source code for the test program is on the CD-ROM in `javadevhdbk\ch03\PolarTest.java` (the bytecode is in `PolarTest.class`) and appears below:

PolarTest.java

```
import      java.awt.*;
import      java.applet.Applet;

public class PolarTest extends Applet
{
    Polar       polar;
    TextField   tf;

    public void init()
    {
        setLayout(new BorderLayout());
          polar = new Polar();
        add("Center", polar);
        tf = new TextField("0, 0");
        add("South", tf);
    }

    public boolean action(Event e, Object ob)
    {
```

```
        if (e.target == polar)
            tf.setText(ob.toString());
        return true;
    }
}
```

Aggregation:
The *ThreeWay* Component

Sometimes absolute precision is required when specifying a number; sometimes a fair approximation is good enough. The `Polar` component of the last example is imprecise, as it receives freehand input and its resolution is limited to radius increments of one pixel. It takes a textfield to really input a number exactly.

The next example offers users a choice of three different levels of precision for entering an int: the complete accuracy of a textfield, the moderate accuracy of a scrollbar, and the vagueness of a set of radio buttons. (The less accurate components will be easier to use.) The resulting component will be called a *threeway*. The `ThreeWay` class goes a few steps beyond the traditional numeric scrollbar coupled with a nearby label or read-only textfield to reflect its value. We want three ways to write a number *and* three ways to read one. Again, the design issues listed in the section *Design Considerations* provide a way in which to move through the process.

Look and Feel

First, consider how the `ThreeWay` should display its value. Of the three elements—scrollbar, textfield, and set of radio button checkboxes—the visually dominant one is the scrollbar. The textfield goes to the right of the scrollbar to conserve screen space. Above the scrollbar is a row of five radio checkboxes. If the component's value is at or near its minimum, the leftmost radio button will be selected, and this button is to be positioned above the left end of the scrollbar, which, of course, is the slider position that represents the scrollbar's own minimum value. The rightmost radio button is positioned above the extreme right-hand position of the scrollbar, and it is selected if the component's value is at or near its maximum. The three radio buttons in the middle designate values that are approximately the half and quarters of the component's range. Simply stated, every subcomponent will do its best to reflect the threeway's current value.

Figure 3.5 below shows a threeway. This screenshot comes from a Windows 95 machine; scrollbar and checkbox appearance vary greatly from platform to platform.

FIGURE 3.5

The ThreeWay component

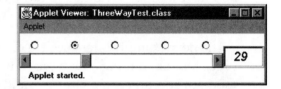

> **WARNING**
> On Motif platforms such as Sun workstations, the triangular arrow buttons of a scrollbar can grow without bounds. A very tall horizontal scrollbar will have very tall arrow buttons, and the buttons are equilateral triangles, so the width will be about .9 times the height. This encroaches on space that would otherwise be available to the slider. A tall scrollbar, no matter how wide it might be, could be useless because its slider's range is only a few pixels, and so it is important to restrict the scrollbar's vertical growth.

> **WARNING**
> On Windows platforms the arrows are well-behaved. They lie inside rectangular boxes, and while the boxes grow taller, the arrows do not; a tall scrollbar has tall, narrow buttons that contain small triangles. Unfortunately, in pre-1.1 releases of the JDK there are several miscellaneous bugs in the Windows implementation of the `Scrollbar` class.

With the manner by which the threeway will display its value established, it is now time to ask how users should interact with the new component. In this example, the answer is simple: users should manipulate the scrollbar, the textfield, and the checkboxes in the expected way, and in no other way.

At this stage of the process a subclassing strategy should be decided on, but in this case it has been obvious from the outset: we will subclass `Panel` and populate it with standard subcomponents. This is the Aggregation strategy, and it has the merit that users interact with familiar devices. The programming task benefits from object reuse; the main task is to get the subcomponents to interact properly, and there is more to this than may be immediately obvious. The components will be referred to by instance variables called `textfield`, `scrollbar`, and `checkboxes[]`.

It is now time to consider programmatically modifying the component's appearance. As with the previous example of the `Polar` class, the `setForeground()`, `setBackground()`, and `setFont()` methods can be made available to clients. There is a bit of work to be done to support `setForeground()` and `setBackground()`. Because subpanels are likely to be used to lay out `ThreeWay`'s components, there will be a modest containment hierarchy, and any intermediate panels—in addition to the main containing panel and the visible components (the scrollbar, the textfield, and the checkboxes)—will need to have their foreground and background colors set. Consider `setForeground()`, which must be overridden. One could simply call `setForeground()` on everything, component by component, but this would introduce a maintenance risk. Somebody could change the containment structure, introducing a new subpanel, and forget to modify `setForeground()` accordingly. Here, a recursive algorithm is used to call `setForeground()` on all components within the threeway panel:

```
public void setForeground(Color color)
{
    super.setForeground(color);
    setForegndRecursive(this, color);
}
```

```
private void setForegndRecursive(Container parent, Color
                                                  color)
{
    Component children[] = parent.getComponents();
    for (int i=0; i<children.length; i++)
    {
        children[i].setForeground(color);
        if (children[i] instanceof Container)
        {
            setForegndRecursive((Container)children[i],
                                                  color);
        }
    }
}
```

We do much the same thing for the overridden setBackground() method. There is no need to go this far for set-Font(), as the only child that actually uses this font is the textfield. Next, consider how to limit input values. The ThreeWay class is not so different from the Scrollbar class; certainly there should be an upper and a lower limit. In the constructor for Scrollbar, the initial value appears before the minimum value, which comes before the maximum. This is the order maintained in ThreeWay's constructor. The constructor's calling sequence is: ThreeWay(int value, int minValue, int maxValue).

The Component's Value

The next issue is storing, setting, and retrieving the component's value. Storing and retrieving are simple. There is a private instance variable called value and a public accessor called getValue():

```
private int      value;
         . . .
public int getValue()
    {
        return(value);
    }
```

Setting requires updating the visible subcomponents. Setting the scrollbar and textfield values is easy. For the checkboxes an instance variable called `spreadPerRadio` is needed to help decide which checkbox is to be turned on. Because there are five checkboxes, the computation of `spreadPerRadio` (performed in the constructor) is:

```
spreadPerRadio = (float)(maxValue-minValue) / 4.0f;
```

The methods to revise the visible components are as follows:

```
private void reviseScrollbar()
    {
        scrollbar.setValue(value);
    }

    private void reviseTextfield()
    {
        textfield.setText((new Integer(value)).toString());
    }

    private void reviseRadios()
    {
        float f = (value - minValue) / spreadPerRadio;
        int nth = Math.round(f);
        if (nth < 0)
        {
            nth = 0;
        }
        else if (nth > 4)
        {
            nth = 4;
        }

        cbgroup.setCurrent(checkboxes[nth]);
    }
```

Next to be addressed is the question of when to deliver action events. Certainly an action from the textfield or the checkboxes should precipitate an action from the `ThreeWay` itself. Because scrollbars do not send action, it stands to reason that `ThreeWay` should not post action when the scrollbar moves. As with the previous example of the

`Polar` class, it is important that the component not send continuous action events. The posting of action provides the opportunity to send some kind of information in the event's `arg` field. The only useful information would be the current value, as an `Integer`.

Is it appropriate to deliver other events besides action? Indeed it is, because clients may want to receive continuous feedback from the scrollbar. From a client programmer's point of view, the most easily understood scheme is to deliver whatever event types are received from the scrollbar. We can still put an `Integer` representing the current value in the event's `arg` field.

Event Posting

The next question is how `ThreeWay` should post events. There is a straightforward approach, which breaks down on inspection. It is tempting to observe that our visible components and invisible subpanels will all return `false` from `action()`, so all actions will ripple out and eventually be handled by the `ThreeWay`. According to this argument, `ThreeWay`'s `action()` method should be responsible for fielding all actions from the subcomponents; the method should revise the internally stored value and update the appearance of those components that did not send the action, so that they reflect the current value. This works with a `ThreeWay`, but what happens if somebody wants to subclass `ThreeWay` to make it self-contained? The subclass will override `action()`, which will no longer maintain appearance and value, but instead will do whatever the subclass' version does. It could be made to work by documenting a lot of instructions about testing `event.target` and calling `super.action()` if the event needs to go to the `ThreeWay` superclass, but whenever subclassing and overriding are this complicated it is an indication of misuse of objects. An object should hide implementation details, not require an understanding of them.

The events will have to be handled before they arrive at the threeway, meaning the visible components will have to take care of them.

And this in turn means subclassing such components as a
SubTextfield, a SubScrollbar, and five SubCheckboxes.

Each self-contained subclass will catch its own events and inform
the threeway, not by delivering an event but by making a method
call. Arguments should specify the caller (as the other components
will have to be updated, but not the caller itself), the triggering event,
and the new value. The method looks like this:

```
void updateValue(Object sender, Event trigger, int newValue)
    {
        value = newValue;

        if (sender != scrollbar)
        {
            reviseScrollbar();
        }
        if (sender != textfield)
        {
            reviseTextfield();
        }
        if (!(sender instanceof Checkbox))
        {
            reviseRadios();
        }

        Event e = copyEvent(trigger, trigger.id,
                            new Integer(newValue));
        deliverEvent(e);
    }
```

The copyEvent() method in the next-to-last line above is taken
directly from the Polar class example. It constructs a new instance
of Event based on an original one. The id and the arg are specified
in the argument list, and the target is set to this—that is, the
instance of ThreeWay. updateValue() revises all visible components except the sender, and then delivers an event to itself.

What should be done when the component resizes? The Polar class
had to adjust its scale factor. The ThreeWay class has no comparable

internal state to revise. The scrollbar has an internal scale factor, but the class takes care of it automatically. Our only responsibility is to ensure that the layout looks reasonable no matter how the ThreeWay gets resized. This means we do not have to override resize() or reshape(), but we do have to build a robust containment hierarchy in our constructor.

As mentioned at the beginning of this section, scrollbars should be constrained in the vertical direction. On the other hand, when the ThreeWay grows horizontally, all the new pixels should be given to the scrollbar; the textfield is always wide enough, and there is no benefit in making it any wider. (See Chapter 4, *Layout Managers*, for more information on layout managers and how they constrain components.) This suggests a border layout manager, with the scrollbar occupying the South region. On the other hand, we need to align a row of checkboxes above the scrollbar, and this suggests a grid layout with two rows of one column. There are probably several feasible solutions (there usually are). Here, the checkboxes are put in a panel (called btnPanel), and the btnPanel is placed above the scrollbar in a 2 x 1 grid.

The btnPanel uses a grid bag layout manager to keep the checkboxes centered in the bottoms of their cells. So far we have the structure shown in Figure 3.6, which introduces a new informal notation. Each container is labeled reasonably close to its upper-left corner. The label's format is *name @ position u layout*, where *name* is the container instance variable handle, *position* is its position within its own container (for example, "N" for north in a border, "2,1" for column 2 row 1 in a grid), and *layout* is the type of layout manager used by the container (B for border, G for grid, F for flow, GB for grid bag, C for card). Noncontainer components are labeled near the center, if at all.

The btnSbarPanel will ensure that the checkboxes stay above the scrollbar, and will be put at South of some other panel, whose only job is to constrain btnSbarPanel from vertical growth. This new panel is called restrictorPanel, and it contains only the single child.

FIGURE 3.6

Containment of
`btnSbarPanel`

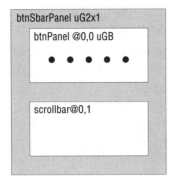

The `restrictorPanel` is put at Center of the `ThreeWay` so that it can grow in both directions: horizontal growth will be passed to `btnSbarPanel`; in the case of vertical growth, `restrictorPanel` will grow taller but `btnSbarPanel` will not—rather, it will stick to the bottom of `restrictorPanel`. This produces the structure shown in Figure 3.7.

FIGURE 3.7

Containment: more
details

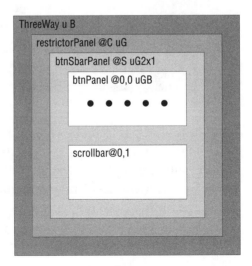

The textfield should go at East, to restrict its horizontal growth (its constructor knows how many digits wide it needs to be, so additional width would be a waste). But it would also be convenient if it could go at South, so that it is horizontally aligned with the scrollbar. An extra panel, called tfPanel, is needed. If tfPanel had to contain several components, a grid bag layout manager might be in order, but in this simple case a border, with the textfield inside tfPanel at South, is sufficient. This completes our design of ThreeWay's containment hierarchy, which is shown in Figure 3.8.

FIGURE 3.8

Complete containment of ThreeWay

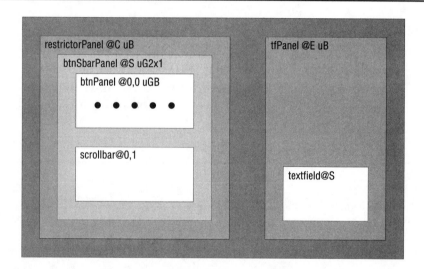

The last step is to make certain that ThreeWay can be subclassed to be self-contained. This is assured, thanks to all the work done in creating subclasses for the visible components. The subclasses do not use the event mechanism to communicate with the ThreeWay, and the ThreeWay does not have a handleEvent() or an action() of its own, so subclasses of ThreeWay can do whatever they like in their own handleEvent() and action() methods.

Here is the full listing of ThreeWay. The code also appears on the CD-ROM, in javadevhdbk\ch03\SubScrollbar.java and

SubScrollbar.class. There are four classes in all: SubScrollbar, SubTextField, SubCheckbox, and ThreeWay.SubScrollbar.java.

SubScrollbar.java

```java
import  java.awt.*;

public class SubScrollbar extends Scrollbar
{
    private ThreeWay        threeWay;

    SubScrollbar(ThreeWay threeWay, int val, int minVal, int maxVal)
    {
        super(Scrollbar.HORIZONTAL, val, 0, minVal, maxVal);
        this.threeWay = threeWay;
    }

    public boolean handleEvent(Event e)
    {
        threeWay.updateValue(this, e, getValue());
        return(true);
    }
}
```

SubTextField.java

```java
import  java.awt.*;

public class SubTextField extends TextField
{
    private ThreeWay        threeWay;

    /*
     * Constructor has to determine maximum number of characters
     * without using any intermediate lines of code, since call
     * to super's constructor must be 1st line of any constructor.
     */
    SubTextField(ThreeWay threeWay, int initVal,
                int minVal, int maxVal)
    {
        super((new Integer(initVal)).toString(),
```

```
                  1+Math.max((new Integer(minVal)).toString().length(),
                            (new Integer(maxVal)).toString().length()));
        this.threeWay = threeWay;
    }

    public boolean action(Event e, Object ob)
    {
        threeWay.updateValue(this, e, Integer.parseInt(getText()));
        return(true);
    }
}
```

SubCheckbox.java

```
import   java.awt.*;

public class SubCheckbox extends Checkbox
{
    private static int       nth = 0;
    private ThreeWay         threeWay;
    private int              value;

    /*
     *  Constructor must determine what value is represented by this
     *  checkbox, based on how many others have previously been
     *  constructed.
     */
    SubCheckbox(ThreeWay threeWay, CheckboxGroup group, boolean state,
                int minVal, int maxVal)
    {
        super("",  group,  state);

        this.threeWay = threeWay;

        if (nth < 4)
        {
            int range = maxVal - minVal + 1;
            value = minVal + nth*range/4;
        }
        else
        {
            value = maxVal;
        }
```

```
            nth++;
    }

    public boolean action(Event e, Object ob)
    {
        threeWay.updateValue(this, e, value);
        return(true);
    }
}
```

ThreeWay.java

```
import      java.awt.*;

public class ThreeWay extends Panel
{
    private SubScrollbar        scrollbar;
    private SubTextField        textfield;
    private CheckboxGroup       cbgroup;
    private SubCheckbox         checkboxes[];
    private int                 minValue;
    private int                 maxValue;
    private int                 value;
    private float               spreadPerRadio;

    ThreeWay(int value, int minValue, int maxValue)
    {
        this.minValue = minValue;
        this.maxValue = maxValue;
        this.value = value;

        checkboxes = new SubCheckbox[5];

        setLayout(new BorderLayout());

        Panel tfPanel = new Panel();
        tfPanel.setLayout(new BorderLayout());
        textfield = new SubTextField(this, value, minValue, maxValue);
        tfPanel.add("South", textfield);
        add("East", tfPanel);

        Panel btnPanel = new Panel();
        GridBagLayout gbl = new GridBagLayout();
```

```
btnPanel.setLayout(gbl);
GridBagConstraints gbc = new GridBagConstraints();
gbc.gridwidth = gbc.gridheight = 1;
gbc.weightx = gbc.weighty = 1;
gbc.gridy = 0;
gbc.fill = GridBagConstraints.NONE;
gbc.anchor = GridBagConstraints.SOUTH;
cbgroup = new CheckboxGroup();
for (int i=0; i<5; i++)
{
    checkboxes[i] = new SubCheckbox(this, cbgroup,
                                    (i==0),
                                    minValue, maxValue);
    gbc.gridx = i;
    if (i > 2)
    {
        gbc.anchor = GridBagConstraints.SOUTHEAST;
    }
    gbl.setConstraints(checkboxes[i], gbc);
    btnPanel.add(checkboxes[i]);
}
spreadPerRadio = (float)(maxValue-minValue) / 4.0f;

Panel btnSbarPanel = new Panel();
btnSbarPanel.setLayout(new GridLayout(2, 1));
btnSbarPanel.add(btnPanel);
scrollbar = new SubScrollbar(this, value, minValue, maxValue);
btnSbarPanel.add(scrollbar);
Panel restrictorPanel = new Panel();
restrictorPanel.setLayout(new BorderLayout());
restrictorPanel.add("South", btnSbarPanel);
add("Center", restrictorPanel);

reviseScrollbar();
reviseTextfield();
reviseRadios();
}

public int getValue()
{
    return(value);
}
```

```
public void setValue(int newValue)
{
    value = newValue;
    reviseScrollbar();
    reviseTextfield();
    reviseRadios();
}

/*
 *  Called by the visible subcomponents when they are selected.
 *  The other components are revised and an event is posted to
 *  this, with the same id as the event which was detected by the
 *  subcomponent.  This will be ACTION_EVENT for the textfield and
 *  checkboxes, and some kind of scrolling event for the scrollbar.
 */
void updateValue(Object sender, Event trigger, int newVal)
{
    value = newVal;

    if (sender != scrollbar)
    {
        reviseScrollbar();
    }
    if (sender != textfield)
    {
        reviseTextfield();
    }
    if (!(sender instanceof Checkbox))
    {
        reviseRadios();
    }

    Event e = copyEvent(trigger, trigger.id, new Integer(newVal));
    deliverEvent(e);
}

/*
 *  Returns a duplicate of the specified event.  Required because
 *  Event's clone() method is protected.  Modifies the clone's id
 *  and arg fields as specified by the caller.  Sets the target to
 *  be this component.
 */
private Event copyEvent(Event eIn, int id, Object arg)
```

```
    {
        Event eOut = new Event(this, id, arg);   // 1st arg is target
        eOut.x = eIn.x;
        eOut.y = eIn.y;
        eOut.when = eIn.when;
        return(eOut);
    }

    private void reviseScrollbar()
    {
        scrollbar.setValue(value);
    }

    private void reviseTextfield()
    {
        textfield.setText((new Integer(value)).toString());
    }

    private void reviseRadios()
    {
        float f = (value - minValue) / spreadPerRadio;
        int nth = Math.round(f);
        if (nth < 0)
        {
            nth = 0;
        }
        else if (nth > 4)
        {
            nth = 4;
        }

        cbgroup.setCurrent(checkboxes[nth]);
    }

    /*
     *  Set background color of everything by setting it on this
     *  container and recursively on all children.
     */
    public void setBackground(Color color)
    {
        super.setBackground(color);
        setBackgndRecursive(this, color);
    }
```

```java
    private void setBackgndRecursive(Container parent, Color color)
    {
        Component children[] = parent.getComponents();
        for (int i=0; i<children.length; i++)
        {
            children[i].setBackground(color);
            if (children[i] instanceof Container)
            {
                setBackgndRecursive((Container)children[i], color);
            }
        }
    }


    /*
     * Set foreground color of everything by setting it on this
     * container and recursively on all children.
     */
    public void setForeground(Color color)
    {
        super.setForeground(color);
        setForegndRecursive(this, color);
    }

    private void setForegndRecursive(Container parent, Color color)
    {
        Component children[] = parent.getComponents();
        for (int i=0; i<children.length; i++)
        {
            children[i].setForeground(color);
            if (children[i] instanceof Container)
            {
                setForegndRecursive((Container)children[i], color);
            }
        }
    }

    public void setFont(Font font)
    {
        textfield.setFont(font);
    }
}
```

Because all the complexity has been encapsulated inside `ThreeWay`, the class is very easy to use. The applet code below updates its textfield with the value of its threeway whenever the user clicks the Show button. The applet is shown in Figure 3.9, followed by the code. It is located on the CD-ROM in the file `javadevhdbk\ch03\ThreeWayTest.java`.

FIGURE 3.9

A simple applet that uses
`ThreeWay`

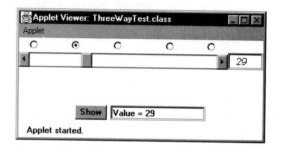

ThreeWayTest.java

```java
import      java.awt.*;
import      java.applet.Applet;

public class ThreeWayTest extends Applet
{
    ThreeWay     threeway;
    Button       button;
    TextField    textfield;

    public void init()
    {
        setLayout(new BorderLayout());
        threeway = new ThreeWay(23, 0, 100);
        threeway.setFont(new Font("Helvetica", Font.ITALIC, 14));
        add("North", threeway);

        Panel panel = new Panel();
        button = new Button("Show");
        panel.add(button);
        textfield = new TextField("Value = 23", 15);
```

```
        panel.add(textfield);
        add("South", panel);
    }

    public boolean action(Event ev, Object ob)
    {
        if (ev.target == button)
        {
            textfield.setText("Value = " + threeway.getValue());
        }
        return true;
    }
}
```

Subclassing a Standard Component: Validating Textfields

Many programs require text validation: information typed in must be numeric, fall within a certain range, or match a certain pattern. The standard AWT `TextField` has no facilities for validation, and so requires that a custom component be created. For this example, three alternatives that offer increasing sophistication will be developed.

Again, the discussion will be guided by the list of questions from the section *Design Considerations*. Many of the questions have obvious answers. The first two issues concern displaying a value and entering a new value. Obviously, a validating textfield should display its value the same way any textfield displays its value, and users should enter new values by typing. The issue of what to do when an invalid value is entered will be addressed later. There is no choice as to subclassing strategy: a single component, `TextField`, requires enhancement. To begin, a `TextField` subclass called `IntTextField`, which only accepts nonnegative integer input, will be created; refinements will be made later.

Programmatically modifying an `IntTextField` appearance is straightforward. Because `IntTextField` is a simple subclass, the `setForeground()`, `setBackground()`, and `setFont()` methods are inherited from `TextField`, and will function as expected without any additional effort.

The next issue is how to restrict values. For now, the class will insist on nonnegative integer values, and that will be the only restriction. When the user types in any character other than one of the ten digits, the input is to be discarded. When an illegal character is typed into an `IntTextField`, the character should be ignored; legal input should be accepted; `keyDown()` will be overridden. The only keyboard events of interest are from arrow keys, control keys (such as Backspace, Delete, Enter, and so on), and of course from the 10 digit keys. If a character is valid, it is passed to the superclass' `keyDown()` so that it can be displayed in the textfield. If the character is not valid, `IntTextField`'s `keyDown()` returns `true`; the event is handled by not doing anything, and neither the superclass nor the container is any the wiser.

NOTE   On all Java platforms, a key value that is less than 32 indicates a control character. Values of 1004 through 1007 represent arrow keys.

Here is `IntTextField`'s `keyDown()` method:

```
public boolean keyDown(Event ev, int key)
{
    char c = (char)key;
    if ((c >= 1004  &&  c <= 1007)  ||          // Arrow key
        c < 32                      ||          // Ctrl char
        (c >= '0'  &&  c <= '9'))               // Digit
        return(super.keyDown(ev, key));
    else
        return(true);                           // Invalid
}
```

The discussion now turns to storing, setting, and retrieving the value. A textfield knows what string it contains, so any instance variable created for this purpose would be redundant. Redundant data representation is a maintenance risk, and unnecessary work besides, so the textfield is allowed to hold the value. Setting the value can happen during construction or during execution. Client programmers need to specify an initial value, and one that is valid. Two constructors are offered below: one takes an int that is the initial value, the other takes an initial value and a field width. If the initial value is negative, it is forced to zero:

```
public IntTextfield(int val)
{
    super((new Integer(val<0 ? 0 : val)).toString());
}

public IntTextfield(int val, int width)
{
    super((new Integer(val<0 ? 0 : val)).toString(), width);
}
```

As for setting the value after construction, there are several alternatives. Programmers expect textfields to have a setText() method. It should be impossible to set an invalid value; setText() is therefore overridden so that it checks the new value. (Methods elsewhere in the class that set the text value take the precaution of calling super .setText() rather than the overridden version.) There are also two versions of a setValue() method available: one takes string input (and is therefore identical to the setText() method), and the other takes int input. Strings that are supposed to represent integers are checked by calling the static parseInt() method of the Integer class.

```
public void setText(String s)
{
    setValue(s);
}

public void setValue(String s)
{
    int     val;
```

```
    try
    {
        val = Integer.parseInt(s);
    }
    catch (NumberFormatException nfex)
    {
        super.setText("0");
        return;
    }

    if (val >= 0)
    {
        super.setText(s);
    }
    else
    {
        super.setText("0");
    }
}

public void setValue(int value)
{
    super.setText((new Integer(value)).toString());
}
```

The value can be retrieved as a string by calling the inherited `getText()` method, but that string most likely would be immediately converted to an int; so an additional accessor called `getValue()` is offered:

```
public int getValue()
{
    return((new Integer(getText())).intValue());
}
```

There is no risk of the Integer constructor's throwing an exception because the text value is restricted to the 10 digit characters.

Now consider when `IntTextField` should send an action event. Because it is a kind of `TextField`, the expectation will be that action is to be sent when the user types **Enter**. The subclass does not need to override `action()`, so this behavior is produced automatically.

Next, look at posting other events. Any events that do not represent invalid input are sent to the superclass, so in this respect `IntTextField` behaves exactly like `TextField`. There is no reason to interfere with this. There is no issue concerning how to deliver events, as this is done by the superclass. Resizing is also not an issue. `IntTextField` resizes just like `TextField`.

Finally, there needs to be assurance that `IntTextField` can be safely subclassed. As far as overriding `action()` is concerned, there is no problem. Because `IntTextField` does not override `action()`, a self-contained subclass can do what it likes in its own `action()`. However, because `IntTextField` overrides `keyDown()`, subclasses should not do so, or should exercise extreme caution in doing so.

Here is the complete listing for `IntTextField` (located on the CD-ROM in `javadevhdbk\ch03\IntTextField.java` and `IntTextField.class`):

IntTextField.java

```java
import        java.awt.*;

public class IntTextField extends TextField
{
    private int         minValue;
    private int         maxValue;

    public IntTextField(int val)
    {
        super((new Integer(val<0 ? 0 : val)).toString());
    }

    public IntTextField(int val, int width)
    {
        super((new Integer(val<0 ? 0 : val)).toString(), width);
    }

    public void setText(String s)
    {
```

```
            setValue(s);
    }

    public void setValue(String s)
    {
        int     val;

        try
        {
            val = Integer.parseInt(s);
        }
        catch (NumberFormatException nfex)
        {
            super.setText("0");
            return;
        }

        if (val >= 0)
        {
            super.setText(s);
        }
        else
        {
            super.setText("0");
        }
    }

    public void setValue(int value)
    {
        super.setText((new Integer(value)).toString());
    }

    public int getValue()
    {
        return((new Integer(getText())).intValue());
    }

    public boolean keyDown(Event ev, int key)
    {
        char c = (char)key;
        if ((c >= 1004  &&  c <= 1007)  ||            // Arrow key
            c < 32                      ||            // Ctrl char
```

```
        (c >= '0'  &&  c <= '9'))                    // Digit
            return(super.keyDown(ev, key));
    else
            return(true);                            // Invalid
    }
}
```

Postvalidation

The `IntTextField` subclass provides keystroke-by-keystroke validation. We might call this *prevalidation*, because characters are checked before they are entered into the textfield. Prevalidation does not consider the state of the component—that is, it only examines the keystroke itself, not what the value of the component *would be* if the keystroke were permitted. If there are conditions to be placed on the entire value of the textfield, not every keystroke can be checked; the value may temporarily need to take on invalid values. For example, if a textfield requires entry of a telephone number, any string of less than seven characters cannot possibly be valid. But the only way to turn a blank textfield into a valid one is to have it contain first one digit (not valid), then two (still not valid), and so on. For more complicated data formats, such as driver's license numbers, transitory user input errors are to be expected. The user should be given a chance to correct the error with backspaces and deletes.

More sophisticated validation requires that validation should occur when the user indicates that the input operation is over. This is called *postvalidation*, because validation happens after the value becomes visible, which suggests validating on Enter. A mechanism should also be provided for validating under arbitrary program control, in case clients need to validate on loss of focus or some other trigger. This just requires making sure the validation method is public.

The next example is a class called `FloatTextField`, which only accepts floating point input. Actually this is not quite accurate— `FloatTextField` uses the `Float` class to parse its input, so our subclass accepts anything `Float` accepts. `Float` accepts a string if it *contains* a float. Extraneous characters do not make the input invalid (usually). Because the subject is component subclassing, not string validation, this is acceptable for now, but the subsequent example shows part of a more rigorous solution.

FloatTextField offers four overloaded methods for setting the value. The different possible input types are string, int, float, and double.

FloatTextField should validate when the user types **Enter**, which causes an action event. But it is better to validate the input in handleEvent(), rather than in action(), because this leaves action() available for overriding by subclasses. handleEvent() passes all nonaction events on to the superclass. An action event requires validation. If the input is not valid, the textfield is restored so that it contains the last known string value that *was* valid, and the event is suppressed by returning true. If the text is valid, the event's arg field is modified, putting in a Float that represents the current value and action() called. Clearly, this works if FloatTextField is not subclassed. A subclass of FloatTextField should leave handleEvent() alone and override action(). When the user types **Enter**, handleEvent() is called. Because the subclass has not overridden, it is FloatTextField's version that gets called. A valid input causes a call to action(), which presumably has been overridden by the subclass.

FloatTextField's handleEvent() looks like this:

```
public boolean handleEvent(Event ev)
{
    String        textValue;

    if (ev.id != Event.ACTION_EVENT)
    {
        return(super.handleEvent(ev));
    }

    textValue = getText();
    if (!validate(textValue))
    {
```

```
            // Invalid input.  Reset text, do not pass the event on.
            super.setText(lastValidTextValue);
            return(true);
        }

        // Valid input.  Modify arg and pass the event on.
        lastValidTextValue = textValue;
        ev.arg = new Float(textValue);
        return(action(ev, ev.arg));
    }
```

Note the use of `lastValidTextValue`, which is an instance variable of type `String`. When a valid input is processed, `lastValidTextValue` is set to that value. When an invalid input is detected, the textfield is reset to `lastValidTextValue`.

The following class listing is located on the CD-ROM in `javadevhdbk\ch03\FloatTextField.java` (the bytecode is in `FloatTextField.class`) and is listed here in its entirety:

FloatTextField.java

```
import        java.awt.*;


public class FloatTextField extends TextField
{
    private String      lastValidTextValue;

    public FloatTextField(double value, int width)
    {
        super((new Double(value)).toString(), width);
        lastValidTextValue = getText();
        if (!validate(lastValidTextValue))
        {
            lastValidTextValue = "0.0";
            setText(lastValidTextValue);
        }
    }

    public void setText(String s)
```

```
    {
        setValue(s);
    }

    public void setValue(String s)
    {
        if (!validate(s))
            s = "0.0";
        lastValidTextValue = s;
        super.setText(s);
    }

    public void setValue(double d)
    {
        String s = (new Double(d)).toString();
        lastValidTextValue = s;
        super.setText(s);
    }

    public void setValue(float f)
    {
        setValue((double)f);
    }

    public void setValue(int i)
    {
        setValue((double)i);
    }

    public double getValue()
    {
        return (new Double(lastValidTextValue)).doubleValue();
    }

    private boolean validate(String s)
    {
        try
        {
            Double.valueOf(s);
        }
        catch (NumberFormatException nfx)
        {
```

```
                    return(false);
                }

            return(true);
        }

        public boolean handleEvent(Event ev)
        {
            String      textValue;

            if (ev.id != Event.ACTION_EVENT)
            {
                return(super.handleEvent(ev));
            }

            textValue = getText();
            if (!validate(textValue))
            {
                // Invalid input.  Reset text, do not pass the event
on.
                super.setText(lastValidTextValue);
                return(true);
            }

            // Valid input.  Modify arg and pass the event on.
            lastValidTextValue = textValue;
            ev.arg = new Float(textValue);
            return(action(ev, ev.arg));
        }
```

There is a sample applet on the CD-ROM at `javadevhdbk\ch03\`
`IntTextFieldTest.java` that just displays an `IntTextField`
and a `FloatTextField`. Readers are invited to run the applet and
verify that the two subclasses behave as expected.

Encapsulated Validation

Sometimes very complex validation is required. A driver's license is
a complicated string, especially if multiple countries and the multiple political units within those countries are taken into account.

Sometimes a valid field is best described by a regular expression, but there is no regular expression pattern matcher in Java. What would be most useful would be a class—called `ValidatingTextField` here—that uses an object of another class to perform validation. The other class could validate in whatever way it chose: regular expression, driver's license, zip code, and so on. That way there would be no need to use only one subclass of `TextField` for every foreseeable input format. The `ValidatingTextField` does not even need to know what kind of validation is being performed. Its constructor is passed an object, and, when needed, the `ValidatingTextField` calls that object's `validate()` method.

The instance of `ValidatingTextField` does not need any knowledge about the validating object—not even its class—provided that there really is a method called `validate()` that takes a `String` and returns a `boolean`. But this one condition must be assured, or the alleged validator will throw an exception when called. There is a way to make the compiler and the runtime environment guarantee that the validator has a `validate()` method; the interface definition is as follows:

```
public interface Validator
{
    public boolean     validate(String s);
}
```

Before constructing an instance of `ValidatingTextField`, the client must construct an instance of some class that implements this interface and pass a reference to this validator into the `Validating-TextField` constructor. The `ValidatingTextField` constructor stores this reference for later use:

```
public class ValidatingTextField extends TextField
{
    private Validator     validator;
    private String        lastValidTextValue;

    public ValidatingTextField(String value, int width,
                                Validator validator)
```

```
        {
            super(value, width);
            lastValidTextValue = value;
            this.validator = validator;
            if (!validator.validate(value))
            {
                lastValidTextValue = "";
                setText(lastValidTextValue);
            }
        }
```

This constructor should seem familiar. It is identical to the constructor for `FloatTextField`, except that it stores the validator and uses the validator's `validate()` method rather than its own.

> **NOTE** Variables need not be declared to be of a class type. It is perfectly acceptable to declare a variable to be of some interface type, as done here with `Validator`. If `Validator` is set to some value that does not declare that it implements `Validator`, the compiler will give an error if it can detect the problem; if it cannot, an exception will be thrown at runtime.

In the example, `Validator` checks for a US-style social security number, whose format consists of runs of three, two, and then four digits, with the runs separated by hyphens. (Of course, the whole point is that it doesn't matter what the validator does.) Here is the listing for class `SSNValidator`, located on the CD-ROM in `javadevhdbk\ch03\SSNValidator.java`, which implements the `Validator` interface:

SSNValidator.java

```
class SSNValidator implements Validator
{
    public boolean validate(String s)
    {
        char        ch;
```

```
        if (s.length() != 11)                    // Check string length
            return false;

        for (int i=0; i<11; i++)
        {
            ch = s.charAt(i);
            if (i == 3  ||  i == 6)              // Hyphen expected
            {
                if (ch != '-')
                {
                    return(false);                // Not a hyphen
                }
            }
            else if (!Character.isDigit(ch))     // Digit expected
            {
                return(false);                    // Not a digit
            }
        }

        return(true);                            // Valid
    }
}
```

The source code for `ValidatingTextField` is on the CD-ROM. We do not present it here because it is identical to `FloatTextField` in all respects but one: the class has no `validate()` method. When a string needs to be validated, a call is made to `validator.validate()`.

The CD-ROM contains a simple test applet that just displays a `ValidatingTextField`. Readers are invited to verify that the class works correctly by typing strings into the textfield and then pressing Enter.

Summary

This chapter has shown that creating a custom component requires a number of detailed considerations. For the sake of users, the component must have a reasonable and intuitive look and feel, and must behave well when resized by a layout manager. For the sake of programmers, the component must do a good job of communicating its value and posting events, and must behave well when subclassed.

The list of issues given in the *Design Considerations* section provides a framework for developing custom component classes that are robust and maintainable.

CHAPTER
FOUR

4

Layout Managers

- Background

- The standard suite of layout managers

- Custom layout managers

- Interdependent layout manager

This chapter shows how to succeed with the standard set of layout managers, and how to create a custom one when the standard set is inadequate. The secret, of course, is to clearly understand how layout managers work and why you need them.

Background

Java's platform independence forces a new philosophy of component layout. From one window system to another, there are minute variations in fonts and moderate variations in component appearance. As a result, a button with a particular label rendered in the default Java font will vary in size from one platform to another. The same principle holds true for the other component types. Dictating absolute component size and position may result in a GUI that looks fine on one platform but unbalanced or even corrupted on another.

Java's solution is the layout manager paradigm. The task of component layout is encapsulated into the `LayoutManager` interface. The paradigm discourages explicit sizing and positioning of components. Instead, a programmer selects a layout manager, which enforces a layout policy. It is the layout manager that takes care of precise size and position issues.

This new paradigm can be frustrating for programmers who are accustomed to exercising complete layout control. In Java, successful GUI programming results from understanding the various policies that are implemented by the various layout managers and surrendering layout control to appropriate layout managers.

What a Layout Manager Does

A layout manager's job is to enforce a layout policy on the components within a container. When a container adds a component to itself it sets a flag, which marks it as invalid. This means that the container is not up to date and must be laid out anew. When the container requires rendering—at initial display time or after resizing—a call is made to the container's `layout()` method; `layout()` tells the layout manager to `layoutContainer()`. Within `layoutContainer()`, the layout manager calls `setBounds()` on the components, specifying whatever size and position best express the layout policy. Figure 4.1 shows the layout calling sequence of a container that uses a flow layout manager to control the display of three buttons.

FIGURE 4.1

Sample layout manager calling sequence

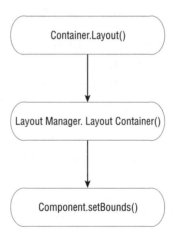

Adding a component is done via the `add()` method of the `Container` class. This method is overloaded. The simplest form takes a component as its single parameter, as in `add(okBtn)`. The container maintains an array, called `component[]`, of child components that appear in the order that they were added to the container. For order-dependent layout managers such as flow and grid, the manager itself does not keep its own list of components. Instead, the manager traverses the container's `component[]` array, positioning components as it encounters them.

Another form of `add()` that may be used with order-dependent layout managers is `add(Component, int)`. The int specifies the component's place in the container's `component[]` array. Subsequent components in the array will be moved down.

More sophisticated layout managers such as border layout use the `add(String, Component)` version. The string specifies the component's position. Layout managers that require this form of `add()` generally ignore the container's `component[]` array. The component is indeed added to the container's array, but more importantly the container calls the layout manager's `addLayoutComponent(String, Component)` method, passing in the string and the component. Typically the layout manager maintains its own list of components, along with the associated strings.

When the container is laid out, the layout manager executes its `layoutContainer()` method, traversing either its own list of components or the container's, and calling `reshape()` on each component. The layout manager must take into account the available space, its particular layout policy, the container's insets, and, if possible, each component's preferred size. An additional consideration is the container's insets, a set of four integers that define how close any component may come to each of the container's four edges of the container. Many layout managers support gaps that specify the distance between adjacent components.

There is no guarantee that all of a container's components will be displayed. If the programmer provides contradictory instructions to the layout manager, some components may be omitted. This happens, for example, if multiple components are added to any of a border layout manager's five regions.

The container, like any other component, may be called on to report its preferred size or its minimum size via the `getPreferredSize()`

and `getMinimumSize()` methods, both of which return an instance of `Dimension`. Often these values should be derived from the preferred or minimum sizes of the child components. Layout managers compute preferred and minimum size with the `preferredLayoutSize(Container)` and `minimumLayoutSize(Container)` methods. The last task of the layout manager is to support removing a component from a container. When a container receives a `remove(Component)` call, the container tells its layout manager to `removeLayoutComponent(Component)`. Although the `LayoutManager` interface supports component removal, it should be noted that there are good reasons for rarely, if ever, taking advantage of this functionality. The next section explores these reasons.

The CD-ROM contains an applet called `LoudLayoutLab` to help readers get an understanding of when a container lays out its components. The applet pops up a frame, because a frame can always be resized manually under any browser. In the middle of the frame is a panel composed of four subpanels. These subpanels appear to be managed, respectively, by a flow, a grid, a border, and a card layout manager, and they contain a variety of buttons. Actually, the layout managers and the buttons are subclasses that record activity in the applet's large text area. The layout managers report when they receive calls to `addLayoutComponent()`, `layoutContainer()`, `preferredLayoutSize()`, and `minimumSize()`. The buttons report when they receive `getPreferredSize()`, `getMinimumSize()`, and `setBounds()`. Because this makes for a cluttered text area, reporting can be disabled via the checkboxes at the top of the frame. To learn more about one of the layout managers, first disable reporting from the others, then clear the text area and resize the frame.

The Case Against Removing Components

At first glance, the rationale for dynamically adding and removing components is sensible: when a component is not relevant to some mode or state of the program, why should the component occupy space on the screen? Isn't the best possible GUI one that configures itself moment by moment to present to the user those controls that are needed and none others? The answer is an emphatic no. The rationale makes sense in theory, but time after time usability studies have found that what users really need in a GUI is stability. Accordingly, modern toolkits allow components to be disabled. A good GUI should deal with an irrelevant control not by removing it, but by graying it out.

When the GUI must be rearranged, it should be rearranged on a large scale, with nothing subtle about it. The user should know, in no uncertain terms, that something is different. Two situations come to mind where a dynamic GUI might be appropriate: displaying completely different content, and adding or removing a toolbar.

In the first situation, a panel may need to display completely different contents. For example, a stock-trading applet might present one screen for buying shares, one for selling, and one for reviewing a customer's portfolio. In this case, there should be buttons outside the main panel so that the user can tell the applet what mode to be in. This can be implemented by laying out the applet with a border layout manager, putting the three mode buttons in a panel at North. The main panel would go at Center and would be managed by a card layout manager. At any moment the main panel would display one of the three major screens: the buying screen, the selling screen, and the portfolio screen. (Readers who are unfamiliar with the border and card layout managers will find them discussed in later sections of this chapter.)

Clicking on a mode button would display the appropriate screen. The mode buttons themselves would always be available, and the three cards would be so different in look that it would be plain to the user what mode the applet was in.

In the second situation, an applet or application may need to add or remove a toolbar. A toolbar is a panel that spans the entire width or height of its window. Generally, no component smaller than a toolbar should be dynamically added or removed from a GUI. When a toolbar is added, the program's working area is correspondingly reduced because the pixels for the toolbar come from the work area. One way to do this in a Java applet is to use a border layout manager and put the toolbars in a toolbar panel at North. This northern toolbar panel should use a grid layout manager, with a single column and with one row per toolbar. The applet's work area is a panel subclass at Center. A toolbar can be added with the following code, which would execute in mid-session in response to a user's request for an additional toolbar.

```
nToolbars++;
toolbarPanel.setLayout(new GridLayout(nToolbars, 1));
toolbarPanel.add(anotherToolbar);
validate();
```

Note the `validate()` call that lays out the entire applet. This ensures that the toolbar panel grows while the work area at Center contracts.

A toolbar can be removed as follows:

```
toolbarPanel.remove(unwantedToolbar);
nToolbars--;
toolbarPanel.setLayout(new GridLayout(nToolbars, 1));
validate();
```

When a component is removed from a container, the container automatically rearranges itself as if `validate()` had been called. Therefore, in regards to the container's interior, it is not necessary to call `validate()` explicitly. However, the container itself may change size as a result of the removal, and this change may cause other components to resize. In our example, the northern toolbar panel must shrink, and the central work area must expand.

The Standard Suite of Layout Managers

There are five layout managers in the AWT package. In the sections that follow, we examine each of these managers and discuss not only what they do but also how to use them appropriately. The standard layout managers are:

- Flow
- Grid
- Border
- GridBag
- Card

We can begin by observing that it is rare to see a full-grown applet or frame that is controlled by a single layout manager. Generally, the applet or frame is subdivided into panels, each of which is controlled by its own layout manager. These smaller panels can contain other panels, and so on.

One of the key facts to know about any layout manager is whether it honors or ignores a component's preferred size. Some component classes should never be laid out in such a way that they can grow without limits. Usually a button, for example, only needs to be large enough to accommodate its label string; anything larger is a waste of pixels. Thus a panel that contains buttons is an unlikely candidate for a grid layout manager, because every button would receive an equal share of the panel's available space. Similarly, sometimes it is desirable for a textfield to be as wide as possible, so using a border layout manager and putting the textfield at North or South is reasonable. However, if the textfield were added at East or West, its height would be unbounded; the upper portion of the textfield would be a blank waste.

We will now examine the standard layout managers one at a time. We will discuss the policies in detail and make recommendations about when it is appropriate to use the various managers.

The Flow Layout Manager

The flow layout manager (`class FlowLayout`) is the default for panels and applets. This layout manager arranges its components in horizontal rows. The preferred size of each component is honored. The height of each row is determined by the height of the tallest component in that row. Within a row, the vertical centers of all components are aligned (not the tops or bottoms). The distance between components in a row is governed by `hgap`, an instance variable in the layout manager that defaults to 5 pixels but may be set in the manager's constructor. The components in a row default in such a way that they clump together in the middle of the row, but the manager can be constructed so they clump together to the right or the left.

Components are added to the top row of the container until that row is full. Subsequent components are added to the second row, then the third, and so on. The distance between rows is governed by `vgap`, another instance variable that defaults to 5 and may be set in the constructor.

The constructors for `FlowLayout` are:

`FlowLayout()` Align components in the center of each row. Horizontal and vertical gaps are both 5.

`FlowLayout(int align)` Align components at the left, in the center, or at the right of each row, according to whether `align` is `FlowLayout.LEFT`, `FlowLayout.CENTER`, or `FlowLayout.RIGHT`. Horizontal and vertical gaps are both 5.

`FlowLayout(int align, int hgap, int vgap)` Align as above. Initialize horizontal and vertical gaps from `hgap` and `vgap`.

The components managed by a flow layout manager are almost always noncontainer components (that is, buttons, textfields, and so on, but not panels). Usually there are not very many of these. A single row of components looks fine on any platform, but a second row will often clash with the first. It is difficult to control where the row will break, and it is undesirable to have one or two components all by themselves in the bottom row when the upper rows are full. More than two rows—and possibly more than one—is an indication that more organization is necessary. For example, the panel could be managed by a grid layout manager with one column (the grid layout manager is discussed in the next section). Each row would then contain a panel, managed by a flow layout manager. Rows would still contain neatly spaced and centered components, but the programmer would have more control over which components went where.

A vertical column of components can be implemented by setting hgap to an extremely large value such as 10,000. Because no container can possibly be this wide, no two components will ever share a row (because there would have to be 10,000 pixels between them).

Often an applet or frame uses a border layout manager, populating only two regions. (The border layout manager is discussed in a subsequent section.) At North is a panel that contains all the program's controls, and at Center is everything else. The panel at North is laid out with a flow layout manager. This is one of the most common uses of flow. For a program with only a few controls, this simple solution looks fine. Even if there is a large number of components in the control panel, this design is helpful during the early stages of development. At this point, the concern is to make the program respond correctly when a button is pressed or a scrollbar is slid, without regard to where the button or scrollbar is situated. Frequent testing of these components will most likely suggest the need for additional components which could not have possibly been anticipated during the early theoretical design phase. There is not much point in designing the perfect layout until all the components have been decided on. Meanwhile, tossing everything into a panel managed by a flow layout manager is perfectly acceptable.

The minimum size of a container using a flow layout manager is found by computing the minimum width and height of every row; the container's minimum width is the largest minimum width of a row, while the container's minimum height is the sum of the minimum heights of each row, plus extra pixels for gaps and insets. The minimum width for any individual row is the sum of the minimum widths of the row's components, plus extra pixels for gaps and insets. The minimum height for a row is the minimum height of that row's tallest component. Preferred size is computed in a similar manner.

The Grid Layout Manager

The grid layout manager divides its container into a rectangular grid of equal-sized cells. Components occupy cells, filling them row by row from left to right in the order they were added to the container (or rather, in their order of appearance in the internal list). It is possible for some number of cells in the bottom row or rows to be empty.

The constructor for `GridLayout` suggests a number of rows and a number of columns. Horizontal and vertical gaps, similar to those used by `FlowLayout`, may be specified optionally; they default to zero. The constructors are:

- `GridLayout(int nrows, int ncols)`
- `GridLayout(int nrows, int ncols, int hgap, int vgap)`

Before it lays out its components, a grid layout manager determines how many rows and columns of cells to implement; these may differ from the values passed into the constructor, especially if the container has only a few components. The row and column count determine the height of every component as a function of the container's height, its top and bottom insets, `nrows`, and `vgap`. The number of columns is just enough to ensure that there is a cell for every component. Layout is rarely affected by `ncols`, which is used for computing minimum and preferred size. To illustrate this, Figure 4.2 shows a four-by-four grid with four buttons. Figure 4.3 shows a four-by-four grid with twenty-three buttons.

FIGURE 4.2

4x4 Grid with four buttons

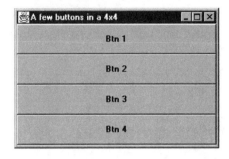

FIGURE 4.3

4x4 Grid with twenty-three buttons

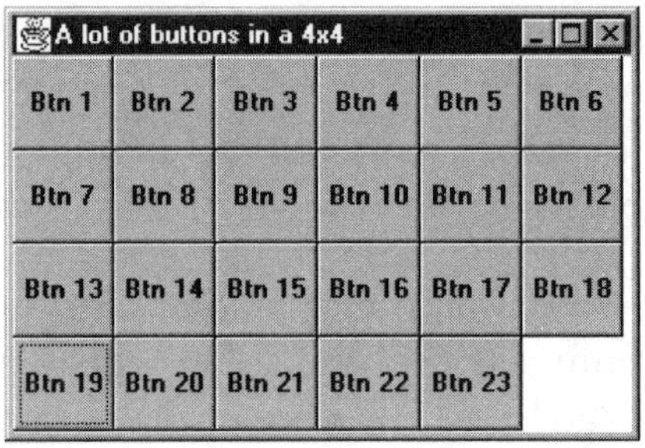

If the nrows parameter passed into the constructor is zero, then there will be exactly ncols columns. If the ncols parameter passed into the constructor is zero, then there will be exactly nrows rows.

Because the grid layout manager fills cells from left to right and top to bottom, there is no explicit way to skip a cell or to place a component in a particular cell. One way to give the illusion of skipping a cell is to insert an empty panel:

```
add(new Panel());
```

As for placing a component in a specific cell, the grid layout manager does not support this. Later in this chapter, in the section titled *SpecificGridLayout*, we develop a custom layout manager that addresses this need.

Because this layout manager generally exerts full control over the size of its contents, there are certain component classes that typically should not be managed by a grid. Buttons, checkboxes, and choices usually should be no larger than their minimum size; they should only appear in a grid-managed container if the container's own size is well controlled. If this can be ensured, it would be reasonable to manage related components this way. For example, radio buttons would look good in a grid if it were just the right size. Textfields and horizontal scrollbars might benefit from unlimited width, but not from unlimited height. (See the warning below for an explanation of why unlimited height for a horizontal scrollbar is a serious problem on Motif platforms.) Panels, canvases, and text areas do not present a problem.

It is common to see grids with just a single row or just a single column. A word-processing program, for example, might have a toolbar panel, managed by a grid layout manager with exactly one column, and one row for each toolbar. Painting programs typically put their toolbars along the left or right edge, and this could be implemented by a grid with one row and a column for each toolbar.

The minimum width of a grid-managed container is `ncols` times the widest child component minimum width, plus extra pixels for gaps and insets. The minimum height is computed similarly, as are the preferred width and the preferred height.

> **WARNING** Motif platforms have a bug that can render scrollbars useless. Motif scrollbars have triangular buttons at each end. These buttons are equilateral triangles whose sides are nearly the thickness of the scrollbar. A horizontal scrollbar that is very tall, or a vertical scrollbar that is very wide, will have triangular buttons that occupy nearly all of the scrollbar's available space; there will be very few pixels left over for the range of the scrollbar's slider. Thus a horizontal scrollbar should not be permitted to grow vertically, and a vertical scrollbar should not be permitted to grow horizontally.

The Border Layout Manager

The border layout manager divides its container into at most five cells. Unlike the grid layout manager, these cells are not arranged in rows and columns. Components must be added using the add(String, Component) version, with the string specifying the name of the cell. The string must be one of the following:

North   The component is placed at the top of the container. Its height is its preferred height. Its width is the entire width of the container.

South   Like North, but the component is placed at the bottom of the container.

East   The component is placed at the right edge of the container. Its width is its preferred width. Vertically it extends up to the bottom of the North component if one is present, or all the way to the top of the panel if there is no North component. Horizontally it extends to the top of the South component if one is present, or all the way to the bottom of the panel if there is no South component.

West   Like East, but the component is placed at the left edge of the container.

Center   All the remaining space once North, South, East, and West have been considered.

The constructor for border layout manager has two forms:

- BorderLayout()
- BorderLayout(int hgap, int vgap)

The border layout manager differentiates between components whose width or height is fixed and those that ought to expand or contract as the container expands or contracts. The typical case is a program with a control panel above a work area. The control panel, which is usually laid out with a flow layout manager, occupies the

North cell, while the work area, usually a subclass of `Panel` or `Canvas`, occupies Center. This arrangement could easily be modified to add a status bar at South, implemented as a read-only textfield.

The example above illustrates the point that panels that use the border layout manager rarely populate all five cells. Another example is a scrolling window, with scrollbars at East and South, and the display area at Center. (Revision 1.1 provides a `ScrollPanel` class to support this appearance.)

Both of these examples have components (the control panel, the status line, the scrollbars) that should be no larger than necessary and work areas at Center that should be as large as possible. This is the situation in which the border layout manager is most useful.

The minimum width of a panel laid out with a border layout manager is the sum of the minimum widths of the West, Center, and East cells (or whichever of these are occupied), plus horizontal gaps and insets. The minimum height is the sum of the minimum heights of the North, Center, and South cells (or whichever of these are occupied), plus vertical gaps and insets. Preferred size is calculated similarly.

The Grid Bag Layout Manager

Of all the standard layout managers, grid bag offers the most control. It is by far the most complicated.

The grid bag layout manager consists of three conceptual layers, as shown in Figures 4.4 through 4.6: the container is divided into a grid; elements of the grid combine to form rectangular cells; and components occupy all or part of a cell.

The constructor does not explicitly state the number of grid rows and columns. The layout manager infers the intended number of grid rows and columns from the per-component layout information supplied by the programmer.

FIGURE 4.4

Grid bag layout manager: the grid

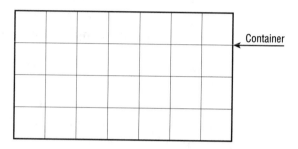

FIGURE 4.5

Grid bag layout manager: cells within the grid

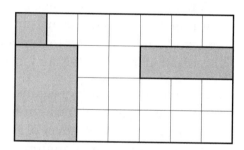

FIGURE 4.6

Grid bag layout manager: components within the cells

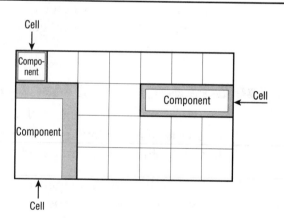

The `GridBagLayout` class uses `GridBagConstraints` as a helper class because describing a component requires more information than can reasonably be expressed in a string. When a component is added, an instance of `GridBagConstraints` must have its instance variables set to the values that describe the component. Then a call must be made to the `GridBagLayout`'s `setConstraints()` method, associating the constraint values with the component:

```
theLayout.setConstraints(okButton, myGridBagConstraints);
```

The layout manager stores a clone of the constraints, so the original may be re-used. This is useful if the constraints for one component are almost the same as those for another.

A `GridBagConstraints` specifies three pieces of information:

- the size and location within the container of the component's cell: width and height may span multiple rows and columns

- the size and location within the cell of the component

- what happens to the cell when the container is resized

Cell size and location are specified in the `gridx`, `gridy`, `gridwidth`, and `gridheight` instance variables of the `GridBag-Constraints`.

The `fill` instance variable determines whether the component's width and height will take their preferred values or completely fill the cell. The `fill` instance variable can take one of four values, which are defined as final ints in `GridBagConstraints` and are described in Table 4.1.

TABLE 4.1   Values for `fill` in `GridBagConstraints`

Fill	Width	Height
None (default)	Preferred	Preferred
Horizontal	Cell Width	Preferred
Vertical	Preferred	Cell Height
Both	Cell Width	Cell Height

If a component does not occupy its entire cell, its position within the cell must be specified. There are nine possibilities, represented by final ints in class `GridBagConstraints`. The default is CENTER, which places the component in the center of the cell. Four other options place it in the cell's corners: NORTHWEST, NORTHEAST, SOUTHEAST, and SOUTHWEST. Four more options place it in the center of the cell's edges: NORTH, EAST, SOUTH, and WEST.

These values are sufficient to dictate components' initial sizes and positions. GridBagLayout allows program control of where extra pixels are allocated when extra space becomes available (when the container resizes, for example). The weightx and weighty instance variables of GridBagConstraints specify what proportion of extra space will be allocated to a cell. These values are not percentages, nor are they proportional to any particular scale. When there are new pixels to be allocated to a row, the total weightx for all the cells in that row is computed; the number of pixels allocated to a cell is in proportion to the contribution its weightx made to the total. Vertical allocation is based on a similar calculation with weighty. This imprecision makes for very easy use. Most often some cells should not grow at all in a particular direction, while others should share equally in any extra pixels that come along. In this case, the cells that do not grow should have weightx or weighty set to zero. Note that if different components have different weights, resizing will result in rows and columns of unequal widths and heights.

Grid bag's computations of minimum and preferred size are similar to grid's. Minimum or preferred size is summed across all rows and all columns.

This is the theory. In practice, grid bag is like the other higher layout managers: in most situations, some features are used and some are not.

The weight feature is useful for the same reason that the border layout manager is useful: when the container resizes, some components should resize, some should resize in just one direction, and some should remain as they are.

Grid bag seems daunting at first, but once understood it is easy to use. The trick is to achieve an intuitive understanding, and this can only come with use. One way to rise up the learning curve is, of course, to write dozens of pieces of trial code. The CD-ROM that comes with this book offers an alternative. The `GridBagLab` applet presents six identical color-coded panels, each of which can be enabled or disabled. The panels contain controls for specifying values of a `GridBagConstraints`. When the Show button is clicked, a frame is displayed which contains one button for each enabled panel. The panel is laid out using a grid bag, and the constraints of each button are set according to the corresponding panel. Any button clicked on in the panel dismisses that panel. A quarter hour of experimentation with `GridBagLab` should be enough to intuitively understand how grid bag works. Figure 4.7 shows `GridBagLab`'s main screen.

FIGURE 4.7

GridBagLab

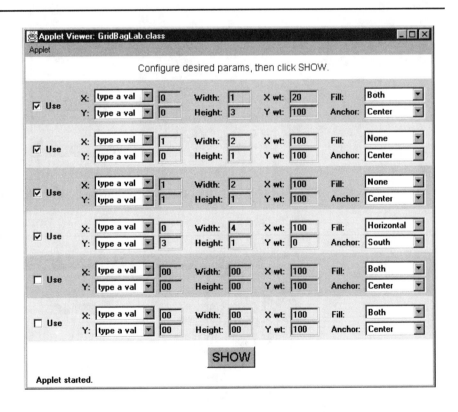

Table 4.2, below, shows sample values for four components. When these values are typed into the text fields in `GridBagLab`, you get the resulting layout is shown in Figure 4.8.

TABLE 4.2   Sample Values for Four Components

X	y	Width	Height	X Weight	y Weight	Fill	Anchor
0	0	1	3	20	100	Both	N/A
1	0	2	1	100	100	None	Center
1	1	2	1	100	100	None	Center
0	3	4	1	100	0	Horizontal	South

FIGURE 4.8

The resulting layout

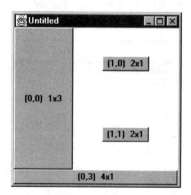

Figure 4.9 shows the same frame after horizontal resizing.

FIGURE 4.9

After resizing

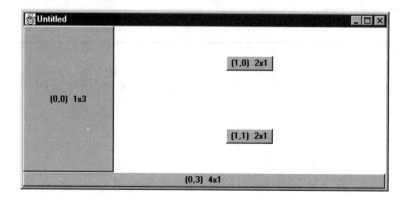

The Card Layout Manager

So far we have looked at layout managers that position their components in 2-D space. The card layout manager positions components in time. That is, if a container uses a card layout manager, then exactly one of the container's components is visible at any moment. The result is similar to tabbed dialogs that are often used for setting options on Windows platforms. Various methods are provided to tell the layout manager to display a different component.

There are two constructors:

`CardLayout()` The default. Both gaps are zero.

`CardLayout(int hgap, int vgap)` Horizontal and vertical gaps are specified. Unlike other layout managers, which manage more than one component at a time, gaps here specify distance from the container's edges, like the container's gaps.

The methods listed below tell the layout manager to display a different component. The first four methods show the next, previous, first, or last component in the container's list, using the order in which they were added. With the last method, a specific component can be displayed. The component must have been added to the container using `add(String, Component)`, so that there is a string handle by which to refer to the desired component.

The following methods display a different component. Note that they are methods in the `CardLayout` class, and they all require the container to be passed in as a parameter:

`next(Container)` Display the container's next child component.

`previous(Container)` Display the container's previous child component.

`first(Container)` Display the container's first child component.

`last(Container)` Display the container's last child component.

`show(Container, String)` Display the component specified by `String`. The component must have been added using `add(String, component)`.

Every child component (or *card*) is resized to fill the container, less gaps and insets. The minimum width is the largest minimum width of any child. The minimum height is the largest minimum height of any child. The preferred width is the largest preferred width of any child. The preferred height is the largest preferred height of any child. (These might be different children.)

The card layout manager is useful whenever the purpose of a region of the screen changes. A text editor application, for example, might use a border layout manager, allocating the North region of its frame for tool panels and the Center region for its work area. A menu item would switch from WYSIWYG editing mode to Print Preview mode. The Center region would be occupied by a panel using a card layout manager which controlled the WYSIWYG and Print Preview panels.

A word of caution from an earlier section of this chapter, *The Case Against Removing Components,* bears repeating here. This layout manager supports a dynamically changing user interface, and GUIs should only be modified with extreme caution. Every card represents a mode of the program. A card change should only happen when the program really changes to a new major state. Each card should look sufficiently different from all the other cards that there can be no mistake on the user's part as to which mode is currently in force. Property sheets are an excellent example of appropriate use of the card layout manager.

No Layout Manager

There is certainly no danger in calling `setLayout(null)`. The `Component` class always checks if it has a null layout manager before calling on the layout manager to do anything. This strategy will not cause a null pointer exception, but there is little to be said in its favor.

The advantage of not using a layout manager is that calling `resize()` and `reshape()` on components actually works. On the other hand, the programmer is responsible for positioning the components, not only at initialization but whenever the container resizes. This requires overriding the container's `reshape()` method, as shown below:

```
public void reshape(int x, int y, int w, int h)
{
        super.reshape(x, y, w, h);
        // (Compute size/position for each child component)
        component1.reshape(x1, y1, w1, h1);
        component2.reshape(x2, y2, w2, h2);

                . . .

}
```

TIP

`Resize(w, h)` **just calls** `reshape(x, y, w, h)` **using the component's current** x **and** y**. It is always sufficient just to override reshape.**

For a very simple layout reshaping is easy, but as the GUI's complexity increases, the chore of laying out becomes increasingly burdensome. The `reshape()` method must implement a layout policy. It is generally easier to implement a custom layout manager because the `LayoutManager` interface provides a framework for ensuring that all layout subtleties are taken care of. (Following this section, the remainder of this chapter deals with custom layout managers.)

That being said, when is it appropriate to set layout to null? The advantage comes when the container contains so few components that, in essence, there is no layout policy to encapsulate in a layout manager. This is rare. One example might be a spreadsheet, where clicking on a cell brings up a panel for viewing or editing the cell's formula.

The spreadsheet can be implemented as a subclass of `Applet`. The subclass' constructor or `init()` calls `setLayout(null)`. The `paint()` method renders the spreadsheet data. A mouse click in a cell reformats the formula panel, reshapes it, and adds it to the spreadsheet panel.

The code for a simplified version of this spreadsheet is below. Cells just display their coordinates, and the formula panel also shows the coordinates. The layout policy can be stated as follows: the formula panel, if it appears, has a constant width and height; if possible it should be centered over the cell it describes, but it should always be at least five pixels from any edge of the spreadsheet.

For the sake of simplicity, this example deliberately uses hard-coded cell width and height. The source code and the applet itself are on the CD-ROM, in javadevhdbk\ch04\NoLayoutSpreadsheet.java.

NoLayoutSpreadsheet.java

```
import        java.awt.*;
import        java.applet.Applet;


public class NoLayoutSpreadsheet extends Applet
{
    static final int      CELL_WIDTH_PIX          = 80;
    static final int      CELL_HEIGHT_PIX         = 60;
    static final int      N_ROWS                  = 5;
    static final int      N_COLS                  = 5;
    static final int      FORMULA_PANEL_WIDTH     = 165;
    static final int      FORMULA_PANEL_HEIGHT    = 80;

    Panel                 formulaPanel;
    TextField             formulaTF;
    Button                formulaOKBtn;


    public void init()
    {
        setBackground(Color.white);
        setLayout(null);
```

```
        // Construct detail panel but do not show it.
        formulaPanel = new Panel();
        formulaPanel.setBackground(Color.lightGray);
        formulaPanel.setLayout(new BorderLayout());
        formulaTF = new TextField(10);
        formulaTF.setEditable(false);
        formulaTF.setFont(new Font("Courier", Font.PLAIN, 40));
        formulaPanel.add("Center", formulaTF);
        Panel p = new Panel();
        formulaOKBtn = new Button("OK");
        p.add(formulaOKBtn);
        formulaPanel.add("South", p);
    }


    public void paint(Graphics g)
    {
        int     i, j, x, y;

        // Draw grid in blue.
        g.setColor(Color.blue);
        for (j=0; j<=N_ROWS; j++)
        {
            y = j * CELL_HEIGHT_PIX;
            g.drawLine(0, y, size().width, y);
        }
        for (i=0; i<=N_COLS; i++)
        {
            x = i * CELL_WIDTH_PIX;
            g.drawLine(x, 0, x, size().height);
        }

        // Draw cell formulas.
        g.setColor(Color.black);
        for (j=0; j<N_ROWS; j++)
        {
            for (i=0; i<N_COLS; i++)
            {
                x = i * CELL_WIDTH_PIX;
                y = j * CELL_HEIGHT_PIX;
                String s = "(" + i + "," + j + ")";
                g.drawString(s, x+18, y+36);
```

```
                    }
                }
            }


        public boolean mouseUp(Event e, int x, int y)
        {
            // Ignore clicks from the formula panel.
            if (e.target != this)
                return true;

            int cellX = x / CELL_WIDTH_PIX;
            int cellY = y / CELL_HEIGHT_PIX;
            formulaTF.setText("(" + cellX + "," + cellY + ")");

            // Determine where the panel should go.
            int panelX = cellX*CELL_WIDTH_PIX + CELL_WIDTH_PIX/2
                            - FORMULA_PANEL_WIDTH/2;
            panelX = Math.max(panelX, 5);
            panelX = Math.min(panelX,
                        size().width - FORMULA_PANEL_WIDTH - 5);
            int panelY = cellY*CELL_HEIGHT_PIX + CELL_HEIGHT_PIX/2
                            - FORMULA_PANEL_HEIGHT/2;
            panelY = Math.max(panelY, 5);
            panelY = Math.min(panelY,
                        size().height - FORMULA_PANEL_HEIGHT - 5);
            formulaPanel.reshape(panelX, panelY,
                        FORMULA_PANEL_WIDTH, FORMULA_PANEL_HEIGHT);
            add(formulaPanel);
            validate();                    // Won't work without this.

            return true;
        }


        public boolean action(Event e, Object ob)
        {
            if (e.target == formulaOKBtn)
                remove(formulaPanel);

            return true;
        }
    }
```

Note that when we add the formula panel in `mouseUp()`, we have to call `validate()`. The `add()` call invalidates—that is, it marks the applet as requiring fresh layout and rendering, but the layout and rendering are not invoked. This is not the case with the `remove()` call in `action()`.

Note also that it is possible to add the formula panel when it has not yet been removed if the user clicks on a new cell while the formula panel is displayed. The `add()` method supports this; it checks to see if the component is already contained in the parent, and if so it removes before adding.

Figure 4.10 shows the spreadsheet with the formula panel displayed.

FIGURE 4.10

A spreadsheet with no layout manager

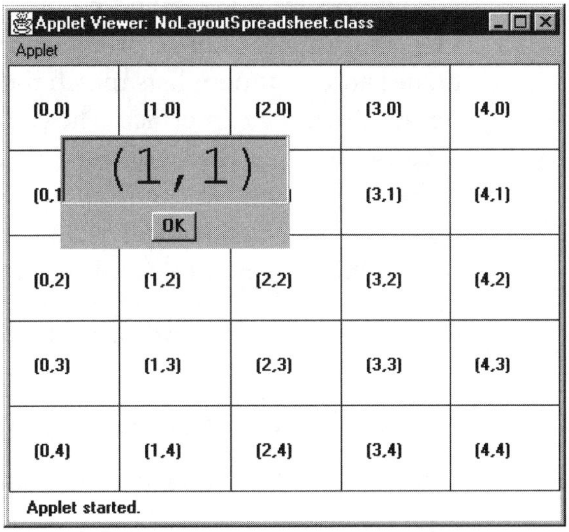

Custom Layout Managers

The next few sections show how to create a new layout manager class, beginning with an examination of the `LayoutManager` interface. Two examples are then developed: The first is like `GridLayout`, but clients specify where in the grid a component is to go. The second is an interdependent layout manager in the spirit of Motif's Form widget, where component positions can be specified relative to other components.

The first example is moderately small. The second is quite long; in fact, it is the longest code example in this book. The code sizes themselves are part of the information. It is hoped that after having read this chapter, the reader will have two good data points for estimating how long it will take to develop a custom layout manager.

The *LayoutManager* Interface

LayoutManager is not a class but an interface. In other words, the various classes share no methods or instance variables. All they have in common are five method names. A class that declares that it implements LayoutManager promises only to provide methods whose names and argument lists match the five methods named in the LayoutManager interface. The code can do anything it pleases. Because interface methods are called blindly, as it were, it is especially important to know what behavior the caller expects. This section details the behavior expected of the methods of the LayoutManager interface. These methods are:

- `public void addLayoutComponent(String, Component)`

- `public void removeLayoutComponent(Component)`

- `public Dimension minimumLayoutSize(Container)`

- `public Dimension preferredLayoutSize(Container)`

- `public void layoutContainer(Container)`

The `addLayoutComponent()` method is called when a component is added to a container by means of the `add(String, Component)` method. The container keeps track of its components but not of the strings passed in with them, so it is the layout manager's job to associate components with strings, typically by storing components in a hashtable that is indexed by the strings. The `add()` and `add(int)` methods of `Container` do not call `addLayoutComponent()`; if the layout manager cares about components added in this fashion, it must find out about them by calling the container's `getComponent()`, `getComponent(int)`, or `getComponents()` method. It is acceptable for a layout manager that uses the strings to ignore components unless it hears about them via `addLayoutComponent()`. This has been observed by everybody who has ever forgotten the North or South parameter when adding with a border layout manager; the component never appears.

The only job of `removeLayoutComponent()` is to remove the component from any storage maintained by the layout manager (such as the hashtable suggested above). It is not necessary to rearrange the remaining components; when the time comes to do that, the container will call `layoutContainer()` explicitly.

The `minimumLayoutSize()` method should return a value based on a geometrical aggregate of the minimum sizes of its components. In practice it is rarely called, and even more rarely does it affect anything, so if computation based on the children's minimum sizes is out of the question, it is reasonable to return some hardwired value. The minimum size is used, not for laying out components within the container, but for reporting the container's own minimum size. There is no guarantee that layout managers will honor a component's minimum size. Layout managers frequently report their preferred layout size (see below) as their minimum layout size. Frequently, this is implemented by calling the next method.

The `preferredLayoutSize()` method should also return a value based on a geometrical consideration of the container's children. This method also is used for computing the container's own preferred size, not for laying out its components. Unlike `minimum-LayoutSize()`, `preferredLayoutSize()` is quite likely to be called, so it is more important to return a reasonable value, unless clients can be warned against using adding the container to a container that uses, for instance, flow or a border layout manager.

> **WARNING** It is tempting to have `minimumLayoutSize()` and `preferred-LayoutSize()` return the container's minimum or preferred size. This seems the courteous thing to do, as if the layout manager is saying to the container, "Oh, I don't much care, what size would *you* prefer?" This usually fails, because the layout manager's `minimumLayoutSize()` and `preferredLayoutSize` methods ordinarily are called by the container's `minimumSize()` and `preferredSize()`, and the result is a back-and-forth call loop that eventually blows its stack. The safe way to defer to the container's size is to return the `size()` of the container.

SpecificGridLayout

The standard grid layout manager insists on populating grid cells in the order in which components appear in the container's internal storage. This example develops a custom manager class called `SpecificGridLayout`, which supports adding components at specific cells. The number of cell rows and columns is specified to the constructor, and that many rows and columns will always be present.

Clients add components with the `add(String, component)` version of `add()`; the string format is x,y, in which x and y are the cell coordinates where the component is to go. The upper-left cell is denoted by the string `0,0`.

The only methods in `SpecificGridLayout` are a pair of constructors (one specifying just grid size, one specifying grid size and gaps) and the five methods of the `LayoutManager` interface. We will go through the entire source file, method by method. The complete source is on the CD-ROM in `javadevhdbk\ch04\` `SpecificGridLayout.java`.

SpecificGridLayout.java

```
import    java.awt.*;
import    java.util.*;


public class SpecificGridLayout implements LayoutManager
{
    int         nrows;
    int         ncols;
    int         hgap;
    int         vgap;
    Hashtable   hash;


    public SpecificGridLayout(int nrows, int ncols)
    {
        this(nrows, ncols, 0, 0);
    }


    public SpecificGridLayout(int nrows, int ncols, int hgap, int vgap)
    {
        this.nrows = nrows;
        this.ncols = ncols;
        this.hgap = hgap;
        this.vgap = vgap;
        hash = new Hashtable();
    }
```

The constructors just initialize the instance variables and construct a new hashtable. The horizontal and vertical gap sizes default to 0.

SpecificGridLayout.java Continued

```
    public void addLayoutComponent(String position, Component component)
    {
        if (!(hash.containsKey(position)))
            hash.put(position, component);
    }
```

When a component is added, it is inserted into the hashtable; the hash key is the position string. If the position string is a duplicate, the new component is not inserted in the hashtable and will not be seen.

SpecificGridLayout.java Continued

```
public void removeLayoutComponent(Component component)
{
    Enumeration keys = hash.keys();
    while (keys.hasMoreElements())
    {
        String key = (String)(keys.nextElement());
        if (hash.get(key) == component)
        {
            hash.remove(key);
            return;
        }
    }
}
```

When a component is to be removed, it is simply removed from the hashtable. Most likely, the removeLayoutComponent() call comes from the container's remove() method, which will later mark the container as invalid and call the layout manager's layoutContainer() method.

SpecificGridLayout.java Continued

```
public Dimension minimumLayoutSize(Container container)
{
    int maxCompMinWidth = 0;
    int maxCompMinHeight = 0;

    Enumeration components = hash.elements();
    while (components.hasMoreElements())
    {
        Component comp = (Component)(components.nextElement());
        Dimension dim = comp.minimumSize();
        if (dim.width > maxCompMinWidth)
            maxCompMinWidth = dim.width;
```

```
        if (dim.height > maxCompMinHeight)
            maxCompMinHeight = dim.height;
    }

    int minWidth =  maxCompMinWidth * ncols  +  hgap * (ncols-1)  +
                    container.insets().left  +
                    container.insets().right;
    int minHeight = maxCompMinHeight * nrows  +  vgap * (nrows-1)  +
                    container.insets().top  +
                    container.insets().bottom;

    return new Dimension(minWidth, minHeight);
}
```

The `minimumLayoutSize()` algorithm calls `minimumSize()` on every component in the hashtable, determining the largest of the minimum widths and heights. The minimum width for the container is the sum of the left and right container insets, plus one maximin component width for every column in the layout, plus one horizontal gap for every gap between columns. The minimum height for the container is computed similarly: it is the sum of the top and bottom container insets, plus one maximin component height for every row in the layout, plus one vertical gap for every gap between rows.

SpecificGridLayout.java Continued

```
public Dimension preferredLayoutSize(Container container)
{
    int maxCompPrefWidth = 0;
    int maxCompPrefHeight = 0;

    Enumeration components = hash.elements();
    while (components.hasMoreElements())
    {
        Component comp = (Component)(components.nextElement());
        Dimension dim = comp.preferredSize();
        if (dim.width > maxCompPrefWidth)
            maxCompPrefWidth = dim.width;
        if (dim.height > maxCompPrefHeight)
            maxCompPrefHeight = dim.height;
    }
```

```
int minWidth =  maxCompPrefWidth * ncols  +  hgap *  (ncols-1)  +
                        container.insets().left  +
                        container.insets().right;
int minHeight = maxCompPrefHeight * nrows  +  vgap *  (nrows-1)  +
                    container.insets().top  +
                    container.insets().bottom;

return new Dimension(minWidth, minHeight);
}
```

The preferredLayoutSize() algorithm is exactly like the minimumLayoutSize() algorithm, except that it operates on each component's preferred size rather than its minimum size.

SpecificGridLayout.java Continued

```
public void layoutContainer(Container container)
{
    // Compute cell width and height.
    Insets insets = container.insets();
    int availableWidth =
            container.size().width - insets.left - insets.right;
    int compWidth = (availableWidth - hgap*(ncols-1)) / ncols;
    int availableHeight =
            container.size().height - insets.top - insets.bottom;
    int compHeight = (availableHeight - vgap*(nrows-1)) / nrows;

    // Position components.
    Enumeration keys = hash.keys();
    while (keys.hasMoreElements())
    {
        String key = (String)(keys.nextElement());
        StringTokenizer st = new StringTokenizer(key, ",");
        int cellx = Integer.parseInt((String)(st.nextToken()).trim());
        int x = insets.left + compWidth*cellx + hgap*(cellx);
        int celly = Integer.parseInt((String)(st.nextToken()).trim());
        int y = insets.top + compHeight*celly + vgap*(celly);
        Component comp = (Component)(hash.get(key));
        comp.reshape(x, y, compWidth, compHeight);
    }
}
} // End of class
```

To lay out its components, the layout manager just computes the component size. Then it iterates through every component in the hashtable, computing x and y and then reshaping the component. Most of the code accounts for insets and gaps. If the layout manager did not support insets and gaps, this method would be reduced to just a few lines.

Figure 4.11 shows an applet laid out using the specific grid layout manager. There are five rows and five columns. This applet is on the CD-ROM in `javadevhdbk\ch04\SpecificGridTest.java`.

FIGURE 4.11

SpecificGridTest

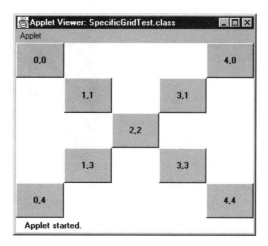

Interdependent Layout Manager

There is one behavior, one very desirable bit of functionality, that is not supported by any of the layout managers of the AWT. It is not possible to specify some attribute of a component's size or position with respect to some other component's size or position. It would be extremely useful if, for example, a programmer could specify to a layout manager that the top edge of the Cancel button is to be 15 pixels below the bottom edge of the OK button; the OK button's width is to be 75 percent of the Cancel button's width, and the two buttons' centers are to be vertically aligned.

Consider a panel with scrollbars at the right and the bottom edges, and the remainder occupied by a canvas depicting some kind of image. This can almost be achieved with a border layout manager, but not quite. With a border layout manager, one scrollbar goes at South and one at East; the canvas goes at Center. The problem is that the bottom scrollbar is too wide. It should not be wider than the canvas. Figure 4.12 illustrates the problem.

FIGURE 4.12

Imperfect bottom scrollbar

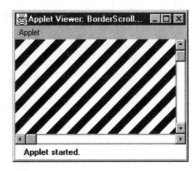

It would be extremely useful if the bottom scrollbar's width could be set in a straightforward manner to be the width of the canvas. Then the panel would appear as in Figure 4.13.

FIGURE 4.13

Bottom scrollbar is just right.

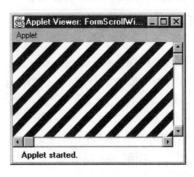

An example of an *interdependent* layout manager will be developed in the remainder of this chapter; an interdependent layout manager is one that supports specifying position or size as functions of another component's position or size. The layout policy will be similar to that of the Motif Form widget, and our new class will be called `FormLayout`. The applet shown in Figure 4.13 was laid out using this custom class. The source for the applet is quite simple and is listed in the section *Using FormLayout* later in this chapter. The source for the layout manager, on the other hand, is not at all simple.

This is a lengthy example. The length itself conveys important information; this is about what it takes to create a layout manager that supports component interdependence.

Three major pieces must be designed before development of the `FormLayout` class can begin:

- The layout policy
- A mechanism for specifying component position and size
- A dependency checker

The layout policy is a statement of the functionality that `FormLayout` is to support.

The specification mechanism in the simplest case would be a code for expressing layout instructions as a string. The string would be passed into the `add(String, Component)` method of a container using the form layout manager. If it should prove too cumbersome to use a string, it will be necessary to create a helper class. This class would play the same role for `FormLayout` that the helper class `GridBagConstraints` plays for `GridBagLayout`.

The dependency checker makes sense out of a hodgepodge of interdependent layout information. Suppose a client program has specified that A goes to the right of B, and B goes to the right of C, and C is attached to the left-hand wall of the container; now something has to figure out that C's layout must be computed first. Only then can B's position be computed, and only after that can A's position be computed.

Each of these, and then the code for the layout manager itself, will be developed in turn. The entire body of code is on the CD-ROM. Because it is just over 1,000 lines long, some of the tedious parts have been abbreviated in the text. It has been made very clear where this is done.

The Layout Policy

The form layout manager's layout policy is designed to be as simple as possible while still being of practical use.

The form layout manager takes the view that there are four attributes that describe a component's horizontal position and size: the position of the left edge, the position of the center, the position of the right edge, and the width. If any two of these are provided by the client program, the layout manager will be able to determine the other two.

Similarly, there are four attributes that describe a component's vertical position and size: the position of the top edge, the position of the center, the position of the bottom edge, and the height. Again, if any two of these are provided by the client program, the layout manager will be able to determine the other two.

Therefore the layout policy is that for each component, the client program must specify two out of the four horizontal attributes and two out of the four vertical attributes.

Because every component has a preferred width, the form layout manager optionally permits clients to specify only one horizontal attribute instead of two, provided that attribute is not the width. In this case, the width will be taken to be the component's preferred width. Similarly, it is permitted to specify only one vertical attribute instead of two, provided that attribute is not the height. In this case, the height will be taken to be the component's preferred height.

The layout policy supports three ways for clients to specify these attributes:

- In absolute pixels: "The right-hand edge of this scrollbar is at pixel coordinate 365."

- In decimal fractions of the container's width or height: "The horizontal center of this button is at 0.25 times the entire width of the container."

- In terms of an attribute of another component: "The bottom edge of this checkbox is aligned with the bottom edge of that label."

Note that the decimal fraction form supports attaching a component to an edge of the container. For example, to attach a component to the top of the container, the client would specify that the top of the component is at 0.0 times the container's height. To attach to the bottom of the container, the client would specify that the bottom of the component is at 1.0 times the container's height.

The layout policy supports one further refinement. Any attribute, having been specified as above, may optionally be given a modification (or *delta*), specified in absolute pixels. Thus a client could tell the layout manager that the left edge of the Cancel button is to be the right edge of the OK button, plus 15 pixels.

The intention of this layout policy is to permit programmers to describe layout relationships in a natural way. How well this is achieved can be gauged by looking at the layout shown in Figure 4.14.

This layout consists of a canvas, a scrollbar, and a button. If you had to describe this layout to somebody over the telephone using only words, you might say the following:

"There is an OK button in the lower-right corner. It is as large as it needs to be and no larger. Above the OK button is a vertical scrollbar. It extends all the way up to the top. It is as wide as the OK button. The remainder of the container is occupied by a canvas."

FIGURE 4.14:

A simple layout

This is not very different from the way a client program would describe the layout to a form layout manager:

- The OK button's right edge is at 1.0 times the container's width. The OK button's width is its preferred width. Its bottom edge is at 1.0 times the container's height. Its height is its preferred height.

- The scrollbar's left edge is the same as the OK button's left edge. Its width is the same as the OK button's width. Its top edge is at the top of the container. Its bottom edge is 5 pixels less than the OK button's top edge.

- The canvas' left edge is at the container's left edge. Its right edge is the same as the scrollbar's left edge. The canvas' top is at the top of the container. Its bottom is at the bottom of the container.

In comparing these two verbal descriptions of the layout, it is clear that the first version (the informal description) is not very different from the second version (the formal description). This suggests that the layout policy will be useful because it supports the way people naturally think and talk about layouts.

Note that even this simple layout description requires 12 sentences, because for each of three components two horizontal attributes and two vertical attributes must be specified. In practice only 10 specifications are required for this example, because the OK button's width and height are to be its preferred width and height, and these are the assumed defaults if no width or height is explicitly requested.

Even so, 10 specifications for 3 components is quite a few. This is unavoidable with interdependent layouts, but it suggests that keeping track of all these specifications will be a major portion of the development task.

Our next step will be to formalize the way client programs will describe layout attributes to the form layout manager.

Specifying Position and Size

In this section a way for clients to express programmatically the desired size and position of components will be developed. We need a way for computers to make statements similar to those in the bullet list of the previous section.

Note that Java's paradigm encourages programmers to express this information in a string if at all possible. The alternative is to develop a helper class along the lines of `GridBagConstraints`. Considering ease of use, readability, and maintainability, using a string is clearly preferable. Client programs will pass the string into a container's `add(String, Component)` method; the container will pass the string along into the form layout manager's `addLayout-Component(String, Component)` method.

Next, observe that many attributes will be specified in terms of attributes of other components. The required specification format will need to refer to other components. We will require that every component be given a unique name.

At this point, at the top level, specifying a component's layout requires three pieces of information: the component's name, its horizontal information, and its vertical information. The general form of a specification string will therefore be:

```
"component_name/horizontal_information/vertical_information"
```

Now a decision about what goes between the slashes needs to be made.

Horizontal specification involves specifying one or two of a component's horizontal attributes (left edge, center, right edge, or width) in one of the three supported formats (absolute pixels, decimal fraction, or relative to another component). The horizontal information part of the formula (the part between the slashes) will be expressed in one of the following formats:

X=*value*   The left edge

C=*value*   The horizontal center

R=*value*   The right edge

X=*value*;C=*value*   The left edge and the horizontal center

X=*value*;R=*value*   The left edge and the right edge

X=*value*;W=*value*   The left edge and the width

C=*value*;R=*value*   The horizontal center and the right edge

C= *value*;W=*value*   The horizontal center and the width

R= *value*;W=*value*   The right edge and the width

These are all the possible combinations (recall that we do not support specifying width only, because this does not provide enough information).

The *value* portion of the formula must support absolute pixel, decimal fraction, and component-relative formats. The supported formats are:

A*int*   The value is an absolute pixel position or size given by *int*.

F*fraction*   The value is a fraction of the container's width. The value of *fraction* is 0, 1, or any fractional number between 0 and 1.

X*other_component*   The value is the X (left edge) of *other_component*.

R*other_component*   The value is the R (right edge) of *other_component*.

C*other_component*   The value is the C (horizontal center) of *other_component*.

W*other_component*   The value is the W (width) of *other_component*.

Because the X's, R's, and so on are capitalized, this format encourages, but does not require, programmers to use lowercase for component names. The result is a quite readable formula.

Any attribute specification may optionally be followed by +*delta* or -*delta*. The following are examples of valid horizontal specifications:

X=A50   The left edge of this component is at 50. The width will be the component's preferred width.

X=Rokbtn+10;R=F1   The left edge of this component is 10 pixels to the right of *okbtn*'s right edge. The right edge of this component is the right edge of the container.

C=A.5   The horizontal center of this component is at half the container's width (thus the component is horizontally centered within its container). Width is preferred width.

Vertical attributes are specified in a similar manner. The vertical portion of the overall formula (the portion after the second slash) must be in one of the following formats:

Y=*value*   The top edge

C=*value*   The vertical center

B=*value*   The bottom edge

Y=*value*;C=*value*   The top edge and the vertical center

Y=*value*;B=*value*   The top edge and the bottom edge

Y=value;H=*value*   The top edge and the height

C=*value*;B=value   The vertical center and the bottom edge

C=*value*;H=*value*   The vertical center and the height

B=*value*;H=*value*   The bottom edge and the height

This completes the formula specification. As an example of the use of the formula, consider the layout pictured in Figure 4.14. (This is the example with the button, the vertical scrollbar, and the canvas.) For reference, we repeat here the formal verbal description of the layout:

- The OK button's right edge is at 1.0 times the container's width. The OK button's width is its preferred width. Its bottom edge is at 1.0 times the container's height. Its height is its preferred height.

- The scrollbar's left edge is the same as the OK button's left edge. Its width is the same as the OK button's width. Its top edge is at the top of the container. Its bottom edge is 5 pixels less than the OK button's top edge.

- The canvas' left edge is at the container's left edge. Its right edge is the same as the scrollbar's left edge. The canvas' top is at the top of the container. Its bottom is at the bottom of the container.

These components would be specified as follows, assuming the components are given the names `okbtn`, `sbar`, and `can`:

```
"okbtn/R=F1/B=F1"
"sbar/X=Xokbtn;W=Wokbtn/Y=A0;B=Yokbtn-5"
"can/X=A0;R=Xsbar/Y=A0;B=F1"
```

The following code fragment shows how these strings might be used to lay out the components (assuming successful development of the rest of the layout manager code!).

```
public class Snippet extends Applet
{
    Button          okButton;
    Scrollbar       sbar;
    Canvas          canvas;


    public void init()
    {
        okButton = new Button("OK");
        scrollbar = new Scrollbar(Scrollbar.VERTICAL);
        canvas = new Canvas();

        setLayout(new FormLayout());
        add("okbtn/R=F1/B=F1", okButton);
        add("sbar/X=Xokbtn;W=Wokbtn/Y=A0;B=Yokbtn-5", scrollbar);
        add("can/X=A0;R=Xsbar/Y=A0;B=F1", canvas);
    }
        . . .
}
```

Now that we have defined a formula for specifying layout information, we need a way to keep track of all that information.

The Dependency Checker

The form layout manager must compute size and position for all its components. Before it can do this, it must decide in what order attributes will be computed.

For example, the layout described in the last section specified that the bottom of the scrollbar should be five pixels above the top of the button. Therefore the button's size and position must be known (at least, its *vertical* size and position must be known) before the layout manager can attempt to lay out the scrollbar.

There are two separate tasks. Clearly the layout manager must compute layout attributes whose values depend on other attributes. In our example, the layout manager knows that the height of the scrollbar depends on the position of the button according to some arithmetical formula. The layout manager must be able to apply the formula and derive the height of the scrollbar. Given any dependent attribute and the values on which that attribute depends, the layout manager must be able to compute the attribute's value.

The second task is knowing which attributes depend on which other attributes. This information must be converted into an ordering of attributes, so that by the time the layout manager attempts to compute an attribute's value, all inputs to the appropriate formula have already been computed.

Another task related to dependencies is *validity checking*. If a Cancel button says that it goes to the right of an OK button, while the OK button goes to the left of the Cancel button, something had better notice and reject this circular dependency or the code is liable to end up in an infinite loop. After all components have been added, something must determine whether or not there is enough information to resolve all dependencies.

At this point it becomes clear that dependency management is a separate task from component layout; it is a task that merits its own class. The class is called `DependencyChecker`. Its API is presented in the next section and its code in the section after that.

The Dependency Checker API

The `DependencyChecker` class knows nothing about layout geometry. It only knows how to maintain a set of dependencies of things on other things. Within the dependency checker, the things being tracked are represented as strings.

In the course of building up the dependency structure, the programmer can tell the dependency checker two kinds of information:

- A depends on B (B must be known before A can be computed).

- Z is known at the outset (there is nothing that Z depends on).

Given two attributes A and B, with A depending on B, A is the *master* and B is the *puppet*. With this terminology the four methods of the `DependencyChecker` class can be defined as follows:

`void add(String puppet, String master) throws InvalidDependencyException` Adds a single dependency relationship. Informs the dependency checker that attribute `puppet` depends on attribute `master`. Throws exception if adding this dependency results in a self-contradictory dependency hierarchy.

`void addKnown(String attribute) throws Invalid-DependencyException` Informs the dependency checker that `attribute` is known; that is, it does not depend on anything. Throws exception if adding this dependency results in a self-contradictory dependency hierarchy.

`void validate() throws InvalidDependencyException` Instructs the dependency checker to check whether its set of dependencies can be completely resolved. Throws exception if invalid; successful return without an exception indicates validity.

`Vector sort() throws InvalidDependencyException` Instructs the dependency checker to determine an order for evaluating its attributes. Returns a vector of strings, which are the attribute names that were passed in via the `add()` and `addKnown()` calls. The order of appearance in the vector is such that if an attribute depends on other attributes (that is, if the attribute is puppet to one or more masters), then all the master attributes (and by recursion *their* masters, and so on) appear in the vector before their puppet appears. Thus attributes may be evaluated in their order of appearance in the vector.

When the dependency checker is used to support the form layout manager, the entities whose dependencies are managed are not components, but rather the layout attributes of components. For example, recall that in the last section the following code was used to add a canvas:

```
add("can/X=A0;R=Xsbar/Y=A0;B=F1", canvas);
```

The layout manager will have to parse the string. In the course of doing so, it will conclude that the *R* of *can* depends on the *X* of *sbar*. The form layout manager represents an attribute of a component by concatenating the attribute with the component's name, using a colon as a delimiter. The *R* of *can* would be represented as "R:can," and the *X* of *sbar* would be represented as "X:sbar." The layout manager will eventually make the following call to the dependency checker:

```
theDependencyChecker.add("R:can", "X:sbar");
```

The canvas' *X* value is specified as an absolute pixel location. It has no dependencies; it is known *a priori*. The layout manager will represent this to the dependency checker by calling

```
theDependencyChecker.addKnown("X:can");
```

NOTE The `DependencyChecker` class manages dependency relationships among strings. It has no knowledge of the meaning of those strings. The dependency checker's client is responsible for calling `sort()` and evaluating the sorted list as it sees fit. In our case, the client is the dependency checker, and its job is to compute layout values. However, the `DependencyChecker` class can be used to manage *any* set of dependency relationships. For example, one could use it to create a make facility for C or C++, where the client specifies which source modules depend on which other source modules. The client would call `sort()` and use the resulting list to dictate order of compilation.

Inside the *DependencyChecker*

This section describes the internals of the DependencyChecker class.

The job of the dependency checker is to represent and analyze relationships among attributes of objects. Implementation is straightforward once it is understood that the way relationships should be represented is backwards from the way client programs wish to specify them. For example, a client would like to say, "His X depends on her Y," while the dependency checker would represent this as "Her Y controls his X." The dependency checker is not concerned with the actual value or meaning of either of these attributes, but only with the dependency relationships between them.

The DependencyChecker class is built around a set of *depnodes*. DepNode is a class which has a vector of strings. Each depnode instance represents a single attribute, and each string in that depnode's vector represents some other attribute that depends on the depnode. Thus the fact that "A controls B" (in other words, "B depends on A") is represented by an entry in the vector of the depnode for "A"; this entry is the string "B."

NOTE It is tempting to implement the depnode class as a subclass of Vector. This would let us add or retrieve dependencies by calling the inherited addElement() and elementAt() methods. This would be poor object-oriented design, however. A depnode is not a kind of vector; it is a class that has a vector, and, indeed, that vector comprises most of depnode's data, but there is no escaping the fact that a depnode is not a vector. The proper relationship is "has a," and not "is a." The depnode class should aggregate Vector, not extend it.

The DepNode class listing is shown below. In addition to the vector (called puppets) there is an instance variable called name, which is the name that was passed into the dependency checker via the add()

or addKnown() methods. The boolean instance variable marked is used for validity checking. The int instance variable refCount is used for validity checking and sorting.

The source code for class DepNode follows. It can be found on the CD-ROM in javadevhdbk\ch04\DepNode.java.

DepNode.java

```java
import java.util.Hashtable;
import java.util.Vector;
import java.util.Enumeration;



/*
 *      A class containing a Vector of strings, one for every node
 *      that depends on this node.
 */

class DepNode
{
    String          name;
    Vector          puppets;
    boolean         marked;
    int                 refCount;

    DepNode(String name)
    {
      this.name = name;
      puppets = new Vector(1, 1);
    }


    // Returns true if this depnode controls the specified puppet.
    boolean controlsPuppet(String puppet)
    {
      for (int i=0; i<puppets.size(); i++)
      {
            if (puppet.equals(puppets.elementAt(i)))
```

```
            {
                    return true;
            }
      }

      return false;
}


int size()
{
  return puppets.size();
}


String attributeAt(int i)
{
  return (String)(puppets.elementAt(i));
}


void addAttribute(String s)
{
  puppets.addElement(s);
}
}
```

The listing for the DependencyChecker class appears below. The discussion will focus on how this class stores dependencies, validates its data, and sorts. The DependencyChecker class is built around a hashtable of depnodes. The keys are strings that represent attributes; the elements themselves are the depnodes that describe the puppets of those attributes. When a client calls add(String puppet, String master), the dependency checker will check the hashtable to see if there is a depnode representing puppet and one representing master. Where there is not, one will be created and added to the hashtable. After ensuring that both the puppet and the master are represented, the dependency checker adds an entry for the puppet in the master's depnode. The result is that client programs tell the dependency checker that "this thing depends on that thing"; the dependency checker stores the fact that "that thing controls this thing."

The dependency checker must also represent known attributes. This is done by creating a depnode at construction time, which is called *the known node* (in the source, its handle is `theKnownNode`). Every string that is added via the `addKnown()` call is registered as a puppet of this node.

The three major tasks of the `DependencyChecker` class are maintaining the dependency list, determining whether or not the dependencies are valid, and creating a sorted list of dependencies. Representation of dependencies has already been examined; the following discussion shows how the dependencies are validated and sorted.

In order for a set of dependencies to be valid, two conditions must hold: it must be possible to derive every attribute's value, and the web of masters and puppets must not contain any loops.

To determine whether every value can be computed, the dependency checker counts root depnodes. These are depnodes that are not puppets of any other depnodes. There ought to be only a single root depnode: the known node. Any other structure is invalid. Finding root depnodes is easy: the dependency checker traverses the depnodes, incrementing a puppet's reference count once for every master that controls it. (This reference count will be useful later when it comes time to sort.) A root depnode is one whose reference count is zero—that is, a depnode not controlled by any other depnode.

If there is only one root depnode, and that one is the known node, then it is time to check for loops. The algorithm starts at the known node and recursively traces every possible downward path, keeping track of path length. Any path longer than the total number of nodes must designate a loop.

The `DependencyChecker` class uses exceptions in the validation process. If an invalid configuration is detected, an `Invalid-DependencyException` is thrown. Several layers of methods declare that they throw `InvalidDependencyException`. This makes the code much more readable, hence maintainable, than if its "train of thought" had to be constantly sidetracked in order to account for possible errors.

In order to sort its depnodes, the dependency checker once again recurses from the known node. The algorithm relies on the reference count in each depnode; this count is now valid, having been set in the validation process described above. A depnode's reference count is the number of masters on which it has a dependency. The sorting algorithm construes a slightly different meaning for the reference count. From now on, the reference count will represent the number of masters that have not yet been added to the sorted list.

The sorted list is implemented as a vector. A depnode is added to the list when the algorithm has determined that its dependencies have been resolved. When a depnode is added, all of its puppets get their reference counts decremented, meaning that each puppet has one fewer unresolved dependency. If a puppet's reference count reaches zero, all its dependencies have been resolved and it too can be added to the sorted list.

Clearly this is a recursive process. The algorithm starts at the known node. Because all puppets of the known node have zero dependencies, they can immediately be added to the sorted list, their reference counts can be zeroed, and their puppets can be recursively visited.

This recursive procedure continues until there are no more puppets (of puppets of puppets, and so on) to check. The validation requirement that there must be no loops ensures that the procedure will terminate. And the validation requirement that every depnode should ultimately descend from the known node, which is where the recursion began, ensures that the procedure will visit every depnode.

It may seem that this discussion has little to do with layout management. It only seems so. Any layout manager that supports positioning components relative to other components cannot escape dependency management. The `DependencyChecker` and `DepNode` classes encapsulate efficient, minimal, maintainable algorithms.

The source code for DependencyChecker appears below. It is found on the CD-ROM in javadevhdbk\ch04\DependencyChecker .java; readers are welcome to use and modify it.

DependencyChecker.java

```
import    java.util.Hashtable;
import    java.util.Vector;
import    java.util.Enumeration;



public class DependencyChecker
{
     private Hashtable          nodes;
     private DepNode            theKnownNode;
     private int                maxPathLength;
     private boolean            valid = false;
     private boolean            sorted = false;
     private Vector             sortedNodes;

     private static final String    KNOWN      = "9";




     /*
      *       Constructs a hashtable with a single node for
      *       representing known values.
      */

     public DependencyChecker()
     {
          nodes = new Hashtable();
          theKnownNode = getNode("9");
     }
```

```
/*
 *      If a node with the specified key exists in the
 *      hashtable,return it.  Otherwise construct one, put
 *      it in the hashtable, and return it.
 */

private DepNode getNode(String key)
{
      DepNode n = (DepNode)(nodes.get(key));
      if (n == null)
      {
            n = new DepNode(key);
            nodes.put(key, n);
      }
      return n;
}



/*
 *      Adds an attribute whose value is known.  This is
 *      represented by a dependency for that attribute on the
 *      "KNOWN" node.
 */

public void addKnown(String puppetName)
    throws InvalidDependencyException
{
      add(puppetName, KNOWN);
}



/*
 *      Adds a dependency for a named component.  Throws if the
 *      dependency already exists.  This involves adding a
 *      String element to the master node's.  This String is the
 *      key in the hashtable of the puppet node.
 */

public void add(String puppetName, String masterName)
    throws InvalidDependencyException
```

```
        {
                DepNode                 masterNode;

                valid = false;
                sorted = false;

                getNode(puppetName);              // Ensure an entry
                if (masterName.equals(KNOWN))
                {
                        masterNode = theKnownNode;
                }
                else
                {
                        masterNode = getNode(masterName);
                }
                if (masterNode.controlsPuppet(puppetName))
                {
                        // Duplicate dependency.
                        throw new InvalidDependencyException(puppetName,
                                                "Duplicate dependency");
                }
                else
                {
                        masterNode.addAttribute(puppetName);
                }
        }


        /*
         *      Resets the "marked" flag and the reference count for
         *      each node, prior to validation and sorting.
         */

        private void clearAll()
        {
                DepNode          node;
                Enumeration              enum;

                enum = nodes.elements();
                while (enum.hasMoreElements())
```

```
        {
                node = (DepNode)(enum.nextElement());
                node.marked = false;
                node.refCount = 0;
        }
}


/*
 *  Returns a Vector containing all the root nodes, i.e., those
 *  on which no other node depends.  Caller should make sure
 *  all reference counts are zero before calling.
 */
private Vector getRootNodes() throws InvalidDependencyException
{
        String          masterName;
        String          puppetName;
        DepNode         masterNode;
        DepNode         puppetNode;
        DepNode         rootNode;
        Enumeration     enum;
        int             i;

        // Count references to each node.
        enum = nodes.elements();
        while (enum.hasMoreElements())
        {
                masterNode = (DepNode)(enum.nextElement());
                masterName = masterNode.name;
                for (i=0; i<masterNode.size(); i++)
                {
                        puppetName = masterNode.attributeAt(i);
                        if (puppetName.equals(masterName))
                        {
                                // A loop!
                                throw new
                                  InvalidDependencyException(masterName,
                                                "Self dependency");
                        }
                        puppetNode = (DepNode)(nodes.get(puppetName));
                        puppetNode.refCount++;
```

```
            }
        }

        // Return array of nodes with zero reference count.
        Vector vec = new Vector();
        enum = nodes.elements();
        while (enum.hasMoreElements())
        {
            rootNode = (DepNode)(enum.nextElement());
            if (rootNode.refCount == 0)
            {
                vec.addElement(rootNode);
            }
        }
        return vec;
    }


/*
 *  Recursively follows all paths from node, checking for length
 *  violation.  The longest legal path is maxPathLength, which
 *  is the total number of nodes.  If a path is longer than
 *  that, at least one node must have been visited at least
 *  twice, indicating a loop.
 */

private void checkNodeForLoops(DepNode node, int depth)
    throws InvalidDependencyException
{
    String              puppetString = null;
    DepNode             puppetNode = null;

    if (++depth > maxPathLength)
    {
        throw new InvalidDependencyException(node.name,
                                             "Loop");
    }

    for (int i=0; i<node.size(); i++)
    {
```

```
            puppetString = node.attributeAt(i);
            puppetNode = (DepNode)(nodes.get(puppetString));
            checkNodeForLoops(puppetNode, depth);
        }
    }


/*
 *      Validates the set of dependencies by verifying that
 *      there are no loops and every dependent node can be
 *      resolved.  Return without an exception means the
 *      structure is valid.
 */

public void validate() throws InvalidDependencyException
{
        Vector              roots;

        valid = false;

        //
        //      Identify root nodes.  For every node to be
        //      resolvable, there must be exactly one root,
        //      namely, the "known" node.
        //
        clearAll();
        roots = getRootNodes();
        if (roots.size() != 1  ||  roots.elementAt(0) !=
                                theKnownNode)
        {
                throw new InvalidDependencyException("???",
                            "Unresolved dependencies");
        }

        //
        //      Everything descends from the known.  Make sure
        //      there are no loops.
        //
        maxPathLength = nodes.size();
```

```
        checkNodeForLoops(theKnownNode, 0);
        valid = true;
}



/*
 *  Returns a Vector of names, in dependency order.
 *  Dependencies may be resolved in order of appearance in the
 *  Vector.
 *
 *  Assumes reference counts are valid.  Recurses through
 *  resolved nodes, decrementing child reference counts.  When a
 *  child's reference count reaches zero, that child is
 *  resolved; it is put in the Vector and recursed upon.
 *
 *  Throws InvalidDependencyException if structure was not
 *  valid.
 */

public Vector sort() throws InvalidDependencyException
{
        if (sorted)
             return sortedNodes;

        if (!valid)
             validate();

        sortedNodes = new Vector();
        sortRecurse(sortedNodes, theKnownNode);
        sorted = true;
        return sortedNodes;
}



/*
 *  Recursively sorts dependencies on a given node, adding
 *  resolved attributes to a Vector.  Assumes the given node
 *  has been resolved.
 */
```

```
private void sortRecurse(Vector vec, DepNode masterNode)
{
      String               puppetName;
      DepNode              puppetNode;
      int                  nNodes;

      nNodes = masterNode.size();
      for (int i=0; i<nNodes; i++)
      {
            puppetName = masterNode.attributeAt(i);
            puppetNode = (DepNode)(nodes.get(puppetName));
            if (-puppetNode.refCount == 0)
            {
                  vec.addElement(puppetNode.name);
                  sortRecurse(vec, puppetNode);
            }
      }
}
```

Inside *FormLayout*

With dependency management encapsulated in its own class, it is now time to look at the implementation of the FormLayout class.

The first thing to realize is that it takes a lot of information to represent a component. Information will have to be stored for each of the eight attributes of every component (horizontal attributes X, R, W, and C; vertical attributes Y, B, H, and C). For each attribute it will be necessary to represent the corresponding substring of the descriptor string, the attribute's dependencies, the formula for deriving the attribute's value, and eventually, it is hoped, the value itself.

Consider the ongoing example of a scrollbar whose descriptor string (as passed into Container.add()) is:

```
"sbar/X=Xokbtn;W=Wokbtn/Y=A0;B=Yokbtn-5"
```

Consider what is required just to represent the coordinate of this scrollbar's bottom edge. The substring of the descriptor is "Yokbtn-5." There is a dependency on the Y value of "okbtn." The formula is the Y value of "okbtn," minus five. The value will have to be stored in an int somewhere.

There is enough going on here that there should be a helper class. It is called `ComponentSpec`, and it encapsulates whatever information and behavior are required to represent a single component. The best way to design this class is to determine what `FormLayout` requires of it, so we begin by considering `FormLayout`.

`FormLayout` has an instance of `DependencyChecker` and maintains a hashtable of its component specs, keyed by descriptor string. The `addLayoutComponent()` method adds the new entry. At some point every descriptor string will have to be parsed, and dependencies will have to be deduced from the string and reported to the dependency checker. `addLayoutComponent()` is an appropriate place to do this. Because a descriptor refers to a single component, it is reasonable to construct a `ComponentSpec` for the component at this time and defer to that class the parsing of the descriptor and the management of dependencies. The layout manager just divides the descriptor string into the name portion (before the first slash) and the remainder, and constructs a component spec. The constructor for the component spec is passed the two pieces of the descriptor string, as well as references to the component, the dependency checker, and the layout manager itself. In the code fragment below, `specs` is the hashtable of component specs.

FormLayout.addLayoutComponent()

```
/*
 *      The descriptor provides 3 fields, separated by slashes.  The
 *      1st field is a name for the component.  The other fields are
 *      descriptors for horizontal and vertical attributes of the
 *      component.
 */
```

```
public void addLayoutComponent(String descriptor,
                                Component component)
{
        ComponentSpec        cspec;
        StringTokenizer      st;
        String               name;
        String               subdesc;

        int slashIndex = descriptor.indexOf("/");
        name = descriptor.substring(0, slashIndex).trim();
        subdesc = descriptor.substring(slashIndex+1).trim();
        cspec = new ComponentSpec(name, component,
                                   subdesc, checker, this);
        specs.put(name, cspec);
}
```

At layout time, the layout manager has to determine the values of each component's attributes in the proper order. There is no sense trying to compute the y coordinate of a button, if that value depends on the height of some scrollbar whose height is not yet known. The dependency checker's job is to tell the layout manager in what order to compute values.

Recall that the strings in the vector returned by the dependency checker's sort() method are in the format *attribute:componentname*. For example, the X coordinate of a component called zipcodetextfield would be represented by the string X:zipcodetextfield. The code below, which is form layout's layoutContainer() method, traverses the vector of sorted attributes. It splits each attribute into a parameter name (the part before the colon, called paramName), and a component name (the part after the colon, called componentName).

At this point, componentName can be used as an index into the form layout manager's hashtable. The hashtable contains specs for the components. Recall that the functionality of the ComponentSpec class has not yet been defined; we are still in the process of figuring out what it needs to do. We now realize that we would like a component spec to be able to compute the value of an attribute; the layout manager will only require a component spec to do so once all the attribute's dependencies have been resolved.

So the first loop in `layoutContainer()` traverses the sorted list of attributes, telling the component that owns the attribute to compute the attribute's value. Once this is done, every component spec will know the x, y, width, and height (as well as the "r," "b," horizontal center, and vertical center) of every component. The second loop in `layoutContainer()` traverses the component specs in the hashtable, instructing each component spec to reshape its corresponding component.

The code for the `layoutContainer()` method is shown below.

FormLayout.layoutContainer()

```
public void layoutContainer(Container parent)
{
        Vector               sorted = null;
        String               nextAttrib;
        String               componentName;
        String               paramName;
        ComponentSpec        cspec;

        this.parent = parent;

        //
        //  Have the dependency checker provide a Vector of sorted
        //  attributes.  All value may safely be computed in the
        //  provided order.
        //
        try
        {
                sorted = checker.sort();
        }
        catch (InvalidDependencyException ex)
        {
                return;
        }

        //
        //        Compute all values.  The elements of sorted are strings
```

```
//        which specify component attributes.
//
for (int i=0; i<sorted.size(); i++)
{
        nextAttrib = (String)(sorted.elementAt(i));
        StringTokenizer st =
            new StringTokenizer(nextAttrib, ":");
        paramName = st.nextToken();
        componentName = st.nextToken();
        cspec = (ComponentSpec)(specs.get(componentName));
        cspec.computeAttributeValue(paramName);
}


//
//        Reshape all components.
//
Enumeration enum = specs.elements();
while (enum.hasMoreElements())
{
      cspec = (ComponentSpec)(enum.nextElement());
      cspec.reshape();
}
}
```

The addLayoutComponent() and layoutContainer() methods are the important ones. The other three methods required by the LayoutManager interface are trivial. removeLayoutComponent() does nothing; component removal is not supported, as it is likely to result in an incomplete set of dependencies. minimumLayoutSize() method and preferredLayoutSize() return hardwired values. This suggests that a panel that uses this layout manager should not be added to a container whose own layout manager will query the panel's preferred size. This restriction is mild. A panel that uses form layout is unlikely to appear in a flow layout, for example, or anywhere except Center of a border layout.

The complete code for FormLayout is listed below, and appears on the CD-ROM in javadevhdbk\ch04\FormLayout.java. A Java 1.1 version of the same code appears on the CD-ROM in javadevhdbk\ch04_1.1.

FormLayout.java

```java
import       java.awt.*;
import       java.util.*;


public class FormLayout implements LayoutManager
{
      Hashtable             specs;
      DependencyChecker     checker;
      Container             parent;


      public FormLayout()
      {
            specs = new Hashtable();
            checker = new DependencyChecker();
      }


      ComponentSpec getComponentSpec(String name)
      {
            return (ComponentSpec)(specs.get(name));
      }


      int parentWidth()
      {
            return parent.size().width;
      }


      int parentHeight()
      {
            return parent.size().height;
      }


      /*
       *      The descriptor provides 3 fields, separated by slashes.  The
       *      1st field is a name for the component.  The other fields are
       *      descriptors for horizontal and vertical attributes of the
```

```
 *      component.
 */

public void addLayoutComponent(String descriptor,
                               Component component)
{
      ComponentSpec      cspec;
      StringTokenizer    st;
      String             name;
      String             subdesc;

      int slashIndex = descriptor.indexOf("/");
      name = descriptor.substring(0, slashIndex).trim();
      subdesc = descriptor.substring(slashIndex+1).trim();
      cspec = new ComponentSpec(name, component,
                                subdesc, checker, this);
      specs.put(name, cspec);
}


public void layoutContainer(Container parent)
{
      Vector             sorted = null;
      String             nextAttrib;
      String             componentName;
      String             paramName;
      ComponentSpec       cspec;

      this.parent = parent;

      //
      // Have the dependency checker provide a Vector of sorted
      // attributes.  All value may safely be computed in the
      // provided order.
      //
      try
      {
          sorted = checker.sort();
      }
      catch (InvalidDependencyException ex)
      {
          return;
      }
```

```
        //
        //      Compute all values.  The elements of sorted are strings
        //      which specify component attributes.
        //
        for (int i=0; i<sorted.size(); i++)
        {
                nextAttrib = (String)(sorted.elementAt(i));
                StringTokenizer st =
                    new StringTokenizer(nextAttrib, ":");
                paramName = st.nextToken();
                componentName = st.nextToken();
            cspec = (ComponentSpec)(specs.get(componentName));
            cspec.computeAttributeValue(paramName);
        }


        //
        //      Reshape all components.
        //
        Enumeration enum = specs.elements();
        while (enum.hasMoreElements())
        {
                cspec = (ComponentSpec)(enum.nextElement());
                cspec.reshape();
        }
    }


    public void removeLayoutComponent(Component c)                { }


    public Dimension preferredLayoutSize(Container parent)
    {
            return(parent.size());
    }


    public Dimension minimumLayoutSize(Container parent)
    {
            return(new Dimension(100, 100));
    }
}
```

The *ComponentSpec* Class

The FormLayout class constructs an instance of ComponentSpec for each component. The instances are stored in a hashtable and keyed by name. The class must be able to parse a descriptor string, report its dependencies to the dependency checker, and eventually compute the values of its attributes. The source for ComponentSpec is on the CD-ROM in javadevhdbk\ch04\ComponentSpec.java. Because it is nearly 600 lines long, we will not present the entire listing here. This section just shows the top-level design of the class, with enough explanation so that understanding the code should be easy.

Every component has eight attributes, four for horizontal information and four for vertical. FormLayout has three eight-element arrays—called descriptors[], deltas[], and values[]—for storing attribute descriptors (substrings of the original descriptor string), deltas (the optional plus-or-minus value), and eventual values. At construction time, the descriptors and deltas are parsed out of the full descriptor string. The values are not computed until the layout manager executes layoutContainer().

For easy array indexing, eight final static ints are defined, with names that correspond to the eight attribute names:

```
final static int    PARAM_X     = 0;
final static int    PARAM_HC    = 1;
final static int    PARAM_R     = 2;
final static int    PARAM_W     = 3;
final static int    PARAM_Y     = 4;
final static int    PARAM_VC    = 5;
final static int    PARAM_B     = 6;
final static int    PARAM_H     = 7;
```

Here and elsewhere, horizontal center ("HC") begins to be distinguished from vertical center ("VC"). Until now we have used "C" to denote both, as a convenience to programmers, and figured out from context which one was intended. From now on they must be distinct.

The `ComponentSpec` class also has int instance variables for the horizontal and vertical "formulas." The formula represents which attributes were specified in the descriptor string. The X formula might be x coordinate only, for example, or x and width. Final static ints are also defined for the nine horizontal formulas and the nine vertical ones:

```
// Values for hFormula.
final static int    H_FORMULA_X     = 0;    // x is specified
final static int    H_FORMULA_C     = 1;    // center is specified
final static int    H_FORMULA_R     = 2;    // right is specified
final static int    H_FORMULA_XR    = 3;    // x, right are specified
final static int    H_FORMULA_XW    = 4;    // x, width specified
final static int    H_FORMULA_RW    = 5;    // right, width specified
final static int    H_FORMULA_CW    = 6;    // center, width specified
final static int    H_FORMULA_XC    = 7;    // x, center specified
final static int    H_FORMULA_RC    = 8;    // right, width specified

// Values for vFormula.
final static int    V_FORMULA_Y     = 0;    // y is specified
final static int    V_FORMULA_C     = 1;    // center is specified
final static int    V_FORMULA_B     = 2;    // bottom is specified
final static int    V_FORMULA_YB    = 3;    // y, bottom are specified
final static int    V_FORMULA_YH    = 4;    // y, height specified
final static int    V_FORMULA_BH    = 5;    // bottom, height specified
final static int    V_FORMULA_CH    = 6;    // center, height specified
final static int    V_FORMULA_YC    = 7;    // top, center specified
final static int    V_FORMULA_BC    = 8;    // bottom, center specified
```

The constructor for `ComponentSpec` gets passed the component's descriptor string; it calls a method called `parseDescriptor()`, which initializes the `descriptors[]` and `deltas[]` arrays.

As an example, consider an OK button whose X is 50, whose right edge is 10 pixels in from the container's right edge, whose top is aligned with the top of a Cancel button, and whose height is one-quarter the height of the container. The descriptor for this button would be:

```
okbtn/X=A50;R=F1-10/Y=Ycancelbtn;H=F.25
```

The formulas would then be H_FORMULA_XR and V_FORMULA_YH. After parsing, the descriptors[] and deltas[] arrays contain the following, as shown in Table 4.3.

TABLE 4.3   descriptor and delta arrays after parsing

Attribute	descriptors[Attribute]	deltas[Attribute]
PARAM_X	A50	0
PARAM_HC		0
PARAM_R	F1	-10
PARAM_W		0
PARAM_Y	Ycancelbtn	0
PARAM_VC .		0
PARAM_B		0
PARAM_H	F25	0

The constructor next calls the method registerDependencies(), which provides information to the dependency checker. This method and its subordinates must consider every possible formula case-by-case, and this is what makes the class so lengthy. For each formula, those parameters that are not provided must still be derived, because values for other components might depend on them. Given any two horizontal attributes, the other two can always be derived (if you know width and R, you can compute X and center). The same holds true for vertical attributes. The programmer must tell the dependency checker that those attributes that are not supplied by the formula string depend on those that are supplied. In the example, HC and W both have dependencies on X and R, while both VC and B depend on Y and H. The calls to add these attributes to the dependency checker might look like this:

```
checker.add("HC:okbtn", "X:okbtn");
checker.add("W:okbtn", "R:okbtn");
checker.add("HC:okbtn", "X:okbtn");
```

```
checker.add("W:okbtn", "R:okbtn");
checker.add("VC:okbtn", "Y:okbtn");
checker.add("B:okbtn", "H:okbtn");
checker.add("VC:okbtn", "Y:okbtn");
checker.add("B:okbtn", "H:okbtn");
```

Three of the attributes (X, R, and H) have their values explicitly stated by the descriptor. These are known values, so they will be passed to the dependency checker using the `addKnown()` method:

```
checker.addKnown("X:okbtn");
checker.addKnown("R:okbtn");
checker.addKnown("H:okbtn");
```

The last attribute to consider is Y, which depends on the Y of some other component. This relationship is communicated to the dependency checker as follows:

```
checker.add("Y:okbtn", "Y:cancelbtn");
```

Eventually all dependencies for all components are reported to the dependency checker. Later, when the layout manager executes `layoutContainer()`, each component spec receives a number of calls to `computeAttributeValue(String attributeName)`. This method inspects the formula for the desired attribute. If the formula begins with "A," the value can be determined from the rest of the formula. If the formula begins with "F," the value can be determined from the rest of the formula and the parent container's size. For all other formats, the value is the value of some other attribute of (possibly) some other component. Because the other component's name is known, its own component spec can be retrieved from the hashtable and the value can be looked up in the `values[]` array. The dependency checker guarantees that what is found in `values[]` is valid.

After the value is computed, the delta is added to it.

Once `computeAttributeValue()` has been called in the proper order for every attribute of every component, all values are known and the components can be reshaped.

Summary of the Design

This example of an interdependent layout manager is typical of the effort involved. Any interdependent layout manager will require a dependency checker. The one developed here (`DependencyChecker.java`) is approximately 350 lines long.

An interdependent layout manager will need a helper class to encapsulate a component's positional information as well as any parsing that may be required. The helper class should be responsible for registering dependencies with the dependency checker. In this example, the `ComponentSpec` helper class is around 600 lines long. The size comes from the large number of input formats supported by the layout policy, and not from any inherent complexity of interdependent layout managers.

The layout manager itself is so well supported by the dependency checker and the component spec that it is just over 100 lines long.

Using FormLayout

In the section titled *An Interdependent Layout Manager*, we showed a screenshot (Figure 4.12) of an imperfect scrolling window that used a border layout manager. We also showed a version (Figure 4.13) that used a form layout manager. That version's scrollbars were correctly aligned. For reference, the correct figure is duplicated here in Figure 4.15.

With so much effort put into developing the form layout manager, there is every right to expect that client code will be simple. This is in fact the case. The code that generates Figure 4.15 is on the CD-ROM in `javadevhdbk\ch04\FormScrollWin.java`.

FIGURE 4.15

Scrolling window with
form layout manager

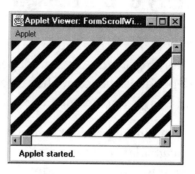

FormScrollWin.java

```
import java.awt.*;
import java.applet.Applet;


public class FormScrollWin extends Applet
{
    public void init()
    {
        Scrollbar      hbar, vbar;
        StripeCanvas   canvas;

        setLayout(new FormLayout());
        hbar = new Scrollbar(Scrollbar.HORIZONTAL);
        vbar = new Scrollbar(Scrollbar.VERTICAL);
        canvas = new StripeCanvas();
        add("view/X=A0;R=Xvert/Y=A0;B=Yhoriz", canvas);
        add("horiz/X=A0;R=Rview/B=F1", hbar);
        add("vert/R=F1/Y=A0;B=Bview", vbar);
    }
}




class StripeCanvas extends Canvas
{
    public void paint(Graphics g)
    {
```

```
        for (int i=0; i<size().width+size().height; i++)
            if ((i/15) % 2 == 0)
                g.drawLine(i, 0, 0, i);
    }
}
```

The *FormLab*

The only difficult thing about using the form layout manager is getting the descriptor string right for each component. One way to get it right is trial-and-error recompilation.

An easier way is to use the `FormLab` applet on the CD-ROM. This applet presents the user with four color-coded panels in which to type descriptor strings. Each panel is activated by a checkbox. When the user clicks the Show button, a frame is displayed, laid out using a form layout manager. The frame contains one button for each activated panel. Clicking on any of these buttons dismisses the frame.

`FormLab` has several pre-packaged sets of descriptor strings; these can be selected via a choice button at the top of the applet. When a set is selected, its descriptor strings are copied into the panels. Users are free to modify the layouts by editing the strings.

Figure 4.16 shows `FormLab`'s main window.

Figure 4.17 shows one of FormLab's pre-packaged options, called *tapering* in the choice button.

The four buttons in this panel were added to their container using the following descriptor strings:

all/C=F.5;W=F1/Y=A5;H=A25

half/C=F.5;W=F.5/Y=Ball+5;H=A25

quarter/C=F.5;W=F.25/Y=Bhalf+5;H=A25

eighth/C=F.5;W=F.125/Y=Bquarter+5;H=A25

FIGURE 4.16

FormLab

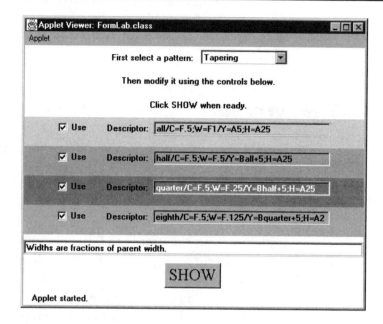

FIGURE 4.17

Tapering

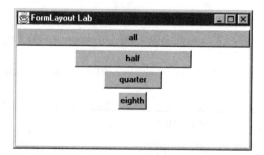

Summary

Java layout managers encapsulate component sizing and positioning. Programmers operate one step removed from precise layout, specifying layout policies, not widths, heights, and positions.

The standard suite of layout managers does a decent job of providing desired functionality. Effective use of the standard layout managers requires an understanding of each manager's algorithm. It is especially important to know when a manager honors a component's preferred size, and when the manager dictates size.

When the standard layout managers are inadequate, it is necessary to create a custom layout manager. This requires implementing the `LayoutManager` interface, which is not especially difficult. The alternative is to use no layout manager at all; usually this is more complicated than it seems, and may be more complicated than creating a custom layout manager class.

Ordinary layout managers may be arbitrarily simple or complicated. Interdependent layout managers, which support positioning components with respect to other components, are moderately complicated. A major portion of the work of developing an interdependent layout manager involves maintaining dependencies. The dependency checker given here can be reused for any dependent layout manager.

CHAPTER

FIVE

5

Portability Issues

- Data representation

- Timing

- Package and class availability

- File system semantics

- Visual aspects

- Local/user configuration

- Network class loading

- Security effects

This chapter discusses the design and implementation considerations that relate to writing genuinely platform-independent Java
code. Platform independence presents some challenges that cannot
be hidden by a language and library set alone.

The entire Java system, both the design of the language and the
libraries, is intended to provide the greatest possible inherent portability. This requires compilers that demand the exact same language
for each platform. The detailed semantics of both the language and
the libraries must be the same on all platforms. The compiler's binary
code output must be independent of the platform. This demands the
use of the runtime interpretation that is provided by the Java Virtual
Machine. Even these rules, which are all that can be imposed at the
language level, do not solve all portability problems.

Despite Java's design, the programmer must still take some care to
avoid writing a program that is not portable. Many problems are
easy to avoid, but some of the potential pitfalls when writing a
portable program are less obvious. The issues that are discussed in
this chapter cover a variety of topics. The underlying platform can
affect the format of data on network connections and in files. Variations in the speed of the CPU and in the thread scheduling scheme of
the host operating system can cause an incorrectly designed program
to fail. Required support classes must be available at runtime and,
although Java can load classes from either the local file system or the
network, these classes must still be accessible and Java has some
rules that define the expected directory layout for classes. The user
interface presented by the Abstract Window Toolkit (AWT) adopts
the look and feel of the host platform and uses the resources of that

platform for fonts and colors. This leads to presentation variations between platforms and optimal behavior might require adjustment or configuration on each platform. This is often best achieved if the program allows the user a means of configuring preferences. Applets run subordinate to security restrictions imposed by the browser. These restrictions are designed to maintain the security and integrity of the host but vary between browsers.

Data Representation

Java requires that data items always appear to have the same representation regardless of the platform or the compiler. An `int`, for example, must always behave as if it were a 32-bit two's complement value. In fact, the standard does not require that this is actually how it is *stored*, but only how it *behaves* and *appears*. These aspects of the language are tightly defined and, in the absence of implementation error, do not cause difficulty when changing platforms.

The representation of characters is defined to appear to be a 16-bit unsigned quantity using the Unicode character set. However, most of the platforms in which Java runs do not support the full Unicode character set. This makes it difficult for the Java runtime system to do so. Because of these difficulties, a quite properly written program might still fail at the I/O level if it uses non-ASCII characters from the Unicode set. Java 1.1 supports those characters in the Unicode set which have direct equivalents on the current host system. For example, a machine running with a French Canadian keyboard and screen configuration is able to support accented characters. In Java 1.1 those characters will be handled correctly, being translated between the local machine representation and Unicode as they pass in and out of the program.

TIP

As additional support, the Java distribution includes the `native2ascii` tool. This command-line tool converts between local character sets and the ASCII-only file format expected by the remainder of the Java tools. The output of this program retains the special characters by translating them into, or from, Unicode escape sequences—the `\uxxxx` literal format. This allows you to edit your Java source programs and support files on a local text editor—using the characters available on your machine—and convert the result to a format suitable for Java. Additionally, `Reader` and `Writer` classes in the `java.io` package perform I/O that includes these conversions in a running program.

When data leave the confines of the Java program, for example being saved in a file or sent over a network, more difficulties can arise. Different systems often have their own ways of coding network or disk information, and these methods are often incompatible. Java can handle these problems in two ways. First, any external data produced or received by Java programs, whether on a network or a disk, will have a format that is independent of the platform. Second, where data is being shared with a non-Java system, such as the conventional platform that is supporting the Java environment, Java allows the necessary control of individual bits and bytes to convert between the formats, provided only that the definition is available for that other format.

NOTE

A common problem that arises when data is shared between platforms is the representation of "end of line." This is done with the line-feed character on UNIX, with line-feed followed by carriage-return in MS-DOS, and carriage-return on Macintosh. The Java libraries hide these problems, but can only do so in Java programs. Files written from Java will still require conversion if taken to a non-Java program on another platform.

> **TIP**
>
> Inside a Java program the ordering of bytes within longer numeric types is effectively invisible; in the absence of pointer manipulation you can only break down an int, say, by using the shift operators (>>, >>> and <<), or the bitwise *and* (&) and *or* (|) operators. When data is moved out of the Java program, however, it is often important to know that the byte ordering used by Java is high byte first, regardless of the conventions of the host platform.

Timing

For many programs the time taken for execution is a matter of user convenience rather than correctness of operation. If the process takes a long time, the delay might be irritating but the answer is usually still right, even when it is late.

However, this is not always the case. In the particular category of program, referred to as *real time*, the time taken for execution is as much a part of the correct operation as any other measure. An everyday example may be found in video player software; that is, MPEG or AVI players, not the kind that sit under TV sets. In this case, the video player software is only operating *correctly* if the frames are updated at the proper rate, and in proper synchronization with the sound output. Although this is a readily understood example, it is just one small example in a whole arena.

Unfortunately, even perfect software cannot make a CPU work any faster than the hardware dictates, so it is always possible that a program that executes perfectly well on one machine might fail on another machine that is operating at a different speed. There are two modes of failure related to timing. In the obvious case, the slower processor is unable to complete a calculation in time and the whole program fails in consequence. This problem can only be addressed in software by improving the algorithm or its implementation. If such improvements are insufficient, then more powerful hardware is required.

The other failure mode relates to the interactions between multiple threads. A loose description of a thread is that it is a mechanism that allows a single program to appear to be doing more than one thing at once. Some machines have multiple CPUs, and these can really do more than one thing at a time. In other systems with only a single CPU, the effect is only an illusion and results are achieved in the same way as by an office worker: by doing a little of one job, then a little of another, and so forth. The term *concurrent* is used to describe multiple threads that are "on the go" simultaneously but are not necessarily actually being worked on by physically separate CPUs. Where different CPUs are working on threads actually at the same time, the threads are said to be running *in parallel*.

In an office, workers who have more than one task in progress might keep working on one job for as long as they can usefully make progress on it, ignoring all others until something prevents further progress, for instance if they need an answer to a question from a colleague. When not more progress can be made, the workers move on to a different job and get on with that instead. This style of working, when applied to threading, approximately describes the idea of a *preemptive* scheduling system. Other workers might take the view that they want to be able to demonstrate steady progress on all tasks. To do so they might do half an hour on one job, if they are able, and then move on to another task even if they could continue with the present one. This style of work, applied to a threading system, describes the idea of a *timesharing* scheduling system.

In a threaded system a number of programming difficulties can arise specifically from the nature of threads. Suppose that a program has two threads that are operating concurrently. They might or might not be timesharing—the Java environment does not specify one behavior rather than the other. If the program is written on a computationally slow machine, it could easily be that a thread involving a great deal of computation might take longer than another thread that is waiting for disk I/O. If the program depends for its correctness on the disk having completed its task before the computation completes, this might work correctly on the slow development machine. If you run the same code on a machine with a comparable disk system, but a faster processor, then the computation thread could complete sooner and thereby cause the whole program fail.

A timing dependency of this type actually constitutes incorrect design or implementation; however, the example of two uncoordinated threads shows again that a portable language and library set is not enough.

> **TIP** The particular issues relating to synchronizing threads and handling the different models are discussed in more detail in Chapter 7, *Threads.*

Java leaves one aspect of the threading model undefined. Given two or more threads of the same priority, all with useful work to perform, some systems might timeshare the CPU between these threads. Other systems allow the current thread to run continuously for as long as it usefully can, only changing to a different thread if a higher priority one becomes runnable or this one cannot proceed. The timesharing system is often considered to be easier to understand, but it is usually less efficient than the second approach. Whatever the relative merits of these approaches in any particular program, code must be correctly designed if it is to work properly on all possible systems.

Package and Class Availability

Java comes with a clearly defined set of core packages, offering a wide base of standard support. Any program, whether it be application or applet, can depend on the availability of the classes in these core packages. More advanced or more unusual programs often require additional support classes and you must take care to ensure that these are available on the target machine.

In addition to core packages, Java also provides support, or non-core, classes. These non-core classes can be considered in three categories. *Required* and *standard extension* are Java terms describing classes. *Third party* refers to additional classes that are not referred to by the specification.

Every implementation of Java, if it is to be given the name *Java*, must include the classes referred to as required. In addition, a number of packages, and groups of classes within packages, are defined by the 1.1 release to be standard extensions, which means that they should be provided by an implementation unless there is some pressing reason that makes this impossible (such as a platform that physically does not have sound equipment).

It is safe to use required classes and entirely reasonable to use standard extension classes for general development. If, however, you use third-party classes, you must decide if these classes become *required support for this product*, or if the program can operate in a reduced way without them. If it is possible, practical, and legal you could supply these support packages with the product. If legal restrictions exist, it might be best to develop alternative classes.

Network speed constraints might make it undesirable to download large volumes of support classes. Further, because of the time taken to set up an individual HTTP connection, transferring large numbers of classes individually will be time consuming even if the classes are small. For this reason, all related class files should be packaged in an archive so they are transferred over the network in a single connection. The standard archive from Java 1.1 is the JAR format. Before 1.1, there was no standard mechanism, and proprietary extensions were offered by both Netscape and Microsoft.

When a class is part of a developer's local support package—in other words, the class is directly accessible from the filesystem of the developer's machine but is not part of the JDK distribution itself—that class must be distributed with any program that uses it. It is very easy to fall into the habit of thinking that class loading happens "by magic" in Java, and that this will be the case over any TCP/IP network too. Packages, and classes in packages, can be distributed along with an applet over the network. For this to happen, however, the package must be correctly installed on the server. This requires a little more thought than simply copying an applet into the classes directory beneath the invoking HTML page.

Locating Classes and Packages

When a browser loads an applet over the Web, that browser has a notion of the classpath from which it was obtained. This is the return value from the applet method `getCodeBase()`. It is the base URL from which the main `Applet` class was loaded. If the applet asks for additional classes, the browser should search the local system—that is, the system that is running the browser—for them first using the `CLASSPATH` or other equivalent mechanism and, if this fails, try to load them from the Web server that supplied the applet. Classes in the unnamed package are taken from the same directory as the codebase. For classes that are members of a package, the codebase is extended by the package name. Hence the class must be located properly on the server. For example, suppose an applet is called `Complex`. It is loaded from a Web page at the URL `http://www.unknown.org/examples/mathematical.html`. If the applet tag that invokes it is `<applet code=Complex.class width=100 height=100>`, then the codebase value is `http://www.unknown.org/examples/` and the file `Complex.class` must be placed in the same directory as the file `mathematical.html`. The diagram in Figure 5.1 shows this.

On the other hand, an applet tag `<applet code=Complex .class codebase=classes width=100 height=100>` would result in a codebase of `http://www.unknown.org/examples/classes/`. The file `Complex.class` should be placed in this subdirectory, beneath the directory containing the HTML file, as shown in Figure 5.2

FIGURE 5.1

Class location for an applet with default `codebase`

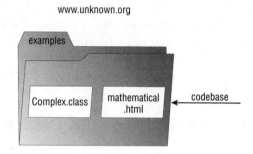

FIGURE 5.2

Class location for an applet with `codebase=classes`

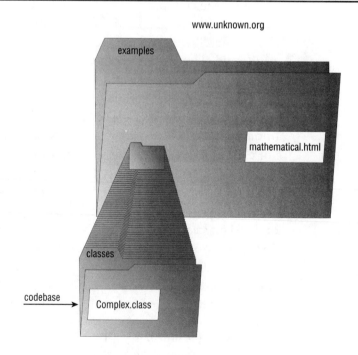

If the `Complex` class requires a support class `unknown.utils`
`.fft`—that is, the class is called `fft` and is a member of the package `unknown.utils`—then the classfile `fft.class` must be placed
in the appropriate directory. In either of these cases, the directory will
be called `utils` and must be located in a directory called `unknown`.
This in turn must be located in the same directory as the applet.
Figures 5.3 and 5.4 show this modification to each of the earlier
examples.

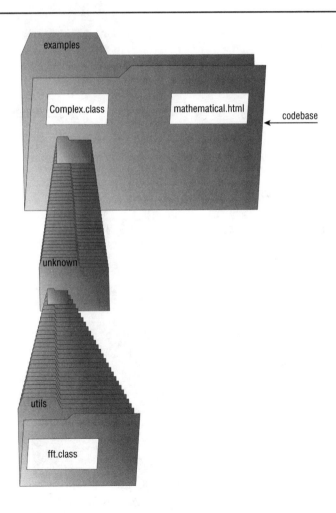

FIGURE 5.4

Location of support class
that is a package mem-
ber with `codebase=
classes`

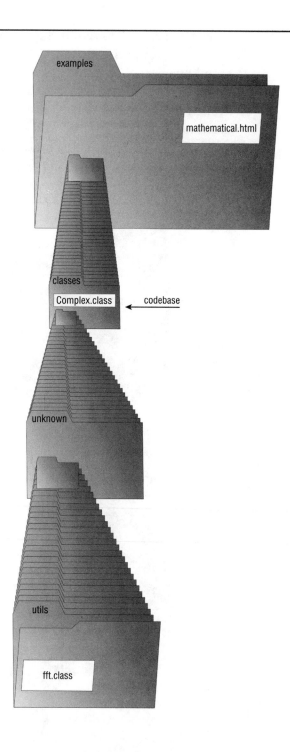

This concept can be extended to applets themselves. Although it is usual for applets to belong to the default or unnamed package, this is not actually required. If an applet is called `unknown.math.Bessel`, then it can still be loaded from a Web server, but a slightly different setup is required.

To load this class properly, the `<applet...>` tag must reflect the proper codebase. The codebase is the directory for classes that belong to the unnamed package. Therefore, the following HTML is required: `<applet code=unknown.math.Bessel.class width=100 height=100>`. In this case, the file `Bessel.class` must be located in a subdirectory called `math`, in a subdirectory called `unknown`, in the directory containing the HTML file. Notice that the `code=xxx` part of the applet tag should really be considered as a class specification rather than a file specification. It is unfortunate, therefore, that the specification describes this as the filename, and requires the `.class` file extension to be present. It is similarly somewhat misleading that the codebase directive is so named rather than being classbase or classpath, either of which would be more consistent with the operation of the command line tools. This is shown in Figure 5.5.

> **NOTE**
>
> The appletviewer programs supplied with both JDK 1.0.x and 1.1 do not reject an `<applet...>` tag if the `.class` part is missing. Omitting it would make the detail of the `<applet...>` tag more consistent with the command line tools, but might result in problems with some other browsers.

In this last example, it is both correct and workable for the `<applet...>` tag to include a `codebase=xxx` specification. In such a case, the directory structure must still reflect the package naming, but the directory containing the directory unknown must be that specified by the codebase directive.

FIGURE 5.5

Class location for an applet that is a package member with default codebase

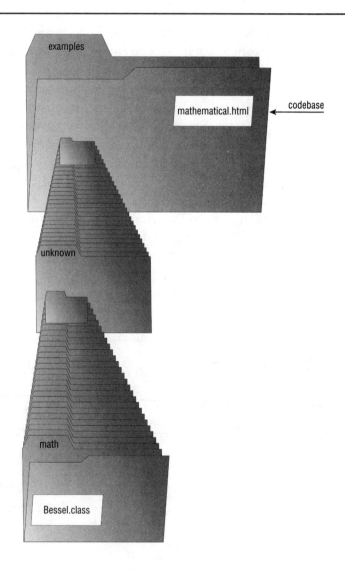

Naming Packages

When classes are to be distributed widely over the Internet, there is great potential for difficulties arising from naming. If an applet tries to load a support class called MyButton, the intention of the programmer is probably that a class defining a customized UI component should be loaded from the same site as the applet. If, however, a class with this name exists on the local classpath, then security rules demand that the local class should be loaded in preference. Because it is unlikely that the two classes will perform exactly comparable functions, with compatible public APIs, the result will almost certainly be the failure of the applet.

Avoiding this difficulty requires a little organization in the allocation of names. Ideally, all publicly distributed classes should belong to a package that uniquely belongs to the author of that class. For Internet-connected organizations this need can be addressed by reversing the domain name and using the result as the first part of the package name. Hence, MyButton created at unknown.org would actually be org.unknown.MyButton. This convention is suggested by the Java documentation.

However, some questions remain with this suggested convention. First, if the unknown organization is large, several programmers might create classes called MyButton. Now there is a potential for local conflict, and for problems when installing these on their Web server. Therefore, in large organizations the domain-package name should be extended with additional naming levels. Appropriate possibilities include the department name or an employee number. For example, the button might be placed in org.unknown.research.MyButton or org.unknown.1234.MyButton. Of course, if two classes are so similarly named, they should be checked for duplication of effort.

Web Server Directory Layout

Web servers that carry many applets requiring support packages might require many directories. For example, if applets are maintained for the support of ten different pages in different directories, and each applet requires three directories in a chain to properly represent package names, this results in a total of 30 specially created directories. The problem is compounded if many supporting classes by different programmers are used. Figure 5.6 exemplifies this problem.

Under these conditions, it might be better to put all Java code in one specific directory tree and use an absolute codebase in the applet tags in the HTML files. For example, `<applet code=org.unknown .research.MyButton.class codebase=/Java width=100 height=100>`. Imagine another applet written by someone in the accounts department, called `HerButton`, shares the use of other supporting classes with `MyButton`. The second applet could be loaded from the tag `<applet code=org.unknown.accounts .HerButton codebase=/Java width=100 height=100>`. Under this layout, far fewer directories are needed, packages are shared, and at most one copy of each classfile is required. Figure 5.7 shows the effect of this modified approach applied to the same example that was used in Figure 5.6.

Despite its many advantages, this approach has two disadvantages. First, there is no clear link between the HTML pages and the applets that they invoke. Second (possibly more tiresome), there is a restriction that affects the loading of sound files into applets. In JDK 1.0.2, a path to an audio file, in the `getAudioClip()` and related methods, cannot have a path that traverses up a directory tree beyond the codebase. There was no good reason for this, and the constraint was removed in 1.1.

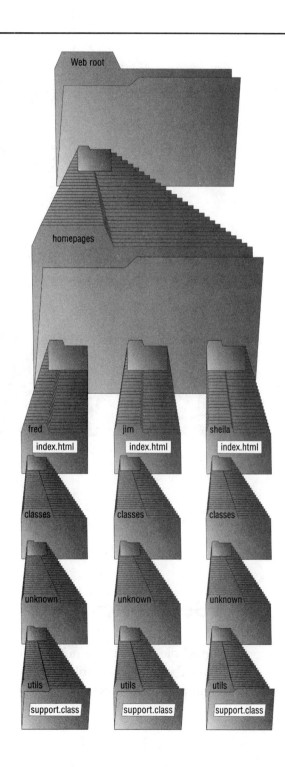

FIGURE 5.6

Cumbersome directory structure and duplication of classes resulting from individual class directories

FIGURE 5.7

Simplified directory
structure with shared
class directories

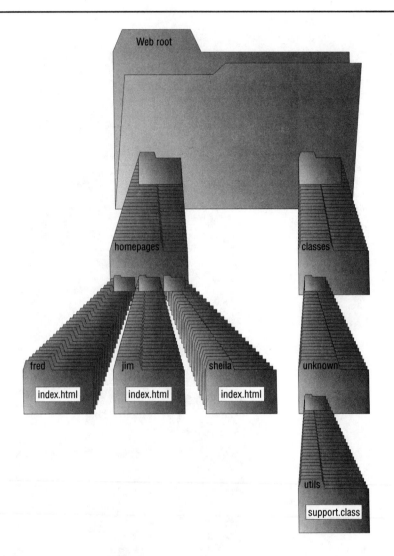

File System Semantics

On the whole, applets are not able to access file systems of the host
that runs them. For portable applications, however, the variety of
different path name conventions does present an issue.

Many of the problems are resolved by the `java.io.File` class. This provides mechanisms that, in principle, allow browsing directory hierarchies without any need to know the local conventions. The following example shows how a directory system can be browsed in a largely platform independent way. The source for this example is located on the CD-ROM in the directory `\javadevhdbk\ch05\Directory.java`.

Directory.java

```java
import java.io.*;
import java.util.*;

public class Directory {
  private File currentDir;

  public Directory() {
    // create any file in current directory
    currentDir = new File("x");
    // get the full path
    currentDir = new File(currentDir.getAbsolutePath());
    // and lose the fake filename.
    currentDir = new File(currentDir.getParent());
  }

  public Directory(String start) throws IOException {
    currentDir = new File(start);
    if (!currentDir.isDirectory()) {
      throw new IOException("Not a directory");
    }
    // this might not be absolute, make it so...
    currentDir = new File(currentDir.getAbsolutePath());
  }

  public File current() {
    return currentDir;
  }

  public static File at(File start, String move) throws IOException {
    if (File.separator.length() != 1) {
```

```
      throw new RuntimeException("Fatal: Unexpected platform." +
        " Multiple character separators not supported");
    }

    StringTokenizer tok = new StringTokenizer(move, File.separator);
    String nextDir = null;

    // Absolute path ignores starting point
    if (File.separator.indexOf(move.charAt(0)) != -1) {
      start = new File(move);
    }
    else {
      // otherwise, work down the move string one element at at time
      while (tok.hasMoreTokens()) {
        nextDir = tok.nextToken();
        // dot is current directory, so no change
        if (nextDir.equals(".")) {
          continue;
        }
        // dot dot is parent, so move up
        else if (nextDir.equals("..")) {
          start = parentOf(start);
        }
        // anything else tries to move down
        else {
          start = new File(start, nextDir);
          // but the result must exist...
          if (!start.exists()) {
            throw new IOException("No such file or directory " + start);
          }
          // and be a directory
          if (!start.isDirectory()) {
            throw new IOException("Not a directory " + start);
          }
        }
      } // end of 'while more path tokens'
    }
    return start;
  }

  public static File parentOf(File child) throws IOException {
    File rv;
```

```
  try {
    rv = new File(child.getParent());
  }
  catch(NullPointerException e) {
    throw new IOException("Already at the top of the tree");
  }
  return rv;
}

public File parentDir() throws IOException {
  return parentOf(currentDir);
}

public void up() throws IOException {
  currentDir = parentDir();
}

public void cd(String dest) throws IOException {
  currentDir = at(currentDir, dest);
}

public String [] dir() {
  return currentDir.list();
}

public String [] dir(String target) throws IOException {
  return at(currentDir, target).list();
}

public static void main(String args[]) {
  boolean finished = false;
  String cmdline = null;
  String command = null;
  String argument = null;
  StringTokenizer tok = null;
  BufferedReader in = new BufferedReader(
                        new InputStreamReader(System.in));
  Directory that;

  if (args.length == 0) {
    that = new Directory();
  }
```

```
      else {
        try {
          that = new Directory(args[0]);
        }
        catch (IOException e) {
          System.out.println("Can't start at " + args[0] + "\n" + e);
          that = new Directory();
        }
      }

      while (!finished) {
        System.out.print(that.current() + "> ");
        System.out.flush();
        try {
          cmdline = in.readLine();
        }
        catch (IOException e) {
          finished = true;
          break;
        }
        tok = new StringTokenizer(cmdline, " \t");
        command = argument = null;
        if (tok.hasMoreTokens()) {
          command = tok.nextToken();
        }
        if (tok.hasMoreTokens()) {
          argument = tok.nextToken();
        }
        if (command == null) {
          continue;
        }
        if (command.equalsIgnoreCase("exit")) {
          finished = true;
        }
        if (command.equalsIgnoreCase("cd")) {
          if (argument == null) {
            System.out.println("Current directory is " + that.current());
          }
          else {
            try {
              that.cd(argument);
            }
```

```
        catch (IOException e) {
          System.err.println("Failed to change directory. " + e);
        }
      }
    }
    if (command.equalsIgnoreCase("up")) {
      try {
        that.up();
      }
      catch (IOException e) {
        System.err.println("Failed to change up directory. " + e);
      }
    }
    if (command.equalsIgnoreCase("dir")) {
      String [] files = null;
      if (argument == null) {
        files = that.dir();
      }
      else {
        try {
          files = that.dir(argument);
        }
        catch (IOException e) {
          System.out.println("Failed to list directory. " + e);
        }
      }
      if (files != null) {
        for (int i = 0; i < files.length; i++) {
          System.out.println(files[i]);
        }
      }
    }
    if (command.equalsIgnoreCase("help")) {
      System.out.println("cd [<directory>]\n" +
        "    Select the specified directory" +
        " or print currently selected directory");
      System.out.println("dir [<directory>]\n" +
        "    List contents of the specified directory" +
        " or the current directory");
      System.out.println("exit\n" +
        "    Quit the program");
      System.out.println("help\n" +
```

```
                  "    Ouputs this message");
              System.out.println("up\n" +
                  "    Select the parent of the current directory");
          }
        }
      }
    }
```

Running the Program

To run the program, change to the CD-ROM directory `javadevhdbk\ch05` and issue one of these two commands:

```
java Directory
```

or

```
java Directory <pathname>
```

The first of these will start the browser in the current directory, while the second will start it in the specified directory.

When the program starts, it will issue a prompt that indicates the current directory. At the prompt the following commands are accepted:

`cd`   echo current directory

`cd <path>`   select new current directory, relative or absolute

`up`   move up one directory

`dir`   list contents of current directory

`dir <path>`   list contents of relative or absolute directory

`exit`   exit the program

`help`   list these commands with brief explanation

The commands cd and dir are similar to their MS-DOS equivalents. By itself, cd is equivalent to the Unix command pwd; with a command-line argument, cd is equivalent to its Unix counterpart of the same name. In Unix, ls performs broadly the same function as dir.

The command up is a shorthand for cd .., and selects the parent of the current directory. The commands exit and help quit the program and provide a brief reminder of these commands, respectively.

On MS-DOS-type systems, the starting path can be specified as a different device, but the program does not operate properly if the root directory of a device is specified. So, the command

```
java Directory C:\somedir
```

works as expected, but the command

```
java Directory C:\
```

fails to work properly and becomes confused. In the latter, the program works properly after the issue of an up command, which resets the current directory to C: without a trailing backslash (\). Unfortunately, the command:

```
java Directory C:
```

fails because it treats C: as a directory name that it expects to find in the current directory of the default device.

The easiest way to start the program in the root directory of a device is to use the form:

```
java Directory C:\.
```

which, because it takes the first form, does work correctly.

Another weakness with this program is that it is not possible to change devices. If it is started on C:, then that is where it will stay.

What It Does

There are two distinct bodies of code in this class. The `main()` method represents a test harness and trivial application, while the class as a whole encapsulates some ideas about directories.

The `main()` method reads commands from the standard input and parses them for the small command set that it recognizes. The `main()` method then invokes the appropriate methods on the instance `that` of the `Directory` class, displaying any appropriate results.

The rest of the class represents a single directory, and provides a number of methods that allow you to move up and down the file system and to list the contents of directories.

The Details

The body of the class provides two static methods that supplement the facilities of the `java.io.File` class. These are called `at()` and `parentOf()`. Each takes a `File` instance as an argument and returns another `File` instance as the result. The `at()` method also takes a `String`. The returned `File` from `at()` describes the directory that results from changing the path of the first argument according to the path given as the second `String`. The `parentOf()` method simply returns a `File` that describes the parent directory of the `File` object supplied. In both cases, erroneous arguments, such as asking for the parent of a root directory or trying to move down through a non-existent path, result in an `IOException` being thrown.

The parsing of path names by the `at()` method handles absolute references and the relative references dot (`.`) and dot dot (`..`). To operate successfully, the `at()` method depends on running on a platform that follows the basic Unix and MS-DOS convention that a fully qualified file name consists of a list of directory names followed by the actual filename, and that the elements of the list are separated by a single, unique character. This character is a forward slash (`/`) in

Unix and a backward one (\)in MS-DOS. If the `Directory` class were used on a VAX/VMS system, which uses a more complex description, it would fail.

TIP

The separator used by the host file system is available from the system properties table. For convenience this information is also available from the `File` class. Two members, called `separator` and `separatorChar` are declared as public static final variables. The `separator` variable is a `String` object which, in principle, might contain multiple characters, although on Windows and Unix platforms it contains only one. The `separatorChar` variable is of type `char` and is the first character from the `separator` variable.

NOTE

The VAX/VMS file system uses a five-part mechanism for specifying a full path to a file. The outline looks like this: `<Node>::<Device>:[<directory.parts>]<filename.ext>;<ver>`. The `<Node>` part specifies a node on a DECNet network at which the file is stored. `<Device>` specifies the name of the device containing the file. The device names are multicharacter. The directory parts describe a hierarchical directory system, and elements of the directory are separated with periods. The whole directory specification is enclosed in square brackets. The filename and extension follows, with a version number after a semicolon. As with most file systems, most parts of these specifications, except the filename itself, are optional.

One aspect of the `at()` method warrants particular mention. The `File` class parses the relative directories dot (`.`) and dot dot (`..`) only partly correctly. For instance, if a `File` object f refers to a directory `x\y\z`, and then a new `File` object f1 is constructed as `f1 = new File(f, "..")`, the result will be that f1 refers to the directory `x\y` as expected.

Although this construction works, it unfortunately appears to be a feature of the underlying operating systems, rather than being behavior built into the `File` class itself. If the `getAbsolutePath()`

method is applied to `f1` it would not return the string `x\y`, but instead `x\y\z\..`, which is rather ugly and might cause comparisons that attempt to determine if two paths are related in some way to fail.

> **NOTE**
>
> One of the security bugs in the alpha releases of the HotJava browser is related to this. HotJava intended that the user be able to specify that files and directories in certain paths could be accessible to untrusted applets. Unfortunately, a file could be specified as, for example, `..\..\autoexec.bat`, and therefore any permitted path could be used to gain access to any part of the disk.

In the `Directory` class example, the `at()` method parses the individual parts of the path modifier and handles the dot (`.`) and dot dot (`..`) as special cases. The result is a path that is tidied up and avoids messy dot and dot dot sequences being left in the path.

> **WARNING**
>
> The parsing of user input splits text on space or tab characters, hence the program will not operate correctly on directories that have spaces in them. This, however, is a limitation of the `main()` method itself and not of the `File` or `Directory` classes.

Based on the two utility routines and the preexisting facilities of the `File` class, a number of features are built into the `Directory` class. Two constructors are provided. The first constructor has no arguments, which extracts the current directory as the default. The second constructor allows the specification of a particular starting path and will throw an `IOException` if this argument does not describe a real path. In addition to the constructors, the `current()` method reports the current directory. The `cd()` method allows changing of the current directory. Two methods called `dir()` allow the contents of either the current or a specified directory to be listed as an array of `Strings`.

Reusing the Example

The major weakness of this code is that it does not properly handle device names such as `C:` in paths. This is tiresome on platforms like Windows that use this form. This problem could be fixed, although the resulting code would be rather fudged and would have to make platform-dependent assumptions about how to distinguish between a directory and a device name. Testing for a colon in the second position is appropriate for DOS/Windows platforms, VMS, and others but, although it is quite general, it is not portable.

The `Directory` class has been written to provide a reasonable basis for reuse, although the `main()` method should probably be cut out if this is to be pursued.

Many applications will require some ability to navigate the file system, and this class can be of assistance where the basic methods of the `File` class are lacking.

Creating a graphical user interface (GUI) for this class would provide a file-management tool.

Appendix C, *Frequently Asked Questions*, gives an example of using the `java.lang.reflection` package to determine if a newly loaded class has a `main()` method and shows how to invoke this method if it exists. It would be a simple exercise to extend the `Directory.java` example to add this behavior. The `java.lang.reflection` package is not available in releases before JDK 1.1.

The example of the `Directory` class has shown that, to a large extent, the standard Java packages allow programs to access the host file system without specific knowledge of its platform. However, some difficulties have to be handled, and some aspects, most notably device names, still present significant barriers to a genuinely platform-independent solution.

Visual Aspects

The visual appearance of a GUI-based program is partly controlled by the programmer, but it is also partly controlled by the host windowing system. Programs are expected to have a look and feel that is comparable with others running in the same environment. In general, each platform that supports Java has a distinct look and feel of its own; Windows 95, Macintosh, and X Windows all have different visual styles. Further, X Windows allows the user to configure the look and feel to a considerable extent, and two distinct versions of Windows NT now exist because the latest version has adopted the look and feel introduced with Windows 95.

Java runtime systems try to adopt the look and feel of the host system; this is important as otherwise users would reject Java programs because of the "culture shock" that results from a strange-looking program. This conformity to the host system has an impact on the programmer. The three aspects of visual appearance that warrant discussion are:

- Fonts
- Colors
- Layout

Fonts

Different platforms support different fonts. Even different installations of the same platform might have different fonts installed. GUIs might require a range of fonts and styles, so it is important that you write a program that is able to determine what fonts are available and is able to use them in an appropriate way without the final result appearing surprising or inappropriate.

You can write a program that extracts a full list of supported font names from the running system, and these fonts can, in principle, be used at any point size and style. Java supports font styles plain, bold, italic, and bold italic.

In addition to polling the running system, a program can be written so the end user is allowed to configure the fonts used for various parts of the GUI.

Obtaining the Available Font List

The list of available fonts can be obtained from the running system via the `Toolkit` object. The `Toolkit` represents the underlying platform-specific windowing system, such as MS Windows or X Windows. Every instance of a `java.awt.Component` has a reference to the `Toolkit` that currently implements it. There is also a static `Toolkit` method called `getDefaultToolkit()` that returns a reference to the default `Toolkit`.

In certain conditions it is possible that the default `Toolkit` might not be used by a particular `Component`. This can occur if the `Component` is not displayed on the local screen or if there are multiple local screens, which frequently occurs in X Windows environments. The `getToolkit()` method, called before the `Component` is actually displayed, will return the default `Toolkit`.

Obtaining a reference to the `Toolkit` from a `Component` is easy once that `Component` has been displayed, but not before that moment. This is awkward because, ideally, the program should be able to determine any information that might impact the displayed appearance before the display occurs. If this determination cannot happen, then when the program is first displayed it is likely to flicker because it has to be redrawn in the light of new information.

In fact, it is possible to extract the required data from the `Component` when it is just about to be displayed. The actual displayable part of a `Component`, known as the *peer*, is created by the method `addNotify()`. Building the peer is called *realizing* the `Component`. The `addNotify()` method may be overridden by a subclass of `Component` and the original method called at the start of the code.

After the return of the parental `addNotify()` method, the return value from the `getToolkit()` method will be valid, and so will the response to any other queries that are made of it. This technique works for other facilities of `Component`, such as `createImage()`, which are unavailable before the realization of the `Component`.

As mentioned earlier, in principle, fonts can be constructed in four styles and any point size. However, the Java system allows itself a little leeway with this; it is possible for a font to be provided that is not precisely the size requested. The tolerance allowed in JDK 1.0.2 is 6 point. Also, a font that is reported by the `getFontList()` method might not actually be available in all the styles.

WARNING Once a Font has been created, the class has methods that return the font name, size, and attributes. It is not usually relevant, but is slightly unfortunate, that the values reflect the constructor arguments, not the actual results. Even obtaining a reference to the `FontPeer` object will not help, because this is different even for two consecutive calls to the `getPeer()` method of the same `Font` object. Hence it is not possible to use these facilities to determine if two fonts are visibly distinguishable. The `FontMetrics` class, described later, can provide some assistance with this problem.

This example provides a basic font-examination tool that generates a list of the font names available on your machine in a Java program. You can select a font and style and immediately see the appearance of that font with a sample of text in the window. This example is located on the CD-ROM in the directory `javadevhdbk\ch05\` `Fontsel.java`. The source file is called `Fontsel.java`. The byte-code is located in the file `Fontsel.class`.

Fontsel.java

```
import java.awt.*;
import java.awt.event.*;
```

```java
public class Fontsel extends Frame
                     implements ActionListener,
                                ItemListener,
                                WindowListener {
  Label sample;
  Choice fontNames;
  TextField fontSize;
  int actualFontSize;
  Checkbox italic;
  Checkbox bold;

  public static void main(String args[]) {
    Fontsel that = new Fontsel();
    that.setVisible(true);
  }

  public Fontsel() {
    super("Font Selection");
    fontNames = new Choice();
    fontSize = new TextField("10", 5);
    actualFontSize = 10;
    Panel topPanel = new Panel();
    topPanel.setLayout(new BorderLayout());
    topPanel.add("West", fontSize);
    topPanel.add("Center", fontNames);
    add("North", topPanel);

    italic = new Checkbox("Italic");
    bold = new Checkbox("Bold");
    Panel leftPanel = new Panel();
    leftPanel.setLayout(new GridLayout(2, 1));
    leftPanel.add(italic);
    leftPanel.add(bold);
    add("West", leftPanel);

    Panel centerPanel = new Panel();
    centerPanel.setLayout(new GridLayout(1, 1));
    sample = new Label("");
    centerPanel.add(sample);
    add("Center", centerPanel);
    pack();
```

```
      italic.addItemListener(this);
      bold.addItemListener(this);
      fontNames.addItemListener(this);

      fontSize.addActionListener(this);

      addWindowListener(this);
  }

  public void addNotify() {
    super.addNotify();
    Toolkit myToolkit = getToolkit();
    String [] fonts = myToolkit.getFontList();
    for (int i = 0; i < fonts.length; i++) {
      fontNames.addItem(fonts[i]);
    }
    showSample();
  }

  public void itemStateChanged(ItemEvent ev) {
    actionPerformed(null);
  }

  public void actionPerformed(ActionEvent e) {
    int guess = 0;
    try {
      guess = Integer.parseInt(fontSize.getText());
    }
    catch (NumberFormatException ex) {
      fontSize.setText("" + actualFontSize);
    }
    if ((guess >= 2) && (guess <= 144)) {
      actualFontSize = guess;
    }
    showSample();
  }


  public void windowClosing(WindowEvent ev) {
      System.exit(0);
  }

  public void windowClosed(WindowEvent ev) {
  }
```

```
public void windowDeiconified(WindowEvent ev) {
}

public void windowIconified(WindowEvent ev) {
}

public void windowOpened(WindowEvent ev) {
}

public void windowActivated(WindowEvent ev) {
}

public void windowDeactivated(WindowEvent ev) {
}

private void showSample() {
  int style = 0;
  if (italic.getState()) {
    style |= Font.ITALIC;
  }
  if (bold.getState()) {
    style |= Font.BOLD;
  }
  Font f = new Font(fontNames.getSelectedItem(), style, actualFontSize);
  sample.setText(f.toString());
  sample.setFont(f);
}
}
```

Running the Program

To run the program, change to the directory containing the classfile and issue the command:

```
java Fontsel
```

The program will start up and launch a new window. Across the top of the window is a TextField in which a font size may be typed (limited to the 2-to-144-point range) and a Choice box that contains the names of all fonts known to Java. Along the left-hand side of the window are two checkboxes, one labeled Italic and the other labeled Bold. An example of the chosen font is shown in the remainder of the window. A screenshot of this program is shown in Figure 5.8.

FIGURE 5.8

The Fontsel program running

Entering a new font size, changing the checkboxes, or choosing a new font from the choices will update the sample text in the lower-right corner of the window.

What It Does

The program starts by creating the GUI layout. A list of fonts is extracted and installed in the Choice. The currently selected font is indicated in the Label area and is updated in both font and text whenever the user changes the values specified by the user interface. The important details of this program relate to the extraction of the font list and the use of the addNotify() method, although the majority of the code relates to building the display.

The Details

In the addNotify() method, just after the invocation of super .addNotify(), the getToolkit() method will return a correct reference to the underlying toolkit. The components are not displayed until after the return of the addNotify() method to its caller. From this Toolkit reference, the getFontList() method returns an array of strings representing the names of the available fonts.

As soon as the list of font names has been obtained, it is used to set up the `Choice` from which the font may be displayed.

Whenever an item or action event callback is received from any of the control AWT elements, the program reacts by constructing the required `Font` and setting the `Label` display to use that `Font`. The text of the `Label` is then set to the text that results from invoking the `toString()` method on the `Font`.

Reusing the Code

The `Fontsel` class is intended to demonstrate principles. It might be a useful utility for determining the available fonts on a platform, but because the bulk of the code provides a GUI for the program and only a line or two is actually of general utility, it is unlikely that this class will be reused.

One aspect is worth noting as a design pattern for use elsewhere; `addNotify()` is used obtain proper connection to the underlying `Toolkit` object before a component is actually visible. This connection is required for a number of facilities—including creating instances of the `Image` class, which is used, amongst other things, for double buffering.

Finding Out about the Font

When a `Font` object has been created and installed in a particular `Component` for use, it is possible to determine information about the dimensions of characters in the `Font`. This information is used by components to determine their own preferred sizes and is useful when coding new components.

To obtain the size information, an instance of the `FontMetrics` class is used. This instance is extracted from the component that uses the font by calling the method `getFontMetrics()`. Using the `FontMetrics` object, a number of methods are available. All the characteristic dimensions of the font are accessible, including the line height and advance width of any single character. *Advance width* describes the space to move forward to get to the position of the next character. One particularly useful method is `getStringWidth()`, which takes a `String` argument and returns the total length of that `String` in units of pixels.

If two `Font`s are visibly different, especially if they are of different point sizes, then it is likely that some detail of the associated `FontMetric` object will differ. This allows the possibility of determining if two `Font`s are actually different from the user's point of view. This can be helpful because the `Font` object methods that return the name, size, and attributes do not report the attributes used on the display; rather, they report the arguments with which the `Font` was constructed.

Colors

When defining a color in a Java program, a 24 + 8-bit true color representation is used at the API. The low-order 24 bits represent three separate 8-bit values. These indicate the intensity of red, green, and blue in the color. Red is the most significant byte and blue is the least significant, with green in between. The extra 8 bits represent an opacity. The opacity is called the *alpha* value and occupies the most significant byte of the full 32-bit integer. An alpha value of 255 indicates that the color is fully opaque, while 0 indicates a fully transparent color. Opacity does not affect a color on the display; rather, it is used for mixing images.

Java programs might be called on to run on platforms with widely differing color capabilities. Monochrome systems still exist, especially in laptops, and certainly not all systems have full 24-bit color facilities. Internally, Java translates this into the best available representation. In some cases, this might not bear much relationship to the original color definition.

It is possible to determine some information about the color system, such as the physical color resolution and the actual colors that are available. Based on this information a program can choose an appropriate behavior when displaying colors. For example, if insufficient color resolution is available for displaying a photograph, a program might use dithering rather than precise color specifications.

NOTE *Dithering* is a technique that uses groups of nearby pixels and color mixing to give the appearance of more colors than are really available. Although this increases the effective color resolution, the effective pixel resolution is reduced.

The `java.awt.Component` class has a method `getColorModel()`. This returns either an instance of `IndexColorModel` or of `DirectColorModel`. Both of these are subclasses of the `java.awt.image.ColorModel` class.

`DirectColorModel` represents a system that has a fixed, evenly distributed number of predefined colors. A range of intensities is available in red, green, and blue, and the three colors can be controlled effectively individually. For example, this model suits 16-bit color or 24-bit true color. The representation of the ranges of each color is done using a number of bits out of a larger value. An 8-bit-per-pixel range is typically treated as 3 bits each of red and green and 2 bits of blue. The range of each color is therefore 0 to 7 for red and green and 0 to 3 for blue. Figure 5.9 shows a typical mapping between red, green, and blue ranges for a `DirectColorModel` with 8 bits per pixel.

FIGURE 5.9

A typical `Direct-ColorModel` using 8 bits per pixel

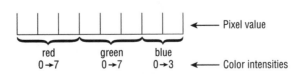

> **TIP**
>
> The human eye is least sensitive to contrast in blue and most sensitive in green. This is why blue is chosen to have the lower resolution when allocating the short number of bits.

The `IndexColorModel` is used for systems that have a palette. This is typical of many X Windows systems and 256-color VGA adapters on IBM PC-type systems. In displays of this type a limited number of different colors can be displayed simultaneously, although each of those colors can be selected from a very large number of colors, allowing smooth graduation of color over a limited range. Figure 5.10 shows an example of a color palette that might be represented by an `IndexColorModel`.

To determine the nature of the color system on the host running a Java program, first obtain the `ColorModel` from a displayed component.

FIGURE 5.10

An example of `Index-ColorModel` palette mechanism

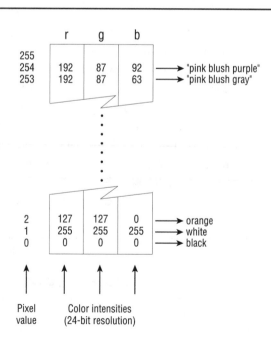

The `instanceof` operator determines which of the two available color models has been returned. The `getPixelSize()` method of the `ColorModel` class returns the number of bits used for each pixel. Assuming all the bits are used, the number of available colors is determined as two raised to the power of the number of bits per pixel. The following example demonstrates this formula. The source for this example is located on the CD-ROM in the directory `javadevhdbk\ch05\ColMod.java`. The corresponding bytecode is in the file `javadevhdbk\ch05\ColMod.class`.

ColMod.java

```java
import java.awt.*;
import java.awt.event.*;
import java.awt.image.*;
import java.applet.*;

public class ColMod extends Applet {
  Label model;
  Label bitsPerPixel;

  public static void main(String args[]) {
    ColModFrame f = new ColModFrame();
    ColMod that = new ColMod();
    f.add("Center", that);
    f.pack();
    f.setVisible(true);
  }

  public ColMod() {
    setLayout(new GridLayout(2, 1));
    model = new Label();
    add(model);
    bitsPerPixel = new Label();
    add(bitsPerPixel);
  }

  public void addNotify() {
    super.addNotify();
    ColorModel m = getColorModel();
    if (m instanceof DirectColorModel) {
```

```
      model.setText("DirectColorModel");
    }
    else if (m instanceof IndexColorModel) {
      model.setText("IndexColorModel");
    }
    else {
      model.setText("Unknown ColorModel " + m.getClass().getName());
    }
    bitsPerPixel.setText(m.getPixelSize() + " Bits per pixel");
  }
}

class ColModFrame extends Frame implements WindowListener {
  public ColModFrame() {
    super("Color Model information");
    addWindowListener(this);
  }

  public void windowClosing(WindowEvent ev) {
    System.exit(0);
  }

  public void windowClosed(WindowEvent ev) {
  }

  public void windowOpened(WindowEvent ev) {
  }

  public void windowIconified(WindowEvent ev) {
  }

  public void windowDeiconified(WindowEvent ev) {
  }

  public void windowActivated(WindowEvent ev) {
  }

  public void windowDeactivated(WindowEvent ev) {
  }
}
```

Running the Program

This example may be run either as an applet or as an application. To run the program as an application, select the directory containing the bytecode and issue the command

```
java ColMod
```

The program launches a new window and reports the `ColorModel` and color range, in terms of bits per pixel, in that window.

To run the program as an applet using the appletviewer, issue the command

```
appletviewer ColMod.html
```

The same HTML file may be launched from any other Java-enabled browser.

What It Does

The bulk of this program creates a basic GUI for displaying the information about the local color system. Three points of interest are the use of `getColorModel()`, applied to the main `Frame` object; the `getPixelSize()` method, applied to the resulting `ColorModel` object; and the use of the `instanceof` operator to determine which particular `ColorModel` was reported.

Reusing the Code

The `ColMod` class serves to demonstrate the use of the methods `getColorModel()` and `getPixelSize()`. Additionally, the use of the `instanceof` operator is exemplified. However, the example is not intended to support reuse.

Determining the Real Color

Objects of the `Color` class represent near-ideal colors and are neither associated with, nor influenced by, a physical display. They describe a full 32-bit value with 24-bit color and 8-bit transparency. The method getRGB() returns the same idealized int value, not the actual color value used to represent it on any particular display. Unfortunately, although it is possible to determine the full list of physical colors available on the system, it is not possible to access the mechanisms used to choose the best match between these colors and any particular target color.

If a DirectColorModel is found, this provides details of the number of bits used to represent red, green, and blue on the display. From this it is possible to determine the exact set of colors available.

TIP

When an IndexColorModel is found, you can extract each entry in the palette in turn using the getRGB() method of this object. Be sure to use the getRGB() method of the IndexColorModel object, not that of a Color object. The argument to this method is the index into the color map palette, typically in the range 0 to 255. The actual number of entries in the color palette is returned from the getMapSize() method but will not be more than 256. This is a limitation imposed by the IndexColorModel class.

Matching the Desktop

When running, a Java program should use display colors that match those of the current host platform. In general, AWT components will handle this directly but, especially if you create your own custom components, you will need to handle this in your code. A number of constants are defined in the Color class that specify the colors in the desktop of the host system. These constants are not defined in the source code of, and compiled into, an implementation, but are determined and configured in the running system when the Color class is loaded.

Several constants are defined that cover the various aspects of the GUI that can be configured independently on Java host platforms. These are listed and described in Chapter 14, *The 1.1 AWT*.

WARNING These constants did not exist in the `Color` class before the release of JDK 1.1. If you wish to produce portable code to run on the widest variety of platforms, remember that there will be a delay before all browsers in use are upgraded to support this program.

Layout

The physical layout of a program's GUI depends in some detail on the sizes of the components that make it up. For this reason it is important to resist any temptation to position components at absolute x,y coordinates. Java provides the *Layout Manager* mechanism to allow layouts to be described in logical terms so the platform can implement the correct absolute positioning required to achieve the desired effect.

Each component is able to express a preference for a particular size in terms of width and height, and is also able to state what minimum size is required for proper operation. If a `LayoutManager` object wishes to, it can inquire for these dimensions and use them in deciding how to lay out the display.

Different systems might use different fonts when running the same program. This typically changes the sizes of text strings and consequently the required space for labels and similar components. In such conditions an absolute layout would be spoiled. Fonts are not the only variations between platforms that might spoil an absolute layout. For example, there are different adornments around different components. On Windows NT, a `TextField` object has a single-pixel wide box around it, whereas on Windows 95, the same component is enclosed in a 3-D box.

For conditions that require a customized layout, it is usually better if you code a special `LayoutManager` class rather than use ad hoc code to perform the layout externally. This provides two benefits.

First, the detail of layout-management calculation does not clutter other parts of the code, which improves the readability and hence maintainability of the work. Second, you can readily reuse the resulting LayoutManager class in other situations. Reuse of code results in re-testing, which in turn results in better quality software. Chapter 4 describes how to write layout managers and includes example implementations of two.

TIP

It is important to realize that a layout manager might coerce either the width, height, or both of each component it lays out. The FlowLayout class controls neither, while the GridLayout class controls both. The BorderLayout class controls the height of the *East* and *West* components, the width of the *North* and *South* components, and both dimensions of the *Center* component. In situations where *either* dimension of component is controlled by the layout manger, the use of setSize() or setBounds() methods will be ineffective as it will be overridden by the layout manager.

Local/User Configuration

Many of the platforms that support Java provide environment variables. These are ways for the user to define certain attributes of environment or preference—such as user name, temporary file directory, or the color of a button—so a program can obtain this information at runtime and behave in a fashion to suit the local user. Not all systems provide this facility, however, and there are no standard conventions for the naming of these attributes. Further, some information that is programmed into environment variables might be sensitive, so applets should not have access to it. Environment variables are commonly used to maintain username, home directory, and perhaps the names of local servers. None of this should be accessible to an applet.

> **WARNING**
>
> Even information that is apparently quite innocuous can be sensitive or dangerous in the hands of someone trying to break into your systems. The type of operating system you are running, for example, would tell the attacker what type of attacks should be tried. Even something as simple as your username and machine name can be used to send unwanted e-mail. For this reason, applets should be denied access to any information that is either not essential to operation or cannot be proven genuinely harmless.

Because environment variables are not platform independent, the Java system provides an alternative mechanism. This alternative is called properties. Some properties are provided by the system itself, and others can be read by applications from both files and the command line. Some browsers support properties, some of which are usually read from a file. If the browser does support properties, they are generally available to applets in that browser. In such circumstances, each request made by an applet to read a property is checked by the security manager, and some accesses are denied for security reasons. Although the full list of properties that are defined depends on the individual browser and version of Java, there is a basic set of standard system properties that are defined in any environment. Table 5.1 shows the names of these properties and indicates if the property value is accessible from an applet.

These properties are actually defined or determined inside the Java runtime. Additional properties are often read from files. The appletviewer, for example, reads the contents of a file called `hotjava` `.properties` to find configuration information for itself. Although many, if not most, of these additional properties are accessible to an applet, they are generally specific to an individual browser, and hence you cannot safely program using them.

The Java interpreter allows *per session* properties to be defined using the `-D` command line option. A command line including the text "`-Dname=value`" provides for a property called `name` to have a value of `value`. The same format, without the `-D` part, is used in property files.

TABLE 5.1   Properties

Property Name	Accessible from Applet?
About the Java distribution	
`java.class.version`	YES
`java.vendor`	YES
`java.vendor.url`	YES
`java.version`	YES
About the Java installation	
`java.class.path`	YES
`java.home`	YES
About the individual user	
`user.dir`	NO
`user.home`	NO
`user.name`	NO
About the host IO system	
`file.separator`	YES
`line.separator`	YES
`path.separator`	YES
About the host operating system	
`os.arch`	YES
`os.name`	YES
`os.version`	YES

The `java.lang` package provides a number of standard methods for obtaining property values of certain types, such as `String`, `int`, and `boolean`, inside programs. These methods are generally encapsulated in the wrapper classes in the `java.lang` package. Hence, the class `java.lang.Boolean` has a method called `getBoolean(String)`.

This method returns a value of true if there is an entry in the property table that has the name specified by the string argument and the value part is set to true. Accessing string properties is done via the getProperty() method of the System class, as all properties are initially defined as String objects, so this property type does not need any conversion.

Properties can be used to control the operation of both applets and applications. Applications are able to load their own property tables from specific files, while applets cannot in general read from files. Because of this, applets usually have to use the property table offered by the browser. In some browsers, this can be extended by the user. Unfortunately, the current implementations of many popular browsers do not allow properties to be set in a file, reducing the utility of the mechanism in the short term.

Although applets cannot generally add their own properties to the system table and cannot read files either, properties can be read from any InputStream object. So, if appropriate, an applet could read properties from a network connection.

The following example application demonstrates some of the fundamentals of using properties. The source for this example is located on the CD-ROM in the directory javadevhdbk\ch05\PropView.java. The corresponding bytecode file, PropView.class, is in the same directory.

PropView.java

```
import java.io.*;
import java.util.*;

public class PropView {
  public static void main(String args[]) {
    Properties properties = System.getProperties();
    System.out.println("The system property table is:");
    properties.list(System.out);

    System.out.println("\nIndividual properties can be obtained" +
```

```
                    "\nThe value of os.name is " + System.getProperty("os.name"));

            if (args.length > 0) {
              FileInputStream in = null;
              boolean success = true;

              try {
                in = new FileInputStream(args[0]);
                properties.load(in);
                success = true;
              }
              catch (IOException ex) { /* do nothing, success remains false */
              }

              if (success) {
                System.out.println("\nThe property table can be extended by " +
                  "applications from an InputStream");
                System.out.println("\nNew system property table is:");
                System.getProperties().list(System.out);
                System.out.println("\nValue of local.animal.defined is " +
                  Boolean.getBoolean("local.animal.defined"));
                System.out.println("\nValue of local.animal.legcount is " +
                  Integer.getInteger("local.animal.legcount"));
              }
              else {
                System.err.println("Unable to open the file " + args[0] +
                  " for reading");
              }
            }
          }
        }
      }
```

Running the Program

To run the program, change to the directory listed above and issue the command

```
java PropView local.prop
```

The argument local.prop refers to a text file that defines a number of additional Properties. This argument is also located in the `javadevhdbk/ch05` directory. To experiment with alternative property sets, you can create your own file and provide the name of it in place of `local.prop`.

What It Does

When the program starts, it prints the defined system properties to the standard output. It then outputs the value of the single property *os.name*, which is used to describe the name of the operating system. Finally, if an argument has been supplied, it is treated as a filename. That file is appended to the system properties and the aggregated table is listed.

The Details

The static `getProperties()` method in the `System` class extracts the table of all system properties. This is an instance of the class `java.util.Properties`. Next, the `list()` method is used on this returned object to write the entire table to the standard output. The static `getProperty()` method of the `System` class is then used, demonstrating a more realistic mode of operation for normal programs. This method extracts from the table a specific system property by name, returning the value as a string.

If an argument has been provided, this is used as the name of a file. That file is then opened for reading. The contents of the file are then appended to the system table, using the `load()` method of the `Properties` class.

If the supplied example file called `local.prop`, which is located in the same directory as the bytecode of this example, has been specified on the command line, then the resulting extended property table has two specific entries: `local.animal` and `local.animal.legcount`. The presence of the command-line argument causes the program to look for these properties using the methods built into the classes `Boolean` and `Integer` and then output the values that it finds.

TIP

Property access methods are also available for several other types, such as `Font` and `Color`. The values returned by these methods have been converted from the original string into an object of the appropriate class. More details of these mechanisms are discussed later, in the sections *Properties and Color* and *Properties and Fonts*.

Effective Use of Properties

You will find that properties are a versatile tool for creating a configurable program so a system administrator, or perhaps a user, can obtain optimal behavior on a specific platform. However, to make the best use of properties, a little advance planning is beneficial.

Each aspect of your program that might be affected by the platform on which it is run should be considered, including fonts, colors, dimensions, label text, default directories, and more. For each aspect, a default value should be chosen along with a property name that is used to allow configuration. The program should be coded so if the property is undefined, the default is used. In some cases this requires checking the return value of a `getXxx()` method. A return of `null` indicates that the property was not defined or the definition could not be interpreted properly. In other cases, a special `getXxx()` method takes a second argument that defines a default value to be returned if the property is not defined.

TIP

Careful use of properties for the messages used in a program can give easy and flexible support for programs that must run in a variety of languages. For example, the error messages issued by the standard Java compiler are defined in a property file that is read when the compiler starts up.

A Generalized Property-Naming Scheme

In the X Windows system, a powerful mechanism called *resources* provides parallel facilities to properties. In that system a hierarchical naming scheme is used. For example, a resource can be defined as

```
*.font: TimesRoman
```

which would cause X programs by default to use the `TimesRoman` font. A specific program can be made to override this by another definition; for example,

```
myProgram.font: Helvetica
```

would cause the program called `myProgram` to ignore the default and use Helvetica instead.

The X resources mechanism is powerful and complex, but the basic principles can be reused in Java via the properties mechanism. Using the example of fonts, you could write a suite of programs to check a series of property names when defining which font to use for warning labels. For example, consider this list:

```
font.mySuite.thisProgram.labels
font.mySuite.any.labels
font.mySuite.thisProgram.any
font.mySuite.any.any
```

The first element of these definitions is a property type. The second part defines the suite or group of related programs. The third element specifies a particular program. The elements beyond this point describe the particular aspect or category of aspects that will be controlled by the definition.

For example, if a program called `thisProgram` in the suite called `mySuite` wishes to know what `Font` to use for a general `Label`, it checks each of the properties listed in turn. As soon as a defined property is found, that property value is used to select the font. If some labels have special functions, such as issuing warnings, then the list could be extended by the addition of even more specific items at the start of the list, for example:

```
font.mySuite.thisProgram.labels.warning
```

The scheme is extensible as far as you require it to be. To define the fonts used for text entry, such as `TextField` or `TextArea`, resources of the form `font.mySuite.thisProgram.textEntry` can be defined. Menu items and any other group of fonts can be handled, and of course the scheme is not restricted to `Font` specifications.

A sample implementation of this concept follows. The source for this example is on the CD-ROM in the directory `javadevhdbk\ch05\Suite.java`. The corresponding bytecode is in the file `Suite.class` in the same directory.

Suite.java

```java
import java.util.*;
import java.io.*;

public class Suite {
  private String suite;
  private String progname;
  private static final boolean TRACE = true;

  public Suite(String suite, String progname) {
    this.suite = suite;
    this.progname = progname;
  }

  public String findBest(String type, String [] matchList) {
    String [] base = new String[3];
    String s, p = null;
    int listElements = matchList.length;

    base[0] = type + "." + suite + "." + progname;
    base[1] = type + "." + suite + ".any";
    base[2] = type + ".any.any";
```

```
    outer:
    for (int b = 0; b < base.length; b++) {
      for (int l = listElements; l >= 0; l--) {
        s = base[b];
        for (int e = 0; e < l; e++) {
          s += "." + matchList[e];
        }
        if (TRACE) {
          System.out.println("checking " + s);
        }
        if ((p = System.getProperty(s)) != null) {
          break outer;
        }
      }
    }
    return p;
  }

  public static void main(String args[]) {
    Properties p = System.getProperties();
    try {
      p.load(new FileInputStream("Suite.prop"));
    }
    catch (IOException e) {
      System.err.println("Failed to open property file Suite.prop");
      System.exit(1);
    }

    if (args.length < 3) {
      System.err.println(
        "Usage: java Suite <suitename> <progname> <propertytype>" +
        " [<specifier>...]");
      System.exit(2);
    }

    Suite that = new Suite(args[0], args[1]);
    String type = args[2];
    String [] s = new String[args.length - 3];
    System.arraycopy(args, 3, s, 0, args.length - 3);

    System.out.println(that.findBest(type, s));
  }
}
```

Running the Program

Run the program with each of the following command lines:

```
java Suite mySuite myProg font label
java Suite mySuite myProg font
java Suite mySuite yourProg font label
```

The output shows the property names that the program looks for and the final decision of the best fit property found.

What It Does

The program appends the contents of a file `Suite.prop` to the system property table. A sample file of the name `Suite.prop` is on the CD-ROM in the same directory as the bytecode of this example. It contains:

```
font.mySuite.myProg=desperate
font.mySuite.myProg.label=labelStuff
font.mySuite.myProg.label.warning=danger
font.mySuite.any=lastDitch
```

The program then takes the first two arguments of the command line and treats them as the name of the suite and the name of this program, respectively. These values are used to create an object of the `Suite` class. The `main()` method, which serves as a test harness, then takes the third argument and an array built from the remaining arguments and asks the `Suite` object for the best fit property from the system property table.

The program performs the search for the best fit by constructing test strings using the details of program and suite name, property type, and the specific details. If the "perfect fit" property is not found, the search proceeds by dropping items from the specific details list and checking for another property. If no match is found by the time the specific details have all been dropped, then the search proceeds again, substituting *any* in place of the program name. If this fails, then *any* is substituted in place of the suite name. Failure at this stage is considered to be complete failure of the match and returns `null`.

To support investigation of the behavior of this example, and to aid understanding the hierarchical definition of these property names, the program prints out each property name as it is sought in the list.

Reusing the Code

`Suite.java` can easily be used in any general program or suite of applications. Removing the `main()` method would improve the space efficiency of the classfile, but is otherwise unnecessary. For real use, the constant definition TRACE should be changed to `false` and the program recompiled. It is not necessary to remove the code block starting `if (TRACE) {` because the compiler optimization removes this block from the bytecode output altogether if TRACE is a constant of the value `false`.

For general use, construct the `Suite` object using an appropriate suite and program name and ensure that a property file that defines the property values is appended to the system properties at startup.

TIP

Although access to local files is generally prohibited to applets, the `load()` method in the `Properties` class expects an `InputStream` instance as its argument. It is therefore perfectly possible to read properties from a URL if this is useful in a particular case. Using the method `getResourceAsStream()` in the `ClassLoader` class, this is directly supported in a way that does not require an applet to be aware of its own origin. This is discussed in the next section.

Locating Properties

The foregoing discussions have considered ways of using properties and of maximizing the convenience they offer to the user. However, the issue of where these properties are located has been left largely open.

As part of their design, some browsers—particularly the appletviewer and HotJava—read specific files for additional resources. It is generally not convenient for either the user, system administrator, or software distributor to have to edit this file as part of software installation. Further, because not all browsers use resources from a file, resources defined in any particular file are not available in all browsers. Finally, because these are browser-configuration files, it would be inappropriate to use the same files in the context of an application.

JDK 1.1 provides a new mechanism that allows general resources to be located by association with packages. The mechanism closely parallels that used for locating classes within packages, and in fact the mechanism is implemented by the class loaders. The mechanism is referred to as *resource location*.

NOTE   A *resource* in Java 1.1 is often a file containing property definitions, but could be any other form of support file as needed in a particular program; for example, an image or sound file.

Recall that the `Properties` class provides a `load()` method that takes an `InputStream` object as its argument. The primary facility provided by the resource mechanism is to return an `InputStream` object suitable for use in this `load()` method. This is done by the `getResourceAsStream()` method in the `Object` class. The argument to the `getResourceAsStream()` method is a `String` object. This string, in the simplest case, is a filename. The `getResourceAsStream()` method attempts to locate the specified file in the same location as that from which the classfile for the requesting object was loaded. In the case of a local class, loaded from the `CLASSPATH`, the file will be sought on each element of the `CLASSPATH`, too. If a class—for example, an `Applet` class—was loaded from a URL, the resource file will be loaded from the same base URL, if it exists.

Earlier in this chapter, the section *Package and Class Availability* described the mechanism that uses package information as a relative directory path when loading classes. A similar approach is taken with the resource mechanism. If a resource is specified using the forward slash (/) character as part of its makeup, then the information up to the last of these will be taken as path information and the search for the resource will be modified accordingly.

WARNING Regardless of the host platform, the forward slash (/) should always be used. In the implementation any necessary translation is handled transparently.

This mechanism allows a convenient way to provide configuration information on a per-class basis. Because an application must be started from a `main()` method in a specific class, this supports application configuration as well.

It is simple to support user-specific resources if required, and it can be achieved in several ways. The username can be made part of the relative path of the resource name or can be the actual resource filename. It might seem convenient to use a dot (`.`) as a part of the `CLASSPATH`, as this would allow the resource file to be loaded from the user's current directory. This approach is probably not to be encouraged because it would potentially result in classes being loaded from the user's directories, too, which would allow the possibility of system attack, either directly by the user seeking to modify the working of the program or by an outsider who managed to breach the user's individual security and place a classfile into his filespace.

TIP In addition to supporting property files via the `getResource-AsStream()` method, the resource mechanism allows arbitrary files to be located in the same way. It can be used via the `getResource-AsStream()` method but can also be used via the `getResourceAs-Name()` method. The `getResourceAsName()` method describes the full path, perhaps including URL protocol information, if appropriate, at which the resource is located. Any appropriate method can then be used to handle the resource directly. This is perhaps particularly appropriate when handling images and sounds.

Properties and Color

Colors can be specified using property values, and a static method in the `Color` class is able to interpret the values directly. The method name is `getColor()`. It takes a string argument that should match the property name. For the mechanism to function correctly, the value of the property should be specified as a 24-bit integral value. This value is interpreted as three bytes. The highest order byte represents red, the middle byte represents green, and the low order byte represents blue. In each case, the color is on a scale of 0-255. The property mechanism for reading integer values allows the use of decimal, hexadecimal, or octal if desired. These formats are represented using the same conventions as source code constants.

TIP

In addition to reading and interpreting the system properties directly, the `Color` class provides the `decode()` method. This is a static method that interprets its argument, which is a `String` object, as a number representing the 24-bit color value. This method can therefore be used to create `Color` objects conveniently from this form of representation. This method was introduced with the release of JDK 1.1.

The CD-ROM has a small example that simply displays a small window and sets the color of that window to a value specified by a property.

ColorProp.java

```java
import java.awt.*;

public class ColorProp extends Frame {
  public static void main(String args[]) {
    ColorProp that = new ColorProp();
    that.setSize(100, 100);
    that.setVisible(true);
  }
```

```
public ColorProp() {
    setBackground(Color.getColor("ColorProp.background"));
}
}
```

Running the Program

The source of this example is on the CD-ROM in the directory `javadevhdbk\ch05\ColorProp.java`. The corresponding byte-code is in the same directory in the file `ColorProp.class`. Try running the program with the following command lines in turn:

```
java -DColorProp.background=0xff0000 ColorProp
java -DColorProp.background=0x00ff00 ColorProp
java -DColorProp.background=0x0000ff ColorProp
```

TIP Remember that an application can read properties from a file, and that is the normal place for properties to be defined. However, the command-line form used here is useful for experimentation because it avoids the need to edit a file before each test run. Instead, you simply change the argument list and run the program again.

What It Does

This program is very simple, and for the purposes of the example only one line is of interest. That is:

```
setBackground(Color.getColor("ColorProp.background"));
```

Within this line, the `Color.getColor()` method is the one that does the interesting work. It attempts to load a property named `ColorProp.background` from the system properties table. If successful, it attempts to treat it as a number and create a new instance of the `Color` class from that number.

The remainder of the program provides a window and sets the background color of that window using the `Color` object returned by the `Color.getColor()` method.

Properties and Fonts

The `Font` class is able to read and interpret properties to define fonts. The static method `getFont()` searches the system properties for a property with the string name that matches the string provided as an argument to the call. If the property name is found, then the value associated with it is interpreted as a font name. Font names contain three parts that define the font's name, style, and point size. The specification of style and size is optional.

To specify only the font name, accepting the default of plain style and 12 point size, you only need to include the name of the font in the property value. If you want to specify either style or size, then the property value should be laid out as three parts, each part being separated by a dash (-) from the others. The font name should be first, followed by the style, and then finally the size. For example, Times Roman 36-point italic is specified with the property value:

```
TimesRoman-italic-36
```

Notice that there are no spaces in this value; the name `TimesRoman` is also a single string with no spaces.

To leave either the size or the style unspecified, both hyphens should be included, but whichever aspect is to take the default value should be left `null`. Hence a default style 24-point Helvetica is indicated as:

```
Helvetica--24
```

This has the same effect as an explicit request for the plain style, which can be made as:

```
Helvetic-plain-24
```

Bold italic style is indicated by the string `bolditalic`. For example:

```
Courier-bolditalic-
```

would indicate a default size Courier typeface with both bold and italic attributes.

TIP

In addition to reading and interpreting the system properties directly, the `Font` class provides the `decode()` method. This is a static method that takes a `String` object as its argument. It interprets the string and returns a new `Font` object constructed according to the rules just described. The `decode()` method was introduced with the release of JDK 1.1.

The following example program reads a property to determine a font. The source and bytecode for this example are on the CD-ROM in the files `FontProp.java` and `FontProp.class` in the directory `javadevhdbk/ch05`.

FontProp.java

```java
import java.awt.*;

public class FontProp extends Frame {
  public static void main(String args[]) {
    FontProp that = new FontProp();
    that.pack();
    that.setVisible(true);
  }

  public FontProp() {
    Font myFont = Font.getFont("FontProp.font");
    setLayout(new FlowLayout());
    setFont(myFont);
    add(new Label(myFont.toString()));
  }
}
```

Running the Program

Try running the program with the following command lines in turn:

```
java -DFontProp.font=TimesRoman-bold-26 FontProp
java -DFontProp.font=TimesRoman-bolditalic-16 FontProp
java -DFontProp.font=Courier-20 FontProp
```

What It Does

As with the `ColorProp.java` example earlier, this is a very simple program. In this case the method that is of interest is called in this line:

```
Font myFont = Font.getFont("FontProp.font");
```

This line attempts to load a property called `FontProp.font` from the system properties table. Provided this is successful, the method treats the resulting value as a font name and creates a new `Font` object based on that value. The rest of the program serves only to present a label using this font.

Security Weakness

A security weakness exists in font allocation on most X Windows platforms. Attempts to create fonts are not restricted by standard security managers. This opens a potentially nasty denial of service attack in X Windows environments.

If a request is made to create a font with a huge point size, the server will take a very long time to create the necessary data structures. This may take several minutes. Unfortunately, most X servers, specifically all those of X11-R5 and older, are single threaded. This means that while the font is being prepared, no other display, keyboard, or mouse activity will be possible. The underlying Unix system will still be running, however, and the problem can be recovered if it is possible to log into the machine from another host and issue a `kill` command.

In addition to hanging the display, the resulting font will take up large amounts of server memory; this might cripple the X server even after the font has been allocated.

Localization of Properties

With the release of JDK 1.1 Java provides significantly more support for localization of programs. Using the idea of a *locale*, the local system administrator or user can specify a preference for the language and other styles, such as currency and data/time format, that the program should use for presenting output.

Several classes have been added or enhanced to provide this functionality. The cornerstone of these facilities is the `Locale` class. The `Locale` class is used to represent a particular set of presentational preferences. There are up to three parts to a locale: the country, language, and a variant.

Country and language are represented both with a readable string and with a code. The country codes are defined in ISO-3166, while the language codes are defined in ISO-639. Variants describe other specific localizations, typically, the platform can be represented as "POSIX," "WIN," or "MAC" for Posix, MS-Windows, or Macintosh respectively.

A `Locale` object that reflects the preference of the user can be obtained using the static method `Local.getDefault()`. Once a `Locale` object has been obtained a number of methods can be used to extract the country, language, and variant from it. The methods `getDisplayCountry()`, `getDisplayLanguage()`, and `getDisplayVariant()` return full strings that are suitable for presentation to the user. Similarly, `getDisplayName()` represents all the locale information in a single string.

Inside programs, short form representations are often more useful. These may be obtained using the methods `getISO3Country()`, `getISO3Language()`, `getCountry()`, `getLanguage()`, and `getVariant()`. The ISO3 versions return the three-character codes specified by the ISO standards, while the `getCountry()` and `getLanguage()` methods return the two-character strings that are normally used instead.

The locale information can be used quite simply to allow localization of properties. If properties are read from a file, then all that is needed is to build the filename to reflect the locale features. In practice, two modifications are made. First, several files should be tried, using the different aspects of the locale as a hierarchical representation. Hence, if the full locale was made up from country Great Britain, language English, variant Windows, then the files from which to load properties might be `prefs`, `prefs_en`, `prefs_en_GB`, and `prefs_en_GB_WIN`.

The second modification is that the classloader in Java 1.1 allows you to obtain a stream from a file located in the same place that the classloader obtains classes. This modification allows applets to obtain properties (and other data) from their Web servers in a platform- and location-independent way.

The following example demonstrates these principles. The source and bytecode files are located on the CD-ROM in the directory `javadevhdbk\ch05`.

LocProp.java

```
import java.applet.*;
import java.awt.*;
import java.io.*;
import java.util.*;


public class LocProp extends Applet {
  TextArea ta = new TextArea(24, 60);
  Properties props = new Properties();
```

```java
Locale loc = Locale.getDefault();
String extras[] = { "Resources",
                    "_" + loc.getLanguage(),
                    "_" + loc.getCountry(),
                    "_" + loc.getVariant() };

public LocProp() {
  setLayout(new BorderLayout());
  add("Center", ta);
}

public void init() {

  ClassLoader c = getClass().getClassLoader();
  String base = "";

  InputStream resStream = null;

  try {
    for (int i = 0; i < extras.length; i++) {
      base += extras[i];
      System.out.print("Looking for " + base);
      if (c != null) {
        resStream = c.getResourceAsStream(base);
      }
      else {
        resStream = ClassLoader.getSystemResourceAsStream(base);
      }
      if (resStream != null) {
        System.out.print(" - found");
        props.load(resStream);
      }
      System.out.println();
    }
    ta.setText("");
    Enumeration pe = props.propertyNames();
    while (pe.hasMoreElements()) {
      String key = (String)(pe.nextElement());
      ta.appendText(key + " = ");
      ta.appendText(props.getProperty(key) + "\n");
    }
  }
```

```
    catch (IOException e) {
      System.err.println("Unexpected exception ");
      e.printStackTrace(System.err);
    }
  }

  public static void main(String args[]) throws Throwable {
    Frame f = new Frame("Localized Properties");
    Applet a = new LocProp();
    f.add("Center", a);
    f.pack();
    f.show();
    a.init();
  }
}
```

Running the Program

This program may be run either as an applet or an application. To run the program as an application, select the directory on the CD-ROM that contains the bytecode and issue the command

```
java LocProp
```

To run the program as an applet, use your browser or the appletviewer to load the HTML file LocProp.html, which is located in the same directory as the classfile.

However it is started, the program will indicate on the standard output the names of four files that it tries to load. These filenames are built from the base name Resources, and each is successively extended with the language, country, and variant information of the current locale. Four resource files are provided in the same directory as this program. These resource files are called Resources, Resources_en_US, Resources_en_GB, and Resources_fr. If your locale is neither US nor British English, and is not French, then you should copy these files, along with the file LocProp.class, onto your hard disk and create a modified resource file that has a name that reflects your locale. Choose one of the filenames that the program reports it is looking for.

After the four resource files have been checked for and loaded if found, the resulting properties will be listed in a text area.

What It Does

This program demonstrates the use of the `ClassLoader` object to obtain a stream from a location that depends on the origin of the class that makes the request. If the program is run as an application, the resource stream will originate from a file located in a directory somewhere on the `CLASSPATH`. If the program is run as an applet, then the resource will originate from a file at the same base URL as the applet classfile itself.

To load a resource in this way, the code first has to locate the class-loader that is to be used. This is done by first using the `getClass()` method on the current object (which is the applet), and then using the `getClassLoader()` method on the `Class` object that was returned. The `getClass()` method is a member of the `Object` class, while the `getClassLoader()` method is a member of the `Class` class.

If a class was loaded from the local system, then it is loaded by the *primordial* classloader—that is, the classloader that is built into the base Java distribution. Calling the `getClassLoader()` method on such a class returns null. Under these conditions, it is necessary to use the static method `ClassLoader.getSystemResourceAsStream()`. For classes loaded from remote systems, however, a non-null `Class-Loader` reference is returned by the `getClassLoader()` method and that reference can be used to invoke the `getResourceAs-Stream()` method.

> **TIP**
>
> Along with the ability to load locally appropriate resources by using elements of the current locale as part of the filename, a generalized mechanism is built into Java 1.1 for internationalization of programs. This internationalization mechanism depends on the locale element names in the same way as has been demonstrated in the `LocProp.java` example. Instead of simply defining properties, however, this mechanism defines whole subclasses and allows arbitrary objects to be written in a variety of locale-dependent ways. At runtime, the correct variant to load is determined according to the locale. This mechanism is embodied in the `java.util.ResourceBundle` class and, as with the `LocProp.java` example, the resources are loaded via the classloader and are therefore sourced from the same location as the class that requests them.

Network Class Loading

Java is highly flexible about the sources from which bytecode can be obtained. Because it is so easy to use a browser and see code being loaded from a Web server or from the browser's own local machine, as required, it is easy to believe that Java has some "magic" and that classes are loaded automatically without any setup or intervention being needed. In reality, the user has this impression because the Web site administrators and developers both of Java and the individual programs, have done their job properly. If you are to distribute your programs successfully, whether they are applets or applications, you will need an understanding of the mechanisms that Java uses to locate a class that it must load. This section discusses those mechanisms and the configuration options that are open to the developer and Web site administrator when installing Java applets for distribution.

To construct an instance of a class, invoke a static method, or access a static variable, the definition for that class must first be loaded into the Java Virtual Machine. A class must also be loaded if it is a superclass of some other class that is also being used.

If an applet refers to several other classes but uses them only in special conditions, then most times the applet runs, these classes are not required at all. It would therefore be a waste of network bandwidth to insist on loading all of the classes every time the applet is loaded. The loading would also delay the startup of the applet.

For these reasons, class loading is deferred until the last possible moment; this is not restricted to applets, but applies to any Java class. So, if an applet has instance variables of types HerClass and HisClass, then the classfiles for these will not be loaded until they are actually required.

It is possible to demonstrate this effect. At the instant a class is loaded, before any constructor or static method can be called, or any static variable accessed, the class undergoes static initialization. This process initializes all the static variables and also invokes any static initializer code blocks. Consider this class skeleton:

```
public class StaticStuff {
   static int x = 7;
   public StaticStuff() {
      // constructor code
   }
   static {
      // this is a static initializer block
      x += 3;
   }
}
```

When the class is loaded, *all* the static initialization is done in sequence, both variable and code blocks. Here, the value of x is first set to 7 and then the body of the static initializer is executed. This increases the value of x by 3, resulting in a value of 10. Multiple static initializer blocks are allowed in a class, although this looks odd, and it is difficult to conceive a reason for wanting to do this.

The static initializer can be used to determine the instant that a class is loaded. The following example demonstrates that classes are only loaded when actually required. The source for this example is

located on the CD-ROM in the directory `javadevhdbk/ch05/C1`
`.java`. The corresponding bytecode is located in the same directory
in the files `C1.class` and `C2.class`.

C1.java

```java
public class C1 {
  C2 that;

  public static void main(String args[]) {
    C2 other;
    System.out.println("I'm started. Pausing for effect....");
    try {
      Thread.sleep(3000);
    }
    catch (InterruptedException e) {
    }
    System.out.println("About to create a C2.");
    other = new C2();
    System.out.println("C2 created, bye.");
  }
}

class C2 {
  static {
    System.out.println("I'm C2 being loaded");
  }
}
```

Running the Program

To run the program, select the directory listed above and issue the
following command:

```
java C1
```

The output of the program is:

```
I'm started. Pausing for effect....
About to create a C2.
I'm C2 being loaded
C2 created, bye.
```

What It Does

The output shows that the static initializer block of the class C2 is not executed until immediately before the call is made to the constructor for that class. This demonstrates the loading of the class has been deferred until the class was actually needed.

Forcing Class Loading

It is possible to force loading of a class even in the absence of an immediately visible requirement for it. This might be done deliberately to enhance running response of a program at the expense of startup time. If the user has a dial-on-demand network connection with a standard modem, this approach might be particularly appropriate. Under such conditions, if the network remains idle for a period, the modem drops the phone line. The connection is reestablished automatically when needed. This reestablishment takes a significant amount of time and, if done regularly, also makes for very inefficient use of modem time.

You can achieve *forced loading* using a static method in the class java.lang.Class called forName(). This method takes a string argument that defines the fully qualified class name, which is the classname with the package name included; it is demonstrated by the following code fragment.

ForceLoad.java

```
public class ForceLoad {
  ForceLoaded that;

  public static void main(String args[]) {
    ForceLoaded other;
    System.out.println("I'm started. Pausing for effect....");
    try {
      Thread.sleep(3000);
    }
```

```
      catch (InterruptedException e) {
      }
      System.out.println("About to create a ForceLoaded.");
      other = new ForceLoaded();
      System.out.println("ForceLoaded created, bye.");
    }

    static {
      try {
        Class.forName("ForceLoaded");
      }
      catch (ClassNotFoundException e) {
        // let it show up later
      }
    }
}

class ForceLoaded {
  static {
    System.out.println("I'm ForceLoaded being loaded");
  }
}
```

This example is deliberately almost identical to the previous example, C1.java. ForceLoad.java. It is located on the CD-ROM in the same directory and may be run in the same way as C1.java, but you will notice that with this example the ForceLoaded class, which parallels the C2 class in the previous example, is actually loaded before any of the mainstream processing occurs.

Security Effects

Java provides a framework for security that allows a user to run an unknown applet with reasonable confidence that the applet will be prevented from performing any malicious actions, such as modifying files or stealing private data. From a programmer's point of view, such prevention can have an impact. For instance, many services that an applet developer might like to use, such as opening a temporary file, will be prohibited. Further, the precise set of operations that are prohibited can vary to an extent between platforms and even between different browsers or different users on the same platform. Because of these considerations, it is important for a developer to understand the background to security and the ways in which the conventional applet restrictions in particular affect the programmer's freedom. This section discusses these points.

Java security is normally discussed in the context of applets. This is because applets, running in browsers, are governed by prewritten security code. However, it is important to be aware that the security mechanism that browsers apply to applets is a general one, and it is possible to design and implement specific security policies on applications. Also, modified security policies can be imposed on existing browsers, although sometimes it might require a specialist's knowledge of the innards of the particular browser—or persistent guesswork.

In general, security has to cover two areas. First, during and after execution of the applet, the machine facilities, CPU, memory, and so forth should remain under the control of, and available to, the legitimate user; "foreign" code should not be able to usurp that control or make runaway use of the system. Second, data stored on the machine and any network companions must be protected against modification, damage, or unauthorized access.

Java, in its current versions, does not actively attempt to ensure the first of these conditions. Attacks in this category are termed *denial of service*. Competent operating systems allocate all resources to user processes on a "fair shares" basis and, as such, no single process should be able to make runaway use of the system. In practice, this assumption is possibly a shade optimistic. It can be very irritating to have a browser's performance reduced by a greedy applet. At the worst, such an attack might necessitate exiting and restarting the browser. Java's fundamental assumption is that the denial of service attacks are irritating but not debilitating. Currently most browsers arrange that the thread that runs an applet's init() method is in a thread group, which limits the maximum priority. However, this alone is not sufficient to protect against a denial of service attack. Future versions of Java are likely to tighten up this situation.

Protection of data is, by contrast, something that Java considers absolutely paramount. Several convenient facilities are strictly prohibited to applets on these grounds.

Data protection can be considered in two categories: protection against unauthorized reading and protection against unauthorized modification. Java browsers go to great lengths to prevent applets from obtaining information that they might be able to misuse. Several properties are unavailable to applets because even knowledge as apparently innocuous as the user's login name on the host machine could be misused. At the low-damage end of the scale, the login name could be used to direct unwanted marketing information via e-mail; at the serious end, it provides an attacker with a target username, which is a valuable first step towards a complete break-in.

It is in the nature of the World Wide Web and other Internet services that it is generally possible for an applet to transmit information to any host that is waiting to receive it. Because it is impossible to prevent an applet from talking to any cooperating remote server, it is therefore vital to restrict the information that it can obtain. You should not, therefore, write applets in such a way that they need to access anything on local file systems, HTML pages, or any other source that might be considered sensitive. To attempt to do so will almost certainly result in an applet that fails to run in a properly platform-independent way.

Protection against unauthorized changes to data is enforced with no less rigor. Again, therefore, applets should be coded in such a way that they do not need to be able to access any local data. For example, any attempt to use the class `FileOutputStream` will normally be rejected.

WARNING   In the controlled environment of an intranet, it might be acceptable to allow applets access to files in certain controlled directories. Some browsers, most notably the appletviewer, are able to support this facility. However, access should not be permitted if the browser has any ability to load applets from untrusted hosts.

Summary

This chapter has discussed a wide variety of topics, all loosely related by their impact on the portability of Java program code. Different platforms run with different native data formats, different file system layouts, different CPU speeds, and different thread-scheduling algorithms. Windowing systems affect the layout, appearance, colors, and size of visible elements of a GUI program. Individuals might want the opportunity to configure a running Java program to their own preferences. Classes must be accessible for loading at runtime, and applets are restricted by the security manager. All these aspects require consideration when a program is being developed if the result is to run smoothly and inconspicuously on all Java platforms.

PART II

Advanced Topics

These chapters introduce topics that are more advanced than those covered in the previous chapters. So far, this book has presented information that is relevant to nearly every Java program. The next nine chapters discuss features that may or may not appear in a program. For example, a program may make heavy use of threads and network communication to query a remote database but have nothing to do with file access or animation; another program might rely on content and protocol handlers to manipulate images and create animations.

CHAPTER

SIX

6

Images

- What an image really is

- Image observers

- The memory image source

- Color models

- Producers, consumers, and filters

Images have a big job to do. It takes a lot to make an image, especially if the source is some file out on the network. The bits that represent the image have to be loaded from the net and stored locally, and all this processing has to take place with a minimum of intrusion. From the user's perspective, dealing with the reality of images should have a minimal impact on performance. From a programmer's perspective, the process of moving pixel information from the net to the window system should be encapsulated in the various classes so that to the greatest extent possible the whole arrangement is hidden.

In practice the whole arrangement is indeed hidden, but in the sense of a slightly fat bear hiding behind a slightly thin tree. There are places where bits stick out into view, alarming the casual passerby. For example, many image-related methods require a mysterious extra parameter of type `ImageObserver`. The `getImage()` method seems to return immediately, even when loading a large image from a slow network. Sometimes you can create an off-screen image and sometimes you cannot.

There are two important things to learn from this chapter. The first, of course, is the way the image infrastructure works. Equally important is an understanding of which parts of that infrastructure can be usefully modified and which are best left alone.

What an Image Really Is

The `Image` class is abstract. You never construct one (that would be impossible because the class is abstract). Instead, you call `createImage()`, which is a method of the `Component` class. Usually the component's `createImage()` method just tells its peer to `createImage()`. The peer is a platform-specific bundle of calls to native methods. Thus the object returned by `createImage()` is a platform-specific subclass of `Image`. Not surprisingly, its methods are primarily calls to native methods.

For example, consider what happens in a `createImage()` call in the `init()` of an applet running on a Solaris/Motif platform. The applet's peer is a subclass of `MComponentPeer` in the `sun.awt.motif` package. The `MComponentPeer` class has its own `createImage()` method that constructs and returns an instance of `X11Image`, which is a concrete subclass of the abstract `Image` class. After much intricate processing, the `X11Image` constructor causes native calls into the Solaris/Motif version of the Java library; eventually a pixel map is created in the X server, and the `X11Image` communicates with this map.

NOTE   This is a perfect example of appropriate polymorphism. As programmers we believe we are using an instance of class `Image`. In fact we are using whatever subclass of `Image` is appropriate to our platform; the chore of deciding which subclass to use is taken care of for us. The entire mechanism is so well encapsulated that we never even need to know about it. Many successful Java programs have been written by people who were not aware that `Image` is abstract.

This is how a fresh image is created. An image can also be loaded from a remote file, via the `getImage()` method of the `Component` class. Here Java goes to great lengths to optimize performance. The simplest strategy would be for `getImage()` to make a connection to the machine that owns the remote graphics file, load the file, parse it, and construct and return an image. This strategy would be adequate in a perfect world, but in reality it could likely introduce extreme delays, for two reasons.

- The connection to the remote machine might be slow. The applet would waste cycles idling while waiting for network response.

- The user might never bring the applet into a state where the image was needed. The time spent in loading the image would have been wasted.

Java therefore enforces the following policies with respect to remote image files:

- All remote images are loaded by asynchronous threads.

- These threads do not begin to load until the corresponding image is used or "observed."

The mechanisms that enforce these policies are almost completely hidden from programmers. Programmatically, the biggest clue that something is going on is the requirement that certain methods require an extra parameter of type ImageObserver. Behaviorally, the biggest clue that Java is doing something complicated is seen when an applet flashes the first time it paints a large image. *Image Observers*, below, examines the image-observer mechanism, explains the flashing, and shows how to eliminate it.

Readers who are unfamiliar with image flashing are invited to run the Flasher applet on the CD-ROM. The first time the program runs in any browser session, the image does not appear all at once on the screen; rather, it grows in vertical chunks, with a repaint flash between chunks. The textfield at the top of the applet indicates that the applet is receiving an extraordinary number of repaint() calls. The code for the applet is quite simple and appears below and on the CD-ROM in javadevhdbk\ch06\Flasher.java. The bytecode is on the CD-ROM in javadevhdbk\ch06\Flasher.class. At the end of the listing is a method that would eliminate the flashing if it were not commented out. The flashing and the fix are explained in *Image Observers*, below.

Flasher.java

```java
import      java.awt.*;
import      java.awt.image.*;
import      java.applet.Applet;


public class Flasher extends Applet
{
    Image           im;
    TextField       tf;
    int             nRepaints;
    int             nPaints;


    public void init()
    {
        setLayout(new BorderLayout());
        tf = new TextField();
        add("North", tf);
        // Load image from server of applet.
        im = getImage(getDocumentBase(), "Hammock.jpg");
    }


    // This is the version of repaint() called by imageUpdate().
    public void repaint(long tm, int x, int y, int w, int h)
    {
        nRepaints++;
        super.repaint(tm, x, y, w, h);
    }


    public void paint(Graphics g)
    {
        nPaints++;
        tf.setText(nRepaints + " repaints, " + nPaints + " paints, "
                + "width = " + im.getWidth(this) +
                    ", height = " + im.getHeight(this));
        g.drawImage(im, 0, 0, this);
    }
```

```
/**** Un-comment this method to eliminate flashing ********
***** without using a MediaTracker. ********************
public boolean imageUpdate(Image img, int flags,
                    int x, int y, int width, int height)
{
    if ((flags & ImageObserver.ALLBITS) != 0)
        repaint();
    return true;
}
************************************************************/
}
```

Image Observers

The image-observer mechanism is an example of the Observer design pattern. The idea is to permit an object to be "observed" by an arbitrary number of other objects. When the object being observed experiences a change that the observers ought to know about, the observed object makes a call to all the observers. The object being observed has the discretion to decide when the observers should be notified.

> **NOTE** For programmers who wish to apply the Observer/Observed paradigm to their own designs, Java offers the interfaces `Observer` and `Observable` in the `util` package. Images do not actually use these interfaces.

In Java's paradigm, the color values for an image are delivered by an object that implements the `ImageProducer` interface, which is covered in detail later in this chapter. For a remote image, the image producer is a thread that communicates via TCP/IP with the server that contains the image file.

Recall Java's policy that the producer thread will run asynchronously (in the background), not beginning its work until the image is observed. For this reason, getImage() returns immediately; the value returned is a reference to an instance of Image with width and height both set to -1. Eventually the width and height will get set to the correct values.

Several methods can make the system decide that the image has been observed. The most common is Graphics.drawImage(), which renders the image onto the screen. This method requires an extra parameter of type ImageObserver, which is an interface, not a class. The Component class implements the interface. The easiest way to call Graphics.drawImage() is to pass as the image observer a reference to the component in which the image is being rendered.

The call to drawImage() causes the image's producer to start producing. Periodically the producer delivers new information to the image and then makes a call to the imageUpdate() method of the image's observer. The meaning of the call is, "The image has changed, and here's how, and you might want to do something about it." The API for imageUpdate() is:

```
public boolean imageUpdate(Image im, int flags,
                           int x, int y, int width, int height)
```

The flags parameter describes the new information being reported by the current imageUpdate() call. The x, y, width, and height parameters specify the bounding box of the image data delivered so far. Not all of these four parameters are valid; validity depends on the value of flags. The flags are described in Table 6.1.

Parameter data cannot be depended on to be valid unless it is referred to by one of the flags. For example, the width parameter should not be used unless the WIDTH bit of the flags is set. Even when set, the value of width is just the current width. In most cases, images are produced row by row so that `width` attains its ultimate value early in the process, but this cannot be guaranteed. Generally, `height` does not get set to its ultimate value until production is all but finished.

TABLE 6.1   Flag Values for `imageUpdate()`

Flag	Meaning
`ImageObserver.WIDTH`	The image's width has been updated and may be read from the `width` parameter or from the image's `getWidth()` method.
`ImageObserver.HEIGHT`	The image's height has been updated and may be read from the `height` parameter or from the image's `getHeight()` method.
`ImageObserver.PROPERTIES`	The image's properties have been updated, and may be read from the image's `getProperties()` method.
`ImageObserver.SOMEBITS`	More pixels have been delivered for an image.
`ImageObserver.FRAMEBITS`	A complete frame of a multiframe image has been delivered.
`ImageObserver.ALLBITS`	The image is complete.
`ImageObserver.ERROR`	An error has occurred in production.
`ImageObserver.ABORT`	Production has been abnormally terminated.

The `imageUpdate()` method of `Component` just calls `repaint()` so that the more complete image gets rendered. This could easily result in several hundred calls to `repaint()`, which does little harm, as most of those calls do nothing. Recall that `repaint()` just requests a call to `update()` in the near future. Most of the calls occur after some other call has already made the request but before the update thread has run, so nothing happens. The hundreds of calls to `repaint()` result in only a few calls to `update()` and `paint()`. Those few calls, however, will produce a visible flashing of the image as `update()` clears the screen and `paint()` draws the incomplete image. The applet Flasher on the CD-ROM illustrates the flashing phenomenon and also displays the number of calls to `paint()` and `repaint()` and the image's size; the source for Flasher is given in *What an Image Really Is*, earlier in this chapter.

One way to eliminate the flashing is to override `imageUpdate()` so it only repaints when the complete image is available. The code below does the trick, and it appears in the source for the Flasher applet, though it is commented out:

```
public boolean imageUpdate(Image img, int flags,
                           int x, int y, int width, int height)
{
    if ((flags & ImageObserver.ALLBITS) != 0)
        repaint();
    return true;
}
```

This fix certainly works, but if there are multiple images the code gets a bit more complicated (it would be desirable to repaint only once, when all images are complete). Moreover, if this is happening in an applet or frame of any complexity, layout considerations may call for subdivision into panels. In this case, some of the logic from `imageUpdate()` must be moved into the subpanel's own `imageUpdate()` method. Overriding `imageUpdate()` is generally not the best strategy for waiting for an image. A much better way is to use the `MediaTracker` class, which is the subject of the next section.

The Media Tracker

It often happens that an applet or application cannot do anything useful until certain images are fully loaded. A prime example is an applet that just presents an animation. If the animation is begun before all frames are available, somewhere there will be a delay or blank frame.

As things stand, this situation is a deadlock. The image is not to be displayed until it is loaded, but the system will not even start to load the image until it tries to display the image.

The `MediaTracker` class solves the problem by providing a sly unseen observer for each image so the pixel-loading thread can be kicked off on demand. This mechanism is hidden from the programmer, who simply registers images with the tracker.

The constructor for `MediaTracker` is

```
MediaTracker(Component target)
```

The `target` parameter can be any component, but for ease of reading, it should be something simple, such as the applet.

After an image is created via `getImage()`, it can be registered with a tracker with the `addImage()` method:

```
tracker.addImage(image, n);
```

Here, `image` is the image to be tracked. The second parameter is an ID or category. The tracker can be asked to load all its images or just those images with a certain ID. The methods are described below:

> `void waitForAll() throws InterruptedException`
> Waits until all registered images are loaded.

> `void waitForID(int id) throws InterruptedException`
> Waits until all images with the specified ID are loaded.

Both methods block the current thread until the images are loaded. The `MediaTracker` supports various other forms of waiting and offers several forms of checking; the 1.1 version also supports unregistering an image. These facilities are straightforward and are adequately documented in the class' API.

NOTE When a method—such as `waitForAll()`—blocks, its thread gives up the CPU and does not become eligible for running until the condition on which it blocked is satisfied (or more rarely, until the call is interrupted). At that point the thread does not necessarily run; it must contend with other runnable threads.

Typically, a program that provides several different animations will use one ID for each animation. All frames (that is, images) for the first animation will use ID = 0, all frames for the second animation will use ID = 1, and so on.

The code to use a media tracker to load an image might look like this (the exception handler has been omitted for simplicity but should be present in any complete robust program):

```
public void init()
{
    MediaTracker tracker = new MediaTracker(this);
    im = getImage(getDocumentBase(), "images/xyz.gif");
    tracker.addImage(im, 0);
    try
    {
        tracker.waitForID(0);
    }
    catch (InterruptedException excep) { }
}
```

Images and Applications

For an applet, the obvious place to create or load an image is in the applet's init() method. Applications do not have init(), but they do have frames, and frames have constructors. As a general rule, tasks that an applet would perform in init() should be done in the constructor of an application's main frame.

This approach does not work with image initialization. Both getImage() and createImage() rely on the image-supporting resources of the underlying window system. In an applet this is no problem; by the time init() is called, the applet has been installed within the browser and its connection with the window system established. This is not the case with a frame in an application.

In Java all components, including applets and frames, are just ones and zeroes somewhere in memory. They remain no more than abstract representations until they are "realized," which happens when a call is made to the component's addNotify() method. At this point the underlying window system is called on (through native methods in the component's peer) to create its own local-style equivalent of the component. It is as if a component that has been realized casts a shadow onto the screen. A component's addNotify() method is most commonly called by the system when its container is realized.

The createImage() method only works if it is executed by a realized component. In an applet, by the time init() is called, the applet has been realized: its addNotify() method has been called, and it has been added into its browser. The applet is already "casting a shadow" onto the screen.

An application's frame is not realized until its show() method is executed. This method, inherited from the Window superclass, calls addNotify(). Before this happens, the frame's createImage() method will return null.

In general, images should be created as soon as possible after addNotify(). The best way to do this is to override addNotify(), calling the superclass' version and then initializing the images. Because there is no guarantee that addNotify() will only be called once, it is a good idea to have a boolean instance variable to ensure that initialization only happens once. The code below implements this strategy:

```
public void addNotify()
{
    super.addNotify();
    if (!imagesInitialized)
    {
        image = createImage(100, 100);
        imagesInitialized = true;
    }
}
```

The Memory Image Source

So far, this chapter has been concerned with loading images from external files. Another source for images is memory: a program can build an int or byte array to represent pixel values and use Java's `MemoryImageSource` class to construct an instance of `Image`.

`MemoryImageSource` has a variety of options for representing colors. Only the simplest option will be used in this section; other ways to specify what Java calls "the color model" will be discussed in the next section.

The input to `MemoryImageSource` in its most simple form is an array of ints. Each int consists of 8 bits (position 0 to 7) to represent blue, 8 bits (8 to 15) to represent green, and 8 bits (16 to 23) to represent red. The most significant 8 bits (24 to 31) are the color's alpha or opacity (see Figure 6.3 later in the chapter).

NOTE True opacity can only be represented on very expensive hardware. Affordable systems render inaccessible transparency combinations the same way they render other inaccessible colors: by dithering.

Life would be easy if the array were two dimensional. Unfortunately, it is one dimensional, with pixel values laid out as might be expected: for an image with *n* columns, the first *n* ints represent the first scan line, the second *n* ints represent the second scan line, and so on.

After the array is formatted, a memory image source can be constructed from the entire array or from a portion of it. The `Memory-ImageSource` constructor needs to be passed the size of the desired image, the int array, an offset into the array, and the width of the hypothetical image represented by the int array. This last parameter is required in case the desired image is to be a subset of the hypothetical full image.

The constructor for `MemoryImageSource` is called as follows:

```
MemoryImageSource(int width, int height, int[] pixels,
                  int arrayOffset, int scanwidth)
```

Figure 6.1 shows how the int array becomes an image. Bear in mind that no instance of `Image` is actually created until the `MemoryImageSource` is told to create one.

FIGURE 6.1

Int array to image

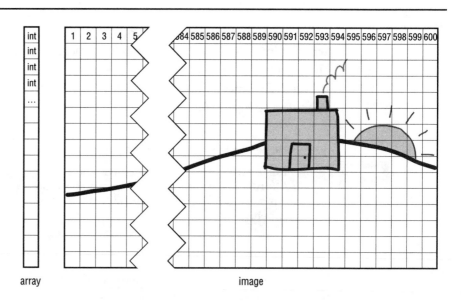

array   image

The Airbrush applet on the CD-ROM uses a `MemoryImageSource` to build nine airbrush images. Each image has pixels of a single color (red, green, and so on), but with an alpha that drops off with distance from the center of the image. The greater the distance from the center, the thinner the paint. The code that populates the nine arrays is as follows:

```
int sources[][] = new int[9][BRUSH_AREA];
for (j=0; j<BRUSH_SIZE; j++)
{
    for (i=0; i<BRUSH_SIZE; i++)
    {
        alpha = getAlpha(i, j);
        alpha <<= 24;
        sources[RED][index]     = 0x00ff0000 + alpha;
        sources[GREEN][index]   = 0x0000ff00 + alpha;
        sources[BLUE][index]    = 0x000000ff + alpha;
        sources[YELLOW][index]  = 0x00ffff00 + alpha;
        sources[MAGENTA][index] = 0x00ff00ff + alpha;
        sources[CYAN][index]    = 0x0000ffff + alpha;
        sources[BLACK][index]   = 0x00000000 + alpha;
        sources[GRAY][index]    = 0x00b8b8b8 + alpha;
        sources[WHITE][index]   = 0x00ffffff + alpha;
        index++;
    }
}
```

The getAlpha() method returns an alpha in the low 8 bits of an int. The alpha drops off with the sixth power of the distance from the center, as that seems to produce the most airbrush-like effect. The code is shown below:

```
int getAlpha(int x, int y)
{
    double deltaX = (double)(x - BRUSH_SIZE/2);
    double deltaY = (double)(y - BRUSH_SIZE/2);
    double distance = Math.sqrt(deltaX*deltaX +
                      deltaY*deltaY);
    double fracDistance = distance / (BRUSH_SIZE/2);
    if (fracDistance > 1.0)
        fracDistance = 1.0;
    fracDistance = 1.0 - fracDistance;
    fracDistance = Math.pow(fracDistance, 6);
    return (int)(255 * fracDistance);
}
```

Figure 6.2 shows a picture created with Airbrush. Of course, this is a monochrome screenshot, and readers are encouraged to create their own on-screen multicolor masterpieces.

FIGURE 6.2

Airbrush special effects

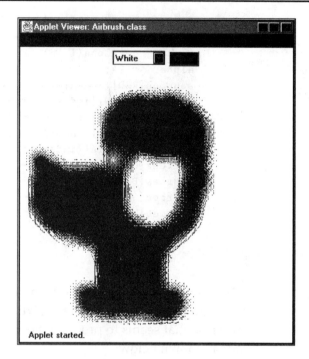

The 1.1 release enhances the MemoryImageSource class by giving it two methods that support multiframe images. The setAnimate() method tells the memory image source that it is to be the source of a multiframe image. The newPixels() method supplies the memory image source with the next frame's pixels.

Color Models

An image is a collection of zeroes and ones. A rendered image is an arrangement of colors. Some sort of convention is required to translate between binary numbers and screen colors. In Java that convention is encapsulated in color models.

Java represents a color as 32 bits. By default there are 8 bits for alpha, 8 for red, 8 for green, and 8 for blue. These values fit conveniently into an int, as shown in Figure 6.3.

FIGURE 6.3

32 bits of color information in an int

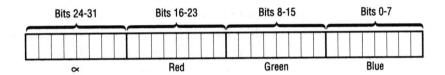

What Figure 6.3 really shows is Java's default color model; in other words, this is the convention by which Java maps bits to colors (and transparencies). When an int is passed to the constructor for a Color, it is expected to be in the format shown above. When an array of ints is passed to the constructor for a MemoryImageSource, all the ints are likewise expected to be in this format.

A program is free to create other color models. The class ColorModel (in package java.awt.image) has two subclasses, which encapsulate the two major categories of color model:

- DirectColorModel supports a custom partition of the 32-bit int into bit positions and numbers of bits to represent alpha, red, green, and blue.

- IndexColorModel supports a lookup table. Colors are represented by bytes, which are used to index into the table. The true color values are ints in the table, which are interpreted according to the default color model.

Direct Color Models

With a direct color model, the program specifies which and how many bits of an int represent which of the four attributes (alpha, red, green, blue). The bits of an attribute must be contiguous and may not overlap the bits of any other attribute.

There are two constructors for class `DirectColorModel`. Both expect an int to specify the width in bits of the model (32 for modern color models, but older systems might only use 8) and one int for each of red, green, and blue. Optionally, a fifth int may be supplied to specify alpha. The API for the constructors is as follows:

- `DirectColorModel(int nbits, int redmask, int greenmask, int bluemask)`

- `DirectColorModel(int nbits, int redmask, int greenmask, int bluemask, int alphamask)`

The masks are just ints with bits set to mark where in the int the corresponding color will be found. For example, a color model that uses 1 bit to represent red, 3 for green, and 20 for blue would be constructed as follows:

```
model = new DirectColorModel(32, 0x800000, 0x700000, 0x0fffff);
```

The applet `DCModelLab`, found on the CD-ROM in `javadevhdbk\ch06\DCModelLab.java` and `DCModelLab.class`, makes it easy to see how an int will be translated into a color via the standard color model and also via a custom direct color model specified by the user. A screenshot is shown in Figure 6.4.

Of course Figure 6.4 is not in color. The reader is invited to run the lab and enter the values shown in the figure. The pixel value is `0xff000f`. With the standard model this means red = 255, green = 0, and blue = 15. This is very close to plain red, and the rectangle on the lower left, representing `0xff000f` as interpreted through the standard color model, is indeed red.

With the custom color model, red is represented by 20 bits, or 5 hex digits. Green and blue only get 2 bits each. The red value is ff000 out of a possible fffff, which amounts to 99.6 percent. Green and blue are both 3 out of a possible 3. Because all three colors are full on, or very nearly so, the result is white.

FIGURE 6.4

DCModelLab

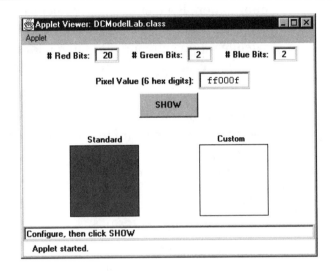

Readers who are developing custom direct color models are invited to use DCModelLab to speed the process of developing their own models.

Indexed Color Models

An indexed model construes the value of a color to be an index into a lookup table of red/green/blue values. In Java, the index is a byte. There are actually three lookup tables, one for each primary color (optionally, a fourth may be used for alpha). Each table entry contains 8 bits that specify color intensity. For example, if the byte 3 is to represent cyan, element 3 in the red table should be 0, and in both the green and blue tables it should be 255. When a byte color is to be rendered, a lookup is made into the tables, and the values retrieved are used to build up 32-bit color value as it would be represented by the default color model.

For images that use relatively few colors, indexed color models provide a convenient mapping mechanism. This mechanism is especially useful when the image to be constructed represents digital information. For example, a weather satellite might generate two-dimensional arrays of ints that represent air pressure. A mapping satellite might generate maps in the form of ints representing altitude. The best way to portray this information visually is to correlate each int value in the map with a color.

Indexed color models are also useful for rendering fractals, for elementary ray tracing, and for other geometrical applications where a pixel's position is mapped to a bounded int, usually by a time-consuming algorithm in the domain of pure mathematics.

The constructor for the `IndexColorModel` class is heavily overloaded. The simplest form is:

```
IndexColorModel(int nbits, int ncolors,
                byte reds[], byte greens[], byte blues[])
```

Here `nbits` is the number of bits used in the index; small models need not use all 8 bits of the byte. `ncolors` is the number of colors in the model, which is the size of the lookup table. The next three parameters are byte arrays that give the red, green, and blue levels; the size of all three arrays should be `ncolors`.

The main benefit of an indexed color model is the encapsulation of the lookup process. A beneficial side effect is that it takes only 8 bits to represent a pixel rather than 32. This is a 75 percent savings, which can mount up impressively if a program uses several large images. Yet another benefit is enhanced image-filtering performance, which is discussed later in this chapter.

The `SquareMIS` applet, found on the CD-ROM in `javadevhdbk\ch06\SquareMIS.java` and `SquareMIS.class`, shows how to use an indexed color model and a memory image source to draw a white box on a blue background. The program is simple enough not to require a screenshot. The listing follows:

SquareMIS.java

```
import  java.awt.*;
import  java.awt.image.*;
import  java.applet.Applet;


public class SquareMIS extends Applet
{
    Image   image;


    public void init()
    {
        ColorModel         model;
        MemoryImageSource  mis;

        // Build the color model.
        //                 color #0    color #1
        //                  white        blue
        byte reds[]   = {(byte)0xff, (byte)0x00};
        byte greens[] = {(byte)0xff, (byte)0x00};
        byte blues[]  = {(byte)0xff, (byte)0xff};
        model = new IndexColorModel(2, 2, reds, greens, blues);

        // Build array of bytes.
        int width = size().width;
        int height = size().height;
        byte pix[] = new byte[width*height];
        int n = 0;
        for (int j=0; j<height; j++)
        {
            for (int i=0; i<width; i++)
            {
                if (i > width/4   &&  i < width*3/4    &&
                    j > height/4  &&  j < height*3/4)
                {
```

```
                                pix[n] = 0;
                        }
                        else
                        {
                                pix[n] = 1;
                        }
                        n++;
                }
        }


        // Build a memory image source and have it build an
        // image.
        mis = new MemoryImageSource(width, height,
                                            model, pix, 0, width);
        image = createImage(mis);
}


public void paint(Graphics g)
{
    g.drawImage(image, 0, 0, this);
}
}
```

Producers, Consumers, Filters

Both the hidden objects that turn a remote gif file into pixel values and the quite visible memory image source are examples of image producers. They implement the ImageProducer interface, which is found in the java.awt.image package. Image producers have the job of delivering pixel values to image consumers. In addition to ImageProducer, there is also an ImageConsumer interface in the java.awt.image package, and the creation of an image is the result of a dialog between producer and consumer.

Java also supports a filter paradigm: between production and consumption there may be any number of filters. Figure 6.5 shows a metaphor for this process.

FIGURE 6.5

Production, consumption, and filtering

The producer

Falling hot water

Falling charcoal-filtered hot water

Falling coffee...

The consumer

First producers and consumers will be discussed, and then filtering.

Producers and Consumers

Programmers are more concerned with creating image producers than with creating image consumers. (Even so, there are many situations where creating a producer is not the best strategy.)

The producer/consumer dialog is initiated by the consumer, which tells the producer to start producing. The producer's appropriate response is to report the size of the image if possible and then to begin computing pixel values (or to begin marshaling them from a file on a remote server). From time to time the producer delivers fresh pixels to the consumer and tells the consumer when that task is done. Figure 6.6 shows schematically the sequence of calls.

FIGURE 6.6

The producer/consumer dialog

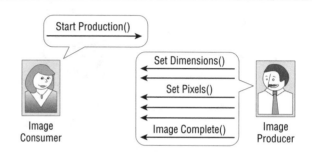

Figure 6.6 is an oversimplification. Both interfaces are more extensive than shown. ImageProducer has methods that permit more than one consumer to register with the producer. ImageConsumer has methods that permit the producer to supply more information about the image and the production process.

The API for ImageProducer is:

void addConsumer(ImageConsumer ic) Registers the consumer with the producer.

boolean isConsumer(ImageConsumer ic) Tells whether the consumer is currently registered with the producer.

void removeConsumer(ImageConsumer ic) Un-registers the consumer with the producer.

void startProduction(ImageConsumer ic) Registers the consumer and directs the producer to begin computing pixel values.

void requestTopDownLeftRightResend(ImageConsumer ic) Requests the producer to resend the pixel data. This is called in the unlikely event that the producer generates pixels in random order. Presumably it has previously generated the image and cached the pixels so now it can very quickly resend everything, row by row. A producer that sends pixels row by row anyway may safely ignore this call.

An image producer is expected to maintain a list of its consumers and report generated information to every consumer.

Image information is reported to image consumers via the calls of the `ImageConsumer` interface, as follows:

`void setDimensions(int width, int height)` Tells the consumer the size of the image.

`void setColorModel(ColorModel cm)` Tells the consumer what color model will be primarily used when pixels are sent. `setPixels()`, which is called arbitrarily many times, is free to use a different color model each call; `setColorModel()` tells the consumer which model will be most commonly used in case the consumer can use this information to improve performance.

`void setHints(int hints)` Tells the consumer how the pixels will be generated in case the consumer can use this information to improve performance. The value of the `hints` parameter is an OR (' | ') of the following constants of ImageConsumer:

`RANDOMPIXELORDER` Pixel values will be delivered in random order.

`TOPDOWNLEFTRIGHT` Pixel values will be delivered row by row, and pixel by pixel within each row.

`COMPLETESCANLINES` Every call to `setPixels()` will deliver complete scan lines.

`SINGLEPASS` Every pixel value will be delivered exactly once (though there might still be multiple calls to `setPixels()`).

SINGLEFRAME   The image consists of one frame, not multiple frames.

void setProperties(Hashtable properties)   Defines a set of properties for the image. Properties are string values associated with string names. The properties parameter is a hashtable of the values keyed by property name. Clients may query properties by calling the getProperty() method of class Image.

void setPixels(int x, int y, int width, int height, ColorModel model, int pixels[], int offset, int scansize)   Delivers more pixels to the consumer. The pixels represent the rectangular area of the image defined by x, y, width, and height. model is the color model of this set of pixels only and is free to change from call to call. pixels[] and offset provide an array, and a starting place within that array, of pixel values. If the color model is indexed, only the low-order byte of each int in pixels[] is used. scansize is the number of pixels in a scan line (row).

void setPixels(int x, int y, int width, int height, ColorModel model, byte pixels[], int offset, int scansize)   Same as above, but pixels[] is an array of bytes rather than ints. The color model is generally an indexed color model, though this method is sometimes seen with direct color model gif image files.

void imageComplete(int status)   Informs the consumer that a frame has been completely delivered or that some problem has occurred. Note that for multiframe images, there could be more frames to deliver, so the method name is misleading in this case. The status parameter is one of the following:

STATICIMAGEDONE   Production is complete.

SINGLEFRAMEDONE   One frame of a multiframe image is complete, but there are more frames to follow.

IMAGEERROR   The producer encountered an error.

IMAGEABORTED   Production has terminated prematurely.

The applet `ProdConLab` on the CD-ROM in `javadevhdbk\ch06\ProdConLab.java` and `ProdConLab.class` uses a memory image source to draw a black circle. The `Memory-ImageSource` class implements the `ImageProducer` interface, and the programmer overrides some of its methods so they will report when called. The applet actually creates a subclass of `MemoryImageSource` called `LoudMIS`, which writes a message to the applet's text area when one of the methods of the `ImageProducer` interface is called. Results will vary from platform to platform. Figure 6.7 shows the applet after it comes up on a Windows 95 machine. The calls to `addConsumer()`, `removeConsumer()`, and `startProduction()` are easily seen.

ProdConLab.java

```
import        java.awt.*;
import        java.awt.image.*;
import        java.applet.Applet;



public class ProdConLab extends Applet
{
    Image       image;
    TextArea    ta;


    public void init()
    {
        LoudMIS        mis;

        // Add a textarea for reporting.
        setLayout(new BorderLayout());
        ta = new TextArea(12, 12);
        add("South", ta);
```

```java
        // Build array to represent 100x100 pixels.
        int blackInt = Color.black.getRGB();
        int whiteInt = Color.white.getRGB();
        int pix[] = new int[100*100];
        int n = 0;
        for (int i=0; i<100; i++)
        {
            for (int j=0; j<100; j++)
            {
                // Formula for a circle
                int r2 = (i-50)*(i-50) + (j-50)*(j-50);
                if (r2 < 1000)
                    pix[n] = blackInt;
                else
                    pix[n] = whiteInt;
                n++;
            }
        }

        // Build a memory image src, and use it to
        // build an image.
        report("\tCREATING Memory Image Source.");
        mis = new LoudMIS(this, 100, 100, pix);
        report("\tCREATING Image.");
        image = createImage(mis);
    }


    public void paint(Graphics g)
    {
        report("\tPAINT()");
        g.drawImage(image, size().width/2 - 50, 5, this);
    }


    void report(String s)
    {
        ta.appendText(s);
        ta.appendText("\n");
    }
}
```

```
class LoudMIS extends MemoryImageSource
{
    ProdConLab        applet;


    LoudMIS(ProdConLab applet, int w, int h, int[] pix)
    {
        super(w, h, pix, 0, w);
        this.applet = applet;
    }


    public void addConsumer(ImageConsumer ic)
    {
        applet.report("addConsumer: " + ic.getClass().getName());
        super.addConsumer(ic);
    }


    public boolean isConsumer(ImageConsumer ic)
    {
        applet.report("isConsumer: " + ic.getClass().getName());
        return super.isConsumer(ic);
    }


    public void removeConsumer(ImageConsumer ic)
    {
        applet.report("removeConsumer: " + ic.getClass().getName());
        super.removeConsumer(ic);
    }


    public void startProduction(ImageConsumer ic)
    {
        applet.report("startProduction: " + ic.getClass().getName());
        super.startProduction(ic);
    }


    public void requestTopDownLeftRightResend(ImageConsumer ic)
    {
```

```
        applet.report("requestTopDownLeftRightResend: "
                    + ic.getClass().getName());
        requestTopDownLeftRightResend(ic);
    }
}
```

FIGURE 6.7

ProdConLab

The next section will examine what it takes to create a custom image producer.

Custom Producer

The code below uses a custom image producer to draw a white box on a blue background. The algorithm and results are identical to those of the memory image source example of the section *Indexed Color Models,* above. This is deliberate. After the listing, the costs and benefits of using a custom image producer are contrasted to those of using an indexed color model with a memory image source.

SquareProducer can be found on the CD-ROM in javadevhdbk\ch06\SquareProducer.java and SquareProducer.class.

SquareProducer.java

```
import      java.awt.image.*;
import      java.awt.Color;
import      java.util.Vector;
import      java.util.Enumeration;


public class SquareProducer implements ImageProducer
{
    private ColorModel      model;
    private int             width, height;
    private byte[]          pix;
    private Vector          consumers;


    public SquareProducer(int width, int height, ColorModel model)
    {
        this.width = width;
        this.height = height;
        this.model = model;
        consumers = new Vector();
        pix = new byte[width];
    }


    public void addConsumer(ImageConsumer ic)
    {
        if (!isConsumer(ic))
        {
            consumers.addElement(ic);
        }
    }


    public boolean isConsumer(ImageConsumer ic)
    {
        return consumers.contains(ic);
    }
```

```
public void removeConsumer(ImageConsumer ic)
{
    consumers.removeElement(ic);
}


public void startProduction(ImageConsumer ic)
{
    ImageConsumer        consumer;
    Enumeration          enum;

    // Add input consumer.
    addConsumer(ic);

    // Set dimensions and hints for all consumers.
    enum = consumers.elements();
    while (enum.hasMoreElements())
    {
        consumer = (ImageConsumer)(enum.nextElement());
        consumer.setDimensions(width, height);
        consumer.setHints(ImageConsumer.TOPDOWNLEFTRIGHT  |
                          ImageConsumer.COMPLETESCANLINES  |
                          ImageConsumer.SINGLEPASS         |
                          ImageConsumer.SINGLEFRAME);
    }

    // Compute pixel values. Set pixels for all consumers.
    for (int j=0; j<height; j++)
    {
        for (int i=0; i<width; i++)
        {
            if (i > width/4   &&   i < width*3/4   &&
                j > height/4  &&   j < height*3/4)
            {
                pix[i] = 0;
            }
            else
            {
                pix[i] = 1;
            }
        }
        enum = consumers.elements();
```

```
        while (enum.hasMoreElements())
        {
            consumer = (ImageConsumer)(enum.nextElement());
            consumer.setPixels(0, j, width, 1,
                               model, pix, 0, width);
        }
    }

    // Send image complete to all consumers.
    enum = consumers.elements();
    while (enum.hasMoreElements())
    {
        consumer = (ImageConsumer)(enum.nextElement());
        consumer.imageComplete(ImageConsumer.STATICIMAGEDONE);
    }

    ic.imageComplete(ImageConsumer.STATICIMAGEDONE);
}


public void requestTopDownLeftRightResend(ImageConsumer ic)
{
    return;
}
}
```

The applet `SquareProdTest`, found on the CD-ROM in `javadevhdbk\ch06\SquareProdTest.java` and `Square-ProdTest.class`, uses the image producer listed above to create an image. The source for `SquareProdTest` is as follows:

SquareProdTest.java

```
import      java.awt.*;
import      java.awt.image.*;
import      java.applet.Applet;


public class SquareProdTest extends Applet
{
    Image    image;
```

```
public void init()
{
    ImageProducer    producer;
    ColorModel       model;
    byte reds[]    = {(byte)0xff, (byte)0x00};
    byte greens[] = {(byte)0xff, (byte)0x40};
    byte blues[]  = {(byte)0xff, (byte)0xff};
    model = new IndexColorModel(8, 2, reds, greens, blues);
    producer = new SquareProducer(size().width, size().height,
                                  model);
    image = createImage(producer);
}


public void paint(Graphics g)
{
    g.drawImage(image, 0, 0, this);
}
}
```

In comparing the above listing to the version that uses a memory image source, one can see that there is very little benefit to be derived from using this image producer. The memory image source implementation must set pixel values in an array, and that is all it has to do. The listing above must not only generate pixel values but also keep track of its consumers and correctly participate in the dialog with those consumers. The MemoryImageSource class merely has to implement ImageProducer, while creating a custom producer requires re-implementing a lot of functionality instead of re-using what has already been provided.

These facts argue for using a MemoryImageSource unless there are compelling reasons not to. On examination of the code above, only one possible reason presents itself. With a custom producer, the producer does not have to allocate one int or byte for every pixel in the image; the example above shows that it is easy to allocate just a small array that contains the current scanline. This could be an issue in programs with large images. With a 500-by-500-pixel image and a direct color model, a custom image producer implementation requires a modest 500 ints, or 2,000 bytes. A memory image source implementation requires 250,000 ints, or 1MB. This is not the total memory requirement, of course (the image itself must be stored somewhere), but just the requirement at the production end of the pipeline.

Filters

By and large, image consumers are invisible to the programmer. Even when a custom image producer is created, the programmer is unaware of the details of the consumers with which the producer has its dialog. Most implementation details, such as the true class of the consumers or when and how they are constructed, are hidden. (Figure 6.7, the screenshot of ProdConLab, shows that on the Windows 95 platform where ProdConLab ran, two consumer classes were involved: ImageInfoGrabber and ImageRepresentation. Neither of these classes is part of the visible portion of the JDK.

One type of image consumer is accessible to the programmer. The ImageFilter class is intended to consume image data, filter it in some way, and pass it on to a producer.

This process is made possible by an auxiliary class called Filtered-ImageSource. The constructor for FilteredImageSource takes as inputs a reference to an image producer and a reference to an image filter. Because Filtered-ImageSource implements the Image-Producer interface, a filtered image can be created as in the following example:

```
SquareProducer prod = new SquareProducer(250, 250, colorModel);
ExampleImageFilter filter = new ExampleImageFilter();
FilteredImageSource filtSrc = new FilteredImageSource(prod, filter);
Image image = createImage(filtSrc);
```

Any number of filters may be chained together to create a highly filtered image. For example, the following code could be used to run an image through a color-to-grayscale filter and then through a contrast-enhancing filter:

```
Image originalImage = getImage(getDocumentBase(), "something.gif");
ImageProducer origProducer = originalImage.getSource();
FilteredImageSource grayProducer =
    new FilteredImageSource(origProducer, grayFilter);
FilteredImageSource contrastSource =
    new FilteredImageSource(grayProducer, contrastFilter);
Image finalImage = createImage(contrastSource);
```

Although this could be done with one filter that performs both functions, creating separate filter classes results in code that is much cleaner and more likely to be reusable.

Filter Subclasses

The ImageFilter class takes care of all image consumer behavior and all interactions with the FilteredImageSource class. It stands to reason that programmers should subclass ImageFilter rather than re-invent it, and in fact the java.awt.image package provides four subclasses for handling major categories of filtering situations.

The first subclass is called CropImageFilter. The constructor is passed x, y, width, and height. The filter extracts the subset of the image specified by these parameters.

The second subclass is RGBImageFilter. This is an abstract class whose abstract method filterRGB(int x, int y, int rgb) must be overridden by subclasses. The x and y parameters are the coordinates of the pixel being filtered, and rgb is the pixel value to be translated. Note that rgb is expressed with respect to the default color model (alpha:red:green:blue). The method should return an int representing the new translated pixel value. Commonly, RGBImage-Filter is subclassed to produce a contextless filter: that is, a filter whose rgb translation algorithm does not depend on the position of the pixel being translated or on the values of any other pixels.

If an `RGBImageFilter` filter truly does not care about a pixel's surroundings (but only on the pixel's color), then the subclass of `RGBImageFilter` can make an important optimization. If the subclass sets the boolean instance variable `canFilterIndexColor-Model` to `true`, then image producers that use an indexed color model do not have to translate every pixel. Instead, only the values in the color model's lookup table need to be translated. This is a significant performance bonus, especially if the translation algorithm is compute-intensive.

Two more filter classes have been added in 1.1: `ReplicateScale-Filter` and `AverageScaleFilter`. The `ReplicateScaleFilter` class is a simple size-scaling filter. Its constructor is passed two ints, which dictate the width and height of the filtered image. The `Average-ScaleFilter` class is a subclass of `ReplicateScaleFilter` that uses a more sophisticated smoothing algorithm than its superclass.

The Pixel Grabber

Some simple filters will be developed in the next section, but first another issue must be addressed: what to do if a filtering algorithm is heavily dependent on a pixel's surrounding pixels as well as on the pixel itself. This is the case in edge-detection and convolution algorithms.

One strategy for handling this situation is to subclass `ImageFilter` so it consumes the entire source image, caching pixel values in an array. When the image is completely cached, the translation algorithm can be applied. The subclass will need code to cache pixels, code to apply the filtering algorithm, and code to participate in the dialog with the `FilteredImageSource`. These are three distinct tasks.

It would be greatly preferable if the filter only had to filter, leaving the other tasks to more appropriate classes. What would be really useful would be a way to convert an image producer to an array of pixel values: a kind of memory image source in reverse. The array could be processed, and then a memory image source could be used to convert it to an image. This strategy bypasses the producer/filter/consumer model because the model is not appropriate to the task at hand.

As it turns out, there is a class that converts images to arrays of ints. The class is `PixelGrabber` in the `java.awt.image` package. There are two constructors for `PixelGrabber`; one takes an image and the other takes an image producer. The version that takes an image producer is more useful for filtering situations. The API for the constructors is as follows:

- `PixelGrabber(ImageProducer producer, int x, int y, int w, int h, int pixels[], int offset, int scansize)`

- `PixelGrabber(Image image, int x, int y, int w, int h, int pixels[], int offset, int scansize)`

In both cases a subset of the image, as defined by x, y, w, and h, is "grabbed" into the entries of array `pixels[]`, starting at `offset`. The array must be allocated and must be large enough. The `scansize` parameter gives the width of the original image.

Once the pixel grabber has been constructed, it can be told to grab pixels into its array of ints. The method is `grabPixels()`, and in its simplest form it takes no arguments. (Release 1.1 introduces a new method, `getPixels()`, which does not require passing a buffer to the constructor and returns an array of bytes or ints.) After calling either `grabPixels()` or `getPixels()`, it is good practice to check for errors by calling the pixel grabber's `getStatus()` method.

Given the ease of use of the `PixelGrabber` class, the cleanest way to apply a contextual filter to the output of an image producer is as shown below:

```
int pixels[] = new int[width*height];
MyImageProducer producer = new MyImageProducer(width, height);
```

```
PixelGrabber grabber = new PixelGrabber(producer, 0, 0,
                                        width, height,
                                        pixels, 0, width);
CustomFilter myFilter = new CustomFilter();
myFilter.filterThis(pixels);
MemoryImageSource mis = new MemoryImageSource(width, height,
                                        pixels, 0, width);
```

Example Filters and FilterLab

Because `PixelGrabber` is so easy to use, the appropriate time to use the filtering mechanism is when the filtering algorithm involves cropping the image or translating pixel values irrespective of the neighboring pixels. In these cases, the `CropImageFilter` and `RGBImageFilter` classes make life even easier than `Pixel-Grabber` does.

The applet `FilterLab`, found on the CD-ROM in `javadevhdbk\ch06\FilterLab.java` and `FilterLab.class`, provides three filters. One crops an image, one converts white to green, and one converts to grayscale. The user may activate any of these filters, or all or none of them, and view the result by clicking the Filter button. The original image is shown on the left, the filtered image on the right. (Combining the white-to-green filter with the grayscale filter may produce a visually counterintuitive result.)

FilterLab uses three filters: one cropping filter and two different custom subclasses of the RGB image filter.

The crop filter is the easiest to create because no subclassing is required. The `CropImageFilter` class constructor takes the position, width, and height of the cropped region, so all that is required is to construct the filter:

```
cropFilter = new CropImageFilter(50, 20, 120, 140);
```

The other two filters require subclassing `RGBImageFilter` so that a new `filterRGB()` method can be provided. The constructors for these subclasses both set `canFilterIndexColorModel` to `true`, so images that use indexed color models may be filtered quickly. This setting can be modified via the checkbox labeled Fast Filter. Even with these fairly small images, a performance decrease should be visible on most platforms if both the white-to-green and the gray-scale filters are enabled.

The `FilterLab` applet uses a gif file for its original image. The gif image used by the applet is indexed, so there is a visible performance difference between using and not using the Fast Filter checkbox to control the value of `canFilterIndexColorModel`. The jpeg format is not indexed, so if FilterLab used a jpeg file for its original image, setting `canFilterIndexColorModel` would not improve performance. The white-to-green filter checks for pixel values whose red, green, and blue levels are all at least 75 percent (`0xC0`). Pixels that pass this test are converted to green (`0xff00ff00`: alpha and green full on, red and blue off). The algorithm is implemented in the `filterRGB()` method as shown below:

```
public int filterRGB(int x, int y, int rgb)
{
    int red   = (rgb & 0x00ff0000) >> 16;
    int green = (rgb & 0x0000ff00) >> 8;
    int blue  = (rgb & 0x000000ff);

    if (blue >= 0xc0  &&  green >= 0xc0  &&  red >= 0xc0)
    {
        return 0xff00ff00;
    }
    else
    {
        return rgb;
    }
}
```

The grayscale filter computes the average of the red, green, and blue intensities and returns a pixel value whose red, green, and blue levels are all set to this average. Its `filterRGB()` method is:

```
public int filterRGB(int x, int y, int rgb)
```

```
{
    int red   = (rgb & 0x00ff0000) >> 16;
    int green = (rgb & 0x0000ff00) >> 8;
    int blue  = (rgb & 0x000000ff);

    int mean = (red+green+blue) / 3;
    return 0xff000000 | mean<<16 | mean<<8 | mean;
}
```

The applet has a method called `filter()`, listed below, which applies filters to the original image's producer. The desired filters are requested via boolean inputs. Note how each producer in turn is used to create the next producer.

```
private void filter(boolean crop, boolean red, boolean gray)
{
    w2gFilter.setFast(fastCbox.getState());
    grayFilter.setFast(fastCbox.getState());

    ImageProducer producer = originalImage.getSource();

    if (crop)
        producer = new FilteredImageSource(producer, cropFilter);
    if (red)
        producer = new FilteredImageSource(producer, w2gFilter);
    if (gray)
        producer = new FilteredImageSource(producer, grayFilter);

    filteredImage = createImage(producer);
}
```

The complete listing for `FilterLab`, which can be found on the CD-ROM in `javadevhdbk\ch06\FilterLab.java` and `FilterLab.class`, follows:

FilterLab.java

```
import    java.awt.*;
import    java.awt.image.*;
```

```java
import      java.applet.Applet;


public class FilterLab extends Applet
{
    Image               originalImage, filteredImage;
    Button              btn;
    Checkbox            cropCbox, w2gCbox, grayCbox;
    Checkbox            fastCbox;
    CropImageFilter     cropFilter;
    WhiteToGreenFilter  w2gFilter;
    GrayFilter          grayFilter;


    public void init()
    {
        // Get original image.
        originalImage = getImage(getDocumentBase(), "emily.gif");
        filteredImage = originalImage;

        // Create filters.
        cropFilter = new CropImageFilter(50, 20, 120, 140);
        w2gFilter = new WhiteToGreenFilter();
        grayFilter = new GrayFilter();

        // Create GUI.
        fastCbox = new Checkbox("Fast Filters");
        fastCbox.setState(true);
        add(fastCbox);
        btn = new Button("FILTER");
        add(btn);
        cropCbox = new Checkbox("Crop");
        w2gCbox = new Checkbox("White to Green");
        grayCbox = new Checkbox("Grayscale");
        add(cropCbox);
        add(w2gCbox);
        add(grayCbox);
    }


    public boolean action(Event ev, Object ob)
    {
```

```
        // Ignore unless button was clicked.
        if (ev.target != btn)
            return true;

        // Create new filteredImage based on checkbox selections.
        filter(cropCbox.getState(),
               w2gCbox.getState(),
               grayCbox.getState());
        repaint();

        return true;
    }


    // Filters the original image using user-selected filters.
    private void filter(boolean crop, boolean red, boolean gray)
    {
        w2gFilter.setFast(fastCbox.getState());
        grayFilter.setFast(fastCbox.getState());

        ImageProducer producer = originalImage.getSource();

        if (crop)
            producer = new FilteredImageSource(producer, cropFilter);
        if (red)
            producer = new FilteredImageSource(producer, w2gFilter);
        if (gray)
            producer = new FilteredImageSource(producer, grayFilter);

        filteredImage = createImage(producer);
    }


    public void paint(Graphics g)
    {
        g.drawImage(originalImage, 10, 50, this);
        g.drawImage(filteredImage, 271, 50, this);

    }
}
```

```
/*
 *  A filter class that translates moderately white pixels to green.
 */

class WhiteToGreenFilter extends RGBImageFilter
{
    public WhiteToGreenFilter()
    {
        canFilterIndexColorModel = true;
    }


    public void setFast(boolean fast)
    {
        canFilterIndexColorModel = fast;
    }


    public int filterRGB(int x, int y, int rgb)
    {
        int red   = (rgb & 0x00ff0000) >> 16;
        int green = (rgb & 0x0000ff00) >> 8;
        int blue  = (rgb & 0x000000ff);

        if (blue >= 0xc0  &&  green >= 0xc0  &&  red >= 0xc0)
        {
            return 0xff00ff00;
        }
        else
        {
            return rgb;
        }
    }
}



/*
 *  A filter that translates to gray.  Each of the red, green, and
 *  blue levels becomes the mean intensity.
 */
```

```
class GrayFilter extends RGBImageFilter
{
    int     nCalls;


    public GrayFilter()
    {
        canFilterIndexColorModel = true;
    }


    public void setFast(boolean fast)
    {
        canFilterIndexColorModel = fast;
    }


    public int filterRGB(int x, int y, int rgb)
    {
        int red   = (rgb & 0x00ff0000) >> 16;
        int green = (rgb & 0x0000ff00) >> 8;
        int blue  = (rgb & 0x000000ff);

        int mean = (red+green+blue) / 3;
        return 0xff000000 | mean<<16 | mean<<8 | mean;
    }
}
```

Summary

Java goes to great lengths to ensure that image manipulation is efficient, platform independent, and well encapsulated. The casual programmer can generally write robust code without knowing anything about producers, consumers, color models, or behind-the-scenes threads.

Beginner image programmers only need to know two tricks: use this wherever an image observer is required, and use a media tracker to coordinate image loading. Eventually curiosity or need leads to further investigation, and the whole complicated infrastructure is revealed. Images are produced, filtered, consumed, and observed. Abstract classes abound, hiding the true type of platform-specific classes.

The image infrastructure is, for the most part, a model of good object-oriented design. The structure is complicated, but everything is there for a reason. The designers have made intelligent subclassing and partitioning decisions throughout.

Programmers who wish to work on the level of the image infrastructure are encouraged to make the most of existing functionality. This chapter has shown an example (the white and blue squares) where creating a custom `ImageProducer` has no advantage over the much simpler approach of using a `MemoryImageSource`. This case is by no means universal, but it is common. This chapter has also made a case for considering a `PixelGrabber` design as an alternative to developing a custom `ImageFilter`.

The image infrastructure is far more complicated than image support on other platform-specific systems, but the complication ensures platform independence and good performance. It is likely that this part of Java will scale easily to new platforms for a long time to come.

CHAPTER

SEVEN

7

Threads

- Creating threads

- Intro to thread scheduling

- More thread control

- Thread groups

- Interaction between threads

- Deadlock

- Threading in AWT

- Designing for multithreading

Traditional programming environments are generally single threaded. Java, however, is multithreaded. Although multithreading is a powerful and elegant programming tool, it is not easy to use correctly and has a number of traps that even experienced threads programmers can fall into. This chapter introduces the ideas of multithreading, describes the tools that Java provides that allow you to create and control threads, and discusses some of the essential programming models you will need to make effective use of threads in your programs.

To better understand threading, think of an office worker analogy. The office worker is likened to a CPU, performing a task according to instructions, which can be thought of as the program for one thread of execution.

In a single-threaded environment, each program is written and executed on the basis that at any one time that program is concerned with only one sequence of processing. In our analogy, this is like an office worker who has been allocated a single task to be performed from start to finish without interruption or distraction.

In a real office, of course, it is highly unusual for a worker to have only one task at a time. Much more commonly, a worker will be called on to work on several tasks at once. The boss gives the tasks to the worker and expects that that worker will do a bit of one task, then a bit of another, and so forth. If progress becomes impossible on one task, perhaps because the worker is waiting for information from another department, the worker will put the task aside and make progress on some other task in the meantime. Generally, the boss expects that the worker will make progress on each job at some point throughout the day.

Multithreaded programming environments are much like this typical office: the CPU is given several tasks, or *threads*, at the same time. Like the office worker, a computer CPU is not actually able to do more than one thing at a time. Instead, time is divided between the various threads so that each one is moved forward a bit at a time. If no progress can be made on one particular thread—for example, if the thread requires keyboard input that has not yet been typed—then work is done on some other thread instead. Typically the CPU switches between threads fast enough to give a human observer the appearance that all the threads are being performed simultaneously. This is not necessarily the case, however, as we will discuss later in this chapter.

There are three key aspects of any processing environment, whether single or multithreaded. The first is the CPU, which actually does the computational activities. The second is the program code that is being executed. The third is the data on which the program operates.

In a multithreaded programming environment, each thread has code to provide the behavior of the thread, and has data for that code to operate upon. It is possible to have more than one thread working on the same code and data. It is equally possible to have different threads each with unique code and data. In fact, the code and data parts are largely independent of each other and can be made available to a thread as needed. Hence it is quite common to have several threads all working with the same code but different data. These ideas can be considered in our office worker analogy. An accountant can be asked to do the books for a single department or for several departments. In any case, the task of *do the books* is the same essential program code, but for each department the data is different. The accountant could also be asked to do the books for the whole company. In this case, there would be several tasks, but some of the data is shared because the company books require figures from each department.

Multithreaded programming environments use a convenient model to hide the fact that the CPU has to switch between jobs. The model allows, in broad principle, the pretense that an unlimited number of CPUs are available. To set up another job, the programmer must ask for another "virtual CPU" and instruct it to start executing a particular piece of code, using a particular data set. Figure 7.1 compares a single CPU with a multiple virtual-CPU computer. Each virtual CPU has one piece of code and one set of associated data.

FIGURE 7.1

Comparing single and
multithreaded program-
ming environments

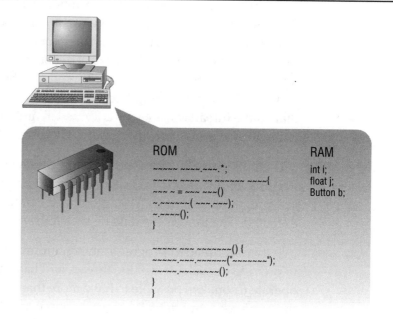

Single computer, single thread

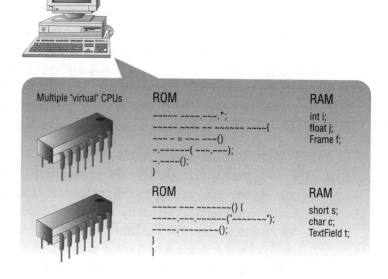

Single computer, multiple thread

In some systems there really are multiple physical CPUs, in much the same way that an office commonly has multiple workers. Using the model of virtual CPUs, multiple threads can be written so they are either executed a bit at a time by a single CPU or genuinely in parallel by multiple physical CPUs, depending on what is actually available at runtime.

Creating Threads

Creating threads in Java is not difficult. Again, the three things that are required are: the code to be executed, the data for that code to operate on, and the virtual CPU that is to execute the code. In Java the virtual CPU is encapsulated in an instance of the `Thread` class.

When a `Thread` object is created, it must be provided with code to execute and data for that code to work on. Java's object-oriented model requires that program code can only be written as member methods of classes. Data can only exist either as automatic (or local) variables inside methods or as class members. These rules require that the code and data we provide for a thread must be in the form of a class instance.

When a thread starts to execute, it does so in a specific method called `public void run()`. This method is the starting point for a thread execution by definition, in much the same way that applications start at `main()` and applets start at `init()`. The local data that the thread operates on are the members of the object that were passed to the thread.

Any class can be used to provide the starting point for the execution of a new thread, and the class can be a subclass of any other single class, if the programmer requires it. The particular requirement is that the class must be declared to implement the interface `Runnable`, and in consequence of this declaration, it must have a nonabstract method called `public void run()`. Because of this interface, a class that provides the code for a thread is often simply referred to as a Runnable.

The following example demonstrates these particular steps. You can find the code on the CD-ROM in the directory javadevhdbk\ch07\ SimpleRunnable.java and SimpleRunnable.class.

SimpleRunnable.java

```java
public class SimpleRunnable implements Runnable {
  private String message;

  public static void main(String args[]) {
    SimpleRunnable r1 = new SimpleRunnable("Hello");
    Thread t1 = new Thread(r1);
    t1.start();
  }

  public SimpleRunnable(String message) {
    this.message = message;
  }

  public void run() {
    for (;;) {
      System.out.println(message);
    }
  }
}
```

First, the main() method constructs an instance of the SimpleRunnable class. Notice that the instance has its own data— in this case a single String, which is initialized to "Hello." Because the instance, r1, is passed to the Thread class constructor, this is the data with which the thread will work when it runs. The code that will be executed will be the instance method run().

Creating a thread by creating an instance of the Thread class, and specifying the code and data using an instance of a Runnable class, allows the creation of multiple threads based on the same Runnable instance—in which case they will all work with the same code and the same data. This could be achieved by simply issuing more lines like this:

```
Thread t2 = new Thread(r1);
Thread t3 = new Thread(r1);
```

This type of behavior is both legitimate and, in some cases, valuable.

WARNING When more than one thread is operating on the same data, some potentially undesirable interactions can occur. *Interaction between Threads*, later in this chapter, expands on these important issues.

The start() method, which is invoked on the threads after they are created, causes them to become runnable. Before this point, the run() method will not be executed. This and other basic thread-control methods are discussed in *Essential Control of Threads*, later in this chapter.

Naming a Thread

Every thread in Java has a name. Java provides different Thread class constructors that allow a particular name to be specified, and if you use a constructor without one of these specific names, then Java automatically provides a unique, if unimaginative, name. Although it is possible, and sometimes useful, to determine the name of a thread in a running program, this facility is most useful in debugging.

To name the thread in the example, a different constructor can be invoked like this:

```
Thread t1 = new Thread(r1, "First Thread");
```

Given an instance of the Thread class, the name can be extracted as a string using the getName() method. For example, this line would print the name of the `Thread` object referred to by the variable `r1`:

```
System.out.println(r1.getName()); // outputs "First Thread".
```

Sharing Code and/or Data

In Java, it is possible to create threads that share program code but have different data to work on. Consider the code below to be a variation of the earlier example. You can find this code on the CD-ROM in the directory `javadevhdbk\ch07\SimpleRunnable2.java` and `SimpleRunnable2.class`.

SimpleRunnable2.java

```java
public class SimpleRunnable2 implements Runnable {
  private String message;

  public static void main(String args[]) {
    SimpleRunnable2 r1 = new SimpleRunnable2("Hello");
    SimpleRunnable2 r2 = new SimpleRunnable2("Goodbye");
    Thread t1 = new Thread(r1);
    Thread t2 = new Thread(r2);
    t1.start();
    t2.start();
  }

  public SimpleRunnable2(String message) {
    this.message = message;
  }

  public void run() {
    for (;;) {
      System.out.println(message);
    }
  }
}
```

In this case, two different instances of the `SimpleRunnable2` class—r1 and r2—are created having different, independent data.

The code that each thread executes is the same `run()` method as before.

To run different code, different `Runnable` classes are usually provided.

```
public class OtherRunnable implements Runnable {
  // constructor, methods, and data items
  public void run() {
    // code to do something useful
  }
}
```

Given this class, it is possible to construct a thread by the following calls:

```
OtherRunnable r3 = new OtherRunnable();
Thread t3 = new Thread(r3);
```

In this case, an entirely new thread is created that shares neither code nor data with the earlier threads created using `SimpleRunnable2` objects.

Sharing Data with Different Code

The local data that is used by a thread is the instance data of its `Runnable` object. These can be primitive types or references to other objects. Sharing data between threads can therefore be achieved simply by placing a reference to a shared object into each `Runnable` object. The following sample code demonstrates this idea:

```
public class TheData {
  int x;
  float f;
  // other member data and methods
}

public class FirstRunnable implements Runnable {
  TheData sharedData;

  public FirstRunnable(TheData toUse) {
```

```
      sharedData = toUse;
  }

  public void run() {
    // do things with 'sharedData'
  }
}

public class SecondRunnable implements Runnable {
  TheData sharedData;

  public SecondRunnable(TheData toUse) {
    sharedData = toUse;
  }

  public void run() {
    // do things with 'sharedData'
  }
}

  // launch from some other method,
  // perhaps main() in another class…
  TheData data = new TheData();
  // set up contents of 'data'
  FirstRunnable f = new FirstRunnable(data);
  SecondRunnable s = new SecondRunnable(data);
  Thread t1 = new Thread(f);
  Thread t2 = new Thread(s);
  // start the threads…
```

Notice that the instance data of the Thread t1 is provided by the instance f of the class FirstRunnable. The code for this Thread is the run() method of that class. The instance data for Thread t2 is provided by the SecondRunnable s. Similarly, the code to execute is the run() method of the class SecondRunnable. In both cases, the instance data has a reference to the single object of class TheData, which was created during the first stage of setting up these threads. In this way, the two threads share common data even though they are using different code from a different class.

The relationship between virtual CPU, code, and data is summarized as follows. A `Thread` encapsulates the virtual CPU. The virtual
CPU starts executing code in the `run()` method of the *class* of
`Runnable` provided to the `Thread` constructor, while the data used
are provided by the *instance* of that `Runnable`.

Different Code in the Same Runnable

It is also possible to share data between threads that are executing
different code by making the `run()` method of a single `Runnable`
class provide multiple different execution paths. Consider this sample:

```
public class TwoPath implements Runnable {
  static Thread t1;
  static Thread t2;
  int a, b;

  public static void main(String args[]) {
    TwoPath r = new TwoPath();
    t1 = new Thread(r);
    t2 = new Thread(r);
    t1.start();
    t2.start();
  }

  public void run() {
    if (Thread.currentThread() == t1) {
      // behavior one
    }
    else {
      // behavior two
    }
  }
}
```

Here the single `run()` method provides two different execution
paths. The selection is made on the basis of which of two threads is

executing it. References to each of the threads are made available to both instances of the Runnable TwoPath via the static variables. The current Thread is determined using the static method Thread.currentThread(), and this value is compared with the stored reference to t1 to determine the appropriate behavior. A similar approach can be worked if you use a string comparison on the name returned from the Thread object getName() method.

Because this approach embeds multiple behavior in a single class, we do not generally recommended it. In most circumstances, it is unlikely to represent a good object-oriented design.

Essential Control of Threads

The execution of a thread can be controlled in a variety of ways. So far, we have only discussed the start() method briefly. This section discusses this method in more detail as well as a few others that provide the fundamental techniques.

Starting a Thread

To start the thread, all you need to provide is an instruction of this form:

```
t1.start();
```

The start() method causes the virtual CPU represented by the Thread object to actually begin executing. Before calling this method, it is as if the program and data memory associated with the CPU have been loaded but the CPU itself has not been switched on. After the start() method is invoked on the Thread instance, the new thread is able to start executing the run() method of the runnable.

WARNING It is important to have a clear understanding of the distinction between `start()` and `run()`. The `start()` method is a member of the `Thread` class and controls the virtual CPU. The `run()` method is a member of the `Runnable` object and provides the code that the thread actually executes. Calling the `run()` method directly is entirely legal in Java, but does not result in a new thread executing the code; rather it constitutes a simple method call like any other. Also, be sure to differentiate between the `start()` method of a `Thread` object and the `start()` method of an applet.

Stopping a Thread

A thread stops executing permanently under some conditions. The first of these is if its `run()` method completes. A thread can also be stopped deliberately by calling its `stop()` method. To achieve this, the method must be invoked on the `Thread` object, not the `Runnable` object. In the earlier example, this code would be effective:

```
t1.stop();
```

However, the following would cause a compiler error because there is no `stop()` method in the class `TwoPath`:

```
r.stop();  // fails to compile
           // no method stop() in class TwoPath...
```

After a thread stops, it is considered to be *dead*. Once dead, the thread cannot execute any further code, even if the `start()` method is called again. The `Thread` object might be subject to garbage collection if no references to it remain.

WARNING The garbage collection of `Thread` objects is not as simple as for other classes. A running `Thread` object must never be garbage collected, but an unreferenced dead one should be. Unfortunately, some versions of Java do not reliably perform this collection.

Pausing Thread Execution

It is possible to temporarily pause a thread in a number of ways. There is a static method called `sleep()` that causes the currently executing thread to stop executing for *at least* a certain period. The time period is specified as the argument to the method. This method is available in two forms allowing specification of either a number of milliseconds or, using two arguments, a number of milliseconds and a number of nanoseconds. The second form allows a more precise specification of the duration of sleep requested.

> **TIP**
>
> The `sleep()` method can throw an `InterruptedException` under some conditions. Because of this, and the compiler's rigid insistence on proper handling of exceptions, `sleep()` is usually coded inside a `try {}` block. Alternatively, the enclosing method can be declared to throw the exception.

> **NOTE**
>
> The sleep time represents the *minimum* time for which the thread will be idle. Later in this chapter, *Introduction to Thread Scheduling* will explain why the thread might be idle for much longer than was requested, and how you can control this effect when the time is critical.

A pair of methods allow a thread to be suspended indefinitely and then awoken by deliberate intervention, rather than after a previously specified period of time. These methods are `suspend()` and `resume()`. Unlike the `sleep()` method, these are instance methods rather than static ones. Hence they can be used to stop the execution of a different thread from that which executes the method.

Like `stop()`, `suspend()` and `resume()` are instance methods that must be invoked on an instance of `Thread`, not of `Runnable`. However, because `sleep()` is a static method that operates on the current `Thread`, it is sufficient to issue the call `Thread.sleep()` without requiring a specific `Thread` reference. If a reference is not readily available, you can determine the current `Thread` using the static method in the `Thread` class called `currentThread()`.

A Real Example

Sufficient groundwork has been covered, and sufficient methods introduced, that a minimal example covering the new material can now be introduced. The source for the following example can be found on the CD-ROM in the directory `javadevhdbk\ch07\ThreadTest.java`. The corresponding bytecode files, `ThreadTest.class` and `FirstRunnable.class`, are in the same directory.

ThreadTest.java

```java
class FirstRunnable implements Runnable {
  public int value = 0;

  public void run() {
    for (;;) {
      try {
        Thread.sleep((int)(Math.random() * 2000));
      }
      catch (InterruptedException e) {
        // ignore and carry on
      }
      value ++;
      System.out.println("Thread " +
        Thread.currentThread().getName() +
          " value is now " + value);
    }
  }
}
```

```
class ThreadTest implements Runnable {
  public FirstRunnable otherData;

  public void run() {
    for (;;) {
      try {
        Thread.sleep((int)(Math.random() * 2000));
      }
      catch (InterruptedException e) {
        // ignore and carry on
      }
      System.out.println("Thread " +
          Thread.currentThread().getName() +
        " value in otherData is currently " +
          otherData.value);

    }
  }

  public ThreadTest(FirstRunnable other) {
    otherData = other;
  }

  public static void main(String args[]) {
    FirstRunnable r1 = new FirstRunnable();
    ThreadTest r2 = new ThreadTest(r1);
    Thread t1 = new Thread(r1, "FirstRunnable, first Thread");
    Thread t2 = new Thread(r1, "FirstRunnable, second Thread");
    Thread t3 = new Thread(r2, "ThreadTest, third Thread");
    t1.start();
    t2.start();
    t3.start();
  }
}
```

Running the Program

To run the program, select the directory listed above and issue the command:

```
java ThreadTest
```

The program will start and begin issuing messages at random intervals on the standard output. The program does not stop unless killed manually, so be ready to do this by typing Ctrl+C or the appropriate kill command for your platform.

What It Does

To ensure clarity of the salient points, `ThreadTest.java` does not do anything either startling or useful in its threads. Three separate threads are created; two of these share an instance of a `Runnable` and hence have the same code and data to work on. The third has an instance of a different `Runnable` and, in addition, has a reference to the `Runnable` used by the other two threads. Each thread executes independently although data is shared, and this fact is demonstrated by the output.

The Details

The startup of `ThreadTest.java`, handled by the `main()` method of the `ThreadTest` class, creates an instance of the class `FirstRunnable`. The single data item in this class, called `value`, is initialized to zero. Actually this explicit initialization is redundant, but it seems to be good style to explicitly perform any initialization on which a program depends. Next, an instance of the `ThreadTest` class is created. Although execution is currently in the `main()` method of this class, no instance of `ThreadTest` exists at this point because `main()` is static.

After `main()` method of the `ThreadTest` class creates the two `runnables`, the three threads are constructed. Each of these is given a separate name that allows the various lines of output to be attributed to its originating thread. Two threads are created from the single `Runnable r1`, and the third is created using `r2`.

When the threads have been started, each enters an infinite loop. The body of the loop pauses for a random period. This is achieved by using the `Math.random()` method to generate a random number in the range 0 to 2000 and using the `sleep()` method to cause the thread to remain idle for at least that many milliseconds. The net result is that the thread remains idle for a random time, somewhere between zero and two seconds. As noted earlier, the `sleep()` method can throw an `InterruptedException`, so this requires the `try {}` construction. In this program there is no possibility that this exception will arise, so it can be ignored.

Each time the threads `t1` and `t2`, executing the `run()` method in the `FirstRunnable` class, awaken from sleep, they increment the contents of `value` and issue a message announcing the name of the current thread and stating the new incremented contents of `value`. The output indicates that both threads are sharing the same data.

When `t3`, executing the `run()` method in the `ThreadTest` class, awakens from sleep, it prints its name and the contents of `value`. This thread does not change the variable `value`, however. This demonstrates that despite running different code, the thread `t3` is able to access the same data as the other runnables.

WARNING Sharing data in this way is generally very risky. This example, `ThreadTest.java`, should be considered as illustrating principles of threading, not as ways to share data. There is a small, but finite, chance you might notice occasional strange behavior, such as the output value failing to increment and then incrementing by two counts. The mechanisms of these problems are potentially platform dependent. Later in this chapter, the section *Interaction between Threads* discusses controlled ways to share data between threads.

Two Ways to Create a Class for Threading

Up to this point, we have only discussed one way to create a thread. That method requires a `Runnable` object to be created, and the `Thread` object is constructed to use that runnable. However, there is an alternative mechanism.

The `Thread` class implements the `Runnable` interface itself; that is, it actually defines a `public void run()` method. In the `Thread` class itself this method is empty, but if another class is a subclass of `Thread`, then it has the opportunity to override the empty definition with a new one. When this is done, creating an instance of the class inherently creates a new `Thread`. All that is needed to start that thread executing is to invoke the `start()` method.

If an object is an instance of some subclass of the `Thread` class, then in the methods of that object the `this` pointer is actually a reference to the currently executing `Thread` object. Because of this reference, `Thread` instance methods such as `suspend()` and `resume()` may be executed directly, without requiring an explicit `Thread` reference.

Despite the ability to execute `Thread` instance methods directly in the context of a `Runnable`, in general it is probably not a good idea to use this approach. Because Java permits only single inheritance, if a class extends `Thread`, it cannot be a subclass of anything else. Other facilities, such as those of the `Applet` class, are only available through subclassing. Therefore, it is unwise to waste this ability when it is not necessary.

There is another reason why extending `Thread` might be considered a poor approach, although the reasoning is rather academic and has no pressing practical significance. In the object-oriented paradigm, subclassing is the mechanism by which a modified version of a predefined "something" is produced. In this way, for example, the object-oriented approach allows modeling of staff in an organization so that an `Employee` class can be specialized, by subclassing, to produce a `Manager` class. Notice that a manager is an employee, but a particular type of employee.

Consider now the original description of the `Thread` class as encapsulating the virtual CPU. The CPU is a separate entity from the code and data on which it operates, hence the proper reason for subclassing a `Thread` is to produce a CPU with new behavior, not to modify the code that it executes. Of course, some designs might actually call for a modified version of the `Thread` class, one with special processing or scheduling characteristics. Under such conditions, it would be not only correct but also necessary to subclass `Thread`.

When Not to Create a Thread

Constructing threads is sufficiently simple that it is easy to get carried away and treat them as disposable items. Creating a new `Thread` object each time a job or service must be performed and letting the thread stop when that service is completed is wasteful. The better approach is to create a single `Thread` object to perform the particular job or service. If the service is needed multiple times, then the same thread should be reused.

In general, constructing instances of classes is a matter of allocating memory space and invoking a constructor to initialize the object. Although the same is broadly true of a `Thread` object, there is an additional aspect for you to consider. Most implementations of Java use the underlying operating system to provide threads. The operating system mechanisms used with threads can involve quite significant overhead. Therefore, setting up a single thread to do a job repeatedly saves CPU time and improves overall efficiency. Usually, it also results in a tidier and more elegant solution.

> **NOTE**
>
> To have a single thread operate in a loop, handling requests as they become available requires a communication mechanism. Somehow the thread must be told that there is work for it to do. See the *Communication between Threads* section later in this chapter.

> **WARNING**
>
> An earlier note pointed out that some versions of JDK have a bug that prevents dead threads from being garbage collected. Because the `Thread` object also keeps a reference to its `Runnable` instance, this `Runnable` instance cannot be garbage collected either. Clearly, under these conditions a potentially severe memory leak could arise if large numbers of threads are left dead.

Introduction to Thread Scheduling

The discussion at the beginning of this chapter suggested that the effect of virtual CPUs is achieved by doing a part of a job and then moving on to do part of another job. The scheme by which decisions are made about which thread is actually executing at any one instant on a physical CPU is called the *Thread Scheduling Model*. In Java, this model is platform dependent, but you will still need some understanding of the various possibilities if you are to program effectively with threads.

This section discusses the two main types of scheduling model: the preemptive scheduler and the time sharing (or time slicing) scheduler. Strictly time slicing is a superset of preemption, but from a programmer's viewpoint there are a number of significant differences that warrant separate description. The preemptive scheduler is described first.

Preemptive Scheduling

In a preemptive scheduling model, each thread is either runnable or not. Threads that are in the *ready to run* state, sometimes called *runnable*, are either running or waiting to run. A thread is not runnable if it needs some condition to be satisfied or some resource—such as input from the user—before it can proceed. The *not ready* state is usually referred to as *blocked*. The physical CPU will execute one of the runnable threads. The next paragraphs consider how a thread is chosen for execution.

Each thread has an associated priority that describes how important the thread is relative to the others. The approach of a preemptive scheduler is that whenever a CPU is available, runnable threads are checked according to priority, and the highest priority runnable thread is chosen for execution. If more than one thread of the same priority tie for this privilege, then usually the one that has been waiting longest is chosen.

The next question is, "When does a thread get taken off a CPU to allow others a chance to run?" The answer is, in a purely preemptive scheduling model the thread is descheduled only under two conditions, the first of which is if a higher priority thread becomes runnable. For example, suppose a thread was blocked and waiting for user input, and that input has now arrived. In such a case, we say that the higher priority thread *preempts* the lower priority one—hence the name of the scheduler. The second condition arises if the original thread is actually unable to continue. This condition might occur if the thread requires an I/O operation or executes the `sleep()` method. Threads in this model can be very selfish and this, at least at first sight, appears to make the pure preemption model a difficult one to program for.

Programming for a Preemptive Scheduler

When threads are working on a common task, the preemptive scheduling model is actually very elegant and easy to use. To illustrate our point, imagine a restaurant. One thread represents a customer, another represents a waiter, and a third represents a chef. Because of the nature of their respective tasks, the chef and waiter threads cannot do anything until the customer thread orders. When the customer thread begins, it prepares some data and then needs to communicate its request to the waiter. At that instant the waiter thread, which has been blocked, waiting for input from the customer, is ready to run. The customer thread then blocks, waiting for the waiter to bring food. Therefore, the waiter thread actually can start to run as the customer is no longer using the CPU. The same kind of interaction occurs between the waiter and the chef.

When this type of dependency exists between threads, the preemptive scheduler is highly efficient. Each thread typically gets the CPU quite soon after it is able to use it, but the overhead of switching between different threads is kept to an absolute minimum.

The following incomplete sample puts this idea into outline Java code for the customer/waiter part of the relationship. Observe how there are specific points at which the control is transferred between the threads, but do not concern yourself with how the communication occurs, as communication techniques have not been discussed, but are the subject of a later section, *Communication between Threads*.

```java
class Customer implements Runnable {
  public void run() {
    chooseFromMenu();      // Uses CPU to think
    waiter.orderMeal();    // Passes information to waiter,
                           // making waiter able to run
    waiter.waitForMeal();  // blocked until waiter returns,
                           // CPU not used here
    eatMeal();             // once food arrives, we can use
                           // the CPU to process chewing,
                           // swallowing, and enjoying food.
  }
}


class Waiter implements Runnable {
  public void run() {
    while (restaurantIsOpen()) {
      waitForCustomerToOrder(); // No CPU time used until
                                // an order is placed
      chef.takeOrder();         // pass the order to the chef
                                // Now the Chef needs the CPU
                                // to be able to do the cooking
      chef.waitForOrder();      // Blocks, releasing CPU (which
                                // the chef will use) until food
                                // is ready.
      takeOrderToCustomer();    // Now the customer can use CPU
                                // and will get it when we loop
                                // round to wait for next order.
    }
  }
}
```

> **NOTE** The programming task becomes harder, and the scheduler less efficient, when threads being coded do not exhibit this type of interdependence. Entirely independent tasks must be given otherwise arbitrary blocking calls, such as the `sleep()` or the `yield()` method discussed in the section *More Thread Control*, later in this chapter.

Time Sharing Scheduling

Although purely preemptive scheduling is elegant and expressive for controlling threads that are working on related aspects of some greater task, there are many situations where threads are working on entirely independent tasks. Therefore, many operating systems provide a means of sharing time between unrelated jobs without those jobs having to give up time voluntarily. This sharing is generally referred to as a *time sharing* or *time slicing scheduler*, and is strictly a superset of the preemptive system. In general, it is easy to construct a time sharing mechanism on the basis of a pure preemption model. All that is required is a high-priority task that deschedules running jobs at intervals.

The potential drawbacks with time sharing are that for interrelated threads, it is generally less efficient than pure preemption, and that the currently executing thread can change without warning or particular reason. Where threads share data, this can give rise to disastrous data corruption. These difficulties are discussed in detail later in this chapter.

Java's Platform Dependence

Our discussion so far has left one important question unaddressed. Just what is the thread-scheduling model used in Java—preeemptive or time sharing? Unfortunately, the specification does not require any particular model. Rather, it is expected that the underlying scheduling system of the host platform will be used. This is a concession to the difficulty of implementing a thread-control scheme outside of an operating system. In general, the degree of interaction between the operating system and the thread scheduler is too great to allow for an efficient implementation if the two aspects are separated.

So, just what is guaranteed by Java? Very little actually, but enough that platform-independent programs can be written, although the result might be rather inefficient. Note, however, that it is very easy to write programs that are platform *dependent* if you make incorrect assumptions about threading models, so a clear understanding of these aspects is important for you to be able to write successful, platform-independent, threaded programs. The following points can be made:

- All Java implementations provide threads.

- The scheduling mechanism is *not* specified.

- Synchronization and communication *are* possible in a platform-independent manner but require techniques that are discussed in the section *Communication between Threads*, later in this chapter.

- Java allows control of thread priorities, but the meaning of *priority* is not specified, is platform dependent, and might not have the effect you expect.

WARNING The usual implication of a priority is that if a task of a particular priority is ready to run, then it will definitely be given the CPU in preference to any task of lower priority. However, this is *not* required of Java implementations. Implementations are at liberty to use the priority value as an indication of the relative amount of time that each thread should receive (sometimes called a *nice* value), or even to ignore the priority specification altogether. For example, the "green threads" provided in JDK for Solaris implement priorities to give exclusive rights to higher priority threads. Windows 95 threads, however, allow lower priority threads to execute, but with a smaller share of CPU time.

The result of this lack of specification is that the programmer must work much harder to produce a reliable portable application. You must not depend on time sharing because this might not be provided. You must not rely on runnable high priority threads preventing lower priority ones from running; this also might not be the case. In consequence, the only definite way to control which of your threads executes at any given time is to use the advanced thread communication and synchronization facilities that are discussed later in this chapter in *Communication between Threads*.

More Thread Control

Java provides several mechanisms for controlling the execution of threads. It is necessary for you to have a proper understanding of all of these mechanisms if programs are to execute correctly under all the scheduling models that are permitted for a Java implementation. This section recaps those which have been introduced so far, fills in details about when these methods should be used, and introduces some additional methods.

The *sleep()* Method

The sleep() method can be used to make a thread cooperate with other threads and allow them a chance to execute. It is most appropriate, however, when a thread must perform an action at regular intervals. To achieve this kind of regular scheduling, a main loop in the thread's run() method should contain a fixed length sleep() call. This call will ensure that the remainder of the body of the loop is executed at regular intervals.

Strictly, this approach does not result in precise timing. There are two reasons for the inaccuracies. The most obvious failing is that the scheduler might well leave the thread in the runnable state for a significant period of time before actually running it again. If the underlying implementation provides meaningful priorities, this effect can be reduced by raising the priority of the thread using the setPriority() method. Of course there might be other considerations that prohibit this particular course of action, in which case you may have to make some compromises.

This approach also fails to take into account the time it takes for the body of the loop itself to execute. If this situation is not corrected, the timing of the thread will tend to *creep* because each time the main loop runs, the timing error will be added, compounding the previous errors. To address this, a high priority thread should be created that performs only a single action in the loop body. This action is to "trigger" the work required. The work must then be performed in another thread. In this way, the incremental error can be limited. Note, however, that this technique is only effective if priorities are meaningful on the host platform and it is not possible to eliminate these timing errors using software alone.

Further improvement can be made to the timing of this loop by marking the absolute start time of the loop and then calculating the target wakeup time each time around. This eliminates incremental creep errors leaving only variations in individual times for the loop. This incomplete sample code demonstrates the idea.

```
public static final int INCREMENT = 50;
public void run () {
  int timevalue = System.gettime();
  for (;;) {
    // loop body
    int targettime = timevalue + INCREMENT;
    int sleeptime = targettime - System.gettime();
    if (sleeptime >0) {
      try {
        Thread.sleep(sleeptime);
      }
      catch (InterruptedException e) {
        // Ignore
      }
    }
  }
}
```

The *yield()* Method

If you use the `sleep()` method to write multiple cooperating threads, then it is possible that CPU time might actually be wasted. This can occur if all the threads are sleeping for cooperation, despite some of them having useful work to perform. Under these conditions, no work gets done by the CPU, even though there is work to be done.

For this reason, cooperating processes should not *all* use the `sleep()` method. If you can choose one that is able to use all the CPU time made available when others are sleeping, but is itself not time critical, then it might be possible to run it without sleeping but at a lower priority. Unfortunately, because you cannot rely on priorities being effective on every platform, this approach is not reliably portable.

In many cases, it is more appropriate to use the `yield()` method to enforce cooperation between threads. This method will cause a thread to be descheduled in favor of some other runnable thread. If no other thread is currently runnable, then this thread continues immediately. Clearly this mechanism has the advantage over the use of `sleep()` because it ensures the CPU is never idle when work can be done.

The *suspend()* and *resume()* Methods

When a program uses a thread to provide a generally continuous service, such as the animation of an applet, it might be necessary to put the behavior on hold from time to time. In the case of an animated applet, this would occur if the applet goes out of context. The `suspend()` and `resume()` methods are appropriate for this type of control. In the case of the animation just described, the animating thread should be suspended when the `stop()` method of the applet is called by the browser. To restart the animating thread, the `resume()` method should be called in the `start()` method of the applet.

A useful feature of the `resume()` method is that it is not an error to resume a thread that has not been suspended. This means, for example, that the `start()` method of an applet can call `resume()` for an animating thread without having to worry if that thread was suspended in the first place.

The *join()* Method

This instance method causes the current thread to stop executing until the thread for which the method is invoked stops. This provides a useful way to wait for the completion of one thread before proceeding in the current one. The following incomplete sample shows how this is achieved.

```
Thread t1 = new Thread(someRunnable);
Thread t2 = new Thread(otherRunnable);
t1.start();
t2.start();
System.out.println("Threads now running");
t1.join();
t2.join();
System.out.println("Threads have now finished");
```

This is a rudimentary form of communication between threads; more control is available using other methods, which are described in *Interaction between Threads*, later in this chapter.

Daemon and User Threads

Threads in the Java system can be marked as either user or daemon threads. A newly created thread inherits this characteristic from the thread that invoked its constructor. The significance of the distinction between the two is that the Java Virtual Machine exits, stopping the entire program, when zero user threads are alive. Hence, creating a user thread prevents the program from exiting until that thread has completed. In contrast, marking the thread as a daemon thread allows the JVM to consider it as being a service provider, without value in the absence of user threads acting as clients of the service.

To create a daemon thread, the `setDaemon()` method should be invoked on the newly created `Thread` object, with the argument `true`, before the thread is started.

Daemon threads are commonly used for housekeeping tasks and services that support a program but are not themselves an active part of that program. In the Java system itself the garbage collector and finalizer are daemon threads. Similarly the threads that are used to load images for the `getImage()` method are daemon threads. Generally, any thread providing a service that is only useful if some other thread exists to use the service is a good contender to be a daemon thread.

> **WARNING** There was a bug in JDK 1.0.2 for 32-bit Windows platforms that prevented the proper exit of a program that has multiple threads. The workaround is to use the `join()` method in `main()` to wait for the completion of one of the threads, and you will often see such code in examples. The bug has been fixed in the 1.1 release.

Thread Groups

Every `Thread` object created in Java is a member of a `ThreadGroup` object. The relationship between a thread and a thread group is very similar to the relationship between a file and a directory. A thread group can contain many instances of both `Thread` and `ThreadGroup` objects in a hierarchical layout.

The thread group mechanism creates an association between related threads. By default a newly created Thread object belongs to the same group as the Thread object that constructs it. Several particular Thread class constructors allow the specification of an explicit ThreadGroup object, overriding this default. The following sections discuss the uses of the thread group mechanism.

Hierarchy—Group Control

Putting threads into thread groups allows the threads to be controlled together, via the ThreadGroup suspend(), resume(), and stop() methods. These methods invoke the corresponding Thread class methods for each Thread object in the group and recursively for all Thread objects in subgroups.

This approach is useful when a number of threads are operating on related work. An applet, for example, could create a new thread group for multiple threads working on a complex simulation. This allows the entire simulation to be suspended if the applet goes off page. All the threads in a group can be stopped in one operation by calling the stop() method of the group.

The following example demonstrates the use of thread groups to provided centralized control over multiple threads. It is located on the CD-ROM in the directory javadevhdbk\ch07\Grp.java and Grp.class.

Grp.java

```java
public class Grp implements Runnable {
  public void run() {
    for (;;) {
      System.out.println("Thread " +
        Thread.currentThread().getName());
      try { Thread.sleep(300); } catch (Exception e) {}
    }
  }
}
```

```
public static void main(String args[]) {
  ThreadGroup g = new ThreadGroup("My Group");
  Runnable r = new Grp();
  Thread t = new Thread(g, r);
  t.start();
  t = new Thread(g, r);
  t.start();
  for (;;) {
    try { Thread.sleep(5000); } catch (Exception e) {}
    g.suspend();
    try { Thread.sleep(5000); } catch (Exception e) {}
    g.resume();
  }
}
}
```

Running the Program

To run the example, simply select the directory containing the byte-code and issue the command

```
java Grp
```

What It Does

This example creates a thread group and two threads that are members of that group. The behavior of the threads is simply to print messages at 300-millisecond intervals, demonstrating that the thread is executing. The main() method, after creating and starting these threads, uses the suspend() and resume() methods at intervals of five seconds. When the threads are running, messages are issued regularly. After five seconds the group is suspended; this causes both threads to be suspended, and no output is seen for the five-second period until the resume() method is issued on the thread group.

Security

A further benefit is offered by the use of thread groups. The security system is able to use the mechanism to decide if one thread should be permitted to operate on another. For example, it would be undesirable for an applet to be able to `suspend()` or `stop()` any thread that controls the browser.

When you execute thread methods, any installed `SecurityManager` object is checked to see if the method is permitted. This mechanism is intended to check if the `Thread` object issuing the call is not a member of the same group or a parent group. If this is not the case, it would be appropriate to reject the attempt and throw a `SecurityException`.

WARNING Although restricting the ability of one thread to manipulate another thread based on the thread group mechanism appears to be a good way to protect browsers from malicious applets that try to deny browser service, the restriction is not implemented in current browsers.

Interaction between Threads

Earlier sections of this chapter have suggested that difficulties can arise when multiple threads share data. This section considers the nature of these difficulties, and following sections discuss solutions for these problems.

Consider the following example. The source code for this example is on the CD-ROM in the directory `javadevhdbk\ch07\Crunch .java`. The bytecode is in the corresponding `.class` file in the same directory.

Crunch.java

```
public class Crunch implements Runnable {
    public int x;
```

```
public static void main(String args[]) {
  Crunch r1 = new Crunch();
  Thread t1 = new Thread(r1);
  Thread t2 = new Thread(r1);
  t1.start();
  t2.start();
}

public void run() {
  int hold;
  for (;;) {
    hold = x + 1;
    try {
      Thread.sleep(1000);
    }
    catch (InterruptedException e) {
    }
    x = hold;
    System.out.println(Thread.currentThread().getName() +
      " value is now " + x);
  }
}
}
```

Running the Program

To run the example, select the directory and issue the command:

```
java Crunch
```

The example starts and begins issuing messages on the standard output. After half a dozen or so messages have been issued, kill the program.

When run, the output of the program looks like this:

```
Thread-1 value is now 1
Thread-2 value is now 1
Thread-1 value is now 2
Thread-2 value is now 2
Thread-1 value is now 3
Thread-2 value is now 3
Thread-1 value is now 4
Thread-2 value is now 4
```

What It Does

The program is intended to increment the value of x in two concurrent threads. However, it fails to achieve this.

The program creates two threads, and these share the data of the Crunch object. At first glance each thread should increment the value of x and output the thread's name and the result of incrementing x.

The Details

Each thread runs by picking up the value of x, adding one to it, and storing the result in a holding variable called hold. The thread then sleeps for one second. After this, the stored value is replaced in the variable x and written to the standard output.

It is clear in Crunch.java that the second thread will pick up the same value of x as the first, and hence the value in each of the two variables called hold will be the same. This happens because of the long delay between picking up the value of x and the moment at which the newly calculated value is written back into x.

Although this example is greatly exaggerated, it demonstrates the essential nature of the problem. Consider a modified run() method:

```
public void run() {
    int hold;
    for (;;) {
      x++;
      System.out.println(Thread.currentThread().getName() +
        "value is now " + x);
    }
  }
```

This time it might appear that the difficulty cannot arise. However, this is not the case. It is true that the problem arises much less often, because the time when the value of x is vulnerable is greatly reduced, but the statement x++ is actually a shorthand for several machine operations. These operations usually take the following general form:

- Load the value from the address of x into a register
- Increment the register
- Store the register value at the address of x

Because these three operations of this *read-modify-write* cycle are quite distinct, and take a finite time to complete, it is possible that the scheduler might change the current thread in the middle of the sequence. In such conditions, the error still arises.

Controlling Multiple Access

Clearly you must avoid the kind of failure that is described in the previous section if multiple threads are to be generally useful. A number of approaches exist, but this discussion will be restricted to the particular solution offered by Java.

The fundamental cause of the difficulty just described is that during manipulation, a data item or group of items might pass through a *delicate* state. This can be a state in which the value is temporarily duplicated in a working variable, a calculation is partially completed, or items in a related data set have been partially changed so the set as a whole is inconsistent. If the current thread happens to stop running while the data are in this delicate state, and some other thread begins instead and also tries to access the data in this delicate state, then a problem arises.

One common feature of all mechanisms that handle these difficulties is that they prevent any other thread from accessing data items while they are in the delicate state. The region of code that has data in a delicate condition like this is known as a *critical section*.

Another common feature of all such mechanisms is that the programmer is responsible for determining the existence of these critical sections and for specifying when the data must be protected.

The Object Lock

Java's protection mechanism hinges on a feature of the Object class called a *lock*. Perhaps somewhat perversely, the object lock may best be described if it is likened to a key. The key fits a particular door that is this grammatical construction:

```
synchronized(obj) {   // enter the door
                      // do delicate work
}                     // leave the door
```

For a thread's execution to proceed inside this block, it must hold the key belonging to obj. Normally the key is held by the obj itself and is available for the asking. However, when a thread holds the key, it is removed from obj. The key behaves like a physical key in that it is only in one place at a time—it is moved rather than copied.

Now suppose that while it is inside the synchronized block, the currently executing thread is descheduled and another thread starts to run. If the second thread tries to pass the door, the key will be missing and the thread cannot pass. At this point, this thread is descheduled and waits for the key to be returned to obj.

If one thread is holding the key inside the synchronized block in the context of one particular object, no other thread can enter that region in the context of the same object until the key is replaced. This happens when the thread that holds the key passes the closing curly brace at the end of the block. When the key is replaced, it is possible for the thread that tried to enter earlier to pick it up and proceed.

TIP

It is vital to realize that the lock is associated with an instance of a class, not with the code itself. It is entirely possible for two different threads to be executing the code of a single synchronized block, provided they are doing so in the context of different instances.

This protection has been coded in the example Crunch2.java. The source and bytecode files for this example are on the CD-ROM in javadevhdbk\ch07, and you can execute the program in the same way as for the earlier example by issuing the command:

```
java Crunch2
```

The only functional change that has been made is to the body of the run() method. Crunch2.java looks like this:

```
for (;;) {
    synchronized(this) {
      hold = x + 1;
      try {
        Thread.sleep(1000);
      }
      catch (InterruptedException e) {
      }
      x = hold;
      System.out.println(Thread.currentThread().getName() +
        "value is now " + x);
    }
  }
```

Given this modification, the output now looks like this:

```
Thread-1 value is now 1
Thread-2 value is now 2
Thread-2 value is now 3
Thread-1 value is now 4
Thread-1 value is now 5
Thread-2 value is now 6
```

Notice that this now increments x successfully each time that a thread executes the body of the main loop. However, the scheduling has changed unexpectedly, and as a result the execution order has changed. The scheduling issues will be addressed later in *Communication between Threads*.

The Object Lock in More Detail

It is worthwhile to consider the significance of the preceding description of the object lock in more detail. The behavior of the object lock and the `synchronized()` instruction can be summarized as follows:

- Every object has a lock. This lock is normally attached to the object itself.

- To execute a statement `synchronized(obj)`, a thread must be able to claim the lock belonging to the object `obj`. Claiming the lock effectively removes it from the object.

- If the lock is not attached to `obj` when a thread begins executing the `synchronized(obj)` instruction, the thread is made to stop running until the lock is returned to the object.

- A thread returns the lock to the object when it leaves the block that originally caused it to take the lock.

Notice that none of this performs any special magic to prevent data from being corrupted; it only provides a mechanism that allows you to protect critical sections against concurrent execution.

To fully protect a data item, additional considerations must be made. Consider the following partial example:

```
public class Crunch3 {
  public int x;
}

    // Threads A and B share an instance of Crunch3 called obj.
    // Thread A executes this:
    synchronized(obj) {
      int hold = x + 1;
      x = hold;
    }

    // Thread B executes this:
    int hold2 = x + 1;
    x = hold2;
```

Suppose that Thread A is executing and is just about to store hold into x. If Thread B is run, interrupting Thread A, then despite the fact that Thread A holds the lock for obj, the data is still corrupted because Thread B had not been programmed to require the lock for obj before starting the delicate operation.

Remember that the synchronized() instruction does not protect data, it only provides a mechanism that allows the programmer to limit to one the number of threads concurrently executing a critical section. To protect the data, you must treat all potentially delicate accesses as critical and guarded by using synchronized() calls.

To protect all accesses to a data item using the synchronized() mechanism, three conditions must be imposed.

1. The data items to be protected must be private members of an object.

2. The object that is used for synchronization is this.

3. You must ensure that any accesses made to these data items must be performed inside a synchronized(this) block.

The data must be private because if not, methods in other classes can be written to access the data directly. This could be done without the protection of synchronized(), breaking the data's protection.

Different objects can require their own critical sections. Just because a thread is doing something to data on one particular instance of a class does not mean that another thread should not operate on data in a different instance of the same class. This means that the lock that should be used is the one associated with the object that contains the data being manipulated.

Because the data must be private, they can only be accessed by methods inside their own class. Therefore, the lock that should be used is the one belonging to the object this.

Finally, having prevented any stray code in other classes from making indelicate access to the data, you must ensure that all accesses in this class are properly protected. You should examine every method in the class to determine whether it has any critical sections. All such sections must then be protected with a synchronized block.

> **TIP**
>
> A popular mechanism for handling critical sections is called a *monitor*. If you are familiar with this concept and its uses, it is important to appreciate that a Java class as a whole is not a monitor in the conventional sense unless *all* its nonprivate methods use `synchronized` to protect all data accesses and all its data items are marked as private.

Synchronized Methods

Because `synchronized` is used most commonly on the `this` object, a convenient shorthand is provided in the language. A method of this form:

```
void method() {
  synchronized(this) {
    // lots of work
  }
}
```

can be shortened, without changing the meaning, to this form:

```
synchronized void method() {
  // lots of work
}
```

> **NOTE**
>
> In the `synchronized` method, the entire method is treated as a critical section. This treatment might result in protecting a larger region of code than is strictly necessary. Although this is often not of consequence, it has the potential to reduce the efficiency of the scheduler.

Nested Synchronization

Sometimes the design of a piece of software might make it desirable to call a method that synchronizes on an object from a method that is already synchronized on that object. In some types of multithreading systems, this can cause a fatal condition called *deadlock*, in which the thread waits forever for itself to release the lock it already holds.

However, Java's synchronization mechanism does not have any difficulty with this scenario. The rules for the behavior of the `synchronized()` call specify that to proceed past the point of the call, the thread must hold the lock. If the thread already holds the lock, then it proceeds without any difficulty.

When a thread exits a `synchronized` block, it returns the lock to the object if, and only if, it first obtained the lock at the entry to this particular block.

NOTE The object-oriented nature of Java makes this feature very valuable. Consider a method in a derived class that is marked as `synchronized`. This method might need to call the method that it overrides, using the construction `super.method()`. If the superclass method is also `synchronized`, this would cause deadlock if the mechanism was not as just described.

Because of these rules, Java's synchronization elegantly avoids the self-deadlock problems that can be tricky to avoid in other systems.

NOTE The causes and avoidance of deadlock is an important topic in its own right and is discussed in *Deadlock*, later in this chapter.

Synchronizing on Other Objects

Java allows the use of object references other than `this` in the synchronized call, which might not be a sound way to create critical sections because it might be impossible to control the use of these other references. However, there are conditions where it is appropriate to synchronize on an object other than `this`.

The simplest way that it can be appropriate and safe to synchronize on an object other than `this` is with private member variables or method local variables that you know refer to objects that are *never* passed outside the `this` object. Under such conditions, you are effectively synchronizing on a subset of `this`. It must, however, be emphasized that it is absolutely crucial to be sure that there are no references to the same object that are accessible outside the `this` object.

There is one other situation where it might be appropriate to issue the `synchronized()` call on an object other than `this`. This situation is discussed in *Communication between Threads*, which describes the communication methods `wait()` and `notify()`.

Synchronization and Static Members

In addition to the ability to synchronize on an object other than `this`, Java allows synchronization on classes. To support this, in addition to the lock associated with every object, there is also a lock associated with each class. In a static method there is no `this` object, and consequently it would not be meaningful to say that the method obtains the lock of the object `this`. In fact, a static synchronized method obtains the lock associated with the class instead.

In a static method, the only data that can normally be accessed are the static members of the class. Provided these members are marked as private, static synchronized methods form critical sections and can provide some protection for those data items. There is a problem, however. Although a static method cannot access instance data items (unless an instance is passed to the method as an argument), the converse is not true. That is, an instance method is fully able to access static data. If an instance method is marked as synchronized, the lock that is obtained is the *instance* lock of the object `this`. This lock is not the same as the *class* lock, and hence concurrent access to the static data items remains possible. Because of this, if static data items require controlled access, instance methods must not access static data items directly; rather, they must do so by calling static synchronized methods to perform the access for them.

TIP

The data items in an object instance can be protected over part of a method using the construction `synchronized(this)`. However, Java does not allow the use of a class name in the `synchronized()` statement. Instead, inside an instance method it is possible to access the class lock by issuing the call: `synchronized(this .getClass())`. This call works because the class lock is actually the instance lock of the class' defining instance of `java.lang.Class`. Unfortunately, the `getClass()` call is an *instance* method of the `Object` class and therefore cannot be invoked inside a static method. Because of this limitation, static methods must be either entirely synchronized or not at all.

Deadlock

The term deadlock has already been introduced, but was not fully explained. This section discusses the nature of this problem and describes broad strategies for avoiding it.

To prevent concurrent access to data items, those data items must be marked private and accessed only via synchronized regions of instance methods in the class itself. To proceed into the critical section, a thread must obtain the lock associated with the object. Suppose a thread requires exclusive access to the data of not one, but two distinct objects. To do so it must obtain two distinct locks—one from each object. So far there are no difficulties with this description. Now suppose that another thread also requires exclusive access to the same two objects. It cannot proceed until it has both locks.

Because both locks are required, a fatal deadlock condition can occur if the programming is not done with care. Imagine that the first thread has obtained the lock for object A and is about to try to get the lock for object B. Meanwhile, the second thread has obtained the lock for object B and is now trying to obtain the lock for object A. Neither thread can proceed because the other holds the lock that it needs. Because neither can proceed, neither can leave the synchronized block that it has already entered. This means that neither can relinquish the lock it now holds.

This particular type of deadlock, where two threads have each grabbed something the other requires to proceed and cannot release it until able to proceed, is called *starvation* and is a classic textbook case of deadlock.

Other types of deadlock can occur, but all have one feature in common. They all reflect a design error that permits a thread to get into a situation in which it cannot proceed without some change in circumstances, and that change will never occur.

Avoiding Deadlock

You can avoid deadlock by careful design. Whenever a thread might block because of some prevailing condition, such as the need for a lock flag, there must be no possibility that the stagnation of the thread might itself prevent that condition from changing.

If multiple resources are to be obtained, such as the locks for two distinct objects, you must create a rule defining the order in which the resources will be obtained. If the locks for objects A and B are always obtained in alphabetical order, then there can be no possibility of the starvation condition just described.

WARNING Because of the nature of the synchronization mechanism and the danger of deadlock conditions, it is unwise to issue `synchronized()` calls on objects that might already be involved in synchronization in unknown ways. That is to say, if the source is not available for a class, its superclasses, and classes that use the same instance of it that you are using, do not synchronize on it. The reason is that if the object is already being used in synchronization, it is not possible to determine if the ordering rules have been adhered to. Additionally, if the class is being used for thread communication, it is possible to break its behavior. For example, it is unsafe to synchronize on an applet because the Abstract Windowing Toolkit (AWT) already does this as part of the painting mechanism.

Threading in AWT

Java makes use of threading to support several features of the runtime system. Garbage collection and object finalization are both performed by low-priority daemon threads that are created when the Virtual Machine starts up. An additional thread is used to handle features of the AWT. This section considers this AWT thread, the way it is controlled, and introduces some cautions relating to effective program design.

The AWT thread handles events and painting. It runs in a loop that waits until an event occurs in the underlying windowing system. Waiting for events blocks a thread, so it is convenient that this is not done in the primary thread of the program. The use of this secondary thread allows the main program design to ignore the problems of *polling* for input; instead of the program having to go looking for the input, the input comes to the program.

The AWT thread spends most of the time idle; blocked, waiting, until there is work for it to do. It wakes up when an event occurs. This event happens in response to user input, such as key presses or mouse movements. It also happens when an area of AWT display has been obscured by another window and is exposed.

When you want an AWT component redrawn, use the `repaint()` method. This method simulates the exposure of the entire region of the component to be redrawn. The simulated exposure causes the AWT thread to wake in the same way as a real exposure would, and hence the component's paint method is called.

To allow the AWT thread to be woken up by the main thread via `repaint()` requires a mechanism for the two threads to communicate. This communication is the subject of *Communication between Threads*, later in this chapter.

Maintaining Responsiveness

In an application there is only one thread handling the AWT behavior, even in a browser that might have many applets displayed simultaneously. There is an important consequence of this fact that is not immediately obvious. Because the AWT thread executes the event handling methods, such as `actionPerformed()`, and all subsidiary methods that might be called, it is important not to tie the AWT thread up with long processing. The same caveat applies inside the `update()` and `paint()` methods.

Suppose an application wishes to perform some processing that takes a significant duration, and this work is to be done in response to clicking the mouse. A good example might be a fractal generator program that allows the user to zoom in on a particular region by clicking the mouse. Consider the flow diagram shown in Figure 7.2.

Normally, the time taken for the AWT thread to service the event, via `actionPerformed()` or similar methods, would be very small in terms of human perception. This would mean that the AWT thread had returned to the block point and would be ready for the next event fast enough for human eyes to perceive the reaction to the next event as instantaneous.

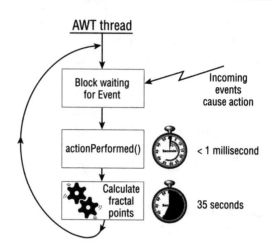

FIGURE 7.2

Flow of control handling
a calculation during
Event handling

Now suppose that the calculation of the fractal points takes 35 seconds, as shown in Figure 7.2. This means that the AWT thread is tied up doing this processing for this amount of time. Crucially, this means that any events that occur during this time will not be serviced until later. The events are not lost, but they cannot be handled until the earlier one completes. One particularly unfortunate consequence of this situation is that if a button is labeled Abort, it will not be possible for this command to take effect until after the earlier behavior completes anyway.

There is a demonstration of this problem on the CD-ROM. The file can be found in the directory `javadevhdbk\ch07\SlowService` `.java`. This code creates a deliberately time-consuming handler for the action of a button. While the `actionPerformed()` method is busy, the example is unable to react effectively to any other events. For example, resizing the frame of the application or attempting to close it down are not acted on until the button press has been serviced completely. Because the example is very simple, it is neither listed nor described in detail here. To run the program, select the ch07 directory and issue the command:

```
java SlowService
```

The program launches a frame containing a button and a label. Try resizing the frame first, and notice that the button and label are redrawn promptly. Next, press the button with the mouse. The program generates numbers on the standard output and takes a significant amount of time to complete the operation. The exact amount of time depends, of course, on the platform. While the output is still counting, try to resize the frame. Notice that the components are not redrawn until after the count is completed. You will notice the same delay if you try to close down the program from the Window Control menu while the count is in progress.

NOTE   An interesting observation can be made about the nature of AWT component peers from this example. Notice that although event handling in general is suspended during the protracted calculations, the button still appears to be reacting to mouse presses. Clicking the mouse over the button causes it to display in the down form and to click back up when the mouse button is released. This behavior is part of the underlying toolkit and is handled by the component peer rather than the AWT thread.

To avoid these difficulties, it is important to avoid using the AWT thread for performing protracted processing. Previous sections have described mechanisms that allow one thread to share information with another; for example, to pass the coordinates of a mouse-click to a thread that will calculate the zoomed image. What is needed to complete the picture is a mechanism that permits one thread to trigger another to start running so it performs the calculations when needed. Figure 7.3 shows, in principle, the flow that must be arranged to implement this design elegantly.

The AWT thread is used only to determine that the recalculation should be made and collect the parameters for that calculation. The work is then done by a separate thread that is dedicated to performing this calculation. In this way, all the remaining features of the user interface remain active, and it is possible to react to an Abort button, if necessary.

FIGURE 7.3

Using a separate thread to handle protracted calculation outside of `handleEvent()`

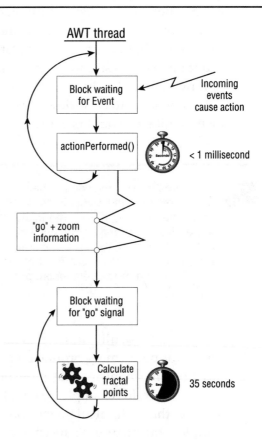

Although in this particular example it would be possible to use `suspend()` and `resume()`, Java provides more elegant techniques with more general application. In the next sections we will discuss and demonstrate these techniques.

Communication between Threads

The simplest way you can arrange communication between threads is using the classes `PipedInputStream` and `PipedOutputStream`. Consider the following example. The source code for this example is on the CD-ROM in the directory `javadevhdbk\ch07\Pipe.java`; the three corresponding bytecode files are in the same directory.

Pipe.java

```java
import java.io.*;

public class Pipe {
  public static void main(String args[]) throws Exception {
    PipedInputStream in = new PipedInputStream();
    PipedOutputStream out = new PipedOutputStream(in);

    Sender s = new Sender(out);
    Receiver r = new Receiver(in);
    Thread t1 = new Thread(s);
    Thread t2 = new Thread(r);
    t1.start();
    t2.start();
    t2.join(); // for Windows/JDK-1.0.2
  }
}

class Sender implements Runnable {
  OutputStream out;

  public Sender(OutputStream out) {
    this.out = out;
  }

  public void run() {
    byte value;

    try {
      for (int i = 0; i < 5; i++) {
```

```
          value = (byte)(Math.random() * 256);
          System.out.print("About to send " + value + ".. ");
          out.write(value);
          System.out.println("..sent..");
          Thread.sleep((long)(Math.random() * 1000));
        }
        out.close();
      }
      catch (Exception e) {
        e.printStackTrace();
      }
    }
  }

class Receiver implements Runnable {
  InputStream in;

  public Receiver(InputStream in) {
    this.in = in;
  }

  public void run() {
    int value;

    try {
      while ((value = in.read()) != -1) {
        System.out.println("received " + (byte)value);
      }
      System.out.println("Pipe closed");
    }
    catch (Exception e) {
      e.printStackTrace();
    }
  }
}
```

Running the Code

To run the example, select the ch07 directory and issue the command:

```
java Pipe
```

What It Does

Pipe.java creates two threads. These communicate over a PipedInputStream/PipedOutputStream pair. The sender thread issues five bytes, chosen at random, at random intervals of less than one second. The receiver thread collects these bytes and prints them out when they arrive.

The Details

The combination of PipedInputStream and PipedOutputStream acts as a conveyer belt for bytes between the two threads. Bytes written into the PipedOutputStream will arrive at the PipedInputStream in the same order they were sent, with none missing. The nature of these streams is that the receiver thread is made nonrunnable while it is waiting for characters and is made runnable again when characters are available.

A typical output from the program looks like this:

```
About to send -8.. ..sent..
received -8
About to send -87.. ..sent..
About to send 24.. ..sent..
received -87
received 24
About to send -52.. ..sent..
About to send 92.. ..sent..
received -52
received 92
Pipe closed
```

Notice that all the bytes that were sent were received in the correct order, and the receiver thread is able to correctly determine when the sender has closed the connection. However, the receiver does not wake up the instant the sender places the output byte into the stream. In some cases, several characters have been written before the receiver gets a chance to run.

> **TIP**
>
> The output shown above was obtained on a Windows 95 system, where priorities are not viewed strictly according to the preemption model, but rather are taken as indications of relative proportion of CPU time. On that platform, raising the priority of the receiver does not significantly change the output seen. By comparison, the Solaris platform does implement preemption style priorities and on that platform the receiver does indeed pick up the bytes immediately if its priority is raised. This example is typical of the type of scheduling differences that occur between different platforms and the kind of effects these differences can have on how a program runs.

Generalized Communication Techniques

Although the `PipedInputStream` and `PipedOuputStream` are easy and convenient to use, they do not suit all situations in which threads need to communicate. In fact, they are not the most fundamental form of thread communication in Java; they are constructed using another mechanism. The following sections discuss these mechanisms and their foundations.

The general approach for all communication between threads is that one thread prepares an item of data, another thread is informed, and then that other thread picks up and uses that item.

Suppose the data item is a simple integer. As a first suggestion, an `int` member variable could be defined in the `Runnable` class of the sender thread, and the `Runnable` class of the receiving thread could be written so it could read that value. Clearly this is not sufficient by itself, because the receiver cannot be informed when the variable contains a value that is valid; that is, some value is always present in the variable, hence the reader cannot distinguish between a proper value it should read and any other value that happens to be in the variable.

This problem can be overcome by the use of a flag variable of some sort. Typically, a `boolean` value could be used. The sender sets this to `true` just after it deposits a value in the variable. This solution has another improvement over the first suggestion, in that the receiver must set the flag back to `false` when it has read the value. This provides a means for the sender to know that the value has been read and hence to know that it is safe to write the next value into the variable.

Consider the following example, which implements this idea. The file can be found on the CD-ROM in the directory `javadevhdbk\ch07\FlagComm.java`. The three corresponding classfiles are located in the same directory.

FlagComm.java

```java
public class FlagComm {
  public static void main(String args[]) {
    FlagSend s = new FlagSend();
    FlagRec r = new FlagRec(s);
    Thread st = new Thread(s);
    Thread rt = new Thread(r);
    rt.setDaemon(true);            // the receiver doesn't die
    st.start();
    rt.start();
    try {
      st.join();                   // for Windows
      while (s.isValid) {          // give receiver a chance to
        Thread.sleep(100);         // read the final value
      }
    }
    catch (InterruptedException e) {
      e.printStackTrace();
    }
  }
}

class FlagSend implements Runnable {
  volatile int theValue;
  volatile boolean isValid;
```

```
    public void run() {
      for (int i = 0; i < 5; i++) {
        while (isValid) {
          Thread.yield();
        }
        theValue = (int)(Math.random() * 256);
        System.out.println("sending " + theValue);
        isValid = true;
      }
    }
}

class FlagRec implements Runnable {
  FlagSend theSender;

  public FlagRec(FlagSend sender) {
    theSender = sender;
  }

  public void run() {
    while (true) {
      while (!theSender.isValid) {
        Thread.yield();
      }
      System.out.println("received " + theSender.theValue);
      theSender.isValid = false;
    }
  }
}
```

Running the Program

To run FlagComm.java, select the ch07 directory and issue the command:

```
java FlagComm
```

The program will start and generate output similar to this:

```
sending 177
received 177
sending 236
```

```
received 236
sending 181
received 181
sending 53
received 53
sending 140
received 140
```

What It Does

The main() method in the FlagComm class creates an instance of each of the classes FlagRec and FlagSend. These instances are then used to create two threads that are run. The sender and receiver threads then communicate using the principles just outlined.

The Details

The two shared variables are theValue and isValid, both in the FlagSend class. When the instance of FlagSend is constructed, these are initialized to zero and false respectively. When the sender wishes to transmit a value, it loops waiting until the value of isValid is false. Because this is the starting condition, the value is written immediately. Once the value has been written, the flag isValid is set to true. The sender then loops round to send the next value. Because isValid is true, it will wait in the loop until this variable is changed by the receiving thread.

When the receiver thread starts, isValid is initially false. This causes it to loop until the sender thread changes this to true. As just described, this happens after the variable theValue has been set to a proper value. At this point, the loop test returns false, and the loop exits. Hence, the receiver thread reads theValue and writes it to the output. After reading this value, the receiver thread sets isValid back to false, which informs the sender thread that it is able to place the next value in theValue.

Notice how the value of isValid is crucial to the correct operation of this program design. It acts as a gate, allowing the sender to write a value without destroying a previous value that has not been used, and it ensures that the receiver is able to read a value without the risk of picking up an old value.

The drawback with this approach is that it is inefficient. Consider a situation in which these two threads communicate rarely, perhaps if the sender thread takes a significant time to prepare the data or the receiver takes time to handle the value sent. Under these conditions, one or the other thread would be looping round testing the value of isValid many times until it finally changed.

> **TIP**
>
> The declarations of theValue and isValid are marked with the modifier volatile. If this marking were not done, the Java compiler would be at liberty to consider the value of these variables as being under the sole control of this thread, hence the compiler could optimize the loop so it does not read the value each time round but remembers the value in a register. This would prevent it from noticing the change. The keyword volatile tells the compiler not to make such assumptions, informing it that the value might be affected unexpectedly from outside the scope of its execution flow analysis.

Communication with *wait()* and *notify()*

Java provides mechanisms that allow a thread, such as the sender and receivers in FlagComm.java, to be idle and wake up at the moment that conditions would allow them to usefully proceed. At first glance this end can be achieved using suspend() and resume(), but in practice this approach is rather cumbersome and presents some difficulties. To get around the problems, Java provides a mechanism specifically for this purpose. The mechanism is built around two methods of the Object class called wait() and notify().

Every object in Java has the ability to keep track of a pool of threads attached to it and in an idle state. A thread joins this pool by issuing the wait() call on the object whose pool it wishes to join. At some later time, another thread can issue the notify() call. If only the one thread was waiting in the pool, and the notify() method was invoked on the same object as the one on which wait() was called, then the first thread leaves the waiting pool.

For reasons that will be discussed later, wait() and notify() must only be issued inside a synchronized block. Making the changes to the earlier FlagComm.java example gives the following code. The source code for this example is located on the CD-ROM in the directory javadevhdbk\ch07\WaitComm.java. The corresponding bytecode files are in the same directory.

WaitComm.java

```java
public class WaitComm {
  public static void main(String args[]) {
    WFlagSend s = new WFlagSend();
    WFlagRec r = new WFlagRec(s);
    Thread st = new Thread(s);
    Thread rt = new Thread(r);
    rt.setDaemon(true);              // the receiver doesn't die
    st.start();
    rt.start();
    try {
      st.join();                     // for Windows
      while (s.isValid) {            // give receiver a chance to
        Thread.sleep(100);           // read the final value
      }
    }
    catch (InterruptedException e) {
      e.printStackTrace();
    }
  }
}

class WFlagSend implements Runnable {
  int theValue;
  boolean isValid;

  public void run() {
    for (int i = 0; i < 5; i++) {
```

```
      synchronized(this) {
        while (isValid) {
          try {
            this.wait();
          }
          catch (InterruptedException e) {
            e.printStackTrace();
          }
        }
      }
      theValue = (int)(Math.random() * 256);
      System.out.println("sending " + theValue);
      synchronized(this) {
        isValid = true;
        this.notify();
      }
    }
  }
}

class WFlagRec implements Runnable {
  WFlagSend theSender;

  public WFlagRec(WFlagSend sender) {
    theSender = sender;
  }

  public void run() {
    while (true) {
      synchronized(theSender) {
        while (!theSender.isValid) {
          try {
            theSender.wait();
          }
          catch (InterruptedException e) {
            e.printStackTrace();
          }
        }
      }
      System.out.println("received " + theSender.theValue);
      synchronized(theSender) {
```

```
        theSender.isValid = false;
        theSender.notify();
      }
    }
  }
}
```

Running the Program

To run `WaitComm.java`, select the `ch07` directory and issue the command:

```
java WaitComm
```

What It Does

The basic algorithm of this example is the same as that used in `FlagComm.java`. The differences are in the handling of the wait phase that each thread has when it is unable to proceed.

The Details

In the case of both the sender and receiver, the threads use the following approach to check the test condition before proceeding. One half of the approach is:

- Enter a synchronized block. This is synchronized on the object that supplies both the flag value and the wait pool.

- Test the flag value.

- If the flag value is such that the thread can properly continue immediately, then do so. Exit the synchronized block on the way out.

- If, on the other hand, the flag value says that the thread cannot proceed, then it calls the `wait()` method on the synchronized object. This causes it to become idle.

The other half of the approach, used by the other thread, is:

- Enter a synchronized block. This is also synchronized on the same object that was used by the other thread; that is, the object that provides the flag value.

- Set the flag to the value that allows the other thread to proceed.

- Call the `notify()` method on the synchronized object. If the other thread was idle in the `wait()` method, this call causes it to stop waiting, which is appropriate because the flag value now has the state required to allow it to proceed.

When either of the threads in `WaitComm.java` is woken up by a `notify()` call, it loops around to check if the state of the flag variable is set to the value required for it to proceed. This is not strictly necessary because, provided the program has been written correctly, the thread only leaves the `wait()` method when the variable has the correct value.

WARNING As the `try{}catch(){}` blocks that surround the `wait()` method call suggest, it is possible for `wait()` to exit under conditions other than receipt of a `notify()`. It is therefore common to see a loop of this form that tests the flag condition and calls the `wait()` method inside the loop. Although this is not necessary if the program is correctly written, the use of imported classes from unknown or untrusted sources, such as Internet servers, make this an unverifiable assumption. Hence, we recommend using a loop as a matter of general course.

TIP The variables `theValue` and `isValid` are not marked as `volatile` in `WaitComm.java`. This is because all accesses are protected by synchronized blocks. These blocks prevent the values of either variable from being accessed or modified by one thread when the other has access to it. Further, the specification of a synchronized block guarantees to write back into main memory any values that have been copied by the thread for optimization.

The Need for Synchronization of *wait()* and *notify()*

The Java language requires that the `wait()` and `notify()` methods must only be called by a thread that holds the lock for the object on which the methods are invoked. In other words, the thread must be synchronized on that object, because the data that control the coordination of the threads must usually be protected from the kind of problems that were described at the beginning of the section *Interaction between Threads*. As an example of the type of problem that can arise, consider the following scenario.

Multiple threads are operating independently but sharing a particular counter value that represents a number of items currently available for use. It does not matter what the items are. A thread that wishes to use one of these items must first check if one is available. If there is, then it must reduce the count and proceed to use that item. After it has finished with the item, it increases the count to reflect this. The `wait()` and `notify()` methods are used to allow a thread that releases one of the items to wake up another thread that might be currently waiting. Consider this nonworkable code fragment, which describes an attempt to address part of this design:

```
int countOfItems = 3;

void useItem() {
  while (countOfItems < 1)
    wait();
  countOfItems —;

  //do the work
  countOfItems++;
  notify();
}
```

The design intention is that a thread that requires to use an item enters this method and loops testing the value of `countOfItems`. If the value is found to be zero, the thread enters the `wait()` method.

When another thread relinquishes one of these items, it increases the count and issues the `notify()` method. At this point, the first thread retests the value of `countOfItems` and determines it is now greater than zero. So far, all is well, but consider what happens if another thread happens to start running and immediately performs the same test: It too will decide that at least one of the shared items is available and will proceed to the section that does the work. There- fore, clearly this implementation has not succeeded in coordinating the threads properly.

The cure for this problem, as described in the earlier discussion, is to place the entire read-modify-write cycle of the access inside a syn- chronized block.

Releasing the Lock in *wait()*

Closer consideration of the use of synchronized blocks around `wait()` and `notify()` calls raises an interesting problem. As we've discussed previously, to enter a synchronized block, a thread must be able to obtain the lock for the object in question. This appears to mean that when one thread blocks inside the `wait()` call, then no other thread can possibly enter the synchronized block to issue the `notify()` call. Clearly, because the example works, there must be some special exception being made here.

When a thread issues a `wait()` call, it actually releases the lock that it holds. This is done deliberately to avoid the kind of deadlock just described. Because the lock is released, the other thread is able to enter its synchronized block and issue the `notify()` call. At this point, it might be expected that the newly notified thread might become runnable, but this is *not* the case. To enforce the semantics of the synchronized block, the thread actually waits to reclaim the lock for the object. Only when the lock is reclaimed does the thread again become runnable.

This means that the significance of the synchronized block is slightly different from the earlier description. It is not actually true to say that the thread holds the lock flag for as long as it is inside the synchronized block, but more precisely it is guaranteed to perform no processing unless it has the lock. Hence, the synchronized block is still an effective way to protect data from multiple concurrent accesses.

WARNING With the sole exception of `wait()`, you should generally avoid using methods that might block a thread inside a synchronized block. If other methods, (such as `suspend()`) are used, the lock is retained during the blocked time, and other threads are locked out of any synchronized blocks. Sometimes this kind of lockout is precisely what you require, but be sure of this before you code such a construction. An example of just this type of behavior is shown in the last example of this chapter, `ReadWrite.java`.

Timing of *wait()* and *notify()*

There is a crucial feature of the `wait()` and `notify()` pair that we have not yet discussed. If no thread is waiting in an object's wait pool at the instant that a `notify()` is issued, then the `notify()` does nothing and is lost. In other words, the next thread to issue the `wait()` call does in fact wait until a further `notify()` is issued. It does not return from `wait()` immediately on the basis of the earlier `notify()`.

This is a further reason that `wait()` and `notify()` are not usually used in isolation, but normally in conjunction with a flag variable of some sort. To keep track of the number of `notify()` calls made, you could use an integer counter.

Handling Timeout Conditions

Sometimes it is necessary for a thread to wait for some condition that might not occur or might not occur soon enough. Under these conditions, it is desirable to be able to cause the wait to be abandoned after a certain period of time. This is generally called a *timeout period*.

Java provides two modified versions of the `wait()` method, which accept arguments indicating a maximum period to wait. After that period the wait is timed out and abandoned. One of these methods accepts a single `long` value that is taken to be a number of milliseconds. The other takes a `long`, indicating milliseconds, and an `int`, indicating additional nanoseconds.

WARNING In principle, the second version of the `wait()` method allows quite precise control over the maximum wait period. In practice, as was the case with the `sleep()` methods that have similar argument choices, the thread will not start running immediately when the `wait()` period expires, but some time later when the scheduler sees fit. Therefore, the higher resolution version is only really meaningful if the target platform and thread scheduling mechanism is known and care is taken, based on that platform knowledge, to ensure that the thread will start executing immediately if the `wait()` times out.

TIP If a `wait()` method times out, there is no indication in the calling thread that the `wait()` ended in a timeout rather than by receipt of a `notify()`. Use of a flag variable will allow this situation to be recognized.

Although Java provides the ability to limit the `wait()` method with a timeout, the same is not true of the `synchronized()` call. In general, the lock for any object should not be held for a protracted period of time. Instead, the `synchronized()` mechanism should be used only to protect data items against the damage caused by concurrent access. The actual communication should be done using variables that are protected in this way. Adopting this approach, combined with the use of `wait()` and `notify()`, to advise threads of when conditions have changed should mean that it is never necessary to hold the lock for long.

Ordering of Exit from *wait()*

As we stated earlier, a thread will awaken from the `wait()` method if it is the only thread waiting on the object notified. If more than one thread is waiting, and a single `notify()` is issued, then only one of the waiting threads will be removed from the wait pool and will start waiting to reclaim the object lock before becoming runnable. In many systems that implement a wait/notify mechanism, the thread that wakes up is the one that has been waiting longest. In other words, threads are placed in a *first in, first out*, or *FIFO*, queue. However, Java does not provide this guarantee. All that is required by the language specification is that when `notify()` is called on an object, if there are threads currently idle in the `wait()` method, one of them will be removed. Nothing is specified about which one. This lack of specification is deliberate to allow Java to be implemented reasonably efficiently on any underlying threading mechanism. Your programs must, therefore, ensure that if multiple threads are waiting on the same object, then they are all equally appropriate choices to be woken by a `notify()` call.

Waking Up Multiple Threads

In most cases, communication between threads is a point-to-point affair. One thread needs some kind of input from some other single thread. However, occasionally it might be that multiple threads are waiting for a condition and some other thread needs to restart them all. This is possible using the method `notifyAll()`.

As with the single `notify()` method, be aware that the threads that are released by `notifyAll()` do not become immediately runnable. Because `wait()` can only be issued in a synchronized block, none of the threads that leave the wait state can become runnable until it regains the object lock. This can happen to only one thread at a time.

Controlling Wake-Up Order

If a design calls for threads to be released in a particular order, then additional efforts must be made to ensure this. To control wake-up order, you must keep track of all the threads that are waiting and the order in which they should be woken. Typically, the desired wake-up order will be the same order in which the threads started to wait. When one is to be notified, that thread's identity is placed in another variable and the `notifyAll()` method is invoked. Each waiting thread is then able to continue execution, subject to reclaiming the lock. When each one does actually start, it checks its own identity against that noted in the variable. If the identities do not match, the thread reenters the `wait()` call.

This approach suffers from the drawback that all waiting threads have to restart and make their own decisions about which should continue. This is wasteful of both CPU and elapsed time. A better approach would be to direct the `notify()` call at the single thread that should be woken. This can be done if each thread issues its `wait()` call on a different object. You can put the objects on which the threads are waiting into a `Vector` object or other appropriate container that maintains the sequence order of the objects it contains.

The following example implements this idea to guarantee that threads are woken in the same order in which they waited. The source code is on the CD-ROM in the directory `javadevhdbk\ch07\Wake.java`. The corresponding classfiles are in the same directory.

Wake.java

```
import java.util.*;

public class Wake {
  private Vector stopped = new Vector();

  public void stopOne() {
    Object myLock = new Object();
    synchronized(myLock) {
      stopped.addElement(myLock);
      try {
        myLock.wait();
      }
      catch (InterruptedException e) {
      }
    }
  }
}
```

```
public void wakeOne() {
  Object theLock = null;
  synchronized(stopped) {
    if (stopped.size() != 0) {
      theLock = stopped.firstElement();
      stopped.removeElementAt(0);
    }
  }
  if (theLock != null) {
    synchronized(theLock) {
      theLock.notify();
    }
  }
}

public static void main(String args[]) {
  Wake queue = new Wake();
  Runnable r = new RunThis(queue);
  Thread t;
  for (int i = 0; i < 10; i++) {
    t = new Thread(r);
    t.start();
  }

  for (int i = 0; i < 11; i++) {
    try {
      Thread.sleep((long)(Math.random() * 1000));
    }
    catch (InterruptedException e) {
    }
    System.out.println("About to wake one thread");
    queue.wakeOne();
  }
}
}

class RunThis implements Runnable {
  Wake w;

  public RunThis(Wake w) {
    this.w = w;
  }
```

```
public void run() {
  System.out.println("Thread starting, name is " +
    Thread.currentThread().getName());
  w.stopOne();
  System.out.println("Thread woken up, name is " +
    Thread.currentThread().getName());
  }
}
```

Running the Program

To run the Wake.java example, select the ch07 directory and issue the command

```
java Wake
```

What It Does

The Wake.main() method creates an instance of the Wake class, which implements the queue mechanism for threads described above. The main() method then creates an instance of the RunThis class, which will be used to create 10 threads. The RunThis object is given a reference to the Wake object so each of the threads can attach to the queue that the Wake class implements.

When the threads are started, they issue a message, announcing their name, and then they attach themselves to the Wake object's queue using the stopOne() method. The main() method proceeds by issuing wakeOne() method calls at intervals. Each of these calls will restart one thread from the queue. When the threads restart, they issue another message announcing their name.

The Details

The important parts of the Wake.java example are the stopOne() and wakeOne() methods.

The stopOne() method starts by creating an Object instance that will be used for the wait() method call. The reference to this object is retained in the variable `myLock`. To thread must be `synchronized()` on `myLock` to allow it to call `myLock.wait()`.

To enforce the order of thread waking, the objects on which the threads wait are placed at the end of a vector. After the object has been appended to the queue, the thread issues the `wait()` method call. At this point the thread ceases executing until after a `notify()` method call has been invoked on the `myLock` object.

The `wakeOne()` method must first determine if there are any objects in the vector. If one is present, it removes the one from position zero, which constitutes the front of the queue. The three methods, `size()`, `firstElement()`, and `removeElementAt()` are invoked in a block that is synchronized on the `stopped` object, which forms the queue. This is done to prevent other threads from modifying the `stopped` vector contents in the middle of this block: The three operations form a critical section of code, operating on the vector.

TIP

Although Java class methods are thread-safe in themselves, the potential problems that can arise if the `size()`, `firstElement()`, and `removeElementAt()` methods are not used in a synchronized block demonstrates the importance of using classes correctly in a threaded program. In this particular case, it would be useful to have a single additional method in the `Vector` class that removes and returns the first element of the `Vector` instance and returns `null` if the vector is empty. A parallel method, called `pop()`, is actually provided in the `Stack` class.

Once an object has been removed from the front of the queue, the `wakeOne()` method synchronizes on that object and then issues the `notify()` method.

Reusing the Code

The `Wake` class can be used for circumstances that require threads to be woken in a strictly first in, first out fashion, and it serves as a style guide for other forms of control. If a particular program required it, you could add priority handling to allow some threads to jump part of the queue. To do this, you would need to create a specific class, rather than using the `Object` class, so the priority of each thread could be marked in the queue.

> **NOTE** Most versions of Java actually implement the wait pool as a FIFO queue, so it may be an acceptable pragmatic solution simply to assume that this behavior will prevail if you simply use `wait()` calls on a single object. However, this cannot be relied on, and bugs arising from this assumption proving false might be very difficult to track down.

Other Thread Communication Mechanisms

Academic textbooks that discuss multithreaded programming usually introduce a variety of communication and synchronization mechanisms. Although most of these mechanisms have some particular advantage, these advantages are generally related to the readability of the resulting solution in a particular circumstance. In general, the methods are interchangeable, and any one mechanism can be written in terms of any other.

One of the mechanisms that is commonly described, and therefore is likely to be familiar to many programmers, is the *semaphore*. A semaphore gets its name from the flag that was used on railroad tracks to ensure that trains did not collide on a section of track. Before the days of electronic communication, in places where a single track was used by trains in both directions, the signalman would have a flag, or semaphore. No train was allowed on the track unless the driver held that flag. When the train passed off the track, the driver returns the flag to the signalman, allowing other trains to use the track. Presumably the signalman had to walk the length of the track if two trains wanted to go in the same direction one after the other.

In computing, a semaphore is usually implemented as a numeric value. Before entering a critical section of code, the programmer issues a down () call. This effectively says: "If the value of the semaphore counter is greater than zero, decrement it and carry on." At the exit from the critical section, you issue an up () call. The up () call says: "Increment the value of the semaphore counter." If the value of the semaphore is already zero when a down () call is issued, the thread is blocked until an up () call is issued by some other thread. In this way, if the semaphore is initialized to a value of one and you are careful always to properly pair the calls to down () and up (), critical sections of code can be protected. The semaphore mechanism is often the main way to protect critical sections in many other programming languages and operating systems, in the same way as using the synchronized mechanism of Java.

Semaphores that change between the values one and zero are called *binary semaphores*, and these are typically used to guard critical sections of code. It is also quite common to work with semaphores that are not restricted to the values one and zero but count from zero up to arbitrarily high numbers. Such a nonbinary semaphore is usually written so the counter is kept non-negative. Operations are provided that can add an amount to the value and subtract an amount from the value. If an attempt to reduce the value of the counter would produce a negative result, then the counter is left unchanged and the thread waits. Whenever the counter value is increased, waiting threads might be restarted if the count increases to the amount required to permit the decrement operation to proceed.

NOTE   The partial example discussed earlier in this chapter, in the section *The Need For Synchronization of* wait () *and* notify (), represents a basic nonbinary semaphore.

The nonbinary semaphore is often used to allocate restricted resources. For example, if three tape devices are available on a computer system, a semaphore could be created and initialized to the value three. If a thread requires use of a tape drive, it must reduce the count in the semaphore by one. This action either "allocates" a tape drive for the exclusive use of that thread or blocks the thread until one can be allocated. After the thread has finished with the tape drive, it increases the semaphore value by one to indicate that another tape drive is now available. Notice that this scheme also works if one thread requires multiple tape drives. It can attempt to decrement the semaphore counter by, say, two. When the thread returns from the decrement call, it knows that two tapes are available. Of course, this example does not consider how the tape drives themselves are allocated, it only considers the availability of the devices.

NOTE
The increment and decrement operations are sometimes referred to in academic papers as "V" and "P." These names are derived from the initials of the Dutch words used for them by their inventor, and as such are not easy to remember. It is more mnemonic to call them *up* and *down*.

Semaphores can be implemented quite easily in Java. The following code does just that. The source code for this example is on the CD-ROM in the directory `javadevhdbk\ch07\Semaphore.java`. The two bytecode files, `Semaphore.class` and `SemTest.class`, are located in the same directory.

Semaphore.java

```
public class Semaphore {
  int value;

  public Semaphore() {
    this(1); // default value of 1
  }

  public Semaphore(int initial) {
    value = initial;
  }
```

```
public void down() {
  down(1);
}

public synchronized void down(int count) {
  while (value < count) {
    try {
      wait();
    }
    catch (InterruptedException e) {
      // ignore it, we test the condition again
    }
  }
  value -= count;
}

public void up() {
  up(1);
}

public synchronized void up(int count) {
  value += count;
  notify();
}
}

class SemTest implements Runnable {
  static Thread pThread;
  static Thread cThread;
  Semaphore theSemaphore;

  public static void main(String args[]) {
    Semaphore theSemaphore = new Semaphore();
    SemTest producer = new SemTest(theSemaphore);
    SemTest consumer = new SemTest(theSemaphore);

    pThread = new Thread(producer);
    cThread = new Thread(consumer);
    pThread.start();
    cThread.start();
  }
```

```java
public SemTest(Semaphore s) {
  theSemaphore = s;
}

public void run() {
  if (Thread.currentThread() == pThread) {
    produce();
  }
  else {
    consume();
  }
}

private void produce() {
  int count;

  while (true) {
    try {
      Thread.sleep((long)(Math.random() * 1000));
    }
    catch (InterruptedException e) {
      // ignore
    }
    count = (int)(Math.random() * 4) + 1;
    System.out.println(
      "producer increasing semaphore by " +
      count);
    theSemaphore.up(count);
  }
}

private void consume() {
  int count;

  while (true) {
    count = (int)(Math.random() * 4) + 1;
    theSemaphore.down(count);
    System.out.println(
      "consumer decremented semaphore by " +
      count);
  }
}
```

Running the Program

To run the example, select the `ch07` directory and issue the command:

```
java SemTest
```

`Semaphore.java` runs in an infinite loop, so after a dozen or so lines of output have been generated, kill the program with the appropriate key sequence for your platform.

What It Does

The `SemTest` class creates two threads; each generates a random number between one and five. One thread attempts to issue a `down()` operation on a semaphore by the amount of its random number. The other thread sleeps for a while and then increases the semaphore value by its random number using the `up()` method. Each thread runs in an infinite loop.

The Details

The keys to `Semaphore.java` are in the methods `down(int)` and `up(int)` in the `Semaphore` class. Both of these are synchronized methods for two reasons. First, these methods perform read-modify-write sequences on the count value. Because this value is shared between multiple threads, it is necessary to handle this modification as a critical section. Additionally, the communication methods `wait()` and `notify()` are issued in the `down()` and `up()` methods, and the `wait()` and `notify()` methods may only be invoked on an object when the thread holds the lock for that object.

The `down()` method starts with a loop. The loop body is executed until the count value is large enough to allow the decrement operation to proceed without resulting in a negative value. The body of the loop effectively contains only a `wait()` call.

The up() method, under the protection of a synchronized block, increases the value of the count and then issues a notify() call. This notify() will awaken at most one thread blocked in a wait() call. The affected thread, if any, will be blocked inside the down() method. Therefore, that thread loops around to test if the count value is now great enough to allow the decrement it wishes to perform. If this is now the case, then the decrement proceeds and the thread returns from the down() method. If the decrement cannot proceed, then the thread goes back into the wait() method where it remains until another notify() is issued, at which point the test is repeated.

Designing for Multithreading

This section describes the main considerations that must be given when producing library code that is required to be thread-safe. Remember that all the Java library code is thread-safe, and programmers are entitled to expect published Java packages to be thread-safe also.

The main issues relate to protecting data against the effects of uncontrolled changes. Several earlier examples, such as Wait.java, have demonstrated the nature of the divisible read-modify-write cycle and described the problems this can cause. Consideration of this concept forms the hub of thread-safe design.

Many data representations require more than one primitive variable. For example, consider the idea of a calendar date. To represent this, several forms are possible, but a likely possibility is to use three integer values, one for the day of month, one for month of year, and the third for the year itself. What happens when a date is incremented? First the day field is incremented. If this results in a value that is greater than the number of days in the indicated month, then the month is incremented and the day is reset to one. Similarly the month and year are modified if the month is increased beyond December.

If two threads simultaneously attempt to modify a date that is represented in this way, it is easy to see that severe difficulties could arise. The algorithm outlined above can be described like this:

```
day++
if (day > days_in_month(month, year)) {
   day = 1;
   month++;
   // handle end of year…
}
```

Now suppose that one thread has just incremented the day and is interrupted by another thread. That second thread enters this method and increments the day again. If this results in a day past the last day of the month, this thread will enter the body of the condition. Suppose the original thread now begins running again. It tests the value of day and finds it to be greater than the number of days in the month. It proceeds by entering the body of the conditional, too. After this scenario, the day will end up set to one, apparently having been incremented once instead of twice, but the month has been incremented twice instead of once. This example is demonstrated in Table 7.1.

TABLE 7.1   How Problems Can Arise When Two Threads Attempt to Increment a Date in the Absence of Proper Protection

Thread 1	Thread 2	Values
		day = 31, month = 1
day++		day = 32
	day++	day = 33
if (day > …) {		true, enter body
	if (day > …) {	true, enter body
day = 1;		day = 1
	day = 1;	day = 1
month++;		month = 2
	month++;	month = 3

Many kinds of data structure exhibit a self-consistency; that is, one part of the data might need to be changed if other parts are changed. Where such a situation exists, the data must be protected using critical sections to ensure that once a thread starts to change a value set, the change proceeds to completion without any other threads breaking in on the incomplete process.

Updating Long and Double Data Items

Most of the primitive data items in Java are *atomic*, that is they are effectively single indivisible items rather than aggregates of several parts, and it is not possible for such data items to be only partially updated when a thread is descheduled. An int, for example, is a single, indivisible value. It is read into the Virtual Machine from memory as a single instruction without any possibility of the thread that performs the read being preempted partway through the operation. The same is true for writing such a value from the Virtual Machine back into memory. However, this is not the case for items of long or double type. These values occupy 64 bits, and the Java specification allows the possibility that they could be read or written in two *separate* 32-bit operations. Further, the specification allows the possibility that the thread performing the operation could be preempted between the two operations. Hence, if a long or double value is to be used in a package, it must be treated the same as a compound data structure and be protected with synchronized blocks if it is to be properly and reliably thread-safe.

Advanced Thread Communication

All the essential details required for successful thread control and communication have now been introduced. All other thread control and communication methods can be constructed on the basis of the basic synchronized block and the wait()/notify() method pair provided by Java. This section will describe one final example of more complex thread interaction.

Multiple Reader, Single Writer Locks

A standard textbook example of more complex thread control is the problem of allowing multiple threads to have concurrent access to a database record for reading, but restricting threads wishing to write. It is generally safe for any number of threads to perform concurrent read operations on a single record, provided that no threads are writing to that record. In the absence of writers, because no data are changing, there is no possibility of reading anything in an inconsistent state.

For any thread to write to a record, that thread must be the only one accessing the record for either read or write. If any other thread attempts to read during the write operation, it might read some parts of the new record and some parts of the old record. If another thread attempts to write at the same time, the record might be committed to the disk with partial information from one thread and partial information from the other.

This problem has a number of standard solutions, and this section implements and describes one of the common solutions.

The source code for this example is on the CD-ROM in the directory `javadevhdbk\ch07\ReadWrite.java`. This file contains two class definitions; the second class is called `TestReadWrite` and is a basic test and demonstration harness for the `ReadWrite` class. The corresponding bytecode files, `ReadWrite.class` and `TestReadWrite.class`, are in the same directory.

ReadWrite.java

```
public class ReadWrite {
  Semaphore db = new Semaphore();
  int readers = 0;

  public synchronized void enterRead() {
```

```
      readers++;
      if (readers == 1) {
        db.down();
      }
    }

    public synchronized void leaveRead() {
      readers--;
      if (readers == 0) {
        db.up();
      }
    }

    public void enterWrite() {
      db.down();
    }

    public void leaveWrite() {
      db.up();
    }
  }

  class TestReadWrite implements Runnable {
    public static final int IDLE = 0;
    public static final int READING = 1;
    public static final int WRITING = 2;

    private static int nextIdx = 0;
    private int stateIdx;
    private static int [] states = {IDLE, IDLE, IDLE, IDLE,
        IDLE, IDLE};
    private ReadWrite controller;


    public static void main(String args[]) {
      ReadWrite that = new ReadWrite();

      Thread t1 = new Thread(new TestReadWrite(that));
      Thread t2 = new Thread(new TestReadWrite(that));
      Thread t3 = new Thread(new TestReadWrite(that));
      Thread t4 = new Thread(new TestReadWrite(that));
      Thread t5 = new Thread(new TestReadWrite(that));
      t1.start();
```

```
    t2.start();
    t3.start();
    t4.start();
    t5.start();
  }

  public TestReadWrite(ReadWrite c) {
    controller = c;
    stateIdx = nextIdx++;
  }

  public void run() {
    String name = Thread.currentThread().getName();
    while (true) {
      if (Math.random() > 0.1) {
        controller.enterRead();
        states[stateIdx] = READING;
        showStates();
        try {
          Thread.sleep(100);
        }
        catch (InterruptedException e) {
        }
        states[stateIdx] = IDLE;
        controller.leaveRead();
        showStates();
      }
      else {
        controller.enterWrite();
        states[stateIdx] = WRITING;
        showStates();
        try {
          Thread.sleep(100);
        }
        catch (InterruptedException e) {
        }
        states[stateIdx] = IDLE;
        controller.leaveWrite();
        showStates();
      }
    }
  }
```

```
private void showStates() {
  for (int i = 0; i < nextIdx; i++) {
    System.out.print(states[i] == IDLE ? " " :
                     (states[i] == READING ? "R" : "W"));
  }
  System.out.println();
}
}
```

Running the Program

To run `ReadWrite.java`, select the `ch07` directory and issue the command:

```
java TestReadWrite
```

What It Does

`ReadWrite.java` creates five threads that each loop continuously. The body of the loop chooses at random either to perform a read or a write operation. The probability of reading is greater than that of writing. To perform the read, the thread calls the `enterRead()` method of the `ReadWrite` object. When the `enterRead()` method returns, the thread sleeps for 100 milliseconds to simulate performing the read operation. After sleeping, the thread calls `leaveRead()`.

If the thread chooses to perform a write operation, a similar sequence is used, but the methods `enterWrite()` and `leaveWrite()` are called instead.

The Details

The main focus of this discussion is the behavior of the four methods in the `ReadWrite` class. An instance of the `Semaphore` class, developed earlier in this chapter, indicates if the database is in use. When the semaphore value is one, the database is idle. In this condition, an attempt to claim read or write access will immediately succeed, reducing the semaphore value to zero. After this has happened, further attempts to reduce the value of the semaphore block in a `wait()` method call until after the value has been restored.

The methods `enterRead()` and `leaveRead()` are both synchronized. This ensures that the value of the variable `readers` can be modified and tested in an atomic fashion. The `Semaphore` object operations that are triggered by the value of this variable are included in the synchronized region to ensure that the condition that caused the operations is not changed before the operation takes place.

When a thread executes the `enterRead()` method, it first increments the value of the counter variable `readers`. If the value becomes one, indicating that no other threads are currently reading, then it proceeds by executing the `down()` method on the database semaphore. If no other threads are currently writing, the `down()` method proceeds immediately; otherwise it blocks. If the thread does block in the `down()` method, then other threads executing the `enterRead()` method will block on entry because the method is synchronized and the other thread still holds the lock. On the other hand, if further threads execute the `enterRead()` method when the first did not block, they will not block, either. They do not block at the entry to the synchronized method because the first thread did not stay in this method; and because the value of `readers` is already nonzero, they do not execute the `down()` operation on the semaphore.

When a thread executes the `leaveRead()` method, provided it is calling it in the correct sequence, no thread can be blocked in the semaphore `down()` operation. Hence, this thread must be able to enter the synchronized region without significant delay. When it does so, it reduces the value of `readers`. If this value becomes zero, then the semaphore `up()` operation is issued, which will potentially unblock a thread currently waiting to write.

Threads entering the `enterWrite()` method simply perform a `down()` operation on the semaphore. If no threads are currently either reading or writing, then the `down()` operation will proceed immediately. If any other kind of access is in progress, then the semaphore value will already be zero and the down() operation will block.

Threads entering the leaveWrite() method simply perform an up() operation on the semaphore. If a thread is waiting either to read or to write, the up() operation will potentially unblock it.

Reusing the Code

The ReadWrite class can be used wherever a single read, multiple write lock is required. However, one crucial aspect of its design must be understood. As with the Semaphore class, it is imperative that the program that uses this class should be correctly designed to pair up calls to the enter and leave methods correctly. If a leave method is called by a thread that has not called the corresponding enter method, the lock will be broken and improper access might be granted to some other thread. Similarly, if a thread fails to call the corresponding leave method after calling an enter method, then the lock becomes sealed permanently against some types of access. Specifically, failing to call leaveRead() will prevent any further write operations, while failure to call leaveWrite() will lock out all access.

Wherever possible, these calls should be wrapped directly around the database-access methods themselves to produce a new compound method. In this way, the danger of incorrect coding can be reduced to a minimum.

Summary

This chapter has introduced the threads mechanism in Java. Some of the ideas are specific to the implementation of Java threads, while most of the ideas relate to threading in any language. Specific discussions have covered creation and control of Java threads and the significance of the AWT event handler thread. Ideas that relate to threading in any environment include the scheduling of threads on platforms that have fewer physical CPUs than threads and the problems of interaction between threads. A substantial discussion, with a number of examples, covered the control of this type of interaction as well as the communication between threads.

CHAPTER
EIGHT

Animation

- ■ In-place animation

- ■ Rubber band techniques

- ■ Ticker-tape animation

- ■ Sprite animation

8

Animation is the display of graphics that change over time. The Java Core API provides limited support for animation. There are no explicit animation classes. However, with a solid understanding of images (Chapter 6) and threads (Chapter 7), a number of animation techniques can be implemented. This chapter investigates some of these techniques; namely, in-place animation, rubber band animation, ticker-tape animation, and sprite animation.

The Core API is unlikely to add animation support in the foreseeable future. The Java Animation API will provide advanced animation support; this code is expected in the latter part of 1997. Macromedia is known to be working on a commercial implementation, as are Intel and SGI.

In-Place Animation

With in-place animation, changing visuals are displayed in a dedicated region of the screen. The individual frames of the animation are generally loaded from external files or generated by software before the animation begins. Either way, the frames are typically stored in an array of images. The job of the animation software is to draw the appropriate image onto the screen at the appropriate time.

In-place animation is, for the most part, straightforward. What requires care is ensuring that the GUI of an animating applet or application continues to be sensitive to user input while the animation is running. This is done with a thread.

In its most common form, in-place animation uses an array of images to store the frames of an animation and an int instance variable to indicate the index in the array of the next frame to be displayed. The animation thread executes an infinite loop in which it sleeps, bumps the index, and calls `repaint()`.

NOTE The example in the next section uses an array of images built from scratch in the `init()` method. Animations that load their images from files should use a media tracker to ensure that all images are fully loaded. See Chapter 6, *Images*, for a discussion of how and why a media tracker is used.

A simple applet that implements in-place animation is listed below. It is assumed that the `initImages()` method somehow initializes the `images[]` array. Code like this is a good first step, but a few important details are overlooked, and as it stands this code is not robust (and therefore does *not* appear on the CD-ROM).

Inadequate In-Place Animation

```
import      java.awt.*;
import      java.applet.Applet;


public class Bogus extends Applet implements Runnable
{
    Image       images[];
    int         index;
    Thread      animator;
```

```
public void init()
{
    images = initImages();
    index = 0;
    animator = new Thread(this);
    animator.start();
}


public void run()
{
    while (true)
    {
        try
        {
            Thread.sleep(100);
        }
        catch (InterruptedException ex) { }
        repaint();
        index = ++index % images.length;
    }
}


public void paint(Graphics g)
{
    g.drawImage(images[index], 0, 0, this);
}

//  . . .
}
```

This design is simple and probably familiar. The animation thread spends most of its time asleep. Every now and then it wakes up, calls repaint(), and bumps the image index. The call to repaint() schedules a call to update(), which calls paint(); all of this happens in a thread separate from the animator thread, which is asleep while the screen refresh is going on.

There are several problems with this code:

First, when the user steps away from the page containing the applet (either by surfing to a different page or by iconifying the browser), the animator thread continues to run, wasting CPU cycles in support of an animation that cannot be seen. There needs to be code to pause and resume the animation at the appropriate times.

Second, it is an oversimplification to assume that the animation really ought to run throughout the lifetime of the applet. The applet itself may want to pause and resume the animation.

Third, because `update()` clears the screen prior to calling `paint()`, there will be a noticeable flicker.

Fourth, and worst, there is a potential problem with the integrity of the `index` instance variable. This variable is written by the animator thread (in `run()`) and read by the update thread (in `paint()`). On a platform with preemptive thread scheduling, the `run()` method might be preempted at any moment, including the moment between incrementing `index` and computing the modulo.

In the next section, a robust example that deals with each of these issues will be developed.

In-Place Animation Example

Our example animation is called `AnimInPlace`, and its source is found on the CD-ROM in `c:\javadev\ch08\AnimInPlace` `.java`. The applet displays a multicolored series of concentric cycloids. The shapes will be familiar to anybody who has played with a Spirograph. The animation begins with just the outermost cycloid. The second frame adds a second cycloid, the third frame adds a third, and so on. Figure 8.1 shows the first frame; Figure 8.2 shows the fourth frame. The cycloid-generating algorithm is irrelevant to the topic at hand, so its code appears on the CD-ROM but is not listed here.

FIGURE 8.1:

First frame

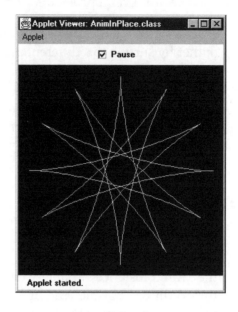

FIGURE 8.2:

Fourth frame

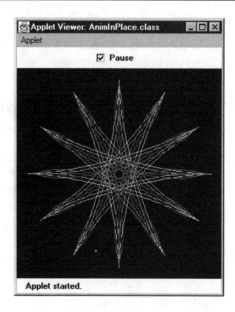

The Pause checkbox is initially not checked. The user may click here at any time to pause the animation; clicking again resumes the animation.

This applet was designed by addressing the four areas where the example of the previous section (*Inadequate In-Place Animation*) falls short.

First, the user will want to pause (and resume) the animation when browsing away from (and returning to) the page containing the applet. The `stop()` and `start()` methods of the `Applet` class are specifically designed to support this functionality. In theory, the intention of `stop()` is to provide hooks for suspending CPU activity that does not contribute to the currently visible page. In practice, `stop()` is most often used for suspending animations and sound clips. The browser should call `stop()` when the user iconifies or browses to a new page; Netscape Navigator products comply with this, but some versions of appletviewer do not. Similarly, the browser should call `start()` when it is de-iconified or when the user revisits an applet's page. Again, Netscape Navigator products comply, and some versions of appletviewer do not. The browser automatically makes one extra call to `start()` at the beginning of execution, shortly after `init()` terminates, which means that the `start()` code cannot assume that a corresponding `stop()` has previously been called.

In the example, `stop()` should simply suspend the animation thread and `start()` should resume it:

```
public void stop()
{
    animator.suspend();
}


public void start()
{
    animator.resume();
}
```

The animator thread will have been started in `init()`. The initial call to `start()` will result in resuming an unsuspended thread, which does no harm.

The applet should support pausing under user control. The Pause checkbox is called `pauseBox`, and it is the applet's only component. The `action()` method should suspend or resume the animator thread, depending on the state of the checkbox:

```
public boolean action(Event ev, Object ob)
{
    if (pauseBox.getState() == true)
        animator.suspend();
    else
        animator.resume();

    return true;
}
```

This causes a problem for the `start()` method. If the user pauses animation by clicking in the checkbox, browses to a different page, and then browses back again, `start()` will resume the animator thread even though the animation should still be paused. This means that `start()` must be refined:

```
public void start()
{
    if (pauseBox.getState() == false)     // if not paused

        animator.resume();
}
```

The next issue is screen flicker. When the animator thread decides that a new image should be shown, it calls `repaint()`, which schedules `update()`, which clears the applet to its background color and then calls `paint()`. For a brief time (after `update()` clears but before `paint()` draws the next animation frame), the applet just shows a solid rectangle. The user will perceive this as a sporadic flash of color, which is more readily noticeable the more the applet's background color differs from the predominant color of the animation frames.

The solution is to override `update()`. This method is inherited from the `Component` class and by default it does the following:

```
public void update(Graphics g)
{
    g.setColor(getBackground());
    g.fillRect(0, 0, width, height);
    g.setColor(getForeground());
    paint(g);
}
```

To eliminate the flash, `update()` needs to be rewritten so that it just calls `paint()`:

```
public void update(Graphics g)
{
    paint(g);
}
```

The last issue is data integrity. The images of the animation are stored in an array called `images[]`, which is indexed by `index`. This index is modified in the `run()` method's infinite loop. The inadequate implementation of `run()` looks like this:

```
public void run()
{
    while (true)
    {
        try
        {
            Thread.sleep(100);
        }
        catch (InterruptedException ex) { }
        repaint();
        index = ++index % images.length;
    }
}
```

The problem is the line `index = ++index % images.length;` this line could be interrupted by the update thread. Consider what happens if the interrupt occurs after `index` is incremented but before the modulo operation. There are 24 frames in the animation, so `index` might be anything from 0 through 23, inclusive. An interrupt when `index` is any value through 22 is no problem. The trouble occurs when `index` is 23. Its value is incremented to 24, and if the interrupt occurs before the modulo operation takes it back down to 0, then `paint()` will find itself accessing `images[24]`, which throws an array index exception.

It is instructive to use `javap`, the Java disassembler, to verify that the code that modifies `index` really is nonatomic. One nice feature of `javap` is that for simple examples it is possible to get valuable information from the disassembled code without actually knowing anything about the JVM's architecture. Begin by building a class that contains a single method that consists of just the line of code to be disassembled:

```
class Atomic
{
    int     index;

    void bump()
    {
        index = ++index % 24;
    }
}
```

Compiling this and then executing `javap -c Atomic` produces the following output (on the Solaris JDK; other compilers may produce different results):

```
Method void bump()
   0 aload_0
   1 aload_0
   2 dup
   3 getfield #3 <Field Atomic.index I>
```

```
 6 iconst_1
 7 iadd
 8 dup_x1
 9 putfield #3 <Field Atomic.index I>
12 bipush 24
14 irem
15 putfield #3 <Field Atomic.index I>
18 return
```

Line 3 loads the value of `index` into a virtual register in the JVM. Line 7 adds 1. Line 9 writes the incremented value from the register back into `index`. Line 14 does the modulo computation (*irem* stands for *integer remainder*), and line 15 stores the final result in `index`. Clearly, a problem interrupt could happen anywhere between lines 9 and 15.

NOTE In the vocabulary of assembly-language programming, an *atomic* operation is one that cannot be interrupted; interrupt requests are not serviced until the atomic operation has completed. In Java, one common interrupt source is thread preemption. Since bumping `index` is not atomic, there is the possibility of being preempted by the update thread in the middle of incrementing and modulo'ing `index`.

There are two ways to resolve this data integrity problem: by making sure that `index` is incremented in an atomic fashion or by synchronizing parts of the code to prevent critical interrupts.

It is not difficult to increment `index` atomically. The following code will work:

```
int temp = index;
temp = ++temp % images.length;
index = temp;
```

JVM specification states that 32-bit writes (such as `index=temp`) are atomic (64-bit writes are not, so it is fortunate that array indices are ints and not longs). This code certainly does the job, but it is a maintenance risk. If the bumping algorithm changes, the person who modifies the code has to know that the new code should be atomic and has to know enough about the JVM to make it so. In the long run it is much safer to synchronize the critical sections of the code.

The synchronization solution requires us to synchronize the code that accesses `index` (the `paint()` method) and the code that modifies `index` (the `run()` method).

The original version of `paint()` is:

```
public void paint(Graphics g)
{
    g.drawImage(images[index], 0, 0, this);
}
```

This version can be synchronized by simply adding the keyword `synchronized` to the method's declaration:

```
public synchronized void paint(Graphics g)
{
    g.drawImage(images[index], 0, 0, this);
}
```

When synchronizing a method, it is important to try to synchronize only the critical portions of the code. In this case the method is only one line long, so this is not an issue.

The original version of `run()` is:

```
public void run()
{
    while (true)
    {
        try
        {
            Thread.sleep(100);
        }
        catch (InterruptedException ex) { }
        repaint();
```

```
        index = ++index % images.length;
    }
}
```

Synchronizing this method would be a disaster: the update thread would never get a chance to run. From the standpoint of maintainability, the most robust solution is to create a new synchronized method just for incrementing `index`; this method can be called from `run()`. Anybody who has to modify the bumping algorithm knows exactly where to go, and no amount of modification of the new synchronized method can break the synchronization.

The new code is as follows:

```
public void run()
{
    while (true)
    {
        try
        {
            Thread.sleep(100);
        }
        catch (InterruptedException e) { }

        bumpIndex();
        repaint();
    }
}


private synchronized void bumpIndex()
{
    index = ++index % images.length;
}
```

The four issues of browser-initiated pausing, user-initiated pausing, screen flicker, and index data integrity have now been addressed. The nearly complete listing follows. The omitted method is `initImages()`, which is not relevant to the topic of animation; the method returns the array of images. The full code, including the class that renders

spirograph-style cycloids in an image, is on the CD-ROM in
`javadevhdbk\ch08`.

AnimInPlace.java

```
import       java.awt.*;
import       java.applet.Applet;



public class AnimInPlace extends Applet implements Runnable
{
    int               index;
    Image             images[];
    Thread            animator;
    Checkbox          pauseBox;
    static final int  IMAGE_SIZE = 300;


    public void init()
    {
        pauseBox = new Checkbox("Pause");
        add(pauseBox);

        index = 0;

        images = initImages(IMAGE_SIZE); //(This method not listed here.)

        animator = new Thread(this);
        animator.start();
    }


    public void stop()
    {
        animator.suspend();
    }


    public void start()
    {
```

```
        if (pauseBox.getState() == false)       // if not paused...
            animator.resume();
    }


    public boolean action(Event ev, Object ob)
    {
        if (pauseBox.getState() == true)
            animator.suspend();
        else
                animator.resume();

        return true;
    }


    public synchronized void paint(Graphics g)
    {
        g.drawImage(images[index], 0, 30, this);
    }


    public void update(Graphics g)
    {
        paint(g);
    }


public void run()
{
    while (true)
    {
        try
        {
            Thread.sleep(100);
        }
        catch (InterruptedException e) { }

        bumpIndex();
        repaint();
    }
}
```

```
private synchronized void bumpIndex()
{
        index = ++index % images.length;
}
}
```

Rubber Band Techniques

Rubber band lines are user-drawn outlines, typically rectangular, of regions of the screen. They are often seen in drawing programs to support user selection of a particular visible object.

Usually a rubber band operation begins when the user presses a mouse button and continues while the mouse is dragged (that is, while the mouse moves with the button still depressed). Through the duration of the operation, a rectangle appears on the screen, tracking the movement of the mouse. One corner of the rectangle is defined by the point where the mouse button went down. The opposite corner is defined by the position of the mouse pointer. Since this corner changes as the mouse moves, the user sees a rectangle that stretches and retracts in response to mouse movement, as if it were made of rubber.

Drawing the rectangle presents no difficulty; drawing rectangles is easy in Java. The trick is to undraw the rectangle when it is time to draw a new one. The pixels that the old rectangle overwrote must be restored. In Java there are two alternative techniques, which will be presented in the next two sections.

Rubber Band with Repainting

This section presents the simplest strategy for implementing rubber banding. The essential points of this strategy are the following:

- When the mouse button goes down, record x and y coordinates in instance variables. This is the "anchor" corner of the rubber band box.

- When the mouse is dragged or its button goes up, record the new x and y coordinates in instance variables. This is the "tracking" corner of the rubber band box. Call `repaint()` so that the screen reflects the proper position of the box.

- In `paint()`, first redraw the entire background; this erases the previous rubber band box no matter where it might have been. Draw the new box as indicated by the instance variables for the anchor and tracking corners.

The major benefit of this approach is its simplicity. Implementation is straightforward and easy to refine. The only drawback is a certain lack of efficiency. In order to erase the previous box, the entire screen (applet, frame, canvas, or panel) is redrawn. Typically this involves rendering tens or hundreds of thousands of pixels, all for the sake of erasing a few hundred. Generally this is not a significant problem; the user is rubber banding in order to tell the program what to do next, and since the program does not yet know what to do next, this is not a time when cycles are precious.

The frequent calls to `repaint()` during mouse drags can result in flicker if the region being painted is of any appreciable size (larger than approximately 200 x 200 pixels on average systems that can run Java). It is advisable to eliminate the flicker by overriding `update()`, as was done in the previous example, so that it calls `paint()` without clearing.

The example below uses this technique to support drawing rubber band boxes on an image. The applet is called `RubberBandRepaint`, and the source is found on the CD-ROM in `c:\javadev\ch08\RubberBandRepaint.java`. The background is an image that is loaded from an external file.

RubberBandRepaint.java

```
import      java.awt.*;
import      java.applet.Applet;
```

```
public class RubberBandRepaint extends Applet
{
    Image        image;
    int          xDown, yDown;
    int          xOpposite, yOpposite;


    public void init()
    {
        // Load the image.
        MediaTracker tracker = new MediaTracker(this);
        image = getImage(getDocumentBase(), "Emily.gif");
        tracker.addImage(image, 0);
        try
        {
            tracker.waitForAll();
        }
        catch (InterruptedException ex) { }
    }


    public void update(Graphics g)
    {
        paint(g);
    }


    public void paint(Graphics g)
    {
        g.drawImage(image, 0, 0, this);

        int x = Math.min(xDown, xOpposite);
        int y = Math.min(yDown, yOpposite);
        int w = Math.abs(xDown-xOpposite);
        int h = Math.abs(yDown-yOpposite);
        g.drawRect(x, y, w, h);
    }


    public boolean mouseDown(Event e, int x, int y)
    {
        xDown = x;
```

```
        yDown = y;
        return true;
    }


    public boolean mouseDrag(Event e, int x, int y)
    {
        xOpposite = x;
        yOpposite = y;
        repaint();
        return true;
    }


    public boolean mouseUp(Event e, int x, int y)
    {
        xOpposite = x;
        yOpposite = y;
        repaint();
        return true;
    }
}
```

One strength of this program is that it follows a very robust design pattern. The event handlers do not directly draw onto the screen. Instead, they record state information in instance variables and then call repaint().

The alternative to this design pattern is to have the event handlers draw directly to the screen. Instead of calling repaint(), a handler such as mouseDrag() would call getGraphics() to get a Graphics object and would use that Graphics object to undraw the old box and draw the new one. It is worthwhile to compare these two approaches.

Centralizing all screen-drawing operations, as is done in the code example above, results in code that is much more maintainable. Consider a program that is 100,000 lines long with a paint() method that is 1,000 lines long. If the screen could be drawn from anywhere in the program, then fixing a screen-related bug or adding a screen-related feature could entail consideration of all 100,000 lines. If, on the other hand, the program follows the guideline of only drawing in `paint()`, only 1,000 lines need to be considered.

The centralized painting approach has a second maintenance benefit. Since the screen's appearance is completely determined by state instance variables, the program has accurate knowledge of the screen's state at every moment. If event handlers modify the screen directly, without the intermediate step of recording all state changes, there is no software record of the screen's appearance. With centralized painting, there is no way to avoid the discipline of storing all screen state information in instance variables.

There is a third advantage to centralized painting. A frame in an application may receive a `paint()` call at any moment in order to repair damage caused by exposure. When an applet is damaged, some browsers repair via a backing store, but others (notably the appletviewer) do not. If a rubber band box is drawn directly in the `mouseDrag()` method and the frame or applet is subsequently hidden and exposed, then a call to `paint()` would not draw the rubber band box. It is uncommon for a frame or browser to get covered and exposed while the user is mouse dragging, but it is certainly possible. For example, many calendar managers spontaneously pop up a dialog box to remind the user of a coming appointment; later the program removes the dialog box. At the moment of removal, whatever was underneath the dialog is damaged.

NOTE   In the vocabulary of windows systems, when two windows overlap and the topmost window is moved to expose new portions of the lower window, the lower window is said to be *damaged*. The pixels that formerly belonged to the topmost window must be redrawn because they now belong to the lower window. This redrawing is known as *repairing*. Some programs (Netscape Navigator browsers, for example) maintain a copy in memory of their window's appearance; this copy is called a *backing store*. Such programs can repair damage very quickly simply by copying pixel values from the backing store. Programs that do not use a backing store must repeat the computations that generated the original pixels.

Rubber Band with XOR

XOR drawing is a technique for drawing graphics in such a way that they may be easily undrawn.

With ordinary drawing (Java calls it *paint mode drawing*), graphic shapes are rendered by setting pixel values without regard to the previous pixel colors. The new pixel value is simply the current color set in the instance of Graphics. With XOR drawing, the new pixel value is (mostly) computed by XORing the current color with the previous color.

To select XOR drawing, call the setXORMode() method of the current instance of Graphics. Subsequent drawing operations will happen in XOR mode until the graphics object executes the setPaintMode() method.

The setXORMode() method takes an instance of Color as an argument, which becomes the XOR color of the graphics object. At this point the result of calling a drawing method (such as draw-Line() or drawRect()) on the graphics object is a function of the current color, the XOR color, and the colors of the pixels being over-written. The formula for the new pixel value is:

new pixel = old pixel ^ current color ^ XOR color

This formula produces several surprising effects:

- Drawing twice in this mode returns any pixel to its original value.

- Drawing over a pixel that is the current color results in the XOR color.

- Drawing over a pixel that is the XOR color results in the current color.

- Drawing over a pixel that is any other color results in some other unpredictable color.

The important point is that drawing twice is the same as not drawing at all. Thus if graphics object gc is in XOR mode, a box can be drawn by calling gc.drawRect(x, y, w, h), and then undrawn with the very same call.

Since colors in XOR mode are determined in part by the color being overwritten, drawing a box over a digitized photograph or any other color-rich background results in a multicolored box, which can be distracting or difficult to see.

The unpredictability of the resulting color can be a problem. Colors cannot really be XORed, after all. The binary numbers that *represent* colors get XORed. These numbers could be true 24-bit red/green/blue values, or they could be indices into color tables. In the latter case, the resulting color is some new arbitrary color table index. There is no guarantee that the resulting color will even be distinct from the previous color.

The applet listed below, RubberBandXOR, illustrates drawing a rubber band box using XOR mode. The box is rendered in XOR mode while the mouse is being dragged and as a solid paint-mode rectangle after the mouse button goes up. The left-hand portion of the applet shows the same digitized image as was used in the previous example; concentric-colored squares appear on the right side of the applet. The applet shows that an XOR box drawn over a color-rich photo is much busier than one drawn over large solid regions.

The code also illustrates the programming overhead required to support this style of rubber band box. The paint() method must perform all drawing, so it needs to know what kind of box is currently displayed (none, plain, or XOR), and what kind of box to draw next. An XOR box can be erased cheaply by redrawing; a plain box must be erased by redrawing the background. The three constants BOX_NONE, BOX_PLAIN, and BOX_XOR are used to indicate box state. The box state variables are lastBoxState and nextBoxState. When a new box is painted, the value in nextBoxState is copied into lastBox-State, so that the next pass will know the prior state.

The applet source is on the CD-ROM in `c:\javadev\ch08\`
`RubberBandXOR.java`.

RubberBandXOR.java

```
import        java.awt.*;
import        java.applet.Applet;


public class RubberBandXOR extends Applet
{
    Image       backgroundImage;
    int         xDown, yDown, xOpposite, yOpposite;
    int         xBox, yBox, wBox, hBox;
    int         lastBoxState, nextBoxState;

    private final static int    BOX_NONE    = 0;
    private final static int    BOX_PLAIN   = 1;
    private final static int    BOX_XOR     = 2;


  public void init()
  {
      Color colors[] = {Color.red, Color.blue, Color.green,
                        Color.yellow, Color.magenta, Color.cyan};

      // Build the background image.
      MediaTracker tracker = new MediaTracker(this);
      Image emily = getImage(getDocumentBase(), "Emily.gif");
      tracker.addImage(emily, 0);
      try
      {
          tracker.waitForAll();
      }
      catch (InterruptedException ex) { }
      backgroundImage = createImage(500, 250);
      Graphics g = backgroundImage.getGraphics();
      g.drawImage(emily, 0, 0, this);
      int x = 270;
```

```
        int y = 0;
        int wh = 210;
        for (int i=0; i<colors.length; i++)
        {
            g.setColor(colors[i]);
            g.fillRect(x, y, wh, wh);
            x += 20;
            y += 20;
            wh -= 40;
        }

        lastBoxState = BOX_NONE;
        nextBoxState = BOX_NONE;
    }


    public void update(Graphics g)
    {
        paint(g);
    }


    public void paint(Graphics g)
    {
        g.drawImage(backgroundImage, 0, 0, this);
        g.setColor(Color.black);

        // Erase any previous xor box.
        if (lastBoxState == BOX_XOR)
        {
            g.setXORMode(Color.white);
            g.drawRect(xBox, yBox, wBox, hBox);
        }

        // No new box to draw.
        lastBoxState = nextBoxState;
        if (nextBoxState == BOX_NONE)
            return;

        // Draw new box if requested.
        xBox = Math.min(xDown, xOpposite);
        yBox = Math.min(yDown, yOpposite);
        wBox = Math.abs(xDown-xOpposite);
```

```
        hBox = Math.abs(yDown-yOpposite);
        if (nextBoxState == BOX_PLAIN)
        {
           g.setPaintMode();
           g.drawRect(xBox, yBox, wBox, hBox);
        }
        else
        {
            g.setXORMode(Color.yellow);
            g.drawRect(xBox, yBox, wBox, hBox);
        }
    }


    public boolean mouseDown(Event e, int x, int y)
    {
        xDown = x;
        yDown = y;
        nextBoxState = BOX_NONE;    // Clear previous box
        repaint();
        return true;
    }


    public boolean mouseDrag(Event e, int x, int y)
    {
        xOpposite = x;
        yOpposite = y;
        nextBoxState = BOX_XOR;     // Request an XOR box
        repaint();
        return true;
    }


    public boolean mouseUp(Event e, int x, int y)
    {
        xOpposite = x;
        yOpposite = y;
        nextBoxState = BOX_PLAIN;   // Request a plain box
        repaint();
        return true;
    }
}
```

Clearly, XOR mode is a trade-off. The benefit of fast erasure is paid for by the additional state variables and the extra logic required in `paint()`. Shapes erased in XOR mode must be erased precisely; any imprecision will show up on the screen.

Ticker-Tape Animation

Ticker-tape animation is a technique for scrolling text horizontally from right to left. The result is similar to the illuminated newsflash billboard in Times Square or the live stock-market displays found in certain trendy Silicon Valley eating establishments.

This kind of animation is useful in any program that has access to real-time textual information. Stock market transactions are a perfect example. This section will demonstrate how to implement ticker-tape animation in Java without considering the source of the information. The result will be a ticker-tape component class that can be told to display arbitrary strings.

Ticker-Tape Requirements and API

The new ticker-tape class will be called `Ticker`. It should have the following characteristics:

First, messages should scroll completely. At first, only the leftmost portion of a message's first character should appear. The message should scroll smoothly across the component and disappear off the left edge; the last part to be seen should be the rightmost portion of the last character.

Second, the component should queue up messages. There should be a reasonable minimum spacing between the end of one message and the beginning of the next.

Third, the component should be efficient. Clearly there will be a thread to manage scrolling as long as there are messages to display. When there are no messages, this thread should not consume any resources.

Fourth, client programs should be able to set the font.

Fifth, the component should compute its preferred height based on its font size. Tickers often appear in border layouts at North or South, where an accurate preferred height is essential.

With these requirements in mind, a simple API can be specified:

`public Ticker()` Constructs a ticker that uses the default font (28-point Times Roman plain).

`public Ticker(Font font)` Constructs a ticker that uses the specified font.

`public void addMessage(String message)` Tells the ticker to display the message.

Ticker-Tape Class Design

The first design consideration for the `Ticker` class is the handling of the animation thread. This thread's `run()` method should execute an infinite loop. The loop should first see if there are any messages to display; if there are not, the thread should be suspended. If there are messages to display, the thread should sleep for a while, then bump some counter that dictates the horizontal position of the message (called `messageInsetRight`), and lastly call `repaint()`.

The `addMessage()` method will need to resume the animation thread if it has been suspended due to lack of messages.

The next issue to consider is how to store the messages. At first glance it seems natural to store them in a vector using the `addElement()`

method. When a message scrolls off the display, it can be removed from the beginning of the vector with a call to removeElementAt(0). This is in fact what is done, but it will be necessary to maintain additional data, as explained below.

If addMessage() is called while the ticker component is idle, it is enough simply to begin displaying the new message. However, if the ticker is already displaying something, the code may need to wait for a while before displaying the new message. One of the requirements of the class is that there should be a minimum spacing between messages. There needs to be a way to determine if and how long a new message has to wait.

One solution to this problem would be to maintain a record of the position of every message on the screen. Given the position and the width of the message (width is determined by using the FontMetrics class), it is possible to find the right-hand edge. If this is too close to the right-hand edge of the component, the new message will have to be delayed.

This approach can be made to work, but it is cumbersome because the position of each message changes with each pass through the animator thread's loop.

Rather than keeping track of each message's position in space, this implementation records the time at which each message started (or will start) to scroll. (After all, Einstein assures us that space and time are equivalent.) The class has two vectors. One, called messages, contains strings. The other, called times, contains times. The unit of time is one iteration through the animation thread's infinite loop. The loop increments a variable of type long, called now; when a new message arrives, the addMessage() method constructs an instance of Long (the wrapper class, not the primitive) based on the current value of now, and adds it to the times vector.

This provides enough information to write the `run()` method used by the animator thread:

```
public void run()
{
    while (true)
    {
        while (messages.size() == 0)
            thread.suspend();    // addMessage() will call resume()
        try
        {
            Thread.sleep(TICK_PERIOD);
        }
        catch (InterruptedException ex) { }
        now++;                      // Bump clock time
        messageInsetRight++;        // Bump leftmost message position
        repaint();
    }
}
```

It is now possible to write the `addMessage()` method. The difficulty here is deciding what value to add to the `times` vector if there are other messages being displayed. Consider the last message in the `messages` vector. The time when it began scrolling is recorded in the last element in the `times` vector; ever since then it has been scrolling to the left at a rate of one pixel per clock tick. The soonest that displaying of the new message can begin is the last time recorded in the vector, plus the width in pixels of the last message, plus the minimum spacing between messages. This total is called `earliestLegal` in the code. If `earliestLegal` is more than the current time (called `now` in the code), then `earliestLegal` is stored in the `times` vector; the new message will be delayed. If `earliestLegal` is less than the current time, then the message may be displayed immediately, with `now` stored in the vector.

The `addMessage()` method looks like this:

```
public void addMessage(String msg)
{
    int size = messages.size();
    if (size == 0)
    {
        // No other messages, start display now.
        times.addElement(new Long(now));
    }
    else
    {
        // Other messages are displayed. May need to delay.
        long lastTime = getArrival(size-1);
        String lastMsg = (String)(messages.elementAt(size-1));
        int lastWidth = metrics.stringWidth(lastMsg);
        long earliestLegal = lastTime + (long)(lastWidth+SPACING);
        long scrollStartTime = Math.max(now, earliestLegal);
        times.addElement(new Long(scrollStartTime));
    }
    messages.addElement(msg);
    thread.resume();    // Could be redundant, does no harm
}
```

The last difficult piece of code is the `paint()` method. It has two jobs:

First, `paint()` has to check the messages at the beginning of the `messages` vector. If any of them have scrolled completely off the screen, they need to be removed from the vector, and their scroll-start times have to be removed from the `times` vector. The `paint()` method maintains an instance variable called `messageInsetRight`, which is the distance from the start of the first message to the component's right-hand edge. If any scrolled-off messages have been deleted, then `messageInsetRight` has to be decremented to reflect the position of the new leftmost message.

Next, of course, `paint()` has to render messages. The vertical position of every message is controlled by the instance variable `messageInsetY`, which is computed in the constructor based on the metrics of the font. The horizontal position of the first message is controlled by `messageInsetY`. The horizontal position of any subsequent messages is controlled by that message's entry in the `times` vector.

The `paint()` method uses a helper method called `getTime()` to retrieve a value from the `times` vector and return it as a long. The method looks like this:

```
public void paint(Graphics g)
{
    int             spacing;
    int             canvasWidth;
    int             msgWidth;
    long            lastTime;
    long            nextTime;
    int             deltaTime;

    // Bail if no messages to display.
    if (messages.size() == 0)
    {
        messageInsetRight = 0;
        return;
    }

    //
    //  Delete any messages that have scrolled off.
    //
    canvasWidth = size().width;
    while (messages.size() > 0)
    {
        String msg = (String)(messages.elementAt(0));
        msgWidth = metrics.stringWidth(msg);
        if (canvasWidth - messageInsetRight + msgWidth >= 0)
        {
            // 1st message in vector is still on screen.
            break;
        }
        // 1st message in vector has scrolled off.
        if (messages.size() >= 2)
        {
            // More messages => adjust messageInsetRight.
```

```
                lastTime = getTime(0);
                nextTime = getTime(1);
                deltaTime = (int)(nextTime - lastTime);
                if (msgWidth + SPACING > deltaTime)
                     messageInsetRight -= msgWidth + SPACING;
                 else
                     messageInsetRight -= deltaTime;
         }
         // Remove 1st message in vector.
         messages.removeElementAt(0);
         times.removeElementAt(0);
    }

    if (messages.size() == 0)
    {
        messageInsetRight = 0;
        return;
    }

    //
    //  Draw messages.
    //
    g.setFont(font);
    int x = canvasWidth - messageInsetRight;
    int y = size().height - messageInsetY;
    for (int i=0; i<messages.size(); i++)
    {
        String msg = (String)(messages.elementAt(i));
        msgWidth = metrics.stringWidth(msg);
        g.drawString(msg, x, y);          // Draw 1 message
        if (i < messages.size()-1)
        {
           // Determine x of next message
           lastTime = getTime(i);
           nextTime = getTime(i+1);
           deltaTime = (int)(nextTime - lastTime);
           if (msgWidth + SPACING > deltaTime)
               x += msgWidth + SPACING;
           else
               x += deltaTime;
        }
```

```
                  if (x > canvasWidth)   // Remaining messages are beyond
                      return;            // right edge
              }
          }
```

The complete listing for the `Ticker` class follows. The code can be found on the CD-ROM in `c:\javadev\ch08\Ticker.java`.

Ticker.java

```
import      java.awt.*;
import      java.util.Vector;



public class Ticker extends Canvas implements Runnable
{
      Font                  font;
      FontMetrics           metrics;
      Vector                messages, times;
      Thread                thread;
      int                   messageInsetRight, messageInsetY;
      long                  now;

      static final int      TICK_PERIOD = 50;     // msecs
      static final int      SPACING = 50;   // pixels


      public Ticker()
      {
          this(new Font("TimesRoman", Font.PLAIN, 28));
      }


      public Ticker(Font font)
      {
          messages = new Vector();
          times = new Vector();

          this.font = font;
          metrics = Toolkit.getDefaultToolkit().getFontMetrics(font);
```

```java
        messageInsetRight = 0;
        messageInsetY = metrics.getMaxDescent() + 2;

        thread = new Thread(this);
        thread.start();
}


public Dimension preferredSize()
{
    int h = metrics.getMaxAscent() + metrics.getMaxDescent() + 4;
    return new Dimension(100, h);
}


public void run()
{
    while (true)
    {
        while (messages.size() == 0)
            thread.suspend();  // addMessage() will call resume()
        try
        {
            Thread.sleep(TICK_PERIOD);
        }
        catch (InterruptedException ex) { }
        now++;                  // Bump clock time
        messageInsetRight++;    // Bump left message position
        repaint();
    }
}


public void addMessage(String msg)
{
    int size = messages.size();
    if (size == 0)
    {
        // No other messages, start display now.
        times.addElement(new Long(now));
    }
    else
```

```
        {
            // Other messages are displayed. May need to delay.
            long lastTime = getTime(size-1);
            String lastMsg = (String)(messages.elementAt(size-1));
            int lastWidth = metrics.stringWidth(lastMsg);
            long earliestLegal = lastTime + (long)(lastWidth+SPACING);
            long scrollStartTime = Math.max(now, earliestLegal);
            times.addElement(new Long(scrollStartTime));
        }
        messages.addElement(msg);
        thread.resume();    // Could be redundant, does no harm
    }


    private long getTime(int i)
    {
        return ((Long)(times.elementAt(i))).longValue();
    }


    public void paint(Graphics g)
    {
        int             spacing;
        int             canvasWidth;
        int             msgWidth;
        long            lastTime;
        long            nextTime;
        int             deltaTime;

        // Bail if no messages to display.
        if (messages.size() == 0)
        {
            messageInsetRight = 0;
            return;
        }

        //
        //  Delete any messages that have scrolled off.
        //
        canvasWidth = size().width;
        while (messages.size() > 0)
```

```
    {
        String msg = (String)(messages.elementAt(0));
        msgWidth = metrics.stringWidth(msg);
        if (canvasWidth - messageInsetRight + msgWidth >= 0)
        {
            // 1st message in vector is still on screen.
            break;
        }
        // 1st message in vector has scrolled off.
        if (messages.size() >= 2)
        {
            // More messages => adjust messageInsetRight.
            lastTime = getTime(0);
            nextTime = getTime(1);
            deltaTime = (int)(nextTime - lastTime);
            if (msgWidth + SPACING > deltaTime)
                messageInsetRight -= msgWidth + SPACING;
            else
                messageInsetRight -= deltaTime;
        }
        // Remove 1st message in vector.
        messages.removeElementAt(0);
        times.removeElementAt(0);
    }

    if (messages.size() == 0)
    {
        messageInsetRight = 0;
        return;
    }

    //
    // Draw messages.
    //
    g.setFont(font);
    int x = canvasWidth - messageInsetRight;
    int y = size().height - messageInsetY;
    for (int i=0; i<messages.size(); i++)
    {
        String msg = (String)(messages.elementAt(i));
        msgWidth = metrics.stringWidth(msg);
        g.drawString(msg, x, y);            // Draw 1 message
```

```
if (i < messages.size()-1)
{
    // Determine x of next message
    lastTime = getTime(i);
    nextTime = getTime(i+1);
    deltaTime = (int)(nextTime - lastTime);
    if (msgWidth + SPACING >  deltaTime)
        x += msgWidth + SPACING;
      else
        x += deltaTime;
}

if (x > canvasWidth)   // Remaining messages are beyond
    return;            // right edge
    }
  }
}
```

Ticker Usage Example

The applet called TickerDemo on the CD-ROM illustrates the use of the `Ticker` class. Users type messages into the textfield. Typing **Enter** in the textfield or clicking on the button causes the textfield's contents to be added to the ticker at the bottom of the applet.

Figure 8.3 shows the `TickerDemo` applet as it begins to show a message.

FIGURE 8.3

`TickerDemo` beginning a message

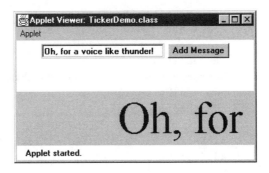

Figure 8.4 shows the `TickerDemo` applet as it finishes showing the same message.

FIGURE 8.4

TickerDemo finishing a message

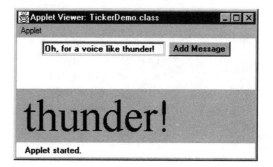

The code for TickerDemo is listed below. It is also on the CD-ROM in `c:\javadev\ch08\TickerDemo.java`.

```
import      java.awt.*;
import      java.applet.Applet;


public class TickerDemo extends Applet
{
    TextField     tf;
    Button        button;
    Ticker        ticker;

    public void init()
    {
        setLayout(new BorderLayout());
        Panel pan = new Panel();
        tf = new TextField(20);
        pan.add(tf);
        button = new Button("Add Message");
        pan.add(button);
        add("North", pan);
        ticker = new Ticker(new Font("TimesRoman", Font.PLAIN, 64));
        ticker.setBackground(Color.lightGray);
        add("South", ticker);
    }
```

```
public boolean action(Event ev, Object ob)
{
    ticker.addMessage(tf.getText());
    return true;
}
}
```

Sprite Animation

Sprites are shapes that move across the screen, often tracking the mouse. Rollover help flags are sprites. So are drag icons in drag-and-drop systems.

The general problem of sprite animation is how to repair a piece of the display after the sprite has moved past that piece. The example developed below demonstrates several techniques for doing this. In the section *Rubber Band with Repainting*, it was necessary to override the update() method in order to eliminate flashing. With sprite animation, elimination of flashing becomes a dominating concern.

The sprite example is a bar chart with rollover details. When the cursor "rolls over" one of the bars, a window pops up to give detailed information about the bar. This window appears at the mouse cursor position and tracks the cursor as it moves.

This example is implemented using two classes. The first, RolloverRegion, is a helper class that represents a single bar of the bar chart. The second class, called Rollover, is an applet that constructs a number of rollover regions and manages the sprite animation.

The *RolloverRegion* Class

The RolloverRegion class represents a single bar of a bar chart. It has a number of instance variables that must be set by the client applet; these include color and position information. There are also two string instance variables: shortLabel appears on the screen just above the bar, and both `shortLabel` and `longLabel` appear in the pop-up image.

The `RolloverRegion` class has two methods:

`public void buildPopupImage(Applet applet)` Builds the offscreen image that will be displayed when the bar is rolled over.

`public void paint(Graphics g)` Paints the bar on the screen using the specified graphics object.

The pop-up image displays the short label above the long label, as shown below in Figure 8.5. Most of the code of the `buildPopup-Image()` method is concerned with computing the size of the image and centering the text. A reference to the pop-up image is stored in the instance variable `popupImage` so that the client applet can access it.

FIGURE 8.5

A pop-up sprite

The `paint()` method is not concerned with the pop-up sprite; it simply paints the vertical bar with a centered label.

The code for the `RolloverRegion` class is listed below. It also appears on the CD-ROM in `c:\javadev\ch08\RolloverRegion.java`.

RolloverRegion.java

```
import      java.awt.*;
import      java.applet.Applet;


class RolloverRegion
{
```

```
Rectangle      bounds;
String         shortLabel;
String         longLabel;
Color          color;
Font           font;
Image          popupImage;
int            popupWidth;
int            popupHeight;


public void buildPopupImage(Applet applet)
{
    FontMetrics     fm;
    Graphics        g;
    int             fontHeight;

    // Create image. Size is a littler bigger than long label.
    fm = Toolkit.getDefaultToolkit().getFontMetrics(font);
    popupWidth = fm.stringWidth(longLabel) + 2*8;
    fontHeight = fm.getHeight();
    popupHeight = (fontHeight + 8) * 2;
    popupImage = applet.createImage(popupWidth, popupHeight);

    // Fill with solid color, bordered in black.
    g = popupImage.getGraphics();
    g.setColor(Color.black);
    g.fillRect(0, 0, popupWidth, popupHeight);
    g.setColor(color);
    g.fillRect(2, 2, popupWidth-4, popupHeight-4);

    // Draw short and long label, centered.
    g.setColor(Color.black);
    int x = (popupWidth - fm.stringWidth(shortLabel)) / 2;
    g.drawString(shortLabel, x, 4+fontHeight);
    g.drawString(longLabel, 8, 8+2*fontHeight);
}

public void paint(Graphics g)
{
    // Draw colored rectangle with a 2-pixel black border.
    g.fillRect(bounds.x, bounds.y, bounds.width, bounds.height);
    g.setColor(color);
```

```
g.fillRect(bounds.x + 2, bounds.y + 2,
         bounds.width - 4, bounds.height - 4);

// Draw short label above colored rectangle and centered.
FontMetrics fm = g.getFontMetrics();
int stringWidth = fm.stringWidth(shortLabel);
int x = bounds.x + (bounds.width-stringWidth)/2;
g.setColor(Color.black);
g.drawString(shortLabel, x, bounds.y-4);

    }
}
```

Sprite Implementation Issues

The top-level design of a rollover sprite program is easy. The mouse-Move() method should be overridden; the new version should determine which rollover region (if any) the mouse cursor is in. The old sprite should be erased, and the new one should then be displayed at the cursor position.

In practice, this approach is unsatisfactory. Appearance is fine when the mouse is stationary; but when it moves, the entire screen, including the sprite, flashes severely. There are three techniques for dealing with this problem:

- Override update().

- Adjust the clip region of the graphics object.

- Buffer the clip region off-screen.

These techniques may be used separately or in combination.

We have already seen how overriding update() eliminates flashing in a rubber-band animation. The technique is to modify update() so that it no longer clears before calling paint().

Adjusting the clip region involves calling the clipRect() method of the Graphics class. The four inputs to this method are the x, y, width, and height of the clipping region. Subsequent graphics operations will only take effect if they fall within the clipping region. As the sprite moves, the only portion of the screen that needs to be refreshed is the union of the old position and the new position. (Fortunately, Java's `Rectangle` class has a `union()` method.) The clip region can be adjusted so that it is the smallest rectangle that contains both the old and the new sprite positions, as illustrated in Figure 8.6.

FIGURE 8.6

Clip region

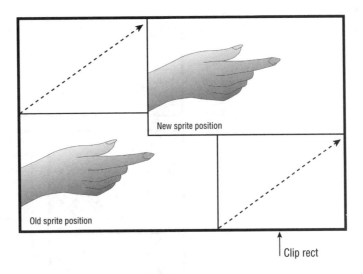

Old sprite position

New sprite position

Clip rect

Adjusting the clip region requires a simple three-step algorithm. First the clip region is set. Then the background image is drawn. Lastly the sprite is drawn at its new position. Clip regions are usually considerably smaller than the entire screen, so relatively very few pixels get modified when the sprite moves, which reduces flashing dramatically but not completely. Every time the sprite moves, the portion of the screen at the new sprite position is first set to the background (in the example, this will be the bar chart). Then the sprite is rendered over the background. The background may be momentarily visible, which causes a small flash that can be eliminated with the buffering technique.

The buffering technique is used in conjunction with clipping. An offscreen image is first cleared to the background; next, the sprite is drawn to the offscreen image. Then the offscreen image is drawn to the screen. Since the screen is only drawn once, there is no flash. Figure 8.7 illustrates the use of the offscreen buffer.

FIGURE 8.7

Offscreen buffer

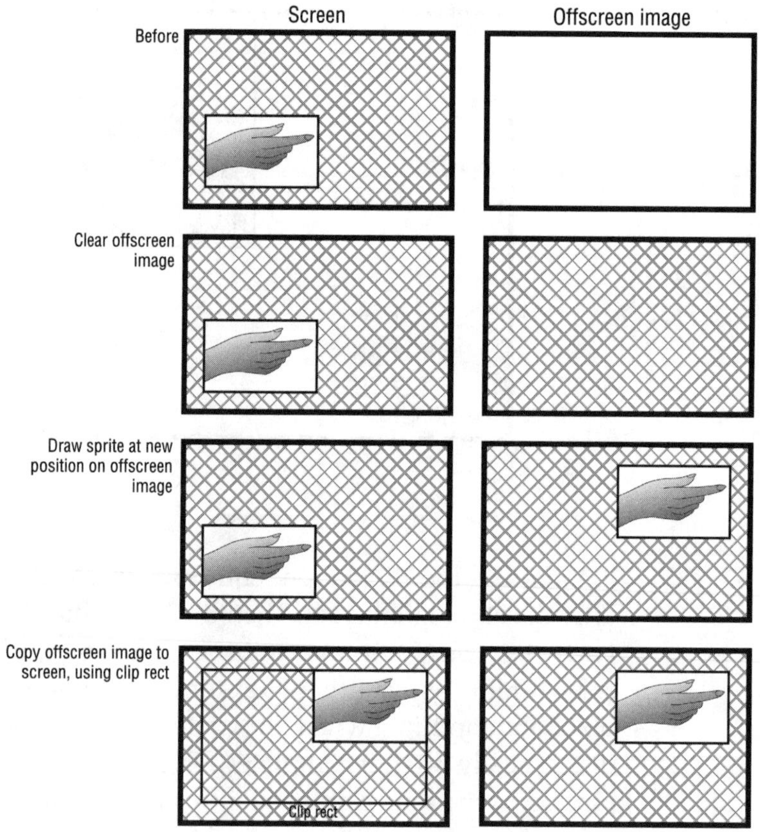

The *Rollover* Applet Class

Figure 8.8 shows the `Rollover` applet.

FIGURE 8.8

The `Rollover` applet

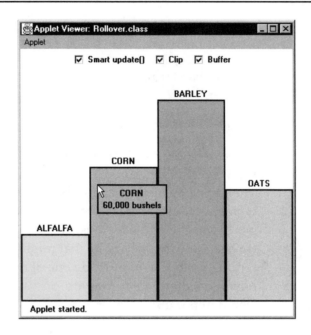

The checkboxes at the top of the applet enable or disable the three techniques discussed in the previous section. For the most satisfactory results, all three boxes should be checked.

The code for the `Rollover` class is about 200 lines long, but for the most part it is straightforward. Prior to the full listing, the `paint()` method will be broken down, beginning as follows:

```
public void paint(Graphics g)
{
    int     regionNum;
    Image   popup;

    // Determine which region, if any, was rolled over.
```

```
for (regionNum=0; regionNum<nRegions; regionNum++)
{
    if (regions[regionNum].bounds.inside(mouseX, mouseY))
    {
        break;
    }
}
if (regionNum == nRegions)        // Not in any region
{                                 // => Just redraw all
    lastPopupRect.x = -1;
    g.drawImage(backgroundImage, 0, 0, this);
    return;
}
popup = regions[regionNum].popupImage;
```

The mouseMove() method records the new mouse position in instance variables mouseX and mouseY, and then calls repaint(). The paint() method begins by traversing the regions[] array, which contains references to all the rollover regions. If the cursor is not inside one of the regions, paint() draws the background image (to erase any defunct sprite that might still be on the screen) and returns. If the cursor is inside one of the regions, the index of the region is stored in regionNum, and a reference to the sprite image is stored in popup.

The next part of paint() sets the clip region if the user has requested this feature:

```
// Clip g if requested.
if (clipCbox.getState())
{
    currentPopupRect.x = mouseX;
    currentPopupRect.y = mouseY;
    currentPopupRect.width = regions[regionNum].popupWidth;
    currentPopupRect.height = regions[regionNum].popupHeight;
    if (lastPopupRect.x == -1)
    {
        // No previous sprite position, clip to current bounds.
        g.clipRect(currentPopupRect.x,
                currentPopupRect.y,
                currentPopupRect.width,
```

```
                    currentPopupRect.height);
    }
    else
    {
        // Clip to union of current and prev sprite positions.
        Rectangle clip = currentPopupRect.union(lastPopupRect);
        g.clipRect(clip.x, clip.y, clip.width, clip.height);
    }
}
```

The clipping functionality software uses the two instance variables currentPopupRect and lastPopupRect to store the past and present location of the pop-up sprite. (At the end of the paint() method, lastPopupRect will get set to currentPopupRect.)

There are two possible cases. If there was no previous sprite (indicated by lastPopupRect = -1), the clipping region is set to the bounds of the new sprite. If there was a previous sprite, the clipping region is set to the union of the old and new bounds.

Next, the sprite is drawn to the screen. Depending on the user's choice, this can happen directly or via the off-screen image called buffer. The graphics object for buffer is called bufferG.

```
// Draw directly to screen.
if (bufferCbox.getState() == false)
{
    g.drawImage(backgroundImage, 0, 0, this);
    // Might see a flash right here.
    g.drawImage(popup, mouseX, mouseY, this);
}

// Draw to screen via buffer.
else
{
    bufferG.drawImage(backgroundImage, 0, 0, this);
    bufferG.drawImage(popup, mouseX, mouseY, this);
    g.drawImage(buffer, 0, 0, this);
}
```

If buffering is not requested, the checkbox state is `false`. The code erases the old sprite by drawing the background image and then draws the new sprite. Note that the graphics object g may or may not have had its clipping region adjusted.

If buffering has been requested, the code draws the background and the sprite to `buffer`. Then `buffer` is drawn to the screen. Again, the graphics object g may or may not have had its clipping region adjusted.

Lastly, `paint()` sets the old popup rect from the current popup rect:

```
        lastPopupRect.x = currentPopupRect.x;
        lastPopupRect.y = currentPopupRect.y;
        lastPopupRect.width = currentPopupRect.width;
        lastPopupRect.height = currentPopupRect.height;
    }
```

The complete listing for the `Rollover` class appears below. It is also on the CD-ROM in `c:\javadev\ch08\RolloverRegion.java`.

Rollover.java

```
import      java.awt.*;
import       java.applet.Applet;



public class Rollover extends Applet
{
    RolloverRegion  regions[];
    Rectangle       lastPopupRect, currentPopupRect;
    Image           backgroundImage, buffer;
    Graphics        bufferG;
    int             nRegions;
    int             mouseX, mouseY;
    Checkbox        smartUpdateCbox, clipCbox, bufferCbox;
```

```
String          shortLabels[] =
                {
                    "ALFALFA",
                    "CORN",
                    "BARLEY",
                    "OATS"
                };
String          longLabels[] =
                {
                    "30,000 bushels",
                    "60,000 bushels",
                    "90,000 bushels",
                    "50,000 bushels"
                };
int             values[] =
                {
                    30, 60, 90, 50
                };
Color           colors[] =
                {
                    Color.yellow, Color.lightGray,
                    Color.cyan, Color.pink
                };


public void init()
{
    int         i;
    int         regionWidth;
    double      valuePerPixel;
    Graphics    backgroundG;

    mouseX = mouseY = -1;
    lastPopupRect = new Rectangle(-1, -1, -1, -1);
    currentPopupRect = new Rectangle(-1, -1, -1, -1);

    // Create background and buffer images.
    backgroundImage = createImage(size().width, size().height);
    backgroundG = backgroundImage.getGraphics();
    buffer = createImage(size().width, size().height);
    bufferG = buffer.getGraphics();
```

```
        // Build GUI.
        smartUpdateCbox = new Checkbox("Smart update()");
        add(smartUpdateCbox);
        clipCbox = new Checkbox("Clip");
        add(clipCbox);
        bufferCbox = new Checkbox("Buffer");
        add(bufferCbox);

        // Create and init regions.
        nRegions = shortLabels.length;
        regions = new RolloverRegion[nRegions];
        int maxValue = 0;
        for (i=0; i<nRegions; i++)
        {
            regions[i] = new RolloverRegion();
            regions[i].shortLabel = shortLabels[i];
            regions[i].longLabel = longLabels[i];
            regions[i].color = colors[i];
            regions[i].font = getFont();
            regions[i].buildPopupImage(this);
            if (values[i] > maxValue)
                maxValue = values[i];
        }

        // Determine drawing scale.  Tell each region where it is.
        regionWidth = size().width / nRegions;
        valuePerPixel = maxValue / (size().height * 0.8);
        for (i=0; i<nRegions; i++)
        {
            int height = (int) ((double)values[i] / valuePerPixel);
            regions[i].bounds = new Rectangle(i * regionWidth,
                                              size().height - height,
                                              regionWidth,
                                              height);
        }

        // Draw each region into the background image.
        for (i=0; i<nRegions; i++)
        {
            regions[i].paint(backgroundG);
        }
    }
```

```
public boolean mouseMove(Event ev, int x, int y)
{
    mouseX = x;
    mouseY = y;
    repaint();
    return true;
}


public boolean mouseExit(Event ev, int x, int y)
{
    mouseX = mouseY = -1;
    repaint();
    return true;
}


public void update(Graphics g)
{
    if (smartUpdateCbox.getState())
        paint(g);
    else
        super.update(g);
}


public void paint(Graphics g)
{
    int     regionNum;
    Image   popup;

    // Determine which region, if any, was rolled over.
    for (regionNum=0; regionNum<nRegions; regionNum++)
    {
        if (regions[regionNum].bounds.inside(mouseX, mouseY))
        {
            break;
        }
    }
    if (regionNum == nRegions)          // Not in any region
    {                                   // => Just redraw all
        lastPopupRect.x = -1;
```

```
        g.drawImage(backgroundImage, 0, 0, this);
        return;
    }
    popup = regions[regionNum].popupImage;

    // Clip g if requested.
    if (clipCbox.getState())
    {
        currentPopupRect.x = mouseX;
        currentPopupRect.y = mouseY;
        currentPopupRect.width = regions[regionNum].popupWidth;
        currentPopupRect.height = regions[regionNum].popupHeight;
        if (lastPopupRect.x == -1)
        {
            // No previous sprite position, clip to current bounds.
            g.clipRect(currentPopupRect.x,
                       currentPopupRect.y,
                       currentPopupRect.width,
                       currentPopupRect.height);
        }
        else
        {
            // Clip to union of current and prev sprite positions.
            Rectangle clip = currentPopupRect.union(lastPopupRect);
            g.clipRect(clip.x, clip.y, clip.width, clip.height);
        }
    }

    // Draw directly to screen.
    if (bufferCbox.getState() == false)
    {
        g.drawImage(backgroundImage, 0, 0, this);
        // Might see a flash right here.
        g.drawImage(popup, mouseX, mouseY, this);
    }

    // Draw to screen via buffer.
    else
    {
        bufferG.drawImage(backgroundImage, 0, 0, this);
        bufferG.drawImage(popup, mouseX, mouseY, this);
```

```
        g.drawImage(buffer, 0, 0, this);
      }

    lastPopupRect.x = currentPopupRect.x;
    lastPopupRect.y = currentPopupRect.y;
    lastPopupRect.width = currentPopupRect.width;
    lastPopupRect.height = currentPopupRect.height;
    }
  }
```

Summary

Java's animation support is limited, but with the four techniques given in this chapter (in-place animation, rubber band animation, ticker-tape animation, and sprite animation), some sophisticated effects can be achieved. And you can look forward to creating really dazzling special effects with the upcoming support of the Animation API.

CHAPTER

NINE

9

File I/O and Streams

- **Abstract superclasses**

- **Low-level file streams**

- **High-level stream classes**

- **The `RandomAccessFile` class**

- **The `StreamTokenizer` class**

Java's file input/output support classes reside in the `java.io` package. Most of these classes support a stream-based model of reading and writing files. There are low-level stream classes for communicating with disk files and high-level classes for organizing the information that moves through the low-level streams. The high-level streams are also useful for organizing information sent to or received from the network; this is discussed in Chapter 10, *Networking*.

This chapter investigates all the low-level and high-level stream classes, as well as the few classes that communicate with disk files without using the streams mechanism.

Streams

A stream can be thought of as a conduit for data, somewhat like a straw or a siphon, with a source at one end and a consumer at the other end. For example, a Java program can read bytes from a disk file with the `FileInputStream` class, as shown below in Figure 9.1.

In the figure, the Java program makes a read call to the file-input stream, which reads bytes from the disk and delivers them to the caller. In Figure 9.2, a program writes to a file with the `FileInput-Stream` class.

In practice, this mechanism is not especially useful. Files usually contain highly structured information. The bytes are to be construed as numbers, text, source code, and so on. Java's `io` package provides a number of high-level input streams that read bytes from a low-level stream and return more sophisticated data. For example, the `Data-InputStream` class consumes bytes and produces Java primitive types and strings, as illustrated in Figure 9.3. The technique of attaching a sophisticated stream to a lower-level one, as shown in the figure, is called *chaining*.

Similarly, writing bytes to a file is cumbersome. Usually a program needs to write structured information to a file. The `DataOutput-Stream` class has methods for writing primitive data types and strings. The data-output stream converts its source data to bytes, which are passed to the stream's output. In Figure 9.4, the data-output stream's output is chained to a file-output stream; the result is that when a program writes primitives to the data-output stream, the corresponding bytes are written to the disk.

FIGURE 9.1

A simple input stream

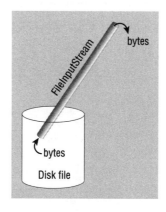

FIGURE 9.2

A simple output stream

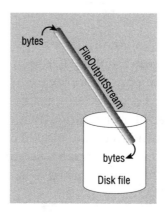

FIGURE 9.3

Two levels of input
stream

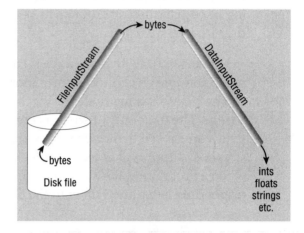

FIGURE 9.4

Two levels of output
stream

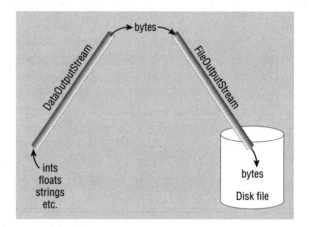

Traditionally, Java's low-level streams have operated on bytes. Release 1.1 of the JDK introduces character-based streams. These stream classes look very similar to their byte-based counterparts, but they permit programmers to operate on a level independent of any character-encoding scheme because all translations between characters and bytes are hidden by the class methods. This makes it easier to develop programs that are simple to internationalize. Moreover, character streams have been optimized for reading and writing multiple characters at a time. For these reasons, it is generally preferable to use character streams rather than byte streams whenever possible.

The next section examines the abstract superclasses of the byte and character input and output stream classes. The remainder of this chapter discusses the various streams available in the `java.io` package, as well as a few miscellaneous classes.

The Abstract Superclasses

Java's byte-oriented input and output streams are derived from the `InputStream` and `OutputStream` abstract classes. The character-oriented classes are derived from `Reader` and `Writer`.

The methods of class `InputStream` are described below. Most of these methods interact with system resources and have the potential for encountering platform-specific system problems and throwing an `IOException`.

`int read() throws IOException` Reads one byte from the data source. Returns the byte in the low-order eight bits of the return value. If the data source has no more data, returns -1. If data is not available at the moment of the call, the calling thread is blocked (see Chapter 7, *Threads*, for more information on blocking).

`int read(byte dest[]) throws IOException` Reads bytes from the data source into the `dest[]` array. Returns when the array is full or when the data source has no more data. The return value is the number of bytes read. Note that an array of bytes can easily be converted to a string by calling the `String(char[], 0)` constructor or the `copyValueOf()` method.

`int read(byte dest[], int offset, int length) throws IOException` Just like `read(byte dest[])` above, but only attempts to read `length` bytes into the portion of the byte array beginning at `offset`. Returns -1 at end of input.

`void close() throws IOException` Releases system resources associated with the data source. For example, on a Unix platform a file-input stream consumes one file descriptor. The `close()` call releases this file descriptor, and the stream then becomes permanently unavailable for reading.

`int available() throws IOException` Returns the number of bytes that may be read immediately without blocking. This call is not reliable on all systems; some implementations of Java are known to return `zero`.

`long skip(long nbytes) throws IOException` Attempts to skip over and discard `nbytes` bytes from the data source. It skips fewer bytes if no more data is available. It returns the number of bytes skipped.

`boolean markSupported()` Returns `true` if the mark/reset mechanism is supported; otherwise, returns `false`. The mark/reset mechanism is described below.

`void mark(int readlimit)` Sets a mark in the input stream. If in the future a `reset()` call is made and `markSupported()` is true, subsequent reads from the input stream will repeat all bytes read since the mark call. If more than `readlimit` bytes are read before the next `reset()` call, the mark is lost.

`void reset() throws IOException` Repositions the stream so that subsequent reads repeat the values read since the last `mark()` call.

The methods of the `OutputStream` class are described below. As with input streams, most of these methods interact with system resources and inform the caller of platform-specific system problems by throwing an `IOException`.

`void write(int b) throws IOException` Writes the byte that appears in the low-order 8 bits of the argument, discarding the higher 24 bits.

`void write(byte b[]) throws IOException`   Writes an array of bytes. Note that a string can be converted to a char array by calling the `getBytes()` method, but any information in the high-order byte of each Unicode character will be lost.

`void write(byte b[],int offset, int length) throws IOException`   Writes the subset of the byte array beginning at `offset` and `length` bytes long.

`void flush() throws IOException`   Writes out any bytes that the stream has buffered.

`void close() throws IOException`   Releases system resources associated with the data source. The stream becomes permanently unavailable for writing. An output stream should be flushed before it is closed.

The character-oriented abstract classes `Reader` and `Writer` both define two constructors in addition to their various methods. The constructors for `Reader` are:

`Reader()`   Constructs an instance of the class.

`Reader(Object lock)`   Constructs an instance of the class. Critical sections of class methods will synchronize on `lock`.

The methods of the `Reader` class are described below. Only two of these methods—`read(char[], int, int)` and `close()`—are abstract and must be supplied by concrete subclasses. All the other methods are implemented.

`int read() throws IOException`   Reads one character from the data source. Returns the byte in the low-order 16 bits of the return value. If the data source has no more data, returns -1. If data is not available at the moment of the call, the calling thread is blocked (see Chapter 7, *Threads*, for more information on blocking).

`int read(char dest[]) throws IOException`   Reads characters from the data source into the `dest[]` array. Returns when the array is full or when the data source has no more data. The return value is the number of characters read, or -1 if there is no more data.

`int read(char dest[], int offset, int length) throws IOException` Just like `read(char dest[])` above, but attempts to read `length` characters into the portion of the character array beginning at `offset`. Returns -1 when there is no more data.

`void close() throws IOException` Releases system resources associated with the data source. For example, on a Unix platform, a file-input stream consumes one file descriptor. The `close()` call releases this file descriptor, and the stream then becomes permanently unavailable for reading.

`long skip(long nchars) throws IOException` Attempts to skip over and discard `nchars` bytes from the data source. It skips fewer bytes if no more data is available. It returns the number of bytes skipped.

`boolean markSupported()` Returns `true` if the mark/reset mechanism is supported; otherwise, returns `false`. The mark/reset mechanism is described below.

`void mark(int readlimit)` Sets a mark in the input stream. If in the future a `reset()` call is made and `markSupported()` returns `true`, subsequent reads from the input stream will repeat all characters read since the mark call. If more than `readlimit` characters are read before the next `reset()` call, the mark is lost.

`void reset() throws IOException` Repositions the stream so that subsequent reads repeat the values read since the last `mark()` call.

`void ready() throws IOException` Returns `true` if the stream has data immediately available, so that a `read()` call will not block. Returns `false` if block prevention cannot be assured.

Like `Reader`, the `Writer` class has an overloaded constructor that offers the option of synchronizing on any arbitrary object. The two constructors for `Writer` are:

`Writer()`   Constructs an instance of the class.

`Writer(Object lock)`   Constructs an instance of the class. Critical sections of class methods will synchronize on `lock`.

The `Writer` methods are described below. Only three of these methods—`write(char[], int, int)`, `flush()`, and `close()`— are abstract and must be supplied by concrete subclasses. All the other methods are implemented.

`void write(int c) throws IOException`   Writes the character that appears in the low-order 16 bits of the argument.

`void write(char c[]) throws IOException`   Writes an array of characters.

`void write(char c[], int offset, int length) throws IOException`   Writes a subset of an array of characters.

`void write(String s) throws IOException`   Writes a string.

`void write(byte b[],int offset, int length) throws IOException`   Writes a subset of a string.

`void flush() throws IOException`   Writes out any characters that the stream has buffered.

`void close() throws IOException`   Releases system resources associated with the data source. The stream becomes permanently unavailable for writing. Writers should be flushed before they are closed.

The Low-Level File Streams

The `java.io` package provides four low-level stream classes for file access. These classes are `FileInputStream` for byte input, `File-OutputStream` for byte output, `FileReader` for character input, and `FileWriter` for character output.

`FileInputStream` class is a byte-based input stream that reads from a file. In addition to the inherited methods described above, this class has three constructors. All three constructors require arguments to specify the file to be opened. The constructors are:

`FileInputStream(String path) throws FileNotFound-Exception`   Attempts to open a stream to the file described by `path`. Throws exception if the file does not exist.

`FileInputStream(File file) throws FileNotFound-Exception`   Attempts to open a stream to the file described by `file`. Throws an exception if the file described by `file` does not exist.

`FileInputStream(FileDescriptor fd)`   Opens a stream to the file described by `fd`.

The `FileOutputStream` class is an output stream that writes to a file. The class has four constructors. The constructors are:

`FileOutputStream(String path) throws IOException` Attempts to open a stream to the file described by `path`.

`FileOutputStream(String path, boolean append) throws IOException`   Attempts to open a stream to the file described by `path`. If `append` is `true`, the file will be opened in append mode; this means that if the file already exists, data will be written to the end of the file, rather than clobbering the file's existing contents.

`FileOutputStream(File file) throws IOException`
Attempts to open a stream to the file described by `file`.

`FileOutputStream(FileDescriptor fd)` Opens a stream to the file described by `fd`.

NOTE In an applet, permission to access files is granted or denied by the browser's security manager. If permission is denied, all the constructors above throw a `SecurityException`. Because `SecurityException` is a type of runtime exception, it does not have to be caught, and it is not mentioned in API listings.

The `FileReader` class is a character-based stream for reading from a file. It is a subclass of the `Reader` and `InputStreamReader` classes, and adds no methods of its own except for the following three constructors:

`FileReader(String path) throws IOException`
Attempts to open a stream to the file described by `path`.

`FileReader(File file) throws IOException` Attempts to open a stream to the file described by `file`.

`FileReader(FileDescriptor fd)` Opens a stream to the file described by `fd`.

The `FileWriter` class is a character-based stream for writing to a file. It is a subclass of the `Writer` and `OutputStreamWriter` classes, and adds no methods of its own except for the following four constructors:

`FileWriter(String path) throws IOException`
Attempts to open a stream to the file described by `path`.

`FileWriter(String path, boolean append) throws IOException` Attempts to open a stream to the file described by `path`. If `append` is `true`, the file will be opened in append mode;

this means that if the file already exists, data will be written to the end of the file, rather than clobbering the file's existing contents.

`FileWriter(File file) throws IOException` Attempts to open a stream to the file described by `file`.

`FileWriter(FileDescriptor fd)` Opens a stream to the file described by `fd`.

Other Low-Level Stream Classes

In addition to `FileInputStream`, the `java.io` package contains several other low-level input stream classes. These classes are `ByteArrayInputStream`, `StringBufferInputStream`, and `PipedInputStream` for byte input; and `CharArrayReader`, `PipedReader`, and `StringReader` for character input. These classes read from sources other than a disk file. Otherwise they are similar to `FileInputStream` and `StringReader`: they inherit from the `InputStream` or `Reader` class, and they read bytes or characters from a data source. A program may use the data directly or chain a high-level input stream for more sophisticated processing.

There are also several low-level output classes in addition to `FileOutputStream`. These are `ByteArrayOutputStream` and `PipedOutputStream` for byte output; and `CharArrayWriter`, `PipedWriter`, and `StringWriter` for character output. These classes write to destinations that are not files. Otherwise they are similar to `FileOutputStream` and `Writer`. They inherit from the `OutputStream` or `Writer` class, and they write bytes or character. A program may write data to any of these classes, or it may chain a higher-level output stream to facilitate writing of more structured information.

The following sections examine these classes in detail.

Stream Classes That Connect to Arrays

The `ByteArrayInputStream` class takes its input from a byte array or from a piece of a byte array. There are two constructors:

`ByteArrayInputStream(byte buf[])`   Constructs an input stream that reads bytes from array `buf`.

`ByteArrayInputStream(byte buf[], int offset, int length)`   Constructs an input stream that reads bytes from a subset of array `buf`. The subset begins at `offset` and is `length` bytes long.

The `ByteArrayOutputStream` class writes to a byte array. The array grows automatically as needed. There are two constructors:

`ByteArrayOutputStream()`   Creates a new instance.

`ByteArrayOutputStream(int size)`   Creates a new instance with an initial destination array of the specified size. If the number of bytes written to the stream exceeds `size`, the destination array will automatically grow.

There are four methods for converting a byte array output stream into more accessible data.

`String toString()`   Returns a `String` consisting of all the bytes written to the stream so far. The high-order byte of each character in the string is `zero`.

`String toString(int highbyte)`   Returns a `String` consisting of all the bytes written to the stream so far. The high-order byte of each character in the string is `highbyte`. Deprecated in 1.1 in favor of the other two forms of this method.

`String toString(ByteToCharConverter btc)`   Returns a `String` using the provided converting mechanism. See *Converting Streams to Readers and Writers*, below, for more information on converters.

`byte[] toByteArray()` Returns an array containing all bytes written to the stream so far. This array is a copy of the stream's contents, so it may be modified without corrupting the original data.

These two classes have character-based analogues that extend the `Reader` and `Writer` abstract superclasses. The `CharArrayReader` class reads characters from a character array; the `CharArray-Writer` class writes characters to a character array. Except for constructors, neither class introduces any new methods beyond those inherited from their respective superclasses.

The constructors for `CharArrayReader` are:

`CharArrayReader(char chars[])` Creates a character array reader from array `chars[]`.

`CharArrayReader(char chars[], int start, int length)` Creates a character array reader from a subset of array `chars[]`.

The constructors for `CharArrayWriter` are:

`CharArrayWriter()` Creates a character array writer.

`CharArrayWriter(int length)` Creates a character array writer whose internal array has initial size `length`.

Stream Classes That Connect to Strings

These classes communicate with Java strings and string buffers. It is important to keep track of which classes communicate with strings and which communicate with string buffers, and the nomenclature can get confusing.

None of these classes adds any methods beyond those inherited from their respective superclasses. The `StringBufferInput-Stream` class reads bytes from a string (*not* a string buffer!); the `StringReader` class reads characters from a string. There is no `StringBufferOutputStream` class; the `StringWriter` class writes characters to a string buffer (*not* a string!).

The `StringBufferInputStream` constructor has the following format:

`StringBufferInputStream(String s)` Constructs an input stream that reads bytes from the specified string.

A string buffer input stream is not very different from a byte array input stream. An important difference is that in Java, a string is immutable. A byte array input stream runs the risk of having its data source accidentally corrupted. There is no such risk with a string buffer input stream.

In the absence of a `StringBufferOutputStream` class, output may be converted to a string by writing to a `ByteArrayOutput-Stream` and calling the `toString()` method, as described in the previous section.

The `StringReader` class is identical to the `StringBuffer-InputStream`, except that it allows you to read characters rather than bytes. Its constructor has the following format:

`StringReader(String s)` Constructs an input stream that reads characters from the specified string.

The `StringWriter` class accumulates its characters in a string buffer. It has two constructors.

`StringWriter()` Constructs a string writer with a default-sized internal buffer.

`StringWriter(int size)` Constructs a string writer with an internal string buffer whose initial size is specified by `size`.

Stream Classes That Connect to Each Other

The `java.io` package contains four *piped* classes that operate pair-wise in tandem. A piped input stream reads bytes that are written to a corresponding piped output stream; a piped reader reads characters that are written to a corresponding piped writer. The most common use for these classes is interthread communications: one thread writes to a piped writer or output stream while another thread reads the same data from a piped reader input stream. It is generally preferable to use a reader/writer pair because those classes are optimized for block transfers. For a deeper discussion on the use of these classes in the context of threads, please see Chapter 7, *Threads*.

Each of these classes has two constructors. The constructors for `PipedInputStream` are:

`PipedInputStream()`   Constructs a piped input stream with no data source. The stream is useless until it is associated with a piped output stream. This is accomplished by calling the `connect(PipedOutputStream)` method.

`PipedInputStream(PipedOutputStream source)`   Constructs a piped input stream whose data source is the bytes written to the `source` output stream.

The constructors for `PipedOutputStream` are:

`PipedOutputStream()`   Constructs a piped output stream with no data receiver. The stream is useless until it is associated with a piped input stream. This is accomplished by calling the `connect(PipedInputStream)` method.

`PipedOutputStream(PipedInputStream receiver)` Constructs a piped output stream whose data is written into the `receiver` piped input stream.

The constructors for `PipedReader` are:

`PipedReader()`   Constructs a piped reader with no data source. The stream is useless until it is associated with a piped writer. This is accomplished by calling the `connect(PipedWriter)` method.

`PipedReader(PipedWriter source)` Constructs a piped reader whose data source is the characters written to the `source` writer.

The constructors for `PipedWriter` are:

`PipedWriter()` Constructs a piped writer with no data receiver. The stream is useless until it is associated with a piped reader. This is accomplished by calling the `connect(PipedReader)` method.

`PipedWriter(PipedReader receiver)` Constructs a piped writer whose data is written into the `receiver` reader.

A stream of any type can be associated with a stream of the opposite type by calling the `connect()` method, as demonstrated below.

There are two ways to create a paired set of piped streams. The first way is to start with a piped input stream:

```
PipedInputStream instream = new PipedInputStream();
PipedOutputStream outstream = new PipedOutputStream(instream);
instream.connect(outstream);
```

The alternative way is to start with a piped output stream:

```
PipedOutputStream outstream = new PipedOutputStream();
PipedInputStream instream = new PipedInputStream(outstream);
outstream.connect(instream);
```

The same principle applies to creating a piped reader/writer pair. One way is to start with a reader:

```
PipedReader reader = new PipedReader();
PipedWriter writer = new PipedWriter(reader);
instream.connect(writer);
```

The alternative is to start with a piped writer:

```
PipedWriter writer = new PipedWriter();
PipedReader reader = new PipedReader(writer);
outstream.connect(instream);
```

The High-Level Stream Classes

High-level input streams take their input from other input streams. High-level output streams direct their output to other output streams.

Each of these classes is constructed by passing as an argument to the constructor an instance of another stream type. The new stream is chained onto the argument stream; a high-level input stream will read bytes from the argument stream, and a high-level output stream will write bytes to the argument stream. The argument stream may itself be a high-level stream.

The following sections discuss each of the high-level input and output stream classes.

The Buffered Classes

The `BufferedInputStream` class maintains an internal array of characters in which it buffers the data it reads from its source. The default size of the buffer is 2048 bytes. The first time one of the `read()` methods is called on the buffered input stream, it fills its buffer from its own data source. Subsequent reads on the buffered input stream return bytes from the buffer until the buffer is empty. At this point the buffered input stream again fills its buffer from the data source.

A buffered input stream is beneficial in situations where reading a large number of consecutive bytes from a data source is not significantly more costly than reading a single byte. For example, when reading from a disk file, a large amount of time is spent in positioning the disk drive's read head and in waiting for the disk to spin into position under the read head. This time expenditure must be made no matter how many consecutive bytes are to be read. In this case it would be advantageous to read an entire block of disk data (512 or 1048 bytes on most systems) and buffer the undesired bytes in case they are needed in the future.

There are two constructors for the BufferedInputStream class. One version creates a buffer with a default size of 2048 bytes; the other version lets the caller specify the buffer size. The constructors are:

BufferedInputStream(InputStream source) Creates a buffered input stream with a 2048-byte buffer. The input stream uses source as its data source.

BufferedInputStream(InputStream source, int bufsize) Creates a buffered input stream with a buffer of bufsize bytes. The input stream uses source as its data source.

The BufferedReader class is the character-based analogue of the buffered input stream. Not surprisingly, there are two constructors:

BufferedReader(Reader source) Creates a buffered reader with a 2048-character buffer. The reader uses source as its data source.

BufferedReader(Reader source int bufsize) Creates a buffered reader with a buffer of bufsize characters. The reader uses source as its data source.

The BufferedOutputStream class also maintains a buffer of bytes. Data written to a buffered output stream is accumulated in the buffer until the buffer is full. Then the bytes are written in a single operation to whatever output stream is chained to the buffered output stream.

Like `BufferedInputStream`, the `BufferedOutputStream` class has two constructors. One version creates a buffer with a default size of 2048 bytes; the other version lets the caller specify the buffer size. The constructors are:

`BufferedOutputStream(OutputStream dest)` Creates a buffered output stream with a 2048-byte buffer. The stream writes its data to `dest`.

`BufferedOutputStream(OutputStream dest, int bufsize)` Creates a buffered output stream with a buffer of `bufsize` bytes. The stream writes its data to `dest`.

The `BufferedWriter` class is analogous:

`BufferedWriter(Writer dest)` Creates a buffered writer with a 2048-byte buffer. The writer writes its data to `dest`.

`BufferedWriter(Writer dest, int bufsize)` Creates a buffered writer with a buffer of `bufsize` characters. The stream writes its data to `dest`.

NOTE The largest network packet size is 64K bytes. If a buffered writer is to be used for network output, there is no benefit to creating it with a larger buffer than 64K.

The *DataInputStream* and *DataOutputStream* Classes

The `DataInputStream` class reads bytes from another stream and interprets them as Java primitives, char arrays, and strings. There is no corresponding character-oriented reader class. The constructor expects to be passed an input stream, as shown below:

`DataInputStream(InputStream source)` Creates a data input stream that takes its data from stream `source`.

In addition to the usual inherited read methods, data-input streams support the following methods:

`boolean readBoolean() throws IOException` Reads a boolean value.

`byte readByte() throws IOException` Reads a signed 2's-complement byte.

`int readUnsignedByte() throws IOException` Reads an unsigned byte, returned as an int.

`short readShort() throws IOException` Reads a signed 2's-complement short. The first byte read is interpreted as the high-order byte of the short value.

`int readUnsignedShort() throws IOException` Reads an unsigned short. The first byte read is interpreted as the high-order byte of the short value.

`char readChar() throws IOException` Reads a two-byte Unicode char. The first byte read is interpreted as the high-order byte of the char.

`int readInt() throws IOException` Reads a signed 2's-complement four-byte Java int. The first byte read is interpreted as the high-order byte of the int.

`long readLong() throws IOException` Reads a signed 2's-complement eight-byte Java long. The first byte read is interpreted as the high-order byte of the long.

`float readFloat() throws IOException` Reads a four-byte representation of a Java float.

`double readDouble() throws IOException` Reads an eight-byte representation of a Java double.

`String readLine() throws IOException` Reads a series of bytes and converts them to a Java string. Each unicode character in the string has its high-order eight bits set to zero. Bytes are read until the data source reports end of file, or until a newline or return character is read. If a newline (`'\n'`) is read, it is discarded; if a return (`'\r'`) is read, then a newline character is appended to the string.

`String readUTF() throws IOException` Reads a series of bytes and interprets them as a Universal Text Format (*UTF*) string. UTF is an emerging international standard that uses one, two, or three bytes to represent each character. There are no string-termination issues because a UTF string includes length information.

`static String readUTF(DataInput din) throws IO-Exception` A static method. Reads a UTF string from the specified input stream.

`void readFully(byte[] dest) throws IOException` Attempts to fill byte array `dest` with bytes from the data source. The executing thread blocks if enough bytes are not available, and it throws an `EOFException` if the data source is depleted before `dest` is filled.

`void readFully(byte[] dest, int offset, int length) throws IOException` Like `readFully()` above, but only attempts to fill a subset of `dest`. The subset begins at index `offset`, and is `length` bytes long.

`void skipBytes(int offset nbytes) throws IOException` Like `readFully()` above, but discards bytes rather than storing them in an array. The executing thread blocks if enough bytes are not available.

The `DataOutputStream` class supports the writing of Java's primitive data types to an output stream. Strings and byte arrays may also be written. There is no analogous character-oriented writer class. The constructor expects to be passed an output stream, as shown below:

`DataOutputStream(OutputStream dest)` Creates a data output stream that writes its data to `dest`.

The data written to a data-output stream is broken up into its constituent bytes, which are written to whatever output stream is chained to the data-output stream. In addition to the various byte-writing methods inherited from its `DataOutput` superclass, the `DataOutputStream` class supports the following methods for writing:

`void writeBoolean(boolean b) throws IOException` Writes a boolean value. A value of `true` is represented by `(byte)0`; a value of `false` is represented by `(byte)1`.

`void writeByte(int i) throws IOException` Writes the low-order byte of `i`.

`void writeShort(int i) throws IOException` Writes the two low-order bytes of `i`. Of the two bytes written, the higher-order byte is written first (bits 8 to 15), followed by the lower-order byte (bits 0 to 7).

`void writeInt(int i) throws IOException` Writes all four bytes of `i`, starting with the highest-order byte (bits 24 to 31).

`void writeLong(long theLong) throws IOException` Writes all four bytes of `theLong`, starting with the highest-order byte (bits 56 to 63).

`void writeFloat(float f) throws IOException` Writes the four-byte representation of `f`.

`void writeDouble(double d) throws IOException` Writes the eight-byte representation of d.

```
void writeBytes(String s) throws IOException
```
Writes s as a series of bytes. Only the low-order byte of each two-byte unicode character is written.

```
void writeChars(String s) throws IOException
```
Writes s as a series of unicode characters. Two bytes are written for each unicode character, starting with the high-order byte.

```
void writeUTF(String s) throws IOException  Writes
```
s as a UTF string.

The *LineNumberInputStream* and *LineNumberReader* Classes

The LineNumberInputStream class maintains an internal count of the number of lines it has read. A line is considered to be any number of bytes, terminated by a return character ('\r'), a newline character ('\n'), or a return followed by a newline.

The constructor expects to be passed an input stream, as shown below:

```
LineNumberInputStream(InputStream source)  Creates
```
a line-number input stream that takes its data from stream source.

The line count may be retrieved or modified with the following methods:

```
int getLineNumber()  Returns the current line number.
```

```
void setLineNumber(int newvalue)  Sets the current line
```
number to newvalue.

NOTE Line number input streams should only be used in programs based on pre-1.1 versions of the JDK. In 1.1, the entire class has been deprecated in favor of line number readers.

The `LineNumberReader` class is the character-based analogue. Its constructors expect to be passed a reader, as shown below:

`LineNumberReader(Reader source)` Creates a line number reader that takes its data from `source`.

`LineNumberReader(Reader source, int size)` Creates a line number reader that takes its data from `source`. The internal buffer size is given by `size`.

This class introduces the following methods:

`int getLineNumber()` Returns the current line number.

`void setLineNumber(int newvalue)` Sets the current line number to `newvalue`.

`Public String readLine() throws IOException` Returns the next line of input.

The Print Classes

The `PrintStream` and `PrintWriter` classes have methods that support printing text. This support consists of data-type conversion and automatic flushing.

The `PrintStream` class has two constructors, as follows:

`PrintStream(OutputStream dest)` Constructs a print stream and chains its output to `dest`. Automatic flushing is not supported.

`PrintStream(OutputStream dest, boolean autoflush)` Constructs a print stream and chains its output to `dest`. The value of `autoflush` determines whether automatic flushing is supported; if this value it `true`, the print stream will be flushed whenever a new-line character is written.

The `PrintStream` class has numerous methods for converting and writing different data types. For each data type, there is a `print()` method, which writes the data as a string, and a `println()` method, which writes the data as a string and appends a newline character. The supported methods are:

`void print(char c)`   Prints a character.

`void println(char c)`   Prints a character followed by a newline character.

`void print(int i)`   Prints an int.

`void println(int i)`   Prints an int followed by a newline character.

`void print(long ln)`   Prints a long.

`void println(long ln)`   Prints a long followed by a newline character.

`void print(float f)`   Prints a float.

`void println(float f)`   Prints a float followed by a newline character.

`void print(double d)`   Prints a double.

`void println(double d)`   Prints a double followed by a newline character.

`void print(boolean b)`   Prints a boolean. If the boolean value is `true`, prints the string `true`, otherwise prints the string `false`.

`void println(boolean b)`   Prints a boolean followed by a newline character.

`void print(char[] c)`   Prints a character array.

`void println(char[] c)` Prints a character array followed by a newline character.

`void print(String s)` Prints a string.

`void println(String s)` Prints a string followed by a newline character.

`void print(Object ob)` Prints an object. The string that is printed is the result of calling `ob.toString()`.

`void println(Object ob)` Prints a character followed by a newline character.

`void println()` Prints a newline character.

NOTE Print streams should only be used in programs based on pre-1.1 versions of the JDK. In 1.1, the entire class has been deprecated in favor of print writers.

The `PrintWriter` class has two constructors:

`PrintWriter(Writer dest)` Constructs a print writer and chains its output to `dest`. Automatic flushing is not supported.

`PrintWriter(Writer dest, boolean autoflush)` Constructs a print writer and chains its output to `dest`. The value of `autoflush` determines whether automatic flushing is supported; if this value is `true`, the print stream will be flushed whenever a newline character is written.

This class' writing methods have names that precisely match those of the `PrintStream` class described above. The only functional difference is that a print writer writes characters rather than bytes.

There is nothing inherent in `PrintStream` or `PrintWriter` that requires that the output be a printing device. A print writer might, for example, be chained to a string writer (which writes to a string buffer, not to a string!); when output to the print writer is completed, the string buffer can be converted to a string and written to a text-area component.

The Pushback Classes

The `PushbackInputStream` and `PushbackReader` classes permits data to be *unread* or *pushed back* into the data source. The classes maintain internal stacks for pushed-back bytes and chars. Read operations pop data from the stack until the stack is empty; only then is the data source accessed again. In pre-1.1 versions of the JDK, only one byte at a time may be pushed back; 1.1 provides constructors for specifying the size of the internal pushback buffer.

The constructors for `PushbackInputStream` are:

`PushbackInputStream(InputStream source)`   Creates a pushback input stream connected to `source`. The stream's buffer accommodates a single byte.

`PushbackInputStream(InputStream source, int buf-size)`   Creates a pushback input stream connected to `source`. The stream's buffer accommodates `bufsize` bytes. This constructor is not supported in pre-1.1 releases of the JDK.

The constructors for `PushbackReader` are:

`PushbackReader(Reader source)`   Creates a pushback reader connected to `source`. The stream's buffer accommodates a single byte.

`PushbackReader(Reader source, int bufsize)`   Creates a reader stream connected to `source`. The stream's buffer accommodates `bufsize` bytes.

For pushback input streams, the methods that support pushing back are:

`void unread(int ch) throws IOException` Stores the low-order byte of `ch` in an internal buffer. The next read operation from the stream will return `ch` as a byte.

`void unread(byte bytes[]) throws IOException` Unreads all the bytes in array `bytes[]`. Not supported in pre-1.1 JDK.

`void unread(byte bytes[], int start, int length) throws IOException` Unreads a subset of array `bytes[]`. Not supported in pre-1.1 JDK.

The pushback methods for pushback readers are:

`void unread(int ch) throws IOException` Pushes back the low-order two bytes of `ch`.

`void unread(char chars[]) throws IOException` Unreads all the characters in array `chars[]`.

`void unread(char bytes[], int start, int length) throws IOException` Unreads a subset of array `chars[]`.

All the pushback methods for both classes throw an `IOException` if the internal pushback buffer does not have space to accommodate the operation. This can happen if the operation pushes more data than the capacity of the buffer or if there have not been enough reads since the last pushback to create sufficient buffer space.

The pushback input classes are useful for finding fields within nondelimited input. To see how this is done, consider first the problem of finding a field within delimited input. Suppose an input stream consists of various nonnumeric data, followed by a single slash character (/), followed by a number. Suppose the stream is currently somewhere in the nonnumeric data, and it is necessary to skip to the numeric field. Because the input is delimited—that is, the fields are separated—this skip is easily done, as shown below. (This code fragment assumes that the input stream is called `instream`.)

```
// Assume instr is somewhere in non-numeric field.
int intchar;
while ((intchar=instr.read()) != -1)
{
    if (intchar == '/')
        break;
}
// Now instr is positioned at 1st char after '/'
```

Unfortunately, not all input is delimited. If the input data does not have a slash between its two fields, it is tempting to do something like the following:

```
int intchar;
while ((intchar=instr.read()) != -1)
{
    if (Character.isDigit((char)intchar))
        break;
}
```

This code fails because by the time the loop is exited, the first character of the numeric field has been read and the input stream is positioned at the second character. The code has to undo the reading of the first numeric character. Reading is undone by chaining a pushback input stream onto `instream`, as shown below.

```
int intchar;
PushbackInputStream pbis = new PushbackInputStream(instr);
while ((intchar=pbis.read()) != -1)
{
    if (Character.isDigit((char)intchar))
    {
        pbis.unread(intchar);
        break;
    }
}
```

The ability to push a single byte back into the data source does not seem impressive, but it permits the easy parsing of structured, non-delimited input.

The *SequenceInputStream* Class

The `SequenceInputStream` class is a mechanism for combining two or more input streams. There is no corresponding character-based reader class. A sequence input stream reads from its first input stream until that stream is exhausted; it then discards the end-of-file exception and reads from its second input stream, and so on until the last input stream is emptied. Only then does a read of the sequence input stream return `-1`.

This class has the following two constructors:

`SequenceInputStream(InputStream s1, InputStream s2)`   Creates a sequence input stream out of `s1` and `s2`.

`SequenceInputStream(Enumeration enum)`   Creates a sequence input stream out of the list of input streams given by `enum`.

The second constructor requires an enumeration—that is, an object that implements the `Enumeration` interface. The easiest way to build an enumeration is to add all the input streams to a vector and then have the vector return an enumeration of its elements. Thus the following code constructs a sequence input stream out of input streams `s1`, `s2`, `s3`, `s4`, and `s5`:

```
Vector vec = new Vector();
vec.addElement(s1);
vec.addElement(s2);
vec.addElement(s3);
vec.addElement(s4);
vec.addElement(s5);
SequenceInputStream sis = new
SequenceInputStream(vec.elements());
```

Converting Streams to Readers and Writers

The InputStreamReader class, when chained onto any subclass of InputStream, reads bytes from the input stream and converts them to characters. The OutputStreamWriter class, when chained onto any subclass of OutputStream, converts characters written to it into bytes and writes the bytes to the output stream. The conversion is illustrated in Figure 9.5.

FIGURE 9.5

InputStreamReader and OutputStreamWriter

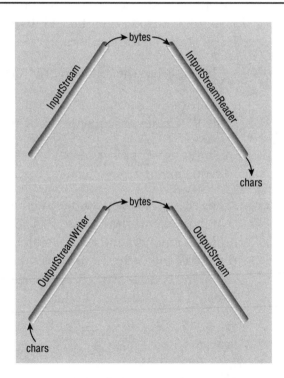

Both classes have to know how to convert between 16-bit characters and 8-bit bytes. Conversion mappings are represented by string names. Either of these classes may be constructed with an optional string argument to specify a mapping other than the default.

The constructors for `InputStreamReader` are:

`InputStreamReader(InputStream source)`   Constructs an input stream reader whose data source is `source`.

`InputStreamReader(InputStream source, String encodingName)`   Constructs an input stream reader whose data source is `source`. Bytes will be converted to chars using the encoding specified by `encodingName`.

The constructors for `OutputStreamWriter` offer the same combinations of options:

`OutputStreamWriter(OutputStream out)`   Constructs an output stream writer connected to `out`.

`OutputStreamWriter(OutputStream out, String encodingName)`   Constructs an output stream writer connected to `out`. Bytes will be converted to chars using the encoding specified by `encodingName`.

Non-Stream Classes

The `io` package contains several classes that are not streams. These include `File`, `FileDescriptor`, `RandomAccessFile`, and `StreamTokenizer`. `File` and `FileDescriptor` are straightforward and are adequately described in Sun's API documentation. The next two sections discuss the `RandomAccessFile` and `StreamTokenizer` classes.

The *RandomAccessFile* Class

The `RandomAccessFile` class supports reading and writing of a file, as well as file-pointer positioning. Because it does not treat the file as an ordered sequence of pure input or pure output, it operates outside of the streams model.

There are two constructors for `RandomAccessFile`:

`RandomAccessFile(String path, String permissions)` Creates a random-access file connected to the file `path`. Access permission is described by the string `permissions`, which must be either `"r"` for read-only permission or `"rw"` for read-write permission.

`RandomAccessFile(File file, String permissions)` Same as above, but the file path is taken from an instance of the `File` class.

Random-access files support a wide variety of methods for reading and writing various data types. These methods have the same names as the methods listed above for the `DataInputStream` and `DataOutputStream` classes.

Unix programmers who are accustomed to the standard I/O library are used to being able to position a file pointer relative to the start of the file, the end of the file, or the current file-pointer position. The `RandomAccessFile` class offers only a single `seek()` method, which positions with respect to the start of the file. In order to achieve the other two modes of seeking, it is necessary to retrieve to file length or the current position, and do an explicit subtraction.

The following methods support positioning:

`void seek(long newPosition)` Sets the file's pointer to `newPosition`.

`long length()` Returns the current length of the file in bytes.

`long getFilePointer()` Returns the current location of the file pointer.

NOTE   Before release 1.1 of the JDK, the only way to append to the end of an existing file was to open a random access file, seek to the end, and write. In 1.1, an easier way is to build a file writer using the `FileWriter(String, boolean)` version of the constructor. If the boolean value is `true`, the file will be opened in append mode.

The *StreamTokenizer* Class

The `StreamTokenizer` class is a parser, useful for analyzing input whose format is similar to Java, C, or C++ source code.

The first step in using a stream tokenizer is, of course, to construct one:

`StreamTokenizer(InputStream instr)`   Constructs a stream tokenizer that takes its input from `instr`.

The next step is to parse the input stream `instr`. Parsing is typically done in a while loop, calling the tokenizer's `nextToken()` method until the end of the input is reached. The `nextToken()` method returns an int that describes the type of the next token. There are four possible return values for `nextToken()`:

`StreamTokenizer.TT_NUMBER`   Indicates that the token just read was a number. The number's value may be read from the tokenizer's `nval` instance variable, which is of type `double`.

`StreamTokenizer.TT_WORD`   Indicates that the token just read was a nonnumerical word (an identifier, for example). The word may be read from the tokenizer's `sval` instance variable, which is of type `String`.

`StreamTokenizer.TT_EOL`   Indicates that the token just read was an end-of-line character.

`StreamTokenizer.TT_EOF`   Indicates that the end of the input stream has been reached.

A stream tokenizer can be customized to recognize caller-specified characters as whitespace, comment delimiters, string delimiters, and other format-specific values. The customizing methods are:

void commentChar(int comment)   Specifies that comment is to denote the first character of a single-line comment. Note that comment is an int, not a byte or a char.

void quoteChar(int quote)   Specifies that quote is to delimit the beginning and end of string constants. Note that quote is an int, not a byte or a char.

void whitespaceChars(int low, int high)   Specifies that all input characters in the range low through high (inclusive) are to be interpreted as whitespace. Note that low and high are ints, not bytes or chars.

void wordChars(int low, int high)   Specifies that all input characters in the range low through high (inclusive) are to be interpreted as word characters. Note that low and high are ints, not bytes or chars.

void ordinaryChar(int ord)   Specifies that ord is an ordinary character and is not a quote delimiter, comment-line delimiter, whitespace character, word character, or number character. Note that ord is an int, not a byte or a char.

void ordinaryChars(int low, int high)   Specifies that all input characters in the range low through high (inclusive) are to be interpreted as ordinary characters. Note that low and high are ints, not bytes or chars.

void eolIsSignificant(boolean flag)   If flag is true, specifies that the parser will recognize end-of-line characters as tokens. If flag is false, end-of-line characters will not be recognized.

void parseNumbers(boolean flag)   If flag is true, specifies that the parser will recognize numbers as tokens. If flag is false, numbers will not be recognized.

`void slashStarComments(boolean flag)` If `flag` is `true`, specifies that the parser will recognize C-style comments. If `flag` is `false`, C-style comments will not be recognized. C-style comments begin with a slash character followed by an asterisk character (`/*`) and end with an asterisk followed by a slash (`*/`); they may span multiple lines.

`void slashSlashComments(boolean flag)` If `flag` is `true`, specifies that the parser will recognize C++-style comments. If `flag` is `false`, C++-style comments will not be recognized. C++-style comments begin with two slash characters (`//`) and end at the end of the current line.

`void resetSyntax()` Resets the significance of all characters to be ordinary.

With the methods described above, the `StreamTokenizer` class can be configured as a flexible and moderately powerful parser for an input stream whose format resembles Java, C, or C++ source code. Parsing of more general formats would require a powerful lexical analyzer and compiler generator, similar to the `lex` and `yacc` tools found in Unix. Such tools are beyond the current scope of the JDK.

Summary

Java's `io` package offers a variety of low-level input and output streams that read or write files, byte arrays, and strings. There are also a number of high-level streams that process or filter data. Streams can be chained together into arbitrarily long sequences.

One common use of streams is for disk file input and output. However, chains of streams can be a powerful solution for any programming problem involving the processing of structured sequential data. A prime example of this situation is network communication; the next chapter shows many ways to use streams for network reading and writing.

CHAPTER

TEN

10

Networking

- Fundamentals of TCP/IP networking

- Network programming basics

- Server design and protocols

- Preexisting protocols

- Implementing a network classloader

- Connection information

- Security considerations

- Using UDP

Java networking uses TCP/IP, the same network system as is used by the Internet. TCP/IP defines a number of protocols for providing services, such as file transfer and remote login, and also several protocols that make up the underlying communication system. The first section of this chapter will discuss some of the fundamental issues that relate to this communication system. An understanding of the nature of the network, along with its strengths and limitations, is crucial when producing programmed systems to run over it. The second part of the chapter will look at programming network systems with Java. Sample code will be described demonstrating client and server programming. Java techniques will be introduced for handling Uniform Resource Locators (URLs) along with the Common Gateway Interface (CGI) mechanisms POST and GET. Java classloaders are described and an example implementation will be shown. The use of the User Datagram Protocol (UDP) is introduced along with examples of both broadcasting and multicasting.

Fundamentals of TCP/IP Networking

The primary function of TCP/IP is to provide a point-to-point communication mechanism. One process on one machine communicates with another process on another machine. This communication appears as two streams of data. One stream carries data from one process to the other, while the other carries data in the other direction. Each process can read the data that have been written by the other, and in normal conditions, the data received are the same, and in the same order, as when they were sent.

To support a point-to-point communication system, each node requires a unique address, which is analogous to a telephone number. In TCP/IP the address takes the form of a 32-bit binary number. Conventionally, because humans do not cope well with long binary numbers, these addresses are represented as four decimal numbers, each in the range 0 to 255. Even with this improvement, humans still have difficulty remembering addresses; for this reason mechanisms have been developed to allow more natural names to be used.

NOTE A name service provides a means of translating between names, which are easy for users to understand, and 32-bit binary numbers, which the machine can understand. Figure 10.1 compares addresses in 32-bit binary format, dotted decimal format, and name service names.

FIGURE 10.1

A comparison of addressing formats used in TCP/IP

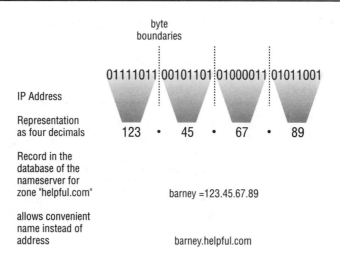

A variety of naming schemes are available and in regular use on private TCP/IP networks, but only one system is accepted for use on the Internet as a whole. That system is called the Domain Name System (DNS).

DNS allows machines to be addressed using textual names instead of numbers. To allow network administrators a degree of autonomy with machine names, a hierarchical approach is used for these names. A DNS name is made up of a number of parts, separated by periods. In the same way that a street address has the city at the end and the individual house number at the beginning, a DNS name has a broad specification at the right, with more detail added with each element to the left. Hence, an address like www.javasoft.com indicates that the machine is called www. That name is known in the context of a zone called javasoft, and the name javasoft is known in the context of a larger zone called com. This domain name format is generally well understood in the area of the Internet.

In addition to the machine addresses provided by the Internet Protocol (IP) part of the network system, TCP/IP has a mechanism for identifying individual processes on a machine, analogous to an office block. The building has a phone number, but each room inside is also identified by an extension number. When a call arrives at the building, it must be connected to the correct room for handling. Payment requests go to accounts payable, orders to sales, and so forth. In the TCP/IP system, the extension numbers are called *ports*, and they are represented by a 16-bit binary number.

NOTE A TCP/IP connection is identified by four numbers: the source and destination machine address, and the source and destination port. Usually only the server port is important for deciding what service is being used, and ports at the client end are allocated according to what is available. Because both port numbers are considered when identifying a connection, the server port can be reused—even from the same client machine—without confusion.

To communicate with the correct part of a particular computer, the sending machine must know both the machine address and the port number to which the message should be sent. The organization of port numbers is rather more rigid than that of telephone extensions.

Most public services use port numbers defined in *Request for Comment* standards (RFCs). A list of these is found in most Unix systems in a file called /etc/services or on Windows systems in \WINDOWS\ SERVICES.

> **TIP** The full set of RFC documents can be obtained from a number of sites, including ftp://nic.ddn.mil/rfc. Relevant RFCs are included on the CD-ROM, accompanying examples later in this chapter.

Recent systems, such as Gopher and the World Wide Web, use URLs to specify individual services. A URL is able to define a port number, protocol, machine, and specific file. Because of this expressiveness, URL-based services are able to use nonstandard port numbers. In most other cases, however, a service will be associated with one particular port. For example, SMTP, the Internet mail service, is found on port number 25, while the Telnet server is found at port 23.

TCP/IP Internals

The TCP/IP system is actually made up of a number of logical layers. Each layer communicates with both its neighbor layers. In this way, clearly defined responsibilities can be allocated to different parts of the system.

The lowest layer handles physical transmission and reception of data from the network cable itself. This is not actually part of the TCP/IP system as such, but is usually provided by another protocol. This layer is sent a block of bytes—conventionally called a *datagram*—by the layer above it and sends the datagram to the network, or it receives data from the network and passes the data to the layer above it.

The first layer service is not expected to know if transmitted data successfully reached the intended destination, nor indeed what the destination was intended to be. When receiving data, this layer is not required to know if this machine is the intended recipient, nor if the data have been received correctly.

> **NOTE** Many implementations of the first layer, such as Ethernet, do actually know if the data is correct and intended for this machine. Although TCP/IP does not require it, it is common for implementations to be optimized to take advantage of these benefits when they are available.

The next layer is the IP, or Internet Protocol, layer. IP knows that it has a physical transport layer available for carrying datagrams. IP takes the data it is to send and adds special control information, called a *header*, to it. The headers describe, amongst other things, the address of the destination machine. In this way, when the IP layer at the receiving machine is passed a datagram by its physical transport layer, it is able to look at the header and decide whether it is the intended recipient. As with the physical transport layer, datagrams are passed down from above to be transmitted (along with the destination address) and received datagrams are passed up when the address has been verified.

IP provides other important services, including routing, but these are not available to Java programmers and hence are not directly relevant to this discussion.

Above the IP layer are a number of other layers at the same level. Two parts of the system occupying this level are interesting here. These are the Transmission Control Protocol (TCP) and the User Datagram Protocol (UDP, often referred to descriptively as the Unreliable Datagram Protocol). In later sections, you will find descriptions of ways to use Java to handle both these services.

TCP and UDP are intended for programs to use when communicating with each other, and they provide one facility in common: port numbers. In the same way that the IP layer built a header and attached it to the front of the data to be transmitted to identify the target machine, TCP and UDP build headers of their own to identify the target port number. When a datagram is passed up to one of these layers by the IP layer, the header is examined so the target port number can be identified and the data passed to the correct process.

NOTE During transmission, each layer of these protocols takes data and control information from the layer above and creates a sort of envelope to wrap the data in. The combined data and control block is passed down to the layer below, where the whole block is regarded simply as data. At the receiving end, each layer in turn "unwraps" the parcel of data, extracting the control information from it. The separated data and control information are then passed up to the layer above. Figure 10.2 illustrates this idea.

FIGURE 10.2

Data blocks are wrapped in envelopes by each successive layer of TCP/IP transmission.

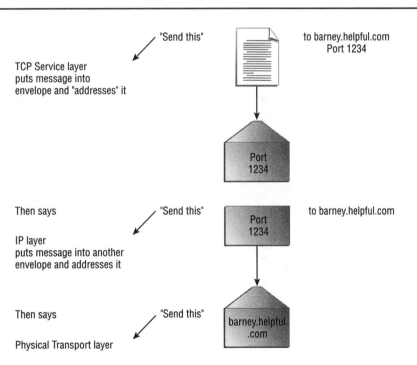

TCP Service layer
puts message into
envelope and "addresses" it

"Send this"

to barney.helpful.com
Port 1234

Port
1234

Then says

"Send this"

Port
1234

to barney.helpful.com

IP layer
puts message into another
envelope and addresses it

Then says

"Send this"

barney.helpful
.com

Physical Transport layer

TCP and UDP have important differences. UDP is called the User Datagram Protocol precisely because it takes the IP layer, which provides a datagram protocol, and provides a programming interface that makes it suitable for use in general programming. So, the user referred to in the name is the user process that makes use of the network system.

UDP has a facility for determining whether the received data has been corrupted, but it is not often used. Even if the data is read incorrectly, UDP does not implement any kind of acknowledgment mechanism, so this layer cannot inform the sender of the failure.

Significantly more facilities are provided by TCP. When a TCP data block, usually called a *segment*, is transmitted, the sender labels it with a *sequence number* and a *checksum*. The sequence number is a label to uniquely identify this segment and its position in the ordered flow of segments. The checksum allows the receiver to determine whether the segment has been received correctly. The data sent are stored along with the time of sending and the sequence number. If the segment is received correctly by the intended recipient and the recipient was ready to receive it, then the recipient sends an acknowledgment. This is a message that says, in effect, "I got your message; it was correct, and it had this label on it." When the sender sees this message, it can discard its copy of the segment data. If the sender does not receive the acknowledgment in a reasonable time, then it retransmits the segment.

NOTE If too many failures occur, the TCP system abandons the attempt on the assumption that there is a physical problem with the network. The program using the TCP system, and in turn the human user, can be informed that a failure has occurred.

Clearly, TCP is the easier system to use from a programming point of view, because the channels it creates can be treated as reliable. That is, unless something catastrophic happens, the bytes that are read and written are known, by both the sender and the receiver, to have been received correctly, in the same order, by the intended process on the intended machine. The sender knows that it will be informed if successful transmission is not possible or cannot be verified. Using UDP, all these questions remain for the programmer to solve.

Despite the added complexity incumbent in its use, UDP is not without appropriate application. It is a simpler protocol, involving less CPU time and less network overhead in terms of additional "management" data. Therefore, on networks that are reasonably reliable, such as most modern LANs, UDP is faster. When using UDP, the programmer must either provide verification and recovery mechanisms or accept the possibility of lost data. If the verification and recovery mechanisms are not carefully designed to match the reliability of the network, the performance of the UDP system will drop. This reduction of performance can be dramatic.

What Java Does Not Provide

There are some facilities offered by traditional TCP/IP programming libraries that are not supported by Java:

Raw sockets allow the programmer to develop new protocol sets, parallel to TCP or UDP. They are also used to implement services that use the Internet Control Message Protocol (ICMP) protocol, such as the `ping` utility.

Out-of-band data allows sending "urgent" messages that jump the queue at the receiver. Normally, a stream of 101 bytes would be passed to the receiver program code in the order sent. If the 101st byte was sent as out-of-band data and the receiver program had only read 5 bytes from its input queue, then the 6th byte read would be the 101st transmitted. The receiver would also be informed that this was urgent data. Some standard Internet services use urgent messages, but it is the exception rather than the rule.

Socket half-close is a little-used facility that allows one end of a connection to close down its transmission while the other end is still sending data in the other direction. In Java, closing either of the streams will close the underlying socket.

DNS, the Domain Name System, allows information about more than just machine names and addresses to be disseminated. Name-to-address translations use an Internet name (IN) record, while address-to-name translations use a pointer (PTR) record: These types of translation are supported by Java. One other record type is particularly important in the Internet but is not supported by Java: the mail exchanger (MX) record. Mail addresses do not usually refer to specific machines; rather they describe a domain. The MX record allows a mail sender to determine from the domain name the most appropriate physical machine to send the mail to so the proper recipient will get it as soon as possible.

Network Programming Basics

The following sections introduce the basics of creating network connections using Java. Rudimentary client and server code is shown describing the fundamentals of the Java networking package.

A Simple TCP Client

The *Daytime* service is a traditional TCP service available on Unix systems. If you have a system that does not provide this service, there is a simulation of the service on the CD-ROM accompanying this book. The Daytime protocol is defined in RFC 867; a copy of this document can be found in the file `javadevhdbk\rfcs\rfc867.txt`.

The Daytime server accepts connections on its designated port and sends to the client a single line of text representing the current date and time. The code for a simple client that connects to this service is listed below:

DayClient1.java

```java
import java.net.*;
import java.io.*;

public class DayClient1 {
  public static final int DAYTIME_PORT = 13;
  String host;
  Socket s;

  public static void main(String args[]) throws IOException {
    DayClient1 that = new DayClient1(args[0]);
    that.go();
  }

  public DayClient1(String host) {
    this.host = host;
  }

  public void go() throws IOException {
    s = new Socket(host, DAYTIME_PORT);
    BufferedReader i = new BufferedReader(
      new InputStreamReader(s.getInputStream()));
    System.out.println(i.readLine());
    i.close();
    s.close();
  }
}
```

Running the Program

You can find the source code for this example in the directory `javadevhdbk\ch10\DayClient1.java`. The bytecode is in the file `javadevhdbk\ch10\DayClient1.class`.

It is not necessary to determine whether your system currently provides a Daytime service. Most Unix systems do, while most other systems do not. Simply attempt to run the Java version of the server: If there is a server already running, the Java version will be unable to use the socket and will fail; otherwise it will start correctly.

Attempt to start the Java server by issuing the command

```
java DayServer1
```

Note that the `DayServer.class` file is located on the CD-ROM along with the `DayClient1.class` file. If no other server is already using port 13, the server will start and run until killed.

In a different window run the example by issuing the command

```
java DayClient1 localhost
```

Be careful to supply a hostname, as this example does not check for it.

TIP There are two ways to refer to the local machine without needing to know its proper name. Traditionally, the name `localhost` is reserved for this purpose. Also, a special address is reserved for a machine to refer to itself: This address is `127.0.0.1`.

If no hostname is given, an `ArrayIndexOutOfBoundsException` will be thrown. (Checks for this error have been omitted to avoid distracting you from the point of the code.) Provided your system networking is correctly installed, the program will run, connect to the server, and read and output the current date and time. The client will exit after this process is completed. If you used the substitute server `DayServer1`, described above, it will continue to run and may be killed after the client has been run.

TIP The Java networking packages insist that hosts must be known by name, otherwise an `IOException` indicating "Unknown host" will be thrown. It is possible to use numeric addresses in string form, but they must match some entry in the name table used by the network. If a numeric address is not listed in the network's name database, it will be rejected.

If your machine is connected to a network, try giving the names of other machines. Some might be running the Daytime service, especially if they are Unix based. On the Internet some publicly accessible systems run the service, including `www.sgi.com` (at the time of writing).

What It Does

The algorithm of the client is very simple. A socket is created and connected to a named host using the command line argument provided. When the connection is established, an input stream reads characters from the network. One line of input is read and copied to the standard output.

The Details

The constructor arguments describe the machine on which the server is located and the port number on which the service is provided. The conventional port number for the Daytime service is 13, and a constant declaration is made for this in the `DayClient1` class. The name of the server host machine is taken from the first command line argument of the program itself. Typically, for this example, use `localhost` to refer to the current machine.

The constructor documentation states that it might throw an `IOException`. This occurs if the hostname provided is not known or if the machine to which it refers is not offering any service on the specified port. This example concentrates on the working of sockets, rather than the failure modes, so the `main()` method is declared to ignore the problem and throw the exception up to the interpreter. In the event of a problem, therefore, the whole program will simply dump an error report and a stack trace, and then stop.

When the constructor is executed, it waits until the connection is established and then returns the new Socket object. At this point, the socket is ready to use. Anyone who has programmed with the traditional sockets libraries (for example, in C) will know that this is a much simpler mechanism.

After the socket is connected, two streams are obtained from it. One is an OutputStream object and the other is an InputStream object. Both streams are connected to the server via the network. Bytes written to the output stream are sent across the network for the server to read. Similarly, bytes transmitted by the server are readable from the client's input stream. This particular program only reads data from the server; no data is output.

Two methods are provided by the Socket class to allow connection to the streams. They are named getInputStream() and getOutputStream(). Rather than use the basic stream interfaces, you would usually plug an addition layer of filtering into them. In this example, this filtering layer is a combination of a BufferedReader and InputStreamReader object. The constructor for this InputStreamReader object takes the feeder InputStream object as an argument and makes the connection automatically. Similarly, the constructor for the BufferedReader object takes the InputStreamReader object as an argument. The final operation of this example is to read the output of the server, using the in.readLine() method of the BufferedReader class. This method collects one line of characters from the stream, and the resulting String object is printed on the standard output channel using the System.out.println() method.

Java streams are generally closed from the top of the stream. This example is no exception. The BufferedReader object is closed, which closes the underlying input stream in the socket. It is important to be aware that closing either the input stream or output stream of a `Socket` object closes that socket entirely.

Reusing the Example

This example can be used to connect to a number of services similar to the Daytime service. Changing the code so it uses a second command-line argument to define the port number for the connection will allow this code to connect to any service that outputs a single line of text.

Further utility can be added by placing the `readLine()` method call inside a loop so multiple lines are read. This requires an additional modification to recognize the end of the communication. The end-of-file condition is indicated by the `readLine()` method returning a null value in this case. Other variations of `read()` methods return -1.

These modifications have been made, and you can find the resulting code in `javadevhdbk\ch10\GeneralClient.java`.

WARNING In JDK versions up to 1.0.2 there was a bug in the `Socket` class implementation under Windows platforms. The bug affected socket closing, so when a socket was closed at one end of the connection, the other end—which should have read an end-of-file indication—remained unaware of the closing until an `IOException` occurred during a `read()`. Many protocols include a specific high-level command indicating that the connection is to be closed. This behavior is useful because it conveniently sidesteps this particular problem.

A Simple TCP Server

It is important to be able to offer services as well as connect to them. To this end, a `ServerSocket` object is used. This section examines the code for a basic server that achieves the same effect as the Daytime service. This code is basically the same server that was used in the preceding section for systems without the Daytime service. In this version, the port number is different to allow the server to coexist with the standard Daytime service on machines that provide it. To operate with this modified server, the client must also use this different port number.

DayServer2.java

```java
import java.io.*;
import java.net.*;
import java.util.*;

public class DayServer2 {
  private ServerSocket ss;

  public static void main(String args[]) throws IOException {
    DayServer2 d = new DayServer2();
    d.go();
  }

  public void go() throws IOException {
    Socket s = null;
    ss = new ServerSocket(DayClient2.DAYTIME_PORT, 5);
    for (;;) {
      s = ss.accept();
      BufferedWriter out = new BufferedWriter(
        new OutputStreamWriter(s.getOutputStream()));
      out.write("Java Daytime server: " +
        (new Date()).toString() + "\n");
      out.close();
      s.close();
    }
  }
}
```

Running the Program

You'll find the source code for this example in javadevhdbk\ ch10\DayServer2.java. The corresponding bytecode is in the file javadevhdbk\ch10\DayServer2.class.

To run the program, change to the directory `javadevhdbk\ch10` and issue the command:

```
java DayServer2
```

The server will start and run until it is killed. In a different window, run the client `DayClient2` by typing the command:

```
java DayClient2 localhost
```

Provided your system networking is correctly set up, the client will run, connect to the server, and print the time and date message that the server transmits.

> **TIP**
>
> Port numbers up to 1024 are reserved for system services. In the case of Unix systems, a program cannot generally use these ports unless it is run by the superuser `root`. Ports in the range 6000 to 6999 are used for X Windows, and a number of services, such as NFS, use ports in the range 2000 to 2999. For these reasons, port numbers cannot be chosen entirely arbitrarily, but must avoid these ranges and any other services running on the local network.

What It Does

The algorithm of this server is very simple. The `ServerSocket` object is created and associated with the chosen port. For this example, the port number 1313 has been chosen from the available ports. When the socket has been created, the program enters an infinite loop. The body of this loop accepts a single connection, extracts the output stream from the resulting `Socket` object and writes the message onto it in ASCII via a buffered writer and output stream writer. The output message is followed by a newline and closure of both the stream and socket as an indication to the client that the message is completed.

The Details

The first argument to the constructor of the `ServerSocket` class is the port number on which connections will be accepted. The second is called *queue depth* or *backlog*. The significance of the second argument is discussed later.

After the `ServerSocket` object has been created, it is able to accept connections from clients. A connection is made by issuing the `accept()` method call. This method blocks the current thread until a client has made a connection. When the connection has been established, `accept()` returns a new `Socket` object. From this object, in the same way as with the client code, `InputStream` and `OutputStream` objects may be obtained. The handling of these streams is identical to that in the client, as discussed above.

Reusing the Example

This trivial server can be easily modified to provide for a variety of simple circumstances. As with the simple client example, reading the port to use from the command line improves the code's versatility.

More general utility may be achieved by modifying the server to read the data to be transmitted from either the command line, a file, or perhaps even a separate program.

TIP Under Unix systems the standard utility `inetd` provides for all these options from a standard facility. The `inetd` utility can be very useful for debugging.

In `javadevhdbk\ch10\GeneralServer.java` you can find the source and bytecode for a modification that implements the port number control and reads the message to be sent from a file. (That file is also named on the command line.) Be aware that the trivial client example

`DayClient1.java`, which expects a single line, will not work properly with the `GeneralServer.java` example if the file specified contains more than a single line. The `GeneralClient.java` example, however, handles multiple lines correctly.

Bidirectional Communications

In the examples shown so far, only the server has transmitted any data and only the client has read data. If you understand the basics of creating client and server sockets, extracting the streams, and passing data from server to client, programming bidirectional communications is easy. Implementing bidirectional communications in Java is simply a matter of extracting the output stream for the client and the input stream for the server. At a design level, a little more thought is needed, and the next section discusses the key issues.

Server Design and Protocols

The basic construction of a network connection between client and server using Java is quite simple, certainly much simpler than with most other programming interfaces. However, once the connection is established, the ensuing communication must be handled and controlled. The following sections will consider these issues.

Server Types

Many servers can handle more than one connection simultaneously, while others, including the examples discussed in the previous sections, accept a single connection, handle it to completion, and then shut down that connection. Only then can a new connection be made. Servers of this type are often called *sequential*, while those that can handle multiple connections are generally described as *parallel*.

Choosing a Server Type

The choice of server type may be made on the basis of timings. A server that keeps itself busy throughout its connection with a client gains nothing from handling multiple connections simultaneously, which would necessarily result in each of the connections taking longer to complete. On the other hand, a server idle for periods while the connection is established could be used to serve another client.

> **TIP**
>
> The forgoing argument captures the essence of the problem, but the reality is somewhat more complex. What, specifically, is meant by the server being idle? At least three components are involved: the CPU, the disk, and the network interface. A fully laden network interface might appear to constitute a busy server, but while the interface is busy, the CPU or disk might be available to prepare more data for another connection. In general, on a modern operating system that schedules the use of its devices, a parallel server will offer some improvement in overall throughput compared with a sequential one.

The sequential server does offer some advantages, but they are in simplicity of design and coding rather than overall throughput. A parallel server requires a threaded implementation, so its design is more complicated, especially if the data used to support the server must be protected from multiple overlapping accesses. If a situation requires a rapid solution then pragmatism might suggest a sequential server.

The practical implementation of a parallel server will be discussed in a later example.

The Queue Depth or Backlog

New connections can only be established if the server program is waiting in the `accept()` call. When this is not the case, however, clients are not refused connection immediately, nor are they left to time out. Rather, the underlying TCP/IP system will hold a number of new clients in a queue. The size of this queue is determined by the second argument to the ServerSocket class constructor, which is called *queue depth* or *backlog*.

NOTE   The queue depth parameter has been incorrectly documented throughout the JDK sources where it is described as a timeout. This error was propagated into the API documentation until later versions of JDK 1.0.2. Server sockets, in the underlying TCP/IP system do *not* generally have a timeout period. Although many servers will apply a timeout to a connected socket if it remains inactive for a long time, the ServerSocket itself, once created and configured, continues to listen for incoming connections until the controlling program shuts it down. There is, however, a timeout facility available on the accept() method. Using the setSoTimeout() method, it is possible to configure the socket so that an accept() that does not receive a connection in a reasonable time will be abandoned. The Java 1.1 documentation correctly reflects all these issues.

If the queue depth is set to five, which happens to be the maximum value most TCP/IP systems permit, the server socket can have at most five connections waiting to be accepted. Current or past connections are not part of this count. If more clients attempt to connect after five are in the queue, the new connections are ignored. If the queue remains full while the client socket retries, the client socket times out and fails. In a Java client program, this causes the Socket object constructor to fail.

NOTE   The period before a client socket timeout occurs is typically around three to five minutes, although this depends on the platform. A Java Socket that fails to make a connection throws an IOException with the message "Connection timed out."

NOTE Although the usual maximum queue depth is five, individual implementations may vary, and some systems, especially Unix-based ones, allow the limit to be reconfigured. However, it is unlikely that any particular server would benefit from an increase in this figure.

Configuring a server socket with enough queue depth to ensure that new clients are never made to wait will generally allow faster service, as the accept() call will not have to wait. If, on the other hand, clients are made to retry because the TCP/IP queue is full, the retries happen at comparatively long intervals, which will result in a greater average waiting time in the accept() method. In a parallel server design, there is less chance that the queue will be needed, because more connections will be handled directly. By contrast, in a sequential server it becomes more important to avoid forcing the clients to retry, as they are less likely to be able to connect the first time to the server itself in this design.

Protocol Issues

If a client and server are to communicate, they must have a prior agreement on how to do so. This agreement is known as a *protocol*. In some cases a protocol can be trivially simple. The Daytime example is one such protocol. In that service the client and server agree that the client will connect on port 13 and listen for one line of output. In most cases such a degree of simplicity is unacceptable.

A common requirement in a client/server relationship is some form of command/response mechanism: the client connects and "asks a question," and the server then determines the proper response and transmits it. Two major decisions must be made in this regard. One is the data format for the communication and the other is the nature of the relationship between request and response.

Stop-and-Wait and Asynchronous Protocols

In order to maintain control of the interaction between client and server, the design must define when each is permitted to send requests or responses and when each should be listening for replies. In a common design pattern, known as *stop-and-wait* or *lockstep*, one end sends a message that the other end must fully process before replying. While the message is being processed, neither end sends anything. Following the response, nothing is transmitted until more is heard from the original station. Such protocols are rather like "walkie-talkie" radio systems and are simple to implement and easy to debug. Probably for these reasons, they are also very common.

Another possibility exists, however, which might be appropriate in some circumstances. Where both client and server are multithreaded, it might be possible for either or both to perform useful actions during times when a stop-and-wait protocol would restrict them from sending network traffic. If those other activities happen to require network support, then the overall use of bandwidth, and possibly the use of CPU resources at one or both ends, could be improved if the stop-and-wait rule were waived.

If a protocol of this type, called *asynchronous,* is to be implemented, a mechanism must be devised to allow a response to be associated with the message, and perhaps thread, that requested it. A number of mechanisms can be employed. If requests are small, responses can reasonably carry copies of the original requests. In circumstances where the requests are large, a *serial number* mechanism might be more appropriate. Clearly, one feature of asynchronous protocols is inevitable: They are more complex to design than the traditional stop-and-wait approach. They can also prove substantially harder to debug in "live" conditions.

There is a limitation in the Java networking libraries that might encourage the design of asynchronous services. Standard TCP/IP sockets allow the transmission of *out-of-band* (OOB) or urgent data.

Messages of this type can *jump the queue* of data waiting to be handled at the receiving end. The `java.net` package does not, however, provide access to these facilities. In traditional stop-and-wait protocols, the out-of-band data mechanism can be used to provide an "emergency stop" facility. Because OOB transmission is not available, an asynchronous protocol with appropriate handling at each end can provide an alternative way to achieve this functionality. This kind of facility can be useful, for example, if a long database request is being handled and the user decides to abort the work while waiting.

Data Formats

The data that are sent over the network may be carried in a number of different formats. Binary and ASCII have been used for many systems in many languages. Java actually raises two more possibilities: Unicode and Universal Transfer Format (UTF), which are not normally considered in other systems. The advantages and disadvantages of each of these formats are considered below.

ASCII   Many of the familiar TCP/IP services use ASCII-based data formats for their communications, which has a number of advantages. Perhaps the most persuasive is that debugging the system becomes much easier. Given an ASCII-based TCP protocol, it is possible to test the server manually using the standard Telnet client. For example, even without a client, the Daytime server can be tested (on a Unix system) simply by issuing the command

```
$ telnet localhost 13
```

which would output date and time information directly to the screen.

Although the Daytime service is sufficiently simple to hide the need for debugging, it is easy to see that in a more typical and complex server, an ASCII-based format can offer great advantages. Commands can be typed at the keyboard and the responses are displayed directly on the console. It is then easy to verify whether the server is working correctly.

NOTE The section *Interlude: Investigation of the SMTP Protocol* uses the Telnet technique to examine a working network server.

In many operating systems, particularly Unix-based ones, it is possible to construct a server using standard operating system services; for example, a server that records the messages sent to it by clients and transmits the contents of a file to a connecting client.

A second advantage of ASCII is that it is platform independent. It is on the back of this aspect that the bulk of the services that built the Internet were constructed.

The disadvantage of ASCII as the basic encoding mechanism for a network connection is that it is rather inefficient in bandwidth terms. As with the design of server type, where a rapid solution is required, the benefits to the developer may make ASCII the most appropriate choice on pragmatic grounds.

Unicode   Because Java uses Unicode for encoding all characters and strings internally, Unicode is clearly a possible choice for network communication. It does not offer the ease of debugging that ASCII does, and it is not necessarily readily supported in systems that are not written using Java. Unicode is a 16-bit representation, which gives it the range it requires but also means that it needs twice the bandwidth of an equivalent ASCII transmission. However, it might be a good choice if a variety of languages are to be handled using the service.

UTF   The Java libraries offer a third possible variation on the theme of text-based communication. Universal Transfer Format (UTF) can represent all the characters in the Unicode set. The representation uses a variable number of bytes for each character. Seven-bit ASCII is represented unchanged. Eight-bit characters and many of the Unicode set are represented using two bytes, while those characters remaining are represented using three bytes. This means that UTF is able to represent non-ASCII characters as comprehensively as Unicode, but, where the bulk of characters are seven-bit ASCII, UTF does not require additional bandwidth. Also, because of its equivalence with seven-bit ASCII, UTF can make some use of Telnet as a debugging tool.

> **TIP** An additional feature of UTF is that it represents record boundaries using a length prefix field rather than by using normal characters. In ASCII systems it is common to use a carriage return or similar character to indicate record boundaries, but this makes it inconvenient to use the delimiter character itself as data for communication. With UTF, however, each message can contain any character, including carriage return, linefeed, null, and so forth.

Binary   Where nontext data is being communicated, the most compact form of data transmission, excluding compression, normally results from direct use of binary. Of course compressed data is binary anyway. This efficiency, especially in conjunction with compression, can make binary the most appropriate choice when large amounts of data is involved. Even for applications that are not handling large data volume, many small transmissions build up to a large bandwidth demand. Hence it is prudent to consider the bandwidth efficiency of any design.

In most designs one of the major disadvantages of using binary communication over a network link is the difficulties that can arise if dissimilar platforms are involved. Different systems commonly have different data formats in terms of byte order and size and representation of primitive types. Java provides an environment in which data formats are consistent between platforms, both in running programs and flowing over streams. Using the various stream, reader, writer, character-to-byte, and byte-to-character conversion classes, two Java programs can be connected over a network and may communicate in binary without concern about data-type mismatches resulting from different platforms.

> **TIP**
>
> The Java standards do not actually require data representations in memory to be the same between platforms, only that the appearance of data items is the standard. For example, it is permitted to use 128-bit values to represent int items, provided the extra resolution is hidden so overflow and all side effects of representation behave as if 32-bit two's complement is used.

A Parallel Server

This section examines the practical implementation of a parallel server and considers some of the issues involved.

In the single-threaded server, the behavior was to accept a connection and handle it to completion before looping round to another `accept()` call. The essence of the parallel server is that several threads are available for handling connections simultaneously.

One common way to approach the parallel server is to create a new thread each time that `accept()` returns a new connection. Code of the following form would achieve this:

```
for (;;) {
  s = ss.accept();
  handler = new ConnectionHandler(s);
  handlerThread = new Thread(handler);
  handlerThread.start();
}
```

In this hypothetical example, the `ConnectionHandler` class implements the `Runnable` interface so it can be used to construct threads. The `run()` method services the connection. The connected `Socket` object is passed into the `ConnectionHandler` instance via its constructor.

This approach, in its simple form, has a major drawback. Some Java garbage collectors do not reclaim the space allocated to any object of the `Thread` class. Further, because the `Thread` is never considered collectable, data to which the `Thread` has access cannot be collected either. If the approach shown above is implemented, the Java Virtual Machine runs steadily out of memory during operation. Chapter 7, *Threads*, has more details of this problem.

Another weakness of the design shown is that it has no mechanism for limiting the number of simultaneous connections. Although the parallel server is likely to produce a higher overall throughput by keeping CPU, network interface, and disk all busy, too many connections will degrade performance. This can happen because of the overhead of switching contexts and because slow servers might cause their clients to retry their requests. Sending a retry to a server already responding slowly only exacerbates the problem by further increasing its load.

To produce a workable solution that does not suffer from the apparent problems of this model, a modified approach must be taken. A fixed number of threads must be launched, each with access to the same `ServerSocket` object. Each of these threads can then run independently, each calling the `accept()` method when it is able to handle another connection.

MultiServe.java

```java
import java.net.*;
import java.io.*;
import java.util.*;

public class MultiServe implements Runnable {
  private ServerSocket ss;

  public static void main(String args[]) throws Exception {
    MultiServe m = new MultiServe();
    m.go();
  }

  public void go() throws Exception {
    ss = new ServerSocket(DayClient2.DAYTIME_PORT, 5);
```

```
Thread t1 = new Thread(this, "1");
Thread t2 = new Thread(this, "2");
Thread t3 = new Thread(this, "3");
t1.start();
t2.start();
t3.start();
}

public void run() {
  Socket s = null;
  BufferedWriter out = null;
  String myname = Thread.currentThread().getName();

  for (;;) {
    try {
      System.out.println("thread " + myname +
        " about to accept..");
      s = ss.accept();
      System.out.println("thread " + myname +
        " accepted a connection");
      out = new BufferedWriter(
            new OutputStreamWriter(s.getOutputStream()));
      out.write(myname + " " + new Date());
      Thread.sleep(10000);
      out.write("\n");
      out.close();
    }
    catch (Exception e) {
      e.printStackTrace();
    }
  }
}
}
```

Running the Program

The source for this example is located on the CD-ROM in the directory `javadevhdbk\ch10\MultiServe.java`. The bytecode is in the file `javadevhdbk\ch10\MultiServe.class`.

To launch the server, select the directory containing the bytecode and issue the command

```
java MultiServe
```

The server provides a multithreaded version of the `DayServer2`
`.java` example, and hence should be run alongside the `DayClient2`
`.java` example. A number of "logging" messages have been added to the output of the server to allow its behavior to be monitored.

When the server is running, select a different window and run the `DayClient2` program. Ideally, several windows should be used and the client program run nearly simultaneously from each.

Messages are issued as each thread goes into the `accept()` statement and again when that statement returns, at which point the thread will be about to send the message to the client. Each successive running of the client will show that the request is served by the next thread in rotation.

What It Does

This example constructs a `ServerSocket` object connected to the same port as was used by the `DayServer2.java` example. The three threads share this `ServerSocket` object. The behavior of the threads is very similar to that of the `DayServer2.java` example. In a loop, a connection is picked up via the `accept()` call and from the `Socket` object that this returns, the `OutputStream` object is extracted, and the date and time message is transmitted to the client.

The Details

A single object of the `MultiServe` class is created. In this object is a member variable of type `ServerSocket`, which is bound to the port chosen for this service.

The `MultiServe` class implements the `Runnable` interface, which allows it to be used as the basis for construction of the three threads.

Because the threads are all built from the same `Runnable` instance, they share the same instance variables; specifically they all share the same `ServerSocket` object. Inside the `run()` method, each thread has its own local variables for `Socket s`, `BufferedWriter out`, and `String myname`.

NOTE It might seem wasteful to create multiple threads before the server's load warrants it. Once created, however, a thread should not be destroyed if there is any chance that it might be needed again. Further, there is a significant CPU overhead to creating a new thread (some operating systems are very poor in this area), and it is generally advantageous to do all this activity once at program startup. Creating a predetermined number of threads in this way is quite common practice in server design, and, if necessary, the number of threads can be controlled with a command line argument, allowing tuning for each installation. If you really need a variable number of threads, you can use the `setSoTimeout()` method to cause `accept()` calls to timeout if they do not receive connections in a reasonable time. This approach would allow you to determine a suitable moment for reducing the number of threads.

The body of the `run()` method determines the behavior of the thread. In this case, this is a loop virtually identical to that which was at the heart of the single-threaded `DayServer2.java` example. A number of logging messages have been added. Each thread prints a message just before it enters the `accept()` method and immediately on its return from that method.

Simulating Long Service Time

This Daytime service provided by `MultiServe.java` does not benefit particularly from a threaded server implementation because the time taken to handle the service is very small. For this reason, a deliberate delay has been introduced into the output. After the main date and time information is sent, the thread is sent to sleep for 10 seconds before it is able to complete the transmission by sending a newline. This delay is deliberately very long to allow for typing the client command in separate windows. Quick typing should prove that the server can in fact handle a new connection before the old one has been completed.

Benefits of This Approach

This approach solves the difficulties of the earlier example server. Multiple simultaneous connections are supported but are limited by the number of threads constructed. Further, because each of the threads is reused, rather than being wasted after handling a single connection, the problems of memory leakage are avoided. The design is not complex either, suggesting that single-threaded servers need only be used for the most basic situations or in circumstances where the data set supporting the server must be protected from concurrent accesses.

Inside the *accept()* Method

Sharing one `ServerSocket` object directly is possible because the implementation of the `accept()` method protects the underlying system from multiple simultaneous access. The Java packages are generally described as *thread-safe*. In the current JDK, the `accept()` method calls a "sister" `accept()` method in the `SocketImpl` class. That method is marked as `synchronized`, which prevents multiple threads from entering the body of the method simultaneously.

Reusing the Code

The overall design of this server can be readily adapted to provide a multithreaded server for any application. A real application should not have the `sleep()` call, as this serves only to demonstrate how the threaded server behaves under load. The number of threads should be controlled via a command-line argument, perhaps with some default built in, to allow balancing resource usage against anticipated load. Remember that as the number of threads increases, the servers throughput increases to a point and then falls off again. Experiment is the only reliable guide for the optimum number of threads in any application on any particular platform. Such experiments should be carried out under live conditions, or the results might be invalid.

Preexisting Protocols

There are many preexisting network services that are commonly available on TCP/IP networks. It is, therefore, appropriate to consider the implications of writing Java code to interface with them.

In general, Java programs for connecting to, or providing, predefined network services are simpler than the equivalent programs written using other languages and libraries. Provided a proper definition of the protocol is available, all that remains is to design and implement code to handle it.

Many of the "core" TCP/IP services use ASCII-based protocols and a stop-and-wait approach to command and response. These features tend to simplify the job of debugging network code regardless of the language or libraries used. This section will discuss the implementation of a basic Java client for the Internet mail service SMTP.

SMTP Mail

The standard protocol used for transporting e-mail over TCP/IP networks is the Simple Mail Transport Protocol (SMTP). Other protocols are used, especially for communication with single-user machines. The Post Office Protocol (POP) is one example.

In common with most of the core TCP/IP services, SMTP uses an ASCII command language. It is instructive to connect to a mail server using Telnet. In this way an insight can be gained into the workings of the protocol. SMTP uses a variety of simple commands, and most servers will actually offer a level of interactive help. This feature makes "manual" operation of the mail service quite easy.

Interlude: Investigation of the SMTP Protocol

If you are familiar with the SMTP protocol, you can safely skip this section and go directly to the description of a simple SMTP client. If not, and you can get access to an SMTP server and a Telnet client, you might find it useful to take a few minutes to investigate its operation.

Connect your Telnet client to the SMTP server using port 25. This will typically mean using one of the following two commands:

```
telnet <serverhost> 25
```

or

```
telnet <serverhost> SMTP
```

Substitute the name of the machine running your SMTP server in place of `<serverhost>`. If the server is running on the machine you are working at, you can use the name `localhost`. Note that 25 is the standard port number of the SMTP protocol as defined by RFC 821.

> **NOTE** The SMTP protocol, like that of Telnet, is defined in RFC documents. A copy of RFCs 821 and 822, the core description of SMTP, are located on the CD-ROM in the files `javadevhdbk\rfcs\rfc821.txt` and `javadevhdbk\rfcs\rfc822.txt`.

After the Telnet client connects, you will see the SMTP server "sign on." Connecting to a system called `freddy.helpful.org` might result in the following output:

```
220 freddy.helpful.org Sendmail SMI-8.6/SMI-SVR4 ready at Wed,
21 Aug 1996 23:56:33 -0100
```

If you then type either **help** or a question mark, followed by return, you should see a list of the commands that the server accepts. Be aware that some servers, especially non-Unix or enhanced-security versions, might not issue help messages. The output might be similar to this:

```
214-Commands:
214- HELO   MAIL   RCPT   DATA   RSET
214- NOOP   QUIT   HELP   VRFY   EXPN
214-For more info use "HELP <topic>".
```

Notice that all the responses from the server start with a three-digit code. These codes describe the status, successful or otherwise, of the command to which the server is responding. Codes starting with a 2 indicate successful completion, while codes starting with a 3 indicate "success so far" of a command that is not yet completed. Other codes indicate difficulties. The full specification is given in the RFCs.

To send a mail message, a signon is first required. The client must introduce itself by using the command HELO. If your local machine is called `talkative`, your signon would be:

```
HELO talkative
```

Note that some security-conscious servers might take the trouble to check the address you gave against your real address, but in general, they will sign the message as being from whatever address the client machine claims.

In response to the client signon, the server will respond. This response generally takes a very friendly format:

```
Hello, talkative, pleased to meet you…
```

After signon, to send a mail message, the SMTP server must be provided with the following three pieces of data:

- The name of the sender
- The name of the recipient
- The body of the message

Each of these items is supplied with a particular command. A new message is introduced by the command MAIL FROM: *sendername*.

Again the server will believe whatever you tell it. This means that you can reasonably expect to be able send mail that shows a name completely different from the real sender's. Mail from `cupid@ olympus.com` or `president@whitehouse.gov` does not necessarily mean that mysterious or powerful forces are trying to tell you something.

The recipient of the message is specified using the `RCPT TO: recipient`. In this case, if the specified recipient is local to the server, the server will attempt to verify that the destination is correct and will issue an error message if it is not.

Finally, the text of the message is sent. The command `DATA` is used to introduce the message text. The message should be sent as lines of text. To indicate that the text has been completed, a single period character (.) should be entered as the only character on a line.

WARNING The definition of SMTP suggests that lines in mail messages should not exceed "about 1,000 characters." This is because long lines might overflow buffers in some implementations. Special error codes should be returned in such conditions, but it is easier to keep lines short than to handle the errors.

NOTE The SMTP protocol is a good example of an ASCII-based stop-and-wait protocol. At each stage, only one machine is listening while the other is allowed to transmit. When the transmission is complete, the other machine is expected to send.

A transcript of a typical, if trivial and fictional, SMTP session is shown below.

```
$ telnet freddy.helpful.org 25
Trying 1.2.3.4...
Connected to freddy.helpful.org.
```

```
Escape character is '^]'.
220 freddy.helpful.org Sendmail V7 ready at Wed, 21 Aug 1996 23:56:33 -0100
helo topsecret.whitehouse.gov
250 freddy.helpful.org Hello topsecret.whitehouse.gov, pleased to meet you
help
214-Commands:
214- HELO  MAIL  RCPT  DATA  RSET
214- NOOP  QUIT  HELP  VRFY  EXPN
214-For more info use "HELP <topic>".
214-smtp
214-For local information contact postmaster at this site.
214 End of HELP info
mail from: president@whitehouse.gov
250 president@whitehouse.gov... Sender ok
rcpt to: simon
250 simon... Recipient ok
data
354 Enter mail, end with "." on a line by itself
Your country needs you! Please report for official
duty tomorrow 5:15am sharp in the oval office.

BC
.
250 ACSE759 Message accepted for delivery
quit
221 freddy.helpful.org closing connection
Connection closed by foreign host.
$
```

A Simple SMTP Mail Client

The SMTP mail client provides for sending, not receiving, mail. A server would be required to receive mail. The mailto protocol type is supported in JDK 1.1. The source of the SMTP mail client is as follows:

SMTP.java

```
import java.net.*;
import java.io.*;
```

```
public class SMTP {
  private String message;
  private String localMachine;
  private String senderName;
  private String recipient;
  private boolean valid_and_unsent = false;

  private BufferedReader in;
  private BufferedWriter out;

  // class constants
  public static final int SMTP_PORT = 25;
  private static final boolean logging = true;

  public SMTP() {
  }

  public SMTP(String sender) {
    int indexOfAtSign = sender.indexOf('@');
    if (indexOfAtSign < 0) {
      throw new RuntimeException("Malformed sender address." +
        " Need full user@host format");
    }
    this.senderName = sender.substring(0, indexOfAtSign);
    this.localMachine = sender.substring(indexOfAtSign + 1);
  }

  public SMTP(String sender, String recipient, String message) {
    this(sender);
    setMessage(recipient, message);
  }

  public void setMessage(String recipient, String message) {
    this.recipient = recipient;
    this.message = message;
    valid_and_unsent = true;
  }

  public void send() throws IOException {
    if (!valid_and_unsent) {
      throw new RuntimeException("Attempt to send incomplete message," +
        " or send message twice");
    }
```

```java
      // if this message is legitimate, continue to extract
      // the remote machine name
      int indexOfAtSign = recipient.indexOf('@');
      if (indexOfAtSign < 0) {
        throw new RuntimeException("Malformed recipient address." +
          " Need full user@host format");
      }
      String destinationMachine = recipient.substring(indexOfAtSign + 1);

      // attempt to make the connection, this might throw an exception
      Socket s = new Socket(destinationMachine, SMTP_PORT);
      in = new BufferedReader(
            new InputStreamReader(s.getInputStream(),"8859_1"));
      out = new BufferedWriter(
            new OutputStreamWriter(s.getOutputStream(),"8859_1"));
      String response;

      // discard signon message, introduce ourselves, and discard reply
      response = hear();
      say("HELO " + localMachine + "\n");
      response = hear();

      say("MAIL FROM: " + senderName + "\n");
      response = hear();
      say("RCPT TO: " + recipient + "\n");
      response = hear();
      say("DATA\n");
      response = hear();
      say(message + "\n.\n");
      response = hear();
      say("QUIT\n");

      // now close down the connection..
      s.close();
  }

  private void say(String toSay) throws IOException {
    out.write(toSay);
    out.flush();
    if (logging) {
      System.out.println(toSay);
    }
  }
}
```

```java
private String hear() throws IOException {
  String inString = in.readLine();
  if ("23".indexOf(inString.charAt(0)) < 0) {
    throw new IOException("SMTP problem: " + inString);
  }
  if (logging) {
    System.out.println(inString);
  }
  return inString;
}

public static void main(String args[]) throws Exception {
  BufferedReader in = new BufferedReader(
                          new InputStreamReader(System.in));
  System.out.print("Your address: ");
  System.out.flush();
  String sender = in.readLine();
  System.out.print("Recipient address: ");
  System.out.flush();
  String recipient = in.readLine();
  String message = "";
  String part;
  System.out.println("Message, end with '.' by itself:");
  for (;;) {
    part = in.readLine();
    if ((part == null) || part.equals(".")) {
      break;
    }
    message += part + "\n";
  }
  SMTP mailer = new SMTP(sender, recipient, message);
  mailer.send();
}
}
```

Running the Program

The source code for this example is located on the CD-ROM in the directory `javadevhdbk\ch10\SMTP.java`. The corresponding bytecode is in the file `javadevhdbk\ch10\SMTP.class`.

To run this program, you will require network access to an SMTP server and knowledge of at least one valid mail account that is accessible to that server. Ideally, the account should be your own, so you can see the results of the mail you send.

Start the mail client by typing

```
java SMTP
```

When the program starts, it prompts for the sender's username and that of the recipient. These should be given in the form `user@machine`. Be sure to give the SMTP server name, not the mail domain if these are different. When both these have been entered, the program prompts for the body of the message. Enter text a line at a time—remembering that there are no editing facilities beyond those of the delete key—and when you have finished the message, type a single period on a line by itself.

When all the input has been given, the program will connect to the SMTP server on the recipient's machine and send the message. The whole protocol transaction will be copied to the standard output so you can see it progress.

NOTE Normally, mail is not sent to a specific machine but to a mail domain. Hence, in the mail address `simon@helpful.org` it is unlikely that `helpful.org` is an actual machine; instead, the DNS name service translates it into a number of machines that act as mailboxes for that domain.

What It Does

The `main()` method of the `SMTP` class is really a test harness. It collects the address information of the sender and recipient and then the body of the message. Given these, a new object of the `SMTP` class is constructed. The method `send()` is then invoked on that object, which goes through the basic SMTP protocol to deliver the message.

The Details

In the SMTP protocol, the client and server remain in *lockstep*. That is, when the connection is established the server is expected to transmit first and the client and server then proceed by taking turns. After that phase has been completed and the receiver has actually read the contents of the buffers, the "right to transmit" changes to the other party. In this approach, unexpected data is not possible, which simplifies the protocol because a main control loop can simply operate by receiving an input, generating the required output, and so forth.

If all is well, the SMTP responses are simply courtesy acknowledgments. However, there are two reasons that the client must read the text of the server's response. First, server implementations sometimes refuse to proceed if their responses have not been read. Perhaps more importantly for a practical mail client, however, the responses carry a numeric status code at the beginning of the line. Numbers starting with a 2 indicate a successful completion, and numbers beginning with a 3 indicate a successful intermediate response, implying "OK so far, go ahead and finish off." Other values indicate some kind of difficulty; for example, if the mail recipient is described as a local user of the server but is not known by the server, the response will be error code 550. This client simply checks that a 2 or 3 starts the response line and throws an exception on everything else. More details of the error status codes are provided in the RFCs on the CD-ROM.

The work of the client is to collect the message data and addresses for recipient and sender. In a production program, the sender's name would be taken from a parameter file and a menu entry would be offered to allow modification of this file. Non-Java systems might use an environment variable, but environment variables are not useful in Java because they are not platform independent and hence are not supported. In this example, for simplicity, the sender's name is also typed in.

TIP Java provides properties that would be entirely suitable as a means of defining the sender's name. The facilities of the `Properties` class are described in Chapter 5, *Portability Issues*.

The SMTP class requires the specification of sender and recipient addresses in `user@hostname` format, and the destination machine address is extracted from that form. The message can be provided as part of the constructor if preferred. When both addresses and a message have been supplied, the `send()` method can be invoked to handle the protocol transfer.

Before making the connection, the recipient address must be split into a machine name and a username. The machine name is then used to connect the client to the server, and the protocol messages are generated in the proper sequence by the body of the `send()` method.

To perform the transfer, two private methods, `say()` and `hear()`, are used. These handle the logging of the transactions. The `hear()` method checks the SMTP return status to determine if any problems have arisen and throws an `IOException` when trouble occurs. To aid in determining the problem, the response that contained the error status is attached, in `String` form, to the exception that is thrown.

NOTE

The `InputStreamReader` and `OutputStreamWriter` objects in the above example are created using an explicit converter to handle the translation between Unicode and byte-character encodings to ensure that the encoding of characters used in the network transactions is fixed. Normally, creating an `InputStreamReader` uses the local default conversion; naturally, this is platform dependent. To avoid this platform dependency, the `SMTP.java` example makes explicit requests to convert between Unicode and ISO 8859-1 encoding. A list of the string names of converters that are supported in Java is provided in the documentation of the `native2ascii` utility.

TIP

The `SMTP` class includes a constant declaration called *logging*. This is set to true in the source, so the class will echo the protocol exchanges to `System.out`. The Java compiler optimizes conditional blocks of code if it sees a constant expression in the condition. Hence, this construction can be used to give conditional compilation, very similarly to the use of `#ifdef` or `#if defined()` in a C or C++ preprocessor.

To provide a useful, self-contained demonstration, the `SMTP` class also contains a `main()` method. If the program is invoked directly, it will prompt for user and destination addresses and a message body. When these have been entered, an instance of the `SMTP` class is constructed, and the message is sent.

Reusing the Code

In general the mail domain name part of an e-mail address is not necessarily a machine name. The Domain Name System provides for the use of MX, or mail-exchanger, records, which provides a means of mapping a single domain name onto several different physical machines. Ideally, the `SMTP` class should be modified to use the MX service and connect to the correct SMTP server accordingly.

Unfortunately, there is no provision for MX record lookup in the `java.net` package at the time of writing.

As an alternative to MX record usage, the client can connect to an intermediate SMTP server and let that system do the work. To do so, the name of the intermediate server must be made available to the SMTP class object, which can be done with a command line argument or a property. Once correctly set up, a property would be less effort for the user.

WARNING An applet is only able to connect to its originating host; therefore, MX lookup facilities would be useless in these conditions. A suitably configured SMTP server on the host that originates the applet should be used to handle mail forwarding as just described.

If desired, it is possible to access DNS MX records from an application by handling the DNS protocol directly. DNS is a UDP-based service; using UDP from Java is described later in this chapter.

To build a serious mail client program, a "proper" user interface should be constructed to allow sensible input of the message, along with some editing facilities. The `java.awt.TextArea` class would provide a good basis for this.

The logging of the protocol transaction to the standard output should be disabled by changing the value of the `public static final boolean` called `logging` to `false` and recompiling.

The URL Class

The URL is a crucial part of the World Wide Web, facilitating navigation for both human and machine alike. The `java.net` package includes two key classes specifically for working with URLs. The classes are called `URL` and `URLConnection`. The following sections discusses these classes.

The most fundamental network facility provided by the `URL` class is the ability to read, as stream, the data to which that `URL` refers. An instance of the `URL` class can be created using a text string that represents the URL; for example,

```
URL theUrl = new URL("http://www.sun.com/");
```

> **NOTE**
>
> This constructor throws an `IOException` if the URL text is malformed, or if the protocol part, `http` in this case, is not known to the system. Because of the validity checks imposed by the compiler, an `IOException` must be either handled via a `try {}` `catch(){}` block, or the calling method must be declared to pass the exception on.

Once the `URL` is constructed, the `openStream()` method provides a simple mechanism for reading the data that the `URL` describes, allowing the input to be handled by any of the standard `InputStream` class facilities, including the chaining of other types of input stream or reader, such as the `DataInputStream` or `InputStreamReader` classes. Other mechanisms permit writing to the server for services such as CGI POST.

Reading a Data Stream from a URL

This section describes an example of the use of the `openStream()` method to load a file over http. This could be a classfile, image, or any other data offered on a Web server. The contents of the URL will be saved to a disk file so they are available locally. This would allow you, for example, to take an applet from a remote site and place it onto your own server without having to obtain the source for it.

WARNING Java code loaded from the local system will be treated as trusted and will bypass all the normal security restrictions. Any other type of executable will also be dangerous, just as if an unknown program is loaded from an FTP site.

GetURL.java

```java
import java.io.*;
import java.net.*;


public class GetURL {
  public static void main(String args[]) {
    if (args.length < 1) {
      System.err.println("Usage: java GetURL <URL>...");
      System.exit(1);
    }
    else {
      for (int i = 0; i < args.length; i++) {
        getURL(args[i]);
      }
    }
  }

  private static void getURL(String urlname) {
    URL url = null;
    InputStream urlstream = null;
    byte [] returned;
    try {
      url = new URL(urlname);
    }
    catch (Exception e) {
      System.err.println("URL " + urlname + " failed, reason is:");
      System.err.println(e.toString());
      return;
    }

    try {
      urlstream = url.openStream();
```

```
      }
      catch (Exception e) {
        System.err.println("URL " + urlname + " failed open, reason is:");
        System.err.println(e.toString());
        return;
      }

      returned = getURLFile(urlstream);

      String filename = (url.getFile()).replace('/', File.separatorChar);
      File f1 = new File(filename);
      filename = f1.getName();
      FileOutputStream f = null;
      try {
        f = new FileOutputStream(filename);

        f.write(returned);
        f.close();
      }
      catch (Exception e) {
        System.err.println("Error handling output file: " + filename);
        return;
      }
  }

  private static byte [] getURLFile(InputStream s) {
    byte [] buffer = new byte [0];
    byte [] chunk = new byte [4096];
    int count;

    try {
      while ((count = s.read(chunk)) >= 0) {
        byte [] t = new byte [buffer.length + count];
        System.arraycopy(buffer, 0, t, 0, buffer.length);
        System.arraycopy(chunk, 0, t, buffer.length,count);
        buffer = t;
      }
    }
    catch (Exception e) {
      System.err.println("Error during reading:" + e);
    }
```

```
    return buffer;
  }
}
```

Running the Program

The source code for this example is located on the CD-ROM in the directory `javadevhdbk\ch10\GetURL.java`. The corresponding bytecode is in the file `javadevhdbk\ch10\GetURL.class`.

To run the program it is not necessary to have a network connection. If required, a `file://` URL may be used. The contents of the URL are not important in themselves but should be something recognizable so when they are copied to the local disk, it will be possible to determine that they have arrived correctly. To run the example, issue the command

```
java GetURL <chosen-URL>
```

The program will start, connect to the URL using the specified protocol, and fetch the data. When the data have been fully loaded, they are written to the disk. The output is placed in a file with the same name as the filename part of the original URL.

What It Does

For each command-line argument, the main method invokes the `getURL()` method. This method constructs a URL from the string supplied by the user and opens the connection to it. When the connection is opened, the data is read into a buffer and then saved to disk.

The Details

Provided the URL constructor is successful, the result is used to execute the method `openStream()`. This method returns an instance of the `InputStream` class from which the data may be read directly. In this example, the resulting stream is passed to the private method `getURLFile()`, which collects data in a buffer. Data is read in chunks of up to 4KB, and each chunk is coalesced with the data that have already been loaded to produce a single larger array. This is done with the two calls to `System.arraycopy()`, which move both the old and new data into the newly allocated buffer.

```
System.arraycopy(buffer, 0, t, 0, buffer.length);
System.arraycopy(chunk, 0, t, buffer.length,count);
```

When loading is completed, the resulting array of bytes is returned by `getURLFile()` to its caller, which then saves the bytes to the disk file.

<table>
<tr><td>**TIP**</td><td>Some servers, for some protocols, can tell the client how much data is to be sent. This information is available in Java if a two-stage process is used to read the URL. First, use the `openConnection()` method of the URL class. This returns an instance of a `URLConnection`. On the `URLConnection` object, use the `getContentLength()` method. To obtain the data from the `URLConnection`, a method called `getInputStream()` is provided. Using the `URLConnection` allows other additional information, such as content type, to be queried.</td></tr>
</table>

The constructor of the URL object might fail if the URL is badly formed. A badly formed URL is reported if some essential part of the URL—such as the ://—is missing or if the protocol specified—FTP, for example—is not known to the running Java system.

If the specified URL is invalid at the server, or the server is not providing a requested service, the `openStream()` call will fail.

<table>
<tr><td>**TIP**</td><td>This example does not use readers or byte-to-character conversion because the data is pure binary bytes, and conversion to Unicode text would be inappropriate and would damage the data.</td></tr>
</table>

Reusing the Code

The `openStream()` method is very easy to use and should not present difficulties for incorporation into other programs. The bulk of this particular piece of example code is dedicated to the file and buffer handling. As such this example might be useful for copying data from Internet servers directly to a disk file, but it is unlikely to form the basis for direct extension into a larger utility.

TIP One aspect that might warrant a moment of attention if the technique is unfamiliar is the use of `System.arraycopy()` and the two buffers in the `getURLFile()` method. The smaller buffer is used to read sizable chunks of data at a time. Each time the `read()` method returns, a new buffer is created that is large enough for all the data so far loaded. The holding buffer is copied to this new buffer and then the newly read data is copied in. Finally, the new buffer becomes the holding buffer.

Further Information

In the next sections, *Handling URL Contents* and *Connecting to CGI*, and also in Chapter 13, *Content and Protocol Handlers*, other techniques are introduced to allow more detailed control over the handing of URLs.

Handling URL Contents

When an HTTP server transmits the data for a URL, it first sends some header information. This information might, but does not always, include the amount of data that is to be sent, a validity time for the data (a kind of electronic sell-by date intended to allow the server a chance to reduce the time for which the client caches the information), and a content type. The content type is expressed as a MIME type string and can be used to allow a Java program, particularly a browser, to handle the data appropriately and automatically.

NOTE   MIME type strings are a hierarchical description of a particular content. The hierarchy is described rather like a directory structure. An HTML document has a MIME type string of `text/html`. Similarly, plain, unformatted text has a type string of `text/plain`. Another hierarchy is used for images, so `image/gif` describes an image file in `.gif` format, while `image/xpm` describes an image in X Windows pixmap form. Unfortunately, in many cases a server will report a MIME type of `content/unknown`, which implies that it does not know what the content type of the document is. Under these conditions, the client is left to guess based on the filename and the actual contents of the data stream. Java's content handling has some hard-coded guesses built in for this purpose.

Content handling in Java is achieved via the URL class method called `getContent()`. When invoked, this method first makes the connection to the server, then fetches the header information to find the MIME content type. If the MIME specification is missing or unknown, then ad-hoc techniques are used to make a guess. Based on this content type, `getContent()` then looks for an appropriate subclass of `ContentHandler`. This `ContentHandler` object is invoked to load the actual data and create a Java object that represents it. In this way, if a URL refers to an image stored in a `.jpeg` file, the content type would be `image/jpeg`. Provided a content handler is available for this, it constructs an object of some subclass of `java.awt.ImageProducer` and returns this object to its caller.

The following example demonstrates loading content from a URL using the `getContent()` method. When an image is fetched in this way, the `getContent()` method returns an object that is a subclass of `ImageProducer`. Given such an object, it is a simple matter to create an `Image`, as is required for display in AWT, using the `createImage()` method in the `Toolkit` class. The `Toolkit` object may be obtained by using `getDefaultToolkit()`, which is a static method in the `Toolkit` class, or directly from any visible AWT Component using the `getToolkit()` method.

GetImage.java

```
import java.awt.*;
import java.awt.image.*;
import java.net.*;

class myCanvas extends Canvas {
  Image i;

  public myCanvas(Image i) {
    this.i = i;
  }

  public void paint(Graphics g) {
    g.drawImage(i, 0, 0, this);
  }
}

public class GetImage {
  String name;
  Frame f;
  Image i;
  myCanvas c;
  MediaTracker m;
  Toolkit t = Toolkit.getDefaultToolkit();

  public static void main(String args[]) {
    if (args.length != 1) {
      System.out.println("Usage: java GetImage <image-URL>");
      System.exit(1);
    }
    GetImage that = new GetImage(args[0]);
    that.go();
  }

  public GetImage(String name) {
    this.name = name;
  }

  public void go() {
    Object o = null;
```

```
f = new Frame("Image from " + name);
URL source = null;
URLConnection con = null;

try {
  source = new URL(name);
  o = source.getContent();
}
catch (Exception e) {
  System.out.println("Problem with URL " + source);
  e.printStackTrace(System.out);
  System.exit(2);
}

if (o instanceof ImageProducer) {
  i = t.createImage((ImageProducer)o);
}
else {
  System.out.println("URL " + source +
                        " didn't give me an ImageProducer");
  System.out.println("but a " + o.getClass().getName() + " instead");
  System.exit(3);
}

c = new myCanvas(i);
m = new MediaTracker(c);
m.addImage(i, 0);
try {
  m.waitForAll();
}
catch (Exception e) { /* do nothing */ }

f.add("Center", c);
c.resize(i.getWidth(c), i.getHeight(c));
f.pack();
f.setVisible(true);
  }
}
```

Running the Program

The source code for this example is located on the CD-ROM in the directory `javadevhdbk\ch10\GetImage.java`. The corresponding bytecode is in the directory `javadevhdbk\ch10\GetImage.java`.

To run the program it is not necessary to have a network connection. If required, a `file://` URL may be used. The contents of the file should be an image in a format that Java understands. The standard release can handle GIF, JPEG, and XBM. To run the class, issue the command

```
java GetImage <image-URL>
```

The program will start, connect to the URL using the specified protocol, and load the image. When the load is completed the resulting image is displayed in a window.

What It Does

This example exploits the built-in handling of image file types. The command line should have a single argument that is taken to be a URL. The program connects to the URL and loads the image. An auxiliary class provides a means of displaying the resulting `Image` object so it can recover from being obscured by other windows.

The Details

The previous example used the URL method `openStream()` to access the data from a URL. In this example, the data is handled automatically, based on its type. For this example to work, the type must be an image in a supported format.

The automatic content handling is performed via the URL method `getContent()`. This method establishes the protocol connection and determines the content type. Content type should ideally be reported by the HTTP server as one of the header fields, but in some cases, especially those where a non-`http://` URL is used, the type may have to be guessed.

When the content type is determined, it is used to select a `ContentHandler` object. The job of a content handler is to load the data and interpret them. The return value of the content handler should be some object that represents the content of the URL. In the case of an image file, the return from the content handler is an instance of the class `ImageProducer`. From this an `Image` object can be created, which in turn can be displayed.

In this example, the content handler's return type is checked at runtime. The `instanceof` method is applied to determine if an `ImageProducer` has indeed been returned. If some other type is found, this program issues an error message, reporting the actual class of the object found.

NOTE   Although Java—and more specifically the HotJava browser—come equipped with some content handlers, there are many content types in use, and new types are added regularly. For this reason, the Java system allows you to add new content handlers. Chapter 13, *Content and Protocol Handlers*, discusses writing and installing content handlers. Most notable is the omission of audio content handling from the core `java api`. The audio handlers are part of the `sun.audio` classes, used by HotJava and the appletviewer.

Reusing the Code

As with the previous example, this code serves mainly to demonstrate the use of a particular method, in this case, `getContent()`. As a result, the body of the code is not of real use as the basis of extension. In some conditions, the support class `myCanvas` might be useful, if a static image is to be displayed and the immediately enclosing part of the GUI is not directly suited to the task of refreshing the image.

Connecting to CGI

In addition to handling conventional noninteractive content types, the URL class can be used to handle CGI connections.

> **TIP**
>
> Common Gateway Interface (CGI) is a well-established mechanism for generating customized output for a Web page. The request carries user originated data with it, and the Web server runs a program to interpret the data and produce a new dynamically created HTML page in response.

CGI requests are made using URLs but come in two varieties. The first form simply encodes the request into the URL text, known as a GET request, and can be handled directly using little more than a URL and the `openStream()` method.

The GET method, although simple, has some technical difficulties. For example, the security of the Web server can be compromised by a request that has a very long argument list. Because of these difficulties an alternative mechanism, called POST, is generally preferred for new CGI programs.

In the POST mechanism, the URL is used to initiate the connection, but then two streams are used. One is an output stream that transmits the parameters to the Web server, while the other is the traditional input stream used to read the results of the request.

Both these forms of CGI are directly supported by Java, and both are simple to implement. The GET mechanism introduces some ground that is common to both approaches and will be described first.

CGI GET Example

In practical use, handling CGI would normally expect the data returned from the server to be presented to the user in an Applet.

This example, for simplicity, will simply dump the output to the standard output channel.

The following is the source:

CGIGet.java

```java
import java.net.*;
import java.io.*;

public class CGIGet {
  public static void main(String args[]) {
    if (args.length <= 1) {
      System.err.println("Usage: java CGIGet <baseURL> <CGI argument>...");
      System.exit(1);
    }

    String fullURL = args[0];
    String arguments = args[1];
    for (int i = 2; i < args.length; i++) {
      arguments += " " + args[i];
    }
    arguments = URLEncoder.encode(arguments);
    fullURL += "?" + arguments;
    InputStream theData = null;

    URL u = null;
    URLConnection uc = null;
    try {
      u = new URL(fullURL);
      uc = u.openConnection();
      theData = uc.getInputStream();
    }
    catch (Exception e) {
      System.err.println("Trouble with URL " + fullURL + " " + e);
      System.exit(1);
    }

    String contentType = uc.getContentType();
    if (contentType.toLowerCase().startsWith("text")) {
```

```
      BufferedReader in = new BufferedReader(
                          new InputStreamReader(theData));
      String line;
      try {
        while ((line = in.readLine()) != null) {
          System.out.println(line);
        }
      }
      catch (IOException e) {
        System.err.println("Trouble with IO" + e);
        System.exit(2);
      }
    }
    else {
      System.out.println("This program only handles text responses");
      System.out.println("I got " + contentType);
    }
  }
}
```

Running the Program

This program requires access to a live network and an HTTP server. Further, the server must offer some GET-type CGI facility. The source is on the CD-ROM in the directory `javadevhdbk\ch10\CGIGet.java`. The corresponding bytecode is in the directory `javadevhdbk\ch10\CGIGet.class`.

Determine the URL of the CGI program you wish to execute and the parameters that it requires. Then issue the command

```
java CGIGet <baseURL> <otherParameters>…
```

Multiple parameters are accepted, but at least one must be provided. When the connection is made, the response type is checked. If a text response is received from the server, then that response will be dumped to the standard output channel. If the response is not text of some sort, a message is issued reporting the difficulty and the reported MIME content type.

What It Does

Each parameter that is supplied is joined using spaces, and the result is converted into the external form required for CGI. This is then joined to the base URL using the ? symbol. Given the resulting composite URL, a stream is opened to collect the server's response. As characters are read from this stream they are copied to the standard output.

The Details

Two aspects of this code are new: the first is the conversion of the URL to the external form, the second is the determination of the content type.

This conversion is handled by the method `encode()`, which is the only method of the `URLEncoder` class. The external form of a URL makes a simple translation designed to minimize the character set used by the transfer and thereby to prevent intermediate programs interpreting characters as special and altering them. Unix shells, for example, would coalesce multiple spaces and treat asterisks and others as wildcard specifications to be expanded.

TIP The conversion process changes spaces to +. Other nonalphanumeric characters are translated to `%xx`, where *xx* represents the hexadecimal ASCII value of the character to be sent.

The content type is determined simply by using the `getContentType()` method on the `URLConnection` object, which returns the MIME type string that the server reported as part of the headers sent as part of an HTTP response.

CGI POST Example

As with the CGI GET example, no effort will be made to handle the data returned from the server, but instead, the standard output will be used.

The source code is as follows:

CGIPost.java

```java
import java.net.*;
import java.io.*;

public class CGIPost {
  public static void main(String args[]) {
    if (args.length <= 1) {
      System.err.println("Usage: java GCIPost
        <baseURL> <GCI argument>...");
      System.exit(1);
    }

    String fullURL = args[0];

    URLConnection conn = null;
    OutputStream theControl = null;
    InputStream theData = null;

    URL u = null;
    try {
      u = new URL(fullURL);
      conn = u.openConnection();
      conn.setDoOutput(true);
      theControl = conn.getOutputStream();
    }
    catch (Exception e) {
      System.err.println("Trouble with URL " + fullURL + " " + e);
      System.exit(1);
    }

    try {
      BufferedWriter out = new BufferedWriter(
                        new OutputStreamWriter(theControl));
```

```
        String encoded = null;
        for (int i = 1; i < args.length; i++) {
          encoded = URLEncoder.encode(args[i]);
          out.write(encoded + "\n");
        }
        out.close();
        theData = conn.getInputStream();

        String contentType = conn.getContentType();
        if (contentType.toLowerCase().startsWith("text")) {
          BufferedReader in = new BufferedReader(
                            new InputStreamReader(theData));
          String line;
          while ((line = in.readLine()) != null) {
            System.out.println(line);
          }
        }
        else {
          System.out.println("This program only handles
            text responses");
          System.out.println("I got " + contentType);
        }
      }
    catch (IOException e) {
      System.err.println("Trouble with IO" + e);
      System.exit(2);
    }
  }
}
```

Running the Program

Like the GET example, this program requires access to a live network and an HTTP server with a POST-type CGI facility. The source for this example is on the CD-ROM in the directory `javadevhdbk\ch10\CGIPost.java`. The corresponding bytecode is located in the directory `javadevhdbk\ch10\CGIPost.java`.

Determine the URL of the CGI program you wish to execute and the parameters that it requires. Then issue the command

```
java CGIPost <baseURL> <otherParameters>…
```

Multiple parameters are accepted, but at least one must be provided. When the connection is made, the response of the server will be dumped to the standard output channel. For this reason, a POST CGI script that produces fairly plain HTML is preferable.

What It Does

This program expects at least two arguments, the base URL and a list of CGI parameters. The URL object is created and used to establish an output stream. The parameters are encoded into the external form and sent to that stream. The response is then read from the input stream and copied to the standard output.

The Details

The crucial detail of this example is that the URL class is very particular about how it should be used when the URL it describes expects to receive input from the client. It is a requirement that the Output-Stream object must be enabled, using the setDoOutput(true) call and the OutputStream object obtained with the call to getOutputStream(). This must happen, in this order, before the InputStream object is obtained. If a URL has obtained its Input-Stream object and the OutputStream object has not previously been opened, the class assumes that this is a traditional input-only URL and will generate an exception if the OutputStream object is requested.

> **WARNING** Although the specifications require that setDoOutput(true) should be issued before getOutputStream(), early versions of JDK did not enforce this rule but instead allowed the OutputStream to be obtained anyway. This behavior was not matched on other platforms, such as Netscape Navigator, leading to platform-dependent behavior. Care should be taken, therefore, to call setDoOutput(true) at the correct point.

Implementing a Network Classloader

This section discusses and develops a rudimentary network-based classloader. Classloaders are used to take an array of bytes and create a new class in the running Virtual Machine. This is the approach by which Java-enabled browsers are able to run code that has been dynamically loaded from the network.

The Mini-Appletviewer

This example uses the URL-based network loading of the earlier sections and develops it into the rudiments of an appletviewer-like program. The example loads class data directly into memory from a URL and creates a new `Class` object in the Java Virtual Machine from it. When the class has been defined, an instance is created, and the reference to it is assigned into a variable of type `java.applet.Applet`. From this variable, the `init()` and `start()` methods will be invoked, so the applet can be given a working environment.

Three classes are used to create this program. The first is the *main* class, which holds the other two together in a workable form. The second class provides an implementation of the `AppletStub` and `AppletContext` interfaces that are required by most applets. The final class is the `Classloader`. This is the one that performs the work of obtaining the data over the network and interacting with the Java Virtual Machine to create the new class. To build up the descriptions from the simple to the complex, the classes will be discussed in the order just outlined.

Because this example is rather larger than others in this chapter, each class will be discussed individually. After each has been listed and described, the overall program will be described.

MinAppletviewer.java

```java
import java.awt.*;
import java.applet.*;
import java.io.*;
import java.net.*;
import java.util.*;

public class MinAppletviewer {
  public static void main(String args[]) {
    URL toload = null;
    String host = null;
    String protocol = null;
    int port = 80;
    String path = null;
    String file = null;

    Applet theApplet = null;
    AppSupport theAppSupport = new AppSupport();
    Frame f;
    Class theAppletClass = null;
    NetworkClassLoader loader = null;

    f = new Frame("Minimum Appletviewer: " + args[0]);
    try {
      toload = new URL(args[0]);
      host = toload.getHost();
      port = toload.getPort();
      protocol = toload.getProtocol();
      path = toload.getFile();
      int join = path.lastIndexOf('/');
      file = path.substring(join + 1);
      path = path.substring(0, join + 1);

      theAppSupport.setCodeBase(
        new URL(protocol, host, port, path));
      theAppSupport.setDocumentBase(theAppSupport.getCodeBase());

      loader = new NetworkClassLoader(theAppSupport.getCodeBase());
      theAppletClass = loader.loadClass(file, true);
```

```
      theApplet = (Applet)(theAppletClass.newInstance());
    }
    catch (Exception e) {
      System.err.println("Problem creating class for " + args[0] +
        "\n Exception: " + e.toString());
      System.exit(1);
    }

    f.add("Center", theApplet);

    theApplet.setStub(theAppSupport);

    f.resize(200, 200);
    f.show();
    theApplet.init();
    theApplet.start();
  }
}
```

What It Does

This is the "glue" class in the mini-appletviewer. It takes the command-line arguments and parses them to produce the components of the supplied URL. These details are used to determine the origin of the `Applet` class that is to be loaded and the classname associated with it. The `main()` method uses this information to configure the other parts of the system.

Provided the classfile is loaded correctly, this part creates the `Applet` instance and simulates its life cycle, providing a window environment and calling the `init()` and `start()` methods. The applet is not provided with a thread of its own.

The Details

The five aspects of the applet's environment whose configuration is controlled from this piece of code are as follows:

- Invoking the classloader to load the classfile and create a new `Class` object

- Instantiating the `Applet` object

- Supplying an `AppletContext` object

- Providing a graphical environment

- Calling the life-cycle methods `init()` and `start()`

The `ClassLoader` object needs to know the URL base from which to load classes. These details are determined by splitting up the supplied URL using the calls `getHost()`, `getPort()`, `getProtocol()`, and `getFile()` on the URL. The `ClassLoader` class expects just the path part of the file information in the constructor, as it is also used to load other classes from the same base URL. This typically happens if the applet requires other support classes. The details of the process of loading classes are discussed after the code for the class loader has been presented.

When the class has been loaded, an instance of it is created by invoking the `newInstance()` method on the `Class` object.

TIP

Notice that the java class called `java.lang.Class`—Class with a capital *C*—is a data structure that *describes* other classes. Given an instance of a `Class`, methods can be invoked to inquire about aspects of the described class, such as its name. The method `newInstance()` invokes the default—that is, zero arguments—constructor of the described class. The `Class` object returned by the `ClassLoader` describes the applet and so creates a new instance of that applet.

The return type of the `newInstance()` method is declared as `Object`. In this case, we expect the new object is actually an applet. If the browser is to be able to handle the object successfully it is required that this be the case.

WARNING It is possible to test if the `Object` is an applet using the `instanceof` operator, but this possibility is omitted in this example. If the loaded class is not in fact of the `Applet` class, then a `ClassCastException` will be thrown when the reference is cast to `Applet`. A full program should check for, and handle gracefully, this exception.

The line

```
theApplet = (Applet)(theAppletClass.newInstance());
```

both creates the instance, casts it to a reference of type `Applet`, and assigns the result to the variable `theApplet`. This, therefore, is the line that might throw a `ClassCastException`.

When running, an applet depends upon a browser features called `AppletContext` and `AppletStub` for a number of services. This `main()` method creates an instance of the supporting class `AppSupport`, which implements these two interfaces. The `Applet` instance method `setStub()` is used to inform the applet of these support services. To find its `AppletContext`, the applet invokes a method in the `AppletStub` called `getAppletContext()`. `AppletStub` and `AppletContext` are used to provide such features as the method `getDocumentBase()`.

Because the `Applet` class is subclassed from `java.awt.Panel` and is essentially graphical in nature, the mini-Appletviewer must provide a GUI environment. This environment is achieved by creating a `Frame` object and using the `add()` method to install the applet in the center region of that `Frame`. The applet is launched in this program without the aid of HTML, so an arbitrary width and height are chosen, in this case 200 pixels square.

After the applet has been loaded, instantiated, and given support and a GUI, the methods `init()` and `start()` are called in turn.

This is possible via the reference theApplet, because the type of this reference is java.applet.Applet.

Reusing the Code

Because this is "glue" code for the mini-Appletviewer, it is more likely that the AppSupport and NetworkClassLoader classes will be reused. However, this example could be extended to provide the basis of a useful tool.

Additional features of this example could also include enhanced command-line parsing. The ability to obtain width and height, or *parameters*—both features that are normally provided by the HTML document—would also be a significant enhancement.

AppSupport.java

```java
import java.applet.*;
import java.awt.*;
import java.net.*;
import java.util.*;
import java.io.*;

public class AppSupport implements AppletStub, AppletContext, Enumeration
{
  private URL codeBase;
  private URL documentBase;

  public AppSupport() {
    URL url = null;
    try {
      url = new URL("file://"+ new File(""));
    }
    catch (Exception e) { /* do nothing. url will remain null */ }

    codeBase = documentBase = url;
  }

  public void appletResize(int w, int h) {
  }
```

```java
   public AppletContext getAppletContext() {
     return (AppletContext)this;
   }

   public URL getDocumentBase() {
     return documentBase;
   }

   public void setDocumentBase(URL url) {
     documentBase = url;
   }

   public URL getCodeBase() {
     return codeBase;
   }

   public void setCodeBase(URL url) {
     codeBase = url;
   }

   public String getParameter(String s) {
     return null;
   }

   public boolean isActive() {
     return true;
   }

// AppletContext parts

   public Applet getApplet(String name) {
     return null;
   }

   public Enumeration getApplets() {
     return (Enumeration)this;
   }

   public AudioClip getAudioClip(URL url) {
     return null;
   }
```

```
  public Image getImage(URL url) {
    return Toolkit.getDefaultToolkit().getImage(url);
  }

  public void showDocument(URL url) {
  }

  public void showDocument(URL url, String target) {
  }

  public void showStatus(String status) {
    System.err.println(status);
  }

// Enumeration parts

  public boolean hasMoreElements() {
    return false;
  }

  public Object nextElement() {
    return null;
  }
}
```

What It Does

To provide environmental support an applet requires an AppletStub and AppletContext. Both of these are interface definitions that may be implemented by the browser directly or by a special class. The AppSupport class provides both these facilities and also implements the Enumeration class to assist in supporting one of the features of the AppletContext.

The Details

The interface AppletStub defines the following six methods:

```
public void appletResize(int w, int h)
public AppletContext getAppletContext()
```

```
public URL getDocumentBase()
public URL getCodeBase()
public String getParameter(String s)
public boolean isActive()
```

These methods provide basic environmental support for the applet. The method `appletResize()` is called to advise the browser that the applet is trying to resize. The method `isActive()` may be used by an applet to determine its state. An active applet is somewhere between a `start()` and `stop()` call in terms of its life cycle. Both these methods are implemented with "dummy" code and hence are effectively nonfunctional for this class.

The method `getParameter()` is used by the applet to extract, by name, any arguments to the applet provided by the HTML document `<param ...>` tags. Again, this example simply returns null from this method. A more advanced mini-appletviewer could be written to parse the command line to extract parameters.

The location of the invoking HTML page and the classfile are available to an applet via the methods `getDocumentBase()` and `getCodeBase()`, respectively. The `AppSupport` class provides two routes for providing this information. The class constructor determines a default for code and document base derived from the current working directory. This is achieved by the code

```
File currentDir = new File("x");
currentDir = new File(currentDir.getAbsolutePath());
String urlpart = currentDir.getParent();
urlpart = urlpart.replace(File.separatorChar, '/');
url = new URL("file://" + URLEncoder.encode(urlpart));
```

The `File` class constructor invoked as `new File("x")` provides a reference to a file in the current directory; it does not matter that this file probably does not exist. When the `getAbsolutePath()` method is invoked on it, this returns a path specification as a `String` object, which includes the full path of the current working directory. This string is used to construct a new `File` object from which the directory part is extracted using the `getParent()` method. Because the getParent() method returns a string that might not use the forward slash character required for URLs, these are then translated using the replace() method. Finally, because the path might include colons or other characters that are not permitted in a URL, the encode() method is used to convert the string so it may be appended to the string constant file:// to produce a valid local URL describing the current directory.

In operation, the MinAppletviewer class does not make use of this facility. Rather, it determines the location of the classfile from the supplied URL and uses the methods setCodeBase() and setDocumentBase() to configure these. Neither of these methods are part of the AppletStub interface definition.

The method getAppletContext() is used by the applet to retrieve a reference to the AppletContext, which provides additional utility methods. In this example, a single class implements both interfaces, so this method simply returns the reference this.

The AppletContext interface defines the following seven methods:

```
public Applet getApplet(String  name)
public Enumeration getApplets()
public AudioClip getAudioClip(URL  url)
public Image getImage(URL  url)
public void showDocument(URL  url)
public void showDocument(URL  url, String  target)
public void showStatus(String  status)
```

The method getApplet() allows one applet to obtain a reference to another applet running in the same browser page, using a name associated with that applet in the HTML document. Because this example only displays a single applet at a time, this method returns null. Similarly, the method getApplets() is intended to return an Enumeration listing all the applets on this page, implemented here by returning a reference to this. Because this class implements the Enumeration interface, this approach is acceptable. When the Enumeration methods are called, they report that no elements are in the list.

The two showDocument() methods are intended to make the browser jump to a new HTML page. These are implemented as empty methods here. Similarly, the showStatus() method is ignored.

The methods getAudioClip() and getImage() provide the applet with convenient methods of loading sounds and pictures. A more generalized but more tedious method would be to use the URL and getContent() methods directly. In the base JDK, there are no mechanisms for handling audio; all audio facilities are embedded in the browser classes in the sun.audio packages. For this reason, the getAudioClip() method simply returns null. Implementing getImage() is not difficult, however, because an exact parallel method is provided by the Toolkit class. The toolkit is the underlying graphics system that supports the AWT. A reference may be obtained to this from any visible AWT Component or from the static method getDefaultToolkit() in the Toolkit class.

Reusing the Code

Although the bulk of the methods in this class are not operational, the class can form the basis of a more comprehensive implementation. Passing parameters into the class from a parsed command line would be a simple but useful extension. Similarly, the showStatus() method could be implemented by adding a label in the "South" region of the browser window and arranging that the method updates the label text.

> **NOTE** If the MinAppletviewer class were modified suitably it would be possible to implement the showDocument() option, although this would require a significant amount of work because a basic parser for HTML would have to be produced.

NetworkClassLoader.java

```java
import java.util.*;
import java.net.*;
import java.io.*;

public class NetworkClassLoader extends ClassLoader {
  private Hashtable cache = new Hashtable();
  private URL myBase;
  private static boolean verbose = Boolean.getBoolean("Debug");

  public NetworkClassLoader(URL myBase) {
    log("NetworkClassLoader: constructor, mybase = " + myBase);
    this.myBase = myBase;
  }

  private synchronized byte[] loadClassData(String name)
    throws ClassNotFoundException {
    log("NetworkClassLoader: loadClassData, name=" + name);
    URL url = null;
    InputStream s = null;
    try {
      url = new URL(myBase, name);
      s = url.openStream();
    }
    catch (Exception e) {
      System.out.println("Stream open to " + url + " failed");
      throw new ClassNotFoundException(name);
    }

    byte [] buffer = new byte [0];
    byte [] chunk = new byte [4096];
    int count;

    try {
      while ((count = s.read(chunk)) >= 0) {
        byte [] t = new byte [buffer.length + count];
        System.arraycopy(buffer, 0, t, 0, buffer.length);
        System.arraycopy(chunk, 0, t, buffer.length, count);
        buffer = t;
      }
    }
```

```
        catch (Exception e) {
          throw new ClassNotFoundException(name);
        }

        return buffer;
      }

      public synchronized Class loadClass(String name, boolean resolve)
        throws ClassNotFoundException {
        log("NetworkClassLoader: loadClass, name=" + name +
            " resolve=" + resolve);
        if (name.charAt(0) == '.') {
          throw new SecurityException("'Absolute' package name");
        }
        if (name.indexOf("..") != -1) {
          throw new SecurityException("Illegal package name");
        }

        Class c = (Class)(cache.get(name));

        if (c == null) {
          try {
            c = findSystemClass(name);
          }
          catch (Exception e) {
            try {
              String path = name.replace('.', '/') + ".class";
              byte data[] = loadClassData(path);
              c = defineClass(name, data, 0, data.length);
              cache.put(name, c);
            }
            catch (ClassFormatError ex) {
              throw new ClassNotFoundException(name);
            }
          }
        }
        if (resolve) {
          resolveClass(c);
        }
        return c;
      }
```

```
private void log(String s) {
  if (verbose) {
    System.err.println(s);
  }
}
}
```

What It Does

The job of a class loader is to convert an array of bytes into an object of class `java.lang.Class`. Given an instance of `Class`, it is possible to construct instances of the class that is described. This code can be found in the file `javadevhdbk\ch10\NetworkClassLoader.java`.

The `NetworkClassLoader` constructor keeps a record of the base URL from which it is to obtain classes. A request to load a class starts by checking for it in a cache. Next the local system is searched, according to the rule that no imported class may be permitted to "masquerade" as a known local one. If the class is still not found, then the loader attempts to obtain the data of a suitably named classfile from the network via the loader's base URL. If this download is successful, the byte array is passed into the system class loader to be converted into a real `Class`.

The resulting `Class` object is placed in the cache and might be resolved if the original argument to the load request specified it. Resolving a class fixes up all the links to other classes such as the parent hierarchy.

The Details

A separate `NetworkClassLoader` object should be constructed for each base URL from which classes are loaded. This is because the class loader used to fetch a class becomes, in effect, part of the resulting class' name. If one class loader is used to obtain all network classes, therefore, an applet loaded from one machine might interfere with the operation of an applet loaded from another machine. This could happen, for example, if they both ask for a support class called `MyThread`, but both wanted different classes from their local authors.

> **NOTE**
>
> Because the loader operates on a specific base URL, the `mini-appletviewer` splits the path name requested in its command-line argument. The base URL is provided to the constructor and only the classname is given to the `loadClass()` method.

> **WARNING**
>
> When the `loadClass()` method is invoked, the loader first checks its local cache, maintained in the hashtable. It is important to cache loaded classes, not only for speed, but because actually loading the same class twice would create two separate instances of the describing `Class` object, resulting in duplicated static variables and class synchronization flags. Both these effects would be potentially disastrous.

If a class request cannot be satisfied from the cache, the class loader next attempts to load it from the local system by simply calling the local class loader using the method `findSystemClass()`. This is a method in the parent class `java.lang.Classloader`. This checks along the CLASSPATH environment variable and returns the `Class` object if it is found locally. Java classloading specifications state that this local search *must* be performed before attempting to load the class from a remote location. This is vital from the security standpoint, as otherwise it would be possible for foreign classes to supersede local ones that might be crucial to the proper operation of other local classes.

In circumstances where the class request has not been satisfied by either the cache or the local system, the class loader proceeds by looking for the class on the network. This is done by constructing the filename of the class, adding the suffix `.class` to the classname itself, and then invoking the local method `loadClassData()`. As part of the preparation of the relative URL from which the class data is loaded, the class is parsed to extract package name information.

WARNING A package name must be handled with some caution—leading or multiple periods should be disallowed. One of the security bugs that has was found and fixed in early versions of Java related to a "fudged" package name that used a leading period. The local `ClassLoader` was persuaded to load classes from an absolute path, bypassing vital aspects of the security model. It is important to treat all aspects of classloading with respect, as errors or ambiguities can easily lead to security problems.

A `byte` array is returned by the `loadClassData()` method, provided the network transaction was successful. The code of this method is essentially the same as the earlier example that loaded the contents of a URL into a local file.

Given an array of bytes representing a class, the method `defineClass()`, which is in the parent class `ClassLoader`, converts this into a real `Class` object, and installs it in the Virtual Machine. As part of this process, the bytecode verifier is run. If the `byte` array does not have the proper format for a classfile or if the bytecode verifier considers the code illegal, then the `defineClass()` method will fail and throw an exception.

The final stage is called *resolution*. All classes depend on their parents for their full definition; `Object` is the only exception to this rule, and the network class loader is not concerned with `java.lang.Object` or any other local class. Resolution ensures that all the parent classes are loaded so that the class is fully defined and may be instantiated.

The resolving process is handled by the parent `ClassLoader` object and the only responsibility of this code is to call the method at the proper time if required.

NOTE The `NetworkClassLoader` class provides a logging facility, which can be enabled by defining a property `Debug` to be `true`. This will cause the output of messages for each call to the loader and for each call to obtain a remote class definition that results.

Reusing the Code

The NetworkClassLoader class can be used in any application that needs to load classes from network connections. It would be a fairly simple modification to validate the base URL against a list of servers known to be local and refuse to load classes from any other hosts. In this way a more tightly controlled applet-execution environment can be created for use in corporate intranet environments.

> **TIP**
>
> If you wish to allow special privilege for classes loaded from your local network, it is generally more appropriate to use the security features provided by signing. Issue certificates to properly authorized classes and configure the client systems to trust those certificates, and you can allocate full privilege to your code. This approach also ensures that only specific classes gain privilege; those written by unauthorized programmers on your network are not included. The signing mechanism is the subject of one of the questions in Appendix C, *Frequently Asked Questions*.

Running the Mini-Appletviewer

Unlike the appletviewer supplied with the JDK distribution, this example does not require an HTML file. In fact, it cannot use one; instead it takes a URL that describes the class to load directly. Also unlike the HTML <applet ...> tag, the URL for this example should not include the .class extension; this is assumed. The absence of an HTML document also means that no dimensions or parameters can be specified.

The source code for this example are on the CD-ROM located in the directory javadevhdbk\ch10, and are called MinAppletViewer .java, AppSupport.java, and NetworkClassLoader.java. The classfiles with corresponding names are in the same directory.

To run the example, choose an applet that does not require additional parameters. The standard JDK demonstrations include a number of these, including one called `CardTest`, which demonstrates the `CardLayout` class, which is a layout manager. Invoke the example by issuing the command

```
java MinAppletViewer <url>
```

For example, to run the `CardTest` demo from the CD-ROM mounted as drive D: in a DOS-like system, issue a command of this form

```
java MinAppletViewer file:///D:/java/demo/CardTest/CardTest
```

Substitute the path to your java installation, and notice that the url ends `.../CardTest`, not `.../CardTest.class`. The `CardTest` applet will start in a window of its own.

> **TIP**
>
> In order to enable the logging output, modify the command with the following:
>
> ```
> java -DDebug=true MinAppletViewer <url>
> ```

Connection Information

The networking facilities provided by the `java.net` package include a variety of informational methods. This section discusses those that allow conversion of network addresses between domain name and numeric IP addresses and those that obtain the addresses and port numbers from a connected socket.

> **NOTE**
>
> The data that support these methods are obtained from the underlying networking system. In an Internet environment DNS is usually responsible for supplying these answers, and in local environments the information might be obtained from text files or some other database system.

Obtaining and Converting Address Information

The package `java.net` includes a class called `InetAddress`, which provides a number of facilities for manipulating addresses in the Internet domain. Two static methods provide conversion from textual domain name format into objects of the `InetAddress` class. These are

```
public static synchronized InetAddress getByName(String host)
  throws UnknownHostException
public static synchronized InetAddress[] getAllByName(String host)
  throws UnknownHostException
```

The first of these takes a DNS type name, such as `www.javasoft.com`, and returns a single instance of the `InetAddress` class that represents a valid IP address of that name. Because it is possible for a name to translate to more than one IP address (to allow redundancy in important servers) the second method provides a means to obtain all the IP addresses associated with a name.

> **NOTE** Multiple IP addresses mean that attempting to connect to a single DNS name, such as `nic.ddn.mil`, might connect to any one of a number of different machines. This allows load distribution. Because a client that fails to connect to one of the listed physical machines can try a different one after the timeout period, a greater service reliability is also achieved.

Where an `InetAddress` object already exists, such as is returned by either of the two methods above, the IP address may be retrieved in the form of an array of bytes (four with the current implementation of IP) so that the numerical form of the address can be manipulated directly. The method that provides this facility is

```
public byte[] getAddress()
```

Another instance method in the `InetAddress` class allows determination of the DNS name for an IP address. The method is

```
public String getHostName()
```

The final method of interest here extracts an `InetAddress` object that refers to the local machine.

WARNING Applets running subject to the security constraints of a browser usually find that the behavior of this method is modified so that the IP address is reported as `127.0.0.1` and the name is reported as `localhost`.

Obtaining Endpoint Addresses

When a `Socket` is connected, three methods allow determination of the connection details. Probably the most useful is

```
public InetAddress getInetAddress()
```

This method reports the IP address of the remote end of the connection. In general, for a client socket this will already be known. However, where this `Socket` object has been extracted from a `ServerSocket` object, the address of the client is not known in advance and this method can be used to obtain it. Using the method `getHostName()` in the `InetAddress` class, the hostname can be extracted.

A connected `Socket` has two port numbers associated with it. One port is associated with each end of a `Socket`. In general, the port number of the client is not of interest, only the port number at the server end is relevant to the service being offered. A method is available for finding each of these port numbers. These methods are

```
public int getPort()
public int getLocalPort()
```

Because the server port number is the one that carries immediate significance, and is also the one that is always known in any program, these methods are not likely to be of general use in TCP programs. They might, however, find use in UDP systems, which are discussed later.

Security Considerations

Java programs, whether applets in a browser or stand-alone applications, are able to load and run code from anywhere. This ability, combined with the fact that many networks now extend into the Internet, and thereby to untrusted machines, opens up massive security concerns. Because the network is the first point of attack, it must also be the first line of defense. Java security measures operate by imposing restrictions on the abilities of running code. Code that tries to perform prohibited operations will fail, so it is important to understand the nature of these restrictions when writing portable programs.

General Network Restrictions Applied to Applets

Security rules are imposed by a `SecurityManager` object. This is not part of the Virtual Machine, but must be installed by an application when it starts up. Until this is done, no restrictions are applied. The unrestricted mode is the usual domain of applications, although it does not have to be. If appropriate, each application can install its own security manager, and hence impose its own set of rules. Browsers should be expected to install a security manager, and the applets they run are therefore subject to its restrictions.

Despite this potential for flexibility, most browsers impose broadly the same security restrictions, and this is likely to remain true. This section will describe the significance of these constraints in relation to network programming.

Sockets and Server Sockets

Network services are often denied to requests that originate from "foreign" machines; these might be machines outside a firewall or perhaps any machine other than a specially chosen list of trusted machines. This security practice substantially reduces the chance that information will be accessed improperly.

If an applet opens a socket to another machine, that socket originates from the machine running the applet not from the machine that provided the applet code. However, the behavior is provided by the applet writer. Unless something else prevents access, this would appear to give an applet the potential to access privileged network-based services that should be denied to the author of the applet. The most draconian approach to this problem, and that taken by early versions of the Netscape Navigator, is to prohibit all network access by any applet. The current convention, adopted by the appletviewer and most Web browsers, is to permit a client socket to be connected to the host from which the applet originated. This is considered safe from the browser host's point of view, as the only information available from services on that host is at the discretion, and under the control, of the supplier of the applet. The security of the machine supplying the applet is not the concern of the browser running the applet or of the local user.

NOTE Because of the requirement that an applet can only connect to the originating host, an applet should always expect to be denied the privilege of creating a server socket. It is in the nature of a server socket that it can accept a connection from anywhere, which would make it impossible to restrict the behavior of the applet.

Name and Address Access

Applets should, in general, be denied access to any information unless they have a legitimate need for it and it can be shown that this information is not considered private. Because knowledge of IP addresses and hostnames can be useful to an attacker, the address access methods of the `InetAddress` class normally return modified information about the local host. Specifically, the address will be returned as `127.0.0.1` and the hostname either as `localhost` or as `127.0.0.1` in text form.

Covert Channels

Although the security restrictions applied to sockets and server sockets are soundly designed, a difficulty remains. Because of the nature of other Internet services, it is impossible to prevent a Java applet from communicating with any host programmed to cooperate with it. In other words, without regard to the host that originated it, the applet is able to covertly send any data to which it has access to any host on the Internet that is cooperating with the subterfuge. It is also able to receive data from any such host. Because of this difficulty, it is important to restrict the information that an applet can obtain in the first place.

There are a number of different mechanisms by which a covert channel can be obtained. A low-bandwidth bidirectional channel can be established simply by using the Domain Name System. An applet is entitled to look up any hostname it needs; this is an essential service for the Internet to be useful. For an applet to communicate the message "hello I am here" to its covert partner, the partner simply needs to run a modified domain name server, and the applet to perform a name lookup on a host called `hello.i.am.here.spy.com`. Because the request for this name translation is passed to the name server for the domain `spy.com`, it is a trivial matter to extract the first part of the message from it. Further, a DNS lookup expects a response, in the form of one or more four-byte IP addresses. It is again simple for this response to be used to return information, which is then accessible in the applet.

The DNS mechanism for covert channels is slow but easy to understand and fairly easy to implement. More importantly, it is not the only available channel. It is therefore vital to address the security of information in terms of preventing an applet from gaining access in the first place. Fortunately, the other Java security mechanisms do achieve a high measure of success.

Using UDP

For most network programs, TCP will be the service of choice, offering reliable, ordered stream connection and relieving the programmer from most of the troublesome work involved in maintaining a connection. Despite this simplicity, there are occasions when UDP might be a more appropriate, or even necessary, choice.

The significant differences between TCP and UDP services are discussed in the background section at the beginning of this chapter. There are two main reasons why UDP might be chosen:

- For preexisting services that use UDP

- For maximum throughput on a fairly reliable network

Using UDP in Java is not difficult, although the problems of reliability and ordering must be addressed. The code examples that follow do not attempt to handle these problems. The nature of the example service is such that even if a large proportion of transmissions were to be lost, the resulting service would be usable, if intermittent.

Daytime Example

This example describes the use of UDP to send date and time information. The standard Daytime service, described in earlier sections of this chapter, does, in fact, have a UDP equivalent. In that service the server waits passively for a message from a client and then responds with time information. In this example, the server transmits time information at one-second intervals, regardless of whether the client is listening. This exemplifies the fundamental difference between TCP and UDP services: there is no concept of a "connection" in the UDP system, and hence transmission of data onto the network does not require any other host to be listening.

There are two classes that make up the UDP-based Daytime system: the server and the client. When started, both client and server continue to run indefinitely. Each time the client notices a new message, it prints it to the standard output channel. If a message is lost, no difficulties arise, but the client's output will pause for more than one second and then jump when a packet is received.

The source of the server class follows:

DayBcast.java

```
import java.net.*;
import java.util.*;

public class DayBcast {
  DatagramSocket ds;
  DatagramPacket dp;
  InetAddress addr;

  public static final int DAYTIME_PORT = 1313;

  public static void main(String args[]) throws Exception {
    DayBcast db = new DayBcast(args[0]);
    db.go();
  }

  public DayBcast(String target) throws Exception {
    addr = InetAddress.getByName(target);
    ds = new DatagramSocket();
  }

  public void go() throws Exception {
    byte [] buff;
```

```
for (;;) {
  Thread.sleep(1000);
  System.out.println("Sending");
  String s = (new Date()).toString();
  buff = s.getBytes();
  dp = new DatagramPacket(buff, buff.length, addr, DAYTIME_PORT);
  ds.send(dp);
}
}
}
```

What It Does

This code has a very simple algorithm. The target address is determined from the command-line argument. An uncommitted `DatagramSocket` object is created and then the code loops, once per second, sending a string representation of the current date and time over the network. Each transmission is accompanied by the message "Sending" on the standard output.

The Details

This code uses port 1313, which is the same port as was used for the unofficial TCP Daytime service. Although TCP and UDP port numbers cover the same range, they are in a different namespace and do not interfere with each other. Because of this, it is possible to have a TCP and UDP server both running simultaneously, using the same port number.

The first step is to construct an `InetAddress` object that describes the remote host to which the date and time information is to be sent, achieved with the method call `InetAddress.getByName(target)`. This call was described in the earlier section *Obtaining and Converting Address Information*. Once the address information has been obtained, the `DatagramSocket` object is created. That the socket is created without a specific port number is the only indication that it is a server program. In UDP it is necessary to specify the port number of the receiver. If this datagram socket were to be used for receiving data, it would need to be configured at a specific port. The absence of this configuration suggests that this datagram socket will be starting the communication, and hence is probably the server end.

When a proper address and socket have been initialized, a Datagram-Packet object must be prepared. The socket is then used to send that packet. The DatagramPacket object is constructed by the line

```
dp = new DatagramPacket(buff, s.length(), addr, DAYTIME_PORT);
```

The first two arguments provide the data to be transmitted (buff) and the length of that data (s.length()). Note that the data length is the length of the String s, not the total capacity of the buffer buff. The argument addr specifies the destination address of this packet, and the final argument DAYTIME_PORT indicates the port number to which the packet is to be sent. Note that this information is provided in the DatagramPacket object rather than the socket.

WARNING In principle, UDP datagrams can be up to 65,536 bytes in length. However, IP implementation standards only require a minimum packet size of 576 bytes. After allowing for the length of headers, this results in a conventional limit on UDP datagrams of 512 bytes.

After the DatagramPacket object has been prepared, the data is transmitted by the call to ds.send(dp);.

The UDP Daytime Client

The client end for this example is no more complex:

DayWatch.java

```
import java.net.*;

public class DayWatch {
```

```
private DatagramSocket ds;
private DatagramPacket dp;

public static void main(String args[]) throws Exception {
  DayWatch d = new DayWatch();
  d.go();
}

public void go() throws Exception {
  byte [] buff = new byte[64];
  String s;
  ds = new DatagramSocket(DayBcast.DAYTIME_PORT);
  dp = new DatagramPacket(buff, buff.length);
  for (;;) {
    dp.setLength(buff.length);
    ds.receive(dp);
    s = new String(dp.getData());
    System.out.println("Time signal received from " +
      dp.getAddress() + "\n  Time is: " + s);
  }
}
}
```

What It Does

This algorithm of this client is even simpler than that of its server. A buffer is created to hold the received characters. A socket is created that is bound to a particular port, and a DatagramPacket object is created to collect the data. The code then enters an infinite loop that receives and then prints data to the standard output.

The Details

The client creates a DatagramSocket object, bound to the port number previously chosen. It also constructs a DatagramPacket object that will be used to hold the received data. To support this reception, the DatagramPacket object is provided with storage space for the received data—this is the array of 64 bytes, which should be more than enough for the date and time string that is expected. In general a buffer size of 512 bytes is a sensible choice as this is the largest UDP packet size that can be handled reliably by all TCP/IP networks.

Once the socket and packet objects are set up, all that is required to receive data is to call the `receive()` method of the `DatagramSocket` class, providing as an argument the `DatagramPacket` object that is to hold the returned data. The client must be in the `receive()` method when the server sends, because there is no connection involved, no way for the sender to know if the receiver got the message, and the protocol does not perform retries.

After the `receive()` method returns, the `DatagramPacket` object will contain the received data. It also has been updated with the address of the sending machine. This address can be extracted with the `getAddress()` method, which returns an `InetAddress` object. This object provides the methods described earlier for manipulating addresses. The `toString()` method of the `InetAddress` class conveniently returns a printable form of the address. If preferred, the `getHostName()` can be used.

NOTE   The method `getHostName()` will not provide a useful text string unless some form of naming service is functioning on your system. Systems without a real network should be expected to return the dotted form of the IP address. This behavior will be found on most systems that are non-Unix and are not connected to a real TCP/IP network.

It is important to appreciate the weaknesses of UDP. Data transmitted by UDP can be lost entirely or duplicated at the recipient. Multiple datagrams can be received in an order different from that in which they were sent. The two benefits of UDP are the reduced overhead that results from the greatly reduced complexity and, to an extent, the record-oriented nature of the system.

Running the Programs

The source code for these examples are located on the CD-ROM in the directory `javadevhdbk\ch10`. The files are called `DayBcast .java` and `DayWatch.java`, respectively. The corresponding class-files are in the same directory.

Using two separate windows, start both parts of the system. Start the server first, by issuing the command

```
java DayBcast <target machine>
```

If you are running both client and server on the same machine, use the name `localhost` to describe the target machine.

To start the client issue the command

```
java DayWatch
```

When the server has started, it will print the message "Sending" on its output at one-second intervals. Some of these might well have been output before you start the client, because there is no "connection" with UDP and so the sender has no way to know whether the packets were lost.

When the client starts, it should print a date and time message each time the server sends. If the server is killed, the client does not exit, but sits waiting for more packets. Indeed, the server can even be restarted, in which case the client will continue to print output messages without noticing the failure or recovery.

Reusing the Code

Because of the simplicity of these examples, they do not readily lend themselves to object-oriented reuse.

Broadcasting

Because UDP does not attempt to set up a connection between the two machines before transmitting data, it is possible to use it to create a broadcast server. The name of the server class in the previous example was a strong indication of this potentially valuable feature of UDP.

In a broadcast message, the destination of the data is not specified as a single machine with a unique address. Instead, a special address, called a *broadcast address*, is given.

Broadcasting can occur in a TCP/IP network on two levels. The data can be sent to all the machines connected to the same subnet as the sender or to all machines on the same network. The first of these is called a *subnet broadcast*.

NOTE The term *subnet* describes a particular collection of local machines, determined by a network parameter called the *subnet mask*. A numerical definition of precisely which machines are members of this collection is given later, although the allocation of subnet masks is beyond the scope of this book.

Broadcasts to an entire network are potentially expensive in terms of bandwidth, as packets might propagate through many bridges and routers. Most bridges and routers provide configuration options to allow broadcast packets to be suppressed, and this option is commonly enabled.

The broadcast address is calculated from other configuration parameters of the local network. For a subnet broadcast, the required data is the local IP address and the subnet mask. If the IP address is I and the subnet mask is M, using bitwise binary logic, the subnet broadcast address A is calculated as

```
A = I or (not M)
```

To put this algebra into words, the local IP address is modified by forcing to "1" all the bits that correspond to a "0" in the subnet mask. For example, if the IP address of a machine is 146.188.4.192 and the subnet mask is 255.255.254.0, the subnet broadcast address is calculated as

```
146.188.4.192 => 10010010 10111100.00000100.11000000
255.255.254.0 => 11111111.11111111.11111110.00000000
```

Forcing to "1" each bit of the IP address corresponding to a "0" in the subnet mask gives:

```
146.188.5.255 => 10010010 10111100.00000101.11111111
                          ^ ^^^^^^^^
```

The caret symbol (^) indicates the bits that have been forced to "1."

A broadcast address for the whole "logical network" is calculated similarly, but instead of using the subnet mask, the default netmask is used for the network. The netmask can be determined from the first byte of the IP address. A first byte in the range 0 to 126 indicates a class A network, the range 128 to 191 indicates a class B network, and the range 192 to 223 indicates class C. For each of these network classes, the default netmask is listed below:

Class	Netmask
A	255.0.0.0
B	255.255.0.0
C	255.255.255.0

Running a Broadcast Example

Using the classes DayBcast and DayWatch from the previous example, a demonstration of UDP broadcasting may be achieved. Set the transmit address used by the server to the local subnet broadcast address. Any machine on the local subnet can then run the DayWatch client successfully.

> **TIP** Although a broadcast UDP packet can be received by multiple machines, it can usually only be received by a single process on each machine. If two clients are started on the same port, one will receive each incoming packet and the other will not see the data.

Multicasting

Broadcasting provides a valuable mechanism for communicating between multiple hosts simultaneously. There are, however, drawbacks in its use:

- The communication must take place between hosts on the local subnet or, at the widest, hosts on the same logical network.

- Every host that receives a broadcast must perform some processing before it is able to determine whether it wants the data or not. This wastes CPU resources on a potentially great number of machines.

- Where a network is divided by bridges or, for logical network broadcasts, routers, the packet must be propagated to every network segment, even if no hosts on that segment are interested. This can add significant network-bandwidth demand. In some cases this forwarding might cause a broadcast packet to reach a network segment that constitutes a security risk.

Multicasting is a mechanism that allows communication between multiple hosts but avoids most of the problems. Multicasting is achieved by using a special range of IP addresses. These addresses are not associated with particular machines; instead, groups of machines associate themselves with a particular address. This association is in addition to the normal IP address for each machine.

> **WARNING** Not all TCP/IP implementations support multicasting. While workstations running Unix will generally be able to handle the service, PC-based implementations might not.

TIP

Although multicast facilities are supplied with the distribution in JDK 1.0.2, they are not supported as such. The facilities are provided in the `sun.net.MulticastSocket` class not in the core `java.net` package. There are also a number of significant but undocumented bugs in the implementation. Users wishing to investigate multicast facilities are advised to do so using JDK 1.1.

For a group of machines to become associated with a particular multicast address, the routers that connect them must all be aware of the associations and the routes between the machines. From this point on, any packet, from any of the machines, that is addressed to the group address will be propagated to each machine in the group. The routers will make directed transmissions so other machines that are not part of the group will not receive the data in the first place and, hence, will not waste CPU time deciding to ignore the packet.

The directed nature of multicast packets addresses all of the difficulties listed for normal UDP broadcast. The packets are not restricted by network topology, CPU time is not wasted rejecting data, and network bandwidth is not used on unnecessary network cable. To an extent, multicasting is also more secure than broadcasting, because the packets are not propagated on irrelevant cable and are not read into machines unnecessarily.

WARNING

As a general point, in the absence of encryption, many LAN technologies are hardly more secure than the cable they use. Because each user's machine is connected to that cable, only good faith or lack of technical knowledge will protect data from other users of the same network cable. Multicasting merely reduces the availability of the data.

Applications of Multicasting

Multicasting is generally suited to any application that requires a number of machines in a distributed group to receive the same data; for example: conferencing, group mail and news distribution, and network management.

A typical application of multicasting is Route Information Protocol-2 or RIP-2. This protocol propagates routing information amongst routers (hosts are sometimes interested too, but less often) to ensure that large dynamic networks have the best possible knowledge of what routes are currently available for traffic. Clearly it would be counterproductive to use extensive broadcasting, with the associated bandwidth demand, for a protocol that attempts to ensure the best network throughput for user applications.

NOTE   Multicasting also has uses in less mundane applications, such as communication between systems in networked multiuser games and simulations. Some games communicate using ordinary broadcast techniques and have become notorious for overloading previously quiet office networks.

Multicast Programming

Programming Java to use multicasting is not difficult in principle. Most of the technique is shared with UDP technology.

Consider the following pair of examples of a multicast server and companion client:

MCastServ.java

```
import java.net.*;
import java.io.*;
import java.util.*;
```

```
public class MCastServ {
  MulticastSocket ms;
  DatagramPacket dp;
  InetAddress addr;

  public static final int MC_DAYTIME_PORT = 1313;

  public static void main(String args[]) throws Exception {
    MCastServ mcs = new MCastServ(args[0]);
    mcs.go();
  }

  public MCastServ(String target) throws Exception {
    addr = InetAddress.getByName(target);
    ms = new MulticastSocket();
    ms.joinGroup(addr);
  }

  public void go() throws Exception {
    byte [] buff = null;
    for (;;) {
      Thread.sleep(1000);
      System.out.println("Sending");
      String s = (new Date()).toString();
      buff = s.getBytes();
      dp = new DatagramPacket(buff, s.length(), addr, MC_DAYTIME_PORT);
      ms.send(dp, (byte)1);
    }
  }
}
```

MCastWatch.java

```
import java.net.*;
import java.io.*;

public class MCastWatch {
  private MulticastSocket ms;
  private DatagramPacket dp;

  public static void main(String args[]) throws Exception {
```

```
        MCastWatch d = new MCastWatch(args[0]);
        d.go();
    }

    public MCastWatch(String groupAddr) throws Exception {
        ms = new MulticastSocket(MCastServ.MC_DAYTIME_PORT);
        ms.joinGroup(InetAddress.getByName(groupAddr));
    }

    public void go() throws Exception {
        byte [] buff = new byte[64];
        String s;
        dp = new DatagramPacket(buff, buff.length);
        for (;;) {
            ms.receive(dp);
            s = new String(dp.getData());
            System.out.println("Time signal received from " +
                dp.getAddress() + "\n  Time is: " + s);
        }
    }
}
```

Running the Programs

The source code for this example is on the CD-ROM in the directory
`javadevhdbk\ch10\MCastServ.java`. The bytecode is in the file
`MCastServ.class` in the same directory.

Note that this example assumes you have JDK 1.1 installed on your
system. If your JDK is 1.0.2, you can edit both files to include the following line at the top of each:

```
import sun.net.*;
```

Recompiling will produce new versions of the programs. Be aware,
however, that the example might well fail depending on your platform, as multicast sockets are not fully supported on JDK 1.0.2.

Next you will need to ensure that a name is associated with a suitable multicast address. This requires access to—and understanding
of—your system's configuration. Add a suitable name, such as

mcast-test and assign it the address 224.1.1.1, which should otherwise be unused.

Now run the server program by issuing the command

```
java MCastServ mcast-test
```

If all is well, if the mcast-test name is successfully installed, and if multicasting is supported by your machine and your version of JDK, you should see the "Sending" message appear at one-second intervals. This suggests that the server is running.

Run the client by issuing the command

```
java MCastWatch mcast-test
```

Note that for this example the address must be provided for both client and server.

You should now see the date and time information being printed at one-second intervals.

What It Does

The basic algorithms of both the server and client, along with much of the code, is taken from the DayBcast.java and DayWatch.java examples in the UDP section. The essential differences are the use of the MulticastSocket class in place of the DatagramSocket class and the need to explicitly join the multicast group address.

The Details

The joinGroup() method of the MulticastSocket class associates the socket with the group IP address and instructs the underlying TCP/IP system to join the group. This must be done on the client as well as the server because, in the multicast scenario, the address is a meeting point rather than a definition of either of the two machines.

The send() method in the MulticastSocket class takes two arguments. The first is the DatagramPacket that is to be transmitted. This aspect is exactly parallel with the use of standard UDP. The second argument is called the *time to live*. This parameter is used to control the number of routers that the packet can be passed through before it is dropped. This precaution ensures that if a packet gets misdirected, perhaps because of the dynamic nature of the multicast group address, the packet does not go bouncing around between routers indefinitely.

In addition to the facilities shown here, there is another important method in the MulticastSocket class: the leaveGroup() method. After joining a group, a program should advise the underlying TCP/IP system that it is no longer interested in the packets. The TCP/IP system informs the routers that ensure packets reach the machine so no more unnecessary traffic is generated.

Reusing the Code

Because this example is purely demonstrative, it is unlikely to form the basis for reuse.

Summary

In this chapter we have introduced a full spectrum of techniques in Java networking. You have seen techniques for programming clients and servers using both TCP and UDP services. URL handling for standard content types and for both POST and GET CGI has been demonstrated. You have also seen the fundamentals of classloading, which is one of the cornerstone capabilities that sets Java apart from most of its predecessors. If you have previous experience of network programming, you will probably agree that Java makes network programming much easier than do most other languages.

CHAPTER

ELEVEN

Database Connectivity (JDBC)

- Java as a database front end

- Database client/server methodology

- Two- and three-tier database design

- The JDBC API

- A JDBC database example

- JDBC drivers

- JDBC-ODBC bridge

- Alternative connectivity strategies

11

In the information age, the database is a tool used to collect and manipulate data. The database forms the foundation of the infra-structure of many companies. While the database system is well-suited to the storage and retrieval of data, human beings need some sort of front-end application in order to see and use the data stored.

The problem is complicated by the heterogeneous nature of the computers in most companies. The art and marketing departments have Macintosh systems, the engineers have high-end Unix worksta-tions and the sales people are using PCs. In order to expose the data in the database, developers must consider all of the various permuta-tions of systems on which they wish to deploy.

This chapter will look at Java as the way to solve the Tower of Babel of database front ends, by providing a single and consistent applica-tion programming interface, the Java Database Connectivity API.

Java as a Database Front End

Java offers several benefits to the developer creating a front-end application for a database server. Java is a "write once, run any-where" language. This means that Java programs may be deployed without change on any of the computer architectures and operating systems that run the Java Virtual Machine. For large corporations, just having a common development platform is a big savings: no longer are programmers required to write to the many platforms a large corporation may have. Java is also attractive to third-party developers—a single Java program can answer the needs of a large corporate customer.

In addition, there is a cost associated with the deployment and maintenance of the hardware and software of any system (client) the corporation owns. Systems such as Windows PCs, Macintosh, and Unix desktop-centric clients (*fat clients*) can cost corporations between $10,000 and $15,000 per installation seat. Java technology now makes it possible for any company to use a smaller system footprint. These systems are based on a Java chip set and can run any and all Java programs from a built-in Java operating system.

Java-based clients (*thin clients*) that operate with a minimum of hard resources and yet run the complete Java environment are expected to cost less than $2,500 per seat. According to various studies, the savings for a corporation moving 10,000 fat client systems to thin clients could be as much as $100 million annually.

It follows, then, that the incentive to create Java-based applications and applets for corporate systems is high. Corporations are extremely interested in shifting their applications from architecture- and operating-system-specific models to network-centric models. Java represents a long-term strategy in saving resource costs.

For the developer, Java represents a huge market opportunity. There are very few medium-to-large organizations that do not use databases for some portion of their business operation, while most use databases for *every* aspect of their business, from human resources to front-line customer sales.

In this chapter, Java Database Connectivity (JDBC) will be examined, including how to use the current JDBC API to connect Java applications and applets to database servers.

Database Client/Server Methodology

The evolution of relational data storage began in 1970 with the work of Dr. E. F. Codd, who proposed a set of 12 rules for identifying relationships between pieces of data. Codd's rules for relational modeling of data formed the basis for the development of systems to manage data. Today, Relational Database Management Systems (RDBMS) are the result of Codd's vision.

Data in an RDBMS are stored as rows of distinct information in tables. A structured language is used to query (retrieve), store, and change the data. The Structured Query Language (SQL) is an ANSI standard, and all major commercial RDBMS vendors provide mechanisms for issuing SQL commands.

The early development of RDBMS applications utilized an integrated model of user interface code, application code, and database libraries. This single binary model ran only on a local machine, typically a mainframe. The applications were simple but inefficient, and did not work over LANs. The model did not scale, and the application and user interface code was tightly coupled to the database libraries. Figure 11.1 illustrates the monolithic single-tier database design.

FIGURE 11.1

The monolithic single-tier database design

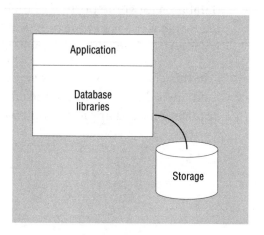

Further, the monolithic approach did not allow multiple instances of the application to communicate with *each other*. So there was often contention between instances of the application.

> **NOTE** It is typical for RDBMS and DBMS (Database Management System) to be used interchangeably because almost all major commercial databases are relational and support some form of SQL to allow the user to query the relations between data tables.

Two-Tier Database Design

Two-tier models appeared with the advent of server technology. Communication-protocol development and extensive use of local and wide area networks allowed the database developer to create an application front end that accessed data through a connection (*socket*) to the back-end server. Figure 11.2 illustrates a two-tier database design, where the client software is connected to the database through a socket connection.

FIGURE 11.2

The two-tier database design

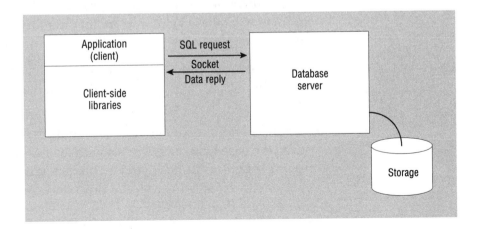

Client programs (applying a user interface) send SQL requests to the database server. The server returns the appropriate results, and the client is responsible for formatting the data. Clients still use a vendor-provided library of functions that manage the communication between client and server. Most of these libraries are written in the C language.

Commercial database vendors realized the potential for adding intelligence to the database server. They created proprietary techniques that allowed the database designer to develop macro programs for simple data manipulation. These macros, called *stored procedures*, can cause problems relating to version control and maintenance. Because a stored procedure is an executable program living on the database, it is possible for the stored procedure to attempt to access named columns of a database table when the table has been changed. For example, if a column with the name id is changed to cust_id, the meaning of the original stored procedure is lost. The advent of *triggers*, which are stored procedures executed automatically upon some action with a particular table or tables, can compound these difficulties when the data returned from a query are not expected. Again, this can be the result of the trigger reading a table column that has been altered.

Despite the success of client/server architectures, two-tier database models suffer a number of limitations:

- They are limited by the vendor-provided library—switching from one database vendor to another requires a rewrite of a significant amount of code to the client application.

- Version control is an issue. When the vendor updates the client-side libraries, the applications that utilize the database must be recompiled and redistributed.

- Vendor libraries deal with low-level data manipulation. Typically the base library only deals with fetches and updates on single rows or columns of data. This can be enhanced on the server-side by creating a stored procedure, but the complexity of the system then increases.

- All of the intelligence associated with using and manipulating the data is implemented in the client application, creating large client-side runtimes. This drives the cost of each client seat up.

Three-Tier Database Design

Today there is a great deal of interest in multitier design. There does not have to be just three tiers, but conceptually this is the next step. In a multitier design, the client communicates with an intermediate server that provides a layer of abstraction from the RDBMS. Figure 11.3 illustrates a three-tier database design.

FIGURE 11.3

A three-tier database design

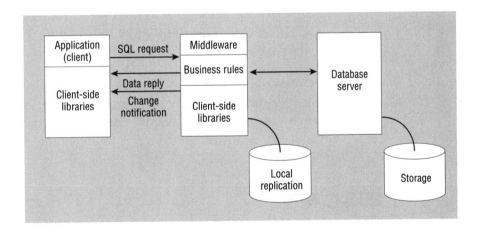

The intermediate layer is designed to handle multiple client requests and manage the connection to one or more database servers. The intermediate tier design provides several advantages over the two-tier design. The middle tier:

- is multithreaded to manage multiple client connections simultaneously

- can accept connections from clients on a variety of vendor-neutral protocols (from HTTP to TCP/IP), then marshal the requests to the appropriate vendor-specific database servers, and return the replies to the appropriate clients

- can be programmed with a set of "business rules" that manage the manipulation of the data; business rules could include anything from restricting access to certain portions of data to making sure that data is properly formatted before being inserted or updated

- prevents the client from becoming too heavy by centralizing process-intensive tasks and abstracting data representation to a higher level

- isolates the client application from the database system and frees a company to switch database systems without having to rework the business rules

- can asynchronously provide the client with a status of a current data table or row

As an example of this last point, suppose that a client application had just completed a query of a particular table. If a subsequent action by another distinct client *changed* that data, the first client could receive notification from an intelligent middle-tier program.

The JDBC API

The JDBC API is designed to allow developers to create database front ends without having to continually rewrite their code. Despite standards set by the ANSI committee, each database system vendor has a unique way of connecting and, in some cases, communicating with their system.

The ability to create robust, platform-independent applications and Web-based applets prompted developers to consider using Java to develop front-end connectivity solutions. At the outset, third-party software developers met the need by providing proprietary solutions, by using native methods to integrate client-side libraries, or by creating a third tier and a new protocol.

JavaSoft, the Sun Microsystems business unit that is responsible for the development of Java products, worked in conjunction with database and database-tool vendors to create a DBMS-independent mechanism that would allow developers to write their client-side applications without concern for the particular database being used. The result is the JDBC API, in its first release, which is part of the core JDK 1.1.

JDBC provides application developers with a *single* API that is uniform and database independent. The API provides a standard to write to, and a standard that takes all of the various application designs into account. The secret is a set of Java interfaces that are implemented by a driver. The driver takes care of the translation of the standard JDBC calls into the specific calls required by the database it supports. In the following figure, the application is written once and moved to the various drivers. The application remains the same; the drivers change. Drivers may be used to develop the middle tier of a multitier database design, also known as *middleware*, as illustrated in Figure 11.4.

In addition to providing developers with a uniform and DBMS-independent framework, JDBC also provides a means of allowing developers to retain the specific functionality that their database vendor offers. JDBC drivers must support ANSI SQL-2 Entry Level, but JDBC allows developers to pass query strings directly to the connected driver. These strings may or may not be ANSI SQL, or SQL at all. The use of these strings is up to the underlying driver. Of course use of this feature limits the freedom of the application developer to change database back ends.

FIGURE 11.4

JDBC database designs

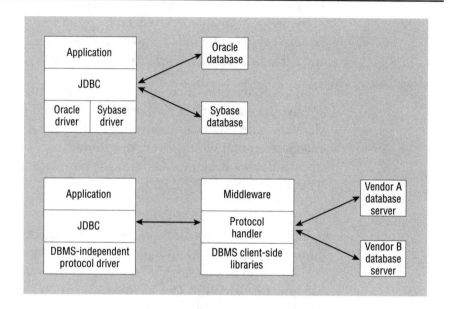

JDBC is *not* a derivative of Microsoft's Open Database Connectivity specification (ODBC). JDBC is written entirely in Java and ODBC is a C interface. However, both JDBC and ODBC are based on the X/Open SQL Command Level Interface (CLI). Having the same conceptual base allows work on the API to proceed quickly and makes acceptance of the API easier. JavaSoft provides a JDBC-ODBC bridge that translates JDBC to ODBC. This implementation, done with native methods, is very small and efficient.

In general, there are two levels of interface in the JDBC API: the Application Layer, where the developer uses the API to make calls to the database via SQL and retrieve the results, and the Driver Layer, that handles all communication with a specific Driver implementation.

Every JDBC application (or applet) must have at least one JDBC driver, and each driver is specific to the type of DBMS used. A driver does not, however, need to be directly associated with a database.

The API Components

As mentioned earlier, there are two distinct layers within the JDBC API: the Application Layer, which database-application developers will use, and the Driver Layer, which driver vendors implement. It is important to understand the Driver Layer, if only to realize that some of the objects that are used at the Application Layer are created by the driver. Figure 11.5 illustrates the connection between the Driver and Application layers.

FIGURE 11.5

JDBC API components

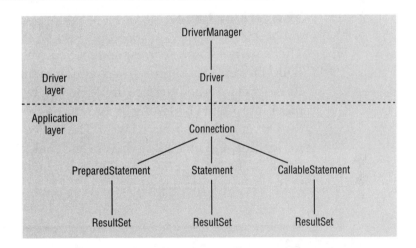

Fortunately, the application developer needs only use the standard API interfaces in order to guarantee JDBC compliance. The driver developer is responsible for developing code that interfaces to the database and supports the JDBC application level calls.

There are four main interfaces that every driver layer must implement, and one class that bridges the Application and Driver layers. The four interfaces are the `Driver, Connection, Statement,` and `ResultSet`. The `Driver` interface implementation is where the connection to the database is made. In most applications, the `Driver` is accessed through the `DriverManager` class—providing one more layer of abstraction for the developer.

The `Connection`, `Statement`, and `ResultSet` interfaces are implemented by the driver vendor, but these interfaces represent the methods that the application developer will treat as real object classes and allow the developer to create statements and retrieve results. So the distinction in this section between Driver and Application layers is artificial—but it allows the developer to create database applications without having to think about where the objects are coming from or worry about what specific driver the application will use.

The Driver Layer

There is a one-to-one correspondence between the database and the JDBC Driver. This approach is common in multitier designs. The `Driver` class is an interface implemented by the driver vendor. The other important class is the `DriverManager` class, which sits above the Driver and Application layers. The `DriverManager` is responsible for loading and unloading drivers and making connections through drivers. The `DriverManager` also provides features for logging and database login timeouts.

NOTE   As shown in Figure 11.4, the driver does not have to connect directly to a database and can support a new protocol for an multitier database design.

The *Driver* Interface   Every JDBC application must have at least one JDBC driver implementation. The `Driver` interface allows the `DriverManager` and JDBC Application layers to exist independently of the particular database used. A JDBC driver is an implementation of the `Driver` interface class.

Drivers use a string to locate and access databases. The syntax of this string is very similar to a URL string. The purpose of a JDBC URL string is to separate the application developer from the driver developer. JavaSoft defines the following goals for driver URLs:

- The name of the driver-access URL should define the type of database being used.

- The user (application developer) should be free from any of the administration of creating the database connection—therefore, any database connection information (host, port, database name, user access, and passwords) should be encoded in the URL.

- A network naming system may be used in order to prevent the user from having to specifically encode the exact hostname and port number of the database.

The URL syntax used by the World Wide Web supports a standard syntax that satisfies these goals. JDBC URLs have the following syntax and structure:

```
jdbc:<subprotocol>:<subname>
```

where `<subprotocol>` defines the type of driver, and `<subname>` provides the network encoded name. For example:

```
jdbc:oracle:products
```

Here the database driver is an Oracle driver and the subname is a local database called `products`. This driver is designed to know how to use the subname when making the connection to the Oracle database.

A network naming service may also be specified as the subprotocol, rather than using a specific database driver name. In this case the subprotocol would define the naming service:

```
jdbc: localnaming:human-resources
```

Here the subprotocol defines a local service that can resolve the subname `human-resources` to a database server. This approach can be very useful when the application developer wants to isolate the user from the actual location, name, database username, and database password. This URL specifies that a driver named `localnaming` be specified; this could be a Java program that contains a simple flat-file lookup, translates `human-resources` into `hrdatabase1.eng:888/personnel`, and knows to use the username `user` and password *matilda*. The details of the connection are kept hidden from the user.

Typically the application developer will know specifically where the database is located and may not wish to use network indirection to locate the database. In this case, the URL may be expanded to include the location of the host and specific port and database information:

```
jdbc:msql://dbserver.eng:1112/bugreports
```

Here an `msql` database driver type is used to locate a server named `dbserver` in the `eng` domain and attempt to connect to a database server on port 1112 that contains a `bugreports` database, using the default username and password to connect.

> **NOTE** Subprotocol names will eventually overlap and there will need to be a registry of reserved names. For more information on registering a JDBC subprotocol name, consult the JDBC Specification.

The `Driver` interface is implemented by the driver vendor by creating methods for each of the following interface methods:

Signature: `interface java.sql.Driver`

> `public abstract Connection connect (String url, Properties info) throws SQLException` The driver implementation of this method should check the subprotocol name of the URL string passed for a match with this driver. If there is a match, the driver should then attempt to make a connection to the database using the information passed in the remainder of the URL. A successful database connection will return an instance of the driver's implementation of a `Connection` interface (object).

The SQLException should be thrown only if the driver recognizes the URL subprotocol but cannot make the database connection. A null is returned if the URL does not match a URL the driver expected. The username and password are included in a container class called Properties.

public abstract boolean acceptsURL (String url) throws SQLException It is also possible to explicitly "ask" the driver if the URL is valid, but note that the implementation of this method (typically) only checks the subprotocol specified in the URL, not whether the connection can be made.

The Driver connect() method is the most important method, and is called by the DriverManager to obtain a Connection object. As previously shown in Figure 11.5, the Connection object is the starting point of the JDBC application layer. The Connection object is used to create Statement objects that perform queries.

The Driver connect() method typically performs the following steps:

- checks to see if the given URL string is valid
- opens a TCP connection to the host and port number specified
- attempts to access the named database table (if any)
- returns an instance of a Connection object

NOTE Connection is a Java interface, so the object returned is actually a reference to an instance of the driver's implementation of the Connection interface.

The *DriverManager* Class The DriverManager class is really a utility class used to manage JDBC drivers. The class provides methods to obtain a connection through a driver, register and de-register drivers, set up logging, and set login timeouts for database access. All of the methods in the `DriverManager` class listed below are static, and may be referenced through the following class name:

Signature: `public class java.sql.DriverManager`

`public static synchronized Connection getConnection (String url, Properties info) throws SQLException` This method (and the other `getConnection()` methods) attempts to return a reference to an object implemented from the `Connection` interface. The method sweeps through a Vector of stored `Driver` classes, passing the URL string and `Properties` object `info` to each in turn. The first `Driver` class that returns a Connection is used. `info` is a reference to a `Properties` container object of tag/value pairs, typically username/password. This method allows several attempts to make an authorized connection for each driver in the Vector.

`public static synchronized Connection getConnection (String url) throws SQLException` This method calls `get-Connection (url, info)` above with an empty `Properties` object (`info`).

`public static synchronized Connection getConnection (String url, String user, String password) throws SQLException` This method creates a `Properties` object (`info`), stores the user and password strings into it, and then calls `getConnection (url, info)` above.

`public static synchronized void registerDriver-(java.sql.Driver driver) throws SQLException` This method stores the instance of the `Driver` interface implementation into a Vector of drivers, along with an instance of `security-Context`, that identifies where the driver came from.

`public static void setLogStream(java.io.Print-Stream out)` This method sets a private static `java.io.PrintStream` reference to the `PrintStream` object passed to the method.

> **TIP**
>
> The driver implementation can make use of two static object references that are stored through set *Type* methods and accessed by the driver through get *Type* methods: an integer that specifies login timeout and a PrintStream object used to log driver information.

Drivers are registered with the DriverManager class either at initialization of the DriverManager class or when an instance of the driver is created.

When the DriverManager class is loaded, a section of static code (in the class) is run, and the class names of drivers listed in a Java property named jdbc.drivers are loaded. This property can be used to define a list of colon-separated driver class names, such as:

```
jdbc.drivers=imaginary.sql.Driver:oracle.sql.Driver:
    weblogic.sql.Driver
```

Each driver name is a class file name (including the package declaration) that the DriverManager will attempt to load through the current CLASSPATH. The DriverManager uses the following call to locate, load, and link the named class:

```
Class.forName(driver);
```

If the jdbc.drivers property is empty (unspecified), then the application programmer must create an instance of a driver class.

In both cases, the Driver class implementation must explicitly register itself with the DriverManager by calling:

```
DriverManager.registerDriver (this);
```

Here is a segment of code from the imaginary Driver (for the Mini-SQL database). The Driver registers itself whenever an instance of the imaginary driver is created:

```
...
public class iMsqlDriver implements java.sql.Driver {
 static {
```

```
try {
  new iMsqlDriver();
}
catch( SQLException e ) {
  e.printStackTrace();
}
}
/**
 * Constructs a new driver and registers it with
 * java.sql.DriverManager.registerDriver() as specified by the
 * JDBC draft protocol.
 */
public iMsqlDriver() throws SQLException {
  java.sql.DriverManager.registerDriver(this);
}
...
```

The primary use of the `DriverManager` is to get a `Connection` object reference through the `getConnection` method:

```
Connection conn = null;
conn = DriverManager.getConnection
("jdbc:sybase://dbserver:8080/billing", dbuser, dbpasswd);
```

This method goes through the list of registered drivers and passes the URL string and parameters to each driver in turn through the driver's `connect()` method. If the driver supports the subprotocol and subname information, a `Connection` object reference is returned.

The `DriverManager` class is not required to create JDBC applications, as it is possible to get a `Connection` object directly from the `Driver`:

```
Connection conn = null;
conn = new
Driver().connect("jdbc:sybase://dbserver:8080/billing", props);
```

This means of obtaining a connection is not as clean, and leaves the application developer dependent on the `Driver` implementation class to provide security checks.

The Application Layer

The Application Layer encompasses three interfaces that are implemented at the Driver Layer, but are used by the application developer. In Java, the interface provides a means of using a general name to indicate a specific object. The general name defines methods that *must* be implemented by the specific object classes. For the application developer, this means that the specific `Driver` class implementation is irrelevant. Just coding to the standard JDBC APIs will be sufficient. This is of course assuming that the driver is JDBC compliant. Recall that this means the database is at least ANSI SQL-2 Entry Level.

The three main interfaces are `Connection`, `Statement`, and `ResultSet`. A `Connection` object is obtained from the driver implementation through the `DriverManager.getConnection()` method call. Once a `Connection` object is returned, the application developer may create a `Statement` object to issue against the database. The result of a `Statement` is a `ResultSet` object, which contains the results of the particular statement (if any).

Connection Basics   The `Connection` interface represents a session with the database connection provided by the `Driver`. Typical database connections include the ability to control changes made to the actual data stored through transactions. A *transaction* is a set of operations that are completed in order. A *commit* action makes the operations store (or change) data in the database. A *rollback* action undoes the previous transaction before it has been committed. On creation, JDBC `Connections` are in an *auto-commit* mode—there is no rollback possible. So after getting a `Connection` object from the driver, the developer should consider setting auto-commit to `false` with the `setAutoCommit(boolean b)` method.

When auto-commit is disabled, the `Connection` will support both `Connection.commit()` and `Connection.rollback()` method calls. The level of support for transaction isolation depends on the underlying support for transactions in the database.

A portion of the `Connection` interface definition follows:

Signature: `public interface Connection`

`Statement createStatement () throws SQLException`
The `Connection` object implementation will return an instance
of an implementation of a `Statement` object. The `Statement`
object is then used to issue queries.

`PreparedStatement prepareStatement (String sql)`
`throws SQLException` The `Connection` object implementation will return an instance of a `PreparedStatement` object that
is configured with the `sql` string passed. The driver may then
send the statement to the database, if the database (driver) handles
precompiled statements. Otherwise the driver may wait until the
`PreparedStatement` is executed by an execute method. An
exception may be thrown if the driver and database do not implement precompiled statements.

`CallableStatement prepareCall (String sql) throws`
`SQLException` The `Connection` object implementation will
return an instance of a `CallableStatement`. `Callable-`
`Statements` are optimized for handling stored procedures. The
driver implementation may send the `sql` string immediately
when `prepareCall()` is complete or may wait until an execute
method occurs.

`void setAutoCommit (boolean autoCommit) throws`
`SQLException` Sets a flag in the driver implementation that
enables commit/rollback (`false`) or makes all transactions commit immediately (`true`).

`void commit () throws SQLException` Makes all changes
made since the beginning of the current transaction (either the opening of the `Connection` or since the last `commit()` or `rollback()`).

`void rollback() throws SQLException` Drops all
changes made since the beginning of the current transaction.

The primary use of the `Connection` interface is to create a statement:

```
Connection msqlConn = null;
Statement stmt = null;

msqlConn = DriverManager.getConnection (url);
stmt = msqlConn.createStatement ();
```

This statement may be used to send SQL statements that return a single result set in a `ResultSet` object reference. Statements that need be called a number of times with slight variations may be executed more efficiently using a `PreparedStatement`. The `Connection` interface is also used to create a `CallableStatement` whose purpose is to execute stored procedures.

Most of the time, the developer knows the database schema beforehand and creates the application based on the schema. However, JDBC provides an interface that may be used to dynamically determine the schema of a database. The `Connection` interface `getMetaData` method will return a `DatabaseMetaData` object. The instance of the class that implements the interface provides information about the database as a whole, including access information about tables and procedures, column names, data types, and so on. The implementation details of `DatabaseMetaData` are dependent on the database vendor's ability to return this type of information.

Statement Basics   A *statement* is the vehicle for sending SQL queries to the database and retrieving a set of results. Statements can be SQL updates, inserts, deletes, or queries (via Select). The `Statement` interface provides a number of methods designed to make the job of writing queries to the database easier.

Signature: `public interface Statement`

> `ResultSet executeQuery(String sql) throws SQLException`   Executes a single SQL query and return the results in an object of type `ResultSet`.

`int executeUpdate(String sql) throws SQLException`
Executes a single SQL query that does not return a set of results, but a count of rows affected.

`boolean execute(String sql) throws SQLException`
A general SQL statement that may return multiple result sets and/or update counts. This method is used to execute stored procedures that return `Out` and `Inout` parameters. The `getResult-Set()`, `getUpdateCount()`, and `getMoreResults()` methods are used to retrieve the data returned.

TIP
> *In parameters* are parameters that are passed into an operation. *Out parameters* are parameters passed by reference; they are expected to return a result of the reference type. *Inout parameters* are *Out* parameters that contain an initial value that may change as a result of the operation. JDBC supports all three parameter types.

`ResultSet getResultSet () throws SQLException`
Returns the current data as the result of a statement execution as a `ResultSet` object. Note that if there are no results to be read or if the result is an update count, this method returns a null. Also note that once read, the results are cleared.

`int getUpdateCount() throws SQLException` Returns the status of an `Update`, `Insert`, or `Delete` query or a stored procedure. The value returned is the number of rows affected. A -1 is returned if there is either no update count or if the data returned is a result set. Once read, the update count is cleared.

`boolean getMoreResults() throws SQLException`
Moves to the next result in a set of multiple results/update counts. This method returns `true` if the next result is a `ResultSet` object. This method will also close any previous `ResultSet` read.

Statements may or may not return a `ResultSet` object, depending on the `Statement` method used. The `executeUpdate()` method, for example, is used to execute SQL statements that do not expect a result (except a row count status):

```
int rowCount;
rowCount = stmt.executeUpdate ("DELETE FROM Customer WHERE
CustomerID = 'McG10233'");
```

SQL statements that return a single set of results can use the `executeQuery()` method. This method returns a single `ResultSet` object. The object represents the row information returned as a result of the query:

```
ResultSet results;
results = stmt.executeQuery ("SELECT * FROM Stock");
```

SQL statements that execute stored procedures (or trigger a stored procedure) may return more than one set of results. The `execute()` method is a general purpose method than can return either a single result set or multiple result sets. The method returns a boolean flag that is used to determine whether there are more result sets. Because a result set could either contain data or the count of an operation that returns a row count, the `getResultSet()`, `getMoreResults()`, and `getUpdateCount()` methods are used.

For example:

```
// Assume SQLString returns multiple result sets
// true if a ResultSet is returned
int count;
if (stmt.execute (SQLstring)) {
    results = stmt.getResultSet();
// false, an UpdateCount was returned
} else {
    count = stmt.getUpdateCount();
}

// Process the first results here ....
```

```
// Now loop until there are no more results or update counts
do {
    // Is the next result a ResultSet?
    if (stmt.getMoreResults()) {
        results = stmt.getResultSet();
    else {
        count = stmt.getUpdateCount();
    }

    // Process next results here ....

} while ((results != null) && (count != -1));
```

The `PreparedStatement` interface extends the `Statement` interface. When there is a SQL statement that requires repetition with minor variations, the `PreparedStatement` provides an efficient mechanism for passing a precompiled SQL statement that uses parameters.

```
public interface PreparedStatement extends Statement
```

`PreparedStatement` parameters are used to pass data into a SQL statement, so they are considered `In` parameters and are filled in by using set*Type* methods:

> **NOTE** The set*Type* methods fill the value of parameters (marked by question marks) in a `PreparedStatement`. These parameters are indexed from 1 to *n*.

```
// Assume priceList is an array of prices that needs
// to be reduced for a 10% off sale, and reducedItems
// is an array of item IDs
int reduction = 10;
PreparedStatement ps = msqlConn.prepareStatment ("UPDATE Catalog
SET Price = ? WHERE ItemID = ?");
// Do the updates in a loop
for (int i = 0; i < reducedItems.length(); i++) {
    // Note that the setType methods set the value of the
    // parameters noted in the SQL statement with question
    // marks (?). They are indexed, starting from 1 to n.
```

```
        ps.setFloat (1, (priceList[i]*((float)(100-reduction)/100)));
        ps.setString (2, reducedItems[i]);
        if (ps.executeUpdate() == 0) {
                throw new SQLException ("No Item ID: " +
                        reducedItems[i]);
        }
}
```

Parameters hold their current values until either a new set*Type* method is called or the method clearParameters() is called for the PreparedStatement object. In addition to the execute methods inherited from Statement, PrepareStatement declares the following set*Type* methods. Each method takes two arguments: a parameter index and the primitive or class type, as illustrated in Table 11.1.

The CallableStatement interface is used to execute SQL stored procedures. CallableStatement inherits from the Prepared-Statement interface, so all of the execute and set*Type* methods are available. Stored procedures have a varying syntax among database vendors, so JDBC defines a standard way for all RDBMSs to call stored procedures.

```
public interface CallableStatement extends PreparedStatement
```

The JDBC uses an escape syntax that allows parameters to be passed as In parameters and Out parameters. The syntax also allows a result to be returned, and if this syntax is used the parameter must be registered as an Out parameter.

Here is an example of a CallableStatement returning an Out parameter:

```
CallableStatement cs = conn.prepareCall ("{call getQuote (?, ?)}");
cs.setString (1, stockName);
// java.sql.Types defines SQL data types that are returned
// as Out parameters
cs.registerOutParameter (2, Types.FLOAT);
stmt.executeUpdate();
float quote = stmt.getFloat (2);
```

TABLE 11.1 *setType* methods

Method Signature	Java Type	SQL Type from the Database
void setByte (int index, byte b)	byte	TINYINT
void setShort (int index, short x)	short	SMALLINT
void setInt (int index, int i)	int	INTEGER
void setLong (int index, long l)	long	BIGINT
void setFloat (int index, float f)	float	FLOAT
void setDouble (int index, double d)	double	DOUBLE
void setBigDecimal (int index, BigDecimal x)	java.math.BigDecimal	NUMERIC
void setString (int index, String s)	java.lang.String	VARCHAR or LONGVAR CHAR
void setBytes (int index, byte x[])	byte array	VARBINARY or LONGVAR BINARY
void setDate (int index, Date d)	java.sql.Date	DATE
void setTime (int index, Time t)	java.sql.Time	TIME
void setTimestamp (int index, Timestamp ts)	java.sql.Timestamp	TIMESTAMP
void setNull (int index, int sqlType)	—	java.sql.Types lists SQL types by number, and NULL is integer 0 (zero)
void setBoolean (int index, boolean b)	boolean	BIT

CallableStatement defines a set of get*Type* methods that convert the SQL types returned from the database to Java types. These methods match the set*Type* methods declared by Prepared-Statement, as shown in Table 11.2.

NOTE The get*Type* methods access data in each column as the result a query. Each column can be accessed by either its position in the row, numbered from 1 to *n* columns, or by its name, like custID.

TABLE 11.2 get*Type* methods

Method Signature	Java Type	SQL Type from the Database
`boolean getBoolean (int index)`	boolean	BIT
`byte getByte (int index)`	byte	TINYINT
`short getShort (int index)`	short	SMALLINT
`int getInt (int index)`	int	INTEGER
`long getLong (int index)`	long	BIGINT
`float getFloat (int index)`	float	FLOAT
`double getDouble (int index)`	double	DOUBLE
`BigDecimal getBigDecimal (int index, int scale)`	`java.math.BigDecimal`	NUMERIC
`String getString (int index)`	String	CHAR, VAR CHAR or LONGVAR CHAR
`byte[] getBytes (int index)`	byte array	BINARY or VARBINARY
`Date getDate (int index)`	`java.sql.Date`	DATE
`Time getTime (int index)`	`java.sql.Time`	TIME
`Timestamp getTimestamp (int index)`	`java.sql.Timestamp`	TIMESTAMP

NOTE Note that it is the responsibility of the JDBC driver to convert the data passed from the database as SQL data types into Java values.

***ResultSet* Basics**   The `ResultSet` interface defines methods for accessing tables of data generated as the result of executing a `Statement`. `ResultSet` column values may be accessed in any order—they are indexed and may be selected by either the name or the number (numbered from 1 to *n*) of the column. `ResultSet` maintains the position of the current row, starting with the first row of data returned. The `next()` method moves to the next row of data.

A partial look at the `ResultSet` interface follows:

Signature: `public interface ResultSet`

`boolean next () throws SQLException`   Positions the `ResultSet` to the next row; `ResultSet` row position is initially just before the first row of the result set.

`ResultSetMetaData getMetaData throws SQLException` Returns an object that contains a description of the current result set: the number of columns, the type of each column, and properties of the results.

`void close () throws SQLException`   Normally a `ResultSet` is closed when another `Statement` is executed, but it may be desirable to release the resources earlier.

As above in the `CallableStatement`, the resulting data can be read through get *Type* methods. For example:

```
// Pass a query to the statement object
ResultSet rs = stmt.executeQuery("SELECT * FROM Stock WHERE quantity = 0");

// Get the results as their Java types
// Note that columns are indexed by an integer starting with 1,
// or by the name of column, as in "ItemID"
```

```
System.out.println ("Stock replenishment list");
while (rs.next()) {

    System.out.println ("Item ID: " + rs.getString("ItemID"));
    System.out.println ("Next ship date: " + rs.getDate(2));
    System.out.println ("");
}
```

ResultSetMetaData   Besides being able to read data from a
`ResultSet` object, JDBC provides an interface to allow the developer
to determine what type of data was returned. The `ResultSet-`
`MetaData` interface is similar to the `DatabaseMetaData` interface
in concept, but is specific to the current `ResultSet`. As with `Data-`
`baseMetaData`, it is unlikely that many developers will use this
interface as most applications are written with an understanding of
the database schema and column names and values. However,
`ResultSetMetaData` is useful in dynamically determining the
`MetaData` of a `ResultSet` returned from a stored procedure.

Sending and Receiving Large Data Chunks   SQL LONG-
VARBINARY and LONGVARCHAR data types can be of arbitrary
size. The `getBytes()` and `getString()` methods can read these
types up to the limits imposed by the driver. The limits can be read
through the `Statement.getMaxFieldSize()` method. For larger
blocks of data, the JDBC allows developers to use `java.io`
`.Input` streams to return the data in chunks.

TIP   Streams must be read immediately following the query execution—
they are automatically closed at the next get of a `ResultSet`.

Sending large blocks of data is also possible using `java.io`
`.OutputStream` as parameters. When a statement is executed the
JDBC driver makes repeated calls to read and transmit the data in
the streams.

Limitations Using JDBC
(Applications vs. Applets)

There are two types of programs in the Java world: applications and applets. Each program type provides benefits and the use of each is generally determined by the way in which the developer wishes the user to access the program.

Applications

Applications are Java programs that are developed as stand-alone executables. The user is expected to have access to the program executable (class file) and the Java interpreter locally. For an Intranet-based database front end, this strategy offers the benefits of faster startup (class files are local) and local disk utilization.

In addition, Java applications are trusted and are allowed greater flexibility with socket connections—making it possible for the client program to access multiple database systems on remote servers.

Java applications are becoming more prevalent as tools become available for GUI development and speed improvements are made possible through Just-In-Time (JIT) compilers/interpreters. Applications can also reduce or eliminate issues with browser security models and the differences in the browser's implementation of Java widgets.

Applets

Applets are mini Java programs that require a Java-enabled browser to run. The browser provides an environment for the applet to run in, including drawing and viewing resources directly on the browser page. When a user moves or "surfs" to a browser page that contains an applet, the applet is automatically executed.

The process includes downloading the necessary Java applet code, including JDBC drivers and application layer software, automatically checking security restrictions on the code, and if ok, running the applet.

Applets provide several key benefits over applications:

Version control It is possible to modify an applet almost on the fly by replacing the class file in the HTML page references.

Easier execution model It takes very little effort to learn to use even the most sophisticated browsers and to execute a front-end client; the user simply navigates to the page where the application is located.

Online help Creating the running program on a browser HTML page makes it extremely easy to embed Help links that can be developed separate from the running program.

A typical use of applets might be for training within a large organization, where the data being delivered is not critical and access can be limited to a two-tier model (three-tier models are possible but involve more complex layering schemes). Another use may be the simple presentation of data to the Internet community, again where the quantity of data is not great and security of the data message is not paramount.

Applets, however, are severely constrained by the browser environment. Applets are not allowed to do the following:

- Access any local files. This limits the use of local caching and table manipulation and storage to in-memory during the life of the applet.

- Connect to arbitrary hosts. Socket connections are only allowed between the applet and the host that the applet originated from.

- Load or run drivers that contain native methods (C language calls).

Additionally there is a considerable performance hit involved in loading applet code across an Internet (wide area) network connection.

Some of these constraints may be lifted or reduced with the introduction of trusted applets and browsers that accept them. Trusted applets may be code signed with a cryptographic key or may be stored in a trusted location. If the browser environment believes that the applets' source is trusted, then for security purposes they may be treated like applications, although there may still be limits regarding the location of databases on an internet that are not related to the Java security manager. Trusted applets are the subject of future consideration in the development of the Java security model.

The other alternative that is more tangible and available today is the use of a three-tier model. In this approach the applet is loaded from a middleware tier that provides both the HTML page and HTTP server, and a multithreaded application (Java, C, or C++) that supports socket connections for multiple clients and, in turn, contacts remote database systems.

Calls to the third tier can be managed by developing a custom (proprietary) protocol, by using Remote Method Invocation (RMI), or by using an Object Request Broker (ORB). See the *Alternative Connectivity Strategies* section in this chapter.

Security Considerations

The JDBC API follows the standard Java security model. In short, applications are considered trusted code, and applets are considered untrusted. In general, the job of writing a secure JDBC driver is left to the driver vendor.

The Java Virtual Machine employs its own well-documented security checks for untrusted applets, including the aforementioned restrictions. However, if a JDBC driver vendor wants to extend the model by adding features to their driver—for example, allowing multiple applets to use the same TCP socket connection to talk to a database—then it becomes the responsibility of the vendor to check that each applet is allowed to use the connection.

In addition to maintaining the integrity of the Java security model, both the JDBC driver vendor and JDBC application developer need to keep in mind that the JDBC API defines a means of executing database calls and does not define a network security model. The data sent over the wire to the database and the resulting table information (for example, to request customer credit card information) are exposed and can be read by any terminal that is capable of snooping the network.

A JDBC Database Example

The following is an example that uses the concepts presented in this chapter; it is artificial, and only meant to illustrate the use of `Statement`, `PreparedStatement`, and `CallableStatement`.

The simple database has a table called *Customers*, which has the schema shown in Table 11.3.

TABLE 11.3   Customer Data Table

CustomerID	VARCHAR
LastName	VARCHAR
FirstName	VARCHAR
Phonenumber	VARCHAR
StreetAddress	VARCHAR
Zipcode	VARCHAR

Table 11.3 is part of a larger database that stores information related to a large catalog ordering system. Here is the definition of a simple

Customer object with two primary methods, insertNewCustomer() and getCustomer():

Signature: `public class Customer`

`public Customer (Connection conn)` is the constructor for the class. The `Customer` constructor receives a `Connection` object, which it uses to create `Statement` references. In addition, the constructor creates a `PreparedStatement` and three `CallableStatements`.

`public String insertNewCustomer (String lname, String fname, String pnum, String addr, String zip) throws insertFailedException, SQLException` creates a new customer record, including a new ID. The ID is created through a stored procedure that reads the current list of customer IDs and creates a new reference. The method returns the new ID created or throws an exception if the insert failed.

`public CustomerInfo getCustomer (String custID) throws selectException, SQLException` returns an object that contains the data in the Customer table. An exception is thrown if the customer ID passed does not exist or is not properly formatted, or if the SQL statement fails.

`public static synchronized boolean validateZip (String zip) throws SQLException` is a utility method to validate the zip code. A `true` value is returned if the zip code exists in the ZipCode table in the database.

`public static synchronized boolean validateID (String id) throws SQLException` is a utility method to validate a customer ID. If the ID exists, the method returns `true`.

The source, found on the CD-ROM in `javadevhdbk\ch08\ Customer.java`, is as follows:

Customer.java

```java
// Customer record class
// This class is used to store and access customer data from the
// database
import java.sql.*;

public class Customer {

    private Connection conn;
    private PreparedStatement insertNewCustomer;
    private CallableStatement getNewID;
    public static CallableStatement checkZip;
    public static CallableStatement checkID;

    // Customer constructor: store a local copy of the
    //                       Connection object
    //                       create statements for use later
    public Customer (Connection c) {
        conn = c;

        try {
            insertNewCustomer = conn.prepareStatement
          ("INSERT INTO Customers VALUES (?, ?, ?, ?, ?, ?)");

            getNewID = conn.prepareCall
                        ("{call getNewID (?)}");

            checkID = conn.prepareCall
                        ("{call checkID (?,?)}");

            checkZip = conn.prepareCall
                        ("{call checkZip (?, ?)}");
        } catch (SQLException e) {
        System.out.println
        ("Unable to create prepared and callable statements");
        }
    }

    // Method for creating a new customer record.
    // The customerID is generated by a stored procedure
    // call on the database
    public String insertNewCustomer (String lname, String fname,
```

```
        String pnum, String addr, String zip)
        throws insertFailedException, SQLException {

            String newID;

            // Get a new customer ID through the stored procedure
            if ((newID = getNewID ()) == null) {
                throw new insertFailedException
                            ("could not get new ID");
            }

            // Insert the new customer ID
            insertNewCustomer.setString (1, newID);
            insertNewCustomer.setString (2, lname);
            insertNewCustomer.setString (3, fname);
            insertNewCustomer.setString (4, pnum);
            insertNewCustomer.setString (5, addr);
            insertNewCustomer.setString (6, zip);

            // Execute the statement
            if (insertNewCustomer.executeUpdate() != 1) {
                throw new insertFailedException
                            ("could not execute insert");
            }
            return (newID);
        }

        // Get a single customer record with this ID
        // Note: this method maps the returned data onto a
        // CustomerInfo container object
        public CustomerInfo getCustomer (String custID)
        throws selectException, SQLException {

            // Check the ID first
            if (!validateID (custID)) {
                throw new selectException
                        ("no customer with ID: " + custID);
            }

            // Create the select statement
            Statement stmt = conn.createStatement();
```

```
        // Get the results
        ResultSet rs = stmt.executeQuery
        ("SELECT *FROM Customer WHERE CustID = " + custID);

        // Create a CustomerInfo container object
        CustomerInfo info = new CustomerInfo ();

        // Populate the CustomerInfo object
        // Columns are indexed starting with 1
        info.CustomerID = rs.getString (1);
        info.LastName = rs.getString (2);
        info.FirstName = rs.getString (3);
        info.PhoneNumber = rs.getString (4);
        info.StreetAddress = rs.getString (5);
        info.Zip = rs.getString (6);

        return (info);
    }


// Method for validation of a customer's zip code
// This method is public so that it can be called from
// a user interface
public static synchronized boolean validateZip (String zip)
throws SQLException {

        // Make call to stored procedure to validate zip code
        checkZip.setString (1, zip);
        checkZip.registerOutParameter (2, Types.BIT);
        checkZip.executeUpdate ();
        return (checkZip.getBoolean(2));

    }


// Method for validating a customer ID
// This method is public so that it can be called from
// a user interface
public static synchronized boolean validateID (String id)
throws SQLException {

        // Make call to stored procedure to validate
        // customer id
        checkID.setString (1, id);
        checkID.registerOutParameter (2, Types.BIT);
```

```
                checkID.executeUpdate();
                return (checkID.getBoolean(2));
        }

        // Method for retrieving a new customer ID from the database
        private String getNewID () throws SQLException {

                // Make call to stored procedure to get
                // customer ID from DB
                getNewID.registerOutParameter (1, Types.VARCHAR);
                getNewID.executeUpdate();
                return (getNewID.getString (1));
        }
}


// Exceptions

// insertFailedException is a general exception for
// SQL insert problems
class insertFailedException extends SQLException {

        public insertFailedException (String reason) {
                super (reason);
        }

        public insertFailedException () {
                super ();
        }
}


// selectException is a general exception for SQL select problems
class selectException extends SQLException {

        public selectException (String reason) {
                super (reason);
        }

        public selectException () {
                super ();
        }
}
```

TIP

The `CustomerInfo` class is a simple container object. Container classes make it easier to pass a complete customer record to and from any method that manipulates the Customer table in the database. Data can be stored in the container class and passed as a single object reference, rather than having to pass each element as a single reference.

The following code can be found in `javadevhdbk\ch11\CustomerInfo.java`.

CustomerInfo.java

```
// A container object for the Customer table
public class CustomerInfo {

        String CustomerID;
        String LastName;
        String FirstName;
        String PhoneNumber;
        String StreetAddress;
        String Zip;

}
```

Finally, to test the simple `Customer` class, here is a simple Java application that illustrates loading a Sybase driver, then making a connection, and passing the `Connection` object returned to a new instance of a `Customer` object.

The code, found on the CD-ROM in `javadevhdbk\ch08\Example.java`, is as follows:

Example.java

```
// A simple Java application that illustrates the use of
// DriverManager,
// Driver, Connection, Statement and ResultSet

import java.sql.*;
import sybase.sql.*;
```

```
public class Example {

    Connection sybaseConn;

    // main
    public static void main (String arg[]) {

        // Look for the url, username and password
        if (arg.length < 3) {
            System.out.println ("Example use:");
            System.out.println
            ("java Example <url> <username> <password>");
            System.exit (1);
        }

        // Create an instance of the class
        Example ex = new Example ();

        // Initialize the connection
        ex.initdb (arg[0], arg[1], arg[2]);

        // Test the connection—write a customer and
        // then read it back
        ex.testdb ();
    }

    // method to initialize the database connection
    // The Connection object reference is kept globally
    public void initdb (String url, String user, String passwd) {
        // Try to open the database and get the connection
        try {

            // Note that this example assumes that
            // Java property "jdbc.drivers"
            // that is loading the appropriate driver(s) for
            // the url passed in the getConnection call.
            // It is possible to explicitly create an
            // instance of a driver as well, for example:
            // new sybase.sql.driver ();

            // Create a connection
            sybaseConn = DriverManager.getConnection
                    (url, user, passwd);
```

```
        } catch (SQLException e) {
            System.out.println
                    ("Database connection failed:");
            System.out.println (e.getMessage());
            System.exit (1);
        }
    }

    // Simple method to test the Customer class methods
    public void testdb () {
        String custID = null;

        // Create the instance of the Customer class
        Customer cust = new Customer (sybaseConn);

        try {
            // Now insert a new Customer
            custID = cust.insertNewCustomer
            ("Jones", "Bill", "555-1234", "5 Main Street",
             "01234");

        } catch (SQLException e) {

            System.out.println ("Insert failed:");
            System.out.println (e.getMessage());
            System.exit (1);
        }

        try {
            // Read it back from the database
            CustomerInfo info = cust.getCustomer (custID);

        } catch (SQLException e) {

            System.out.println ("Read failed:");
            System.out.println (e.getMessage());
            System.exit (1);
        }
    }
}
```

This example illustrates the use of the `CallableStatements` to issue stored procedure calls that validate the zip code and validate the customer ID, and the `PreparedStatement` to issue an Insert SQL statement with parameters that will change with each insert.

This example also illustrates code that will run with any JDBC driver that will support the stored procedures used in the `Customer` class. The driver class names are loaded from the `jdbc.drivers` property so code recompilation is not required.

JDBC Drivers

One of the real attractions of the JDBC API is the ability to develop applications knowing that all of the major database vendors are working in parallel to create drivers. A number of drivers are available both from database vendors and from third-party developers. In most cases it is wise to shop around for the best features, cost, and support.

Drivers come in a variety of flavors according to their construction and the type of database they are intended to support. JavaSoft categorizes database drivers four ways:

1. A JDBC-ODBC bridge driver, shown in Figure 11.6, implemented with ODBC binary code and in some cases a client library as well. The bridge driver is made up of three parts: a set of C libraries that connect the JDBC to the ODBC driver manager; the ODBC driver manager; and the ODBC driver.

2. A native library-to-Java implementation, as shown in Figure 11.7. This driver uses native C language library calls to translate JDBC to the native client library. These drivers use C language libraries that provide vendor-specific functionality and tie these libraries (through native method calls) to the JDBC. These drivers were the first available for Oracle, Sybase, Informix, DB2, and other client-library-based RDBMSs.

FIGURE 11.6

JDBC-ODBC bridge
driver

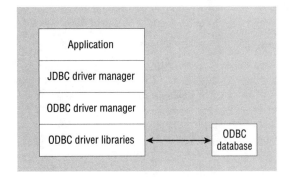

FIGURE 11.7

Native library-to-Java
driver

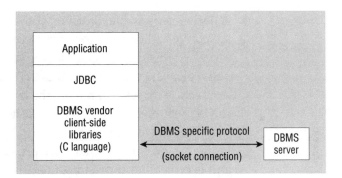

3. A network-protocol Java driver, as shown in Figure 11.8. JDBC calls are translated by this driver into a DBMS-independent protocol and sent to a middle-tier server over a socket. The middle-tier code contacts a variety of databases on behalf of the client. This approach is becoming the most popular and is by far the most flexible. This approach also deals specifically with issues relating to network security, including passing data through firewalls.

FIGURE 11.8

DBMS-independent
network protocol driver

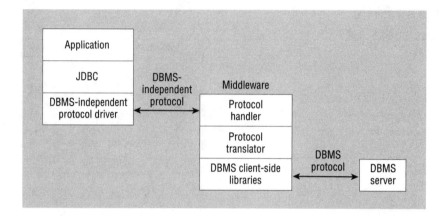

4. A native-protocol Java driver, shown in Figure 11.9. JDBC calls
   are converted directly to the network protocol used by the DBMS
   server. In this driver scenario, the database vendor supports a
   network socket, and the JDBC driver communicates over a socket
   connection directly to the database server. The client-side code
   can be written in Java. This solution has the benefit of being one
   of the easiest to implement and is very practical for Intranet use.
   However, because the network protocol is defined by the vendor
   and is typically proprietary, the driver usually comes only from
   the database vendor.

FIGURE 11.9

DBMS-protocol all-Java
driver

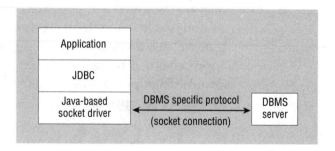

JDBC-ODBC Bridge

The JDBC-ODBC bridge is a JDBC driver that provides translation of JDBC calls to ODBC operations. There are a number of DBMSs that support ODBC—when a company the size of Microsoft creates a standard for database access, there are sure to be vendors that follow, and in fact there are more than 50 different ODBC drivers available.

As mentioned earlier, both JDBC and ODBC are based upon the X/Open CLI, so the translation between JDBC and ODBC is relatively straightforward. ODBC is a client-side set of libraries and a driver that is specific to the client's operating system and, in some cases, machine architecture.

From the developer's perspective, using a JDBC-ODBC bridge driver is an easy choice—applications will still speak directly to the JDBC interface classes, so it is exactly the same as using any other JDBC driver. However, the implementation of a JDBC-ODBC bridge requires that the developer be aware of what is required to run the application. Because ODBC calls are made using binary C calls, the client must have a local copy of the ODBC driver, the ODBC driver manager, and the client-side libraries.

For these reasons, JavaSoft makes the recommendation that the JDBC-ODBC bridge not be used for Web-based database access. For Intranet access, the developer must distribute the Java program to the client machines as either a Java application or Java applet (which would run as a trusted source from the local client file system).

Current JDBC Drivers

JDBC drivers are being released from so many vendors and at such a rapid rate that a definitive list is just not practical and would be obsolete by the time it was printed. For information on current driver vendors, their product names, and what databases they support, a good source is:

`http://splash.javasoft.com/jdbc/jdbc.drivers.html`

Alternative Connectivity Strategies

JDBC represents a very easy way to save time and future investment when developing database applications. The API guarantees that a client program written to the JDBC standard will work with any JDBC-compliant driver and database combination. The next section discusses two alternative technologies coming from JavaSoft that also provide a flexible way to preserve a development investment: Remote Method Invocation (RMI) and the Common Object Request Broker Architecture (CORBA).

Remote Method Invocation (RMI)

Both RMI and CORBA can also be used to connect client applications to databases, although there are some caveats to consider. RMI is analogous to Remote Procedure Calls (RPC), but while RPC was not designed for distributed object systems, this is RMI's strength. RMI is designed to allow client applications to execute the methods of objects that exist on a remote server, and execute these methods in such a way that it *appears* that the objects are local.

For database connectivity, this means that the developer can create an application that accesses database objects directly, even though these objects are actually implemented on the database server host. Because RMI provides mechanisms for allowing objects to be passed as serialized streams, it also supports protocols for passing these streams through firewalls.

Because RMI is a Java-to-Java solution, it is also possible to combine the best of JDBC and RMI for a multitier solution. For example, if the JDBC driver is written using RMI, then it becomes possible to write to a standard database interface definition *and* use object persistence and remote method calls via RMI, thereby extending the JDBC model.

> **NOTE** For more information on RMI, consult the following JavaSoft Web page: `http://chatsubo.javasoft.com/current/rmi/`.

The Common Object Request Broker Architecture (CORBA)

The Common Object Request Broker Architecture (CORBA) is the result of years of work by the Object Management Group (OMG). The OMG is a consortium of more than 500 companies that have compiled a specification for a communications infrastructure that allows different computer languages on different computer architectures to access a distributed collection of objects.

For the database application developer, CORBA provides the ultimate flexibility in a heterogeneous development environment. The server could be developed in C or C++ and the client could be a Java applet. Currently JavaSoft is in the process of providing a Java Interface Definition Language (IDL) compiler that takes a CORBA 2.0 IDL file and creates the necessary stub files for a client implementation.

CORBA is a standard (at version 2.0 as of this writing) that defines a definition language that is vendor- and language-neutral. The IDL is used to create a contract between a client and server implementation. IDL is not an implementation language itself; it merely describes object services and operations that may be performed on an implementation of the those services.

At the core of CORBA is the Object Request Broker (ORB). The ORB is the principal component for the transmission of information (requests for operations and their results) between the client and server of a CORBA application. The ORB manages marshaling requests, establishes a connection to the server, sends the data, and executes the requests on the server side. The same process occurs when the server returns the results of the operation.

The CORBA 2.0 specification also defines an Internet interoperability protocol (IIOP) that defines the protocol of the connection between the client and server through the ORB. This allows developers to choose a client IDL compiler and server IDL compiler from two different vendors.

Besides JavaSoft, there are several vendors that provide CORBA 2.0 compliance, including IIOP and Java IDL compilers.

NOTE   For a closer look at CORBA and a wealth of information on the OMG consortium, consult the following Web page: http://www .omg.org/.

Connectivity to Object Databases

Besides RMI and CORBA, another alternative is to use an object database, specifically one that supports Java's object model. There are several object database products for Java, but currently there are no existing standards. Fortunately, there is an object database standards committee, the Object Database Management Group (ODMG) that is working on a standard API for Java object databases. The ODMG 2.0 release is expected to be published sometime in 1997.

> **NOTE**
> For more information on ODMG work on a standard Java object database, consult the following Web page: `http://www.odmg.org/java.html`.

Connectivity with Web-Based Database Systems

While not specifically JDBC, and not always related to Java, there is another alternative to accessing databases from Web pages. It is possible to use HTML pages to send information to Common Gateway Scripts (CGI). The CGI scripts then in turn connect to the database and return results to the HTML page. Vendors in the Web-based database market have a variety of strategies for improving the performance of CGI with multithreaded applications written in C or C++ that handle the database connection and queries.

JavaSoft is also working to provide a technology that exceeds the performance of CGI. The Jeeves API presents a collection of classes that allow applets to execute small *servlets* (also written in Java) on a server to perform a task. The servlet can be instructed to open a database connection, retrieve a result, and return the data to the applet.

> **NOTE**
> For more information on servlet technology, consult the following Web page: `http://java.sun.com/products/jeeves/`.

> **NOTE**
> You can also visit the following Web page, which has a listing of Web-based database connectivity products, both free and commercial: `http://www.stars.com/Vlib/Providers/Database.html`.

Summary

The interest in Java has created a number of new strategies for moving data between the database system and the front-end user. In this chapter the Java Database Connectivity API was presented as the primary technique for connecting Java applications to database systems. The JDBC solves the problem of connecting a single application to a multitude of database systems by isolating the interface that the developer uses and the driver that is used to connect to the database.

In addition, the chapter looked briefly at alternative connectivity strategies like Remote Method Invocation (RMI) and the Common Object Request Broker Architecture (CORBA).

CHAPTER

TWELVE

Persistence and Remote Method Invocation

- Object persistence

- Remote Method Invocation

- The RMI architecture

The 1.1 release of the Java Developer's Kit includes support for object persistence and for making method calls on remote objects. This chapter explains these two concepts, discusses Java's support for them, and shows how they are related.

Object Persistence

A Java object ordinarily lasts no longer than the program that created it. An object may cease to exist during runtime if it gets reaped by the garbage collector. If it avoids that fate, it still goes away when the user terminates the browser (for an applet) or the object's runtime environment (for an application).

In this context, *persistence* is the ability of an object to record its state so it can be reproduced in the future, perhaps in another environment. For example, a persistent object might store its state in a file. The file can be used to *restore* the object in a different runtime environment. It is not really the object itself that persists, but rather the information necessary to construct a replica of the object.

Serialization

An object records itself by writing out the values that describe its state. This process is known as *serialization* because the object is represented by an ordered series of bytes. Java provides classes that write objects to streams and restore objects from streams.

The main task of serialization is to write out the values of an object's instance variables. If a variable is a reference to another object, the referenced object must also be serialized. This process is recursive; serialization may involve serializing a complex tree structure that consists of the original object, the object's objects, the object's object's objects, and so on. An object's ownership hierarchy is known as its *graph*.

Not all classes are capable of being serialized. Only objects that implement the `Serializable` or `Externalizable` interfaces may successfully be serialized. Both interfaces are in the `java.io` package. A serializable object can be serialized by an external object, which in practice is a type of output stream; an externalizable object must be capable of writing its own state, rather than letting the work be done by another object.

The `Serializable` interface does not have any methods. When a class declares that it implements `Serializable`, it is declaring that it participates in the serializable protocol. When an object is serializable, and the object's state is written to a stream, the stream must contain enough information to restore the object. This must hold true even if the class being restored has been updated to a more recent (but compatible) version.

You can serialize any class as long as the class meets the following criteria:

- The class, or one of its superclasses, must implement the `java.io.Serializable` interface.

- The class must participate with the `writeObject()` method to control data that is being saved and append new data to existing saved data.

- The class must participate with the `readObject()` method to read the data that was written by the corresponding `writeObject()` method.

If a serializable class has variables that should not be serialized, those variables must be marked with the `transient` keyword; the serialization process will ignore them. In general, references to AWT classes that rely on system peers should be marked as transient.

The `Externalizable` interface identifies objects that can be saved to a stream but that are responsible for their own states. When an externalizable object is written to a stream, the stream is only responsible for storing the name of the object's class; the object must write its own data. The `Externalizable` interface is defined as:

```
public interface Externalizable extends Serializable {

    public void writeExternal (ObjectOutput out)
        throws IOException;

    public void readExternal (ObjectInput in)
        throws IOException, ClassNotFoundException;
}
```

An externalizable class must adhere to this interface by providing a `writeExternal()` method for storing its state during serialization and a `readExternal()` method for restoring state during deserialization.

Object Output Streams

Objects that can serialize other objects implement the `ObjectOutput` interface from the `java.io` package. This interface is intended to be implemented by output stream classes. The interface's definition is:

```
public interface ObjectOutput extends DataOutput {
    public void writeObject(Object obj)
        throws IOException;
    public void write (int b) throws IOException;
    public void write(byte b[]) throws IOException;
    public void write(byte b[], int off, int len)
        throws IOException;
    public void flush() throws IOException;
    public void close() throws IOException;
}
```

The essential method of the interface is `writeObject(Object obj)`, which writes `obj` to a stream. Static and transient data of `obj` is ignored; all other variables, including private ones, are written.

Exceptions can occur while accessing the object or its fields or when attempting to write to the storage stream. If these occur, the stream that the interface is built on will be left in an unknown and unusable state. If this happens, the external representation of the object is corrupt.

The `ObjectOutput` interface extends the `DataOutput` interface. `DataOutput` methods support writing of primitive data types. For example, the `writeDouble()` method writes data of type `double`, and `writeBoolean()` writes data of type `boolean`. These primitive-type writing methods are used for writing out an object's primitive instance variables.

The primary class that implements the `ObjectOutput` interface is `ObjectOutputStream`. This class is similar to other output stream classes, which are discussed in Chapter 9, *File I/O and Streams*. Readers who have read that chapter will recognize the techniques discussed below. Note that objects are represented as streams of bytes, rather than characters, so they are represented by streams rather than character-oriented writers.

When an object is to be serialized to a file, the first step is to create an output stream that talks to the file:

```
FileOutputStream fos = new FileOutputStream("obj.file");
```

The next step is to create an object output stream and chain it to the file output stream:

```
ObjectOutput objout = new ObjectOutputStream(fos);
```

The object output stream automatically writes a header into the stream; the header contains a magic number and a version. This data is written automatically with the `writeStreamHeader()` method when the object output stream is created. Later in this chapter, we

Chapter 12 • Persistence and Remote Method Invocation

will demonstrate how an object input stream reads this header and verifies the object before returning its state.

After writing the header, the object output stream can write the bit representation of an object to the output stream using the `writeObject()` method. For example, the following code constructs an instance of the `Point` class and serializes it:

```
objout.writeObject(new Point(15, 20));
objout.flush();
```

This example shows that serializing an object to a stream is not very different from writing primitive data to a stream. The next section investigates restoring serialized objects from input streams. The example writes objects to a file, but the output stream can just as easily be chained to a network connection stream.

Deserialization and Object Input Streams

The `ObjectInputStream` class deserializes a serialized stream. It is responsible for maintaining the state of the stream and all of the objects that have been serialized to the stream. By using the methods of this class, a program can restore a serialized object from the stream along with the entire tree of objects referred to by the primary object. Primitive data types may also be read from an object input stream.

There is only one class constructor in the `ObjectInputStream` class:

```
public ObjectInputStream(InputStream in) throws IOException,
StreamCorruptedException
```

The constructor calls the class's `readStreamHeader()` method to verify the header and the version that were written into the stream by the corresponding object output stream. If a problem is detected with the header or the version, a `StreamCorruptedException` is thrown.

The primary method of the `ObjectInputStream` class is `read-Object()`, which deserializes an object from the data source stream. The deserialized object is returned as an `Object`; the caller is responsible for casting it to the correct type.

During deserialization, a list is maintained of objects that have been restored from the stream. This list is called the *known objects table*.

If the data being maintained is of a primitive type, it is simply treated as a a sequence of bytes and restored from the input stream. If the data being restored is a string, it is read using the string's UTF encoding; the string will be added to the known objects table. If the object being restored is an array, the type and length of the array are determined. Next, memory for the array is allocated, and each of the elements contained in the array is read using the appropriate read method. Once the array is reconstructed, it is added to the known objects table; if it is an array of objects (as opposed to primitives), then each object is deserialized and added to the known objects table. When an ordinary object (that is, not a string and not and array) is restored, it is added to the known objects table; then the objects to which the original object refers are restored recursively and added to the known objects table.

Once an object has been retrieved from a stream, it must be validated so it can become a full-fledged object and be used by the program that deserialized it. The `validateObject()` method is called when a complete graph of objects has been retrieved from a stream. If the primary object cannot be made valid, the validation process will stop, and an exception will be thrown.

Security

Serialization can involve storing an object's data on a disk file or transmitting the data across a network. In both cases there is a potential security problem because the data is located outside the Java runtime environment, beyond the reach of Java's security mechanisms.

The `writeExternal()` method is public, so any object can make an externalizable or serializable object write itself to a stream. Caution should be exercised when deciding whether or not `write-External()` should serialize sensitive private data. When an object is restored via an ordinary `readExternal()` call, its sensitive values are restored back into private variables and no harm is done. However, while the serialized data is outside the system, an attacker could access the data, decode its format, and obtain the sensitive values. A similar form of attack would involve modifying data values so, for example, a password is replaced or a bank balance is incremented. A less precise attack would simply corrupt the serialized data.

When an object is serialized, all the reachable objects of its ownership graph are potentially exposed. For example, a serialized object might have a reference to a reference to a reference to an instance of the `FileDescriptor` class. An attacker could reserialize the file descriptor and gain access to the file system of the machine where the serialized object originated.

The best protection for an object that has fields that should not be stored is to label those fields with the `transient` keyword. Transient fields, like static fields, are not serialized and are therefore not exposed.

If a class cannot be serialized in a manner that upholds the integrity of the system containing it, then it should avoid implementing the `Serializable` interface. Moreover, it should not be referred to by any class that will be serialized.

Externalizable objects (that is, ones that take care of writing their own data) often use the technique of including invariant data among their instance variables. These invariants serve no useful purpose during normal operation of the class. They are inspected after deserialization; an unexpected value indicates that the external serialized representation has been corrupted.

Serialization Exceptions

There are seven types of exceptions that can be thrown during serialization or deserialization of an object. All seven types are extensions of `ObjectStreamException`, which is an extension of `IOException`. The exceptions are described below.

`InvalidClassException`   This exception is typically thrown when the class type cannot be determined by the reserializing stream or when the class that is being returned cannot be represented on the system retrieving the object. The exception is also thrown if the deserialized class is not declared public, or if it does not have a public default (no-argument) constructor.

`NotSerializableException`   This exception is typically thrown by externalizable objects (which are responsible for their own reserialization) on detection of a corrupted input stream. The corruption is generally indicated by an unexpected invariant value.

`StreamCorruptedException`   This exception is thrown when a stored object's header or control data is invalid.

`NotActiveException`   This exception is thrown if the `registerValidation()` method is not called during a call to `readObject()`.

`InvalidObjectException`   This exception is thrown when a restored object cannot be made valid after deserialization.

`OptionalDataException`   This exception is thrown when a stream is supposed to contain an object in it, but it actually only contains primitive data.

`WriteAbortedException`   This exception is thrown during reserialization (reading), when an input stream detects that its data is incomplete because of abnormal termination of the writing process.

Writing and Reading an Object Stream

Writing an object to a stream is a simple process, similar to the process of writing any other kind of high-level structure. This process is explained in detail in Chapter 9, *File I/O and Streams*. You must create a low-level output stream to provide access to the external medium (generally file or network). Next, a high-level stream is chained to the low-level stream; for serialization, the high-level stream is an object output stream.

The following code fragment constructs an instance of `Point` and writes it to a file called `point.ser` on the local file system:

```
Point p = new Point(13, 10);
FileOutputStream f = new FileOutputStream("Point.ser");
ObjectOutputStream s = new ObjectOutputStream (f);
try
{
    s.writeObject (p);
    s.flush ();
} catch (IOException e) { }
```

Restoring the object involves opening a file input stream on the file and chaining an object input stream to the file input stream. The point object is read by calling `readObject()` from the object input stream; the return value is of type `Object` and must be cast by the caller. The following code fragment shows how all this is done:

```
Point p = null;
FileInputStream f = new FileInputStream("Point.ser");
ObjectInputStream s = new ObjectInputStream (f);
try
{
    p = (Point)s.readObject ();
}
catch (IOException e) {}
```

The next section develops a simple example program that saves and restores an object.

Serialization Example

In this section we develop a simple painting program that can store its display list to a file. (A display list is a data structure that contains an abstract description of what should appear on the screen.) The program allows the user to draw rectangles with the mouse; pressing down on the mouse button defines one corner of a rectangle, and releasing the button defines the opposite corner. The display list is a vector that contains two instances of the Point class for each rectangle. One point represents the mouse-down corner of the rectangle.

The PersisTest application is a subclass of Frame. A panel across the top of the frame contains four control buttons. The frame's paint() method clears the screen to white and then traverses the display list vector, drawing one black rectangle for each pair of points in the vector.

The four control buttons support clearing, saving, restoring, and quitting. The handler for the Save button uses the writing technique discussed in the previous section, *Writing and Reading an Object Stream*, to store the display list vector in a file. The file name must be specified in the command-line argument. The handler for the Restore button deserializes a vector, replacing the old display list with the new vector.

To test the application, invoke it with a file name as a command-line argument:

```
java PersisTest filename
```

Then use the mouse to draw some rectangles. Next, click on the Save button to write the display list to the file. Clear the screen or draw more rectangles. Finally, click on the Restore button. The display will change back to the state it was in when the Save button was clicked. You can even terminate the application and restart it; it will still restore correctly from the external file.

This example could achieve the same result by opening a data output stream instead of an object output stream and writing four ints for each rectangle. The benefit to using serialization lies in the dramatic improvement in program maintainability. If you were to store and restore the display list by using data input and output streams, any change in the format of the display list would force a change in both the writing and the reading code. With serialization, the display list data format is irrelevant.

The source code for the following example program is located on the CD-ROM in the directory `javadevhkbk\ch12\PersisTest.java`.

PersisTest.java

```java
import java.awt.*;
import java.awt.event.*;
import java.io.*;
import java.rmi.*;
import java.util.Vector;


public class PersisTest extends Frame
implements MouseListener, ActionListener
{
    Vector      displayList;
    String      pathname;
    Button      clearBtn, saveBtn, restoreBtn, quitBtn;


    public static void main(String args[])
    {
        if (args.length == 0)
        {
            System.out.println("Usage: java PersisTest filename");
            System.exit(0);
        }

        PersisTest that = new PersisTest(args[0]);
        that.show();
    }
```

```
public PersisTest(String pathname)
{
    this.pathname = pathname;
    displayList = new Vector();

    // Handle our own mouse clicks.
    addMouseListener(this);

    // Build the GUI. Make this object a listener for all actions.
    setLayout(new BorderLayout());
    Panel pan = new Panel();
    clearBtn = new Button("Clear");
    clearBtn.addActionListener(this);
    pan.add(clearBtn);
    saveBtn = new Button("Save");
    saveBtn.addActionListener(this);
    pan.add(saveBtn);
    restoreBtn = new Button("Restore");
    restoreBtn.addActionListener(this);
    pan.add(restoreBtn);
    quitBtn = new Button("Quit");
    quitBtn.addActionListener(this);
    pan.add(quitBtn);
    add("North", pan);

    resize(350, 200);
}


public void paint(Graphics g)
{
    // Clear to white.
    g.setColor(Color.white);
    g.fillRect(0, 0, getSize().width, getSize().height);

    // Traverse display list, drawing 1 rect for each 2 points
    // in the vector.
    g.setColor(Color.black);
    int i = 0;
    while (i < displayList.size())
    {
```

```
            Point p0 = (Point)(displayList.elementAt(i++));
            Point p1 = (Point)(displayList.elementAt(i++));
            int x = Math.min(p0.x, p1.x);
            int y = Math.min(p0.y, p1.y);
            int w = Math.abs(p0.x - p1.x);
            int h = Math.abs(p0.y - p1.y);
            g.drawRect(x, y, w, h);
        }
}


public void mousePressed(MouseEvent e)
{
    // Store x and y in display list vector.
    Point p = new Point(e.getX(), e.getY());
    displayList.addElement(p);
}


public void mouseReleased(MouseEvent e)
{
    // Store x and y in display list vector, and request repaint.
    Point p = new Point(e.getX(), e.getY());
    displayList.addElement(p);
    repaint();
}


// Unused methods of MouseListener interface.
public void mouseClicked(MouseEvent e) { }
public void mouseEntered(MouseEvent e) { }
public void mouseExited(MouseEvent e)  { }


public void actionPerformed(ActionEvent e)
{
    if (e.getSource() == clearBtn)
    {
        // Repaint with an empty display list.
        displayList = new Vector();
        repaint();
    }
```

```
else if (e.getSource() == saveBtn)
{
    // Write display list vector to an object output stream.
    try
    {
        FileOutputStream fos = new FileOutputStream(pathname);
        ObjectOutputStream oos = new ObjectOutputStream(fos);
        oos.writeObject(displayList);
        oos.flush();
        oos.close();
        fos.close();
    }
    catch (Exception ex)
    {
        System.out.println("Trouble writing display list vector");
    }
}
else if (e.getSource() == restoreBtn)
{
    // Read a new display list vector from an object input stream.
    try
    {
        FileInputStream fis = new FileInputStream(pathname);
        ObjectInputStream ois = new ObjectInputStream(fis);
        displayList = (Vector)(ois.readObject());
        ois.close();
        fis.close();
        repaint();
    }
    catch (Exception ex)
    {
        System.out.println("Trouble reading display list vector");
    }
}
else if (e.getSource() == quitBtn)
{
    hide();
    dispose();
    System.exit(0);
}
    }
}
```

Remote Method Invocation

Java's *Remote Method Invocation* (*RMI*) feature enables a program running on a client computer to make method calls on an object located on a remote server machine. In the remainder of this chapter we discuss RMI, beginning with a look at the relationship between object persistence and RMI.

The Remote Method Invocation feature gives Java programmers the ability to distribute computing across a networked environment. Object-oriented design requires that every task be executed by the object most appropriate to that task. RMI takes this concept one step further by allowing a task to be performed on the *machine* most appropriate to the task.

RMI defines a set of remote interfaces that can be used to create remote objects. A client can invoke the methods of a remote object with the same syntax that it uses to invoke methods on a local object. The RMI API provides classes and methods that handle all of the underlying communication and parameter referencing requirements of accessing remote methods. RMI also handles the serialization of objects that are passed as arguments to methods of remote objects.

The `java.rmi` and the `java.rmi.server` packages contain the interfaces and classes that define the functionality of the Java RMI system. These packages and interfaces provide the building blocks for creating server-side objects and client-side object stubs. A stub is a local representation of a remote object. The client makes calls to the stub, which automatically communicates with the server.

Object Persistence and Remote Method Invocation

When a Java program makes a remote method invocation, method parameters must be transmitted to the server, and a return value must be sent back to the client. Primitive values can simply be sent byte by byte. However, passing objects, either as parameters or return values, present a problem.

Object persistence is a useful feature in its own right. It is also indispensable for remote invocation. The server-side object needs access to a parameter object's entire graph of referenced objects. The remote method might construct and return a complicated object that owns references to other objects. If this occurs, the entire graph must be returned.

If the remote method invocation feature is to support passing and returning objects as well as primitives, there has to be a full-featured object-serialization system, which is why serialization and persistence are generally discussed together. Any object passed to or returned from a remote method must implement either the `Serializable` or the `Externalizable` interface.

NOTE Remote method invocation is similar to the *Remote Procedure Call* (RPC) feature that Sun introduced in 1985. RPC also required a way to serialize parameter and return value data, although the situation was simpler because of the absence of objects. Sun developed a system called *External Data Representation* (XDR) to support data serialization. One significant difference between RPC and RMI is that RPC uses the fast but less-than-reliable UDP protocol; RMI uses the slower but more reliable TCP/IP protocol.

The RMI Architecture

The RMI consists of three layers: the stubs/skeleton layer, the remote reference layer, and the transport layer. The relationships among these layers are shown in Figure 12.1.

When a client invokes a remote method, the request starts at the top with the stub on the client side. The client references the stub as a proxy for the object on the remote machine; all the underlying functionality shown in Figure 12.1 is invisible to the client. The stub code is generated with the `rmic` compiler and uses the *Remote Reference Layer* (RRL) to pass method invocation requests to the server object.

FIGURE 12.1

Architecture overview

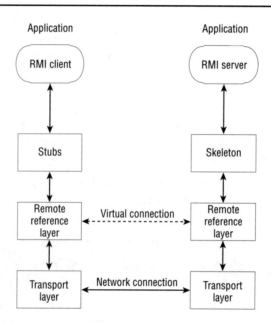

Stubs

The stub is the client-side proxy representing the remote object. Stubs define all of the interfaces that the remote object implementation supports. The stub is referenced as any other local object by a program running on the client machine. It looks like a local object on the client side; it also maintains a connection to the server-side object. The Remote Reference Layer on the client side returns a *marshal stream* to the stub. The marshal stream is used by the RRL to communicate to the RRL on the server side. The stub serializes parameter data, passing the serialized data into the marshal stream.

After the remote method has been executed, the RRL passes any serialized return values back to the stub, which is responsible for deserializing.

The Skeleton

The skeleton is the server-side construct that interfaces with the server side RRL. The skeleton receives method invocation requests from the client side RRL. The server side RRL must unmarshal any arguments that are sent to a remote method. The skeleton then makes a call to the actual object implementation on the server side. The skeleton is also responsible for receiving any return values from the remote object and marshaling them onto the marshal stream.

Remote Reference Layer

The Remote Reference Layer (RRL) is responsible for maintaining an independent reference protocol that is not specific to any stub or skeleton model. This flexibility allows you to change the RRL if desired without affecting the other two layers. The RRL deals with the lower-level transport interface and is responsible for providing a stream to the stubs and skeleton layers.

The RRL uses a server-side and a client-side component to communicate via the transport layer. The client-side component contains information specific to the remote server. This information is passed to the server-side component and therefore is dependent only on the server-side RRL. The RRL on the server side is responsible for the reference semantics and deals with those semantics before delivering the remote method invocation to the skeleton. The communication between client- and server-side components is handled by the transport layer.

The Transport Layer

The transport layer is responsible for creating and maintaining connections between the client and server. The transport layer consists of four abstractions:

- An *endpoint* is used to reference the address space that contains a Java Virtual Machine (JVM). An endpoint is a reference to a specific transport instance.

- A *channel* is the pathway between two address spaces. This channel is responsible for managing any connections from the client to the server and vice versa.

- A *connection* is an abstraction for transferring data (arguments and return values) between client and server.

- The *transport* abstraction is responsible for setting up a channel between a local address space and a remote endpoint. The transport abstraction is also responsible for accepting incoming connections to the address space containing the abstraction.

The transport layer sets up connections, manages existing connections, and handles remote objects residing in its address space.

When the transport layer receives a request from the client-side RRL, it locates the RMI server for the remote object that is being requested. Then the transport layer establishes a socket connection to the server. Next, the transport layer passes the established connection to the client-side RRL and adds a reference to the remote object to an internal table. At this point the client is connected to the server.

The transport layer monitors the "liveness" of the connection. If a significant amount of time passes with no activity on the connection, the transport layer is responsible for shutting the connection down. The timeout period is 10 minutes.

RMI Example

This section steps you through the making, compiling, and running of an RMI application. To create an application that is accessible to remote clients, there are a number of steps that you must follow:

1. Define interfaces for the remote classes.

2. Create and compile implementation classes for the remote classes.

3. Create stub and skeleton classes using the `rmic` command.

4. Create and compile a server application.

5. Start the RMI Registry and the server application.

6. Create and compile a client program to access the remote objects.

7. Test the client.

In this chapter we develop a detailed example, using the steps listed above as a framework. The example will model a very simple credit card system. The server will support creating a new account, as well as performing transactions against an existing account. Because the intention of the example program is to show you how to use RMI, there will not be a client-side user interface; the client will simply make a few hard-coded invocations.

All the source code modules for this example are located on the CD-ROM in the directory `javadevhdbk\ch12`. The individual file names are listed with the code.

Step 1:
Define Interfaces for Remote Classes

The program will use two remote classes. The `CreditCardImpl` class will maintain the user name, balance, available credit, and personal ID signature number for a single credit card account. The `CreditManager` will maintain a list of `Account` objects and create new ones when necessary. The server-side application will construct a single instance of `CreditManagerImpl` and make it available to remote clients.

Each of these classes must be described by an interface (`Credit-Card` and `CreditManager`). The client-side stubs will implement these interfaces. The stub classes will be created in a later step by the `rmic` utility. Note that `rmic` requires that the interfaces must be public and extend the `Remote` interface; each method must throw `RemoteException`; and the stub and implementation code must reside in a package.

All sources listed below appear on the CD-ROM in `javadevhdbk\ch12`. (There are four trivial exception classes that appear on the CD-ROM but are not listed here; they extend `Exception` without adding new data or methods.) The definition of `CreditCard` is:

CreditCard.java

```
package credit;

import credit.*;
import java.rmi.*;

public interface CreditCard extends java.rmi.Remote {

    /** This method returns a credit card's credit line. */
    public float getCreditLine() throws java.rmi.RemoteException;

    /** This method allows a card holder to pay all or some
        of a balance. Throws InvalidMoneyException if the
        money param is invalid. */
    public void payTowardsBalance(float money) throws
        java.rmi.RemoteException, InvalidMoneyException;

    /** This method allows the cardholder to make purchases
        against the line of credit. Throws
        CreditLineExceededException
        if the purchase exceeds available credit. */
```

```
public void makePurchase(float amount, int signature) throws
    java.rmi.RemoteException, InvalidSignatureException,
    CreditLineExceededException;

/** This method sest the card's personal i.d. signature. */
public void setSignature(int pin)throws java.rmi.RemoteException;
}
```

The structure of `AccountManager` is similar, though it only defines a single method:

CreditManager.java

```
package credit;

import credit.*;
import java.rmi.*;
import java.rmi.RemoteException;

public interface CreditManager extends java.rmi.Remote {

    /** This method finds an existing credit card for a given customer
        name. If the customer does not have an account, a new card will
        be "issued" with a random personal i.d. signature and a $5000
        starting credit line. */
    public CreditCard findCreditAccount(String Customer) throws
        DuplicateAccountException, java.rmi.RemoteException;


    /** This method creates a new Cedit Account with a random
        personal i.d. signature and a $5000 starting credit line. */
    public CreditCard newCreditAccount(String newCustomer) throws
        java.rmi.RemoteException;
}
```

Step 2: Create and Compile Implementation Classes

The implementation classes are server-side classes that implement the interfaces listed above.

The CreditCard interface that was defined earlier is implemented by the CreditCardImpl class. This class must implement all of the methods in the CreditCard interface, and it must extend Unicast-RemoteObject. The UnicastRemoteObject class defines the remote object as a *unicast* object, which means that only a single instance of the object can exist on a single server. (Distinguish this from the MulticastRemoteObject, which will be able to be replicated across multiple servers. To date, however, there is no support for multicast objects.)

Both interfaces and both classes declare that they belong to the credit package. All four sources should be compiled with the -d <directoryname> option to specify a destination directory. Within the destination directory, the compiler will automatically create a subdirectory called credit (if one does not already exist); the class files will be created in the credit subdirectory. The destination directory supplied to the -d option should be in the classpath. An easy way to compile the interfaces and classes is to specify the current working directory as the destination directory, as follows:

```
javac -d . CreditCard.java
javac -d . CreditCardImpl.java
javac -d . CreditManager.java
javac -d . CreditManagerImpl.java
```

The source code for the CreditCardImpl class appears below.

CreditCardImpl.java

```
package credit;

import java.rmi.*;
import java.rmi.server.*;
import java.io.Serializable;

/** This class is the remote object that will referenced by the skeleton
    on the server side and the stub on the client side. */
```

```java
public class CreditCardImpl
    extends UnicastRemoteObject
    implements CreditCard, Serializable
{

    private float currentBalance = 0;
    private float creditLine = 5000f;
    private int signature = 0;          // Like a p.i.n. number
    private String accountName;         // Name of owner

    /** Class constructor generates an initial pin.*/
    public CreditCardImpl(String customer) throws
    java.rmi.RemoteException, credit.DuplicateAccountException {
        accountName = customer;
        signature = (int)(Math.random() * 10000);
    }


    /** Returns credit line. */
    public float getCreditLine() throws java.rmi.RemoteException {
        return creditLine;
    }


    /** Pays off some debt. */
    public void payTowardsBalance(float money) throws
    java.rmi.RemoteException, credit.InvalidMoneyException {
        if (money <= 0) {
            throw new InvalidMoneyException ();
        } else {
            currentBalance -= money;
        }
    }


    /** Changes signature. */
    public void setSignature(int pin) throws java.rmi.RemoteException
{
        signature = pin;
    }


    /** Makes a purchase. Makes sure enough credit is available,
        then increments balance and decrements available credit. */
    public void makePurchase(float amount, int signature) throws
    java.rmi.RemoteException, credit.InvalidSignatureException,
    credit.CreditLineExceededException {
```

```
            if (signature != this.signature) {
                throw new InvalidSignatureException();
            }
            if (currentBalance+amount > creditLine) {
                throw new CreditLineExceededException();
            } else {
                currentBalance += amount;
                creditLine -= amount;
            }
        }
    }
}
```

The CreditManagerImpl class is responsible for creating and storing new accounts (as CreditImpl objects). This class uses a hashtable to store the account objects, keyed by owner name.

CreditManagerImpl.java

```
package credit;

import java.rmi.*;
import java.rmi.server.*;
import java.util.Hashtable;

public class CreditManagerImpl extends UnicastRemoteObject
implements CreditManager {
    private static transient Hashtable accounts = new Hashtable();

    /** This is the default class constructor that does nothing
        but implicitly call super(). */
    public CreditManagerImpl() throws RemoteException { }

    /** Creates a new account. Puts the customer name and the customer's
        credit card in the hashtable. */
    public CreditCard newCreditAccount(String customerName)
    throws java.rmi.RemoteException {
        CreditCardImpl newCard = null;
        try {
            newCard = new CreditCardImpl(customerName);
        } catch (DuplicateAccountException e) {
            return null;
        }
```

```
        accounts.put(customerName, newCard);
        return newCard;
    }


    /** Searches the hashtable for an existing account. If no account
        for customer name, one is created and added to hashtable.
        Returns the account. */
    public CreditCard findCreditAccount(String customer)
    throws DuplicateAccountException, RemoteException {
        CreditCardImpl account = (CreditCardImpl)accounts.get(customer);
        if (account != null) {
            return account;
        }
        // Create new account. Add credit card to hashtable.
        account = new CreditCardImpl(customer);
        accounts.put(customer, account);
        return account;
    }
}
```

Step 3:
Create Stub and Skeleton Classes

Once the implementation classes are compiled, the next step is to
create the stub and skeleton class files that are used to access the
implementation classes. The stub classes are used by client code to
communicate with the server skeleton code.

The rmic command automatically creates stub and skeleton code
from the interface and implementation class definitions. The syntax
of the command is:

```
rmic [options] package.interfaceImpl ...
```

For our example, the following command would create the stubs
and skeletons for the CreditCard and CreditManager remote
classes:

```
rmic -d . credit.CreditCardImpl credit.CreditManagerImpl
```

Note that the command requires specification of the package in which the class files reside; this is why all the source modules listed above under Step 2 declared that they belonged to the `rmi.atm` package.

The `rmic` command creates four class files in the `credit` package directory:

- `CreditCardImpl_Skel.class`
- `CreditCardImpl_Stub.class`
- `CreditManagerImpl_Skel.class`
- `CreditManagerImpl_Stub.class`

Now that the stubs and skeletons have been created, the next step is to create a server-side application that makes these classes available to clients for remote invocation.

Step 4: Create and Compile the Server Application

Everything is now in place to create the server-side application. It will be an application class called `CardBank`, whose main job is to construct an instance of `CreditManager`. Except for the line that calls the `CreditManager` constructor, all the rest of the `CardBank` code involves making the credit manager object available to remote clients. The details of this process are explained after the following code listing.

CardBank.java

```
package credit;

import java.util.*;
import java.rmi.*;
import java.rmi.RMISecurityManager;
```

```
public class CardBank {

    public static void main (String args[]) {
        //  Create and install a security manager.
        System.setSecurityManager(new RMISecurityManager());

        try {
            // Create an instance of our Credit Manager.
            System.out.println
                ("CreditManagerImpl: create a CreditManager");
            CreditManagerImpl cmi = new CreditManagerImpl();

            // Bind the object instance to the remote registry. Use the
            // static rebind() method to avoid conflicts.
            System.out.println("CreditManagerImpl: bind it to a name");
            Naming.rebind("cardManager", cmi);

            System.out.println("CreditManager is now ready");

        } catch (Exception e) {
            System.out.println("An error occured");
            e.printStackTrace();
            System.out.println(e.getMessage());
        }
    }
}
```

Applications, by default, run without security managers. The `setSecurityManager()` call enforces an RMI security manager.

The server "publishes" an object instance by binding a specified name to the instance and registering that name with the RMI Registry. There are two methods that allow an instance to be bound and registered:

- `public static void bind(String name, Remote obj) throws AlreadyBoundException, MalformedUrlException, UnknownHostException, RemoteException`

- `public static void rebind(String name, Remote obj) throws MalformedUrlException, UnknownHost-Exception, RemoteException`

Notice that both methods are static and ask for a name to reference the object, as well as the actual remote object that is bound to the name. In the current example, the object name is `cardManager`; any reachable machine on the network can refer to this object by specifying the host machine and the object name.

The `name` argument required by both `bind()` and `rebind()` is a URL-like string. This string can be in the format `protocol://host:port/bindingName`. Here `protocol` should be `rmi`, `host` is the name of the RMI server, `port` is the port number on which the server should listen for requests, and `bindingName` is the exact name that should be used by a client when requesting access to the object. If just a name is given in the string, then default values are used. The defaults are: `rmi` for the protocol, `localhost` for server name, and `1099` for the port number.

Both `bind()` and `rebind()` associate a name with an object. They differ in their behavior when the name being bound has already been bound to an object. In this case `bind()` will throw `AlreadyBound-Exception`, and `rebind()` will discard the old binding and enforce the new one.

Step 5: Start the RMI Registry and the Server Application

The RMI Registry is an application that provides a simple naming lookup service. When the `AtmServer` calls `rebind()`, it is the Registry that maintains the binding. The Registry is an independent program, and it must be running before the server-side application is invoked. The program resides in the `java/bin` directory. It can be invoked by simply typing **rmiregistry** at the command line.

The following two command lines invoke the Registry and start up the card bank server:

```
rmiregistry
java credit.CardBank
```

The card bank application prints several status lines as it starts up the service. If there are no errors, you should see the following output:

```
CreditManagerImpl: create a CreditManager
CreditManagerImpl: bind it to a name
CreditManager is now ready
```

Once an object has been passed to the Registry, a client may request that the RMI registry provide a reference to the remote object. The next section shows how this is done.

Step 6:
Create and Compile the Client Program

The Shopper application needs to find a credit manager object on the remote server. The program assumes that the server name has been passed in as the first command-line argument. This name is used to create a URL-like string of the format rmi://<hostname>/atmManager. The string is passed to the static lookup() method of the Naming class. The lookup() call communicates with the server and returns a handle to the remote object that was constructed and registered in Step 5, above. (More accurately, what is returned is a handle to a stub that communicates with the remote object.)

The return type from lookup() is Remote, which is the parent of all stub interfaces. When the return value is cast to type Credit-Manager, the methods of CreditManager can be invoked on it. The following sample code, titled Shopper.java, shows how this is done.

The client expects two command-line arguments and an optional third. The first argument specifies the server. (For testing on a single machine, specify *localhost* for the server name.) The second argument is a string that provides an account name. The client program asks the server-side credit manager object for a handle to the credit card object that represents this customer's account. (If the customer has no account yet, one will be created.) The initial random pin number is modified to something a user will find easier to remember. The client program then makes several purchases and one payment, reporting the available credit after each transaction. The client code is as follows:

Shopper.java

```
package credit;

import java.rmi.*;
import java.rmi.RMISecurityManager;

public class Shopper {

    public static void main(String args[]) {

        CreditManager cm = null;
        CreditCard account = null;

        // Check the command line.
        if (args.length < 2) {
            System.err.println("Usage:");
            System.err.println("java Shopper <server> <account name>");
            System.exit (1);
        }

        // Create and install a security manager.
        System.setSecurityManager(new RMISecurityManager());

        // Obtain reference to card manager.
        try {
            String url = new String ("//" + args[0] + "/cardManager");
```

```
        System.out.println ("Shopper: lookup cardManager, url = "
                            + url);
        cm = (CreditManager)Naming.lookup(url);
    } catch (Exception e) {
        System.out.println("Error in getting card manager" + e);
    }

    // Get user's account.
    try {
        account = cm.findCreditAccount(args[1]);
        System.out.println ("Found account for " + args[1]);
    } catch (Exception e) {
        System.out.println("Error in getting account for " + args[1]);
    }

    // Do some transactions.
    try {
        System.out.println("Available credit is: "
                            + account.getCreditLine());
        System.out.println("Changing pin number for account");
        account.setSignature(1234);
        System.out.println("Buying a new watch for $100");
        account.makePurchase(100.00f, 1234);
        System.out.println("Available credit is now: " +
                            account.getCreditLine());
        System.out.println("Buying a new pair of shoes for $160");
        account.makePurchase(160.00f, 1234);
        System.out.println("CardHolder: Paying off $136 of balance");
        account.payTowardsBalance(136.00f);
        System.out.println("Available credit is now: "+
                            account.getCreditLine());
    } catch (Exception e) {
        System.out.println("Transaction error for " + args[1]);
    }

    System.exit(0);
  }
}
```

Step 7:
Test the *AtmClient*

The final step, of course, is to execute the client code. It can be run from any computer that has access to the server and to the supporting classes. Here is a sample session output on a Unix machine, with the remote service running on a host named `sunbert` (the first line is the invocation; the rest is output):

```
% java credit.Shopper sunbert pogo
Shopper: lookup cardManager, url = //sunbert/cardManager
Found account for pogo
Available credit is: 5000.0
Changing pin number for account
Buying a new watch for $100
Available credit is now: 4900.0
Buying a new pair of shoes for $160
CardHolder: Paying off $136 of balance
Available credit is now: 4740.0
```

After the client program has finished running, the remote objects are still alive. The execution shown above created a new account for the customer. A second invocation of the client will work with that account; the available credit numbers in the listing below reflect the current state of the account:

```
% java credit.Shopper sunbert pogo
Shopper: lookup cardManager, url = //sunbert/cardManager
Found account for pogo
Available credit is: 4740.0
Changing pin number for account
Buying a new watch for $100
Available credit is now: 4640.0
Buying a new pair of shoes for $160
CardHolder: Paying off $136 of balance
Available credit is now: 4480.0
```

Summary

Java's persistent object support provides a very useful facility for storing and reconstituting objects. This feature is valuable in its own right; moreover, it plays an essential role in remote object invocation. Both features are moderately intricate, and successful programming (especially for RMI) involves a number of steps. However, the individual steps are not difficult. The example code listed in this chapter and provided on the CD-ROM provides a template for development.

Sun introduced Remote Procedure Call support in 1985. To this day, RPC is an essential building block of many distributed applications. It seems likely that RMI will play a vital role in distributed Java applications, where the distributed code will benefit from platform independence.

CHAPTER
THIRTEEN

13

Content and Protocol Handlers

- Protocol and handler types

- Protocols and the URL

- Approaches to content and protocol handling

- The daytime protocol handler

- In-stream protocols

- Content handling

- Server side handlers

The Internet, mainly in the guise of the World Wide Web, allows data to be shifted around in a wide variety of formats. Despite appearances, the Internet has many more components besides HTTP and the World Wide Web. In fact, a wide variety of different protocols—such as FTP, Telnet, and Gopher—exist on the Internet and are quite well known. Java programs may be required to handle any or all of these protocols and data formats. This chapter looks at the issues that are raised by these requirements and the mechanism that is built into the Java core packages for coping with the variety. The first sections discuss the background issues and consider how problems are handled in other related systems. Later sections describe the implementation and installation of Java content and protocol handlers.

Protocol and Content Types

The Internet contains information resources in a wide variety of formats. A corporate Intranet also offers the benefit of a wide variety of formats, including all those that are normally found on the Internet. For example, it might be advantageous to publish figures using the native format of a spreadsheet application, which would also allow the work to be modified and might even result in smaller files when compared to, for example, PostScript files. Each of these different formats constitutes a different *content type*.

Two things are required to support multiple content types and to be able to view them in a Web browser without user intervention. First, the browser must be able to recognize the content type in some way. Second, it must be able to invoke code that handles the content correctly.

It has long been a tradition to use an extension, such as `.txt` or `.cmd`, in a filename to indicate the nature of the contents of a file. In a Web environment, especially one with many dissimilar platforms, this mechanism is not sufficiently expressive nor widely standardized. Problems can easily arise when such mnemonic extensions are reused by different applications for incompatible files. This situation is handled on the Web by making more detailed content type information available as part of the protocol. The nature of a data set is described using a string called the MIME content type.

Describing Content Type with MIME

MIME, the Multipurpose Internet Mail Extensions system, was first invented, as the name suggests, to facilitate sending files representing images and sounds over Internet mail links. Strictly speaking, Internet e-mail is a 7-bit ASCII-only protocol; therefore, sending binary files directly is not possible. MIME, in the mail context, addresses two separate issues: first, how to represent 8-bit binary data using only 7-bit ASCII; and second, how to describe the significance of the files that are being transmitted. It is this second facility that is important in this discussion.

A number of general, or "top-level," categories are defined by MIME, including `text`, `audio`, `image`, and `video`. These categories are further subdivided to indicate the particular type of encoding used. So, for example, normal Web pages are encoded using HTML, and the MIME type string representing that is `text/html`. Notice that the parts that make up the type are separated by a forward slash, in a fashion similar to that used to separate elements of a URL.

TIP
Like all Internet protocols, MIME is defined by *Request For Comment* documents (RFCs). In this case, the documents are RFC 1521 and 1522. These are on the CD-ROM in the directory `javadevhdbk\rfcs`.

Protocols and the URL

Identifying the protocol to be used for a data transfer is at least as important as identifying the contents of that transfer. In a URL, the protocol to be used is defined by the part of the URL immediately before the first colon. So a URL that starts with `http:` specifies the use of the HTTP protocol, while a URL that starts with `telnet:` indicates that Telnet is the protocol to be used.

Each protocol has a default port number associated with it, but this can be overridden in the body of the URL by adding a number, prefixed with a full colon (:) between the end of the target machine domain name and the start of the path part of the URL. For example, if an HTTP connection is to be made using port 8080 rather than the default port of 80, to a machine `www.fred.com`, the URL would start like this:

```
http://www.fred.com:8080/
```

A number of well-known protocols exist, and the URL concept allows the possibility of added new ones. Such additions might be particularly appropriate in a closed environment like a corporate Intranet.

Approaches to Content and Protocol Handling

Modern browsers must handle the wide variety of content types and protocols that exist on the Internet. Ideally, it should be possible to enhance them to cope with new standards that arise without having to upgrade the whole browser. The same extensibility is required in Java.

Whatever technique is used to provide this extensibility, the software that handles a particular content type is referred to as a *content handler*, while the software that handles a particular protocol is called a *protocol handler*. This section discusses some of the approaches that are used by browsers to achieve the flexible content and protocol handling, and then describes Java's approach.

Helper Programs

One of the earliest techniques for extending a browser was to allow the configuration of an external "helper" program that could be used when an otherwise unsupported protocol or content type was encountered. This approach does not allow the resulting data to be displayed in the same browser window as the rest of the data being loaded, but it is easy to implement in a variety of systems. Its limitations are that the browser must be configured manually for each new content type or protocol, and the handling program must be obtained separately.

Dynamic Linking

A browser can, in principle, be designed to be extended by means of additional code modules provided after the original browser has been written. This extensibility eliminates the need to load and run external programs to work with additional protocols and content types. This code-module approach is the principle underlying the plug-ins used by the Netscape Navigator browser.

The Java Virtual Machine provides a mechanism for loading code into a running program. This dynamic-linking idea is fundamental to the design of Java and is ideally suited to the particular case of content or protocol handlers.

Superclasses and Extensibility in Java

The key to creating a program that can be readily extended later lies in a well-thought-out object-oriented design. Consider a drawing program that is being created to handle lines, circles, and rectangles. If it is coded so that these items are handled explicitly, then a later extension will require changes to the source, recompilation, and redistribution of the whole program. On the other hand, if the program deals instead with a more generalized object of a class called, for example, Drawable, then it can quite easily be extended to handle any other subclass of Drawable without needing recompilation.

For this to work in practice, two things must be done. First, the Drawable class must be designed carefully to ensure that it provides an interface flexible enough to allow any future ideas to be expressed, at least as far as possible within the broad context of drawing. Second, a mechanism must be provided for the program to determine which implementations of Drawable are available for use at runtime. These must be able to express their names and make themselves available via the user interface.

In the case of a drawing program, it is reasonable to arrange that all specific Drawable classes be placed in one particular directory. The program can then scan that directory to determine the names of the Drawable classes that are available to it.

Protocol and Content Handler Extensions

In the case of both content and protocol handers, the mechanism by which the program determines the availability of the handler code is quite simple. If a particular handler is required, there is a convention that determines what the names of both the package and the class should be based on the name of the protocol or content type in question. Given this convention, it is a simple matter for the browser program to ask for the handler by name. If the attempt to load that driver fails, then the protocol or content type is unsupported.

> **NOTE**
>
> Java's framework for locating content and protocol handlers allows, in principle, for these handlers to be loaded from the same Web server that supplies the data. However, in the current implementations of appletviewer and HotJava this ease of loading is not possible. Current browsers only support searching for either type of handler on the local machine CLASSPATH, which is a significant limitation.

Locating a Protocol Handler

In a URL, the protocol name is specified as the first part of the URL text string immediately before the :// separator. It is easy to extract this, and the mechanism for doing so is consistent regardless of the protocol. Furthermore, the URL class in the java.net package provides a built-in method for this purpose.

Because the protocol name is part of the URL, the primary responsibility for locating handler code for any particular protocol rests with the URL class. When the method openConnection() is called on a URL object, a protocol handler is located, if possible, and invoked. The protocol handler returns a URLConnection object over which the data can be transferred.

The URL class provides three routes for obtaining a protocol handler, which are:

- Locate a Handler class using the local CLASSPATH and a package name built using the protocol name and a predefined prefix.

- Locate a Handler class using the local CLASSPATH and a package name built using the protocol name and a user-specified prefix.

- Invoke a *factory*. A factory takes a protocol name and attempts to return an instance of a ProtocolHandler. It can use any algorithm to achieve this, limited only by the programmer's imagination.

> **NOTE**
>
> You will see later that the factory concept is also employed in content handling.

Whatever the name of the protocol, the handler class for it is conventionally called `Handler`. To allow handlers for a variety of protocols to be installed, each `Handler` class is placed in a package that reflects the protocol name. For example, given the textual name of a protocol, `finger`, the `Handler` class is located in a subpackage called `finger`. This subpackage is located in a particular parent package which is called, by default, `sun.net.www`.

> **NOTE**
>
> The `finger` protocol, where available, allows you to find out information about users on other machines. Conventionally, `finger` would report the full name, last login time, and related personal information about either users currently logged in or about an individual specified by login name. The `finger` service is often disabled, as this kind of information is of potential use to malicious hackers.

It is possible to override this parent package name. If a property called `java.handler.protocol.pkgs` is defined, it is taken to be a list of package names. The elements of the list should be separated with the vertical bar character (|). For each element of this list, a tentative package name is created by appending the protocol name. If a class called `Handler` is found within the package, and it is a protocol hander, then it will be used. If, for example, the property was defined to have the value `myhandlers`, then a `finger` protocol handler could be found first in the class `myhandlers.finger.Handler`, or, if that failed, in the default class `sun.net.www.finger.Handler`.

> **NOTE**
>
> This mechanism, based on the property `java.handler.protocol.pkgs`, was added to the URL class in Java 1.1.

Using a Factory

The forgoing discussions describe the default mechanisms in Java. These mechanisms build a package name using the protocol name and search for a standard class in the resulting package. This describes the behavior of the appletviewer too. As was stated, a third option exists in the URL class, although the standard security manager prohibits its use by applets, so it is only possible in applications. The third option is to use a factory.

The interface URLStreamHandlerFactory defines a single method called createURLStreamHandler(). This method takes a String argument, which names the protocol. The return from the method is an instance of a protocol handler (URLStreamHandler class). The method can make whatever decisions are required to choose a protocol handler and can load it from anywhere it deems suitable.

To use a factory as a source of protocol handlers, an application must create an object that implements the URLStreamHandlerFactory interface. Once this has been created, it can be installed in the system by invoking the static method of the URL class URL.setURLStream-HandlerFactory(). The URLStreamHandlerFactory class is passed to this method as its single argument.

TIP The setURLStreamHandlerFactory() method can only be issued once and cannot be called by untrusted code, such as an applet. Therefore, an application can only have a single factory, which must be able to locate all the protocol handlers that are not located according to the package name conventions.

If the factory fails to find an appropriate protocol handler, then the search proceeds with the mechanisms described earlier, involving packages defined by the property java.handler.protocol.pkgs and the default package sun.net.www.

> **NOTE**   An example of creating and installing a `URLStreamHandlerFactory` is given in *Server Side Handlers*, toward the end of this chapter.

Writing a Protocol Handler

The search process results in the selection of a single class that will support handling of the protocol. This will be a subclass of `URL-StreamHandler`, as that is the defined return type of the `create-URLStreamHandler()` method in the handler factory. This object itself is not expected to handle the protocol; rather, it acts as an intermediary and is called on to create other objects that actually handle the protocol. The method that is called to do this is `openConnection()`. The return type of this method is `URLConnection`. The actual returned object is a subclass of this method, written to handle the protocol.

The `URLConnection` object has a number of methods that might be of interest, and there is one that is particularly important. `URL-Connection` itself is an abstract class, and the method `connect()` must be overridden to make the connection. Doing so generally involves creating and connecting the socket that will actually handle the data transfer and performing any required protocol transactions that might be needed to set up or configure the connection.

The methods `getInputStream()` and `getOutputStream()` of the `URLConnection` class can also be overridden, if appropriate. They allow the actual streams to be obtained by the program. Typically, these methods simply return the `InputStream` and `Output-Stream`, respectively, from the socket that is handling the data transfers. In some cases, this behavior is modified. Protocols that provide only unidirectional communication will not want to provide access to one stream or the other. In such a case, the parental method is left without being overridden. The effect of this situation is to throw an `UnknownServiceException` if the method is called.

> **TIP** Unidirectional communication usually means reading from the server, in which case the `getOuputStream()` method will be left unchanged. However, the `getInputStream()` method will be overridden.

There are a series of methods for accessing information about the nature of the data to be transferred. These methods have a strong flavor of HTML about them, but they provide a useful mechanism for requesting general information about the connection. Standard HTTP header fields that can be queried are: content-type, content-length, content-encoding, date, expires, and last-modified. These specific query methods use a general method that simply takes a string to indicate the name of the field to be returned. This method can be overridden to provide any information that might be required for a particular protocol. In the absence of an overriding method, the base method returns `null` for any field inquiry.

> **TIP** If you use the Netscape Navigator, you can see the HTTP headers that apply to a page by selecting the View ➤ Document Info menu item.

The Daytime Protocol Handler

This section looks at development of a simple but complete protocol handler. The daytime protocol is used for this example. The daytime protocol is quite simple and is discussed in Chapter 10, *Networking*. In that chapter, a server is developed for this protocol, and that server will be used here to support the protocol handler we develop.

Using the daytime protocol, a client connects to the server and reads one line of ASCII data. The protocol specifies that the service is normally provided on port 13, but to avoid clashing with the built-in daytime service of some operating systems, the one we develop here uses port 1313.

Class Layout

This example uses the default mechanism for locating a protocol handler, which is to use a package name that starts with `sun.net.www` followed by the protocol name. This protocol is called *daytime*, so the essential class must be called `sun.net.www.daytime.Handler`. This class must extend the `URLStreamHandler` class.

The job of the `Handler` class is to return a reference to a newly constructed subclass of `URLConnection`. This, by convention, should be located in the same package as the `Handler` class. This example will adopt that convention.

The name of the `URLConnection` subclass is not important, although it is conventional for the name to reflect the protocol that is handled and to end with the word *Connection*. Again, this example sticks with the conventions, and the class is called `DaytimeConnection`.

TIP It is a convention that classnames start with a capital letter. So although the protocol is called *daytime* with a lowercase *d*, this class is called `DaytimeConnection` with a capital *d*.

The Daytime Protocol Example

Handler.java

```
package sun.net.www.protocol.daytime;

import java.net.*;
import java.io.*;
```

```
public class Handler extends URLStreamHandler {
  public URLConnection openConnection(URL u) {
    return new DaytimeConnection(u);
  }
}
```

DaytimeConnection.java

```
package sun.net.www.protocol.daytime;

import java.net.*;
import java.io.*;

public class DaytimeConnection extends URLConnection {
  Socket s;

  protected DaytimeConnection(URL u) {
    super(u);
  }

  public void connect() throws IOException {
    int port;
    String host;

    if (connected) {
      return;
    }

    if ((port = url.getPort()) == -1) {
      port = 13;
    }

    if ((host = url.getHost()) == null) {
      host = "localhost";
    }

    s = new Socket(host, port);
    connected = true;
  }

  public InputStream getInputStream() throws IOException {
    if (!connected) {
      connect();
    }
```

```
      return s.getInputStream();
    }

    public String getHeaderField(String fieldName) {
      if ("content-type".equalsIgnoreCase(fieldName)) {
        return "text/plain";
      }
      else {
        return null;
      }
    }
  }
}
```

Running the Program

Because this code provides a protocol handler, it can only be run indirectly. There are two convenient ways to invoke it that do not require any software other than that available in the base JDK. First, a protocol handler is invoked automatically by the appletviewer if it encounters a URL that requires it. Second, an applet or application can create and use a URL that requires it.

First investigate the behavior of the appletviewer in the absence of a protocol handler for the daytime protocol. Ensure that you have *not* selected the directory for ch13, as this makes the handler unavailable. Then invoke the appletviewer like this:

```
appletviewer daytime://localhost:1313/
```

The appletviewer should fail, complaining that daytime: is not a known protocol. The message looks like this:

```
Bad URL: daytime: (unknown protocol: daytime)
```

Next, select the CD-ROM directory javadevhdbk\ch13. Notice that this directory contains a tree of subdirectories sun\net\www\protocol\daytime and that in this subdirectory are two classfiles: Handler.class and DaytimeConnection.class. These correspond to the source files Handler.java and DaytimeConnection.java, which are located in the ch13 directory.

TIP

The Java compiler, `javac`, provides a useful command-line switch for compiling classes that are members of explicit packages. Using `-d <path>` will cause the compiler to place the output files in a directory that properly reflects the package hierarchy. The compiler will even create the directory hierarchy for you if it does not already exist. You might, however, have to use the `-classpath <path-list>` switch as well to ensure that imports are correctly located. For example, to compile the files `Handler.java` and `DaytimeConnection.java`, the command `javac -d . Handler .java DaytimeConnection.java` is appropriate, provided that the two source files are in the current directory, the current directory (referred to by the period after `-d`) will be on the classpath, and that the current directory is on a normal hard disk rather than the CD-ROM.

Having selected the `ch13` directory, invoke the appletviewer as before. This time, although nothing useful happens, notice that the URL is no longer rejected. You will see a message like this instead:

```
I/O exception while reading: 127.0.0.1
Is daytime: the correct URL?
```

NOTE

127.0.0.1 is the address defined in the TCP/IP protocols for referring to the local machine, which is why the error report refers to that address even though you asked to load the applet from `localhost` by name.

This indicates that the URL was considered valid, which means that the protocol handler was located successfully. The problem this time is that the connection failed, which happened because no server is available.

Now, using a different window, start the `DayServer` program from Chapter 10, *Networking*, by issuing the command

```
java DayServer
```

Then run the appletviewer again. This time you will see a new error message:

```
Warning: No Applets were started, make sure the input contains an <applet> tag.
use: appletviewer [-debug] url|file ...
```

This indicates that the URL was recognized as valid and that the connection to the server was opened. The problem this time is that the DayServer program returns a date and time string, not an HTML file. Therefore, the appletviewer is unable to proceed.

Although appletviewer is not able to make real use of the daytime protocol, it is a simple matter to use it from within an applet or an application, as demonstrated in the next example, DayApplet.java.

The Details

The first class, Handler, is very simple. It serves only to satisfy the naming conventions required by the protocol-handling mechanisms. It accepts the URL object and returns a newly constructed instance of DaytimeConnection, based on the object.

The DaytimeConnection class has rather more work to do. First, using the facilities of its parent class URLConnection, it keeps a referenct to the URL object that it is to work on. The URLConnection class has a protected variable called url, which is set up by the URLConnection constructor. That constructor is invoked by the super(u) call issued in the DaytimeConnection constructor.

The constructor for DaytimeConnection is marked as protected. It could be public but is not for security reasons. The protected constructor is only accessible to members of the same package and sub-classes. In this case, that is the sun.net.www.protocol.daytime package. By default the security manager will not allow imported classes to reside in the sun.* package hierarchies. The constructor is still accessible to the `Handler` class, which is the only place that it should be constructed because `Handler` is part of the same package.

The bulk of the work is done in the `connect()` method. Connection is performed only the first time it is asked for; subsequent attempts are quietly ignored. A `boolean` variable called `connected` is inherited from the `URLConnection` class and is used to keep track of connection attempts. Because many of the methods in the `URLConnection` class that have not been overridden make use of this variable, it must be used.

To perform the connection, the URL is parsed to determine whether a specific host and port number have been specified. These default to `localhost` and `13`, respectively, in this protocol. Although there is no requirement to supply a default, it is normal to at least provide a default port. If a default will not be provided, then a `MalformedURLException` should be thrown in the absence of a specification.

> **TIP**
>
> The documentation for the `connect()` method indicates that it should throw an `IOException`. In fact, `MalformedURLException` is a subclass of `IOException`.

Once the host and port have been determined, the `Socket` object that actually handles the data transfer is created. Notice that the `Socket` constructor might throw an `Exception`, but this is simply passed up to the caller of this `connect()` method. Some protocols may have a mechanism for attempting to handle such difficulties, perhaps retrying, or trying alternate servers, before failing completely.

The `connect()` method does nothing with the connection aside from establishing it. The next job is to get the data from the URL so it can be handled locally. The getInputStream() method returns some subclass of InputStream that allows access to that data. In fact, two methods are defined in the URLConnection class: these are getInputStream() and getOutputStream() because some protocols involve sending user data, as distinct from protocol messages, outward to the server. The input and output methods are separate to allow for the possibility that a protocol might be read only, write only, or read-write. The definition of these methods in the URLConnection class simply throws an UnknownServiceException. Because of this, it is important to override both methods where a protocol requires both input and output.

In this example, the InputStream returned by the getInputStream() method is simply the one extracted from the Socket object. This implies that the data stream does not require any processing as part of the protocol. In many cases, the protocol is not so simple. To perform processing on the data stream, a subclass of FilterInputStream must be created to handle the aspects of the protocol that are involved in the data transfer. The returned InputStream should then be an instance of that filter connected to the socket. For example, if a TelnetInputStream class had been created to handle the Telnet line protocols, the last line of the connect() method would look like this:

```
return new TelnetInputStream(s.getInputStream());
```

Because it is legitimate, and actually normal, to call the getInputStream() method on a URLConnection object before it has been connected, it is necessary to conditionally perform the connect() method at the start of the getInputStream() method.

This example also overrides the getHeaderField() method. This method relates mainly to the HTTP protocol, where it is used to extract certain standard bits of header information, such as the content type. Although the daytime protocol does not have such header information, it is valuable to pretend that the content type field is supported because the content handler mechanism, discussed later in this chapter, determines which content handler to use based on the content type. If no information is available, automatic content handling will not work. The type `text/plain` is a suitable default for any protocol that returns plain text. Other content types should either be recognized MIME types or should use the approach specified for "experimental" additions in the MIME standard.

Testing the Daytime Protocol Handler

To run the protocol handler code, you will need some other example that will invoke it. This section presents a simple applet that connects to a URL and presents the returned data to the user in a label.

DayApplet.java

```
import java.applet.*;
import java.awt.*;
import java.net.*;
import java.io.*;

public class DayApplet extends Applet {
  Label l;

  public void init() {
    String source = getParameter("source");
    if (source == null) {
      source = "daytime://localhost:1313/";
    }
    URL u = null;
    URLConnection c = null;

    try {
      u = new URL(source);
    }
    catch (Exception e) {
```

```
      System.out.println("Problem creating URL: " + source);
      e.printStackTrace();
      return;
    }

    try {
      c = u.openConnection();
    }
    catch (Exception e) {
      System.out.println("Problem connecting to URL: " + source);
      e.printStackTrace();
      return;
    }

    BufferedReader in = null;
    String value = null;
    try {
      in = new BufferedReader(
        new InputStreamReader(c.getInputStream(), "8859_1"));
      value = in.readLine();
    }
    catch (Exception e) {
      System.out.println("Problem with input stream:");
      e.printStackTrace();
      return;
    }

    if (1 == null) {
      1 = new Label(value);
      add(1);
    }
    else {
      1.setText(value);
    }
  }
}
```

Running the Program

This example, located on the CD-ROM in the `javadevhdbk\ch13` directory, runs as an applet. The supporting HTML file is called `DayApplet.html` and is in the same directory.

The applet can be run in any Java-enabled browser provided that the `CLASSPATH` variable is set to include the `ch13` directory and is available from the Web pages of the CD-ROM. The daytime server program should be running on your local machine. To run under appletviewer, select the `ch13` directory and issue the command

```
appletviewer DayApplet.html
```

The applet will start and display a single text string with the output message of the daytime server.

What It Does

The `DayApplet` class reads a parameter called `source` if it is defined in the HTML file. If no such definition is found, which is the case in the supplied HTML, then a default is used instead. The resulting `String` is used to construct a URL object. To demonstrate the use of the protocol handler, this URL object should be based on the daytime protocol, hence the default is `daytime://localhost:1313/`, which is intended to connect to the `DayServer.java` example used earlier.

Once the URL object has been constructed, which requires that the URL class be able to locate an appropriate protocol handler, the resulting `URLConnection` is connected, and the `InputStream` is extracted. Any errors that arise in this process cause exceptions that are caught and displayed.

Provided the `InputStream` is successfully obtained, one line of data is read through a `DataInputStream` and is displayed in the label in the body of the applet.

In-Stream Protocols

The daytime protocol described so far requires only that a connection be made to a particular port and a single line of plain ASCII read from it. In many protocols, this is not sufficient. Some protocols, such as HTTP, require an initial configuration phase where the client expresses a particular need to the server. The server might return some preliminary status information, too, such as the size of the data to be transferred.

One requirement that is quite common is the handling of in-band protocol data, which appears, for example, in the Telnet protocol. This protocol allows the negotiation of certain facilities, such as whether characters typed at the keyboard should automatically be echoed by the terminal or by the remote computer. These options can be renegotiated and modified during the lifetime of the connection.

Protocols of this type are quite common and should be handled in subclasses of `FilterInputStream`. Bidirectional protocols require a matching pair of input and output filters. The next example demonstrates these ideas by implementing a minimal Telnet protocol handler.

Interlude: Discussion of the Telnet Protocol

The Telnet protocol addresses a number of requirements. The first is bidirectional communication, in that both client and server can transmit information. This type of communication is simple in Java and requires only the extraction of both `InputStream` and `OutputStream` from the `Socket`. Second, Telnet provides a control facility that allows the protocol to handle a variety of programmable options. For example, it allows the server to specify that characters should not be echoed to the screen when they are typed. Transmitting commands and data over the same connection requires a mechanism to distinguish between them. This idea, known as *escaping*, is a fundamental part of the control mechanism design.

NOTE

The Telnet protocol, like all core TCP/IP services, is defined in an RFC. RFCs may be obtained from `ftp://nic.ddn.mil/ftp`. RFC854, which describes the core Telnet protocol, is on the CD-ROM in the file `javadevhdbk\rfcs\rfc854.txt`.

Unlike many standard services in the TCP/IP suite, Telnet does not use ASCII for commands, but binary. A prefix (the byte value 255) is used to indicate that a command follows. Immediately following this byte value is a command of some form. If either system actually needs to send a real 255 value, then it is sent as two 255 bytes in sequence. This type of command escape mechanism is quite common in binary protocols.

A variety of commands are defined in the Telnet protocol; many are used for *option negotiation*. Option negotiation consists of requests for, or offers of, particular facilities. These messages pass both ways between server and client. Requests for an option to be enabled are made using the DO message, while an offer to use an option is made using the WILL message. Each of these is followed by further data indicating the particular facility to which the message relates.

The possible responses to a DO message are either WILL or WONT, while the responses to a WILL message are DO or DONT. This protocol is elegantly designed so that if one end offers a service the other is simultaneously requesting, each end sees the other's request as a positive acknowledgment of its own message.

The Table 13.1 lays out the possibilities. Notice the same format is used for an offer and a positive acknowledgment of a request, and vice versa. If a DONT or WONT is received, the facility *must* be disabled. This feature ensures that a common service set will always be found, even if this is the most basic communication with all features disabled.

TABLE 13.1 Option Negotiation Possibilities

Request received:	Means:	To say:	Send this:
`DO xxxx`	I would like you to use `xxxx` mode.	I am willing and able to do `xxxx`.	`WILL xxxx`
		NO, sorry, I cannot or do not wish to do `xxxx`.	`WONT xxxx`
`WILL xxxx`	I am willing and able to use `xxxx` mode.	I would like you to use `xxxx` mode.	`DO xxxx`
		Please do not use `xxxx` mode.	`DONT xxxx`

Many facilities can be controlled using this option-negotiation scheme, and it is transparently extensible to allow future enhancements. Typical of the type of facility that can be controlled is the local echoing of typed characters to the screen. A server might ask for this to be turned off when passwords are entered. It is permissible for either end to say that it WONT do something that it has been asked to DO. Under these conditions, the end that issued the request is aware of the limitation and is expected to make the best of it.

A Simple Telnet Example

To demonstrate a more complete protocol-handling scheme than the one shown in the previous daytime example, this section implements a simple Telnet client. All the aspects previously shown—a handler and connection class located in the `sun.net.www.protocol.telnet` package—are required for this client. Additionally, stream protocol handling is required.

This particular client reacts to any `DO` or `WILL` message by issuing a `WONT` or `DONT` reply without even examining what service is being requested. The important part of the example is that although the services are unimplemented, the protocol itself is implemented. Hence, the code serves as an example and as a starting point for enhancement. No matter what facilities are offered, the Telnet protocol specification requires that the connection must be able to operate in this fundamental mode. This minimal behavior is known as an NVT (Network Virtual Terminal).

The minimal Telnet client is made up of several classes. Each class will be discussed individually. After each class has been listed and described, the overall program will be described.

TelnetDefs.java

```java
package sun.net.www.protocol.telnet;

public class TelnetDefs {
  public static final int IAC   = 255;
  public static final int DONT  = 254;
  public static final int DO    = 253;
  public static final int WONT  = 252;
  public static final int WILL  = 251;
  public static final int SB    = 250;
  public static final int GA    = 249;
  public static final int EL    = 248;
  public static final int EC    = 247;
  public static final int AYT   = 246;
  public static final int AO    = 245;
  public static final int IP    = 244;
  public static final int BRK   = 243;
  public static final int DM    = 242;
  public static final int NOP   = 241;
  public static final int SE    = 240;
  public static final int EOR   = 239;
  public static final int ABORT = 238;
  public static final int SUSP  = 237;
  public static final int EOF   = 236;
}
```

What It Does

This class provides definitions of the standard commands used by the Telnet protocol. Most of these facilities are not, in fact, supported by the minimal client.

The meaning of these commands is described in the RFCs. Five elements are actually used in this example. IAC stands for *Introduces a Command,* while DO, DONT, WILL, and WONT are the commands that have been discussed in the theoretical section.

TelnetOutputStream.java

```
package sun.net.www.protocol.telnet;

import java.io.*;

public class TelnetOutputStream extends FilterOutputStream {

  public TelnetOutputStream(OutputStream out) {
    super(out);
  }

  public void sendCommand(int cmd)
    throws IOException{
    out.write(TelnetDefs.IAC);
    out.write(cmd);
  }

  public void sendCommand(int cmd, int arg)
    throws IOException {
    sendCommand(cmd);
    out.write(arg);
  }

  public void write(int b) throws IOException {
    // Data bytes of IAC need to be doubled
    if ((b & TelnetDefs.IAC) == TelnetDefs.IAC) {
      out.write(TelnetDefs.IAC);
    }
    out.write(b);
  }
}
```

What It Does

This class is a subclass of FilterOutputStream, modifying a flow of characters to suit the demands of the Telnet protocol. When a data byte in the flow is the same as IAC, it must be doubled to distinguish it from a real command introduction. The class provides two convenience methods, called `sendCommand()`, which allow the sending of one- or two-byte commands with the Telnet IAC flag in front of them.

The Details

The `TelnetOuputStream` class, like any `FilterOutputStream`, must be constructed with an `OutputStream` argument. It is used to write the combined data and command stream.

TelnetInputStream.java

```java
package sun.net.www.protocol.telnet;

import java.io.*;

public class TelnetInputStream extends FilterInputStream {
  protected TelnetOutputStream outChannel;

  public TelnetInputStream(InputStream source,
                           TelnetOutputStream out) {
    super(source);
    outChannel = out;
  }

  public int read() throws IOException {
    int b = in.read();
    // If we have a command introducion, go into
    // the processing body
    while (b == TelnetDefs.IAC)
    {
      // start by fetching the follow on byte
      b = in.read();
      // the byte after IAC is the command byte
      switch (b)
      {
        // another IAC implies that we have a data byte of 255
        case TelnetDefs.IAC:
          return b;
```

```
                    // break; not reached..
            case TelnetDefs.WILL:
              b = in.read();
              outChannel.sendCommand(TelnetDefs.DONT, b);
              break;
            case TelnetDefs.WONT:
              b = in.read();
              break;
            case TelnetDefs.DO:
              b = in.read();
              outChannel.sendCommand(TelnetDefs.WONT, b);
              break;
            case TelnetDefs.DONT:
              b = in.read();
              break;
          }
          b = in.read();
        }
        return b;
    }
}
```

What It Does

This class is a `FilterInputStream`, which reads a flow of characters and separates commands in the Telnet protocol from the data stream. `IAC` control bytes are recognized, and `WILL` and `DO` commands that are found result in a `DONT` or `WONT` reply. `WONT` or `DONT` messages that are received are not acknowledged because the protocol definition requires ignoring instructions to set a mode that is already current.

The Details

When this class is constructed it is given a reference to an `InputStream`, which is used as the character source from the remote end of the connection. A `TelnetOutputStream` object, connected to the outgoing channel of the network connection, should be provided. This object is used to send responses to the protocol commands.

When a WILL or DO command is recognized, the option byte is collected and a corresponding negative acknowledgment, DONT or WONT, is constructed and sent by the TelnetOutputStream object. If WONT or DONT commands are received, these do not require acknowledgment because the Telnet protocol does not permit refusal of them.

GlassTTY.java

```java
import java.awt.*;
import java.io.*;

public class GlassTTY extends Canvas implements Runnable {
  private Font font;
  private FontMetrics metrics;

  private InputStream in;
  private OutputStream out;
  private Thread inHandler;

  private char [][] display = new char[24][80];
  private char[] blankLine = new char[display[0].length];
  private int x, y;

  public GlassTTY() {
    for (int i = 0; i < blankLine.length; i++) {
      blankLine[i] = ' ';
    }
    font = new Font("Courier", Font.PLAIN, 10);
    setFont(font);
  }

  public void connect(InputStream source, OutputStream dest) {
    in = source;
    out = dest;
    inHandler = new Thread(this, "input handler");
    inHandler.start();
  }

  public Dimension preferredSize() {
    return minimumSize();
  }
```

```java
public Dimension minimumSize() {
  int x = 0;
  int y = 0;

  if (metrics != null) {
    x = display[0].length * metrics.charWidth(' ');
    y = display.length * metrics.getHeight();
  }
  return new Dimension(x, y);
}

public void addNotify() {
  super.addNotify();
  metrics = getToolkit().getFontMetrics(font);
  for (int y = 0; y < display.length; y++) {
    for (int x = 0; x < display[y].length; x++) {
      display[y][x] = ' ';
    }
  }
}

public void join() {
  boolean success = true;
  do {
    try {
      inHandler.join();
    }
    catch (InterruptedException e) {
      success = false;
    }
  } while (!success);
}

public void run() {
  int c = 0;

  for (;;) {
    try {
      c = in.read();
      if (c == -1) {
        break;
      }
    }
```

```
          catch (IOException e) {
            e.printStackTrace();
            System.exit(1);
          }
          switch(c) {
          case 0x08:
            doBS();
            break;
          case 0x0a:
            doCR();
          case 0x0d:
            doLF();
            break;
          default:
            newChar(c);
            break;
          }
          repaint();
      }
  }

  private synchronized void doBS() {
    if (x > 0) {
      x--;
    }
  }

  private synchronized void doLF() {
    if (y < display.length - 1) {
      y++;
    }
    else {
      for (int y = 0; y < display.length - 1; y++) {
        System.arraycopy(display[y+1], 0, display[y], 0,
                         display[y].length);
      }
      System.arraycopy(blankLine, 0, display[y], 0, display[y].length);
    }
  }

  private synchronized void doCR() {
    x = 0;
  }
```

```
private synchronized void newChar(int c) {
  display[y][x] = ((char)c);
  if (++x >= display[y].length) {
    x = 0;
    doLF();
  }
}

public void paint(Graphics g) {
  for (int y = 0; y < display.length; y++) {
    g.drawChars(display[y], 0, display[y].length,
                0, (y * metrics.getHeight()) +
                metrics.getLeading() +
                metrics.getAscent());
  }
  putCursor(g);
}

public void putCursor(Graphics g) {
  int x, y, w, h;
  Rectangle r = cursor();
  x = r.x;
  y = r.y;
  w = r.width;
  h = r.height;
  g.drawRect(x, y, w, h);
}

private Rectangle cursor() {
  return new Rectangle(x * metrics.charWidth(' '),
                y * metrics.getHeight(),
                metrics.charWidth(' ') - 1,
                metrics.getHeight() - 1);

}

public boolean handleEvent(Event ev) {
  if (ev.id == Event.KEY_PRESS) {
    try {
      switch (ev.key) {
      case '\n':
        doLF();
        doCR();
```

```
              break;
            case 8:
              doBS();
              newChar(' ');
              doBS();
              break;
            default:
              newChar(ev.key);
              break;
          }
          repaint();
          out.write(ev.key);
        }
        catch (IOException e) {
          e.printStackTrace();
          System.exit(1);
        }
      }
      return super.handleEvent(ev);
    }

    public void ec() {
      display[y][x] = (' ');
      repaint();
    }

    public void el() {
      System.arraycopy(blankLine, 0, display[y], 0, display[y].length);
    }

    public static void main(String args[]) throws Exception {
      PipedInputStream i = new PipedInputStream();
      PipedOutputStream o = new PipedOutputStream(i);
      Frame f = new Frame("GlassTTY test");
      GlassTTY that = new GlassTTY();
      f.add("Center", that);
      f.pack();
      f.show();
      that.connect(i, o);
    }
  }
```

What It Does

This class provides a basic *glass teletype,* or crude terminal program. It takes keystrokes and transmits them to an `OutputStream`. Characters received from an `InputStream` are pasted onto the 80-by-24-character display. To support the basic NVT mode of Telnet, characters typed at the keyboard are echoed to the display as well as being sent to the output.

The Details

To support the two streams simultaneously, this class creates a separate `Thread`, which is used to read characters from the `InputStream`. Characters typed at the keyboard cause calls to the `handleEvent()` method and are processed and sent to the output channel from there.

The display is maintained very crudely. A two-dimensional array holds 24 rows of 80 characters. Whenever the display requires updating, this entire array is copied to the screen. The `minimumSize()` and `preferredSize()` methods use the `FontMetrics` for the Courier font to provide size information so that a `LayoutManager` can properly display this window.

GlassTelnet.java

```java
import java.awt.*;
import java.net.*;
import java.io.*;

public class GlassTelnet
{
  public static void main(String args[]) throws Exception
  {
    URL u = new URL((args.length > 0) ? args[0] : "telnet://localhost/");
    URLConnection c = u.openConnection();
    GlassTTY glass = new GlassTTY();
    glass.connect(c.getInputStream(), c.getOutputStream());
```

```
   Frame f = new Frame("GlassTelnet to " + args[0]);
   f.add("Center", glass);
   f.pack();
   f.show();
   glass.join();
   System.out.println("Connection closed. Press <return> to exit");
   System.in.read();
   System.exit(0);
 }
}
```

What It Does

This class provides the glue that holds the previous classes together in a workable example. It creates the network connection and the other objects.

The Details

The command-line argument, if any, should be a URL. To exercise this example, the URL should use the `telnet:` protocol and may include an optional port number. A URL is created based on that argument or on the default `telnet://localhost/` if no argument has been supplied. This requires that the Telnet protocol handler be found by the underlying system. Once the URL has been created, it is connected, and a `GlassTTY` is created based on the input and output streams of the resulting `URLConnection`.

After all the parts have been constructed, a `Frame` is built, and the `GlassTTY` object is added to it. The `Frame` is sized and shown. After that, the main thread waits for the `GlassTTY` object to kill its input thread. It is killed when the input stream to that object returns -1, indicating the end of the file.

Running the Program

The source (`telnetExample.java`) and bytecode (`telnetExample.class`) files for this example are located on the CD-ROM in the directory `javadevhdbk\ch13`. You will recall that the protocol handler mechanisms require that the handler be a class called `Handler`. Because Java requires public classes be declared in a file with a name that matches the classname, the source file is therefore always called `Handler.java`, regardless of the actual protocol. This subdirectory has been used to avoid a name clash with the `Handler.java` source file used in the daytime example.

To run the program, you must have a network service to connect to. Although the program will work adequately as a general client, the Telnet protocol parts will not be exercised at all unless the program connects to a Telnet server. If you have a network connection to a Unix machine, you can log into that. If you have an Internet connection, there are a number of services that allow you to use a Telnet client. A service called Hytelnet was set up some time ago to attempt to organize these services. A Web search for *hytelnet* should yield an interesting example server to connect to. Some of these services require specific terminal emulation, which the Telnet client cannot offer. You should therefore select one that allows the use of a *glass TTY*.

When a suitable server has been located, start the Telnet client by issuing the command:

```
java GlassTelnet <remoteURL>
```

The program will run, set up the connection, and display the terminal window. The server will usually issue a login prompt first, and from that point the operation is governed by the remote server.

WARNING Because of the absence of controls in this client, passwords entered using it will be echoed. It should not be used for any serious applications without being modified.

Reusing the Code

Although this is quite a large example, it implements only the absolute minimum requirements of the Telnet protocol. To make a useful program, the user interface should be extended to support some of the options that are most commonly used. The `Telnet-InputStream` and `TelnetOutputStream` classes must be modified to respond appropriately to inquiries and commands relating to the options that are implemented.

The `GlassTTY` class can be enhanced in a number of ways. First, the screen update can be made much more efficient. At present, any single character change on the display results in the entire 80-by-24 matrix being redrawn, including all the blanks at the ends of lines. This situation could be improved by keeping track of where characters have been changed and only refreshing those areas under normal conditions. Be careful to ensure that exposure is properly handled, however.

Additional terminal emulation could be added, allowing direct cursor control and other capabilities. If this is done, it would be sensible to implement one of the commonly used terminals, such as the VT series, so that the resulting work is as useful as possible.

Content Handling

A number of the ideas discussed for protocol handling are broadly applicable to content handling. As we saw before, the content type must be determined before getting started. Based on that information, an appropriate content handler is sought. As with protocol handlers, either a factory can be used or a specific named package can be checked. If a content handler is located, it is then responsible for receiving and decoding the data that comes to it. The results of that decoding operation must be made available to the caller in a useful form.

Locating a Content Handler

Content handlers are invoked by objects of the URLConnection class. When the getContent() method is called, the URLConnection determines the content type of the connection it represents; this is done via the protocol handler getContentType() method. Based on that type, a content handler is sought.

A similar approach to that taken for the protocol handler search is adopted. Generally, content handlers are found in a class named after the content type, in a package called sun.net.www.content. So, for example, the handler for audio/wav would be located in the class sun.net.www.content.audio.wav. Notice that the slash character (/) has been converted into a dot, indicating that the hierarchy of content types has been translated into a hierarchy of packages.

TIP Many content types—for example, application/mac-binhex40 and video/x-msvideo, which are used for HQX and AVI files, respectively—include the hyphen character and other nonalphanumeric characters. The specification says that all slash characters are converted to dots and all other nonalphanumeric characters are converted into underscore (_). This point is particularly important because the hyphen, and many other nonalphanumeric characters, are not legal in class names.

Using a Factory

As with the search for a protocol handler, it is possible to install a content handler factory using the static method of the URLConnection class setContentHandlerFactory(). If this method has been used, the content handler factory method createContentHandler() will be called with the MIME type string as its argument. If this fails, the standard package and classname search described above is pursued.

Writing a Content Handler

Content handlers must be subclasses of `ContentHandler`. This subclass defines a single method, `getContent()`, which takes a URLConnection as its argument and from that obtains the `InputStream`, which supplies the data to be handled.

It is in the nature of a content handler that the work involved be mainly decoding the actual data passed over from the server. To produce an example that is not unduly cumbersome and overloaded with handling code that would obscure the essential point, the example used handles, which are a tiny subset of HTML.

The content type is called `text/tml`. The format of the data for `tml` is similar to HTML, except that the only tags that are understood are `<hr>` and `<br>`, which generate a horizontal rule and a newline, respectively.

Two classes make up the content handler, and a third describes a trivial test applet. These sources are described individually in the following sections. Descriptions of how the classes work together to produce a complete example content handler and how to run the test follow each individual class description.

TmlStream.java

```java
package sun.net.www.content.text;

import java.io.*;

public class TmlStream {
  public static final int  PLAIN = 0;
  public static final int  TAG   = 1;
  public static final int ENDED = -1;

  private static final String HLINE =
    "\n...................." +
    "....................\n";
  private static final String NEWLINE = "\n";
```

```java
private int lastType = PLAIN;
private String lastString;
private int state = PLAIN;

BufferedReader source;
StringBuffer buildup = new StringBuffer();


public TmlStream(InputStream in) throws IOException {
  source = new BufferedReader(
    new InputStreamReader(in, "8859_1"));
}

public int nextToken() throws IOException {
  int c;
  boolean lastWasSpace = false;
  boolean completed = false;

  if (state == PLAIN) {
    do {
      c = source.read();
      if (Character.isWhitespace((char)c)) {
        if (lastWasSpace) {
          while (Character.isWhitespace((char)(c = source.read())))
            ;
          lastWasSpace = false;
        }
        else {
          c = ' ';
          lastWasSpace = true;
        }
      }
      else {
        lastWasSpace = false;
      }

      if ((c != '<') && (c != -1)) {
        buildup.append((char)c);
      }
      else {
        completed = true;
        lastType = PLAIN;
```

```
          lastString = buildup.toString();
          buildup.setLength(0);
          if (c == '<') {
            state = TAG;
          }
          else if (c == -1) {
            state = ENDED;
          }
        }
    } while (!completed);
}
else if (state == TAG) {
    do {
      c = source.read();
      if (Character.isWhitespace((char)c)) {
        if (lastWasSpace) {
          while (Character.isWhitespace((char)(c = source.read())))
            ;
          lastWasSpace = false;
        }
        else {
          c = ' ';
          lastWasSpace = true;
        }
      }
      else {
        lastWasSpace = false;
      }

      if (c == -1) {
        state = ENDED;
        throw new IOException("TML format error, EOF inside tag");
      }
      else if (c != '>') {
        buildup.append((char)c);
      }
      else {
        lastType = TAG; // tentative
        state = PLAIN;
        completed = true;
        lastString = buildup.toString();
        lastString = lastString.trim().toLowerCase();
```

```
        if (lastString.equals("br")) {
          lastString = NEWLINE;
          lastType = PLAIN;
        }
        else if (lastString.equals("hr")) {
          lastString = HLINE;
          lastType = PLAIN;
        }
        buildup.setLength(0);
      }
    } while (!completed);
  }
  else if (state == ENDED) {
    lastType = ENDED;
  }
  return lastType;
}

public String tokenValue() {
  return lastString;
}
}
```

What It Does

This class takes a character stream as its input and parses it to produce a sequence of tokens. To drive the parser, the nextToken() method is called. This method returns an integer value that indicates whether the collected token is plain text, a token, or the end of the input.

After the next token has been assembled, and its type reported by the nextToken() method, calling the tokenValue() method returns the actual token value. This action is appropriate provided that the token type was not ENDING, which indicates that the end of input has been reached.

Tokens are returned as String objects; they are either plain text strings or the contents of a tag. Two specific tags, <br> and <hr>, are recognized by the parser. When one of these is found, it is converted into a plain text representation, either a newline or a newline followed by a string of 80 hyphens, followed by another newline. These two tokens, therefore, loosely mimic the effect of the same tokens in normal HTML. Any other token that is found is collected and then stripped of the leading and trailing < and > symbols and any spaces. Finally, the token is converted to lowercase before being returned.

While collecting characters to form a token, multiple whitespace characters are coalesced into a single-space character. So newlines, for example, are ignored and, where specifically required, must be encoded in the source by the token <br>. This coding is like normal HTML.

This class is not a subclass of FilterInputStream; it has more similarities with the StringTokenizer class. This dissimilarity is not a problem, as the classes that will use this class do not need to be written to use an InputStream as such, provided they are written correctly to use whatever API is available to them.

The TmlStream class is a member of the sun.net.www.content .text package simply to group it with the rest of this example; there is no specific need for this placement.

tml.java

```java
package sun.net.www.content.text;

import java.io.*;
import java.net.*;
import java.awt.*;

public class tml extends ContentHandler {
  public Object getContent(URLConnection c) throws IOException {
    StringBuffer sb = new StringBuffer();
    InputStream source = c.getInputStream();
    TmlStream i = new TmlStream(source);

    int tokType;
    while ((tokType = i.nextToken()) != TmlStream.ENDED) {
      if (tokType == TmlStream.PLAIN) {
```

```
            sb.append(i.tokenValue());
        }
        else if (tokType == TmlStream.TAG) {
          System.out.println("\nUNKNOWN TAG <" + i.tokenValue() + ">");
        }
      }
    return new TextArea(sb.toString());
    }
}
```

What It Does

This class is the actual content handler that is used to handle content of type text/tml. It must therefore fulfill two requirements. First, it must be a subclass of ContentHandler. Second, it must have precisely the correct package and classname in order to be located by the default rules for content handlers. In this case, the class must be called tml and be located in the package sun.net.www.content.text.

> **WARNING** Although it is the convention to begin classnames with a capital letter, this must not be done in this case. If a capital is used, the class will not be recognized as a handler for the text/tml content type, but instead be mistaken for the text/Tml content type.

The behavior of the content handler is embedded in the getContent() method, and the data that is to be decoded is supplied by the stream encapsulated in the URLConnection argument to that method. In this case, the InputStream source is extracted from the URLConnection and used to construct an instance of TmlStream that will parse the input.

After the input streams have been set up, the getContent() method proceeds by collecting all the tokens into a StringBuffer. Tags other than <br> and <hr> are wrapped up on a line by themselves with the UNKNOWN TAG message. All plain strings, including the converted values used for `<br>` and `<hr>`, which appear as simple text, are appended to the `StringBuffer` as is.

Once the input is completely read, the contents of the `StringBuffer` are converted to a `String`, which is used to initialize a `TextArea`. This `TextArea` is then returned from the `getContent()` method.

TmlTest.java

```
import java.applet.*;
import java.awt.*;
import java.net.*;

public class TmlTest extends Applet {
  public void init() {
    setLayout(new BorderLayout());
    String u = getParameter("url");
    if (u == null) {
      u = "TmlTest.tml";
    }
    URL url = null;
    Object o = null;
    try {
      url = new URL(getDocumentBase(), u);
      o = url.getContent();
    }
    catch (Exception e) {
      e.printStackTrace();
      throw new RuntimeException("URL trouble: " + e);
    }
    if (!(o instanceof Component)) {
      o = new Label("Can't handle content type: " +
                    o.getClass().getName());
    }
    add("Center", (Component)o);
  }
}
```

What It Does

This applet tests the content handler for the `text/tml` content type. Notice that it does not refer directly to either of the classes that are involved in this content handling, rather those classes are invoked automatically without intervention by the applet.

First, the applet has to decide on the URL to fetch. If the HTML from which the applet is loaded defines a parameter `url`, then that value is used as a starting point; otherwise, a default of `TmlTest.tml` is used. The URL that is determined in this way is treated as relative to the document base from which the HTML file was loaded. This treatment allows an absolute URL to be given if desired; or a relative one may be used, if preferred. No matter what is chosen for loading, a URL object is constructed, and the `getContent()` method is invoked on that. Notice that no intermediate `URLConnection` is created; creating one is possible but not necessary in this case. The URL object will handle that aspect.

The returned value from the `getContent()` method will, if the `text/tml` content handler has been invoked successfully, be a `TextArea`. This applet simply checks to see if the class of the returned object is an instance of the `Component` class, and if not, it creates a label with an error message indicating the class of the object that was returned. The resulting `Component` is then added to the applet display in the Center region. Notice that the applet has been configured to use a `BorderLayout` rather than the default `FlowLayout`.

The input file `TmlTest.tml` contains the following text:

TmlTest.tml

```
hello
   there
      this
is a test<br>This should be a new line
<hr>and this should
be beneath a rule
```

When everything is running properly, this input results in the appletviewer display shown in Figure 13.1.

FIGURE 13.1

The appletviewer showing the `TmlTest` applet running

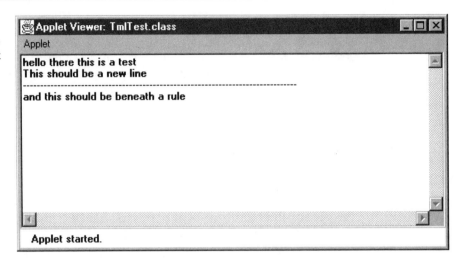

Running the Program

This applet is quite demanding to run properly. The reason is that the content type for the file `TmlTest.tml` must be specified as `text/tml`, which does not occur by recognition of the file extension, but rather by means of having a properly configured HTTP server. If you do not have a Web server available to you, you cannot run this example.

If you do have a Web server, you will need to copy the following files into a directory from which the server can make them available for HTTP access: `TmlTest.class`, `TmlTest.html`, and `TmlTest.tml`. Once you have located these, configure your Web server to report files with the extension `.tml` as having the MIME type `text/tml` and start the server if necessary.

When the server is configured and running, start appletviewer to load, via HTTP, the `TmlTest.html` file. Appletviewer should be started from the directory `javadevhdbk\ch13` so the `sun\net\www\content\text` subdirectory containing the elements of the content handler is located in the current directory. You also need to ensure that the current directory is on your CLASSPATH; this is the case by default unless you explicitly set up a CLASSPATH value.

> **TIP**
>
> If you do not have a Web server, there are several suitable ones available at no cost for evaluation. A search on the Web will locate several, such as JavaSoft's own server *Jeeves* or O'Reilly's *Website*.

Server Side Handlers

One of the opportunities that Java originally offered was for *server side* content and protocol handlers. If a Web site wanted to provide a new content type or use a specialist protocol for some reason, the expectation was that Java would allow the handlers for those services to be loaded transparently over the network when the browser needed them.

This action is still possible in principle, but as we have mentioned, it is not supported under the current browsers. This section discusses the nature of this limitation and the difficulties in overcoming it. Given an understanding of the issues involved, it is possible, although not trivial, to create a browser that does handle server side content and protocol handlers.

Dynamic Classloading

When an applet runs in a Java browser, it can load supporting classes. When a class is needed, the classloader first searches for it on the local system to ensure the best possible response time and to maintain the integrity of the system classes so they are not usurped by imported classes that appear to have the same name. If the class is not found locally, the classloader used to load the applet proceeds to look for that class on the same system that provided the applet itself.

If a class is a member of a named package, then the URL from which the classloader attempts to load it is modified by the package name in the same way that a locally loaded class would be. If an applet has been loaded from `http://www.xyz.com/interesting/myjava` `.class`, and that class attempts to load a class called `mysupport` `.math.Complex`, then the classloader will attempt to load from the URL `http://www.xyz.com/interesting/mysupport/math/` `Complex.class`. This behavior appears to suggest that it would be possible to load content or protocol handlers from a server simply by placing them in the required directory structure, reflecting the package name `sun.net.www.…` according to the particular conditions. In fact, a number of problems arise when this is attempted.

The first difficulty is that packages starting with `sun…`, `java…`, or `netscape…` are protected by the security manager by default so that imported code cannot be added to them. This is done by a general mechanism. Defining two properties in the `.hotjava/properties` file called `package.restrict.access.sun` and `package` `.restrict.definition.sun`, and setting the values to `false` will remove this restriction. Unfortunately, it also removes an important part of the security barrier that protects your system. Most notably, these changes allow an applet, or other imported code, to create and use arbitrary parts of the `sun.` package hierarchy. One part of this, the `sun.tools.debug` package, would be particularly sensitive because it would potentially allow an applet to bypass all other security restrictions.

In Java 1.1 an alternative might be to redefine the property `java.handler.protcol.pkgs`, but this would be installation dependent. Handler loading would require that this value be set up to correspond to the configuration of the server.

Another difficulty comes up because the content and protocol handlers are not loaded by the applet; they are loaded by system classes, specifically the URL and URLConnection classes. Whenever a class asks to use another class, the class is loaded by the same classloader that loaded the class that is making the request, unless the first class specifically requests otherwise. Here, the URL and URLConnection classes have been loaded by the system classloader, which never loads from anywhere except the local system. So the content and protocol handlers are only sought on the local machine.

It might appear that the way around this problem is to have an applet load the handlers. Unfortunately, this fails too. Classes are loaded into namespaces that are controlled by the classloader that loaded them. So it turns out that if a content or protocol handler is loaded by an applet, it is not visible to the URL and URLConnection classes that need to use it.

In fact, even if this last approach is taken, there are two other difficulties. The first of these is that content and protocol handlers should be available to the browser itself, not just to the applets. It is inconvenient to have to load an applet on a page to support a particular content type used within that page. The applet would also probably be loaded too late to work properly.

The second problem with the last approach has to do specifically with protocol handlers. Any Java code that is not loaded by the system classloader is considered untrusted. The security manager does not operate solely on applets. Rather, any and all imported code is restricted. One of the key restrictions is that a network connection can only be made to the same host that supplied the code. Because protocol handlers must create the Socket objects that communicate with the remote host, an imported protocol handler can only connect to its originating site. Of course, this does not, of itself, make the protocol handler useless, but it does continue to reduce its facility even after the other difficulties have been overcome. If the restrictions on creating sockets are not imposed completely, there is a danger of a security breach, and the browser is left wide open to attack. So the rule must not be waived.

Additional difficulties arise when using a browser that is not "pure" Java, such as Netscape Navigator or Microsoft's Internet Explorer. In such systems, the Java Virtual Machine is only invoked specifically to run applets and not to handle arbitrary bits of HTML. In these cases, there is clearly no immediate possibility of installing Java content or protocol handlers from remote sites.

Approaching a Solution

One approach that can be taken to make server side handler loading a possibility is to install factories for content and protocol handlers. These allow the URL and URLConnection classes to use a more flexible approach to finding the handlers they need. To achieve this, the browser code itself must be modified because factories cannot be installed by imported code, for obvious security reasons. Instead, they must be installed once and only once by the local classes of the application.

If a factory is to be used, it must be able to communicate with the browser to determine the URL from which the current document has been loaded. Based on this, the factory can then determine the full URL from which to attempt to load any handlers required to support that particular page.

Alternatives to Server Side Handlers

Clearly, it is not trivial to implement server side handlers. Perhaps the biggest problem is that the result is nonstandard, which means that, at least until a commercial grade browser implements the facility and clearly documents the requirements it makes of the server, server side handlers will be nothing more than an interesting academic discussion topic.

The question remains of how the promise of Java can be fully realized. There are two answers to this, and both are quite simple. First, in a controlled environment such as a corporate intranet, the handlers can be made available along with other company-wide software simply by using file-sharing systems such as the Network File System (NFS). In an open environment, such as the Internet, the only solution is to embed the handling into an applet in an ad hoc way. This approach, although it lacks the elegance of the built-in content and protocol handling, can still be tidy, extensible, reusable, and elegant. This approach depends only on having a good object-oriented design that considers the needs of the protocols and the applets that will use them.

Implementing Server Side Handlers

Because of the dynamic nature of Java, it is possible to take existing code and put wrappers around it in such a way that a modified version of a program can be produced without ever recompiling any of the original. This ability will be used in this example to produce a modified version of the appletviewer program that will implement a rudimentary server side loading of protocol handlers. The example could be extended to deal with content handlers, but that has not been implemented in the interest of simplicity.

The standard appletviewer is actually implemented as a Java program created out of a number of classes in the package `sun.applet`. Issuing a command in this form:

```
appletviewer myexample.html
```

is actually only a convenient shorthand replacement for:

```
java sun.applet.AppletViewer myexample.html
```

It turns out that the `main()` method of the class `AppletViewer` is responsible for parsing the command-line arguments given to the program. Each argument is used to construct a full URL. If a partial

URL is given on the command line, then `file://` and the current working directory are added to create a full one. For each of these URLs, the `AppletViewer` class' static method `parse()` is called. This method creates and launches the appletviewer window and does all the real work.

Because of these aspects of the appletviewer's design, it is possible to create a new class that selects just the elements of the `AppletViewer` class that are needed. This example, which is built on the appletviewer of JDK 1.0.2, uses this approach.

To install a protocol handler factory, you must first create a factory class. A protocol handler factory is actually just a class that implements the interface `URLStreamHandlerFactory`. Because the amount of code involved in implementing the single method required by this is small, a single class will be created to serve as both the modified appletviewer and the factory.

SuperApplet.java

```
package sun.applet;

import java.net.*;
import java.io.*;

public class SuperApplet implements URLStreamHandlerFactory {
  AppletClassLoader acl;

  public static void main(String args[]) throws Exception {
    URL url = null;
    if (args.length != 1) {
      System.out.println("Usage: SuperApplet <URL>");
      System.out.println("Exactly one full URL must be given");
    }
    else {
      url = new URL(args[0]);
      SuperApplet that = new SuperApplet();
      that.acl = new AppletClassLoader(url);
      URL.setURLStreamHandlerFactory(that);
      AppletViewer.parse(url);
```

```
      }
    }

    public URLStreamHandler createURLStreamHandler(String protocol) {
      String handlerClass = "sun.net.www.protocol." + protocol + ".Handler";
      System.out.println("Protocol factory trying to load " +
        "handler from class " + handlerClass);

      Class cl = null;
      try {
        cl = acl.loadClass(handlerClass);
        if (cl != null) {
          Object o = cl.newInstance();
          if (o instanceof URLStreamHandler) {
            System.out.println(":-) Load was successful.");
            return (URLStreamHandler)o;
          }
        }
      }
      catch (Exception e) {
      }

      System.out.println(":-( Load was unsuccessful.");
      return null;
    }
  }
```

What It Does

The code performs two functions. First, it serves to parse the command-line arguments, set up the factory, and launch the standard appletviewer under modified conditions. The second function is that performed by the factory itself.

The Details

The SuperApplet class is a member of the package sun.applet, which is necessary because it must be able to create an instance of the AppletClassLoader class, which is a nonpublic class in that package. This requirement does not present a problem as this is a local class.

To serve as a factory, as well as the main entry point for the modified appletviewer, the class must implement the interface `URLStream-HandlerFactory`. This interface requires that a method `public URLStreamHandler createURLStreamHandler(String protocol)` be defined; this method is described later in the chapter.

The class has as a member variable an instance of the `Applet-ClassLoader` class, which is the classloader used by the appletviewer itself. Instances of this must be given a URL from which classes are to be loaded. This URL is supplied as the argument to the constructor. After stripping out any specific filename part so that it ends with a /, the URL is stored in the `AppletClassLoader` in a nonpublic variable called `base`. In principle, it would be possible to modify it so that the classloader could be used to load from different sources. Modification is not recommended, however, as it might compromise the security manager's integrity.

The `main()` method of the class starts by checking that exactly one argument has been given. Unlike the standard appletviewer, this version can only handle a single URL. That URL must be complete. For the sake of simplicity, this code does not attempt to take a simple filename and add the `file:` protocol part and the current directory to it. Provided this URL is valid—which means that it cannot involve any nonlocal protocols because the factory has not been installed yet—an `AppletClassLoader` is created based on it.

The reference to the new classloader is stored in the `acl` variable in the instance `that` of the `SuperApplet` class so it will be accessible to the factory method, which is invoked as an instance rather than a static method.

The method call `URL.setURLStreamHandlerFactory(that)` installs the factory so when a new protocol handler is needed, the method `createURLStreamHandler()` will be invoked. Finally, the

`AppletViewer.parse()` method is invoked using the URL provided. This launches the appletviewer with the new factory in place.

The factory method `createURLStreamHandler()` first uses the protocol name to create a fully qualified classname for the handler that is to be sought. The convention of using a class `sun.net.www` `.protocol.<protocol-name>.Handler` is reused here as there is no real benefit in changing the name. Once the name has been created, the `AppletClassLoader` is called to try to load the class. Notice that if the class exists on the local path, it will be loaded from there rather than from the remote system.

Provided the `loadClass()` method returns a `Class` object, the factory proceeds by attempting to create an instance of the newly loaded class. After that, if an `Object` is returned, the `instanceof` operator tests whether that object really is a `URLStreamHandler`. If all these conditions are met, the factory method returns this new instance.

During the loading and instantiating process, a number of exceptions can arise. Any difficulties simply result in the factory returning `null` so the `catch() {}` block does not attempt any recovery.

To provide basic tracing of the activity of this factory, three `System` `.out.println()` method calls are made. These demonstrate whether the factory has been successfully called and indicate the protocol for which it has been called.

Running the Program

The source code for this example is located on the CD-ROM in the directory `javadevhdbk\ch13\ServerSide`. The corresponding classfile is in the subdirectory `sun\applet` within that, which reflects its package. It is important that this directory not include the protocol handler material for the daytime protocol.

First you should satisfy yourself that the standard appletviewer is not able to locate the daytime protocol handler via the applet base

URL. To do so, start the `DayServer2.java` program from Chapter 10, *Networking*. The source code is located on the CD-ROM in the directory `javadevhdbk\ch10`. Select the `ch10` directory and issue the command

```
java DayServer2
```

Then, in a separate window, verify the server operation by selecting the `ch10` directory and issuing the command

```
java DayClient2 localhost
```

This should produce the date and time string. If this test shows that all is well with the server, select the `javadevhdbk\ch13\ServerSide` directory and issue this command:

```
appletviewer file:/javadevhdbk/ch13/DayApplet.html
```

This command attempts to run the `DayApplet.java` example. This attempt should fail with an error indicating that the protocol is unknown. The output you can expect is:

```
Problem creating URL: daytime://localhost:1313/
java.net.MalformedURLException: unknown protocol: daytime
```

Now run the modified version of appletviewer by issuing the following command:

```
java sun.applet.SuperApplet
file:/javadevhdbk/ch13/DayApplet.html
```

This time, the appletviewer should start up, and the date and time string should be displayed in the label. The factory method issues messages indicating the work that it does. The messages look like this:

```
Protocol factory trying to load handler from class
sun.net.www.protocol.daytime.Handler
:-) Load was successful.
```

If you have a Web server, you can use an `http:`-based URL to load the applet. This approach will require that the protocol handler also be loaded via the Web server. If you run the example, you will see that the Web server access logs indicate that the protocol handler classes were in fact loaded this way.

Summary

This chapter has discussed the nature of protocols and content types. MIME was introduced as the preferred mechanism for identifying content type. Different mechanisms for handling content and protocols were discussed in the light of the organic nature of the Internet.

The mechanisms of protocol handlers, and the ways in which they can be located by a browser or application needing them were introduced along with a basic example. A second example showed the beginnings of a Telnet handler. It also described the approach to handling protocols, which require the manipulation of stream data—as distinct from those where the protocol simply requires a preliminary configuration before producing pure data.

Content handlers have been introduced, and the mechanisms for locating the handlers were discussed. An example demonstrated a severely stripped down version of HTML being handled automatically by the appletviewer.

Finally, the promise and difficulties of server side handlers were discussed and a rudimentary server side protocol handler mechanism was implemented on top of the standard appletviewer tool.

The 1.1 AWT

- Data transfer

- Desktop colors

- Event delegation

- Mouseless operation

- Pop-up menus

- Printing

- The `ScrollPane` class

- The `Polar` component revisited

The 1.1 release of the Java Developer's Kit includes major enhancements to the AWT package. Many classes have been expanded, some classes have been changed, and a number of sub-packages have been introduced.

The enhancements fall into seven categories:

Data Transfer   These enhancements support a clipboard paradigm and provide hooks for future drag-and-drop functionality.

Desktop Colors   These enhancements enable a Java program to detect a desktop color scheme.

Event Delegation   The event-handling model has been substantially expanded to support more flexible and maintainable components.

Mouseless Operation   These enhancements support keyboard focus traversal and keyboard menu shortcuts.

Pop-up Menus   The 1.1 release supports pop-up menus for applets and applications.

Printing   These enhancements support printing of components and component hierarchies.

Scrolling Pane   The new ScrollPane class provides a scrolling window.

Each of these new features will be examined in this chapter. At the end of the chapter, one of the detailed custom-component examples from Chapter 3, *Creating Custom Components*, will be reworked to take advantage of the new event-delegation model.

Data Transfer

The two major models of data transfer are clipboard operations and drag-and-drop operations. Release 1.1 only supports clipboard data transfer; drag-and-drop will not be seen until a future release. This section discusses the current implementation of clipboard support and the planned future implementation of drag-and-drop.

The classes that support data transfer are in a new package called `java.awt.datatransfer`.

Transferable Objects

Both the current clipboard model and the future drag-and-drop model rely on the concept of a *transferable object*. This is a representation of the data that is to be cut/copied/pasted or dragged-and-dropped.

A transferable object contains not only the data to be transferred, but also information concerning the various formats in which the data can be presented. For example, when text is copied from a word processor, consumers of the text may want to access it in plain ASCII or in Rich Text Format (RTF). In the first case, font information is lost. In the second case, font information is maintained.

The data-transfer API uses the term *flavor* to indicate a possible format of transferred data. An individual flavor is represented by an instance of the `DataFlavor` class. A data flavor object may represent a MIME type or an instance of a Java class. In either case, the data type is represented internally as a MIME string; for Java classes, the MIME format is simply extended, as explained below.

For a standard MIME type, the flavor's MIME string is the standard MIME string. For example, a data flavor that represents Rich Text Format would have a MIME string of `"application/rtf."` When data is transferred using this flavor, the entity requesting the data is returned an `InputStream` from which to read and parse the data.

When a data flavor represents a Java class, the flavor's MIME string is derived from the class name. For example, a flavor representing a canvas would have a MIME string of `"application/ x-javaserializedobject; class=java.awt.Canvas."` When data is transferred using this flavor, the entity requesting the data is returned an instance of the `Canvas` class.

There are two constructors for the `DataFlavor` class, one to be used when the flavor represents a MIME type and one to be used when the flavor represents a Java class. Both versions require a *human presentable name*, which is suitable for presentation in a GUI. The constructors are:

`DataFlavor(String mimeType, String humanName)` Constructs a flavor representing data in the specified MIME type. Any requests for data of this flavor will receive an `InputStream` for reading and parsing via the `getTransferData()` method described below.

`DataFlavor(Class class, String humanName)` Constructs a flavor representing data of a specified class. Any requests for data of this flavor will receive an instance of the class via the `getTransferData()` method described below.

The API indicates that two commonly used flavors will be plain text and Java strings. Two corresponding instances of `DataFlavor` are available as static instance variables of the `DataFlavor` class. They are `DataFlavor.plainTextFlavor` and `DataFlavor.stringFlavor`.

Any class of object that wishes to be transferred must maintain an internal list of data flavors that it supports. The API provides the `java.awt.datatransfer.Transferable` interface, which classes must implement in order to be transferred. The interface has the following three methods:

`Object getTransferData(DataFlavor flavor) throws UnsupportedFlavorException, IOException` Returns the data in the format described by `flavor`. If the requested flavor is not supported, an exception is thrown. If the flavor is a regular MIME type, the returned object is an instance of `InputStream`; otherwise, the flavor is a Java class, and the returned object is an instance of that class. This method call must be made in a try/catch block because the exception types are not runtime exceptions.

`DataFlavor[] getTransferDataFlavors()` Returns an array of supported flavors. The array should be sorted in descending order of flavor richness.

`boolean isDataFlavorSupported(DataFlavor flavor)` Returns a boolean indicating whether or not the specified flavor is supported.

Any instance of a class that implements this interface may be cut, copied, and pasted with the 1.1 clipboard API. In the future, it may be dragged and dropped.

It is reasonable to anticipate that a great proportion of data transfers within Java programs will simply involve Java bytecode strings. The API provides a transferable class called `java.awt.datatransfer.StringSelection`. This class implements the `Transferable` interface and only supports the Java string flavor (as represented by `DataFlavor.stringFlavor`). Its constructor takes a Java string as an argument.

Clipboard Data Transfer

The clipboard is represented by the `java.awt.datatransfer.Clipboard` class. The toolkit has an instance of a clipboard that interacts with the local desktop. This instance can be retrieved by calling the `getSystemClipboard()` method on the toolkit.

Any class that will be writing to the clipboard must implement the `java.awt.datatransfer.ClipboardOwner` interface. This interface has a single method:

```
void lostOwnership(Clipboard clipboard, Transferable contents)
```

The clipboard makes this call back to the owner to inform it that new data has been copied to the clipboard.

The Clipboard class supports writing of data with the following method:

```
void setContents(Transferable data, ClipboardOwner owner)
```

The data must implement the Transferable interface as described in the previous section.

The StringSelection class described in the previous section implements the ClipboardOwner interface (in addition to the Transferable interface), so it is especially convenient as the first (data) argument of the Clipboard.setContents() method. The following code fragment writes the string "abcde" to the clipboard, using the StringSelection class:

```
StringSelection data = new StringSelection("abcde");
Clipboard clipboard =
    Toolkit.getDefaultToolkit().getSystemClipboard();
clipboard.setContents(data, data);
```

Data can be retrieved from the clipboard by calling its getContents() method. This method takes as an argument an instance of Object; this should always be the object requesting the data. The following code fragment retrieves clipboard data into the variable stringData.

```
Clipboard clipboard =
Toolkit.getDefaultToolkit().getSystemClipboard();
Transferable clipboardData = clipboard.getContents(this);
try
{
    String stringData =
        (String)
        (clipboardData.getTransferData(DataFlavor
        .stringFlavor));
}
catch (IOException e) { }
catch (UnsupportedFlavorException e) { }
```

Drag-and-Drop Data Transfer

All information in this section is preliminary and subject to change, and, as such, is only an attempt to provide an overview. The functionality described here is not part of the 1.1 release.

Drag-and-drop functionality will be supported by the `java.awt.dnd` package. Components that wish to be capable of being dragged must implement the `java.awt.dnd.DragSource` interface. Components that wish to be capable of being dropped on must implement the `java.awt.dnd.DropTarget` interface.

The `DragSource` interface contains the following three methods:

`DragContext dragBegin(int x, int y)` This method is called when a drag might be beginning. The method should determine whether it is permissible for a drag to begin. If so, it should return an instance of the `DragContext` class; this is a convenience class that describes allowable drop targets and their corresponding actions. The actions are represented by integer class constants.

`boolean dragOver(DragContext context, int suggestedAction)` This method is called when the drag source is being dragged over a valid drop target. The `suggestedAction` parameter is one of the ints from the drag context. If the default drag cursor appearance is desired, this method should simply return `false`; otherwise the method should enforce its desired custom drag cursor and return `true`.

`void dragEnd(DragContext context, int actionTaken)` This method is called when a drag operation is complete.

The `DropTarget` interface contains the following six methods:

`int dropEnter(DropContext context)` This method is called when a drag enters a drop target region. The `context` parameter is an instance of the `java.awt.dnd.DropContext` class; this class contains information about actions supported by the drag source. The return value is an int representing the action to be taken should the drop occur.

int dropOver(DropContext context)   This method is called whenever a drag is over the drop target. The return value is an int representing the action to be taken should the drop occur.

int drop(DropContext context)   This method is called whenever a drag is actually dropped over the drop target. The return value is an int representing the action to be taken.

Insets getScrollInsets()   For targets that support drop scrolling, this method returns the insets from the target's edges of the scrolling region.

void dropScroll(DropContext context, int hIncr, int vIncr)   For targets that support drop scrolling, this method suggests scrolling directions. The hIncr and vIncr parameters control horizontal and vertical scrolling respectively and should be set to either -1 (scroll left or up), 0 (do not scroll), or 1 (scroll right or down).

int drop(DropContext context)   This method is called whenever a drag leaves the drop target or when a drop has occurred on the target.

Desktop Colors

Many modern windows systems support desktop color schemes. The new desktop colors features allow Java programs to detect the various colors of the current color scheme. These features include, for example, highlight and shadow colors, the window border color, and the color of the desktop itself. In 1.1, the standard component classes are modified to present themselves in the desktop colors.

Programmers may determine the settings of the colors by reading new final static instance variables in the `java.awt.SystemColor` class. These are all of subclasses of class `Color`. The variable names are:

`activeCaption`   Caption background color (The *caption* is the window's title bar area.)

`activeCaptionBorder`   Caption border color

`activeCaptionText`   Caption text color

`control`   Control (noncontainer component) background color

`controlDkShadow`   Control dark shadow color

`desktop`   Desktop's background color

`controlHighlight`   Control regular highlighting color

`controlLtHighlight`   Control light highlighting color

`controlShadow`   Control shadow color

`controlText`   Control text color

`inactiveCaption`   Inactive caption background color

`inactiveCaptionBorder`   Inactive caption border color

`inactiveCaptionText`   Inactive caption text color

`info`   Spot-help background color

`infoText`   Spot-help text color

`menu`   Menu background color

`menuText`   Menu text color

`scrollbar`   Scrollbar background color

`textHighlight`   Background text highlighting color

`textHighlightText`   Foreground text highlight color

`textInactiveText`   Text color for disabled controls

`textText`   Text color in text components

`window`   Window background color

`windowBorder`   Window border color

`windowText`   Text color inside windows

Not every color scheme model supports all these symbolic colors. Unsupported symbolic colors will be set to reasonable values.

The values of these colors are set when the `java.awt.Toolkit` class is loaded. There is no guarantee that they will be revised if the user selects a new color scheme in mid-execution of a Java program.

Consider a custom component that subclasses `Canvas` and that incorporates a text label. Before 1.1, the `paint()` method of such a component might have looked like this:

```
public void paint(Graphics g)
{
    g.setColor(Color.black);
    g.drawString(labelstring, x, y);
    // Other rendering code …
}
```

With desktop colors, this code might be rewritten as follows:

```
public void paint(Graphics g)
{
    g.setColor(SystemColor.controlText);
    g.drawString(labelstring, x, y);
    // Other rendering code …
}
```

> **WARNING**
>
> The `equals()` method does not work with system colors. To compare two system colors `sc1` and `sc2`, do *not* use `if (sc1.equals(sc2))`. Instead, convert the colors to RGB values: `if (sc1.getRGB() == sc2.getRGB())`.

Event Delegation

Release 1.1 makes substantial changes to the way events are handled. Under the new model there are many classes of event, and events may be sent to a wide variety of recipients. This model removes some of the limitations of the previous model and provides a robust base of support for Java Beans (see Chapter 15, *Java Beans API*). The new classes are to be found in the `java.awt.event` package.

Backward compatibility is a major goal of the new model. The old model, in which events propagate outward through a component's containment hierarchy, will still be supported. Thus existing code need not be modified. Developers of new code may choose between the old and the new models (though the new model is preferable, being more robust and current). The only restriction is that the two models may not be combined within a single program.

The paradigm of the new model is that an *event source* fires off events to one or more *event listeners*. An event source is most often a component. A listener is an object that implements an `EventListener` interface. (This interface is defined in the `java.util` package and has a number of sub-interfaces in the `java.awt.event` package.)

Under the old model, a single event class (`java.awt.Event`) encapsulates all information about an event. The new model introduces many new event classes, and many corresponding event listener interfaces. These will be examined in detail in the sections that follow.

The New Event Classes

The new model introduces 10 event classes, all in the `java.awt` `.event` package. Each class represents a small set of related events. The classes are:

`ComponentEvent`   Indicates that a component has been moved, resized, shown, or hidden.

`FocusEvent`   Indicates that a component has received or lost focus.

`KeyEvent`   Indicates that a component has received keyboard input.

`MouseEvent`   Indicates that a component has received mouse input.

`ActionEvent`   Indicates that a component has been activated (e.g., a button has been clicked; this activity would post an action event under the 1.0 model).

`AdjustmentEvent`   Indicates that a scrollbar or similar nonstandard component has been moved.

`ItemEvent`   Indicates that a new item has been selected in a list, checkbox group, choice, or similar nonstandard component.

`WindowEvent`   Indicates that a window has received a window level event.

`ContainerEvent`   Indicates that a component has been added to or removed from a container.

`TextEvent`   Indicates that a change has happened to a text field or text area. The change could be initiated by the user (typing, cutting, or pasting) or by the program.

The first four classes (component, focus, key, and mouse events) are called *low-level events*; they represent fairly raw user input. The last four classes (action, adjustment, item, and window events) are called *semantic events*; they represent higher-level GUI semantics. A semantic event is composed of a series of low-level events (for example, a button action happens because the mouse clicked down and then up inside the button), but this is all taken care of by the peer system. As far as Java is concerned, low-level and semantic events are treated equally.

Each of these classes encapsulates information that describes the event. A common superclass (`java.awt.event.AwtEvent`) provides a `getId()` method that returns an int; this int provides event-specific identity. Each class also has class-specific methods that give further information.

For example, the `MouseEvent` class defines seven static final ints to be returned by `getId()`. These are:

- `MouseEvent.MOUSE_CLICKED`
- `MouseEvent.MOUSE_PRESSED`
- `MouseEvent.MOUSE_RELEASED`
- `MouseEvent.MOUSE_MOVED`
- `MouseEvent.MOUSE_ENTERED`
- `MouseEvent.MOUSE_EXITED`
- `MouseEvent.MOUSE_DRAGGED`

The `MouseEvent` class also has methods for retrieving further information:

`int getX()` Returns the x coordinate of the event.

`int getY()` Returns the y coordinate of the event.

`Point getPoint()` Returns the x and y coordinates of the event.

`void translatePoint(int x, int y)` Translates the event's position (as accessed by the three methods above) by `(x,y)`.

`int getClickCount()` Returns the number of mouse clicks associated with the event.

`boolean isPopupTrigger()` Returns whether or not the event is the pop-up menu trigger for the current platform.

The other event classes are structured similarly. Constants describe specifically what kind of event took place; these are to be returned by `getId()`. Additional getter methods return additional type-specific information.

Event Listeners

There are 11 event-listener interfaces. They all are in the `java.awt` `.event` package, and they extend `java.util.EventListener`. The interfaces are:

- `ComponentListener`
- `FocusListener`
- `KeyListener`
- `MouseListener`
- `MouseMotionListener`
- `WindowListener`
- `ActionListener`
- `AdjustmentListener`
- `ItemListener`
- `ContanerListener`
- `TextListener`

Each interface lists a number of methods that can be called when an event takes place of the corresponding type. For example, the

`MouseMotionListener` interface has the following two methods:

- `void mouseMoved(MouseEvent)`
- `void mouseDragged(MouseEvent)`

An object that implements this interface (event listener) can register itself with a component (event source). Subsequently, whenever the event source experiences mouse motion, it will call the listener's `mouseMoved()` or `mouseDragged()` method. The `MouseEvent` parameter can be queried for additional information by calling its `getId()` method or any of the various type-specific getter methods described in the previous section.

Event Sources

An event source maintains a list of interested event listeners. When mouse or keyboard activity occurs within the event source, the source invokes a method on every registered event listener, passing as a parameter an instance of the appropriate event class.

For example, a canvas might have two registered mouse motion event listeners. When the mouse moves within the canvas, each listener receives a `mouseMoved()` call; the parameter of the call is an instance of the `mouseEvent` class. Each listener can now determine the mouse position by calling `getX()` and `getY()` on the mouse event object.

Some of the event classes have methods that could enable the listener to modify the event's values. If one of these events is to be passed, the event source passes a copy of the event, so that no listener can spoil the data for any other listener.

A listener registers with an event source via one of nine methods. Each method name has the format `addXXXListener()`, where `XXXListener` is the name of one of the event listener interfaces. The parameter of each of these methods is a listener of the appropriate interface type.

A component type only supports those `addXXXListener()` calls that are relevant to the event types it can fire. The listener-registering methods supported by the various standard component types are listed below.

Component

- `void addComponentListener(ComponentListener listener)`

- `void addFocusListener(FocusListener listener)`

- `void addKeyListener(KeyListener listener)`

- `void addMouseListener(MouseListener listener)`

- `void addMouseMotionListener(MouseMotion-Listener)`

Dialog

- `void addWindowListener(WindowListener listener)`

Frame

- `void addWindowListener(WindowListener listener)`

Button

- `void addActionListener(ActionListener listener)`

Choice

- `void addItemListener(ItemListener listener)`

Checkbox

- `void addItemListener(ItemListener listener)`

CheckboxMenuItem

- `void addItemListener(ItemListener listener)`

List

- `void addActionListener(ActionListener listener)`
- `void addItemListener(ItemListener listener)`

MenuItem

- `void addActionListener(ActionListener listener)`

Scrollbar

- `void addAdjustmentListener(AdjustmentListener listener)`

TextArea

- `void addTextListener(TextListener listener)`

TextField

- `void addActionListener(ActionListener listener)`
- `void addTextListener(TextListener listener)`

There is no guarantee about the order in which an event source will make event calls to its listeners.

The above list does not reflect inheritance.

Adapters

Any event listener is required by the compiler to implement every method of its interface. The `java.awt.event` package provides six abstract convenience *adapter* classes that make it easier to write event listener code.

Each adapter class provides every method specified by the corresponding listener interface. None of these methods does anything. Thus each class implements its interface without providing any functionality. The adapter classes are:

- `ComponentAdapter`

- `ContainerAdapter`

- `FocusAdapter`

- `KeyAdapter`

- `MouseAdapter`

- `MouseMotionAdapter`

- `WindowAdapter`

Thanks to adapters, an easy way to create an event listener is to subclass the appropriate adapter class, overriding the appropriate methods. For example, the following code implements a mouse motion adapter that reacts to mouse-drag events and ignores mouse-moved events.

```
class ExampleAdapter extends MouseMotionAdapter
{
    public void mouseDragged(MouseEvent e)
    {
        int x = e.getX();
        int y = e.getY();
        // Do something here with x and y.
    }
}
```

The following code fragment constructs a canvas and uses the class listed above to catch mouse drag events:

```
Canvas theCanvas = new Canvas();
ExampleAdapter theAdapter = new ExampleAdapter();
theCanvas.addMouseMotionListener(theAdapter);
```

Subclassing Components without Listeners

It is possible to create component subclasses that handle their own events while bypassing the event delegation model. Such subclasses do not need to implement any listener interfaces and are therefore spared the necessity of implementing do-nothing stubs for irrelevant interface methods.

A listener-free subclass must execute the `enableEvent()` method, passing as a parameter a mask from the `AWTEvent` class. For example, to enable self-handling of item events, a component needs to execute the following call:

```
enableEvent(AWTEvent.ITEM_EVENT_MASK);
```

Subsequently, any item events generated by the component will be initially delivered to the component's `processItemEvent()` method. Ordinarily it is the job of this method to notify item listeners of the event by calling their `itemStateChanged()` methods, but the subclass can provide its own event processing by overriding `processItemEvent()`. It is good practice to call `super.process-ItemEvent()` at the end of the subclass' version, in case any objects other than the component itself are registered listeners.

A listener-free subclass of `Checkbox`, `CheckboxMenuItem`, or `Choice` should pass `AWTEvent.ITEM_EVENT_MASK` into `enable-Event()` and catch events by overriding `processItemEvent()`. A listener-free subclass of `Button`, `List`, `MenuItem`, or `TextField` should pass `AWTEvent.ACTION_EVENT_MASK` into `enableEvent()` and catch events by overriding `processActionEvent()`. A listener-free subclass of `Frame` should pass `AWTEvent.WINDOW_EVENT_MASK` into `enableEvent()` and catch events by overriding `processWindowEvent()`. A listener-free subclass of `Scrollbar` should pass `AWTEvent.ADJUSTMENT_EVENT_MASK` into `enable-Event()` and catch events by overriding `processAdjustmentEvent()`.

The code listed below shows how to subclass `Choice` so it handles its own item events. The choice contains the names of the nine planets. The `processItemEvent()` method prints out the current selection. The source code appears on the CD-ROM in `javadevhdbk\ch12\NoListenerChoice.java`.

NoListenerChoice.java

```java
import java.awt.*;
import java.awt.event.*;

public class NoListenerChoice extends Choice
{
    public static void main(String args[])
    {
        Frame frame = new Frame("No-Listener Example");
        frame.resize(200, 60);
        frame.setLayout(new FlowLayout());
        frame.add(new NoListenerChoice());
        frame.show();
    }

    public NoListenerChoice()
    {
        addItem("Mercury");
        addItem("Venus");
        addItem("Earth");
        addItem("Mars");
        addItem("Jupiter");
        addItem("Saturn");
        addItem("Uranus");
        addItem("Neptune");
        addItem("Pluto");

        enableEvents(AWTEvent.ITEM_EVENT_MASK);
    }


    public void processItemEvent(ItemEvent e)
    {
```

```
        System.out.println(getSelectedItem());
        super.processItemEvent(e);      // Notify any listeners
    }
}
```

Advantages of the Event Delegation Model

A major benefit of the new model is that it supports Java Beans. For programmers this is not a direct benefit, though the advantages will make themselves known over time as Beans-based GUI builders come onto the market. (See Chapter 15, *Java Beans API*, for an explanation of this API.)

The new model also offers programmers some immediate benefits. There are two reasons why event delegation makes it easier to write large robust Java programs.

First, the 1.0 containment ripple model offers many opportunities for erroneous event handling. Even moderately simple programs, such as the ThreeWay aggregate component presented in Chapter 3, *Creating Custom Components*, must handle events very carefully. Overriding the handleEvent() method is especially risky because every event is exposed to the overriding code. The new model is more intricate and requires more knowledge and planning, but there is very little risk of mishandling events.

Second, the new model permits better partitioning of work among classes. Under the old model, a program with many components must either create many component subclasses or catch all events at the frame or applet level. Neither option is ideal from the point of view of object-oriented design. The object-oriented approach dictates that all processing of information, including event handling, ought to be handled by the most appropriate class. A side effect of this approach is that in well-designed systems, classes tend to specialize in a single portion of the task at hand. The old model forces component classes, which should specialize in being components, to moonlight as competent event handlers as well.

These benefits may seem theoretical, as they are most evident in large programs. Not very many large applets or applications have been created in Java yet. But as Java evolves, and large programming teams spend greater amounts of time in development, the new event model will prove increasingly worthwhile.

Mouseless Operation

Mouseless operation allows users to type instead of using the mouse. This reduces hand movement for expert users. The two main categories of mouse action that are emulated on the keyboard are *focus traversal* and *menu input shortcuts*.

Focus Traversal

Typical GUIs might have several components (textfields and textareas, for example) that can accept text input. At any moment, there is one component to which all keyboard events are delivered; this component is said to have *keyboard focus*. On some systems, the user selects a new component to receive keyboard focus by moving the mouse pointer into the component. On other systems, the mouse must be clicked inside the new component. This is a nuisance in a GUI with many text components, such as a form with many input fields.

Modern systems support the concept of a traversal order among components that can accept focus. To relieve the user of the burden of reaching for the mouse in order to move focus, typing the Tab key moves focus to the next component in the traversal order. Typing Shift+Tab moves focus to the previous component.

Java's focus-traversal model leverages the traversal support of the underlying window system so applets and applications will have a familiar look and feel for traversal on any platform. The result is a certain amount of behavior variation from platform to platform. For example, different systems have different algorithms for determining traversal order. Also, certain component types (buttons, for example) may receive focus on certain platforms and not on others.

Focus traversal is supported by the addition of a new method in the Component class. This method is:

```
public boolean isFocusTraversable()
```

A component should return true from this method if the component can accept focus. In 1.1, the standard AWT components have been modified to return appropriate values, so a GUI composed of just these standard components will automatically support focus traversal. The only issue for developers is how to create custom components that behave appropriately.

A custom component that does not support keyboard input should simply override isFocusTraversable() so that it returns false. A custom component that is capable of receiving focus must do three things:

- First, the component should override isFocusTraversable() so that it returns true. This ensures that the component will accept focus when the underlying windows system offers it.

- Second, the component should make sure that it takes input focus when the user clicks in it. (This is the case where focus is transferred via mouse activity, rather than via the traversal mechanism.) A component grabs focus by calling the request-Focus() method.

- Third, when the component receives input focus via either mechanism, it should change its appearance to provide a visual cue that it has focus. When a component receives focus, it receives a GOT_FOCUS event. The way to detect focus receipt depends on the program's event model. With the 1.0 model (which many 1.1 programs will retain), the component's handleEvent() method should be overridden to detect an event whose ID is `Event.GOT_FOCUS`. With the new 1.1 event delegation model, a focus event is fired. The *Event Delegation* section earlier in this chapter discusses the new event-delegation model.

Menu Shortcuts

Menu shortcuts are conspicuous by their absence from the pre-1.1 JDK. Under 1.1 a menu item is given a shortcut character via a new version of the constructor:

`MenuItem(String label, MenuShortcut shortcut)`

The shortcut argument is an instance of the new `Shortcut` class, which encapsulates the accelerator character. This class has two constructors:

`MenuShortcut(char accelerator)`   Constructs a shortcut based on the specified accelerator `char`.

`MenuShortcut(char accelerator, boolean shift)` Same as above, but the accelerator key must be shifted or unshifted according to the value of `shift`.

Any menu item that has a shortcut will automatically be triggered when the user types the shortcut character while holding down the menu-shortcut-modifier key. The menu-shortcut-modifier key varies from platform to platform. On Windows and Motif machines, it is the Ctrl key. On Macintoshes, it is the Command key.

Pop-Up Menus

The 1.1 release supports pop-up menus. The new class `java.awt.PopupMenu` extends the familiar `java.awt.Menu` class. A pop-up menu is constructed in exactly the same manner as an ordinary menu;

one simply omits the final step of adding the menu into a menu bar.
For example:

```
PopupMenu popmen = new PopupMenu("File");
popmen.add(new MenuItem("New..."));
popmen.add(new MenuItem("Open..."));
popmen.addSeparator();
popmen.add(new CheckboxMenuItem("Print Preview Mode"));
popmen.add(new MenuItem("Exit"));
```

The paradigm for popping up a menu varies from system to system.
On Windows platforms, a menu is popped up when mouse button #2
goes up. In Motif, a menu is popped up when mouse button #3 goes
down, and remains on-screen if mouse button #3 goes up again within
a brief interval.

After a pop-up menu is built, it must be associated with a *parent*
component via a new version of the add() method of the Component
class:

```
add(PopupMenu popup);
```

The association may be terminated by calling

```
remove(PopupMenu popup);
```

NOTE This version of the add() method is implemented in the Component
class, *not* in Container. The component to which the pop-up gets
added does not have to be some kind of container; it could, for
example, be a button or a canvas. If the component is indeed a
container (a panel, for example), the pop-up menu is *not* added to
the container's containment hierarchy or positioned by the container's layout manager.

A pop-up menu may be popped up over its parent component or
over any component within the parent's containment hierarchy. The
method that displays the menu is

```
show(Component origin, int x, int y);
```

The `origin` parameter is the component above which the menu will be displayed. The `x` and `y` parameters are with respect to the origin component; this component must be either the menu's parent or a child within the parent's containment hierarchy.

The 1.1 `Event` and `MouseEvent` classes (which support, respectively, the old and new event propagation models) have flags to indicate that the local platform-specific menu pop-up trigger has occurred. This flag is defined as `Event.POPUP_TRIGGER`. The following code fragment shows how an applet would catch a pop-up trigger event in order to display a pop-up called `myPopup`.

```
public boolean handleEvent(Event e)
{
    if (e.flags & Event.POPUP_TRIGGER)
    {
        myPopup.show(this, e.x, e.y);
        return true;
    }
    return super.handleEvent(e);
}
```

Note that this code works correctly even if the trigger event happened in a subcomponent of the applet (for example, in a canvas within a panel within a panel) because the `x` and `y` fields of the `Event` object are translated to the coordinate system of the component that receives the `handleEvent()` call. This code always pops up the menu at the mouse position.

WARNING The `POPUP_TRIGGER` constant does not appear in beta 1 or 2 of 1.1; however, it is described in the AWT Enhancements Design Specification. It is hoped that a future release will provide this capability, or a reasonable alternative.

Printing

In the 1.1 model, a Java program prints by using an instance of the new java.awt.PrintGraphics interface, which is a subclass of java.awt.Graphics. The intention of this model is that an applet or application will detect a print request from the user, obtain a print graphics instance, and call its paint() method, passing in the print graphics instance. Thus existing programs can be upgraded to support printing without any modification to the existing paint() method. Permission to print is granted or denied by the security manager, if one is present.

The first step of the printing cycle is to obtain an instance of the new PrintJob class from the toolkit. The Toolkit class has a method called getPrintJob():

```
PrintJob getPrintJob(Frame frame, String jobname, Properties
props);
```

The frame parameter is a print dialog. The jobname parameter is an arbitrary string that can be useful for printer administration. The props parameter permits programmatic specification of printer-configuration parameters such as the printer name or the page order.

The next step of the printing cycle is to obtain a print graphics object from the print job via the following call:

```
PrintGraphics getGraphics();
```

The third step is to make drawing calls on the print graphics object. The most straightforward way to do this is to call the print() method of the component to be printed, passing in the print graphics object; this method simply calls paint(). If the component to be printed is a container, the entire containment hierarchy can be printed by calling printAll() instead of print().

Finally, the program should flush the page through the printer by calling `dispose()` on the print graphics object and then submit the print job by calling `end()` on the print job object.

Some print operations will generate more than a single page. It is the program's responsibility to manage pagination. The `PrintJob` class has two methods that provide the necessary information:

- `Dimension getPageDimension()`
- `int getPageResolution()`

For each page, the program should call `getGraphics()`, render the component's appearance onto the page, and then call `dispose()` on the print graphics object. When all pages have been printed, the program should submit the print job by calling `end()` on the print job object.

The *ScrollPane* Class

The `ScrollPane` class is a new component type that provides a scrolling view of a single child component. The scrollbars and all scrolling operations are taken care of by the class. Most importantly, programmers do not need to catch `handleEvent()` calls from scrollbars.

The `ScrollPane` constructor takes a single int argument that describes the desired style of scrollbar support. The possible values for this int are:

`ScrollPane.SCROLLBARS_AS_NEEDED`   The component displays horizontal/vertical scrollbars only when they are needed (when the size of the child exceeds the horizontal/vertical size of the scrollpane).

`ScrollPane.SCROLLBARS_ALWAYS`   The component always displays horizontal/vertical scrollbars, even when the component completely fits horizontally/vertically within the scrollpane's display region.

`ScrollPane.SCROLLBARS_NEVER`   The component never displays scrollbars. Positioning of the child within the scrollpane's display region is entirely the program's responsibility.

The scrollpane is given its child via the `add()` method. The code fragment below illustrates how an applet would create a small scrollpane to display a large instance of a canvas subclass called `GameBoard`.

```
public class ScrollPaneDemo extends Applet
{
    ScrollPane      spane;
    GameBoard       board;

    public void init()
    {
        board = new GameBoard();
        board.resize(600, 600);
        spane = new ScrollPane(ScrollPane.SCROLLBARS_AS_NEEDED);
        spane.add(board);
        spane.resize(75, 75);
        add(spane);
    }
}
```

The Polar Component Revisited

Chapter 3, *Creating Custom Components*, presented three models for designing custom components. One of these models involved subclassing the `Canvas` class. The job of the subclass was to keep the appearance of the canvas up to date, to handle all mouse input, and to post events when appropriate.

The chapter developed an example called the Polar class, which enabled a user to input a two-dimension point in polar coordinates. In this section, the Polar class is modified to take advantage of the 1.1 event-propagation model. The new version of the class will be called NewPolar. Readers are encouraged to review the original example from Chapter 3 before continuing.

Chapter 3 presents a long list of design issues for custom components. These relate to look, feel, event handling, event passing, and subclassing. Look-and-feel issues are not affected by the choice of event model, although they could take advantage of the new System-Color class for improved appearance. The next section restates the event and subclassing issues in the context of the 1.1 event model.

Design Issues

When designing a custom component under the 1.1 event model, it is useful to consider the following issues:

- Which events do the custom component class need to catch?

- Should the events be caught by the component class or by a separate class?

- If the component class will be catching events (that is, if an adapter class will not be used), what listener interfaces will the component class need to implement?

- What events should the component class send to its clients?

The sections that follow investigate these issues as they apply to the NewPolar component.

Design Decisions: Catching Events

The use model for the NewPolar component has not changed from 1.0 to 1.1: users input new values by pressing, dragging, and releasing the mouse.

Pressing the mouse button causes the canvas to send `mouse-Pressed()` to its mouse listener. Dragging causes the canvas to send `mouseDragged()` to its mouse *motion* listener. Releasing causes the canvas to send `mouseReleased()` to its mouse listener. These are the events that the `NewPolar` class will have to deal with.

Under the 1.1 model, the `NewPolar` class can delegate these events to any object at all, provided that object implements the methods `mousePressed()`, `mouseDragged()`, and `mouseReleased()`. Alternatively, `NewPolar` can delegate the events to itself. With 1.1, the design of any event-generating Java program requires deciding which object or objects will receive event notification.

Two considerations should inform this decision. If handling events involves a significant amount of code, it may well be appropriate to factor out the event-processing task into a separate class; this is simply good object-oriented design. On the other hand, if handling events requires a significant amount of access to the component's data and methods, it is probably appropriate not to create a separate class because that class would be too tightly coupled to the `NewPolar` class.

In practice, very little processing is required for handling mouse events. However, this processing is tightly coupled to the the `New-Polar` class' data and methods, particularly the `value` instance variable and the `repaint()` method. It is therefore doubly appropriate for the class itself to handle mouse input, rather than delegate to a separate object.

Because the `NewPolar` class will do its own event processing, it will register itself as its own mouse listener (for mouse pressed and released events) and its own mouse motion listener (for mouse dragged events). (Alternatively, the class could enable mouse events and override `processMouseEvent()`, as illustrated in the section *Subclassing Components without Listeners*, earlier in this chapter.) Listener registration is set up with the following calls:

```
addMouseListener(this);
addMouseMotionListener(this);
```

`Panel` inherits these two methods from its `Component` superclass. The definitions of these methods are:

- `public void addMouseListener(MouseListener listener)`

- `public void addMouseMotionListener(MouseMotion-Listener listener)`

The `NewPolar` class will pass a reference to itself as the argument to both these calls:

```
addMouseListener(this);
addMouseMotionListener(this);
```

The `NewPolar` class has to implement the `MouseListener` interface so it can pass itself into `addMouseListener()`. It also has to implement the `MouseMotionListener` interface so it can pass itself into `addMouseMotionListener()`. Thus, the signature for the `NewPolar` class is:

```
public class NewPolar extends Canvas
        implements MouseListener, MouseMotionListener
```

Implementing these interfaces obligates the `NewPolar` class to provide all the methods of both interfaces. In addition to the three desired methods (`mousePressed()`, `mouseDragged()`, and `mouseReleased()`), the class has to provide the remaining mouse listener method (`mouseClicked()`) and the remaining mouse motion listener methods (`mouseEntered()`, `mouseExited()`, and `mouseMoved()`). The component is not affected by these events, so the methods should not do anything:

```
public void mouseClicked(MouseEvent e)     { }
public void mouseEntered(MouseEvent e)     { }
public void mouseExited(MouseEvent e)      { }
public void mouseMoved(MouseEvent e)       { }
```

The handlers for the three event types that `NewPolar` actually cares about all have similar tasks: they should update the component's value, update its appearance, and send some kind notification to the component's client. This list of tasks brings up the topic of which events the component should send, which is the topic of the next section.

Design Decisions: Posting Events

The 1.0 implementation that was developed in Chapter 3 posts a scroll absolute event in response to mouse drag input, and an action event in response to mouse up input. In 1.1, posting action events is simple; however, posting scroll events is surprisingly complicated.

In 1.1, action events are posted to action listeners. As with all listener types, a component may have any number of action listener types. A client registers a listener with a client by calling `addAction-Listener(ActionListener)`; the component maintains an internal list of its action listeners. In the present example, the `NewPolar` class implements its internal list as a vector, called `actionListeners`. The `addActionListener()` method is as follows:

```
public void addActionListener(ActionListener al)
{
    actionListeners.addElement(al);
}
```

When circumstances call for sending action events, the code should traverse the vector of action listeners. For each listener, an instance of `ActionEvent` should be constructed and passed to the listener via the `actionPerformed(ActionEvent)` method. (Each listener should have its own copy of the event object so that each listener can modify its event without interfering with the other listeners.) The code that sends an action event to each action listener is as follows:

```
/*
 *  Post an action event to each registered action listener.
 */
private void postAction()
{
```

```
ActionListener        listener;
ActionEvent           event;

int size = actionListeners.size();
if (size == 0)
    return;            // No listeners

for (int i=0; i< size; i++)
{
    listener = (ActionListener)(actionListeners.elementAt(i));
    // Each listener gets its own event.
    event = new ActionEvent(this,
                            ActionEvent.ACTION_PERFORMED,
                            null);
    listener.actionPerformed(event);
}
}
```

Just as action events are sent to action listeners, scroll events are sent to adjustment listeners. The `AdjustmentListener` interface only defines one method:

- `public void adjustmentValueChanged (AdjustmentEvent event)`

Thus, if `NewPolar` is to post adjustment events to adjustment listeners, there will have to be code, similar to `postAction()` above, to construct and dispatch the events. This is where the difficulty arises. The only appropriate constructor for `AdjustmentEvent` is:

- `public AdjustmentEvent(Adjustable source, id, type, int value)`

The source should be the object sending the event—that is, the New-Polar component itself. Unfortunately, the constructor requires that the source implement the `Adjustable` interface, which has 14 methods, other than `addAdjustmentListener()`. So if the `NewPolar` class is to post adjustment events, it will have to implement stubs for all these methods, none of which contributes anything to the class.

The logical conclusion is that it is not appropriate for the NewPolar class to send adjustment events. Still, it would be convenient if New-Polar components could send some kind of continuous notification to listeners. The solution is for NewPolar to provide an optional continuous-update mode. When the component is in this mode, an action event is sent when the mouse is dragged or released; otherwise, action is only sent when the mouse is released. The mode is controlled by the boolean instance variable continuousUpdate; clients turn the mode on or off via the following method:

```
public void setContinuousUpdate(boolean b)
{
    continuousUpdate = b;
}
```

The handler for mouse pressed events does not send any events of its own; it just updates the component's value and refreshes the screen to reflect the value:

```
/*
 * Update current value and repaint, but do not send any events.
 */
public void mousePressed(MouseEvent e)
{
    xyToPolarPoint(e.getX(), e.getY(), value);
    repaint();
}
```

The handler for mouse dragged events also updates the component's value and appearance; it also sends an action event to each action listener, provided the component is in continuous-update mode:

```
/*
 * Refresh the screen.  Post an ActionEvent if continuous
 * updates have been requested.
 */
public void mouseDragged(MouseEvent e)
{
    dragging = true;
    xyToPolarPoint(e.getX(), e.getY(), value);
```

```
        repaint();
        if (continuousUpdate)
            postAction();
    }
```

The handler for mouse released events also updates the component's value and appearance. It unconditionally sends action events to all action listeners.

```
/*
 *  Refresh the screen and post an ActionEvent.
 */
public void mouseReleased(MouseEvent e)
{
    dragging = false;
    xyToPolarPoint(e.getX(), e.getY(), value);
    repaint();
    postAction();
}
```

Source Code for *NewPolar*

The complete listing for the new version of the polar component appears below. It can also be found on the CD-ROM in javadevhdbk\ch14\NewPolar.java. Just like the 1.0 version, the class uses class PolarPoint to represent its value. PolarPoint does not require modification, but it is reproduced and is on the CD-ROM in javadevhdbk\ch14\PolarPoint.java.

NewPolar.java

```
import   java.awt.*;
import   java.awt.event.*;
import   java.util.Vector;


/*
 *  1.1 version of our home-made component for specifying a point
 *  in polar coordinates.  Gives constant graphical and textual
```

```
 *    feedback of its current value.  Sends an ActionEvent on mouse up.
 *    Optionally sends continuous ActionEvents on mouse drag.
 */

public class NewPolar extends Canvas
implements MouseListener, MouseMotionListener
{
    private PolarPoint          value;
    private double              maxRho;
    private double              unitsPerPixel;
    private boolean             dragging = false;
    private Color               dragColor = Color.blue;
    private boolean             showTextValue = true;
    private boolean             continuousUpdate = false;
    private Vector              actionListeners;


    public NewPolar()
    {
        this(100.0, 0.0, 100.0);
    }


    public NewPolar(double initRho, double initTheta, double maxRho)
    {
        value = new PolarPoint(initRho, initTheta);
        this.maxRho = maxRho;
        setBackground(Color.white);
        actionListeners = new Vector();
        addMouseListener(this);
        addMouseMotionListener(this);
    }


    public void setDragColor(Color c)
    {
        dragColor = c;
    }


    public void enableText(boolean b)
    {
```

```
        showTextValue = b;
    }


    public void setValue(PolarPoint newValue)
    {
        value = newValue;
        repaint();
    }


    public void setContinuousUpdate(boolean b)
    {
        continuousUpdate = b;
    }


    public void setValue(double newRho, double newTheta)
    {
        setValue(new PolarPoint(newRho, newTheta));
    }


    public PolarPoint getValue()
    {
        return((PolarPoint)(value.clone()));
    }


    public void addActionListener(ActionListener al)
    {
        actionListeners.addElement(al);
    }


     /*
      *  Adjust scale so that the largest permissible value takes up
      *  not quite the entire component.
      */
    private void adjustScale(int w, int h)
    {
```

```
        unitsPerPixel = 2.0 * maxRho / Math.min(w, h);
        unitsPerPixel *= 1.1;
    }



    /*
     *  When the component resizes, we need to adjust our scale.
     *  Note that we do not need to override resize(), because
     *  resize() calls reshape().
     */
    public void setBounds(int x, int y, int w, int h)
    {
        adjustScale(w, h);
        super.setBounds(x, y, w, h);
    }



    public void paint(Graphics g)
    {
        int     radiusPix;
        int     centerX;
        int     centerY;

        radiusPix = (int)(value.rho / unitsPerPixel);
        centerX = size().width / 2;
        centerY = size().height / 2;
        int ulx = centerX - radiusPix;
        int uly = centerY - radiusPix;

        // Draw axes in light gray.
        g.setColor(Color.lightGray);
        g.drawLine(centerX, 0, centerX, size().height);
        g.drawLine(0, centerY, size().width, centerY);

        // Draw label string in upper-left corner.
        g.setColor(getForeground());
        if (showTextValue)
        {
            g.drawString((value.rho + ", " + value.theta),
                         5, size().height-5);
        }
```

```
        // If dragging, subsequent drawing will use the drag color.
        if (dragging)
        {
            g.setColor(dragColor);
        }

        // Draw ring.
        g.drawOval(ulx, uly, 2*radiusPix, 2*radiusPix);

        // Draw dot.
        int arrowTipX = centerX +
                        (int)(radiusPix * Math.cos(value.theta));
        int arrowTipY = centerY -
                        (int)(radiusPix * Math.sin(value.theta));
        g.fillOval(arrowTipX-3, arrowTipY-3, 7, 7);

        // Draw line from center to dot, space permitting.
        if (radiusPix > 5)
        {
            g.drawLine(centerX, centerY, arrowTipX, arrowTipY);
        }
    }


    /*
     * Converts pixel coordinates x and y to polar coordinates,
     * storing the result in dest,
     */
    private void xyToPolarPoint(int x, int y, PolarPoint dest)
    {
        int deltaX = x - size().width/2;
        int deltaY = size().height/2 - y;
        double deltaLen = Math.sqrt(deltaX*deltaX + deltaY*deltaY);
        dest.rho = unitsPerPixel * deltaLen;
        dest.rho = Math.min(dest.rho, maxRho);
        dest.theta = Math.atan2(deltaY, deltaX);
        while (dest.theta < 0.0)
            dest.theta += 2*Math.PI;
    }
```

```
/*
 *  Update current value and repaint, but do not send any events.
 */
public void mousePressed(MouseEvent e)
{
    xyToPolarPoint(e.getX(), e.getY(), value);
    repaint();
}



/*
 *  Refresh the screen.  Post an ActionEvent if continuous
 *  updates have been requested.
 */
public void mouseDragged(MouseEvent e)
{
    dragging = true;
    xyToPolarPoint(e.getX(), e.getY(), value);
    repaint();
    if (continuousUpdate)
        postAction();
}



/*
 *  Refresh the screen and post an ActionEvent.
 */
public void mouseReleased(MouseEvent e)
{
    dragging = false;
    xyToPolarPoint(e.getX(), e.getY(), value);
    repaint();
    postAction();
}



/*
 *  Post an action event to each registered action listener.
 */
private void postAction()
{
```

```
    ActionListener       listener;
    ActionEvent          event;

    int size = actionListeners.size();
    if (size == 0)
        return;          // No listeners

    for (int i=0; i<actionListeners.size(); i++)
    {
        listener =
            (ActionListener)(actionListeners.elementAt(i));
        // Each listener gets its own event.
        event = new ActionEvent(this,
                                ActionEvent.ACTION_PERFORMED,
                                null);
        listener.actionPerformed(event);
    }
}


public Dimension minimumSize()
{
    return(new Dimension(50, 50));
}


public Dimension preferredSize()
{
    return(new Dimension(50, 50));
}


/*
 *  Method stubs to fulfill interfaces.
 */
public void mouseClicked(MouseEvent e)      { }
public void mouseEntered(MouseEvent e)      { }
public void mouseExited(MouseEvent e)       { }
public void mouseMoved(MouseEvent e)        { }
}
```

Test Applet for *NewPolar*

The following program implements a simple test applet for the New-Polar class. The test applet constructs an instance of NewPolar, a checkbox, and a text field. The checkbox takes the NewPolar in and out of continuous-update mode. Whenever the polar component sends an action event (the applet registers itself as an action listener), the new value of the polar component is written to the text field.

The source code for the test applet appears below and can be found on the CD-ROM in javadevhdbk\ch14\NewPolarTest.java.

NewPolarTest.java

```
import     java.awt.*;
import     java.awt.event.*;
import     java.applet.Applet;


public class NewPolarTest extends Applet implements
ActionListener, ItemListener
{
    NewPolar        polar;
    TextField       tf;
    Checkbox        cbox;


  public void init()
  {
        setLayout(new BorderLayout());
        polar = new NewPolar();
        add("Center", polar);
        polar.addActionListener(this);

        Panel pan = new Panel();
        pan.setLayout(new GridLayout(2, 1));
        tf = new TextField(polar.getValue().toString());
        tf.setEditable(false);
        pan.add(tf);
        cbox = new Checkbox("Continuous Update");
```

```
                    cbox.addItemListener(this);
                    pan.add(cbox);
                    add("South", pan);
            }


        public void actionPerformed(ActionEvent e)
        {
                tf.setText(polar.getValue().toString());
        }


        public void itemStateChanged(ItemEvent e)
        {
            polar.setContinuousUpdate(cbox.getState());
        }
    }
```

Figure 14.1 shows the test applet.

FIGURE 14.1

Test Applet for *NewPolar*

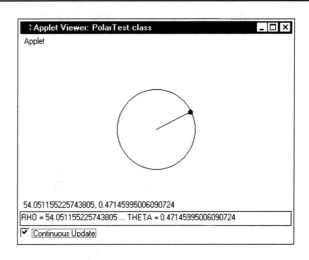

54.05155225743805, 0.47145995006090724

RHO = 54.051155225743805 ... THETA = 0.47145995006090724

☑ Continuous Update

Summary

The 1.1 AWT enhancements address a number of short-term and long-term needs. The Desktop color, pop-up menu, printing, and scrollpane features provide support for making user interfaces more intuitive. Existing applets and applications can be easily modified to take advantage of these features. The new drag-and-drop support is an infrastructure that will not be completed until some time in the future; programs that are currently in the design phase should be organized in such as way that adding drag-and-drop functionality in the future will be painless. Lastly, the new event-delegation model facilitates the clean, maintainable design of large GUIs. Because GUIs grow over time, new applets and applications would be well advised to use the new model.

PART III

New APIs

The next three chapters present information concerning some of the new APIs that Sun is introducing for release 1.1 of the JDK: Java Beans, The Java Electronic Commerce Framework, and Servlets.

CHAPTER
FIFTEEN

15

Java Beans API

- The Java "Bean"

- Bean introspection and customization

- The `BeanInfo` interface

- Bean persistence

- The Beans Development Kit (BDK)

- Creating a new Bean

- Integrating Beans in other technologies

One of the real goals of software development is to recoup the investment made in code by making it possible for the code to be reused in other development efforts, either in the same company, or in other companies. In recent years, programmers have expended great energy on creating reusable software. The early efforts spent on object-oriented programming are now coming full circle with the development of a programming language like Java, where the software will run on a variety of platforms without any additional effort.

However, Java does not automatically allow software to be reusable. Java code may be well written, and thus allow another developer to make changes to the code easily, but the goal of reusable software is to allow developers to use the code *without* having to recompile the code. Further, true reuse implies that developers can integrate code pieces into their designs without having to recompile *their* code either.

These are the goals of the Java Beans API, and the focus of this chapter. The Java Beans API is not yet a formal part of the language, but enough of the design is available to make it possible for developers to get started with this very exciting and powerful technology.

Overview

The Java Beans API describes a software component model for Java. The model is specifically designed to allow third-party vendors to create and sell Java components that are integrated into other software products by other developers.

An application developer will purchase off-the-shelf components from a vendor, drag-and-drop them onto a developer tool container, make any necessary modifications to each component, test, and revise as necessary without needing to write and compile code. Within the Java model, components may be modified and/or combined with other components to create new components or complete applications.

At runtime, the end user may also modify components through properties that the component designer (or application developer) built in. These may be simple properties, like color or shape, or more sophisticated properties that affect the overall behavior of the component.

The component model specified by the Java Beans 1.00-A Specification defines five major services:

Introspection A mechanism that allows components to publish the operations and properties they support and a mechanism to support the discovery of such mechanisms in other components.

Communication An event handling mechanism for creating or "raising" an event to be received as a message by other components.

Persistence A means of storing the state of a component.

Properties Control over the layout of a component. This includes the physical space that a component takes and the relationship of the component to other components when they are placed together on a container.

Customization A mechanism for allowing developers control over changes that each component requires. Components should provide visibility for properties and operations (behavior) to a builder application. The application can then provide a developer with a means for modifying the component pieces in order to construct the appropriate application.

The component model allows software to be designed for modification. Each piece of software contains a set of properties, operations, and event handlers. Combining several components can create the specific runtime behavior a designer/developer wants. Components are held together in a container or toolkit, which provides the context for the application.

The Java "Bean"

A Java "Bean" is a single reusable software component. Beans are manipulated in a builder's tool (container) to provide specific operational behavior. Beans are building blocks for creating applications. The most common Bean will most likely be a small-to-medium control program, but it is also possible to create a Bean that encompasses a complete application and to embed that Bean into a compound document. For example, Figure 15.1 illustrates a container panel that is holding three components.

FIGURE 15.1

A set of Bean components on a container

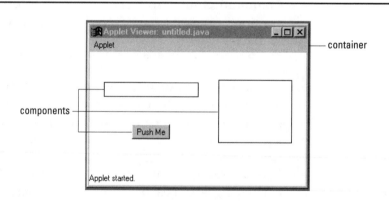

In general, Beans can be represented by simple GUIs—they can be button components, sliders, menu lists, and so on. These simple components provide a straightforward means of letting the user know what a Bean does. However, it is possible to create "invisible" Beans that are used to receive events and work behind the scenes. In any case, it is easiest to think of Beans as component building blocks designed to receive an event and process it so that some operation is carried out.

A Bean is neither a class library nor a programmatic API like JDBC (see Chapter 11, *Database Connectivity (JDBC)*, for more information on this topic). While JDBC provides a means of querying databases, the Beans API connects the user to the JDBC queries. For example, a Bean may be used to provide a simple Select button on an application-user interface. This may in turn be a Bean that composes the appropriate database select statement and issues the request. Visually then, the Bean used in this case would resemble a Java button (as shown in Figure 15.2).

Bean Architecture

Beans are composed of three parts, as shown in Figure 15.3: properties, methods, and events.

Bean properties describe the state attributes of the Bean, including its physical representation. Bean properties are the primary mechanisms

FIGURE 15.2

A simple Java Bean

FIGURE 15.3

Bean architecture

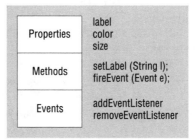

of change within a Bean, and are set or retrieved through methods. In addition, methods are used to fire and receive events, the mechanism by which Beans communicate. Multiple Beans, connected by event methods, make up a complete system or application, as shown in Figure 15.1.

Bean Event Model

Bean events are the mechanism for notification between Beans, and between Beans and containers. A Bean uses an event to notify another Bean to take an action or to inform the Bean that a state change has occurred. An event is registered or published by the source and propagated (through a method call) to one or more target listeners.

Bean events are passed as an object, an instance of a class that extends from `java.util.EventObject`. The event can be created directly from this class, as in the following example:

```
public class MyEvent extends java.util.EventObject {
    public MyEvent (Object source) {
        super (source);
    }
}
```

The Java Beans API closely models the JDK 1.1 AWT Event model. This is helpful because many Bean components are visual GUI elements that are part of the AWT hierarchy. At the lowest level, events are sent as the result of some change, input, or other occurrence on the visual component. The AWT defines the low-level hierarchy as follows:

```
java.util.EventObject
    java.awt.AWTEvent
        java.awt.event.ComponentEvent
        java.awt.event.FocusEvent
        java.awt.event.InputEvent
        java.awt.event.KeyEvent
        java.awt.event.MouseEvent
```

The AWT Event hierarchy also defines a set of events that are used to provide events that occur at the higher level of the user interface. These higher-level events apply to multiple component types, as in the following:

```
java.util.EventObject
    java.awt.AWTEvent
        java.awt.event.ActionEvent
        java.awt.event.AdjustmentEvent
        java.awt.event.ItemEvent
```

Beans send events as the single parameter to an event method of the target bean. However, events encapsulate elements that may be used by the recipient of the event. For example:

```
public void fireAction (String command) {
    if (listener != null) {
        ActionEvent actionEvt =
            new ActionEvent(this, 0, command);
        listener.actionPerformed(actionEvt);
    }
}
```

Here an event object with a `String` command is sent to the listener object, and the event method to be triggered is the `action-Performed()` event.

Event Sources and Targets

The event model in Java Beans is defined by event sources and event targets. The event source identifies itself as the initiator of an event by registering one or more event targets. Both the event source and the event target establish a set of methods that the event source will use to call on event listeners.

An event source attempts to send a desired event to an arbitrary collection of event targets. This mode is the default behavior of the event source and is called *multicast*: the event source keeps track of the event listeners for each kind of event it fires and notifies each target when an event is fired.

A multicast event allows a source object to notify several event listeners all at once, which is accomplished by keeping the state of every event listener registered in a Vector class:

```
private Vector listenerList = new Vector ();

public synchronized void addActionListener (ActionListener 1) {
    listenerList.addElement (1);
}

public synchronized void removeActionListener (ActionListener 1)
{
    listenerList.removeElement (1);
}
```

NOTE The add/remove ActionListener **pair are typically synchronized to avoid multithread race conditions.**

Event sources may also be *unicast* sources, where the event source is required to keep track of a single target listener for each type of event it fires. A unicast event is sent to the specific single target listener.

The unicast event allows only one listener to be registered; otherwise, an exception, java.util.TooManyListenersException, is thrown. The unicast event listener stores just one instance of a listener:

```
private ActionListener 1;

public synchronized void addActionListener (ActionListener 1)
    throws java.util.TooManyListenersException {
    if (1 == null) {
        this.1 = 1;
    } else {
        throw new java.util.TooManyListenersException ();
    }
}

public synchronized void removeActionListener (ActionListener 1) {
    1 = null;
}
```

The event target is an instance of a class that implements some (or all) of the `EventListener` interface—specifically, the event methods that class is interested in.

Each event type is tied to a single method, and event methods are typically grouped by their application. For example:

```java
import java.awt.event.*;
public class MyActionEventListener implements ActionListener {

    // Provide an event method for the actionPerformed event
    public void actionPerformed (ActionEvent e) {

        // Pull the command out of the event
        String command = e.getActionCommand ();

        if (command.equals ("add")) {
            . . .
        }
    }
}
```

The following is an example use of a multicast event source and event listener. This example illustrates how an event listener is registered with an event source and how the event source sends an event to each of the listeners registered.

```java
import java.util.Vector;
import java.awt.event.*;
public class MyApp {
    private Vector listenerList = new Vector ();
    private MyActionEventListener myListener;

    public MyApp () {
        myListener = new MyActionEventListener ();
        addActionListener (myListener);
    }

    public synchronized void addActionListener(ActionListener l)
    {
        listenerList.addElement (l);
    }
```

```
public synchronized void removeActionListener
  (ActionListener l) {
    listenerList.removeElement (1);
}

public void fireAction (String command) {
    Vector targets;
    synchronized (this) {
        targets = (Vector) listenerList.clone();
    }
    ActionEvent actionEvt =
            new ActionEvent(this, 0, command);
    for (int i = 0; i < targets.size(); i++) {
        ActionListener target =
                (ActionListener)targets.elementAt(i);
        target.actionPerformed(actionEvt);
    }
}
...
}
```

In some cases, the event target cannot implement the interface directly, and an instance of an event-adapter class may be used to interpose between the source and one or more listeners.

The event adapter implements one or more listener interfaces and allows a developer to use a single event to be sent to two different adapter classes that interpose between the source and listener.

Besides allowing a developer to use a single event with multiple event sources to a single listener, adapters are useful for filtering events and implementing advanced features like event queues.

Properties

The *properties* of a Bean describe attributes associated with the Bean, such as color, size, or the string to be used as a label.

Properties may be used in a number of ways, depending on the environment that the bean is accessed in. Properties can be changed at runtime through their getter and setter methods; through a scripting environment; or in a property sheet that is part of a Beanbuilder/customization tool.

They are changed by the end user through a pair of `get`/`set` methods that are specific to the property. For example, there may be a color property for the Bean, and the end user changes the color of the Bean through a properties dialog box provided with the Bean. The Bean provides two methods to allow the private color property to be changed:

```
public Color getFillColor (); // This Bean's object fill color
public void setFillColor (Color c);
```

Properties may be indexed to support a range of values, where the indexes are specified by ints. Indexed properties have four access signatures where the arrays of values may be accessed by either a single element or by the entire array:

```
void setLabel (int index, String label);
String getLabel (int index);
void setLabel (String [] labels);
String [] getLabel ();
```

The indexed methods should check array bounds and throw `java .lang.ArrayIndexOutOfBoundsException` if the index is outside the array bounds.

Other property types include bound properties and constrained properties. A bound property sends a notification of a change in property to other Beans and/or the container when a property change occurs. A bound property will raise an event when a change is made.

A bound property sends a notification that a change has been made. The notification process occurs by *binding* the property type to a `PropertyChangeListener` event listener. A Bean that wishes to notify either itself, some other Bean, or the Bean container tool will include a pair of multicast event listener registration methods:

```
public void addPropertyChangeListener (PropertyChangeListener 1);
public void removePropertyChangeListener (PropertyChangeListener 1);
```

The Java Beans API provides a class that supports bound properties. This class may be used to display a property sheet editor for a particular property. For example:

```
private PropertyChangeSupport changes =
    new PropertyChangeSupport(this);

public void setFillColor (Color newColor) {
    Color oldColor = currColor;
    currColor = newColor;
    changes.firePropertyChange ("color", oldColor, newColor);
    ...
}
```

The firePropertyChange() method above will call the property-Change() method on the object that implements the Property-ChangeListener interface. Typically, this object would be part of a builder tool and would call an appropriate property sheet method to open a property editor.

Constrained properties are validated internally and rejected if they are inappropriate. The user/developer is notified of a rejected property through an exception. For example:

```
public Dimension getSize () {
    return currSize;
}
public void setSize (Dimension d)
    throws SizeChangeRejectedException (){
    // Check the size and throw an exception
    // if it exceeds some preset value
    ...
}
```

Constrained properties use the `VetoableChangeListener` interface to validate changes. These are implemented in the Bean by including a pair of add/remove methods:

```
public void addVetoableChangeListener (VetoableChangeListener v);
public void removeVetoableChangeListener (VetoableChangeListener v);
```

Naturally, the Bean property method should fire an event before the property is changed. For example:

```
private VetoableChangeSupport vetos =
    new VetoableChangeSupport(this);

public void setSize (Dimension newSize)
    throws PropertyVetoException {
    Dimension oldSize = currSize;
    vetos.fireVetoableChange ("size", oldSize, newSize);
    // No one vetoed, make the change
    currSize = newSize;
    changes.firePropertyChange ("size", oldSize, newSize);
    ...
}
```

Methods

Bean methods are the operations that are called from other components (that have an instance of the Bean), the container, or from a scripting environment. Bean methods may be exported by making them public; this makes it possible to view the methods with a builder tool using Java introspection (more on this later).

Methods are used to set/get properties and fire/catch events. Bean methods may be either public or private. Methods that are private may not be seen or modified by builder tools.

Bean Storage

Beans are stored in a Java Archive (JAR) format. Essentially, JAR files are Zip-formatted archive files with an optional component called a manifest file that can contain additional information about the contents of the JAR file. For more information, look at Chapter 11, *Packaging*, of the Java Beans Specification, version 1.00-A, and at the JAR HTML file in the Beans Development Kit under `<installation directory>/beans/doc/jar.html`.

> **NOTE** Applications that use Beans are not required by the Java Beans Specification to use JAR files or even to store beans as JAR files; however, the specification does propose that Beans are shipped as JAR files initially.

Bean Introspection and Customization

Beans will be received as pieces of software from vendors or developed internally within companies. A Bean is likely to be developed as a generic component; that is, designed to be customized by the developer at application creation. The way this happens is through two Java technologies that are maturing with the Java Beans API. The first is the Java Reflection API, a set of classes that are used to look into a class file and discover the properties (variables) and methods of the class. The second is the Java Serialization API, which is used to create a permanent storage of a class, including its current state.

These two technologies are used to allow Beans to be investigated and discovered by a builder tool, then modified and stored for a particular application use. The Java Bean Introspection process exposes the properties, methods, and events of a Bean. The introspection process is actually quite rote: Bean classes are assumed to have properties if there are methods that either set or get a property type:

```
public <PropertyType> get<PropertyName> ();
public void set<PropertyName> (<PropertyType p>);
```

If only one of the `get`/`set` methods is discovered, then `Property-Name` is determined to be read-only or write-only.

Properties that are `boolean`—that is, return a `boolean` type—may also have a `boolean` method:

```
public boolean is<PropertyName> ();
```

Indexed properties are also discovered when the method signatures include indexed properties:

```
public <PropertyElement> get<PropertyName> (int a);
public void set<PropertyName> (int a, <PropertyElement> b);
```

These are replaced by the four access signatures described earlier.

Events are discovered by a pair of add/remove event methods. These are assumed to begin with `add` and `remove` and take an `<EventListenerType>` argument that extends the `java.util.EventListener` interface, where the type name ends with `Listener`. For example:

```
public void add<EventListenerType> (<EventListenerType> a);
public void remove<EventListenerType> (<EventListenerType> a);
```

Methods are discovered if the method access is public. This includes all of the property and event methods.

The *BeanInfo* Interface

The Java Bean API also provides an explicit interface to allow Bean designers to expose the properties, events, methods and any global information about a Bean. A Bean vendor provides a `BeanInfo` interface by providing a class that extends the `BeanInfo` interface and appends `BeanInfo` to the classname:

```
public class myBeanBeanInfo implements java.util.BeanInfo {...
```

The `BeanInfo` interface provides a series of methods to access Bean information, but a Bean developer can also provide private description files that the `BeanInfo` class uses to define Bean information. By default a `BeanInfo` object is created when introspection is run on the Bean.

The process follows the following steps to discover the inner workings of a Bean:

- Walk the class and superclass chain of each target class.

- Look for a `BeanInfo` classname (the classname with `BeanInfo` appended to the end of the name).

- Use low-level reflection to study the class and create a `BeanInfo` object with the results.

Bean Persistence

Java Beans are components that rely on state. When a Bean receives a state change, the Bean designer may desire to store, or *persist*, the changed state. State changes may occur as the result of some action, either during runtime or development.

Beans may be stored in one of two ways: automatically through the Java Object Serialization mechanism, or through a future externalization stream mechanism that will allow the Bean object complete control over the writing of its state, including the ability to mimic arbitrary existing data formats.

Normally a Bean will store away the parts of its internal state that would be used to define the Bean on re-creation. Typically these are the Bean's look and feel and the Bean's behavior. A Bean that references other Beans may wish to store these references, but this activity is inherently dangerous because it assumes the *referenced* Beans are also saved. Instead, references to other Beans should be rebuilt during the re-creation process. In this way Beans may mark references as "transient" to specify that the reference is volatile and will be rebuilt as necessary.

The Beans Development Kit (BDK)

In the early part of December 1996, JavaSoft announced the Java Developer's Kit version 1.1 Beta release, followed four days later by a minor update of the JDK to 1.1 Beta 2. At the same time, JavaSoft announced a Beta version (currently at Beta 3) of the Beans Development Kit (BDK). The BDK is not intended as a commercial product by JavaSoft; instead, BDK provides a first look at Beans: how they are constructed and how they are applied through a simple and easy-to-use builder application.

The BDK is a 100 percent Java application that allows Java developers to create Beans that use the Bean event model. The BDK is dependent only on the current release of the JDK 1.1, and it is available for both Solaris Unix and Win32 platforms. The latest BDK is available from `http://splash.javasoft.com/beans/`; the latest JDK 1.1 release is available from `http://www.javasoft.com:80/products/JDK/1.1/`. The final (first customer ship) BDK is planned for the first quarter of 1997.

The Beta BDK is a complete system and contains source code for all of the applications, examples, and documentation. The BDK also contains a sample Bean builder and customizer application called BeanBox.

The Beta BDK is downloaded as either a Bourne shell executable (`bdk_beta3.sh`) for Solaris Unix or as a Win32 exe file (`bdk_beta3.exe`) for Windows 95 and NT systems. For Solaris Unix, the BDK is unpacked by running the shell executable:

```
% sh bdk_beta3.sh
```

For Win32 systems the BDK is installed by copying the `bdk_beta3.exe` file into a folder and double-clicking it. This will unpack the distribution and create a setup batch script. To continue the installation, this script is also double-clicked.

Both installations ask the user to agree to the terms of the distribution license agreement and then create a `beans` directory that contains the following subdirectories:

`apis`   the source code for the Bean API

`beanbox`   the sample Bean builder tool

`classes`   the compiled Bean class files

`demo`   the location of the sample Beans in the beanbox

`doc`   HTML files that describe the Bean API, the beanbox, and examples

`jars`   the JAR files of the example Beans that the beanbox application will read and load

To use the BDK Beta, the current JDK 1.1 Beta must also be loaded, and the `CLASSPATH` environment variable should include: `<installation directory>/beans/classes`.

The *BeanBox*

The BDK BeanBox application (located in the `beanbox` directory under the beans installation directory) is a simple test container that allows Bean components to be

- dropped onto a composition window
- resized and moved
- altered with property sheets
- customized with a `customizer` application
- connected together
- saved through serialization

It is also possible to add new Beans to the BeanBox and then use existing components to create simple applications. In *The TrafficLight Bean*, later in this chapter, an example Bean called the `Traffic Light` is presented.

Using the BeanBox

Figure 15.4 shows the BeanBox composition window (center), ToolBox palette (left), and Property Sheet window (right). The ToolBox palette displays the Beans that are available to be dropped onto the composition window. When a Bean is selected, the Property Sheet window displays the properties of the Bean that are available for editing.

FIGURE 15.4

The BeanBox application

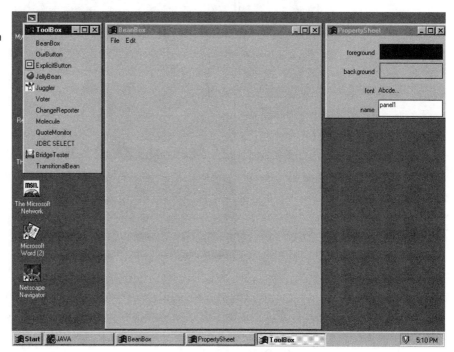

To place a Bean on the composition window, the Bean is selected from the Bean's icon or name on the ToolBox palette, then placed on the composition window by clicking the mouse down on the location where the center of the Bean will go. The Bean is then drawn onto the composition window with a black-and-white-hashed boundary as shown in Figure 15.5. Note that the property sheet shows the properties available for the selected Bean. In this case, the Bean selected was the Juggler Bean, so the property sheet shows the color, foreground, background, a `priceInCents` property, font, and component name.

FIGURE 15.5

A Juggler Bean drawn on the BeanBox

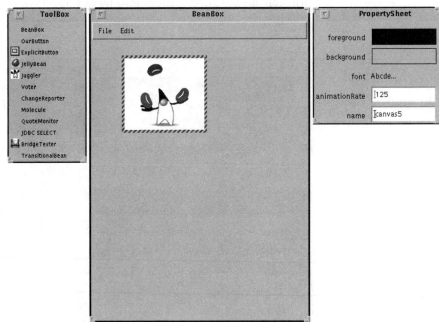

The File menu item at the top left of the BeanBox composition window allows the current composition to be saved, cleared, or exited. The Load item under the File menu is used to restore the state of a saved composition.

The Edit menu item is used to change the currently selected Bean (or the composition window if no Bean is selected). The Edit item supports Cut, Copy, and Paste of selected Beans. Depending on the Bean selected, the Edit item will also list the Events option, which allows you to "connect" Beans together.

The Sample Beans

The BeanBox comes with a set of 12 sample Beans. Each of these has a different function and provides an example of various aspects of the Java Beans API. The Beans provided with the BeanBox are listed in the ToolBox palette:

BeanBox   This composition window itself is a Bean, and a Bean-Box can be nested inside another.

OurButton   A simple button component, this Bean is a subclass of a `java.awt.Canvas`. This Bean is the simplest button GUI component, and when clicked will send a standard AWT `action-Performed` method. OurButton exposes four properties: (label, fontSize, largeFont, and debug) in addition to the standard `java.awt.Component` properties. These properties illustrate the use of getter/setter methods for `String`, `int`, `Font` class, and `boolean` parameter types.

ExplicitButton   The ExplicitButton Bean is a simple subclass of the OurButton Bean, and illustrates the effect that a `BeanInfo` class can have. The `ExplicitButtonBeanInfo` class includes a `Property-Descriptor` method that defines default values for the `label`, `fontSize`, `largeFont`, and `debug` parameters. The `Explicit-ButtonBeanInfo` class also illustrates how to define icons that will appear to the left of the Bean name in the ToolBox palette and makes use of a simple `customizer` class, the `OurButtonCustomizer` class. This `customizer` appears in the Edit menu item when this Bean is selected and allows the developer to edit the button label.

JellyBean   This is a simple visual component that draws a colored oval "jelly bean." This Bean illustrates the use of bound and constrained properties. The color property is a bound component and notifies the JellyBean when a change is made to the component. The `priceInCents` property is an example of a constrained property.

Juggler   This Bean component represents a threaded animation component that may be started and stopped by connecting a button-push event from an ExplicitButton or OurButton to the start-and-stop event methods supported by the Juggler Bean.

Voter   The Voter Bean is designed to handle a `vetoableChange` event. By default the Bean will reject all change requests (it is initially set to NO), but change requests will be accepted if the `vetoAll` property is set to `false`.

ChangeReporter   This Bean is a `TextField` component that can be used to display `PropertyChange` events.

Molecule   This Bean is similar to Juggler in concept. The Bean displays a 3-D representation of a molecule and accepts mouse input to rotate the molecule. It is also possible to rotate the molecule by attaching buttons to the `rotateX()` and `rotateY()` methods.

QuoteMonitor   This Bean, applying additional Java technology, uses Remote Method Invocation (RMI) to contact a remote (or local) quote server and request a real or imaginary stock quote value. The RMI server is started by changing directories to the `demo` directory and executing `gnumake -f quote,gmk run &` on Solaris Unix or `start nmake -f quote,mk run` from a DOS prompt on a Win32 system.

JDBC SELECT   This is a Bean that uses the JDBC API to connect to a database at a specified URL and issue a select statement. It is complex and requires its own `customizer` to configure the JDBC URL string, database username, and password.

BridgeTester   This Bean provides a set of property types and events that may be used to test other Bean components.

TransitionalBean   This is a Bean that uses the JDK 1.0.2 Event model and will work with both JDK 1.1 and JDK 1.0.2.

Connecting Beans

Beans are connected visually in the BeanBox tool. Figure 15.6 shows the Juggler Bean with two ExplicitButton Beans. The next step in making a simple animation application is to connect one of the buttons to the `start()` event method on the Juggler Bean and connect the other to a `stop()` event method.

FIGURE 15.6

The Juggler application

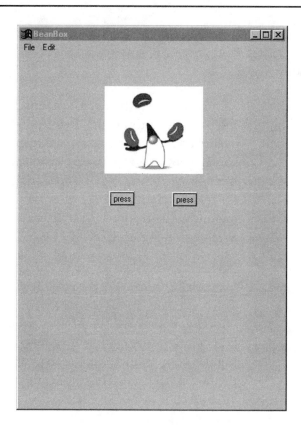

After selecting one of the ExplicitButton Beans, the Edit menu item is selected and opened to button Push, and then to `actionPerformed` as shown in Figure 15.7.

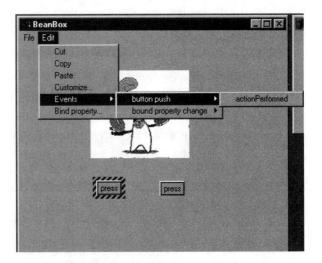

Once selected, the BeanBox will draw a rubber banding line from the ExplicitButton Bean. This line illustrates the event source. The event target (listener) is selected by clicking on the Bean that the event source should go to. In this case, the Juggler Bean will receive an `actionPerformed` event. The Juggler Bean supports two methods that can receive an `actionPerformed` event: the `start` and `stop` methods. These appear in an `EventTargetDialog` pop-up window as shown in Figure 15.8.

Selecting the start method will connect the ExplicitButton's `actionPerformed` event to the start method of the Juggler Bean. The two Beans are now connected. Clicking on the ExplicitButton with the mouse will send the event to the Juggler Bean, and the Bean will begin the animation. To connect the other ExplicitButton to the Juggler `stop()` method, the steps above are repeated, and the `stop()` method is selected. The application is now completely functional after just a few mouse clicks.

To complete the application, the two buttons are labeled to indicate what actions they will have on the Juggler Bean, as shown in Figure 15.9.

FIGURE 15.8

The EventTarget-
Dialog for Juggler

FIGURE 15.9

The completed Juggler
application

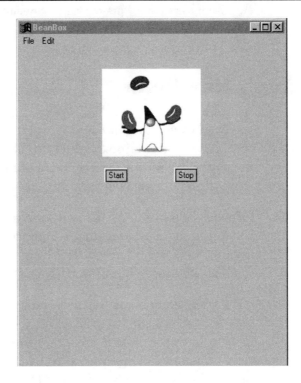

Saving and Restoring Bean Applications

Bean applications created in the BeanBox can be saved in their current state (including running or stopped as in the case of the Juggler application) by selecting the File menu item and then the Save item. A dialog box will open that is used to specify the name of the file that the current set of beans in the composition window is saved to.

The application is restored through the Load item on the File menu.

NOTE
The current BeanBox composition window is in a Beta state and not intended for commercial use. There are two important things to note: the Clear and Load items under the File menu will clear the current set of Beans on the composition window without any warning, even if they are not already saved. Also, the Save item will not ask to overwrite any current Bean application.

Creating a New Bean

The Bean Development Kit also provides a means for new Beans to be added to the BeanBox and tested. This section will outline the steps required for the development of new Beans and highlight the propagation of new events in the JDK 1.1 Event model.

The new Bean will emulate the operation of a traffic signal light. The traffic signal is a rectangular component with three colored circles: red, yellow, and green. These are meant to emulate the functions of a real-life traffic signal; stop, slow, and go.

The traffic component will respond to a signal from a Walk button to cycle between its current state (either red or green; yellow is a transient state) to allow someone to cross the street. In the interest of simplicity, the component will be represented by a two-dimensional rectangle. Figure 15.10 illustrates the proposed traffic light Bean component.

FIGURE 15.10

The traffic light Bean
component

This component is a visual component, so it will need to subclass from an AWT component. In addition to responding to a signal from the Walk button, the component should signal or support a second traffic light slave that would appear at a four-way intersection.

The TrafficLight Bean

The BDK provides a directory where it stores the example source code and a set of make files that are used to create the JAR files that the BeanBox requires. This directory is just below the installation directory of the BDK in a directory named demo.

This directory contains the GNU and nmake files for Solaris and Win32 systems. There is also a directory sun/demo, where the source files for the example Beans are stored. For simplicity, here is where the directory containing TrafficLight is created; it's called tlight. Using this directory path and structure makes it possible to copy one of the existing make files in the BDK demo directory.

The TrafficLight Bean subclasses a java.awt.Canvas component. TrafficLight exposes two properties, defaultLight, which is a String representing the starting color of the light in its resting state, and a boolean debug property, which may be turned on or off through a property sheet in order to see the result of events as they are passed to and from the TrafficLight component.

Here is the source code, which is located on the CD-ROM in javadevhdbk\ch15\TrafficLight.java and Traffic-Light.class, for the TrafficLight component:

TrafficLight.java

```
package sun.demo.tlight;

import java.awt.*;
import java.awt.event.*;
import java.awt.image.*;
import java.beans.*;

// A Simple bean - represents a traffic light component

public class TrafficLight extends Canvas implements Runnable {

    private ActionListener l = null;

    private Thread me = null;

    private String defaultLight = "RED";
    private String currLight = defaultLight;

    private boolean debug = false;

    // Set the size of the Bean display
    public TrafficLight () {
        setSize (100, 200);
    }

    // Turn debugging on/off
    public void setDebugging (boolean state) {
        debug = state;
    }

    public boolean getDebugging () {
        return debug;
    }
```

```
// Methods for get/set of the default light state
public synchronized String getDefaultLightState () {
    return defaultLight;
}

public void setDefaultLightState (String state) {
    defaultLight = state;
    currLight = state;
    repaint();
}

// Display the current traffic light state
public void paint (Graphics g) {

    // Put a black border around it
    g.setColor (Color.black);
    g.drawRect (1, 1, 98, 198);

    // Paint the outline of the traffic light
    g.setColor (Color.white);
    g.fillRect (2, 2, 96, 196);

    // Paint the outline of the lights
    g.setColor (Color.black);
    g.drawOval (30, 30, 40, 40);
    g.drawOval (30, 80, 40, 40);
    g.drawOval (30, 130, 40, 40);

    // Debug
    if (debug) {
        System.out.println
            ("Current light state is: " + currLight);
    }
```

```java
        // Which light is on?
        if (currLight.equals("RED")) {
            g.setColor (Color.red);
            g.fillOval (30, 30, 40, 40);
        } else {
            if (currLight.equals("YELLOW")) {
                g.setColor (Color.yellow);
                g.fillOval (30, 80, 40, 40);
            } else    {
                if (currLight.equals("GREEN")) {
                    g.setColor (Color.green);
                    g.fillOval (30, 130, 40, 40);
                }
            }
        }

    }


    // Send a message to the light to start a cycle
    public void start (ActionEvent x) {
        // Debug
        if (debug) {
            System.out.println ("Got a start Event!");
        }
        startCycle ();
    }


    // Start a light cycle
    private synchronized void startCycle () {
        // Don't bother unless there is no cycle running already
        if (me == null) {
            me = new Thread (this);
            me.start ();
        }
    }
```

```
// The run method
public void run () {
    // Debug
    if (debug) {
        System.out.println ("Started cycle");
    }

    while (me != null) {
        try {
            me.sleep (3000);
        } catch (InterruptedException e) {
        }

        // Get the current light state
        if (currLight.equals ("RED")) {
            // Cycle to green
            currLight = "GREEN";
            fireAction(currLight);
        } else {
            if (currLight.equals("GREEN")) {
                // Cycle through yellow to red
                currLight = "YELLOW";
            } else {
                // Otherwise, we are at YELLOW,
                // so cycle to RED
                currLight = "RED";
                fireAction(currLight);
            }
        }
        repaint ();
        // Break the cycle when the default state is reached
        if (currLight.equalsdefaultLight) {
            me = null;
        }
    }

}
```

```
// Get an event that indicates a light
// Change from another light
// In which case, we will act as slave
public void lightChange (ActionEvent x) {
    // Check the state of this event
    String command = x.getActionCommand();
    // Debug
    if (debug) {
        System.out.println
            ("Received event from traffic light: "
            + defaultLight + " command: go to " + command);
    }

    // If the other light went red, then check our default
    if (command.equals ("RED")) {
        if (currLight.equals ("GREEN")) {
            // ok, do nothing
        } else {
            // Cycle
            currLight = "GREEN";
            repaint ();
        }
    } else {
        if (command.equals ("GREEN")) {
            if (currLight.equals ("RED")) {
                // ok, do nothing
            } else {
                // Cycle
                currLight = "YELLOW";
                repaint ();
                try {
                    Thread.sleep (3000);
                } catch (InterruptedException e) {}
                currLight = "RED";
                repaint ();
            }
        }
    }
}
```

```
// The fireAction method sends an Event to the
// slave TrafficLight to tell it we are changing
// state.
public void fireAction (String s) {
    // Debug
    if (debug) {
        System.out.println ("Firing action event");
    }

    if (1 != null) {
        ActionEvent actionEvt = new ActionEvent(this, 0, s);
        1.actionPerformed(actionEvt);
    }
}

// List ourselves as the source of an event
// Just use Action for now...
public void addActionListener (ActionListener 1)
    throws java.util.TooManyListenersException
{
    // Debug
    if (debug) {
        System.out.println ("Registering a listener");
    }

    // Is there an Event listener already?
    if (this.1 != null) {
        throw new java.util.TooManyListenersException ();
    }
    this.1 = 1;
}

public void removeActionListener (ActionListener 1) {
    1 = null;
}
}
```

How It Works

The TrafficLight component uses a pair of set/get methods to expose the Debugging and DefaultLightState properties. The paint() method for the component paints a white rectangle and three empty circles to indicate the red, yellow, and green lights for the TrafficLight Bean.

Public methods that take an ActionEvent argument may be connected to an actionPerformed event (like the Juggler example Bean above). The TrafficLight Bean supports two such methods: a start() method that calls a private startCycle() method that in turn creates a thread and begins the cycle of changing the TrafficLight from its current state to its opposite state and back again. This method is intended to support the Walk button.

The lightChange() method is used to support a second traffic light slave. This method is used to connect two TrafficLight Beans. When one light is cycling, the other is notified through an event that the light should change. For example, if the first traffic light changes from green to red, then the second light (on the other intersection) will change from red to green.

The fireAction() method is used to notify another TrafficLight Bean that is registered as an ActionListener. Note that the Traffic-Light Bean is an example of a unicast event source and therefore does not support more than a four-way intersection.

Compiling the TrafficLight Bean

The BDK provides a set of make files that make it easier to compile Bean components and place them in the appropriate classes directory, as well as making them into JAR files that the BeanBox can read.

The following listing is an example of a GNU make file copied and modified from one of the existing make files in the demo directory below the installation directory of the BDK.

tlight.gmk

```
CLASSFILES= \
    sun/demo/tlight/TrafficLight.class
#    sun/demo/tlight/TrafficLightBeanInfo.class

#GIFFILES= \
#    sun/demo/tlight/TrafficLightIcon.gif

JARFILE= ../jars/tlight.jar

all: $(JARFILE)

# Create a JAR file with a suitable manifest.

$(JARFILE): $(CLASSFILES) $(GIFFILES)
    echo "Manifest-Version: 1.0" > manifest.tmp
    echo "" >> manifest.tmp
    echo "Name: sun/demo/tlight/TrafficLight.class" >> manifest.tmp
    echo "Java-Bean: True" >> manifest.tmp
    jar cfm $(JARFILE) manifest.tmp sun/demo/tlight/*.class
$(GIFFILES)
    @/bin/rm manifest.tmp

%.class: %.java
    export CLASSPATH; CLASSPATH=../classes:.; \
    javac $<

clean:
    /bin/rm -f sun/demo/tlight/*.class
    /bin/rm -f $(JARFILE)
```

> **NOTE**
>
> For a Win32 system, the `make` file for TrafficLight should be a copy of one of the `.mk` files, and the `nmake` utility is used to compile the `make` file.

To compile and create a JAR file (under Solaris Unix) the make file is compiled with gnumake, a GNU make utility:

```
% cd Beans/demo
% gnumake tlight.gmk
```

Once compiled correctly, the make file will create a manifest file for the TrafficLight.class file and create an appropriate JAR file. The new JAR file is then copied into the jars directory, where the BeanBox can read it.

Inserting the New Bean into the BeanBox

When the BeanBox is started through its make file, the BeanBox application will load the JAR files that are located in the jars directory. So, to add the tlight JAR file created by the make file above, the BeanBox application is started through the make file:

```
%cd beans/beanbox
%gnumake run
```

> **NOTE** For a Win32 system, the BeanBox will reload the JAR files with the command **nmake run**.

This forces the BeanBox to reload the JAR files in the jars directory and re-create the ToolBox palette with the TrafficLight component as shown in Figure 15.11.

FIGURE 15.11

The ToolBox with the TrafficLight Bean

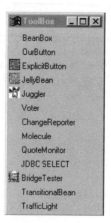

Using the TrafficLight Bean

To test the TrafficLight Bean, two instances of the new Bean and one instance of an ExplicitButton (for the Walk signal) are placed on the composition window as shown in Figure 15.12.

Using the Edit menu and Event item, the ExplicitButton `action-Performed` event is connected to the `start()` event method of the first TrafficLight Bean. When the button is clicked with the mouse, the TrafficLight Bean will cycle to green, yellow, and then back to red, with a brief (3-second) delay between light changes.

Both TrafficLight Beans are in a RED state by default, so the second Bean's `defaultLightState` is changed to GREEN by entering the string **GREEN** on the property sheet for the second Bean.

Next, the first traffic light gets connected to the second traffic light through an `actionPerformed` method to the second traffic light's `lightChange()` method. This is done by repeating the steps above for connecting the ExplicitButton. First select the first TrafficLight Bean, then choose the Edit menu item; drag down to Events, drag across to action, and then to the `actionPerformed` event. When the

FIGURE 15.12

Testing the Traffic-Light Bean

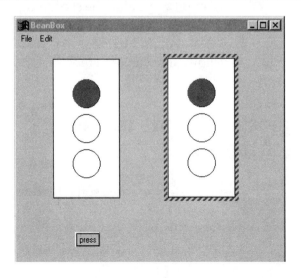

EventTargetDialog appears, select the lightChange method and click the OK button.

As a final step, the label property of the ExplicitButton is changed from Press to Walk as shown in Figure 15.13.

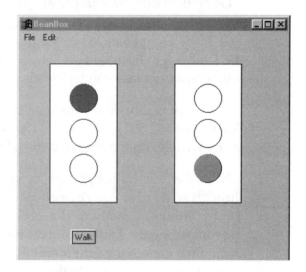

When the Walk button is clicked with the mouse, the first traffic light sends a signal to the second light to change and then begins its own change cycle. The second light changes from green to yellow, and then red, as the first traffic light changes from red to green, then to yellow, and finally to red.

Integrating Beans in Other Technologies

Besides being reusable software components, Beans also will allow developers to integrate their code with other technologies, including access to Microsoft's ActiveX API, AppleSoft's OpenDoc technology, and Netscape's JavaScript and LiveConnect technologies.

Java Beans will allow developers to create controls for ActiveX through COM events. The result is that the Bean will run in the ActiveX environment without any knowledge of the underlying environment and without having to create any C++ code or tie the Bean development into any Microsoft tools. The projected date for the first release of the ActiveX bridge is January 1997, with a ship date projected as March 1997.

Beans under OpenDoc will run as OpenDoc parts, and it will be possible to create a Bean that acts as an OpenDoc container. Beans under Netscape will be able to fire events to JavaScript, and JavaScript will be able to make property changes on Beans. These technologies are currently under development by their respective companies.

In addition to integration with other technologies, the Java Bean specification has several authors and partners from other industries, including Borland (J Builder), IBM (Visual Age for Java), Penumbra Software (Mojo), SunSoft (Java Workshop and Java Studio), Symantec (Visual Café), and others. These partners are creating builder tools that facilitate Bean development and deployment.

Summary

The Java development environment continues to add more functionality and features. The Java language has gone from being an interesting departure from C++ to a serious multiplatform development language. The Java Beans specification and the Bean Development Kit will move Java into a next-generation tool, allowing developers to concentrate on writing code that is cross-platform and truly reusable.

TIP **For additional information on Beans, the slides from the first Java Beans conference at Long Beach are available from** `http://splash` `.javasoft.com/beans/LongBeach/`.

The Java Electronic Commerce Framework (JECF)

- JECF's Merchant Applet layer

- JECF's Wallet layer

- JECF's Cassette layer

The Java Electronic Commerce Framework (JECF) provides support for applet-based shopping and other financial transactions. Pre-Java shopping sites on the World Wide Web have tended to standardize on the metaphor of a shopping cart. Users click on items they wish to purchase to add the items to a virtual shopping cart. At the end of the shopping session, the user specifies a payment instrument (typically a credit card), clicks on a Pay button, and hopes that the goods arrive a few days later.

The JECF standardizes computer-aided shopping (CASH) and provides a rich infrastructure for making the shopping experience seamless, intuitive, and secure. The JECF also provides functionality for applets to charge for their use and for banks and other financial institutions to offer Web-based services.

The JECF architecture is based on a three-layer structure: the Merchant Applet layer, Wallet layer, and Cassette layer. This chapter briefly examines each of these layers.

The Merchant Applet Layer

The JECF's Merchant package (`java.commerce.merchant`) is simply a set of subclasses of `java.applet.Applet`. Merchants (that is, providers of Web-based shopping services) may use these applets for easy and standard support of the common shopping functions.

The applet subclasses in this layer fall into four families:

- Shopping Cart

- Identity

- Tally

- Payment Instrument Selection

These applet subclasses are discussed in the following sections.

The Shopping Cart Applet

Shopping Cart applets implement the metaphor of adding desired merchandise to a virtual shopping cart. This is the first phase of the user's experience. Sophisticated online shopping sites may offer dozens or even hundreds of Web pages of merchandise description. As the user browses these pages, he or she can click on any desired products, thus adding them to the user's shopping cart.

Eventually, the product-selection phase of the shopping trip is over, and the user clicks on a Pay button. When this happens, the applet code must verify the user's identity and access a private database containing transaction information specific to the user. This functionality is supported by the Wallet and Cassette layers, which are described in the next two sections.

The Identity, Tally, and Payment Instrument Selection Applets

After verifying identity and opening the database, the Shopping Cart applet typically will display a single Web page containing three applets:

Identity applet   Verifies the identity of the seller. The Identity applet establishes that the seller is the entity it claims to be in the applet. This makes it difficult for counterfeit sites to pretend to be reputable merchants.

Tally applet   Describes the merchandise in the user's virtual shopping cart, along with quantity and price. It is common at this point to offer the user the opportunity to modify the desired quantity of any item. The Tally applet also displays the total price of the user's purchases.

> **NOTE** There is a clear advantage to having an applet handle the tallying chore, as opposed to using CGI (Common Gateway Interface) scripts. With a CGI solution, any change to the shopping cart (for example, deciding after all not to buy a certain product) must fire off a script. This script consumes CPU cycles on the server and results in loading a new page into the browser. With a JECF applet, minor adjustments are all handled locally without the server's involvement.

Payment Instrument Selection applet   Allows the user to select the method of payment. The shopper's private database contains information from which the JECF is able to build a "wallet" that contains, among other things, representations of the various electronic payment instruments that have been issued to the shopper. Because this applet has access to the contents of the shopper's wallet, it can format a personalized screen so that the shopper can select from among those instruments that have actually been issued to that user. A user who does not have a VISA card, for example, need not be shown an option to charge the purchases to a VISA card. A user with four VISA cards may choose which of these credit cards to use.

Somewhere in these three applets (most likely in Payment Instrument Selection), there is an ultimate OK or Apply button. Clicking on this button brings up one final screen. Unlike the previous applets, which are customized by the merchant and provided on the merchant's Web pages, this final screen is brought up by the JECF. This screen is called the *final confirmation window*. If the user confirms one last time that the purchase is desired, the JECF code initiates the sequence of electronic financial transactions that will cause the payment instrument to be debited and will notify the merchant that the purchase has taken place. The vital payment instrument information (VISA card number and expiration date, for example) is not visible to the merchant.

The final step in the process is for the JECF to display a verification page to the user. This page documents the shopping transaction that just took place. This information is also stored in the shopper's private database, in an entity called the user's *transaction register*. The JECF provides support for service software that can analyze the transaction register.

The Wallet Layer

As described in the previous section, the JECF extends the shopping-cart metaphor to include the act of opening a wallet, looking inside, and selecting an instrument of payment. Two very important characteristics of real-world wallets are that they are personal and they are private. A JECF wallet is built on a user's individual database. The information within the wallet—and most especially the information that grants permission to spend the user's money—is guarded by security mechanisms that are new in revision 1.1 of the JDK. The JECF security apparatus relies heavily on the digital signature mechanism.

> **NOTE** Digital signatures are part of the Java 1.1 Security API. Signatures are based on a public key/private key encryption scheme. With such a scheme, entities (people and organizations) have public and private keys. These keys are large numbers that are mathematically related according to a complicated algorithm. The private key is known only to the entity; the public key is published. The public key is used to verify that a digital signature has been generated by the owner of the private key. The advantage of this scheme is that it is impossible (or nearly impossible) to deduce the private key from the public key.

A wallet is a collection of cassettes, or instruments, which are signed collections of Java class packages. Cassettes are described in the next section.

The Cassette Layer

The JECF uses the cassette mechanism to represent payment instruments and financial service applications. Payment instruments include the following:

- Credit cards

- Debit cards

- Pre-authorized payments

- Electronic checks

- Frequent flier miles

- Coupons

Service applications include the following:

- Accounting

- Budgeting and household management

- Tax analysis

- Banking

- Stock and bond brokerage

A *cassette* is a collection of Java packages. These packages are combined into a compressed Java Archive file (JAR file) and signed by a trusted authority. This trusted authority might be the issuer of the credit card represented by the cassette. The JECF uses the identity of the authority to grant access permissions to the user's private database.

Cassette Identity

As a security safeguard, every JECF cassette must have an *identity*. An identity is a subclass of the new `CassetteIdentifier` class (in package `java.commerce.cassette`). The organization that signs the cassette puts identical `CassetteIdentifier` classes in each package in the cassette. The cassette specification requires every package to have an identity, and the Java language specifies that every class name within a package must be unique. Thus, it is impossible for an attacker to insinuate a counterfeit identity into a cassette's package.

The `CassetteIdentifier` class (and therefore its subclasses) provides methods that describe the signer. The following are some of the methods of the `CassetteIdentifier` class:

`String getName()`   Returns the identity's common name.

`String getVersion()`   Returns the version of the identity.

Along with an identity, the JECF uses the digital-signature method for authentication.

Roles and Access Control

The JECF uses a design model of *roles*, *ultimate objects*, and *permit objects* to enforce access control. The `Ticket.stamp()` method tells whether an object plays a particular role. Tickets are discussed in the next section.

To understand the role mechanism and the JECF access control model, consider two cassettes. One implements a credit card payment instrument, and it will need to both read and write the user's private database. The other cassette implements a budget-analysis service. It will certainly need to read the database, but there is no reason for it to write the database. Clearly, the first cassette should have read/write permission on the database; the second should have read-only permission. In the vocabulary of roles, the credit card payment instrument cassette plays a *modifier* role with respect to the database, and the budget-analysis service cassette plays a *reader* role with respect to the database.

The JECF uses a design pattern called Capability to provide a flexible permission scheme that is extremely robust. To extend the example of the two cassettes accessing the user's database, suppose that access to the database is provided by an object called userDB. In the Capability design pattern, userDB is known as the *ultimate object*. An additional layer is created between the cassettes and the database, but it is userDB that the cassettes ultimately wish to access.

The extra layer is called the *permit* layer. Cassettes never make direct method calls to the userDB object. Instead, they obtain an object from the permit layer and make calls to that permit object; it is the permit object that makes calls to the userDB object. Each permit type corresponds to a role. In our example there are two roles: *database modifier* and *database reader*.

Permits are interfaces, not classes. This allows the JECF to take advantage of the fact that interfaces may have multiple inheritance.

NOTE   It is illegal in Java to define a class that extends two or more superclasses. It is perfectly legal, however, to do this with interfaces. Thus there is nothing wrong with the following declaration:

```
interface A extends B, C, D, E, F { … }.
```

The example needs to have one permit type that supports database reading and writing, and another that supports only reading. The JECF style would be to create three interfaces: one to support reading, one to support writing, and one to support both. The last interface would simply inherit from the first two. The code below shows how this would be done, assuming the existence of a class called `Data` that represents information to be read or written.

```
interface DBReadPermit
{
    Data read();
}

interface DBWritePermit
{
    void write(Data d);
}

interface DBReadWritePermit extends DBReadPermit, DBWritePermit
{
    // Nothing in here; all methods are inherited.
}
```

Consider the budget-analysis cassette. It never receives a handle to the `userDB` object, which is the ultimate object. Because its role is database reader, it can only receive a handle to some object that implements the `DBReadPermit` interface. This permit object forbids writing to the database because it has no methods that write. This is the essence of the Capability design pattern.

The next section examines the mechanism for providing appropriate permits.

Tickets, Gates, and Permits

Access permission for a particular JECF resource is based on the identity of the client code (the client being the software entity that wishes to access the resource) and the role played by that client. In the example, one client is the credit card payment instrument. The resource is the database, and the role is database modifier. The JECF uses a ticket/gate architecture to ensure that clients receive access permits that correspond to their roles.

A *ticket* is an object that describes an identity and a role. Anyone can create a *role*, which is essentially a public/private key pair. The role's public key could be embedded in the financial institution's cassette. Clients could then use these tickets to prove their identity and role. In particular, tickets are used as inputs to *gate* methods, which return permits. In the example, there would be three gate methods:

```
DBReadPermit dataBase_ReadPermit(Ticket t, // other params)
DBWritePermit dataBase_WritePermit(Ticket t, // others)
DBReadWritePermit dataBase_ReadWritePermit(Ticket t, // others)
```

The form of each of these would be similar to the first:

```
DBReadPermit dataBase_ReadPermit (Ticket t) Throw SecurityException {
    if (t.stamp (ReadDBRole))
        return new DBReadPermit();
    else
        throw new SecurityException();
```

TIP
The JECF uses very specific naming conventions for permits, tickets, and gate methods. Sun has posted documents that detail these conventions on the Java Commerce Home Page at http://www.javasoft.com/products/commerce/.

The gate methods inspect the tickets to determine whether the client may access the requested resource. (The resource is specified in the other input parameters to the gate methods, designated by `// other params` in the list above.) If the resource request is legitimate, the gate method returns a permit object to the client; otherwise, a `SecurityException` is thrown. This permit object provides methods that support the operations permitted to the client; operations forbidden to the client are not supported by the permit object.

Summary

The JECF provides support for applet-based shopping and other financial transactions. The three layers in the JECF architecture are the Merchant Applet layer, Wallet layer, and Cassette layer.

The JECF is both secure and extensible. New payment instruments and new online financial services will likely be invented as electronic shopping and other forms of Internet commerce become an accepted part of everyday life. These instruments and services can be implemented as JECF cassettes and will be able to take advantage of the Java security apparatus.

Java Servlets

- Advantages of servlets

- Servlet classes and methods

- Java Web Server configuration for servlets

- Server-side includes

- Communication between servlets

The Java Web Server, formerly known as Jeeves, is JavaSoft's own Web server. The Java Web Server is just a part of a larger framework, intended to provide you not just with a Web server, but also with tools to build customized network servers for any Internet or Intranet client-server system. The most interesting part of the Java Web Server distribution, from a programmer's point of view, is the Servlet API. Servlets are to a Web server what applets are to the browser.

This chapter discusses the Servlet API and the origin of the servlet as an improved form of CGI (Common Gateway Interface). The examples demonstrate the use of servlets in HTTP environments, and the key Servlet API mechanisms are introduced.

Although, as programmers, you will be mainly concerned with the techniques for coding servlets, the chapter also covers some of the basic elements of the Java Web Server configuration. This knowledge will allow you to set up the server for servlet support and install and try out the examples.

In addition to the fundamental facilities of servlets and the supporting Web server configuration, this chapter also discusses the server-side include (SSI) mechanism as it applies to servlets, as well as a number of techniques for arranging communication between servlets.

CGI Limitations

When HTML and the World Wide Web were first invented, the content of each displayed page was essentially static. Each URL referred directly to either a fixed page or a fixed element of a page. To allow for the possibility of more interaction, and hence for pages that are tailored to an individual request, the CGI mechanism was introduced.

CGI allows a URL to contain a basic reference, which is not to a page of HTML, but to a program. In addition to that basic reference, parameters to control the execution can also be passed from the browser into the CGI program.

Although CGI is quite simple to use, both from the user's and the server administrator's point of view, it has a number of weaknesses:

Low performance   Most CGI programs are written using interpreted languages such as Unix shell scripts and PERL. This is not a requirement of the CGI specification, but appears to be the popular option. Using compiled languages improves speed but tends to raise platform-dependency issues.

Startup time   CGI programs run as separate processes, which generally involves significant startup time. This overhead occurs each time the program is invoked. The startup time is compounded if you are using an interpreter.

Poor inter-CGI communication   Because each invocation of a CGI program starts a separate process, communicating between invocations must usually be done via files, and hence can be quite slow. Communicating between different CGI programs on the same server is similarly cumbersome.

Security   Some variations of CGI have suffered from significant security weaknesses. Even when more recent standards and relatively safe languages like PERL are used, the system does not have a basic security framework, but relies instead on a collection of ad hoc rules.

A number of enhancements have been made to CGI to address these limitations. FastCGI avoids the process-startup overhead by using persistent processes, but using FastCGI interprocess communication is still slow. Some C language APIs allow for programs to run inside the server, but these APIs are platform dependent and difficult to secure; they also tend to be rather complex.

Another choice that you now have is to use a servlet. Servlets can do the things that CGI is used for, and they have many advantages over CGI scripts.

Introducing Servlets and the Java Web Server

Since the arrival of Java, applets have provided a mechanism for Web pages to have not just tailored information, but actually interactive and dynamic content. As you've learned, with an applet, the process is run on the browser's own machine. In general, this configuration is an advantage because it improves response time and reduces network bandwidth requirements. But this configuration might present problems if your program has either of these requirements:

Privileged access to server facilities   An applet generally does not have any special access to services and information on a server. Even the server that supplied the applet cannot, in the absence of something like a digital signature, distinguish between a request from an applet that it might want to trust and any other request. Hence, an applet cannot be granted the right to read, say, a database on the server unless full access to that database is given to any HTTP request.

Protection of proprietary algorithms   In a number of ways, Java's bytecode is easier to reverse-engineer than other machine languages. This is partly because it is difficult to generate obfuscated bytecodes—the demands of the bytecode verifier will reject as illegal many forms of code that are not straightforward. Because of this fact, a proprietary algorithm of significant value should generally not be entrusted to an applet.

If either of these considerations applies, a servlet might be the better choice. With a servlet approach, the server can grant full access to local facilities, such as databases, and trust that the servlet itself will control the amount and precise nature of access that is effectively afforded to external users. So, for example, the rate at which requests can be made could be limited, and the origin of requests can be monitored and verified. If a proprietary algorithm is built into a servlet, the code never passes beyond the boundaries of the server; only the results that it produces do. If the code is not passed to the client, it cannot be saved and disassembled.

A servlet and applet can be used as a pair to gain both the benefits of servlets and of the interactive nature of applets. This paired approach can also be used to provide optimization of the data stream, possibly involving actual compression, and, if desired, encryption. The data streams can be optimized in many cases simply by appropriate use of the binary methods of the `DataInputStream` and `DataOutputStream` classes in the `java.io` package, or by using object serialization. Encryption is typically handled by classes such as `SSLSocket`, which implements a Secure Sockets Layer for use in a Java program.

To accompany the introduction of the new servlet standard, a new Web server has been produced. The Java Web Server is JavaSoft's Web server, written in Java, which supports the use of servlets. It is not part of the JDK distribution, but you can download it from the JavaSoft site: http://jeeves.javasoft.com. Because Java Web Server is written in Java, it can be used on any Java-capable platform. It also provides the security reassurances of Java in a networked environment. Other servers are already starting to announce support for this mechanism. For example, support for Netscape Enterprise and FastTrack 2.x is provided, with Microsoft IIS 2.x/3.x and Apache expected in the next release.

NOTE

Running servlets requires a degree of administrative effort. Early versions of the Java Web Server had very few administrative support tools, requiring that all configuration be done with a text editor. More recently, interactive GUI-based administration tools have been added. Other Web servers have their own configuration mechanisms, which are likely to be similar to the ones in JavaSoft's Web server. Configuration for the Java Web Server is discussed in this chapter. If you will be using another type of Web server with your Java servlets, see the documentation for your system for configuration information.

The Java Servlet Development Kit

Before creating any servlets, you need to install JavaSoft's Java Servlet Development Kit (JSDK). The kit includes the `java.servlet` and `sun.servlet` packages, sample servlets, and, for Windows 95 and NT, ServletRunner, which is an appletviewer-like tool to test servlets.

TIP

For more information about the Windows-specific ServletRunner, refer to the online documentation provided with the JSDK.

In order for your servlets to find the servlet packages, you need to add their location to your `CLASSPATH` environment variable. For example, on a Windows 95 or NT system, with the JSDK installed in the default location, the following will do the trick:

```
set CLASSPATH=%CLASSPATH%;C:\Program Files\JSDK\lib\classes.zip
```

The Servlet API

At a superficial level, a servlet is much like an applet. It does not run as an application or start at a static `main()` method; rather, it is loaded, and an instance is created. When the instance exists, it is given an environment from which it can determine details, such as the parameters with which it has been invoked.

In an `Applet` class, the behavior is largely determined by a few methods, which are called by the browser. These methods are `init()`, `start()`, `stop()`, `destroy()`, and `paint()`. In a `Servlet` class, the same basic concept is used, but the particular methods of interest are slightly different.

When a `Servlet` instance is created, its `init()` method is called. This closely parallels the life cycle of an applet and is intended to allow the servlet to initialize itself.

TIP

> The general rule with the `Applet` class is that `init()` should be called only once, just after construction. A number of browsers have slightly different behaviors in this respect, so that in some environments `init()` might be called several times for less-than-obvious reasons. This situation is best handled by writing `init()` in such a way that it is only necessary to run it once, and if it is called again, it simply reinitializes the applet. This condition is easy to achieve with careful use of the constructor. It seems a sensible precaution to treat `init()` in a `Servlet` class in the same way.

A servlet does not need to become active or inactive in the way that an applet does when it moves in and out of the current page. Also, a servlet does not have a GUI of its own. The `Servlet` class, therefore, does not define the `start()`, `stop()`, or `paint()` methods. The main behavior of the servlet is required in response to a new connection at the server, and that connection results in a call to the `service()` method of the servlet.

The `service()` method takes two parameters. These are defined by interface types called `ServletRequest` and `ServletResponse`. These interface types provide accessor methods that allow the servlet to examine its environment, determine how it has been executed, and then decide what request it has received and what to do to provide a proper response. In particular, the input and output streams that are connected to the browser client are accessible through these parameters.

NOTE The `Servlet` class is declared as abstract because the `service()` method is actually undefined. Hence, to implement a servlet, it is essential to override this method. The nature of the servlet is such that it could not actually perform useful work otherwise.

The basic `Servlet` class is not protocol-specific. However, because a large proportion of servlets are likely to use HTTP as the basis of their communication, a subclass of the `Servlet` class, the `HttpServlet` class, is provided to give additional support methods that are useful when handling this protocol. Most of the examples in this chapter use the `HttpServlet` class.

Two additional support interfaces are defined for use with the `HttpServlet` class: the `HttpServletRequest` interface and the `HttpServletResponse` interface. These interfaces extend the `ServletRequest` and `ServletResponse` interfaces, and provide definitions of additional accessor methods for handling HTTP-specific aspects of a servlet's environment, such as the header information that forms the initial part of an HTTP transaction.

The information that may be read from an `HttpServletRequest` includes the details of the request, such as the path and query string, along with authorization type and header fields. The `HttpServlet-Response` class supports sending of HTTP-specific errors and also of redirects.

A Simple Servlet Example

The following example demonstrates the working environment of an `HttpServlet` object, reporting the values of significant parameters as supplied by the call it receives.

```
import java.io.*;
import java.util.*;
import java.servlet.*;
import java.servlet.http.*;
public class HelloServlet extends HttpServlet {
   public void init() {
      System.out.println("HelloServlet got an init()!");
      File f = new File("");
      f = new File(f.getAbsolutePath());
      System.out.println("HelloServlet current directory is " + f);
   }
   public void service(HttpServletRequest req,
                       HttpServletResponse resp) {
      try {
         ServletOutputStream out = resp.getOutputStream();
         resp.setContentType("text/html");
         resp.setStatus(HttpServletResponse.SC_OK);
         out.println ("<html>");
         out.println ("<head><title>Hello World</title></head>");
         out.println ("<body>");
         out.println ("<H1>Hello World!</H1>");
         out.println ("<H2>This servlet was invoked with:</H2>");
         out.println ("<dl>");
         Enumeration e = req.getHeaderNames();
         while (e.hasMoreElements()) {
            String name = (String)e.nextElement();
            out.println ("<dt>" + name + "</dt><dd>" +
               req.getHeader(name) + "</dd>");
         }
         out.println ("<dt>Request method:</dt><dd>" +
            req.getMethod() + "</dd>");
         out.println ("<dt>Translated Request path info:</dt><dd>" +
            req.getPathTranslated() + "</dd>");
         out.println ("<dt>Request query string:</dt><dd>" +
            req.getQueryString() + "</dd>");
```

```
        out.println ("</dl>");
        out.println ("</body></head></html>");
    } catch (IOException e) {
        // Ignore it. Let the client worry...
    }
  }
}
```

Running the Servlet

To run any servlets, you need a Web server that supports them. This chapter describes the use of JavaSoft's Java Web Server, but any other servlet-enabled server will work. To run a servlet, follow this sequence of actions:

1. Start your Web server, if it is not already running.

2. Configure the server to install the servlet (the servlet must be installed in the Web server).

3. Start your Web browser.

4. Direct the browser to the particular URL that refers to the new servlet.

NOTE Some servers might require that you restart them after installing a new servlet, but this is not the case with JavaSoft's server when using the Web-based interactive administration tools. If you have a server that requires restarting after a servlet is installed, you should perform step 2 before step 1 in the above list.

You will find the source code and bytecode files for this servlet on the CD-ROM. If you are using JavaSoft's server and are unfamiliar with its configuration for running servlets, see the "Servlet Configuration," section later in this chapter. Install the servlet into the Web server and direct your browser to this URL:

```
http://localhost:8080/servlet/HelloServlet?Hello+World
```

Notice that this assumes that you have configured your server to use port 8080. This is the default for the early releases of JavaSoft's server, and it is a sensible choice in any case because it allows the server to run on Unix systems without requiring root privilege.

When the browser has loaded, the page should show a heading and several entries in a list. Figure 17.1 shows an example of the kind of output you can expect to see.

FIGURE 17.1

Typical output from HelloServlet

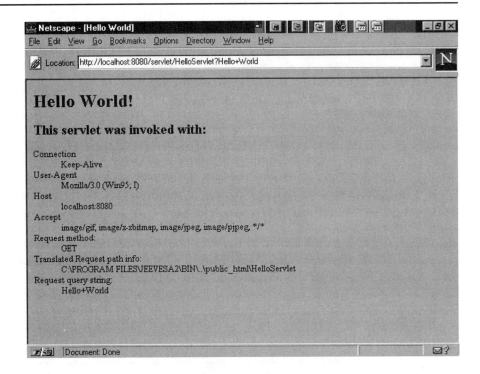

Changing the Query String You can experiment with modifications to the URL. The first part, which describes the protocol, host, port, and path, cannot be changed. The parts after the query character (?) form the *query string*.

The query string is qualifying information that may be changed within certain restrictions. You should not put spaces or nonalphanumeric characters in this string, except for the plus symbol (+), which signifies a space. If you need to represent any other characters, you should find the appropriate ASCII code for the character, in hexadecimal, and use that with a percent symbol (%) as a prefix. For example, the percent symbol itself is represented as %25.

When you change the query string, observe that all the output, except for the last line, remains the same. If you omit the query string entirely and simply use the following:

```
URL http://localhost:8080/servlet/HelloServlet
```

the output reports the request query string as null, which results from attempting to convert a null reference to a `String` object in the servlet itself.

HelloServlet's Classes and Methods

The `HelloServlet` example simply extracts some of the available environment information from the `HttpServletRequest` and `HttpServletResponse` objects that are provided to it as the arguments to its `service()` method. HTML-formatted output is then returned to the caller via the output stream supplied by the server.

The `HelloServlet` class is a subclass of the `HttpServlet` class, rather than a direct subclass of the `GenericServlet` class, because a number of useful utility methods and definitions are provided by the `HttpServlet` class, and most servlets will use HTTP as their protocol. If you wish to write a servlet that uses some other—perhaps entirely proprietary—protocol, you should extend the `GenericServlet` class.

> **NOTE**
>
> The Java Web Server is part of the much larger Server Toolkit. This kit allows you to build your own network server for arbitrary protocols, including ordinary client/server systems; it is not limited to HTTP and Web-related services. However, HTTP servlets provide good examples of the essence of any servlet and are the focus of this chapter. If you will be writing servlets for radically different services, see Chapter 10, which covers network programming. It describes other useful aspects of writing client/server systems with Java.

The GenericServlet class, or more precisely the Servlet interface, defines a method called service(), which takes two arguments that are objects that implement the ServletRequest and Servlet-Response interfaces, respectively. The HttpServlet class defines a new method called service() that takes different argument types. These two arguments are objects that implement the HttpServlet-Request and HttpServletResponse interfaces, respectively. The new service() method therefore overloads the method name, rather than overriding it. Because the Web server thinks of the servlet simply as an object that implements the Servlet interface, and the Web server knows nothing about the HttpServlet class, it will call only the first service() method. In the HttpServlet class, this original service() servlet method is written to pass the call to the new service() method instead.

Inside a servlet, two streams are available for communication with the remote client. This example produces only a page of HTML; it does not read input from the client. Therefore, it requires only the output stream. In either a ServletResponse object or—as is the case with an HttpServlet class like the HelloServlet example—an HttpServletResponse object, you can extract the output stream using the getOutputStream() method. If you are implementing bidirectional communication, such as is required for the POST protocol, you will also need to use the getInputStream() method on the ServletRequest object.

The output from the servlet has two broad parts, which can be thought of as the status part and the content part. In the status part, this example specifies that the content type of its reply is text/html and the status is OK. Both of these operations use methods of the HttpServletResponse object. The first, setContentType(), takes an argument of the String class, which is used to specify the MIME-type string of the response that is to be sent. The status is specified using the setStatus() method, although for a reply of OK, this method is actually redundant.

> **NOTE**
> The `setContentType()` method is actually a member of the parent class `ServletResponse`, and is therefore available for use in servlets using protocols other than HTTP. The `setStatus()` method, however, is defined in the `HttpServletResponse` class and not in its parent class.

After setting up the status parts of the reply, `HelloServlet` then generates the HTML text, which is presented to the user in the client browser window. The output stream obtained from the `HttpServletResponse` object is an instance of the `java.servlet.ServletOutputStream` class, which defines `println()` methods with a variety of overloads supporting different argument types. For this reason, it is not necessary to create an intervening `DataOutputStream`, `PrintStream`, or `PrintWriter` object, although this would be typical practice in similar situations where a stream has been obtained from an underlying service.

There is a minor irritation with the `ServletOutputStream` class, which is that it declares the `println()` method as throwing an `IOException` if trouble occurs with the connection. The `println()` method of the more familiar `PrintStream` class hides this exception from the caller. Because of this exception, the bulk of the body of this `service()` method is wrapped in a `try` block. If the exception occurs in this example, it is simply ignored. In a servlet intended for production use rather than a simple example, the error would probably be logged. Later sections of this chapter examine the log mechanisms available to servlets.

Once the output stream has been obtained, the servlet must construct the page to provide to the client browser. Normally, this will involve some form of calculated or conditional response; otherwise, the page should be defined by a simple HTML text file. The `HelloServlet` object will return an HTML page, which is a typical action, especially for servlets that are constructed based on the `HttpServlet` class. The HTML page is generated through a series of `println` statements.

An earlier version of the development kit included a package of HTML-generation support classes, but that was removed from the current beta release. If they return in the final release, they will make your life easier.

After the initial page headings, a definition list is created. A *definition list* in HTML takes a series of entries, which are headings and body text pairs. The corresponding HTML tags used to define entries in such a list are <DT> and <DD>. The result has the general form of the latter part of this servlet's output, as shown earlier.

Construction of the list does not require any arguments, because the HTML definition list does not have a title of its own, only separate elements. After it has been constructed, the individual elements are added by lines like this one:

```
out.println ("<dt>Request method:</dt><dd>" +
   req.getMethod() + "</dd>");
```

Notice that two arguments are supplied. The first is the title part of the list element, and the second is the text that follows.

The information provided in this particular list is obtained from the request information carried by the first argument of the service() method. This argument is an instance of the HttpServletRequest class. In the HelloServlet example, several pieces of information are extracted and placed into the list; the first few pieces of information that are added are the header values.

An HTTP request has a number of attendant headers that define general aspects of the connection. The precise set of headers will depend on the browser being used to issue the request. You can see from the sample output of this servlet that information describing the actual browser forms one of the header fields. To obtain the headers, a servlet can use one of a number of getHeader() methods. This example, because it is simply going to output all the headers, uses the variation that fetches the enumeration of header names and loops until no more are found.

Normally, a particular header—such as the Accept list, which describes the preferred response types—would be required, and for this purpose another overloaded `getHeader()` method is provided. This method accepts a `String` object as an argument and attempts to find the particular header specified by name in that argument. If any of these `getHeader()` methods cannot find the requested header, they simply return null.

In addition to accessing the headers, several other data items are available to the servlet. The `HelloServlet` example demonstrates three of them, which are obtained using the `getMethod()`, `getPathTranslated()`, and `getQueryString()` methods.

The `getMethod()` method returns the request type. This type is almost always one of the three strings `GET`, `POST`, or `HEAD`, although some other strings are permitted by the definition of HTTP. These strings name the type of request that the Web server received. The method used for general requests from a browser is `GET`. This type of request carries all the information from the browser to the server as part of the URL string. Requests from HTML forms commonly use the `POST` method, which sends the bulk of its data to the server as a stream rather than as part of the URL. In a servlet, this data stream is the input stream obtained from the `ServletRequest` object using the `getInputStream()` method. In the standard JDK HTTP protocol handler, opening the output stream from the client applet automatically makes the request into a `POST` type. The `HEAD` method constitutes a request for header information only, and it is typically used to determine if a cache entry can be reused or if it should be replaced with newer information.

The path information, returned from the `getPathTranslated()` method, describes the path on the server machine from which the servlet was loaded. Hence, for this example, the path information returned, which is specific to the particular installation of the server, is `C:\JEEVES\BIN\..\public_html\HelloServlet`. This information might be very useful if a servlet needs to read from support files.

> **NOTE**
>
> Also related to paths is the `getPathInfo()` method, which returns the path part of the original URL. In the conditions of this example, the `getPathInfo()` method returns `/HelloServlet`, treating the `servlet` part of the original URL as a server directive, not as part of the path itself. This treatment is entirely consistent because it is not actually a directory name (for instance, in the Java Web Server, servlets are typically placed in a directory called servlets, and a translation takes place to convert the /servlet part of the URL). In general, the `getPathInfo()` method is less useful because it does not relate directly to the local file system.

In many conventional requests to CGI services, the URL carries additional argument information that qualifies the particular request. The sample output shown earlier resulted from the full URL:

```
http://localhost:8080/servlet/HelloServlet?Hello+World
```

and, in this case, the query string was reported as `Hello+World`.

The `getQueryString()` method returns the full text of the query string from the invoking URL. Notice that the returned value is still in the URL-encoded format and might need to be converted before it is used.

> **NOTE**
>
> At the time of writing, no standard method existed to facilitate decoding a URL-encoded string, which is surprising because the `URLEncoder` class exists to encode the string in the first place. It is also unfortunate because, although the decoding is a simple operation, it is still one more step you need to take.

Finally, after the definition list has been constructed, the closing HTML statements are added.

Other Important Servlet Methods

The preceding section described the basic use of the `HttpServlet` class and a number of supporting classes. A considerable number of additional methods are provided in the various classes that support servlets.

General Servlet Methods

When the server needs a servlet for the first time, it starts by loading the class, then creating an instance of it. The next step is to call the `init()` method, which can be used for general initialization of the servlet. You should ensure that only initialization is performed in the `init()` method, because it might be called to reset the servlet after it has been used, as explained earlier in this chapter.

Web servers generally keep records about the accesses they receive, and servlets have the opportunity to do so, too. The `log()` method of the `ServletContext` interface takes a `String` argument with which it builds an entry that is written to the server's log file. Logs are generally written into a directory called logs under the server's home directory.

Information about the Request

Five more methods supply additional details about the request itself: `getContentLength()`, `getContentType()`, `getProtocol()`, and the pair `getParameter()` and `getParameterNames()`. These are all member methods of the `ServletRequest` object.

The `getContentLength()` method returns the number of bytes of input that are to be supplied, or `-1` in the event that this number is unknown. It is not good practice to allow a servlet to depend functionally on the content length that is reported, because the responsibility for providing this information rests with the client browser, and therefore the accuracy of the content length information is beyond your control. In general, input on an HTTP connection to a servlet will occur with a `POST` type request, so this value can be ignored for `GET` requests.

The `getContentType()` method returns a string that contains the MIME content type for the data that is to be sent to the servlet from the client browser. If no type has been specified by the client, or the connection is not issuing any data for use by the server, this method returns null. Some browsers specify content types of `text/plain` to indicate that the data is of no special type, some use `content/unknown`, and some use `application/octet-stream`. In general, it is likely that most servlets will expect a fairly specific type of data and may be written to handle just that. It also is likely that one particularly common input type will be argument values from a `POST` request. Form results in a `POST` request are normally reported using the MIME-type `application/x-www-form-urlencoded`.

The protocol used, which will typically be some version of HTTP, is reported by the `getProtocol()` method. This method returns a string of the form `<Protocol>/<major_version>.<minor_version>`. `HTTP/1.0` is a typical return value from a Web browser client, although older browsers still exist that use `HTTP/0.9`. If the browser does not explicitly state the protocol type that it is using, the default (`HTTP/0.9`) is assumed and reported by the `getProtocol()` method.

CGI requests commonly include parameter information encoded onto the end of the URL itself in the form of `name=value` assignments. Multiple parameters should be separated using the ampersand character (`&`). Note that neither the equals symbol nor the ampersand should be converted to the external form using the percent (%) representation discussed earlier, or they will lose their special meaning as separators and simply become part of the query string. Such information can be accessed by a servlet by using the `getParameterNames()` and `getParameter()` methods. If a particular named parameter is expected, it is sufficient to use the `getParameter()` method, which takes a string argument specifying the name of the parameter to match and returns a string that represents the associated value. For example, given a URL like this:

```
http://localhost:8080/servlets/getparameter?quantity=maximum
```

the method call `getParameter("quantity")` would return the `String` value `maximum`. As with applets, all parameters are returned as `String` objects. If your servlet expects, say, an `int`, you must convert it.

In some servlets, it might be inconvenient or impossible to predict the parameter names that are acceptable in advance of the call. In these circumstances, the `getParameterNames()` method is useful. This method returns an enumeration of the strings representing the names, but not the values, of the parameters that have been passed. For each of these names, the associated value can be obtained by calling the `getParameter()` method.

Information about the Client

The request also carries information about the host of the client browser. The `getRemoteAddr()` method returns the IP address of the remote host, and the `getRemoteHost()` method returns its name.

> **WARNING** You should not attribute trust to any remote machine based solely on its name as extracted from either the `getRemoteAddr()` or `getRemoteHost()` method. Such a name will have been obtained from a reverse DNS lookup—a translation of the address into a name—and this process can be subverted by untrusted outsiders. If you need to allocate trust to particular hosts, either look up the name you trust and verify that the remote address you have matches one of those returned, or simply use addresses directly. Forward DNS lookups—that is, name-to-address translation—and actual IP addresses are much more difficult to subvert, especially when the machines are in the same network.

Length of Reply

In addition to the `getOutputStream()` and `setContentType()` methods, the `ServletResponse` object also provides a method for specifying the length of content that is to be returned.

The `setContentLength()` method takes an integer argument that specifies the number of bytes of data that will be returned. Nothing in this method constrains the actual amount of data sent, so be careful to ensure that the value specified is correct. It is not necessary to use this method to set any value if it is difficult or inconvenient to calculate the correct value. However, if you choose not to use the `setContent-Length()` method, the client browser will not be able to display a progress monitor.

TIP
Determining the size of a dynamically constructed page is easiest if the whole page is constructed in a buffer and then transmitted as a whole when complete. This strategy allows the size to be taken from the buffer size.

Accessing HTTP Header Information

A variety of headers are meaningful in the HTTP environment, and these can be accessed using methods in the `HttpServletRequest` and `HttpServletResponse` classes. Header values can be read using methods in the `HttpServletRequest` class. The `Hello-Servlet` example uses the `getHeaderNames()` method; this accesses the headers by their order. Another `getHeader()` method takes a `String` object as an argument and allows searching for specific headers.

Both the `getHeader()` method and `getHeaderNames()` return strings, or an enumeration of strings. Convenience methods are provided to interpret these strings into either integer or date format.

When generating a reply, the headers may be set using a similar set of methods. In this case, the methods are members of the `HttpServlet-Response` object. The basic `setHeader()` method takes two strings as arguments: the first names the header field, and the second specifies the value to be associated with the header. The `setIntHeader()` and `setDateHeader()` methods are convenience methods that take an `int` and a `long` representing a date, respectively.

Servlet Initialization Parameters

When a servlet is first loaded into a server, it can be configured via initialization parameters. These parameters are set by the administrator and are used for localization and installation of the servlet rather than configuration of a particular request. The initialization parameters are named, and the values associated with them can be read into the servlet from the `ServletContext` object—which is an interface to the server itself—by the method `getInitParameter()`. This method takes a string argument that should match the string name of the parameter in question. To obtain a list of all the parameters that have been configured, use the `getInitParameterNames()` method.

Servlet Configuration

In JavaSoft's Java Web Server, a servlet cannot be loaded or executed without prior configuration from the administrator. This is an important security feature. This section briefly outlines how to configure the Java Web Server to enable a servlet.

The Java Web Server is supplied with a collection of servlets and an applet to support configuration from the browser interface. Two particular views within the administration applet are of interest for servlet configuration: the log-in view and the servlet-loading view. The main entry to the administration system is via the URL http://localhost :9090applet.html and is accessed via a Java-enabled browser (port 9090 is the administration port).

In the log-in view, two text fields and a Log in button are presented, as shown in Figure 17.2. The text fields prompt for a username and a password. By default, the administration login uses the username and password `admin`. Entering these into the text fields and selecting the Log in button changes the view to a supervisory control-panel view. This view has a list of the available services. Selecting the Web Page Service choice and clicking on the Manage button displays the administration functions. Selecting the Servlets button changes the view again. Figure 17.3 shows this form.

FIGURE 17.2

Logging in to the Java
Web Server

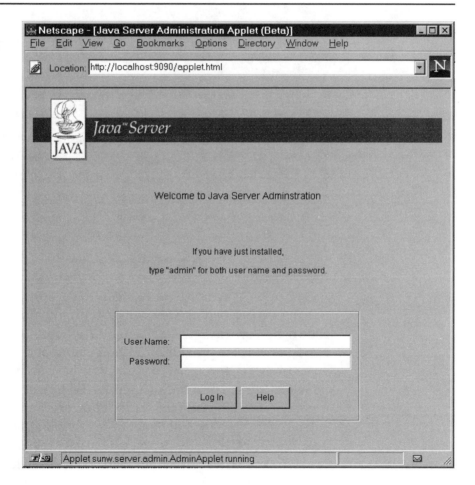

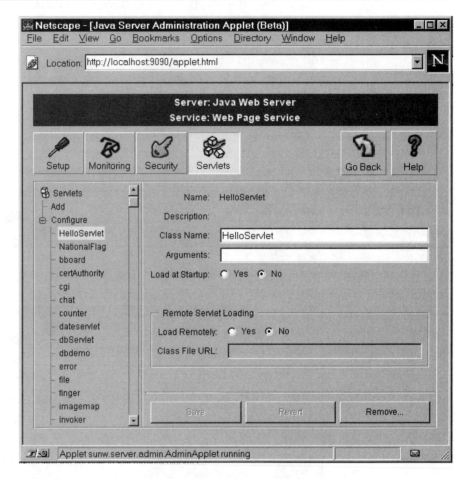

In the servlet-loading view, a list of currently known servlets is
shown along with Add and Configure options. With the Add option,
two text fields are provided for servlet name and class name. After
you add a servlet, you can configure it to have arguments and possibly
remote loading. The name of a servlet can be a descriptive name and
is not restricted to being the same as the class name. The class name
entered should be the fully qualified class name, and the path should
describe the base of any package hierarchy that should be searched.
For HelloServlet, just place **HelloServlet** in both fields, since the servlet
is in the default package.

In configure mode, a pair of radio buttons allow you to indicate whether the servlet should be loaded automatically when the server starts. If this option is not selected, the servlet will be loaded in response to the first client request for its service. Once loaded, a servlet will remain resident in the server until it is shut down. Therefore, most servlets should be loaded at startup unless there is a real possibility that the servlet will not be invoked at all during a server session.

The administration servlets actually act on underlying configuration files, which are maintained in the form of properties in a file called servlets.properties in the server installation's admin\properties\process\javawebserver\adminservice directory. A servlet is defined primarily by an entry of the form *servletname.code=classname*. For example, if a servlet referred to as Useful is defined in a class called Use1, the entry in the servlets.properties file would be Useful .code=Use1. Such an entry represents, in a single record, both the servlet name and the class that is to be loaded.

The code base for a servlet defaults to the servlets directory of the server installation but may be overridden by an entry of the form *servletname.codebase=URL*.

Arguments to the servlet are specified in the servlets.properties files by an entry of the form *servletname.initArgs=comma_separated_list*. For example, if two arguments called one and two are to be specified for a servlet called Test, and the arguments are to have the values yes and maybe, respectively, the servlet .properties file would contain the entry Test.initArgs=one=yes, two=maybe.

A Fuller Example of a Servlet

Now you are ready for a fuller servlet example. The following servlet combines a number of techniques to return an image representing the national flag of the country in which the host is apparently located. Of course, this idea is not entirely reliable, because many multinational and US-based companies use the .com top-level domain for all their offices, regardless of geographical location. Hence, a connection from a Sun Microsystems office in the United Kingdom would appear as being from sun.com and be treated as if it were of US origin. However, despite this limitation, the example demonstrates a number of interesting and useful techniques.

```java
import java.io.*;
import java.util.*;
import java.servlet.*;
import java.servlet.http.*;

public class NationalFlag extends HttpServlet {
    File flagDir;
    Hashtable flags = new Hashtable();

    private static final int SUFFIX      = 0;
    private static final int FILENAME    = 1;
    private static final int CONTENTTYPE = 2;

    private String defflagname[] = {
        "us",    "usa-flag.jpg", "image/jpeg"
    };

    private String flagnames[][] = {
        {"nl",   "nl-flag.jpg",   "image/jpeg"},
        {"fr",   "fr-flag.jpg",   "image/jpeg"},
        {"uk",   "uk-flag.jpg",   "image/jpeg"}
    };

    public void init() throws ServletException {
        String fileDir = getInitParameter("flagDirectory");
        if (fileDir == null) {
            fileDir = "servlets" + File.separator;
        }
        flagDir = new File(fileDir);
        if (!(flagDir.exists() && flagDir.isDirectory())) {
            log("Invalid flagDirectory value specified");
            throw new ServletException("Can't find flag Directory");
        }
```

```java
    else {
       File f = new File(flagDir, defflagname[FILENAME]);
       if (!(f.exists() && f.canRead())) {
          log("can't find default flag ");
          throw new ServletException("Can't find default flag");
       }
    }
    for (int i = 0; i < flagnames.length; i++) {
       flags.put(flagnames[i][0], flagnames[i]);
    }
}


public void service(HttpServletRequest req,
                             HttpServletResponse resp)
    throws IOException {
    String country = null;
    if (req.getParameter("country") != null) {
       country = req.getParameter("country");
    }
    else {
       country = req.getRemoteHost();
       int i = country.lastIndexOf('.');
       if (i != -1) {
          country = country.substring(i + 1);
       }
    }

    String [] flagdef = (String [])(flags.get(country));
    if (flagdef == null) {
       flagdef = defflagname;
    }

    try {
       resp.setContentType(flagdef[2]);
       File f = new File(flagDir + flagdef[1]);

       int size = (int)f.length();
       resp.setContentLength(size);

       byte [] buffer = new byte[size];
       FileInputStream in = new FileInputStream(f);
       in.read(buffer);
```

```
            resp.getOutputStream().write(buffer);
        }
        catch (IOException e) {
            log("Trouble: " + e);
            throw e;
        }
        finally {
            resp.getOutputStream().close();
        }
    }
}
```

Running the Servlet

To run this example, you need a running Web server that supports the servlet mechanism. Copy the class file from the CD-ROM into the appropriate directory in your server hierarchy.

This example requires the flag image files, too. Copy all the .jpg files from the CD-ROM into the servlet directory of your server.

In operation, this servlet must be able to locate the flag files. Although it uses the initialization parameter `flagDirectory` to allow these to be placed anywhere convenient, the servlet calculates a default directory if this parameter is not set. Provided your servlet directory is called servlets and is a subdirectory beneath the server's default directory, you will not need to set this parameter. (Note that this default directory might change between releases.)

Once the files are in the correct places, configure the server to load this servlet and then load the servlet from a browser. Typically, this would mean loading the URL:

```
http://localhost:8080/servlet/NationalFlag
```

If you have completed the installation according to the needs of your server, you should expect to see a flag. It will probably be the Stars and Stripes, as the local connection suggested here will probably not advertise your full domain name, even if you are in a non-US domain. However, you might see a representation of another national flag.

Because it is difficult in most cases to test this servlet from different geographical locations—or even to simulate the effect by modifying naming tables—and because the genuine local host name will be hidden in many installations, this example checks for a parameter that overrides the host name in controlling the choice of flag to return. The parameter is called country, and it may be set to any of the values usa, uk, nl, or fr. These are the only countries that are supported by the image files on the CD-ROM. Test other countries by directing your browser to a URL of this form:

```
http://localhost:8080/servlet/NationalFlag?country=uk
```

You should find that the flag displayed changes to one appropriate to the country parameter value. In this particular case, you should see the Union Jack.

In normal use, this servlet would be embedded in a page using the IMG tag. A sample Web page is located on the CD-ROM in the file NatFlag.html.

Copy this file into a suitable subdirectory in a public directory of your server and direct your browser to that URL. Provided you installed the NationalFlag servlet so that it is at the URL used above, you will see the Stars and Stripes embedded in a normal HTML page. If your servlet installation is different, you will need to edit the NatFlag.html file to reflect the particulars of your installation.

The NationalFlag Servlet's Classes and Methods

The first part of the NationalFlag servlet is its init() method. This method determines the directory from which image files are to be loaded and verifies that the default flag can be found in that directory. The init() method completes by building a hashtable containing the other flags that are available.

Each time the servlet is invoked, it tests to see whether the country parameter has been supplied; if it has, this value is used to determine which flag to return. If not, the host name of the client is used instead. Once the flag has been chosen, it is loaded into a buffer. The content type and length are set appropriately, and then the image data is sent to the client.

The servlet comprises two parts: the `init()` method and the `service()` method itself. The `init()` method performs the one-time initialization. First, it checks whether an initialization parameter called `flagDirectory` has been set. This parameter may be used to specify the directory in which the supporting flag image files are located. If no value is found for the `flagDirectory` variable, a default is assumed, which is the subdirectory servlets beneath the servlet's default directory. For the Java Web Server, the current working directory of a running servlet is the base directory of the server, and hence is the parent directory of the servlets directory.

Once a directory has been chosen as a string, a `File` object is constructed to represent it. Using that object, the `init()` method checks whether the file it describes is an existing directory. If it isn't, a log entry is made indicating the nature of the problem, and a servlet exception is thrown.

Provided the directory chosen exists, the `init()` method proceeds by checking whether it contains a readable file for use as the default flag. The name for this file is taken from the `defflagname` array of strings. As before, if this is found not to be the case, a log entry is made, and a servlet exception is thrown to indicate the problem.

If the `init()` method has found the default flag file, a `Hashtable` object is filled with descriptions of each known country, the associated flag filename, and the content type that describes the file. In this example, the `Hashtable` is filled from a predefined array, but in a production implementation, it could be filled using either properties or some other external file. Such an approach would allow greater flexibility and, hence, permit the addition of new flags without requiring recompilation.

NOTE

The definitions of the `init()` method in the `Servlet` interface, the `GenericServlet` class, and the `HttpServlet` class allow the method to throw a `ServletException` object if required. This allowance is important because it provides a means for the servlet to indicate to the server that the initialization has failed. If no exception is thrown, the `init()` method would be incorrectly deemed to have completed successfully, and the servlet would be called whenever a request was received. This would then need to be rejected each time by the `service()` method.

The `service()` method must determine which flag image should be returned. If a `country` parameter is set for the request, the value of that parameter is used to determine the flag. However, if no `country` parameter is defined, the host name of the client is looked up, and the last part, following the last occurrence of a period, is used. The intention is that if a connection is received from a machine with, for example, the host name `jaques.delores.fr`, the `fr` part is extracted and taken to represent the connection's country of origin.

Once a country value has been determined, either from the end of the host name or from a parameter, it is used as the key to look up the corresponding flag in the hashtable of known flags. If no match is found in that table, the default flag is used. Note that in the NationalFlag example, the default flag is not actually entered in the `Hashtable` itself, which means that the handling of US connections is indistinguishable from the handling of undetermined connections. If you change this behavior under default conditions to return a special image indicating an unrecognized connection, all the various US suffixes (.com, .edu, and so forth) should be added to the `Hashtable`.

Each entry in the hashtable is an array of three strings. These describe the country identifier, the name of the flag file, and the MIME content type of the file. The country identifier is used as the key for the hashtable because this is the value that must be looked up to determine which flag is required. When a country has been identified, the MIME content type of the response is specified using the third of these strings from the hashtable entry. A `File` object is also created using the directory that was determined by the `init()` method and the individual filename from the second element of the hashtable entry. This `File` object is used to determine the actual size in bytes of the flag file, and this value is used to set the content length of the response. The length allows the client browser to indicate correctly the progress of the download.

A buffer is allocated using the indicated file size, and the whole file is read in via a `FileInputStream` object. Once this buffer has been filled, it is written to the output stream of the `HttpServletResponse` object, and thereby to the client.

During the execution of the `service()` method, a number of different methods are called that might cause an `IOException` object to be thrown. Any of these would be very difficult to recover from effectively, so in this servlet any such problem simply causes a log entry and is passed back to the server.

Regardless of any exceptions that might occur, the output channel is closed before the servlet returns. Any exception that occurs during this closure is simply passed to the server and otherwise ignored.

Server-Side Includes

The Java Web Server has the ability to perform a *server-side include* (SSI) using a servlet. With server-side inclusion, the server converts a placeholder in an HTML document into alternative dynamically calculated text each time the document is served to a client.

A server-side include is requested in two ways:

- The document carries the extension .shtml rather than the normal .html.

- The point at which the inclusion should be made is marked with a special tag.

Most servers, other than the Java Web Server, have adopted an HTML comment format to indicate the point of inclusion. In Java-Soft's server, the servlet tag is used. The format of the servlet tag is similar to the applet tag, and in its minimum form looks like this:

```
<servlet name=ServletName>
</servlet>
```

The servlet itself does not have a user interface at the client; therefore, a servlet tag, unlike an applet tag, does not require, and in fact cannot have, a width or height parameter. Furthermore, because the servlet is conventionally referenced by a name other than its class name, it is not necessary to specify a class name in this tag. If both a name and the class name are specified in the servlet tag, and the named servlet is already loaded in the server, that servlet will be invoked by its name. But if the servlet tag in an .shtml file has only the servlet name part, without a class name specified, the server checks all loaded servlets for the name given. If the servlet is not found preloaded, the tag is simply ignored.

However, with an appropriate servlet tag, it is not always necessary for a servlet to be preloaded. If the class name and servlet name are specified in the servlet tag, and the servlet is not found by name, it will be loaded using the specified class name and registered in the server for future use by the name given. If a class name part, but no servlet name part, is specified in the tag, the servlet will be reloaded every time the include is requested, which should be avoided.

The full format for specifying a server-side included servlet is:

```
<servlet name=ServletName code=ServletCode
    initParam1=initArg1 initParam2=initArg2 ...>
    <param name=param1 value=val1>
</servlet>
```

Notice that named parameters can be specified, using a format that exactly mimics the one used for applet parameters. Also, initialization parameters can be specified as part of the main part of the servlet tag.

Inter-Servlet Communication

One of the difficulties with standard CGI is that of communication. With traditional CGI mechanisms, communication between different CGI scripts tends to be rather slow because it involves either reading and writing files, or perhaps using pipes to communicate between different processes.

Servlets are persistent in that once the server starts one, the servlet remains in existence to service all future requests, and, also, servlets all exist in the same Virtual Machine (VM) and hence in the same process space. These two considerations make it possible for different servlets to communicate conveniently and efficiently.

To effect communication between two servlets, the servlets must be able to obtain references to each other and must be designed to communicate. This section discusses these two aspects. Of course, the servlets must also have something useful to say to each other.

Finding a Servlet

When a servlet runs, it does so inside a Web server. The server provides a number of facilities to the servlets it runs, including the ability to locate other servlets on the same server. The Web server, from the API point of view, is encapsulated in the `ServletContext` interface, similar in principle to `AppletContext`. The servlet itself can obtain a reference to the Web server by issuing a call to the `getServletContext()` method. Note that this method is not defined in the `Servlet` interface, but in the `GenericServlet` class.

Once the servlet context has been obtained, two methods are available for locating servlets:

`getServlets()` Returns an enumeration of all the servlets in the server. Inside a servlet, this method cannot return an empty enumeration, because the servlet itself must be included in the list.

`getServlet()`   Takes a string argument and returns a reference to the servlet named by that string. This method will return null if the server does not know about the servlet that was requested.

Both the `getServlets()` and `getServlet()` methods will return only those servlets that are currently loaded. Neither will cause the server to load any servlet, even if its name is known. For this reason, it is usually required that if servlets are to communicate, they be marked as loaded at startup in the administration system.

Communicating between Servlets

You can implement communication between servlets in several different ways. These are methods that allow programs of various types to communicate, and are not specific to servlets.

Calling Each Other's Methods

If the two servlets are written at the same time and are able to know each other's public API when they are compiled, they can call each other's methods. This situation would allow, for example, each servlet to implement a `getInfo()` and `setState()` method—the actual names are unimportant—so that each can call the appropriate method to control the other.

Using Stream Classes

It might be appropriate to use the `PipedInputStream` and `PipedOutputStream` classes. These classes are discussed in Chapter 15 as one of the ways that different threads can communicate, and their use is equally appropriate for servlets. To set up such a communication, each servlet must be able to obtain a handle on the streams of the other. One possible approach is described by the following code fragments:

```
public class TalkerServlet extends GenericServlet {
    public final PipedOutputStream myOutput = new PipedOutputStream();
```

```
// body of class…
}

public class ListenerServlet extends GenericServlet {
    private PipedInputStream myInput = null;
    public void service(ServletRequest req,
                        ServletResponse resp)
        throws ServletException {
        if (myInput == null) {
            ServletContext context = getServletContext();
            Servlet theTalker = context.getServlet("TalkerServlet");
            if ((theTalker == null) ||
              !(theTalker instanceof TalkerServlet)) {
                throw new ServletException("Cannot find Talker");
            }
            TalkerServlet ts = (TalkerServlet)theTalker;
            try {
                    myInput = new PipedInputStream(ts.myOutput);
            }
            catch (IOException io) {
                    myInput = null; // ?
            }
        }
        // main body of service()
    }
}
```

In this scheme, one end of the input/output stream pair must be created first; in this case, the output has been chosen, and it is created at the moment the TalkerServlet object is instantiated. Some time later, the other end of the stream can be created. In this example, the other end of the stream is not created in an init() method because there would be a risk of the servlets being created in the wrong order. To avoid this problem, the other end of the stream is created during the first call to the service() method of the ListenerServlet object. Provided that both the talker and the listener are loaded at server startup, this approach will work safely.

This approach is equally applicable for bidirectional communication. Although this sample code shows only one stream being set up, it would be simple to add an instance of the PipedInputStream class to the `TalkerServlet` class and attach that to an output stream in the listener in the same way.

Using Static Variables

It is possible to use static variables as the basis for communication between classes. For example, using input and output streams, the mechanism shown in the previous section could be modified to use a static variable to provide access to the output stream. In this way, it would not be necessary to use the `ServletContext` object to obtain a handle on the other `Servlet` object. Consider the following code fragments:

```
public class TalkerServlet extends GenericServlet {
   public static final PipedOutputStream myOutput;

   static {
     try {
        myOutput = new PipedOutputStream();
     }
     catch (IOException e) {
     }
   // body of class…
}


public class ListenerServlet extends GenericServlet {
   private PipedInputStream myInput;
public ListenerServlet() throws IOException {
      myInput = new PipedInputStream(
TalkerServlet.myOutput);
   }
   // main body of class
}
```

Usually, the fact that the value of a static variable is shared between all instances makes this type of variable subject to misuse and misunderstanding in a fashion similar to global variables in non–object-oriented languages. However, in this case, because only one instance of a servlet is ever created in a Web browser environment, these particular difficulties do not arise.

By using the static variable, observe that the `TalkerServlet` class can create and advertise its `PipedOutputStream` object at the moment the class is loaded, which ensures that the `ListenerServlet` object can refer to that output stream immediately. The approach also avoids the earlier requirement of ensuring that the servlets be loaded by the server at startup, because the VM itself will resolve any dependencies between the classes, as the language clearly defines the proper behavior. So if the `ListenerServlet` class refers to the `TalkerServlet` class in this way, the system, rather than the browser, ensures that the `TalkerServlet` class will be loaded if it is not already loaded.

Using Once Objects

A variation on the static variable idea is the concept of a *once* object. The once object is effectively an object that is created and advertised as a static variable but that has some protection against corruption from outside the class. You can set up a once object by adhering to the following guidelines:

- Declare at least one constructor and mark all constructors for the class as private.

- Declare a private static variable of the same type as the class itself.

- Declare a nonprivate synchronized static method, which returns an instance of the class.

- In the static method, if the private variable described above is non-null, simply return it. However if the variable is null, create an instance of the class (remember, the private constructors are accessible to this method) and put the reference to the new object into the variable. Now return the value of that variable.

A code fragment following these guidelines looks like this:

```
public class Once {
    private static Once myself;
    private Once() {
```

```
      // set me up
   }
   public static synchronized Once newOnce() {
      if (myself == null) {
         myself = new Once();
      }
      return myself;
   }
}
```

Now if two servlets need to communicate, they can both have instances variables that are of this Once class. The variables themselves do not need to be static, and can be private, but they will necessarily both refer to the same object. The classes would look like this:

```
public class XXXXServlet extends HttpServlet {
   private Once myOnce = Once.newOnce();
   // rest of class
}
```

This approach is effectively just syntactic sugar on the basic idea of a static variable in the classes, but has the—potentially great—advantage of loosening the coupling between the talker and listener classes. When you use static variables directly, one of these classes must know about, and use explicitly, the other class and the variable name within it. Such coupling reduces maintainability of the classes. With the once object approach, this coupling is significantly reduced. The talker class could change its name and function entirely, the variable in which it stores its reference to the shared object could be changed or even deleted entirely, and the listener class would be unaffected.

TIP The applicability of the once object approach is not restricted to servlets. It is a powerful design pattern in general object-oriented programming, also known as Singleton. Its value derives from its ability to loosen the coupling between components as just described.

Summary

This chapter started by explaining the limitations of using CGI, an earlier mechanism for dynamically calculated content. Then it described the relative advantages of using servlets and a Java-capable Web server for providing these services.

You have learned how to use the Servlet API classes and methods for creating servlets, including the `service()` method and the `HttpServletRequest` and `HttpServletResponse` classes.

Next, you learned how to configure the Java Web Server, JavaSoft's Web server, to support your servlets. Other Java-based Web servers are available, and it is likely that they will need similar configuration to support servlets.

Finally, a number of possible mechanisms for implementing communication between servlets were described. These mechanisms are appropriate for a variety of purposes and can actually be used for communication between all sorts of classes, not just servlets.

If you expect to be writing extensive network-based services, the Java Web Server and the Servlet API are likely to reward your study. In addition, if those services will connect to corporate databases, you should ensure that you are familiar with the general techniques of one of the database interface mechanisms, such as JDBC (Java Database Connectivity), which is used for relational database interfacing. For more information about JDBC, see Chapter 11.

The 1.1 APIs

This appendix lists the APIs of all the classes and interfaces of the 1.1 Java Developer's Kit. This chapter is intended as a reference, not as instructional material, so data and method signatures are given without additional textual explanation. (Sun's online API Web pages are freely distributed, and the explanations go into reasonable depth. To repeat that information here would require several hundred additional pages.)

The packages are presented in alphabetical order. Within each package, the classes and interfaces are presented in alphabetical order. Within each class and interface, the public data, public constructors, and public methods are presented in alphabetical order. In the data section, static variables appear first, followed by instance variables. In the methods section, static methods appear first, followed by non-static methods. Non-public data and methods are omitted, again in the spirit of creating a useful reference rather than a complete manual that would require hundreds of additional pages.

NOTE These APIs were generated by software that read and parsed the source code for the Beta 3 release of the 1.1 JDK. (The software is available for a reasonable licensing fee; please send e-mail to authorph@sgsware.com for more details.) Everything below comes directly from the source.

The *java.applet* Package

The *Applet* Class

```
public Class Applet extends Panel
```

Methods

```
public void destroy();
public AppletContext getAppletContext();
public String getAppletInfo();
public AudioClip getAudioClip(URL url);
public AudioClip getAudioClip(URL url, String name);
public URL getCodeBase();
public URL getDocumentBase();
public Image getImage(URL url);
public Image getImage(URL url, String name);
public Locale getLocale();
public String getParameter(String name);
public String[][] getParameterInfo();
public void init();
public boolean isActive();
public void play(URL url);
public void play(URL url, String name);
public void resize(Dimension d);
public void resize(int width, int height);
public final void setStub(AppletStub stub);
public void showStatus(String msg);
public void start();
public void stop();
```

The *AppletContext* Interface

```
public Interface AppletContext
```

Methods

```
Applet getApplet(String name);
```

```
Enumeration getApplets();
AudioClip getAudioClip(URL url);
Image getImage(URL url);
void showDocument(URL url);
public void showDocument(URL url, String target);
void showStatus(String status);
```

The *AppletStub* Interface

```
public Interface AppletStub
```

Methods
```
void appletResize(int width, int height);
AppletContext getAppletContext();
URL getCodeBase();
URL getDocumentBase();
String getParameter(String name);
boolean isActive();
```

The *AudioClip* Interface

```
public Interface AudioClip
```

Methods
```
void loop();
void play();
void stop();
```

The *java.awt* Package

The *AWTError* Class

```
public Class AWTError extends Error
```

Constructors
```
public AWTError(String msg);
```

The *AWTEvent* Class

```
public abstract Class AWTEvent extends EventObject
```

Data

```
public final static long ACTION_EVENT_MASK = 0x80;
public final static long ADJUSTMENT_EVENT_MASK = 0x100;
public final static long COMPONENT_EVENT_MASK = 0x01;
public final static long CONTAINER_EVENT_MASK = 0x02;
public final static long FOCUS_EVENT_MASK = 0x04;
public final static long ITEM_EVENT_MASK = 0x200;
public final static long KEY_EVENT_MASK = 0x08;
public final static long MOUSE_EVENT_MASK = 0x10;
public final static long MOUSE_MOTION_EVENT_MASK = 0x20;
public final static long TEXT_EVENT_MASK = 0x400;
public final static long WINDOW_EVENT_MASK = 0x40;
```

Constructors

```
public AWTEvent(Event event);
public AWTEvent(Object source, int id);
```

Methods

```
public int getId();
public String paramString();
public String toString();
```

The *AWTEventMulticaster* Class

```
public Class AWTEventMulticaster extends Object implements
   ComponentListener, ContainerListener, FocusListener,
   KeyListener, MouseListener, MouseMotionListener,
   WindowListener, ActionListener, ItemListener,
   AdjustmentListener, TextListener
```

Methods

```
public static ActionListener add(ActionListener a,
   ActionListener b);
public static AdjustmentListener add(AdjustmentListener a,
   AdjustmentListener b);
```

```
public static ComponentListener add(ComponentListener a,
  ComponentListener b);
public static ContainerListener add(ContainerListener a,
  ContainerListener b);
public static FocusListener add(FocusListener a,
  FocusListener b);
public static ItemListener add(ItemListener a,
  ItemListener b);
public static KeyListener add(KeyListener a, KeyListener b);
public static MouseListener add(MouseListener a,
  MouseListener b);
public static MouseMotionListener add(MouseMotionListener a,
  MouseMotionListener b);
public static TextListener add(TextListener a,
  TextListener b);
public static WindowListener add(WindowListener a,
  WindowListener b);
public static ActionListener remove(ActionListener l,
  ActionListener oldl);
public static AdjustmentListener remove(AdjustmentListener l,
  AdjustmentListener oldl);
public static ComponentListener remove(ComponentListener l,
  ComponentListener oldl);
public static ContainerListener remove(ContainerListener l,
  ContainerListener oldl);
public static FocusListener remove(FocusListener l,
  FocusListener oldl);
public static ItemListener remove(ItemListener l,
  ItemListener oldl);
public static KeyListener remove(KeyListener l,
  KeyListener oldl);
public static MouseListener remove(MouseListener l,
  MouseListener oldl);
public static MouseMotionListener remove(MouseMotionListener
  l, MouseMotionListener oldl);
public static TextListener remove(TextListener l,
  TextListener oldl);
public static WindowListener remove(WindowListener l,
  WindowListener oldl);
public void actionPerformed(ActionEvent e);
public void adjustmentValueChanged(AdjustmentEvent e);
```

```
public void componentAdded(ContainerEvent e);
public void componentHidden(ComponentEvent e);
public void componentMoved(ComponentEvent e);
public void componentRemoved(ContainerEvent e);
public void componentResized(ComponentEvent e);
public void componentShown(ComponentEvent e);
public void focusGained(FocusEvent e);
public void focusLost(FocusEvent e);
public void itemStateChanged(ItemEvent e);
public void keyPressed(KeyEvent e);
public void keyReleased(KeyEvent e);
public void keyTyped(KeyEvent e);
public void mouseClicked(MouseEvent e);
public void mouseDragged(MouseEvent e);
public void mouseEntered(MouseEvent e);
public void mouseExited(MouseEvent e);
public void mouseMoved(MouseEvent e);
public void mousePressed(MouseEvent e);
public void mouseReleased(MouseEvent e);
public void textValueChanged(TextEvent e);
public void windowActivated(WindowEvent e);
public void windowClosed(WindowEvent e);
public void windowClosing(WindowEvent e);
public void windowDeactivated(WindowEvent e);
public void windowDeiconified(WindowEvent e);
public void windowIconified(WindowEvent e);
public void windowOpened(WindowEvent e);
```

The *AWTException* Class

```
public Class AWTException extends Exception
```

Constructors

```
public AWTException(String msg);
```

The *Adjustable* Interface

```
public Interface Adjustable
```

Data
```
public static final int HORIZONTAL = 0;
public static final int VERTICAL = 1;
```

Methods
```
void addAdjustmentListener(AdjustmentListener 1);
int getBlockIncrement();
int getMaximum();
int getMinimum();
int getOrientation();
int getUnitIncrement();
int getValue();
int getVisibleAmount();
void removeAdjustmentListener(AdjustmentListener 1);
void setBlockIncrement(int b);
void setMaximum(int max);
void setMinimum(int min);
void setUnitIncrement(int u);
void setValue(int v);
void setVisibleAmount(int v);
```

The *BorderLayout* Class

```
public Class BorderLayout extends Object implements
   LayoutManager2, java.io.Serializable
```

Data
```
public static final String CENTER = "Center";
public static final String EAST = "East";
public static final String NORTH = "North";
public static final String SOUTH = "South";
public static final String WEST = "West";
```

Constructors

```
public BorderLayout();
public BorderLayout(int hgap, int vgap);
```

Methods

```
public void addLayoutComponent(Component comp, Object
  constraints);
public void addLayoutComponent(String name, Component comp);
public int getHgap();
public float getLayoutAlignmentX(Container parent);
public float getLayoutAlignmentY(Container parent);
public int getVgap();
public void invalidateLayout(Container target);
public void layoutContainer(Container target);
public Dimension maximumLayoutSize(Container target);
public Dimension minimumLayoutSize(Container target);
public Dimension preferredLayoutSize(Container target);
public void removeLayoutComponent(Component comp);
public void setHgap(int hgap);
public void setVgap(int vgap);
public String toString();
```

The *Button* Class

```
public Class Button extends Component
```

Constructors

```
public Button();
public Button(String label);
```

Methods

```
public void addActionListener(ActionListener 1);
public void addNotify();
public String getActionCommand();
public String getLabel();
public void removeActionListener(ActionListener 1);
public void setActionCommand(String command);
public synchronized void setLabel(String label);
```

The *Canvas* Class

```
public Class Canvas extends Component
```

Constructors
```
public Canvas();
```

Methods
```
public void addNotify();
public void paint(Graphics g);
```

The *CardLayout* Class

```
public Class CardLayout extends Object implements
    LayoutManager2, java.io.Serializable
```

Constructors
```
public CardLayout();
public CardLayout(int hgap, int vgap);
```

Methods
```
public void addLayoutComponent(Component comp, Object
    constraints);
public void addLayoutComponent(String name, Component comp);
public void first(Container parent);
public int getHgap();
public float getLayoutAlignmentX(Container parent);
public float getLayoutAlignmentY(Container parent);
public int getVgap();
public void invalidateLayout(Container target);
public void last(Container parent);
public void layoutContainer(Container parent);
public Dimension maximumLayoutSize(Container target);
public Dimension minimumLayoutSize(Container parent);
public void next(Container parent);
public Dimension preferredLayoutSize(Container parent);
public void previous(Container parent);
public void removeLayoutComponent(Component comp);
public void setHgap(int hgap);
```

```
public void setVgap(int vgap);
public void show(Container parent, String name);
public String toString();
```

The *Checkbox* Class

```
public Class Checkbox extends Component implements
    ItemSelectable
```

Constructors

```
public Checkbox();
public Checkbox(String label);
public Checkbox(String label, boolean state);
public Checkbox(String label, boolean state, CheckboxGroup
    group);
public Checkbox(String label, CheckboxGroup group, boolean
    state);
```

Methods

```
public void addItemListener(ItemListener 1);
public void addNotify();
public CheckboxGroup getCheckboxGroup();
public String getLabel();
public Object[] getSelectedObjects();
public boolean getState();
public void removeItemListener(ItemListener 1);
public void setCheckboxGroup(CheckboxGroup g);
public synchronized void setLabel(String label);
public void setState(boolean state);
```

The *CheckboxGroup* Class

```
public Class CheckboxGroup extends Object implements
    java.io.Serializable
```

Constructors

```
public CheckboxGroup();
```

Methods

```
public Checkbox getCurrent();
```

```
public Checkbox getSelectedCheckbox();
public synchronized void setCurrent(Checkbox box);
public synchronized void setSelectedCheckbox(Checkbox box);
public String toString();
```

The *CheckboxMenuItem* Class

```
public Class CheckboxMenuItem extends MenuItem implements
   ItemSelectable
```

Constructors
```
public CheckboxMenuItem();
public CheckboxMenuItem(String label);
public CheckboxMenuItem(String label, boolean state);
```

Methods
```
public void addItemListener(ItemListener 1);
public void addNotify();
public synchronized Object[] getSelectedObjects();
public boolean getState();
public String paramString();
public void removeItemListener(ItemListener 1);
public synchronized void setState(boolean b);
```

The *Choice* Class

```
public Class Choice extends Component implements
   ItemSelectable
```

Constructors
```
public Choice();
```

Methods
```
public synchronized void add(String item);
public synchronized void addItem(String item);
public void addItemListener(ItemListener 1);
public void addNotify();
public int countItems();
public String getItem(int index);
```

```
public int getItemCount();
public int getSelectedIndex();
public synchronized String getSelectedItem();
public synchronized Object[] getSelectedObjects();
public synchronized void insert(String item, int index);
public synchronized void remove(int position);
public synchronized void remove(String item);
public synchronized void removeAll();
public void removeItemListener(ItemListener l);
public synchronized void select(int pos);
public synchronized void select(String str);
```

The *Color* Class

```
public Class Color extends Object implements
   java.io.Serializable
```

Data

```
public final static Color black = new Color(0, 0, 0);
public final static Color blue = new Color(0, 0, 255);
public final static Color cyan = new Color(0, 255, 255);
public final static Color darkGray = new Color(64, 64, 64);
public final static Color gray = new Color(128, 128, 128);
public final static Color green = new Color(0, 255, 0);
public final static Color lightGray = new Color(192,
   192, 192);
public final static Color magenta = new Color(255, 0, 255);
public final static Color orange = new Color(255, 200, 0);
public final static Color pink = new Color(255, 175, 175);
public final static Color red = new Color(255, 0, 0);
public final static Color white = new Color(255, 255, 255);
public final static Color yellow = new Color(255, 255, 0);
```

Constructors

```
public Color(int r, int g, int b);
public Color(int rgb);
public Color(float r, float g, float b);
```

Methods

```
public static Color decode(String nm) throws
    NumberFormatException;
public static Color getColor(String nm);
public static Color getColor(String nm, Color v);
public static Color getColor(String nm, int v);
public static Color getHSBColor(float h, float s, float b);
public static int HSBtoRGB(float hue, float saturation, float
    brightness);
public static float[] RGBtoHSB(int r, int g, int b, float[]
    hsbvals);
public Color brighter();
public Color darker();
public boolean equals(Object obj);
public int getBlue();
public int getGreen();
public int getRed();
public int getRGB();
public int hashCode();
public String toString();
```

The *Component* Class

```
public abstract Class Component extends Object implements
    ImageObserver, MenuContainer, Serializable
```

Data

```
public static final float BOTTOM_ALIGNMENT = 1.0f;
public static final float CENTER_ALIGNMENT = 0.5f;
public static final float LEFT_ALIGNMENT = 0.0f;
public static final Object LOCK = new Object();
public static final float RIGHT_ALIGNMENT = 1.0f;
public static final float TOP_ALIGNMENT = 0.0f;
```

Methods

```
public boolean action(Event evt, Object what);
public synchronized void add(PopupMenu popup);
public synchronized void
    addComponentListener(ComponentListener 1);
```

```
public synchronized void addFocusListener(FocusListener 1);
public synchronized void addKeyListener(KeyListener 1);
public synchronized void addMouseListener(MouseListener 1);
public synchronized void
  addMouseMotionListener(MouseMotionListener 1);
public void addNotify();
public Rectangle bounds();
public int checkImage(Image image, ImageObserver observer);
public int checkImage(Image image, int width, int height,
  ImageObserver observer);
public boolean contains(int x, int y);
public boolean contains(Point p);
public Image createImage(ImageProducer producer);
public Image createImage(int width, int height);
public void deliverEvent(Event e);
public void disable();
public void doLayout();
public void enable();
public void enable(boolean b);
public float getAlignmentX();
public float getAlignmentY();
public Color getBackground();
public Rectangle getBounds();
public ColorModel getColorModel();
public Component getComponentAt(int x, int y);
public Component getComponentAt(Point p);
public Cursor getCursor();
public Font getFont();
public FontMetrics getFontMetrics(Font font);
public Color getForeground();
public Graphics getGraphics();
public Locale getLocale();
public Point getLocation();
public Point getLocationOnScreen();
public Dimension getMaximumSize();
public Dimension getMinimumSize();
public String getName();
```

```
public Container getParent();
public ComponentPeer getPeer();
public Dimension getPreferredSize();
public Dimension getSize();
public Toolkit getToolkit();
public final Object getTreeLock();
public boolean gotFocus(Event evt, Object what);
public boolean handleEvent(Event evt);
public void hide();
public boolean imageUpdate(Image img, int flags, int x, int y,
    int w, int h);
public boolean inside(int x, int y);
public void invalidate();
public boolean isEnabled();
public boolean isFocusTraversable();
public boolean isShowing();
public boolean isValid();
public boolean isVisible();
public boolean keyDown(Event evt, int key);
public boolean keyUp(Event evt, int key);
public void layout();
public void list();
public void list(PrintStream out);
public void list(PrintStream out, int indent);
public void list(PrintWriter out);
public void list(PrintWriter out, int indent);
public Component locate(int x, int y);
public Point location();
public boolean lostFocus(Event evt, Object what);
public Dimension minimumSize();
public boolean mouseDown(Event evt, int x, int y);
public boolean mouseDrag(Event evt, int x, int y);
public boolean mouseEnter(Event evt, int x, int y);
public boolean mouseExit(Event evt, int x, int y);
public boolean mouseMove(Event evt, int x, int y);
public boolean mouseUp(Event evt, int x, int y);
```

```
public void move(int x, int y);
public void nextFocus();
public void paint(Graphics g);
public void paintAll(Graphics g);
public boolean postEvent(Event e);
public Dimension preferredSize();
public boolean prepareImage(Image image, ImageObserver
    observer);
public boolean prepareImage(Image image, int width, int
    height, ImageObserver observer);
public void print(Graphics g);
public void printAll(Graphics g);
public synchronized void remove(MenuComponent popup);
public synchronized void
    removeComponentListener(ComponentListener 1);
public synchronized void removeFocusListener(FocusListener 1);
public synchronized void removeKeyListener(KeyListener 1);
public synchronized void removeMouseListener(MouseListener 1);
public synchronized void
    removeMouseMotionListener(MouseMotionListener 1);
public void removeNotify();
public void repaint();
public void repaint(int x, int y, int width, int height);
public void repaint(long tm);
public void repaint(long tm, int x, int y, int width, int
    height);
public void requestFocus();
public void reshape(int x, int y, int width, int height);
public void resize(Dimension d);
public void resize(int width, int height);
public void setBackground(Color c);
public void setBounds(int x, int y, int width, int height);
public void setBounds(Rectangle r);
public synchronized void setCursor(Cursor cursor);
public void setEnabled(boolean b);
public synchronized void setFont(Font f);
public void setForeground(Color c);
```

```
public void setLocale(Locale l);
public void setLocation(int x, int y);
public void setLocation(Point p);
public void setName(String name);
public void setSize(Dimension d);
public void setSize(int width, int height);
public void setVisible(boolean b);
public void show();
public void show(boolean b);
public Dimension size();
public String toString();
public void transferFocus();
public void update(Graphics g);
public void validate();
```

The *Container* Class

```
public abstract Class Container extends Component
```

Methods
```
public Component add(Component comp);
public Component add(Component comp, int index);
public void add(Component comp, Object constraints);
public void add(Component comp, Object constraints, int
    index);
public Component add(String name, Component comp);
public void addContainerListener(ContainerListener l);
public void addNotify();
public int countComponents();
public void deliverEvent(Event e);
public void doLayout();
public float getAlignmentX();
public float getAlignmentY();
public Component getComponent(int n);
public Component getComponentAt(int x, int y);
public Component getComponentAt(Point p);
public int getComponentCount();
```

```
public Component[] getComponents();
public Insets getInsets();
public LayoutManager getLayout();
public Dimension getMaximumSize();
public Dimension getMinimumSize();
public Dimension getPreferredSize();
public Insets insets();
public void invalidate();
public boolean isAncestorOf(Component c);
public void layout();
public void list(PrintStream out, int indent);
public void list(PrintWriter out, int indent);
public Component locate(int x, int y);
public Dimension minimumSize();
public void paint(Graphics g);
public void paintComponents(Graphics g);
public Dimension preferredSize();
public void print(Graphics g);
public void printComponents(Graphics g);
public void remove(Component comp);
public void remove(int index);
public void removeAll();
public void removeContainerListener(ContainerListener l);
public void removeNotify();
public void setLayout(LayoutManager mgr);
public void validate();
```

The *Cursor* Class

```
public Class Cursor extends Object implements java.io
  .Serializable
```

Data

```
public static final int CROSSHAIR_CURSOR = 1;
public static final int DEFAULT_CURSOR = 0;
public static final int E_RESIZE_CURSOR = 11;
public static final int HAND_CURSOR = 12;
```

```
public static final int MOVE_CURSOR = 13;
public static final int N_RESIZE_CURSOR = 8;
public static final int NE_RESIZE_CURSOR = 7;
public static final int NW_RESIZE_CURSOR = 6;
public static final int S_RESIZE_CURSOR = 9;
public static final int SE_RESIZE_CURSOR = 5;
public static final int SW_RESIZE_CURSOR = 4;
public static final int TEXT_CURSOR = 2;
public static final int W_RESIZE_CURSOR = 10;
public static final int WAIT_CURSOR = 3;
```

Constructors

```
public Cursor(int type);
```

Methods

```
static public Cursor getDefaultCursor();
static public Cursor getPredefinedCursor(int type);
public int getType();
```

The *Dialog* Class

```
public Class Dialog extends Window
```

Constructors

```
public Dialog(Frame parent);
public Dialog(Frame parent, boolean modal);
public Dialog(Frame parent, String title);
public Dialog(Frame parent, String title, boolean modal);
```

Methods

```
public void addNotify();
public synchronized void addWindowListener(WindowListener 1);
public String getTitle();
public boolean isModal();
public boolean isResizable();
public synchronized void removeWindowListener
    (WindowListener 1);
public void setModal(boolean b);
```

```
public synchronized void setResizable(boolean resizable);
public synchronized void setTitle(String title);
public void show();
```

The *Dimension* Class

```
public Class Dimension extends Object implements
  java.io.Serializable
```

Data
```
public int height;
public int width;
```

Constructors
```
public Dimension();
public Dimension(Dimension d);
public Dimension(int width, int height);
```

Methods
```
public boolean equals(Object obj);
public Dimension getSize();
public void setSize(Dimension d);
public void setSize(int width, int height);
public String toString();
```

The *Event* Class

```
public Class Event extends Object implements
  java.io.Serializable
```

Data
```
public static final int ACTION_EVENT = 1 + MISC_EVENT;
public static final int ALT_MASK = 1 << 3;
public static final int BACK_SPACE = '\b';
public static final int CAPS_LOCK = 1022;
public static final int CTRL_MASK = 1 << 1;
public static final int DELETE = 127;
public static final int DOWN = 1005;
public static final int END = 1001;
```

```
public static final int ENTER = '\n';
public static final int ESCAPE = 27;
public static final int F1 = 1008;
public static final int F10 = 1017;
public static final int F11 = 1018;
public static final int F12 = 1019;
public static final int F2 = 1009;
public static final int F3 = 1010;
public static final int F4 = 1011;
public static final int F5 = 1012;
public static final int F6 = 1013;
public static final int F7 = 1014;
public static final int F8 = 1015;
public static final int F9 = 1016;
public static final int GOT_FOCUS = 4 + MISC_EVENT;
public static final int HOME = 1000;
public static final int INSERT = 1025;
public static final int KEY_ACTION = 3 + KEY_EVENT;
public static final int KEY_ACTION_RELEASE = 4 + KEY_EVENT;
public static final int KEY_PRESS = 1 + KEY_EVENT;
public static final int KEY_RELEASE = 2 + KEY_EVENT;
public static final int LEFT = 1006;
public static final int LIST_DESELECT = 2 + LIST_EVENT;
public static final int LIST_SELECT = 1 + LIST_EVENT;
public static final int LOAD_FILE = 2 + MISC_EVENT;
public static final int LOST_FOCUS = 5 + MISC_EVENT;
public static final int META_MASK = 1 << 2;
public static final int MOUSE_DOWN = 1 + MOUSE_EVENT;
public static final int MOUSE_DRAG = 6 + MOUSE_EVENT;
public static final int MOUSE_ENTER = 4 + MOUSE_EVENT;
public static final int MOUSE_EXIT = 5 + MOUSE_EVENT;
public static final int MOUSE_MOVE = 3 + MOUSE_EVENT;
public static final int MOUSE_UP = 2 + MOUSE_EVENT;
public static final int NUM_LOCK = 1023;
public static final int PAUSE = 1024;
public static final int PGDN = 1003;
```

```
public static final int PGUP = 1002;
public static final int PRINT_SCREEN = 1020;
public static final int RIGHT = 1007;
public static final int SAVE_FILE = 3 + MISC_EVENT;
public static final int SCROLL_ABSOLUTE = 5 + SCROLL_EVENT;
public static final int SCROLL_BEGIN = 6 + SCROLL_EVENT;
public static final int SCROLL_END = 7 + SCROLL_EVENT;
public static final int SCROLL_LINE_DOWN = 2 + SCROLL_EVENT;
public static final int SCROLL_LINE_UP = 1 + SCROLL_EVENT;
public static final int SCROLL_LOCK = 1021;
public static final int SCROLL_PAGE_DOWN = 4 + SCROLL_EVENT;
public static final int SCROLL_PAGE_UP = 3 + SCROLL_EVENT;
public static final int SHIFT_MASK = 1 << 0;
public static final int TAB = '\t';
public static final int UP = 1004;
public static final int WINDOW_DEICONIFY = 4 + WINDOW_EVENT;
public static final int WINDOW_DESTROY = 1 + WINDOW_EVENT;
public static final int WINDOW_EXPOSE = 2 + WINDOW_EVENT;
public static final int WINDOW_ICONIFY = 3 + WINDOW_EVENT;
public static final int WINDOW_MOVED = 5 + WINDOW_EVENT;
public Object arg;
public int clickCount;
public Event evt;
public int id;
public int key;
public int modifiers;
public Object target;
public long when;
public int x;
public int y;
```

Constructors

```
public Event(Object target, long when, int id, int x, int y,
    int key, int modifiers, Object arg);
public Event(Object target, long when, int id, int x, int y,
    int key, int modifiers);
public Event(Object target, int id, Object arg);
```

Methods

```
public boolean controlDown();
public boolean metaDown();
public boolean shiftDown();
public String toString();
public void translate(int x, int y);
```

The *EventQueue* Class

```
public Class EventQueue extends Object
```

Methods

```
public static EventQueue getEventQueue();
public synchronized Object getNextEvent() throws
    InterruptedException;
public synchronized Object peekEvent();
public synchronized Object peekEvent(int id);
public synchronized void postEvent(AWTEvent theEvent);
public synchronized void postEvent(Event theEvent);
```

The *EventSource* Interface

```
public Interface EventSource
```

Methods

```
boolean postEvent(Event e);
```

The *FileDialog* Class

```
public Class FileDialog extends Dialog
```

Data

```
public static final int LOAD = 0;
public static final int SAVE = 1;
```

Constructors

```
public FileDialog(Frame parent);
public FileDialog(Frame parent, String title);
public FileDialog(Frame parent, String title, int mode);
```

Methods

```
public void addNotify();
public String getDirectory();
public String getFile();
public FilenameFilter getFilenameFilter();
public int getMode();
public synchronized void setDirectory(String dir);
public synchronized void setFile(String file);
public synchronized void setFilenameFilter(FilenameFilter
    filter);
public void setMode(int mode);
```

The *FlowLayout* Class

```
public Class FlowLayout extends Object implements
    LayoutManager, java.io.Serializable
```

Data

```
public static final int CENTER = 1;
public static final int LEFT = 0;
public static final int RIGHT = 2;
```

Constructors

```
public FlowLayout();
public FlowLayout(int align);
public FlowLayout(int align, int hgap, int vgap);
```

Methods

```
public void addLayoutComponent(String name, Component comp);
public int getAlignment();
public int getHgap();
public int getVgap();
public void layoutContainer(Container target);
public Dimension minimumLayoutSize(Container target);
public Dimension preferredLayoutSize(Container target);
public void removeLayoutComponent(Component comp);
public void setAlignment(int align);
public void setHgap(int hgap);
```

```
public void setVgap(int vgap);
public String toString();
```

The *Font* Class

```
public Class Font extends Object implements
  java.io.Serializable
```

Data
```
public static final int BOLD = 1;
public static final int ITALIC = 2;
public static final int PLAIN = 0;
```

Constructors
```
public Font(String name, int style, int size);
```

Methods
```
public static Font decode(String str);
public static Font getFont(String nm);
public static Font getFont(String nm, Font font);
public boolean equals(Object obj);
public String getFamily();
public String getName();
public FontPeer getPeer();
public int getSize();
public int getStyle();
public int hashCode();
public boolean isBold();
public boolean isItalic();
public boolean isPlain();
public String toString();
```

The *FontMetrics* Class

```
public abstract Class FontMetrics extends Object implements
  java.io.Serializable
```

Methods
```
public int bytesWidth(byte data[], int off, int len);
```

```
public int charsWidth(char data[], int off, int len);
public int charWidth(char ch);
public int charWidth(int ch);
public int getAscent();
public int getDescent();
public Font getFont();
public int getHeight();
public int getLeading();
public int getMaxAdvance();
public int getMaxAscent();
public int getMaxDecent();
public int getMaxDescent();
public int[] getWidths();
public int stringWidth(String str);
public String toString();
```

The *Frame* Class

```
public Class Frame extends Window implements MenuContainer
```

Data

```
public static final int CROSSHAIR_CURSOR =
  Cursor.CROSSHAIR_CURSOR;
public static final int DEFAULT_CURSOR =
  Cursor.DEFAULT_CURSOR;
public static final int E_RESIZE_CURSOR =
  Cursor.E_RESIZE_CURSOR;
public static final int HAND_CURSOR = Cursor.HAND_CURSOR;
public static final int MOVE_CURSOR = Cursor.MOVE_CURSOR;
public static final int N_RESIZE_CURSOR =
  Cursor.N_RESIZE_CURSOR;
public static final int NE_RESIZE_CURSOR =
  Cursor.NE_RESIZE_CURSOR;
public static final int NW_RESIZE_CURSOR =
  Cursor.NW_RESIZE_CURSOR;
public static final int S_RESIZE_CURSOR =
  Cursor.S_RESIZE_CURSOR;
public static final int SE_RESIZE_CURSOR =
  Cursor.SE_RESIZE_CURSOR;
```

```
public static final int SW_RESIZE_CURSOR =
  Cursor.SW_RESIZE_CURSOR;
```

```
public static final int TEXT_CURSOR = Cursor.TEXT_CURSOR;
```

```
public static final int W_RESIZE_CURSOR =
  Cursor.W_RESIZE_CURSOR;
```

```
public static final int WAIT_CURSOR = Cursor.WAIT_CURSOR;
```

Constructors

```
public Frame();
```

```
public Frame(String title);
```

Methods

```
public void addNotify();
```

```
public synchronized void addWindowListener(WindowListener 1);
```

```
public synchronized void dispose();
```

```
public int getCursorType();
```

```
public Image getIconImage();
```

```
public MenuBar getMenuBar();
```

```
public String getTitle();
```

```
public boolean isResizable();
```

```
public synchronized void remove(MenuComponent m);
```

```
public synchronized void removeWindowListener
  (WindowListener 1);
```

```
public synchronized void setCursor(int cursorType);
```

```
public synchronized void setIconImage(Image image);
```

```
public synchronized void setMenuBar(MenuBar mb);
```

```
public synchronized void setResizable(boolean resizable);
```

```
public synchronized void setTitle(String title);
```

The *Graphics* Class

```
public abstract Class Graphics extends Object
```

Methods

```
public abstract void clearRect(int x, int y, int width, int
  height);
```

```
public abstract void clipRect(int x, int y, int width, int
  height);
```

```
public abstract void copyArea(int x, int y, int width, int
  height, int dx, int dy);
```

```
public abstract Graphics create();

public abstract void dispose();

public abstract void drawArc(int x, int y, int width, int
    height, int startAngle, int arcAngle);

public abstract boolean drawImage(Image img, int x, int y,
    ImageObserver observer);

public abstract boolean drawImage(Image img, int x, int y, int
    width, int height, ImageObserver observer);

public abstract boolean drawImage(Image img, int x, int y,
    Color bgcolor, ImageObserver observer);

public abstract boolean drawImage(Image img, int x, int y, int
    width, int height, Color bgcolor, ImageObserver observer);

public abstract boolean drawImage(Image img, int dx1, int dy1,
    int dx2, int dy2, int sx1, int sy1, int sx2, int sy2,
    ImageObserver observer);

public abstract boolean drawImage(Image img, int dx1, int dy1,
    int dx2, int dy2, int sx1, int sy1, int sx2, int sy2, Color
    bgcolor, ImageObserver observer);

public abstract void drawLine(int x1, int y1, int x2, int y2);

public abstract void drawOval(int x, int y, int width, int
    height);

public abstract void drawPolygon(int xPoints[], int yPoints[],
    int nPoints);

public abstract void drawPolyline(int xPoints[], int
    yPoints[], int nPoints);

public abstract void drawRoundRect(int x, int y, int width,
    int height, int arcWidth, int arcHeight);

public abstract void drawString(String str, int x, int y);

public abstract void fillArc(int x, int y, int width, int
    height, int startAngle, int arcAngle);

public abstract void fillOval(int x, int y, int width, int
    height);

public abstract void fillPolygon(int xPoints[], int yPoints[],
    int nPoints);

public abstract void fillRect(int x, int y, int width, int
    height);

public abstract void fillRoundRect(int x, int y, int width,
    int height, int arcWidth, int arcHeight);

public abstract Shape getClip();

public abstract Rectangle getClipBounds();

public abstract Color getColor();

public abstract Font getFont();
```

```
public abstract FontMetrics getFontMetrics(Font f);
public abstract void setClip(int x, int y, int width, int
    height);
public abstract void setClip(Shape clip);
public abstract void setColor(Color c);
public abstract void setFont(Font font);
public abstract void setPaintMode();
public abstract void setXORMode(Color cl);
public abstract void translate(int x, int y);
public Graphics create(int x, int y, int width, int height);
public void draw3DRect(int x, int y, int width, int height,
    boolean raised);
public void drawBytes(byte data[], int offset, int length, int
    x, int y);
public void drawChars(char data[], int offset, int length, int
    x, int y);
public void drawPolygon(Polygon p);
public void drawRect(int x, int y, int width, int height);
public void fill3DRect(int x, int y, int width, int height,
    boolean raised);
public void fillPolygon(Polygon p);
public void finalize();
public Rectangle getClipRect();
public FontMetrics getFontMetrics();
public String toString();
```

The *GridBagConstraints* Class

```
public Class GridBagConstraints extends Object implements
    Cloneable, java.io.Serializable
```

Data
```
public static final int BOTH = 1;
public static final int CENTER = 10;
public static final int EAST = 13;
public static final int HORIZONTAL = 2;
public static final int NONE = 0;
public static final int NORTH = 11;
public static final int NORTHEAST = 12;
```

```
public static final int NORTHWEST = 18;
public static final int RELATIVE = -1;
public static final int REMAINDER = 0;
public static final int SOUTH = 15;
public static final int SOUTHEAST = 14;
public static final int SOUTHWEST = 16;
public static final int VERTICAL = 3;
public static final int WEST = 17;
public int anchor, fill;
public int gridx, gridy, gridwidth, gridheight;
public Insets insets;
public int ipadx, ipady;
public double weightx, weighty;
```

Methods

```
public GridBagConstraints ();
public Object clone ();
```

The *GridLayout* Class

```
public Class GridLayout extends Object implements
   LayoutManager, java.io.Serializable
```

Constructors

```
public GridLayout();
public GridLayout(int rows, int cols);
public GridLayout(int rows, int cols, int hgap, int vgap);
```

Methods

```
public void addLayoutComponent(String name, Component comp);
public int getColumns();
public int getHgap();
public int getRows();
public int getVgap();
public void layoutContainer(Container parent);
public Dimension minimumLayoutSize(Container parent);
public Dimension preferredLayoutSize(Container parent);
public void removeLayoutComponent(Component comp);
```

```
public void setColumns(int cols);
public void setHgap(int hgap);
public void setRows(int rows);
public void setVgap(int vgap);
public String toString();
```

The *IllegalComponentStateException* Class

```
public Class IllegalComponentStateException extends
    IllegalStateException
```

Constructors
```
public IllegalComponentStateException();
public IllegalComponentStateException(String s);
```

The *Image* Class

```
public abstract Class Image extends Object implements
    java.io.Serializable
```

Data
```
public static final int SCALE_AVERAGE = 16;
public static final int SCALE_DEFAULT = 1;
public static final int SCALE_FAST = 2;
public static final int SCALE_REPLICATE = 8;
public static final int SCALE_SMOOTH = 4;
public static final Object UndefinedProperty = new Object();
```

Methods
```
public abstract void flush();
public abstract Graphics getGraphics();
public abstract int getHeight(ImageObserver observer);
public abstract Object getProperty(String name, ImageObserver
    observer);
public abstract ImageProducer getSource();
public abstract int getWidth(ImageObserver observer);
public Image createScaledImage(int width, int height,
    int hints);
```

The *Insets* Class

```
public Class Insets extends Object implements Cloneable,
    java.io.Serializable
```

Data

```
public int bottom;
public int left;
public int right;
public int top;
```

Constructors

```
public Insets(int top, int left, int bottom, int right);
```

Methods

```
public Object clone();
public boolean equals(Object obj);
public String toString();
```

The *ItemSelectable* Interface

```
public Interface ItemSelectable
```

Methods

```
public void addItemListener(ItemListener l);
public Object[] getSelectedObjects();
public void removeItemListener(ItemListener l);
```

The *Label* Class

```
public Class Label extends Component
```

Data

```
public static final int CENTER = 1;
public static final int LEFT = 0;
public static final int RIGHT = 2;
```

Constructors

```
public Label();
public Label(String text);
```

```
public Label(String text, int alignment);
```

Methods

```
public void addNotify();
public int getAlignment();
public String getText();
public synchronized void setAlignment(int alignment);
public synchronized void setText(String text);
```

The *LayoutManager* Interface

```
public Interface LayoutManager
```

Methods

```
void addLayoutComponent(String name, Component comp);
void layoutContainer(Container parent);
Dimension minimumLayoutSize(Container parent);
Dimension preferredLayoutSize(Container parent);
void removeLayoutComponent(Component comp);
```

The *LayoutManager2* Interface

```
public Interface LayoutManager2 extends LayoutManager
```

Methods

```
void addLayoutComponent(Component comp, Object constraints);
public float getLayoutAlignmentX(Container target);
public float getLayoutAlignmentY(Container target);
public void invalidateLayout(Container target);
public Dimension maximumLayoutSize(Container target);
```

The *List* Class

```
public Class List extends Component implements ItemSelectable
```

Constructors

```
public List();
public List(int rows);
public List(int rows, boolean multipleMode);
```

Methods

```
public void add(String item);
public synchronized void add(String item, int index);
public void addActionListener(ActionListener 1);
public void addItem(String item);
public synchronized void addItem(String item, int index);
public void addItemListener(ItemListener 1);
public void addNotify();
public boolean allowsMultipleSelections();
public synchronized void clear();
public int countItems();
public synchronized void delItem(int position);
public synchronized void delItems(int start, int end);
public synchronized void deselect(int index);
public String getItem(int index);
public int getItemCount();
public synchronized String[] getItems();
public Dimension getMinimumSize();
public Dimension getMinimumSize(int rows);
public Dimension getPreferredSize();
public Dimension getPreferredSize(int rows);
public int getRows();
public synchronized int getSelectedIndex();
public synchronized int[] getSelectedIndexes();
public synchronized String getSelectedItem();
public synchronized String[] getSelectedItems();
public Object[] getSelectedObjects();
public int getVisibleIndex();
public boolean isIndexSelected(int index);
public boolean isMultipleMode();
public boolean isSelected(int index);
public synchronized void makeVisible(int index);
public Dimension minimumSize();
public Dimension minimumSize(int rows);
public Dimension preferredSize();
public Dimension preferredSize(int rows);
```

```
public synchronized void remove(int position);
public synchronized void remove(String item);
public void removeActionListener(ActionListener 1);
public synchronized void removeAll();
public void removeItemListener(ItemListener 1);
public void removeNotify();
public synchronized void replaceItem(String newValue, int
   index);
public synchronized void select(int index);
public synchronized void setMultipleMode(boolean b);
public synchronized void setMultipleSelections(boolean b);
```

The *MediaTracker* Class

```
public Class MediaTracker extends Object implements
   java.io.Serializable
```

Data
```
public static final int ABORTED = 2;
public static final int COMPLETE = 8;
public static final int ERRORED = 4;
public static final int LOADING = 1;
```

Constructors
```
public MediaTracker(Component comp);
```

Methods
```
public void addImage(Image image, int id);
public synchronized void addImage(Image image, int id, int w,
   int h);
public boolean checkAll();
public synchronized boolean checkAll(boolean load);
public boolean checkID(int id);
public synchronized boolean checkID(int id, boolean load);
public synchronized Object[] getErrorsAny();
public synchronized Object[] getErrorsID(int id);
public synchronized boolean isErrorAny();
public synchronized boolean isErrorID(int id);
public synchronized void removeImage(Image image);
```

```
public synchronized void removeImage(Image image, int id);
public synchronized void removeImage(Image image, int id, int
   width, int height);
public synchronized int statusAll(boolean load);
public synchronized int statusID(int id, boolean load);
public void waitForAll() throws InterruptedException;
public synchronized boolean waitForAll(long ms) throws
   InterruptedException;
public void waitForID(int id) throws InterruptedException;
public synchronized boolean waitForID(int id, long ms) throws
   InterruptedException;
```

The *Menu* Class

```
public Class Menu extends MenuItem implements MenuContainer
```

Constructors
```
public Menu();
public Menu(String label);
public Menu(String label, boolean tearOff);
```

Methods
```
public synchronized MenuItem add(MenuItem mi);
public void add(String label);
public void addNotify();
public void addSeparator();
public int countItems();
public MenuItem getItem(int index);
public int getItemCount();
public synchronized void insert(MenuItem menuitem, int index);
public void insert(String label, int index);
public void insertSeparator(int index);
public boolean isTearOff();
public String paramString();
public synchronized void remove(int index);
public synchronized void remove(MenuComponent item);
public synchronized void removeAll();
public void removeNotify();
```

The *MenuBar* Class

```
public Class MenuBar extends MenuComponent implements
   MenuContainer
```

Constructors
```
public MenuBar();
```

Methods
```
public synchronized Menu add(Menu m);
public void addNotify();
public int countMenus();
public void deleteShortcut(MenuShortcut s);
public Menu getHelpMenu();
public Menu getMenu(int i);
public int getMenuCount();
public MenuItem getShortcutMenuItem(MenuShortcut s);
public synchronized void remove(int index);
public synchronized void remove(MenuComponent m);
public void removeNotify();
public synchronized void setHelpMenu(Menu m);
public synchronized Enumeration shortcuts();
```

The *MenuComponent* Class

```
public abstract Class MenuComponent extends Object implements
   java.io.Serializable
```

Methods
```
public Font getFont();
public String getName();
public MenuContainer getParent();
public MenuComponentPeer getPeer();
public boolean postEvent(Event evt);
public void removeNotify();
public void setFont(Font f);
public void setName(String name);
public String toString();
```

The *MenuContainer* Interface

```
public Interface MenuContainer
```

Methods
```
Font getFont();
boolean postEvent(Event evt);
void remove(MenuComponent comp);
```

The *MenuItem* Class

```
public Class MenuItem extends MenuComponent
```

Constructors
```
public MenuItem();
public MenuItem(String label);
public MenuItem(String label, MenuShortcut s);
```

Methods
```
public void addActionListener(ActionListener 1);
public void addNotify();
public void deleteShortcut();
public synchronized void disable();
public synchronized void enable();
public void enable(boolean b);
public String getActionCommand();
public String getLabel();
public MenuShortcut getShortcut();
public boolean isEnabled();
public String paramString();
public void removeActionListener(ActionListener 1);
public void setActionCommand(String command);
public synchronized void setEnabled(boolean b);
public synchronized void setLabel(String label);
public void setShortcut(MenuShortcut s);
```

The *MenuShortcut* Class

```
public Class MenuShortcut extends Event
```

Constructors
```
public MenuShortcut(int key);
public MenuShortcut(int key, boolean useShiftModifier);
```

Methods
```
public boolean equals(MenuShortcut s);
public int getKey();
public String toString();
public boolean usesShiftModifier();
```

The *Panel* Class

```
public Class Panel extends Container
```

Constructors
```
public Panel();
public Panel(LayoutManager layout);
```

Methods
```
public void addNotify();
```

The *Point* Class

```
public Class Point extends Object implements
  java.io.Serializable
```

Data
```
public int x;
public int y;
```

Constructors
```
public Point();
public Point(Point p);
public Point(int x, int y);
```

Methods
```
public boolean equals(Object obj);
```

```
public Point getLocation();
public int hashCode();
public void move(int x, int y);
public void setLocation(int x, int y);
public void setLocation(Point p);
public String toString();
public void translate(int x, int y);
```

The *Polygon* Class

```
public Class Polygon extends Object implements Shape,
    java.io.Serializable
```

Data
```
public int npoints = 0;
public int xpoints[] = new int[4];
public int ypoints[] = new int[4];
```

Constructors
```
public Polygon();
public Polygon(int xpoints[], int ypoints[], int npoints);
```

Methods
```
public void addPoint(int x, int y);
public boolean contains(int x, int y);
public boolean contains(Point p);
public Rectangle getBoundingBox();
public Rectangle getBounds();
public boolean inside(int x, int y);
public void translate(int deltaX, int deltaY);
```

The *PopupMenu* Class

```
public Class PopupMenu extends Menu
```

Constructors
```
public PopupMenu();
public PopupMenu(String label);
```

Methods

```
public synchronized void addNotify();
public void show(Component origin, int x, int y);
```

The *PrintGraphics* Interface

```
public Interface PrintGraphics
```

Methods

```
public PrintJob getPrintJob();
```

The *PrintJob* Class

```
public abstract Class PrintJob extends Object
```

Methods

```
public abstract void end();
public abstract Graphics getGraphics();
public abstract Dimension getPageDimension();
public abstract int getPageResolution();
public abstract boolean lastPageFirst();
public void finalize();
```

The *Rectangle* Class

```
public Class Rectangle extends Object implements Shape,
    java.io.Serializable
```

Data

```
public int height;
public int width;
public int x;
public int y;
```

Constructors

```
public Rectangle();
public Rectangle(Rectangle r);
public Rectangle(int x, int y, int width, int height);
```

```
public Rectangle(int width, int height);
public Rectangle(Point p, Dimension d);
public Rectangle(Point p);
public Rectangle(Dimension d);
```

Methods

```
public void add(int newx, int newy);
public void add(Point pt);
public void add(Rectangle r);
public boolean contains(int x, int y);
public boolean contains(Point p);
public boolean equals(Object obj);
public Rectangle getBounds();
public Point getLocation();
public Dimension getSize();
public void grow(int h, int v);
public int hashCode();
public boolean inside(int x, int y);
public Rectangle intersection(Rectangle r);
public boolean intersects(Rectangle r);
public boolean isEmpty();
public void move(int x, int y);
public void reshape(int x, int y, int width, int height);
public void resize(int width, int height);
public void setBounds(int x, int y, int width, int height);
public void setBounds(Rectangle r);
public void setLocation(int x, int y);
public void setLocation(Point p);
public void setSize(Dimension d);
public void setSize(int width, int height);
public String toString();
public void translate(int x, int y);
public Rectangle union(Rectangle r);
```

The *ScrollPane* Class

```
public Class ScrollPane extends Container
```

Data
```
public static final int SCROLLBARS_ALWAYS = 1;
public static final int SCROLLBARS_AS_NEEDED = 0;
public static final int SCROLLBARS_NEVER = 2;
```

Constructors
```
public ScrollPane();
public ScrollPane(int scrollbarDisplayPolicy);
```

Methods
```
public Component add(Component comp, int pos);
public void addNotify();
public void doLayout();
public Adjustable getHAdjustable();
public int getHScrollbarHeight();
public int getScrollbarDisplayPolicy();
public Point getScrollPosition();
public Adjustable getVAdjustable();
public Dimension getViewportSize();
public int getVScrollbarWidth();
public void layout();
public String paramString();
public void printComponents(Graphics g);
public final void setLayout(LayoutManager mgr);
public void setScrollPosition(int x, int y);
public void setScrollPosition(Point p);
```

The *Scrollbar* Class

```
public Class Scrollbar extends Component implements Adjustable
```

Data
```
public static final int HORIZONTAL = 0;
public static final int VERTICAL = 1;
```

Constructors

```
public Scrollbar();

public Scrollbar(int orientation);

public Scrollbar(int orientation, int value, int visible, int
  minimum, int maximum);
```

Methods

```
public void addAdjustmentListener(AdjustmentListener 1);

public void addNotify();

public int getBlockIncrement();

public int getLineIncrement();

public int getMaximum();

public int getMinimum();

public int getOrientation();

public int getPageIncrement();

public int getUnitIncrement();

public int getValue();

public int getVisible();

public int getVisibleAmount();

public void removeAdjustmentListener(AdjustmentListener 1);

public synchronized void setBlockIncrement(int v);

public void setLineIncrement(int v);

public synchronized void setMaximum(int newMaximum);

public synchronized void setMinimum(int newMinimum);

public synchronized void setOrientation(int orientation);

public void setPageIncrement(int v);

public synchronized void setUnitIncrement(int v);

public synchronized void setValue(int newValue);

public synchronized void setValues(int value, int visible, int
  minimum, int maximum);

public synchronized void setVisibleAmount(int newAmount);
```

The *Shape* Interface

```
public Interface Shape
```

Methods

```
public Rectangle getBounds();
```

The *SystemColor* Class

```
public Class SystemColor extends Color implements
    java.io.Serializable
```

Data

```
public final static int ACTIVE_CAPTION = 1;

public final static int ACTIVE_CAPTION_BORDER = 3;

public final static int ACTIVE_CAPTION_TEXT = 2;

public final static SystemColor activeCaption = new
    SystemColor((byte)ACTIVE_CAPTION);

public final static SystemColor activeCaptionBorder = new
    SystemColor((byte)ACTIVE_CAPTION_BORDER);

public final static SystemColor activeCaptionText = new
    SystemColor((byte)ACTIVE_CAPTION_TEXT);

public final static int CONTROL = 17;

public final static SystemColor control = new
    SystemColor((byte)CONTROL);

public final static int CONTROL_DK_SHADOW = 22;

public final static int CONTROL_HIGHLIGHT = 19;

public final static int CONTROL_LT_HIGHLIGHT = 20;

public final static int CONTROL_SHADOW = 21;

public final static int CONTROL_TEXT = 18;

public final static SystemColor controlDkShadow = new
    SystemColor((byte)CONTROL_DK_SHADOW);

public final static SystemColor controlHighlight = new
    SystemColor((byte)CONTROL_HIGHLIGHT);

public final static SystemColor controlLtHighlight = new
    SystemColor((byte)CONTROL_LT_HIGHLIGHT);

public final static SystemColor controlShadow = new
    SystemColor((byte)CONTROL_SHADOW);

public final static SystemColor controlText = new
    SystemColor((byte)CONTROL_TEXT);

public final static int DESKTOP = 0;

public final static SystemColor desktop = new
    SystemColor((byte)DESKTOP);

public final static int INACTIVE_CAPTION = 4;

public final static int INACTIVE_CAPTION_BORDER = 6;

public final static int INACTIVE_CAPTION_TEXT = 5;

public final static SystemColor inactiveCaption = new
    SystemColor((byte)INACTIVE_CAPTION);
```

```
public final static SystemColor inactiveCaptionBorder = new
  SystemColor((byte)INACTIVE_CAPTION_BORDER);
public final static SystemColor inactiveCaptionText = new
  SystemColor((byte)INACTIVE_CAPTION_TEXT);
public final static int INFO = 24;
public final static SystemColor info = new
  SystemColor((byte)INFO);
public final static int INFO_TEXT = 25;
public final static SystemColor infoText = new
  SystemColor((byte)INFO_TEXT);
public final static int MENU = 10;
public final static SystemColor menu = new
  SystemColor((byte)MENU);
public final static int MENU_TEXT = 11;
public final static SystemColor menuText = new
  SystemColor((byte)MENU_TEXT);
public final static int NUM_COLORS = 26;
public final static int SCROLLBAR = 23;
public final static SystemColor scrollbar = new
  SystemColor((byte)SCROLLBAR);
public final static int TEXT = 12;
public final static SystemColor text = new
  SystemColor((byte)TEXT);
public final static int TEXT_HIGHLIGHT = 14;
public final static int TEXT_HIGHLIGHT_TEXT = 15;
public final static int TEXT_INACTIVE_TEXT = 16;
public final static int TEXT_TEXT = 13;
public final static SystemColor textHighlight = new
  SystemColor((byte)TEXT_HIGHLIGHT);
public final static SystemColor textHighlightText = new
  SystemColor((byte)TEXT_HIGHLIGHT_TEXT);
public final static SystemColor textInactiveText = new
  SystemColor((byte)TEXT_INACTIVE_TEXT);
public final static SystemColor textText = new
  SystemColor((byte)TEXT_TEXT);
public final static int WINDOW = 7;
public final static SystemColor window = new
  SystemColor((byte)WINDOW);
public final static int WINDOW_BORDER = 8;
public final static int WINDOW_TEXT = 9;
```

```
public final static SystemColor windowBorder = new
    SystemColor((byte)WINDOW_BORDER);
public final static SystemColor windowText = new
    SystemColor((byte)WINDOW_TEXT);
```

Methods

```
public int getRGB();
public String toString();
```

The *TextArea* Class

```
public Class TextArea extends TextComponent
```

Data

```
public static final int SCROLLBARS_BOTH = 0;
public static final int SCROLLBARS_HORIZONTAL_ONLY = 2;
public static final int SCROLLBARS_NONE = 3;
public static final int SCROLLBARS_VERTICAL_ONLY = 1;
```

Constructors

```
public TextArea();
public TextArea(String text);
public TextArea(String text, int rows, int columns);
public TextArea(String text, int rows, int columns, int
    scrollbars);
public TextArea(int rows, int columns);
```

Methods

```
public void addNotify();
public synchronized void append(String str);
public void appendText(String str);
public int getColumns();
public Dimension getMinimumSize();
public Dimension getMinimumSize(int rows, int columns);
public Dimension getPreferredSize();
public Dimension getPreferredSize(int rows, int columns);
public int getRows();
public int getScrollbarVisibility();
```

```
public synchronized void insert(String str, int pos);
public void insertText(String str, int pos);
public Dimension minimumSize();
public Dimension minimumSize(int rows, int columns);
public Dimension preferredSize();
public Dimension preferredSize(int rows, int columns);
public synchronized void replaceRange(String str, int start,
    int end);
public void replaceText(String str, int start, int end);
public void setColumns(int columns);
public void setRows(int rows);
```

The *TextComponent* Class

```
public Class TextComponent extends Component
```

Methods

```
public void addTextListener(TextListener l);
public int getCaretPosition();
public synchronized String getSelectedText();
public synchronized int getSelectionEnd();
public synchronized int getSelectionStart();
public synchronized String getText();
public boolean isEditable();
public void removeNotify();
public void removeTextListener(TextListener l);
public synchronized void select(int selectionStart, int
    selectionEnd);
public synchronized void selectAll();
public void setCaretPosition(int position);
public synchronized void setEditable(boolean b);
public synchronized void setSelectionEnd(int selectionEnd);
public synchronized void setSelectionStart(int
    selectionStart);
public synchronized void setText(String t);
```

The *TextField* Class

```
public Class TextField extends TextComponent
```

Constructors
```
public TextField();
public TextField(String text);
public TextField(String text, int columns);
public TextField(int columns);
```

Methods
```
public void addActionListener(ActionListener 1);
public void addNotify();
public boolean echoCharIsSet();
public int getColumns();
public char getEchoChar();
public Dimension getMinimumSize();
public Dimension getMinimumSize(int columns);
public Dimension getPreferredSize();
public Dimension getPreferredSize(int columns);
public Dimension minimumSize();
public Dimension minimumSize(int columns);
public Dimension preferredSize();
public Dimension preferredSize(int columns);
public void removeActionListener(ActionListener 1);
public void setColumns(int columns);
public void setEchoChar(char c);
public void setEchoCharacter(char c);
```

The *Toolkit* Class

```
public abstract Class Toolkit extends Object
```

Methods
```
public static synchronized Toolkit getDefaultToolkit();
public static String getProperty(String key, String
    defaultValue);
```

```
public abstract void beep();

public abstract int checkImage(Image image, int width, int
    height, ImageObserver observer);

protected abstract ButtonPeer createButton(Button target);

protected abstract CanvasPeer createCanvas(Canvas target);

protected abstract CheckboxPeer createCheckbox(Checkbox
    target);

protected abstract CheckboxMenuItemPeer
    createCheckboxMenuItem(CheckboxMenuItem target);

protected abstract ChoicePeer createChoice(Choice target);

protected abstract DialogPeer createDialog(Dialog target);

protected abstract FileDialogPeer createFileDialog(FileDialog
    target);

protected abstract FramePeer createFrame(Frame target);

public abstract Image createImage(byte[] imagedata, int
    imageoffset, int imagelength);

public abstract Image createImage(ImageProducer producer);

protected abstract LabelPeer createLabel(Label target);

protected abstract ListPeer createList(List target);

protected abstract MenuPeer createMenu(Menu target);

protected abstract MenuBarPeer createMenuBar(MenuBar target);

protected abstract MenuItemPeer createMenuItem(MenuItem
    target);

protected abstract PanelPeer createPanel(Panel target);

protected abstract PopupMenuPeer createPopupMenu(PopupMenu
    target);

protected abstract ScrollbarPeer createScrollbar(Scrollbar
    target);

protected abstract ScrollPanePeer createScrollPane(ScrollPane
    target);

protected abstract TextAreaPeer createTextArea(TextArea
    target);

protected abstract TextFieldPeer createTextField(TextField
    target);

protected abstract WindowPeer createWindow(Window target);

public abstract ColorModel getColorModel();

public abstract String[] getFontList();

public abstract FontMetrics getFontMetrics(Font font);
```

```
protected abstract FontPeer getFontPeer(String name, int
   style);
public abstract Image getImage(String filename);
public abstract Image getImage(URL url);
public abstract PrintJob getPrintJob(Frame frame, String
   jobtitle, Properties props);
public abstract int getScreenResolution();
public abstract Dimension getScreenSize();
public abstract Clipboard getSystemClipboard();
public abstract boolean prepareImage(Image image, int width,
   int height, ImageObserver observer);
public abstract void sync();
public Image createImage(byte[] imagedata);
public int getMenuShortcutKeyMask();
```

The *Window* Class

```
public Class Window extends Container
```

Constructors
```
public Window(Frame parent);
```

Methods
```
public void addNotify();
public void dispose();
public Component getFocusOwner();
public Locale getLocale();
public Toolkit getToolkit();
public final String getWarningString();
public void pack();
public boolean postEvent(Event e);
public void show();
public void toBack();
public void toFront();
```

The *java.awt.datatransfer* Package

The *Clipboard* Class

```
public Class Clipboard extends Object
```

Constructors

```
public Clipboard(String name);
```

Methods

```
public synchronized Transferable getContents(Object
  requestor);
public String getName();
public synchronized void setContents(Transferable contents,
  ClipboardOwner owner);
```

The *ClipboardOwner* Interface

```
public Interface ClipboardOwner
```

Methods

```
public void lostOwnership(Clipboard clipboard, Transferable
  contents);
```

The *DataFlavor* Class

```
public Class DataFlavor extends Object
```

Data

```
public static DataFlavor plainTextFlavor;
public static DataFlavor stringFlavor;
```

Constructors

```
public DataFlavor(Class representationClass, String
  humanPresentableName);
public DataFlavor(String mimeType, String
  humanPresentableName);
```

Methods

```
public boolean equals(DataFlavor dataFlavor);
```

```
public String getHumanPresentableName();
public String getMimeType();
public Class getRepresentationClass();
public final boolean isMimeTypeEqual(DataFlavor dataFlavor);
public boolean isMimeTypeEqual(String mimeType);
public void setHumanPresentableName(String
    humanPresentableName);
```

The *StringSelection* Class

```
public Class StringSelection extends Object implements
    Transferable, ClipboardOwner
```

Constructors

```
public StringSelection(String data);
```

Methods

```
public synchronized Object getTransferData(DataFlavor flavor)
    throws UnsupportedFlavorException, IOException;
public synchronized DataFlavor[] getTransferDataFlavors();
public boolean isDataFlavorSupported(DataFlavor flavor);
public void lostOwnership(Clipboard clipboard, Transferable
    contents);
```

The *Transferable* Interface

```
public Interface Transferable
```

Methods

```
public Object getTransferData(DataFlavor flavor) throws
    UnsupportedFlavorException, IOException;
public DataFlavor[] getTransferDataFlavors();
public boolean isDataFlavorSupported(DataFlavor flavor);
```

The *UnsupportedFlavorException* Class

```
public Class UnsupportedFlavorException extends Exception
```

Constructors

```
public UnsupportedFlavorException(DataFlavor flavor);
```

The *java.awt.event* Package

The *ActionEvent* Class

```
public Class ActionEvent extends AWTEvent
```

Data

```
public static final int ACTION_FIRST = 1001;
public static final int ACTION_LAST = 1001;
public static final int ACTION_PERFORMED = ACTION_FIRST;
public static final int ALT_MASK = Event.ALT_MASK;
public static final int CTRL_MASK = Event.CTRL_MASK;
public static final int META_MASK = Event.META_MASK;
public static final int SHIFT_MASK = Event.SHIFT_MASK;
```

Constructors

```
public ActionEvent(Object source, int id, String command);
public ActionEvent(Object source, int id, String command, int
  modifiers);
```

Methods

```
public String getActionCommand();
public int getModifiers();
public String paramString();
```

The *ActionListener* Interface

```
public Interface ActionListener extends EventListener
```

Methods

```
public void actionPerformed(ActionEvent e);
```

The *AdjustmentEvent* Class

```
public Class AdjustmentEvent extends AWTEvent
```

Data

```
public static final int ADJUSTMENT_FIRST = 601;
```

```
public static final int ADJUSTMENT_LAST = 601;

public static final int ADJUSTMENT_VALUE_CHANGED =
  ADJUSTMENT_FIRST;

public static final int BLOCK_DECREMENT = 3;

public static final int BLOCK_INCREMENT = 4;

public static final int TRACK = 5;

public static final int UNIT_DECREMENT = 2;

public static final int UNIT_INCREMENT = 1;
```

Constructors

```
public AdjustmentEvent(Adjustable source, int id, int type,
  int value);
```

Methods

```
public Adjustable getAdjustable();

public int getAdjustmentType();

public int getValue();

public String paramString();
```

The *AdjustmentListener* Interface

```
public Interface AdjustmentListener extends EventListener
```

Methods

```
public void adjustmentValueChanged(AdjustmentEvent e);
```

The *ComponentAdapter* Class

```
public abstract Class ComponentAdapter extends Object
  implements ComponentListener
```

Methods

```
public void componentHidden(ComponentEvent e);

public void componentMoved(ComponentEvent e);

public void componentResized(ComponentEvent e);

public void componentShown(ComponentEvent e);
```

The *ComponentEvent* Class

```
public Class ComponentEvent extends AWTEvent
```

Data

```
public static final int COMPONENT_FIRST = 100;

public static final int COMPONENT_HIDDEN = 3 +
    COMPONENT_FIRST;

public static final int COMPONENT_LAST = 103;

public static final int COMPONENT_MOVED = COMPONENT_FIRST;

public static final int COMPONENT_RESIZED = 1 +
    COMPONENT_FIRST;

public static final int COMPONENT_SHOWN = 2 + COMPONENT_FIRST;
```

Constructors

```
public ComponentEvent(Component source, int id);
```

Methods

```
public Component getComponent();

public String paramString();
```

The *ComponentListener* Interface

```
public Interface ComponentListener extends EventListener
```

Methods

```
public void componentHidden(ComponentEvent e);

public void componentMoved(ComponentEvent e);

public void componentResized(ComponentEvent e);

public void componentShown(ComponentEvent e);
```

The *ContainerAdapter* Class

```
public abstract Class ContainerAdapter extends Object
    implements ContainerListener
```

Methods

```
public void componentAdded(ContainerEvent e);

public void componentRemoved(ContainerEvent e);
```

The *ContainerEvent* Class

```
public Class ContainerEvent extends ComponentEvent
```

Data

```
public static final int COMPONENT_ADDED = CONTAINER_FIRST;
public static final int COMPONENT_REMOVED = 1 +
    CONTAINER_FIRST;
public static final int CONTAINER_FIRST = 300;
public static final int CONTAINER_LAST = 301;
```

Constructors

```
public ContainerEvent(Component source, int id, Component
    child);
```

Methods

```
public Component getChild();
public Container getContainer();
public String paramString();
```

The *ContainerListener* Interface

```
public Interface ContainerListener extends EventListener
```

Methods

```
public void componentAdded(ContainerEvent e);
public void componentRemoved(ContainerEvent e);
```

The *FocusAdapter* Class

```
public abstract Class FocusAdapter extends Object implements
    FocusListener
```

Methods

```
public void focusGained(FocusEvent e);
public void focusLost(FocusEvent e);
```

The *FocusEvent* Class

```
public Class FocusEvent extends ComponentEvent
```

Data

```
public static final int FOCUS_FIRST = 1004;
public static final int FOCUS_GAINED = FOCUS_FIRST;
public static final int FOCUS_LAST = 1005;
public static final int FOCUS_LOST = 1 + FOCUS_FIRST;
```

Constructors

```
public FocusEvent(Component source, int id, boolean
  temporary);
public FocusEvent(Component source, int id);
```

Methods

```
public boolean isTemporary();
public String paramString();
```

The *FocusListener* Interface

```
public Interface FocusListener extends EventListener
```

Methods

```
public void focusGained(FocusEvent e);
public void focusLost(FocusEvent e);
```

The *InputEvent* Class

```
public abstract Class InputEvent extends ComponentEvent
```

Data

```
public static final int ALT_MASK = Event.ALT_MASK;
public static final int BUTTON1_MASK = 1 << 4;
public static final int BUTTON2_MASK = 1 << 5;
public static final int BUTTON3_MASK = 1 << 6;
public static final int CTRL_MASK = Event.CTRL_MASK;
public static final int META_MASK = Event.META_MASK;
public static final int SHIFT_MASK = Event.SHIFT_MASK;
```

Methods

```
public void consume();
public int getModifiers();
public long getWhen();
public boolean isAltDown();
public boolean isConsumed();
public boolean isControlDown();
public boolean isMetaDown();
public boolean isShiftDown();
```

The *ItemEvent* Class

```
public Class ItemEvent extends AWTEvent
```

Data

```
public static final int DESELECTED = 2;
public static final int ITEM_FIRST = 701;
public static final int ITEM_LAST = 701;
public static final int ITEM_STATE_CHANGED = ITEM_FIRST;
public static final int SELECTED = 1;
```

Constructors

```
public ItemEvent(ItemSelectable source, int id, Object item,
    int stateChange);
```

Methods

```
public Object getItem();
public ItemSelectable getItemSelectable();
public int getStateChange();
public String paramString();
```

The *ItemListener* Interface

```
public Interface ItemListener extends EventListener
```

Methods

```
void itemStateChanged(ItemEvent e);
```

The *KeyAdapter* Class

```
public abstract Class KeyAdapter extends Object implements
  KeyListener
```

Methods

```
public void keyPressed(KeyEvent e);
public void keyReleased(KeyEvent e);
public void keyTyped(KeyEvent e);
```

The *KeyEvent* Class

```
public Class KeyEvent extends InputEvent
```

Data

```
public static final char CHAR_UNDEFINED = 0x0;
public static final int KEY_FIRST = 400;
public static final int KEY_LAST = 402;
public static final int KEY_PRESSED = 1 + KEY_FIRST;
public static final int KEY_RELEASED = 2 + KEY_FIRST;
public static final int KEY_TYPED = KEY_FIRST;
public static final int VK_0 = 0x30;
public static final int VK_1 = 0x31;
public static final int VK_2 = 0x32;
public static final int VK_3 = 0x33;
public static final int VK_4 = 0x34;
public static final int VK_5 = 0x35;
public static final int VK_6 = 0x36;
public static final int VK_7 = 0x37;
public static final int VK_8 = 0x38;
public static final int VK_9 = 0x39;
public static final int VK_A = 0x41;
public static final int VK_ADD = 0x6B;
public static final int VK_ALT = 0x12;
public static final int VK_B = 0x42;
public static final int VK_BACK_QUOTE = 0xC0;
public static final int VK_BACK_SLASH = 0x5C;
public static final int VK_BACK_SPACE = '\b';
```

```
public static final int VK_C = 0x43;
public static final int VK_CANCEL = 0x03;
public static final int VK_CAPS_LOCK = 0x14;
public static final int VK_CLEAR = 0x0C;
public static final int VK_CLOSE_BRACKET = 0x5D;
public static final int VK_COMMA = 0x2C;
public static final int VK_CONTROL = 0x11;
public static final int VK_D = 0x44;
public static final int VK_DECIMAL = 0x6E;
public static final int VK_DELETE = 0x7F;
public static final int VK_DIVIDE = 0x6F;
public static final int VK_DOWN = 0x28;
public static final int VK_E = 0x45;
public static final int VK_END = 0x23;
public static final int VK_ENTER = '\n';
public static final int VK_EQUALS = 0x3D;
public static final int VK_ESCAPE = 0x1B;
public static final int VK_F = 0x46;
public static final int VK_F1 = 0x70;
public static final int VK_F10 = 0x79;
public static final int VK_F11 = 0x7A;
public static final int VK_F12 = 0x7B;
public static final int VK_F2 = 0x71;
public static final int VK_F3 = 0x72;
public static final int VK_F4 = 0x73;
public static final int VK_F5 = 0x74;
public static final int VK_F6 = 0x75;
public static final int VK_F7 = 0x76;
public static final int VK_F8 = 0x77;
public static final int VK_F9 = 0x78;
public static final int VK_G = 0x47;
public static final int VK_H = 0x48;
public static final int VK_HELP = 0x9C;
public static final int VK_HOME = 0x24;
public static final int VK_I = 0x49;
public static final int VK_INSERT = 0x9B;
```

```java
public static final int VK_J = 0x4A;
public static final int VK_K = 0x4B;
public static final int VK_L = 0x4C;
public static final int VK_LEFT = 0x25;
public static final int VK_M = 0x4D;
public static final int VK_META = 0x9D;
public static final int VK_MULTIPLY = 0x6A;
public static final int VK_N = 0x4E;
public static final int VK_NUM_LOCK = 0x90;
public static final int VK_NUMPAD0 = 0x60;
public static final int VK_NUMPAD1 = 0x61;
public static final int VK_NUMPAD2 = 0x62;
public static final int VK_NUMPAD3 = 0x63;
public static final int VK_NUMPAD4 = 0x64;
public static final int VK_NUMPAD5 = 0x65;
public static final int VK_NUMPAD6 = 0x66;
public static final int VK_NUMPAD7 = 0x67;
public static final int VK_NUMPAD8 = 0x68;
public static final int VK_NUMPAD9 = 0x69;
public static final int VK_O = 0x4F;
public static final int VK_OPEN_BRACKET = 0x5B;
public static final int VK_P = 0x50;
public static final int VK_PAGE_DOWN = 0x22;
public static final int VK_PAGE_UP = 0x21;
public static final int VK_PAUSE = 0x13;
public static final int VK_PERIOD = 0x2E;
public static final int VK_PRINTSCREEN = 0x9A;
public static final int VK_Q = 0x51;
public static final int VK_QUOTE = 0xDE;
public static final int VK_R = 0x52;
public static final int VK_RIGHT = 0x27;
public static final int VK_S = 0x53;
public static final int VK_SCROLL_LOCK = 0x91;
public static final int VK_SEMICOLON = 0x3B;
public static final int VK_SEPARATER = 0x6C;
public static final int VK_SHIFT = 0x10;
```

```
public static final int VK_SLASH = 0x2F;
public static final int VK_SPACE = 0x20;
public static final int VK_SUBTRACT = 0x6D;
public static final int VK_T = 0x54;
public static final int VK_TAB = '\t';
public static final int VK_U = 0x55;
public static final int VK_UNDEFINED = 0x0;
public static final int VK_UP = 0x26;
public static final int VK_V = 0x56;
public static final int VK_W = 0x57;
public static final int VK_X = 0x58;
public static final int VK_Y = 0x59;
public static final int VK_Z = 0x5A;
```

Constructors

```
public KeyEvent(Component source, int id, long when, int
    modifiers, int keyCode, char keyChar);
public KeyEvent(Component source, int id, long when, int
    modifiers, int keyCode);
```

Methods

```
public static String getKeyModifiersText(int modifiers);
public static String getKeyText(int keyCode);
public char getKeyChar();
public int getKeyCode();
public boolean isActionKey();
public String paramString();
public void setKeyCode(int keyCode);
public void setModifiers(int modifiers);
```

The *KeyListener* Interface

```
public Interface KeyListener extends EventListener
```

Methods

```
public void keyPressed(KeyEvent e);
public void keyReleased(KeyEvent e);
public void keyTyped(KeyEvent e);
```

The *MouseAdapter* Class

```
public abstract Class MouseAdapter extends Object implements
  MouseListener
```

Methods

```
public void mouseClicked(MouseEvent e);
public void mouseEntered(MouseEvent e);
public void mouseExited(MouseEvent e);
public void mousePressed(MouseEvent e);
public void mouseReleased(MouseEvent e);
```

The *MouseEvent* Class

```
public Class MouseEvent extends InputEvent
```

Data

```
public static final int MOUSE_CLICKED = MOUSE_FIRST;
public static final int MOUSE_DRAGGED = 6 + MOUSE_FIRST;
public static final int MOUSE_ENTERED = 4 + MOUSE_FIRST;
public static final int MOUSE_EXITED = 5 + MOUSE_FIRST;
public static final int MOUSE_FIRST = 500;
public static final int MOUSE_LAST = 506;
public static final int MOUSE_MOVED = 3 + MOUSE_FIRST;
public static final int MOUSE_PRESSED = 1 + MOUSE_FIRST;
public static final int MOUSE_RELEASED = 2 + MOUSE_FIRST;
```

Constructors

```
public MouseEvent(Component source, int id, long when, int
  modifiers, int x, int y, int clickCount, boolean
  popupTrigger);
```

Methods

```
public int getClickCount();
public Point getPoint();
public int getX();
public int getY();
public boolean isPopupTrigger();
public String paramString();
public synchronized void translatePoint(int x, int y);
```

The *MouseListener* Interface

```
public Interface MouseListener extends EventListener
```

Methods

```
public void mouseClicked(MouseEvent e);
public void mouseEntered(MouseEvent e);
public void mouseExited(MouseEvent e);
public void mousePressed(MouseEvent e);
public void mouseReleased(MouseEvent e);
```

The *MouseMotionAdapter* Class

```
public abstract Class MouseMotionAdapter extends Object
    implements MouseMotionListener
```

Methods

```
public void mouseDragged(MouseEvent e);
public void mouseMoved(MouseEvent e);
```

The *MouseMotionListener* Interface

```
public Interface MouseMotionListener extends EventListener
```

Methods

```
public void mouseDragged(MouseEvent e);
public void mouseMoved(MouseEvent e);
```

The *PaintEvent* Class

```
public Class PaintEvent extends ComponentEvent
```

Data

```
public static final int PAINT = PAINT_FIRST;
public static final int PAINT_FIRST = 800;
public static final int PAINT_LAST = 801;
public static final int UPDATE = PAINT_FIRST + 1;
```

Constructors

```
public PaintEvent(Component source, int id, Graphics g);
```

Methods

```
public Graphics getGraphics();
public String paramString();
```

The *TextEvent* Class

```
public Class TextEvent extends AWTEvent
```

Data

```
public static final int TEXT_FIRST = 900;
public static final int TEXT_LAST = 900;
public static final int TEXT_VALUE_CHANGED = TEXT_FIRST;
```

Constructors

```
public TextEvent(Object source, int id);
```

Methods

```
public String paramString();
```

The *TextListener* Interface

```
public Interface TextListener extends EventListener
```

Methods

```
public void textValueChanged(TextEvent e);
```

The *WindowAdapter* Class

```
public abstract Class WindowAdapter extends Object implements
    WindowListener
```

Methods

```
public void windowActivated(WindowEvent e);
public void windowClosed(WindowEvent e);
public void windowClosing(WindowEvent e);
public void windowDeactivated(WindowEvent e);
```

```
public void windowDeiconified(WindowEvent e);
public void windowIconified(WindowEvent e);
public void windowOpened(WindowEvent e);
```

The *WindowEvent* Class

```
public Class WindowEvent extends ComponentEvent
```

Data

```
public static final int WINDOW_ACTIVATED = 5 + WINDOW_FIRST;
public static final int WINDOW_CLOSED = 2 + WINDOW_FIRST;
public static final int WINDOW_CLOSING = 1 + WINDOW_FIRST;
public static final int WINDOW_DEACTIVATED = 6 + WINDOW_FIRST;
public static final int WINDOW_DEICONIFIED = 4 + WINDOW_FIRST;
public static final int WINDOW_FIRST = 200;
public static final int WINDOW_ICONIFIED = 3 + WINDOW_FIRST;
public static final int WINDOW_LAST = 206;
public static final int WINDOW_OPENED = WINDOW_FIRST;
```

Constructors

```
public WindowEvent(Window source, int id);
```

Methods

```
public Window getWindow();
public String paramString();
```

The *WindowListener* Interface

```
public Interface WindowListener extends EventListener
```

Methods

```
public void windowActivated(WindowEvent e);
public void windowClosed(WindowEvent e);
public void windowClosing(WindowEvent e);
public void windowDeactivated(WindowEvent e);
public void windowDeiconified(WindowEvent e);
public void windowIconified(WindowEvent e);
public void windowOpened(WindowEvent e);
```

The *java.awt.image* Package

The *AverageScaleFilter* Class

```
public Class AverageScaleFilter extends ReplicateScaleFilter
```

Constructors
```
public AverageScaleFilter(int width, int height);
```

Methods
```
public void setHints(int hints);
public void setPixels(int x, int y, int w, int h, ColorModel
   model, byte pixels[], int off, int scansize);
public void setPixels(int x, int y, int w, int h, ColorModel
   model, int pixels[], int off, int scansize);
```

The *ColorModel* Class

```
public abstract Class ColorModel extends Object
```

Constructors
```
public ColorModel(int bits);
```

Methods
```
public static ColorModel getRGBdefault();
public abstract int getAlpha(int pixel);
public abstract int getBlue(int pixel);
public abstract int getGreen(int pixel);
public abstract int getRed(int pixel);
private native void deletepData();
public void finalize();
public int getPixelSize();
public int getRGB(int pixel);
```

The *CropImageFilter* Class

```
public Class CropImageFilter extends ImageFilter
```

Constructors
```
public CropImageFilter(int x, int y, int w, int h);
```

Methods

```
public void setDimensions(int w, int h);

public void setPixels(int x, int y, int w, int h, ColorModel
    model, byte pixels[], int off, int scansize);

public void setPixels(int x, int y, int w, int h, ColorModel
    model, int pixels[], int off, int scansize);

public void setProperties(Hashtable props);
```

The *DirectColorModel* Class

```
public Class DirectColorModel extends ColorModel
```

Constructors

```
public DirectColorModel(int bits, int rmask, int gmask, int
    bmask);

public DirectColorModel(int bits, int rmask, int gmask, int
    bmask, int amask);
```

Methods

```
final public int getAlpha(int pixel);

final public int getAlphaMask();

final public int getBlue(int pixel);

final public int getBlueMask();

final public int getGreen(int pixel);

final public int getGreenMask();

final public int getRed(int pixel);

final public int getRedMask();

final public int getRGB(int pixel);
```

The *FilteredImageSource* Class

```
public Class FilteredImageSource extends Object implements
    ImageProducer
```

Constructors

```
public FilteredImageSource(ImageProducer orig,
    ImageFilter imgf);
```

Methods

```
public synchronized void addConsumer(ImageConsumer ic);
public synchronized boolean isConsumer(ImageConsumer ic);
public synchronized void removeConsumer(ImageConsumer ic);
public void requestTopDownLeftRightResend(ImageConsumer ic);
public void startProduction(ImageConsumer ic);
```

The *ImageConsumer* Interface

```
public Interface ImageConsumer
```

Methods

```
void imageComplete(int status);
void setColorModel(ColorModel model);
void setDimensions(int width, int height);
void setHints(int hintflags);
void setPixels(int x, int y, int w, int h, ColorModel model,
   byte pixels[], int off, int scansize);
void setPixels(int x, int y, int w, int h, ColorModel model,
   int pixels[], int off, int scansize);
void setProperties(Hashtable props);
```

The *ImageFilter* Class

```
public Class ImageFilter extends Object implements
   ImageConsumer, Cloneable
```

Methods

```
public Object clone();
public ImageFilter getFilterInstance(ImageConsumer ic);
public void imageComplete(int status);
public void resendTopDownLeftRight(ImageProducer ip);
public void setColorModel(ColorModel model);
public void setDimensions(int width, int height);
public void setHints(int hints);
public void setPixels(int x, int y, int w, int h, ColorModel
   model, byte pixels[], int off, int scansize);
```

```
public void setPixels(int x, int y, int w, int h, ColorModel
    model, int pixels[], int off, int scansize);
public void setProperties(Hashtable props);
```

The *ImageObserver* Interface

```
public Interface ImageObserver
```

Data

```
public static final int ABORT = 128;
public static final int ALLBITS = 32;
public static final int ERROR = 64;
public static final int FRAMEBITS = 16;
public static final int HEIGHT = 2;
public static final int PROPERTIES = 4;
public static final int SOMEBITS = 8;
public static final int WIDTH = 1;
```

Methods

```
public boolean imageUpdate(Image img, int infoflags, int x,
    int y, int width, int height);
```

The *ImageProducer* Interface

```
public Interface ImageProducer
```

Methods

```
public void addConsumer(ImageConsumer ic);
public boolean isConsumer(ImageConsumer ic);
public void removeConsumer(ImageConsumer ic);
public void requestTopDownLeftRightResend(ImageConsumer ic);
public void startProduction(ImageConsumer ic);
```

The *IndexColorModel* Class

```
public Class IndexColorModel extends ColorModel
```

Constructors

```
public IndexColorModel(int bits, int size, byte r[], byte g[],
    byte b[]);
```

```
public IndexColorModel(int bits, int size, byte r[], byte g[],
    byte b[], int trans);
public IndexColorModel(int bits, int size, byte r[], byte g[],
    byte b[], byte a[]);
public IndexColorModel(int bits, int size, byte cmap[], int
    start, boolean hasalpha);
public IndexColorModel(int bits, int size, byte cmap[], int
    start, boolean hasalpha, int trans);
```

Methods

```
final public int getAlpha(int pixel);
final public void getAlphas(byte a[]);
final public int getBlue(int pixel);
final public void getBlues(byte b[]);
final public int getGreen(int pixel);
final public void getGreens(byte g[]);
final public int getMapSize();
final public int getRed(int pixel);
final public void getReds(byte r[]);
final public int getRGB(int pixel);
final public int getTransparentPixel();
```

The *MemoryImageSource* Class

```
public Class MemoryImageSource extends Object implements
    ImageProducer
```

Constructors

```
public MemoryImageSource(int w, int h, ColorModel cm, byte[]
    pix, int off, int scan);
public MemoryImageSource(int w, int h, ColorModel cm, byte[]
    pix, int off, int scan, Hashtable props);
public MemoryImageSource(int w, int h, ColorModel cm, int[]
    pix, int off, int scan);
public MemoryImageSource(int w, int h, ColorModel cm, int[]
    pix, int off, int scan, Hashtable props);
public MemoryImageSource(int w, int h, int pix[], int off, int
    scan);
public MemoryImageSource(int w, int h, int pix[], int off, int
    scan, Hashtable props);
```

Methods

```
public synchronized void addConsumer(ImageConsumer ic);

public synchronized boolean isConsumer(ImageConsumer ic);

public void newPixels();

public synchronized void newPixels(byte[] newpix, ColorModel
    newmodel, int offset, int scansize);

public synchronized void newPixels(int x, int y, int w, int
    h);

public synchronized void newPixels(int x, int y, int w, int h,
    boolean framenotify);

public synchronized void newPixels(int[] newpix, ColorModel
    newmodel, int offset, int scansize);

public synchronized void removeConsumer(ImageConsumer ic);

public void requestTopDownLeftRightResend(ImageConsumer ic);

public synchronized void setAnimated(boolean animated);

public synchronized void setFullBufferUpdates(boolean
    fullbuffers);

public void startProduction(ImageConsumer ic);
```

The *PixelGrabber* Class

```
public Class PixelGrabber extends Object implements
    ImageConsumer
```

Constructors

```
public PixelGrabber(Image img, int x, int y, int w, int h,
    int[] pix, int off, int scansize);

public PixelGrabber(ImageProducer ip, int x, int y, int w, int
    h, int[] pix, int off, int scansize);

public PixelGrabber(Image img, int x, int y, int w, int h,
    boolean forceRGB);
```

Methods

```
public synchronized void abortGrabbing();

public synchronized ColorModel getColorModel();

public synchronized int getHeight();

public synchronized Object getPixels();

public synchronized int getStatus();

public synchronized int getWidth();
```

```
public boolean grabPixels() throws InterruptedException;
public synchronized boolean grabPixels(long ms) throws
   InterruptedException;
public synchronized void imageComplete(int status);
public void setColorModel(ColorModel model);
public void setDimensions(int width, int height);
public void setHints(int hints);
public void setPixels(int srcX, int srcY, int srcW, int srcH,
   ColorModel model, byte pixels[], int srcOff, int srcScan);
public void setPixels(int srcX, int srcY, int srcW, int srcH,
   ColorModel model, int pixels[], int srcOff, int srcScan);
public void setProperties(Hashtable props);
public synchronized void startGrabbing();
public synchronized int status();
```

The *RGBImageFilter* Class

```
public abstract Class RGBImageFilter extends ImageFilter
```

Methods

```
public abstract int filterRGB(int x, int y, int rgb);
public IndexColorModel filterIndexColorModel(
   IndexColorModel icm);
public void filterRGBPixels(int x, int y, int w, int h, int
   pixels[], int off, int scansize);
public void setColorModel(ColorModel model);
public void setPixels(int x, int y, int w, int h, ColorModel
   model, byte pixels[], int off, int scansize);
public void setPixels(int x, int y, int w, int h, ColorModel
   model, int pixels[], int off, int scansize);
public void substituteColorModel(ColorModel oldcm, ColorModel
   newcm);
```

The *ReplicateScaleFilter* Class

```
public Class ReplicateScaleFilter extends ImageFilter
```

Constructors

```
public ReplicateScaleFilter(int width, int height);
```

Methods

```
public void setDimensions(int w, int h);
public void setPixels(int x, int y, int w, int h, ColorModel
    model, byte pixels[], int off, int scansize);
public void setPixels(int x, int y, int w, int h, ColorModel
    model, int pixels[], int off, int scansize);
public void setProperties(Hashtable props);
```

The *java.awt.peer* Package

The *ButtonPeer* Interface

```
public Interface ButtonPeer extends ComponentPeer
```

Methods
```
void setLabel(String label);
```

The *CanvasPeer* Interface

```
public Interface CanvasPeer extends ComponentPeer
```

The *CheckboxMenuItemPeer* Interface

```
public Interface CheckboxMenuItemPeer extends MenuItemPeer
```

Methods
```
void setState(boolean t);
```

The *CheckboxPeer* Interface

```
public Interface CheckboxPeer extends ComponentPeer
```

Methods
```
void setCheckboxGroup(CheckboxGroup g);
void setLabel(String label);
void setState(boolean state);
```

The *ChoicePeer* Interface

```
public Interface ChoicePeer extends ComponentPeer
```

Methods

```
void add(String item, int index);
void addItem(String item, int index);
void remove(int index);
void select(int index);
```

The *ComponentPeer* Interface

```
public Interface ComponentPeer
```

Methods

```
int checkImage(Image img, int w, int h, ImageObserver o);
Image createImage(ImageProducer producer);
Image createImage(int width, int height);
void disable();
void dispose();
void enable();
ColorModel getColorModel();
FontMetrics getFontMetrics(Font font);
Graphics getGraphics();
Point getLocationOnScreen();
Dimension getMinimumSize();
Dimension getPreferredSize();
java.awt.Toolkit getToolkit();
void handleEvent(AWTEvent e);
void hide();
boolean isFocusTraversable();
Dimension minimumSize();
void paint(Graphics g);
Dimension preferredSize();
boolean prepareImage(Image img, int w, int h,
    ImageObserver o);
void print(Graphics g);
```

```
void repaint(long tm, int x, int y, int width, int height);
void requestFocus();
void reshape(int x, int y, int width, int height);
void setBackground(Color c);
void setBounds(int x, int y, int width, int height);
void setCursor(Cursor cursor);
void setEnabled(boolean b);
void setFont(Font f);
void setForeground(Color c);
void setVisible(boolean b);
void show();
```

The *ContainerPeer* Interface

```
public Interface ContainerPeer extends ComponentPeer
```

Methods
```
void beginValidate();
void endValidate();
Insets getInsets();
Insets insets();
```

The *DialogPeer* Interface

```
public Interface DialogPeer extends WindowPeer
```

Methods
```
void setResizable(boolean resizeable);
void setTitle(String title);
```

The *FileDialogPeer* Interface

```
public Interface FileDialogPeer extends DialogPeer
```

Methods
```
void setDirectory(String dir);
void setFile(String file);
void setFilenameFilter(FilenameFilter filter);
```

The *FontPeer* Interface

```
public Interface FontPeer
```

The *FramePeer* Interface

```
public Interface FramePeer extends WindowPeer
```

Methods
```
void setIconImage(Image im);
void setMenuBar(MenuBar mb);
void setResizable(boolean resizeable);
void setTitle(String title);
```

The *LabelPeer* Interface

```
public Interface LabelPeer extends ComponentPeer
```

Methods
```
void setAlignment(int alignment);
void setText(String label);
```

The *LightweightPeer* Interface

```
public Interface LightweightPeer extends ComponentPeer
```

The *ListPeer* Interface

```
public Interface ListPeer extends ComponentPeer
```

Methods
```
void add(String item, int index);
void addItem(String item, int index);
void clear();
void delItems(int start, int end);
void deselect(int index);
Dimension getMinimumSize(int rows);
Dimension getPreferredSize(int rows);
```

```
int[] getSelectedIndexes();
void makeVisible(int index);
Dimension minimumSize(int v);
Dimension preferredSize(int v);
void removeAll();
void select(int index);
void setMultipleMode(boolean b);
void setMultipleSelections(boolean v);
```

The *MenuBarPeer* Interface

```
public Interface MenuBarPeer extends MenuComponentPeer
```

Methods
```
void addHelpMenu(Menu m);
void addMenu(Menu m);
void delMenu(int index);
```

The *MenuComponentPeer* Interface

```
public Interface MenuComponentPeer
```

Methods
```
void dispose();
```

The *MenuItemPeer* Interface

```
public Interface MenuItemPeer extends MenuComponentPeer
```

Methods
```
void disable();
void enable();
void setEnabled(boolean b);
void setLabel(String label);
```

The *MenuPeer* Interface

```
public Interface MenuPeer extends MenuItemPeer
```

Methods

```
void addItem(MenuItem item);
void addSeparator();
void delItem(int index);
```

The *PanelPeer* Interface

```
public Interface PanelPeer extends ContainerPeer
```

The *PopupMenuPeer* Interface

```
public Interface PopupMenuPeer extends MenuPeer
```

Methods

```
void show(Event e);
```

The *ScrollPanePeer* Interface

```
public Interface ScrollPanePeer extends ContainerPeer
```

Methods

```
void childResized(int w, int h);
int getHScrollbarHeight();
int getVScrollbarWidth();
void setScrollPosition(int x, int y);
void setUnitIncrement(Adjustable adj, int u);
void setValue(Adjustable adj, int v);
```

The *ScrollbarPeer* Interface

```
public Interface ScrollbarPeer extends ComponentPeer
```

Methods

```
void setLineIncrement(int 1);
void setPageIncrement(int 1);
void setValues(int value, int visible, int minimum, int
    maximum);
```

The *TextAreaPeer* Interface

```
public Interface TextAreaPeer extends TextComponentPeer
```

Methods
```
Dimension getMinimumSize(int rows, int columns);
Dimension getPreferredSize(int rows, int columns);
void insert(String text, int pos);
void insertText(String txt, int pos);
Dimension minimumSize(int rows, int cols);
Dimension preferredSize(int rows, int cols);
void replaceRange(String text, int start, int end);
void replaceText(String txt, int start, int end);
```

The *TextComponentPeer* Interface

```
public Interface TextComponentPeer extends ComponentPeer
```

Methods
```
int getCaretPosition();
int getSelectionEnd();
int getSelectionStart();
String getText();
void select(int selStart, int selEnd);
void setCaretPosition(int pos);
void setEditable(boolean editable);
void setText(String 1);
```

The *TextFieldPeer* Interface

```
public Interface TextFieldPeer extends TextComponentPeer
```

Methods
```
Dimension getMinimumSize(int columns);
Dimension getPreferredSize(int columns);
Dimension minimumSize(int cols);
Dimension preferredSize(int cols);
```

```
void setEchoChar(char echoChar);
void setEchoCharacter(char c);
```

The *WindowPeer* Interface

```
public Interface WindowPeer extends ContainerPeer
```

Methods
```
void toBack();
void toFront();
```

The *java.io* Package

The *BufferedInputStream* Class

```
public Class BufferedInputStream extends FilterInputStream
```

Constructors
```
public BufferedInputStream(InputStream in);
public BufferedInputStream(InputStream in, int size);
```

Methods
```
public synchronized int available() throws IOException;
public synchronized void mark(int readlimit);
public boolean markSupported();
public synchronized int read() throws IOException;
public synchronized int read(byte b[], int off, int len)
    throws IOException;
public synchronized void reset() throws IOException;
public synchronized long skip(long n) throws IOException;
```

The *BufferedOutputStream* Class

```
public Class BufferedOutputStream extends FilterOutputStream
```

Constructors
```
public BufferedOutputStream(OutputStream out);
public BufferedOutputStream(OutputStream out, int size);
```

Methods

```
public synchronized void flush() throws IOException;
public synchronized void write(byte b[], int off, int len)
    throws IOException;
public synchronized void write(int b) throws IOException;
```

The *BufferedReader* Class

```
public Class BufferedReader extends Reader
```

Constructors

```
public BufferedReader(Reader in, int sz);
public BufferedReader(Reader in);
```

Methods

```
public void close() throws IOException;
public void mark(int readAheadLimit) throws IOException;
public boolean markSupported();
public int read() throws IOException;
public int read(char cbuf[], int off, int len) throws
    IOException;
public String readLine() throws IOException;
public boolean ready() throws IOException;
public void reset() throws IOException;
public long skip(long n) throws IOException;
```

The *BufferedWriter* Class

```
public Class BufferedWriter extends Writer
```

Constructors

```
public BufferedWriter(Writer out);
public BufferedWriter(Writer out, int sz);
```

Methods

```
public void close() throws IOException;
public void flush() throws IOException;
public void newLine() throws IOException;
public void write(char cbuf[], int off, int len) throws
    IOException;
```

```
public void write(int c) throws IOException;
public void write(String s, int off, int len) throws
    IOException;
```

The *ByteArrayInputStream* Class

```
public Class ByteArrayInputStream extends InputStream
```

Constructors

```
public ByteArrayInputStream(byte buf[]);
public ByteArrayInputStream(byte buf[], int offset, int
    length);
```

Methods

```
public synchronized int available();
public synchronized int read();
public synchronized int read(byte b[], int off, int len);
public synchronized void reset();
public synchronized long skip(long n);
```

The *ByteArrayOutputStream* Class

```
public Class ByteArrayOutputStream extends OutputStream
```

Constructors

```
public ByteArrayOutputStream();
public ByteArrayOutputStream(int size);
```

Methods

```
public synchronized void reset();
public int size();
public synchronized byte toByteArray()[];
public String toString();
public String toString(int hibyte);
public String toString(String enc) throws
    UnsupportedEncodingException;
public synchronized void write(byte b[], int off, int len);
public synchronized void write(int b);
public synchronized void writeTo(OutputStream out) throws
    IOException;
```

The *CharArrayReader* Class

public Class CharArrayReader extends Reader

Constructors
public CharArrayReader(char buf[]);

public CharArrayReader(char buf[], int offset, int length);

Methods
public void close();

public void mark(int readAheadLimit) throws IOException;

public boolean markSupported();

public int read() throws IOException;

public int read(char b[], int off, int len) throws
  IOException;

public boolean ready() throws IOException;

public void reset() throws IOException;

public long skip(long n) throws IOException;

The *CharArrayWriter* Class

public Class CharArrayWriter extends Writer

Constructors
public CharArrayWriter();

public CharArrayWriter(int initialSize);

Methods
public void close();

public void flush();

public void reset();

public int size();

public char toCharArray()[];

public String toString();

public void write(char c[], int off, int len);

public void write(int c);

public void write(String str, int off, int len);

public void writeTo(Writer out) throws IOException;

The *CharConversionException* Class

```
public Class CharConversionException extends
  java.io.IOException
```

Constructors

```
public CharConversionException();
public CharConversionException(String s);
```

The *DataInput* Interface

```
public Interface DataInput
```

Methods

```
boolean readBoolean() throws IOException;
byte readByte() throws IOException;
char readChar() throws IOException;
double readDouble() throws IOException;
float readFloat() throws IOException;
void readFully(byte b[]) throws IOException;
void readFully(byte b[], int off, int len) throws IOException;
int readInt() throws IOException;
String readLine() throws IOException;
long readLong() throws IOException;
short readShort() throws IOException;
int readUnsignedByte() throws IOException;
int readUnsignedShort() throws IOException;
String readUTF() throws IOException;
int skipBytes(int n) throws IOException;
```

The *DataInputStream* Class

```
public Class DataInputStream extends FilterInputStream
  implements DataInput
```

Constructors

```
public DataInputStream(InputStream in);
```

Methods

```
public final static String readUTF(DataInput in) throws
    IOException;
public final int read(byte b[]) throws IOException;
public final int read(byte b[], int off, int len) throws
    IOException;
public final boolean readBoolean() throws IOException;
public final byte readByte() throws IOException;
public final char readChar() throws IOException;
public final double readDouble() throws IOException;
public final float readFloat() throws IOException;
public final void readFully(byte b[]) throws IOException;
public final void readFully(byte b[], int off, int len) throws
    IOException;
public final int readInt() throws IOException;
public final String readLine() throws IOException;
public final long readLong() throws IOException;
public final short readShort() throws IOException;
public final int readUnsignedByte() throws IOException;
public final int readUnsignedShort() throws IOException;
public final String readUTF() throws IOException;
public final int skipBytes(int n) throws IOException;
```

The *DataOutput* Interface

```
public Interface DataOutput
```

Methods

```
void write(byte b[]) throws IOException;
void write(byte b[], int off, int len) throws IOException;
void write(int b) throws IOException;
void writeBoolean(boolean v) throws IOException;
void writeByte(int v) throws IOException;
void writeBytes(String s) throws IOException;
void writeChar(int v) throws IOException;
void writeChars(String s) throws IOException;
void writeDouble(double v) throws IOException;
void writeFloat(float v) throws IOException;
```

```
void writeInt(int v) throws IOException;
void writeLong(long v) throws IOException;
void writeShort(int v) throws IOException;
void writeUTF(String str) throws IOException;
```

The *DataOutputStream* Class

```
public Class DataOutputStream extends FilterOutputStream
    implements DataOutput
```

Constructors

```
public DataOutputStream(OutputStream out);
```

Methods

```
public void flush() throws IOException;
public final int size();
public synchronized void write(byte b[], int off, int len)
    throws IOException;
public synchronized void write(int b) throws IOException;
public final void writeBoolean(boolean v) throws IOException;
public final void writeByte(int v) throws IOException;
public final void writeBytes(String s) throws IOException;
public final void writeChar(int v) throws IOException;
public final void writeChars(String s) throws IOException;
public final void writeDouble(double v) throws IOException;
public final void writeFloat(float v) throws IOException;
public final void writeInt(int v) throws IOException;
public final void writeLong(long v) throws IOException;
public final void writeShort(int v) throws IOException;
public final void writeUTF(String str) throws IOException;
```

The *EOFException* Class

```
public Class EOFException extends IOException
```

Constructors

```
public EOFException();
public EOFException(String s);
```

The *Externalizable* Interface

```
public Interface Externalizable extends java.io.Serializable
```

Methods

```
void readExternal(ObjectInput in) throws IOException,
   ClassNotFoundException;
void writeExternal(ObjectOutput out) throws IOException;
```

The *File* Class

```
public Class File extends Object implements
   java.io.Serializable
```

Data

```
public static final String pathSeparator =
   System.getProperty("path.separator");
public static final char pathSeparatorChar =
   pathSeparator.charAt(0);
public static final String separator =
   System.getProperty("file.separator");
public static final char separatorChar = separator.charAt(0);
```

Constructors

```
public File(String path);
public File(String path, String name);
public File(File dir, String name);
```

Methods

```
private native String canonPath(String p) throws IOException;
public boolean canRead();
private native boolean canRead0();
public boolean canWrite();
private native boolean canWrite0();
public boolean delete();
private native boolean delete0();
public boolean equals(Object obj);
public boolean exists();
private native boolean exists0();
```

```
public String getAbsolutePath();
public String getCanonicalPath() throws IOException;
public String getName();
public String getParent();
public String getPath();
public int hashCode();
public native boolean isAbsolute();
public boolean isDirectory();
private native boolean isDirectory0();
public boolean isFile();
private native boolean isFile0();
public long lastModified();
private native long lastModified0();
public long length();
private native long length0();
public String[] list();
public String[] list(FilenameFilter filter);
private native String[] list0();
public boolean mkdir();
private native boolean mkdir0();
public boolean mkdirs();
public boolean renameTo(File dest);
private native boolean renameTo0(File dest);
private native boolean rmdir0();
public String toString();
```

The *FileDescriptor* Class

```
public Class FileDescriptor extends Object
```

Data

```
public static final FileDescriptor err = initSystemFD(new
  FileDescriptor(),2);
public static final FileDescriptor in = initSystemFD(new
  FileDescriptor(),0);
public static final FileDescriptor out = initSystemFD(new
  FileDescriptor(),1);
```

Methods

```
private static native FileDescriptor
  initSystemFD(FileDescriptor fdObj, int desc);
public native void sync() throws SyncFailedException;
public native boolean valid();
```

The *FileInputStream* Class

```
public Class FileInputStream extends InputStream
```

Constructors

```
public FileInputStream(String name) throws
  FileNotFoundException;
public FileInputStream(File file) throws
  FileNotFoundException;
public FileInputStream(FileDescriptor fdObj);
```

Methods

```
public native int available() throws IOException;
public native void close() throws IOException;
public final FileDescriptor getFD() throws IOException;
private native void open(String name) throws IOException;
public native int read() throws IOException;
public int read(byte b[]) throws IOException;
public int read(byte b[], int off, int len) throws
  IOException;
private native int readBytes(byte b[], int off, int len)
  throws IOException;
public native long skip(long n) throws IOException;
```

The *FileNotFoundException* Class

```
public Class FileNotFoundException extends IOException
```

Constructors

```
public FileNotFoundException();
public FileNotFoundException(String s);
```

The *FileOutputStream* Class

```
public Class FileOutputStream extends OutputStream
```

Constructors

```
public FileOutputStream(String name) throws IOException;
public FileOutputStream(String name, boolean append) throws
   IOException;
public FileOutputStream(File file) throws IOException;
public FileOutputStream(FileDescriptor fdObj);
```

Methods

```
public native void close() throws IOException;
public final FileDescriptor getFD() throws IOException;
private native void open(String name) throws IOException;
private native void openAppend(String name) throws
   IOException;
public void write(byte b[]) throws IOException;
public void write(byte b[], int off, int len) throws
   IOException;
public native void write(int b) throws IOException;
private native void writeBytes(byte b[], int off, int len)
   throws IOException;
```

The *FileReader* Class

```
public Class FileReader extends InputStreamReader
```

Constructors

```
public FileReader(String fileName) throws
   FileNotFoundException;
public FileReader(File file) throws FileNotFoundException;
public FileReader(FileDescriptor fd);
```

The *FileWriter* Class

```
public Class FileWriter extends OutputStreamWriter
```

Constructors

```
public FileWriter(String fileName) throws IOException;
```

```
public FileWriter(String fileName, boolean append) throws
    IOException;
public FileWriter(File file) throws IOException;
public FileWriter(FileDescriptor fd);
```

The *FilenameFilter* Interface

```
public Interface FilenameFilter
```

Methods

```
boolean accept(File dir, String name);
```

The *FilterInputStream* Class

```
public Class FilterInputStream extends InputStream
```

Methods

```
public int available() throws IOException;
public void close() throws IOException;
public synchronized void mark(int readlimit);
public boolean markSupported();
public int read() throws IOException;
public int read(byte b[]) throws IOException;
public int read(byte b[], int off, int len) throws
    IOException;
public synchronized void reset() throws IOException;
public long skip(long n) throws IOException;
```

The *FilterOutputStream* Class

```
public Class FilterOutputStream extends OutputStream
```

Constructors

```
public FilterOutputStream(OutputStream out);
```

Methods

```
public void close() throws IOException;
public void flush() throws IOException;
public void write(byte b[]) throws IOException;
```

```
public void write(byte b[], int off, int len) throws
   IOException;
public void write(int b) throws IOException;
```

The *FilterReader* Class

```
public abstract Class FilterReader extends Reader
```

Methods

```
public void close() throws IOException;
public void mark(int readAheadLimit) throws IOException;
public boolean markSupported();
public int read() throws IOException;
public int read(char cbuf[], int off, int len) throws
   IOException;
public boolean ready() throws IOException;
public void reset() throws IOException;
public long skip(long n) throws IOException;
```

The *FilterWriter* Class

```
public abstract Class FilterWriter extends Writer
```

Methods

```
public void close() throws IOException;
public void flush() throws IOException;
public void write(char cbuf[], int off, int len) throws
   IOException;
public void write(int c) throws IOException;
public void write(String str, int off, int len) throws
   IOException;
```

The *IOException* Class

```
public Class IOException extends Exception
```

Constructors

```
public IOException();
public IOException(String s);
```

The *InputStream* Class

```
public abstract Class InputStream extends Object
```

Methods

```
abstract public int available() throws IOException;
public abstract int read() throws IOException;
public void close() throws IOException;
public synchronized void mark(int readlimit);
public boolean markSupported();
public int read(byte b[]) throws IOException;
public int read(byte b[], int off, int len) throws
    IOException;
public synchronized void reset() throws IOException;
public long skip(long n) throws IOException;
```

The *InputStreamReader* Class

```
public Class InputStreamReader extends Reader
```

Constructors

```
public InputStreamReader(InputStream in);
public InputStreamReader(InputStream in, String enc) throws
    UnsupportedEncodingException;
```

Methods

```
public void close() throws IOException;
public String getEncoding();
public int read() throws IOException;
public int read(char cbuf[], int off, int len) throws
    IOException;
public boolean ready() throws IOException;
```

The *InterruptedIOException* Class

```
public Class InterruptedIOException extends IOException
```

Data

```
public int bytesTransferred = 0;
```

Constructors

```
public InterruptedIOException();
public InterruptedIOException(String s);
```

The *InvalidClassException* Class

```
public Class InvalidClassException extends
   ObjectStreamException
```

Data

```
public String classname;
```

Constructors

```
public InvalidClassException(String reason);
public InvalidClassException(String cname, String reason);
```

Methods

```
public String getMessage();
```

The *InvalidObjectException* Class

```
public Class InvalidObjectException extends
   ObjectStreamException
```

Constructors

```
public InvalidObjectException(String reason);
```

The *LineNumberInputStream* Class

```
public Class LineNumberInputStream extends FilterInputStream
```

Constructors

```
public LineNumberInputStream(InputStream in);
```

Methods

```
public int available() throws IOException;
public int getLineNumber();
public void mark(int readlimit);
public int read() throws IOException;
public int read(byte b[], int off, int len) throws
   IOException;
```

```
public void reset() throws IOException;
public void setLineNumber(int lineNumber);
public long skip(long n) throws IOException;
```

The *LineNumberReader* Class

```
public Class LineNumberReader extends BufferedReader
```

Constructors
```
public LineNumberReader(Reader in);
public LineNumberReader(Reader in, int sz);
```

Methods
```
public int getLineNumber();
public void mark(int readAheadLimit) throws IOException;
public int read() throws IOException;
public int read(char cbuf[], int off, int len) throws
    IOException;
public String readLine() throws IOException;
public void reset() throws IOException;
public void setLineNumber(int lineNumber);
public long skip(long n) throws IOException;
```

The *NotActiveException* Class

```
public Class NotActiveException extends ObjectStreamException
```

Constructors
```
public NotActiveException(String reason);
public NotActiveException();
```

The *NotSerializableException* Class

```
public Class NotSerializableException extends
    ObjectStreamException
```

Constructors
```
public NotSerializableException(String classname);
public NotSerializableException();
```

The *ObjectInput* Interface

```
public Interface ObjectInput extends DataInput
```

Methods
```
public int available() throws IOException;

public void close() throws IOException;

public int read() throws IOException;

public int read(byte b[]) throws IOException;

public int read(byte b[], int off, int len) throws
  IOException;

public Object readObject() throws ClassNotFoundException,
  IOException;

public long skip(long n) throws IOException;
```

The *ObjectInputStream* Class

```
public Class ObjectInputStream extends InputStream implements
  ObjectInput, ObjectStreamConstants
```

Constructors
```
public ObjectInputStream(InputStream in) throws IOException,
  StreamCorruptedException;
```

Methods
```
private static native Object allocateNewArray(Class aclass,
  int length);

private static native Object allocateNewObject(Class aclass,
  Class initclass) throws InstantiationException,
  IllegalAccessException;

public int available() throws IOException;

public void close() throws IOException;

public final void defaultReadObject() throws IOException,
  ClassNotFoundException, NotActiveException;

private native void inputArrayValues(Object o, Class
  currclass) throws InvalidClassException,
  StreamCorruptedException, ClassNotFoundException,
  IOException;

private native void inputClassFields(Object o, Class cl, int[]
  fieldSequence) throws InvalidClassException,
  StreamCorruptedException, ClassNotFoundException,
  IOException;
```

```
private native boolean invokeObjectReader(Object o, Class
   aclass) throws InvalidClassException,
   StreamCorruptedException, ClassNotFoundException,
   IOException;
private native Class loadClass0(Class cl, String classname)
   throws ClassNotFoundException;
public int read() throws IOException;
public int read(byte[] data, int offset, int length) throws
   IOException;
public boolean readBoolean() throws IOException;
public byte readByte() throws IOException;
public char readChar() throws IOException;
public double readDouble() throws IOException;
public float readFloat() throws IOException;
public void readFully(byte[] data) throws IOException;
public void readFully(byte[] data, int offset, int size)
   throws IOException;
public int readInt() throws IOException;
public String readLine() throws IOException;
public long readLong() throws IOException;
public final Object readObject() throws OptionalDataException,
   ClassNotFoundException, IOException;
public short readShort() throws IOException;
public int readUnsignedByte() throws IOException;
public int readUnsignedShort() throws IOException;
public String readUTF() throws IOException;
public synchronized void
   registerValidation(ObjectInputValidation obj, int prio)
   throws NotActiveException, InvalidObjectException;
public int skipBytes(int len) throws IOException;
```

The *ObjectInputValidation* Interface

```
public Interface ObjectInputValidation
```

Methods

```
public void validateObject() throws InvalidObjectException;
```

The *ObjectOutput* Interface

```
public Interface ObjectOutput extends DataOutput
```

Methods

```
public void close() throws IOException;

public void flush() throws IOException;

public void write(byte b[]) throws IOException;

public void write(byte b[], int off, int len) throws
    IOException;

public void write(int b) throws IOException;

public void writeObject(Object obj) throws IOException;
```

The *ObjectOutputStream* Class

```
public Class ObjectOutputStream extends OutputStream
    implements ObjectOutput, ObjectStreamConstants
```

Constructors

```
public ObjectOutputStream(OutputStream out) throws
    IOException;
```

Methods

```
private static native int getRefHashCode(Object obj);

public void close() throws IOException;

public final void defaultWriteObject() throws IOException;

public void flush() throws IOException;

private native boolean invokeObjectWriter(Object o, Class c)
    throws IOException;

private native void outputArrayValues(Object o, Class
    currclass) throws IOException, InvalidClassException;

private native void outputClassFields(Object o, Class cl,
    int[] fieldSequence) throws IOException,
    InvalidClassException;

public void reset() throws IOException;

public void write(byte b[]) throws IOException;

public void write(byte b[], int off, int len) throws
    IOException;

public void write(int data) throws IOException;
```

```
public void writeBoolean(boolean data) throws IOException;
public void writeByte(int data) throws IOException;
public void writeBytes(String data) throws IOException;
public void writeChar(int data) throws IOException;
public void writeChars(String data) throws IOException;
public void writeDouble(double data) throws IOException;
public void writeFloat(float data) throws IOException;
public void writeInt(int data) throws IOException;
public void writeLong(long data) throws IOException;
public final void writeObject(Object obj) throws IOException;
public void writeShort(int data) throws IOException;
public void writeUTF(String data) throws IOException;
```

The *ObjectStreamClass* Class

```
public Class ObjectStreamClass extends Object implements
    java.io.Serializable
```

Methods

```
private static native int getClassAccess(Class aclass);
private static native int getFieldAccess(Class aclass, String
    fieldsig);
private static native String[] getFieldSignatures(Class
    aclass);
private static native int getMethodAccess(Class aclass, String
    methodsig);
private static native String[] getMethodSignatures(Class
    aclass);
private static native long getSerialVersionUID(Class cl);
private static native boolean hasWriteAndReadObject(Class cl);
public static ObjectStreamClass lookup(Class cl);
public Class forClass();
private native ObjectStreamField[] getFields0(Class cl);
public String getName();
public long getSerialVersionUID();
public String toString();
```

The *ObjectStreamException* Class

```
public abstract Class ObjectStreamException extends
   IOException
```

The *OptionalDataException* Class

```
public Class OptionalDataException extends
   ObjectStreamException
```

Data

```
public boolean eof;
public int length;
```

The *OutputStream* Class

```
public abstract Class OutputStream extends Object
```

Methods

```
public abstract void write(int b) throws IOException;
public void close() throws IOException;
public void flush() throws IOException;
public void write(byte b[]) throws IOException;
public void write(byte b[], int off, int len) throws
   IOException;
```

The *OutputStreamWriter* Class

```
public Class OutputStreamWriter extends Writer
```

Constructors

```
public OutputStreamWriter(OutputStream out, String enc) throws
   UnsupportedEncodingException;
public OutputStreamWriter(OutputStream out);
```

Methods

```
public void close() throws IOException;
public void flush() throws IOException;
public String getEncoding();
```

```
public void write(char cbuf[], int off, int len) throws
   IOException;
```

```
public void write(int c) throws IOException;
```

```
public void write(String str, int off, int len) throws
   IOException;
```

The *PipedInputStream* Class

```
public Class PipedInputStream extends InputStream
```

Methods

```
public PipedInputStream ();
```

```
public PipedInputStream (PipedOutputStream src) throws
   IOException;
```

```
public synchronized int available() throws IOException;
```

```
public void close() throws IOException;
```

```
public void connect(PipedOutputStream src) throws IOException;
```

```
public synchronized int read() throws IOException;
```

```
public synchronized int read(byte b[], int off, int len)
   throws IOException;
```

The *PipedOutputStream* Class

```
public Class PipedOutputStream extends OutputStream
```

Constructors

```
public PipedOutputStream(PipedInputStream snk) throws
   IOException;
```

```
public PipedOutputStream();
```

Methods

```
public void close() throws IOException;
```

```
public void connect(PipedInputStream snk) throws IOException;
```

```
public synchronized void flush() throws IOException;
```

```
public void write(byte b[], int off, int len) throws
   IOException;
```

```
public void write(int b) throws IOException;
```

The *PipedReader* Class

```
public Class PipedReader extends Reader
```

Constructors

```
public PipedReader();
public PipedReader(PipedWriter src) throws IOException;
```

Methods

```
public void close() throws IOException;
public void connect(PipedWriter src) throws IOException;
public int read(char cbuf[], int off, int len) throws
    IOException;
```

The *PipedWriter* Class

```
public Class PipedWriter extends Writer
```

Constructors

```
public PipedWriter();
public PipedWriter(PipedReader sink) throws IOException;
```

Methods

```
public void close() throws IOException;
public void connect(PipedReader sink) throws IOException;
public void flush() throws IOException;
public void write(char cbuf[], int off, int len) throws
    IOException;
```

The *PrintStream* Class

```
public Class PrintStream extends FilterOutputStream
```

Constructors

```
public PrintStream(OutputStream out, boolean autoFlush);
```

Methods

```
public PrintStream (OutputStream out);
public boolean checkError();
public void close();
```

```
public void flush();
public void print(char c);
public void print(char s[]);
public void print(double d);
public void print(float f);
public void print(int i);
public void print(long 1);
public void print(Object obj);
public void print(String s);
public void println(boolean x);
public void println(char x);
public void println(char x[]);
public void println(double x);
public void println(float x);
public void println(int x);
public void println(long x);
public void println(Object x);
public void println(String x);
public void write(int b);
public void print(boolean b);
public void println();
public void write(byte buf[], int off, int len);
```

The *PrintWriter* Class

```
public Class PrintWriter extends Writer
```

Constructors
```
public PrintWriter(Writer out, boolean autoFlush);
public PrintWriter(OutputStream out);
public PrintWriter(OutputStream out, boolean autoFlush);
```

Methods
```
public PrintWriter (Writer out);
public boolean checkError();
public void close();
public void flush();
```

```
public void print(char c);
public void print(char s[]);
public void print(double d);
public void print(float f);
public void print(int i);
public void print(long l);
public void print(Object obj);
public void print(String s);
public void println(boolean x);
public void println(char x);
public void println(char x[]);
public void println(double x);
public void println(float x);
public void println(int x);
public void println(long x);
public void println(Object x);
public void println(String x);
public void write(int c);
public void print(boolean b);
public void println();
public void write(char buf[], int off, int len);
public void write(char buf[]);
public void write(String s, int off, int len);
public void write(String s);
```

The *PushbackInputStream* Class

```
public Class PushbackInputStream extends FilterInputStream
```

Constructors

```
public PushbackInputStream(InputStream in, int size);
public PushbackInputStream(InputStream in);
```

Methods

```
public int available() throws IOException;
public boolean markSupported();
public int read() throws IOException;
```

```
public int read(byte[] b, int off, int len) throws
    IOException;
public void unread(byte[] b, int off, int len) throws
    IOException;
public void unread(byte[] b) throws IOException;
public void unread(int b) throws IOException;
```

The *PushbackReader* Class

```
public Class PushbackReader extends FilterReader
```

Constructors

```
public PushbackReader(Reader in, int size);
public PushbackReader(Reader in);
```

Methods

```
public void close() throws IOException;
public boolean markSupported();
public int read() throws IOException;
public int read(char cbuf[], int off, int len) throws
    IOException;
public boolean ready() throws IOException;
public void unread(char cbuf[], int off, int len) throws
    IOException;
public void unread(char cbuf[]) throws IOException;
public void unread(int c) throws IOException;
```

The *RandomAccessFile* Class

```
public Class RandomAccessFile extends Object implements
    DataOutput, DataInput
```

Constructors

```
public RandomAccessFile(String name, String mode) throws
    IOException;
public RandomAccessFile(File file, String mode) throws
    IOException;
```

Methods

```
public native void close() throws IOException;
public final FileDescriptor getFD() throws IOException;
```

```
public native long getFilePointer() throws IOException;

public native long length() throws IOException;

private native void open(String name, boolean writeable)
    throws IOException;

public native int read() throws IOException;

public int read(byte b[], int off, int len) throws
    IOException;

public int read(byte b[]) throws IOException;

public final boolean readBoolean() throws IOException;

public final byte readByte() throws IOException;

private native int readBytes(byte b[], int off, int len)
    throws IOException;

public final char readChar() throws IOException;

public final double readDouble() throws IOException;

public final float readFloat() throws IOException;

public final void readFully(byte b[]) throws IOException;

public final void readFully(byte b[], int off, int len) throws
    IOException;

public final int readInt() throws IOException;

public final String readLine() throws IOException;

public final long readLong() throws IOException;

public final short readShort() throws IOException;

public final int readUnsignedByte() throws IOException;

public final int readUnsignedShort() throws IOException;

public final String readUTF() throws IOException;

public native void seek(long pos) throws IOException;

public int skipBytes(int n) throws IOException;

public void write(byte b[]) throws IOException;

public void write(byte b[], int off, int len) throws
    IOException;

public native void write(int b) throws IOException;

public final void writeBoolean(boolean v) throws IOException;

public final void writeByte(int v) throws IOException;

private native void writeBytes(byte b[], int off, int len)
    throws IOException;

public final void writeBytes(String s) throws IOException;

public final void writeChar(int v) throws IOException;

public final void writeChars(String s) throws IOException;
```

```
public final void writeDouble(double v) throws IOException;
public final void writeFloat(float v) throws IOException;
public final void writeInt(int v) throws IOException;
public final void writeLong(long v) throws IOException;
public final void writeShort(int v) throws IOException;
public final void writeUTF(String str) throws IOException;
```

The *Reader* Class

```
public abstract Class Reader extends Object
```

Methods

```
abstract public void close() throws IOException;
abstract public int read(char cbuf[], int off, int len) throws
    IOException;
public void mark(int readAheadLimit) throws IOException;
public boolean markSupported();
public int read() throws IOException;
public int read(char cbuf[]) throws IOException;
public boolean ready() throws IOException;
public void reset() throws IOException;
public long skip(long n) throws IOException;
```

The *SequenceInputStream* Class

```
public Class SequenceInputStream extends InputStream
```

Constructors

```
public SequenceInputStream(Enumeration e);
public SequenceInputStream(InputStream s1, InputStream s2);
```

Methods

```
public int available() throws IOException;
public void close() throws IOException;
public int read() throws IOException;
public int read(byte buf[], int pos, int len) throws
    IOException;
```

The *Serializable* Interface

```
public Interface Serializable
```

The *StreamCorruptedException* Class

```
public Class StreamCorruptedException extends
  ObjectStreamException
```

Constructors
```
public StreamCorruptedException(String reason);
public StreamCorruptedException();
```

The *StreamTokenizer* Class

```
public Class StreamTokenizer extends Object
```

Data
```
public static final int TT_EOF = -1;
public static final int TT_EOL = '\n';
public static final int TT_NUMBER = -2;
public static final int TT_WORD = -3;
public double nval;
public String sval;
public int ttype;
```

Constructors
```
public StreamTokenizer(InputStream I);
public StreamTokenizer(Reader I);
public void commentChar(int ch);
public void eolIsSignificant(boolean flag);
public int lineno();
public void lowerCaseMode();
public int nextToken() throws IOException;
public void ordinaryChar(int ch);
public void ordinaryChars(int low, int hi);
public void parseNumbers();
public void pushback();
```

```
public void quoteChar(int ch);
public void slashSlashComments(boolean flag);
public void slashStarComments(boolean flag);
public String toString();
public void whitespaceChars(int low, int hi);
public void wordChars(int low, int hi);
```

The *StringBufferInputStream* Class

```
public Class StringBufferInputStream extends InputStream
```

Constructors
```
public StringBufferInputStream(String s);
```

Methods
```
public synchronized int available();
public synchronized int read();
public synchronized int read(byte b[], int off, int len);
public synchronized void reset();
public synchronized long skip(long n);
```

The *StringReader* Class

```
public Class StringReader extends Reader
```

Constructors
```
public StringReader(String s);
```

Methods
```
public void close();
public void mark(int readAheadLimit) throws IOException;
public boolean markSupported();
public int read() throws IOException;
public int read(char cbuf[], int off, int len) throws
  IOException;
public boolean ready();
public void reset() throws IOException;
public long skip(long ns) throws IOException;
```

The *StringWriter* Class

```
public Class StringWriter extends Writer
```

Constructors
```
public StringWriter();
```

Methods
```
public void close();
public void flush();
public StringBuffer getBuffer();
public String toString();
public void write(char cbuf[], int off, int len);
public void write(int c);
public void write(String str);
public void write(String str, int off, int len);
```

The *SyncFailedException* Class

```
public Class SyncFailedException extends IOException
```

Constructors
```
public SyncFailedException(String desc);
```

The *UTFDataFormatException* Class

```
public Class UTFDataFormatException extends IOException
```

Constructors
```
public UTFDataFormatException();
public UTFDataFormatException(String s);
```

The *UnsupportedEncodingException* Class

```
public Class UnsupportedEncodingException extends IOException
```

Constructors
```
public UnsupportedEncodingException();
public UnsupportedEncodingException(String s);
```

The *WriteAbortedException* Class

```
public Class WriteAbortedException extends
  ObjectStreamException
```

Data
```
public Exception detail;
```

Constructors
```
public WriteAbortedException(String s, Exception ex);
```

Methods
```
public String getMessage();
```

The *Writer* Class

```
public abstract Class Writer extends Object
```

Methods
```
abstract public void close() throws IOException;
abstract public void flush() throws IOException;
abstract public void write(char cbuf[], int off, int len)
  throws IOException;
public void write(char cbuf[]) throws IOException;
public void write(int c) throws IOException;
public void write(String str) throws IOException;
public void write(String str, int off, int len) throws
  IOException;
```

The *java.lang* Package

The *AbstractMethodError* Class

```
public Class AbstractMethodError extends
  IncompatibleClassChangeError
```

Constructors
```
public AbstractMethodError();
public AbstractMethodError(String s);
```

The *ArithmeticException* Class

```
public Class ArithmeticException extends RuntimeException
```

Constructors
```
public ArithmeticException();
public ArithmeticException(String s);
```

The *ArrayIndexOutOfBoundsException* Class

```
public Class ArrayIndexOutOfBoundsException extends
   IndexOutOfBoundsException
```

Constructors
```
public ArrayIndexOutOfBoundsException();
public ArrayIndexOutOfBoundsException(int index);
public ArrayIndexOutOfBoundsException(String s);
```

The *ArrayStoreException* Class

```
public Class ArrayStoreException extends RuntimeException
```

Constructors
```
public ArrayStoreException();
public ArrayStoreException(String s);
```

The *Boolean* Class

```
public Class Boolean extends Object implements
   java.io.Serializable
```

Data
```
public static final Boolean FALSE = new Boolean(false);
public static final Boolean TRUE = new Boolean(true);
public static final Class TYPE =
   Class.getPrimitiveClass("boolean");
```

Constructors
```
public Boolean(boolean value);
public Boolean(String s);
```

Methods

```
public static boolean getBoolean(String name);
public static Boolean valueOf(String s);
public boolean booleanValue();
public boolean equals(Object obj);
public int hashCode();
public String toString();
```

The *Byte* Class

```
public Class Byte extends Number
```

Data

```
public static final byte MAX_VALUE = 127;
public static final byte MIN_VALUE = -128;
public static final Class TYPE =
  Class.getPrimitiveClass("byte");
```

Constructors

```
public Byte(byte value);
public Byte(String s) throws NumberFormatException;
```

Methods

```
public static Byte decode(String nm) throws
  NumberFormatException;
public static byte parseByte(String s) throws
  NumberFormatException;
public static byte parseByte(String s, int radix) throws
  NumberFormatException;
public static String toString(byte b);
public static Byte valueOf(String s, int radix) throws
  NumberFormatException;
public static Byte valueOf(String s) throws
  NumberFormatException;
public byte byteValue();
public double doubleValue();
public boolean equals(Object obj);
public float floatValue();
```

```
public int hashCode();
public int intValue();
public long longValue();
public short shortValue();
public String toString();
```

The *Character* Class

```
public Class Character extends Object implements
  java.io.Serializable
```

Data

```
public static final int MAX_RADIX = 36;
public static final char MAX_VALUE = '\uffff';
public static final int MIN_RADIX = 2;
public static final char MIN_VALUE = '\u0000';
public static final Class TYPE =
  Class.getPrimitiveClass("char");
public static final byte UNASSIGNED = 0, UPPERCASE_LETTER = 1,
  LOWERCASE_LETTER = 2, TITLECASE_LETTER = 3, MODIFIER_LETTER
  = 4, OTHER_LETTER = 5, NON_SPACING_MARK = 6, ENCLOSING_MARK
  = 7, COMBINING_SPACING_MARK = 8, DECIMAL_DIGIT_NUMBER = 9,
  LETTER_NUMBER = 10, OTHER_NUMBER = 11, SPACE_SEPARATOR = 12,
  LINE_SEPARATOR = 13, PARAGRAPH_SEPARATOR = 14, CONTROL = 15,
  FORMAT = 16, PRIVATE_USE = 18, SURROGATE = 19,
  DASH_PUNCTUATION = 20, START_PUNCTUATION = 21,
  END_PUNCTUATION = 22, CONNECTOR_PUNCTUATION = 23,
  OTHER_PUNCTUATION = 24, MATH_SYMBOL = 25, CURRENCY_SYMBOL =
  26, MODIFIER_SYMBOL = 27, OTHER_SYMBOL = 28;
```

Constructors

```
public Character(char value);
```

Methods

```
public static int digit(char ch, int radix);
public static char forDigit(int digit, int radix);
public static int getNumericValue(char ch);
public static int getType(char ch);
public static boolean isDefined(char ch);
public static boolean isDigit(char ch);
```

```
public static boolean isIdentifierIgnorable(char ch);
public static boolean isISOControl(char ch);
public static boolean isJavaIdentifierPart(char ch);
public static boolean isJavaIdentifierStart(char ch);
public static boolean isJavaLetter(char ch);
public static boolean isJavaLetterOrDigit(char ch);
public static boolean isLetter(char ch);
public static boolean isLetterOrDigit(char ch);
public static boolean isLowerCase(char ch);
public static boolean isSpace(char ch);
public static boolean isSpaceChar(char ch);
public static boolean isTitleCase(char ch);
public static boolean isUnicodeIdentifierPart(char ch);
public static boolean isUnicodeIdentifierStart(char ch);
public static boolean isUpperCase(char ch);
public static boolean isWhitespace(char ch);
public static char toLowerCase(char ch);
public static char toTitleCase(char ch);
public static char toUpperCase(char ch);
public char charValue();
public boolean equals(Object obj);
public int hashCode();
public String toString();
```

The *Class* Class

```
public Class Class extends Object implements
  java.io.Serializable
```

Methods

```
public static native Class forName(String className) throws
  ClassNotFoundException;
static native Class getPrimitiveClass(String name);
public Class[] getClasses();
public native ClassLoader getClassLoader();
public native Class getComponentType();
public Constructor getConstructor(Class[] parameterTypes)
  throws NoSuchMethodException, SecurityException;
```

```
private native Constructor getConstructor0(Class[]
  parameterTypes, int which);
public Constructor[] getConstructors() throws
  SecurityException;
private native Constructor[] getConstructors0(int which);
public Class[] getDeclaredClasses() throws SecurityException;
public Constructor getDeclaredConstructor(Class[]
  parameterTypes) throws NoSuchMethodException,
  SecurityException;
public Constructor[] getDeclaredConstructors() throws
  SecurityException;
public Field getDeclaredField(String name) throws
  NoSuchFieldException, SecurityException;
public Field[] getDeclaredFields() throws SecurityException;
public Method getDeclaredMethod(String name, Class[]
  parameterTypes) throws NoSuchMethodException,
  SecurityException;
public Method[] getDeclaredMethods() throws SecurityException;
public Class getDeclaringClass();
public Field getField(String name) throws
  NoSuchFieldException, SecurityException;
private native Field getField0(String name, int which);
public Field[] getFields() throws SecurityException;
private native Field[] getFields0(int which);
public native Class[] getInterfaces();
public Method getMethod(String name, Class[] parameterTypes)
  throws NoSuchMethodException, SecurityException;
private native Method getMethod0(String name, Class[]
  parameterTypes, int which);
public Method[] getMethods() throws SecurityException;
private native Method[] getMethods0(int which);
public native int getModifiers();
public native String getName();
public java.net.URL getResource(String name);
public InputStream getResourceAsStream(String name);
public native Object[] getSigners();
public native Class getSuperclass();
public native boolean isArray();
public native boolean isAssignableFrom(Class cls);
```

```
public native boolean isInstance(Object obj);
public native boolean isInterface();
public native boolean isPrimitive();
public native Object newInstance() throws
    InstantiationException, IllegalAccessException;
native void setSigners(Object[] signers);
public String toString();
```

The *ClassCastException* Class

```
public Class ClassCastException extends RuntimeException
```

Constructors
```
public ClassCastException();
public ClassCastException(String s);
```

The *ClassCircularityError* Class

```
public Class ClassCircularityError extends LinkageError
```

Constructors
```
public ClassCircularityError();
public ClassCircularityError(String s);
```

The *ClassFormatError* Class

```
public Class ClassFormatError extends LinkageError
```

Constructors
```
public ClassFormatError();
public ClassFormatError(String s);
```

The *ClassLoader* Class

```
public abstract Class ClassLoader extends Object
```

Methods
```
public static final java.net.URL getSystemResource(String
    name);
```

```
private static native String getSystemResourceAsName0(String
    name);
public static final InputStream
    getSystemResourceAsStream(String name);
private static native InputStream
    getSystemResourceAsStream0(String name);
protected abstract Class loadClass(String name, boolean
    resolve) throws ClassNotFoundException;
private native Class defineClass0(String name, byte data[],
    int offset, int length);
private native Class findSystemClass0(String name) throws
    ClassNotFoundException;
public java.net.URL getResource(String name);
public InputStream getResourceAsStream(String name);
private native void init();
public Class loadClass(String name) throws
    ClassNotFoundException;
private native void resolveClass0(Class c);
```

The *ClassNotFoundException* Class

```
public Class ClassNotFoundException extends Exception
```

Constructors

```
public ClassNotFoundException();
public ClassNotFoundException(String s);
```

The *CloneNotSupportedException* Class

```
public Class CloneNotSupportedException extends Exception
```

Constructors

```
public CloneNotSupportedException();
public CloneNotSupportedException(String s);
```

The *Cloneable* Interface

```
public Interface Cloneable
```

The *Compiler* Class

```
public Class Compiler extends Object
```

Methods

```
public static native Object command(Object any);
public static native boolean compileClass(Class clazz);
public static native boolean compileClasses(String string);
public static native void disable();
public static native void enable();
private static native void initialize();
```

The *Double* Class

```
public Class Double extends Number
```

Data

```
public static final double MAX_VALUE =
    1.79769313486231570e+308;
public static final double MIN_VALUE = longBitsToDouble(1L);
public static final double NaN = 0.0d / 0.0;
public static final double NEGATIVE_INFINITY = -1.0 / 0.0;
public static final double POSITIVE_INFINITY = 1.0 / 0.0;
public static final Class TYPE =
    Class.getPrimitiveClass("double");
```

Constructors

```
public Double(double value);
public Double(String s) throws NumberFormatException;
```

Methods

```
public static native long doubleToLongBits(double value);
static public boolean isInfinite(double v);
static public boolean isNaN(double v);
public static native double longBitsToDouble(long bits);
public static String toString(double d);
public static Double valueOf(String s) throws
    NumberFormatException;
static native double valueOf0(String s) throws
    NumberFormatException;
```

```
public byte byteValue();
public double doubleValue();
public boolean equals(Object obj);
public float floatValue();
public int hashCode();
public int intValue();
public boolean isInfinite();
public boolean isNaN();
public long longValue();
public short shortValue();
public String toString();
```

The *Error* Class

```
public Class Error extends Throwable
```

Constructors
```
public Error();
public Error(String s);
```

The *Exception* Class

```
public Class Exception extends Throwable
```

Constructors
```
public Exception();
public Exception(String s);
```

The *ExceptionInInitializerError* Class

```
public Class ExceptionInInitializerError extends LinkageError
```

Constructors
```
public ExceptionInInitializerError();
public ExceptionInInitializerError(Throwable thrown);
public ExceptionInInitializerError(String s);
```

Methods
```
public Throwable getException();
```

The *Float* Class

```
public Class Float extends Number
```

Data

```
public static final float MAX_VALUE =
    3.40282346638528860e+38f;
public static final float MIN_VALUE = 1.40129846432481707e-
    45f;
public static final float NaN = 0.0f / 0.0f;
public static final float NEGATIVE_INFINITY = -1.0f / 0.0f;
public static final float POSITIVE_INFINITY = 1.0f / 0.0f;
public static final Class TYPE =
    Class.getPrimitiveClass("float");
```

Constructors

```
public Float(float value);
public Float(double value);
public Float(String s) throws NumberFormatException;
```

Methods

```
public static native int floatToIntBits(float value);
public static native float intBitsToFloat(int bits);
static public boolean isInfinite(float v);
static public boolean isNaN(float v);
public static String toString(float f);
public static Float valueOf(String s) throws
    NumberFormatException;
public byte byteValue();
public double doubleValue();
public boolean equals(Object obj);
public float floatValue();
public int hashCode();
public int intValue();
public boolean isInfinite();
public boolean isNaN();
public long longValue();
public short shortValue();
public String toString();
```

The *IllegalAccessError* Class

```
public Class IllegalAccessError extends
  IncompatibleClassChangeError
```

Constructors

```
public IllegalAccessError();
public IllegalAccessError(String s);
```

The *IllegalAccessException* Class

```
public Class IllegalAccessException extends Exception
```

Constructors

```
public IllegalAccessException();
public IllegalAccessException(String s);
```

The *IllegalArgumentException* Class

```
public Class IllegalArgumentException extends RuntimeException
```

Constructors

```
public IllegalArgumentException();
public IllegalArgumentException(String s);
```

The *IllegalMonitorStateException* Class

```
public Class IllegalMonitorStateException extends
  RuntimeException
```

Constructors

```
public IllegalMonitorStateException();
public IllegalMonitorStateException(String s);
```

The *IllegalStateException* Class

```
public Class IllegalStateException extends RuntimeException
```

Constructors

```
public IllegalStateException();
public IllegalStateException(String s);
```

The *IllegalThreadStateException* Class

```
public Class IllegalThreadStateException extends
   IllegalArgumentException
```

Constructors
```
public IllegalThreadStateException();
public IllegalThreadStateException(String s);
```

The *IncompatibleClassChangeError* Class

```
public Class IncompatibleClassChangeError extends LinkageError
```

Constructors
```
public IncompatibleClassChangeError(String s);
```

Methods
```
public IncompatibleClassChangeError ();
```

The *IndexOutOfBoundsException* Class

```
public Class IndexOutOfBoundsException extends
   RuntimeException
```

Constructors
```
public IndexOutOfBoundsException();
public IndexOutOfBoundsException(String s);
```

The *InstantiationError* Class

```
public Class InstantiationError extends
   IncompatibleClassChangeError
```

Constructors
```
public InstantiationError();
public InstantiationError(String s);
```

The *InstantiationException* Class

```
public Class InstantiationException extends Exception
```

Constructors
```
public InstantiationException();
public InstantiationException(String s);
```

The *Integer* Class

```
public Class Integer extends Number
```

Data
```
public static final int MAX_VALUE = 0x7fffffff;
public static final int MIN_VALUE = 0x80000000;
public static final Class TYPE =
    Class.getPrimitiveClass("int");
```

Constructors
```
public Integer(int value);
public Integer(String s) throws NumberFormatException;
```

Methods
```
public static Integer decode(String nm) throws
    NumberFormatException;
public static Integer getInteger(String nm);
public static Integer getInteger(String nm, int val);
public static Integer getInteger(String nm, Integer val);
public static int parseInt(String s, int radix) throws
    NumberFormatException;
public static int parseInt(String s) throws
    NumberFormatException;
public static String toBinaryString(int i);
public static String toHexString(int i);
public static String toOctalString(int i);
public static String toString(int i, int radix);
public static String toString(int i);
public static Integer valueOf(String s, int radix) throws
    NumberFormatException;
```

```
public static Integer valueOf(String s) throws
    NumberFormatException;
public byte byteValue();
public double doubleValue();
public boolean equals(Object obj);
public float floatValue();
public int hashCode();
public int intValue();
public long longValue();
public short shortValue();
public String toString();
```

The *InternalError* Class

```
public Class InternalError extends VirtualMachineError
```

Constructors

```
public InternalError();
public InternalError(String s);
```

The *InterruptedException* Class

```
public Class InterruptedException extends Exception
```

Constructors

```
public InterruptedException();
public InterruptedException(String s);
```

The *LinkageError* Class

```
public Class LinkageError extends Error
```

Constructors

```
public LinkageError();
public LinkageError(String s);
```

The *Long* Class

```
public Class Long extends Number
```

Data

```
public static final long MAX_VALUE = 0x7fffffffffffffffL;
public static final long MIN_VALUE = 0x8000000000000000L;
public static final Class TYPE =
  Class.getPrimitiveClass("long");
```

Constructors

```
public Long(long value);
public Long(String s) throws NumberFormatException;
```

Methods

```
public static Long getLong(String nm);
public static Long getLong(String nm, long val);
public static Long getLong(String nm, Long val);
public static long parseLong(String s, int radix) throws
  NumberFormatException;
public static long parseLong(String s) throws
  NumberFormatException;
public static String toBinaryString(long i);
public static String toHexString(long i);
public static String toOctalString(long i);
public static String toString(long i, int radix);
public static String toString(long i);
public static Long valueOf(String s, int radix) throws
  NumberFormatException;
public static Long valueOf(String s) throws
  NumberFormatException;
public byte byteValue();
public double doubleValue();
public boolean equals(Object obj);
public float floatValue();
public int hashCode();
public int intValue();
public long longValue();
public short shortValue();
public String toString();
```

The *Math* Class

```
public Class Math extends Object
```

Data

```
public static final double E = 2.7182818284590452354;
public static final double PI = 3.14159265358979323846;
```

Methods

```
public static double abs(double a);
public static float abs(float a);
public static int abs(int a);
public static long abs(long a);
public static native double acos(double a);
public static native double asin(double a);
public static native double atan(double a);
public static native double atan2(double a, double b);
public static native double ceil(double a);
public static native double cos(double a);
public static native double exp(double a);
public static native double floor(double a);
public static native double IEEEremainder(double f1,
    double f2);
public static native double log(double a);
public static double max(double a, double b);
public static float max(float a, float b);
public static int max(int a, int b);
public static long max(long a, long b);
public static double min(double a, double b);
public static float min(float a, float b);
public static int min(int a, int b);
public static long min(long a, long b);
public static native double pow(double a, double b);
public static synchronized double random();
public static native double rint(double a);
public static long round(double a);
public static int round(float a);
```

```
public static native double sin(double a);
public static native double sqrt(double a);
public static native double tan(double a);
```

The *NegativeArraySizeException* Class

```
public Class NegativeArraySizeException extends
    RuntimeException
```

Constructors

```
public NegativeArraySizeException();
public NegativeArraySizeException(String s);
```

The *NoClassDefFoundError* Class

```
public Class NoClassDefFoundError extends LinkageError
```

Constructors

```
public NoClassDefFoundError();
public NoClassDefFoundError(String s);
```

The *NoSuchFieldError* Class

```
public Class NoSuchFieldError extends
    IncompatibleClassChangeError
```

Constructors

```
public NoSuchFieldError();
public NoSuchFieldError(String s);
```

The *NoSuchFieldException* Class

```
public Class NoSuchFieldException extends Exception
```

Constructors

```
public NoSuchFieldException();
public NoSuchFieldException(String s);
```

The *NoSuchMethodError* Class

```
public Class NoSuchMethodError extends
    IncompatibleClassChangeError
```

Constructors
```
public NoSuchMethodError();
public NoSuchMethodError(String s);
```

The *NoSuchMethodException* Class

```
public Class NoSuchMethodException extends Exception
```

Constructors
```
public NoSuchMethodException();
public NoSuchMethodException(String s);
```

The *NullPointerException* Class

```
public Class NullPointerException extends RuntimeException
```

Constructors
```
public NullPointerException();
public NullPointerException(String s);
```

The *Number* Class

```
public abstract Class Number extends Object implements
    java.io.Serializable
```

Methods
```
public abstract double doubleValue();
public abstract float floatValue();
public abstract int intValue();
public abstract long longValue();
public byte byteValue();
public short shortValue();
```

The *NumberFormatException* Class

```
public Class NumberFormatException extends
    IllegalArgumentException
```

Methods

```
public NumberFormatException ();
public NumberFormatException (String s);
```

The *Object* Class

```
public Class Object extends Object
```

Methods

```
protected native Object clone() throws
    CloneNotSupportedException;
public boolean equals(Object obj);
public final native Class getClass();
public native int hashCode();
public final native void notify();
public final native void notifyAll();
public String toString();
public final void wait() throws InterruptedException;
public final native void wait(long timeout) throws
    InterruptedException;
public final void wait(long timeout, int nanos) throws
    InterruptedException;
```

The *OutOfMemoryError* Class

```
public Class OutOfMemoryError extends VirtualMachineError
```

Constructors

```
public OutOfMemoryError();
public OutOfMemoryError(String s);
```

The *Process* Class

```
public abstract Class Process extends Object
```

Methods

```
abstract public void destroy();
abstract public int exitValue();
abstract public InputStream getErrorStream();
abstract public InputStream getInputStream();
abstract public OutputStream getOutputStream();
abstract public int waitFor() throws InterruptedException;
```

The *Runnable* Interface

```
public Interface Runnable
```

Methods

```
public abstract void run();
```

The *Runtime* Class

```
public Class Runtime extends Object
```

Methods

```
public static Runtime getRuntime();
public static void runFinalizersOnExit(boolean value);
private static native void runFinalizersOnExit0(boolean
    value);
private native String buildLibName(String pathname, String
    filename);
public Process exec(String command) throws IOException;
public Process exec(String command, String envp[]) throws
    IOException;
public Process exec(String cmdarray[]) throws IOException;
public Process exec(String cmdarray[], String envp[]) throws
    IOException;
private native Process execInternal(String cmdarray[], String
    envp[]) throws IOException;
public void exit(int status);
```

```
private native void exitInternal(int status);
public native long freeMemory();
public native void gc();
public InputStream getLocalizedInputStream(InputStream in);
public OutputStream
  getLocalizedOutputStream(OutputStream out);
private synchronized native String initializeLinkerInternal();
public synchronized void load(String filename);
private native int loadFileInternal(String filename);
public synchronized void loadLibrary(String libname);
public native void runFinalization();
public native long totalMemory();
public native void traceInstructions(boolean on);
public native void traceMethodCalls(boolean on);
```

The *RuntimeException* Class

```
public Class RuntimeException extends Exception
```

Constructors
```
public RuntimeException();
public RuntimeException(String s);
```

The *SecurityException* Class

```
public Class SecurityException extends RuntimeException
```

Constructors
```
public SecurityException();
public SecurityException(String s);
```

The *SecurityManager* Class

```
public abstract Class SecurityManager extends Object
```

Methods
```
public void checkAccept(String host, int port);
public void checkAccess(Thread g);
```

```
public void checkAccess(ThreadGroup g);
public void checkAwtEventQueueAccess();
public void checkConnect(String host, int port);
public void checkConnect(String host, int port, Object
    context);
public void checkCreateClassLoader();
public void checkDelete(String file);
public void checkExec(String cmd);
public void checkExit(int status);
public void checkLink(String lib);
public void checkListen(int port);
public void checkMemberAccess(Class clazz, int which);
public void checkMulticast(InetAddress maddr);
public void checkMulticast(InetAddress maddr, byte ttl);
public void checkPackageAccess(String pkg);
public void checkPackageDefinition(String pkg);
public void checkPrintJobAccess();
public void checkPropertiesAccess();
public void checkPropertyAccess(String key);
public void checkRead(FileDescriptor fd);
public void checkRead(String file);
public void checkRead(String file, Object context);
public void checkSecurityAccess(String provider);
public void checkSetFactory();
public void checkSystemClipboardAccess();
public boolean checkTopLevelWindow(Object window);
public void checkWrite(FileDescriptor fd);
public void checkWrite(String file);
protected native int classDepth(String name);
protected native int classLoaderDepth();
protected native ClassLoader currentClassLoader();
private native Class currentLoadedClass0();
protected native Class[] getClassContext();
public boolean getInCheck();
public Object getSecurityContext();
public ThreadGroup getThreadGroup();
```

The *Short* Class

```
public Class Short extends Number
```

Data

```
public static final short MAX_VALUE = 32767;
public static final short MIN_VALUE = -32768;
public static final Class TYPE =
  Class.getPrimitiveClass("short");
```

Constructors

```
public Short(short value);
public Short(String s) throws NumberFormatException;
```

Methods

```
public static Short decode(String nm) throws
  NumberFormatException;
public static short parseShort(String s) throws
  NumberFormatException;
public static short parseShort(String s, int radix) throws
  NumberFormatException;
public static String toString(short s);
public static Short valueOf(String s, int radix) throws
  NumberFormatException;
public static Short valueOf(String s) throws
  NumberFormatException;
public byte byteValue();
public double doubleValue();
public boolean equals(Object obj);
public float floatValue();
public int hashCode();
public int intValue();
public long longValue();
public short shortValue();
public String toString();
```

The *StackOverflowError* Class

```
public Class StackOverflowError extends VirtualMachineError
```

Constructors

```
public StackOverflowError();
public StackOverflowError(String s);
```

The *String* Class

```
public Class String extends Object implements
    java.io.Serializable
```

Constructors

```
public String();
public String(String value);
public String(char value[]);
public String(char value[], int offset, int count);
public String(byte ascii[], int hibyte, int offset, int
    count);
public String(byte ascii[], int hibyte);
public String(byte bytes[], int offset, int length, String
    enc) throws UnsupportedEncodingException;
public String(byte bytes[], String enc) throws
    UnsupportedEncodingException;
public String(byte bytes[], int offset, int length);
public String(byte bytes[]);
```

Methods

```
public static String copyValueOf(char data[], int offset, int
    count);
public static String copyValueOf(char data[]);
public static String valueOf(boolean b);
public static String valueOf(char data[]);
public static String valueOf(char data[], int offset, int
    count);
public static String valueOf(char c);
public static String valueOf(double d);
public static String valueOf(float f);
```

```
public static String valueOf(int i);
public static String valueOf(long l);
public static String valueOf(Object obj);
public String (StringBuffer buffer);
public char charAt(int index);
public int compareTo(String anotherString);
public String concat(String str);
public boolean endsWith(String suffix);
public boolean equals(Object anObject);
public boolean equalsIgnoreCase(String anotherString);
public byte[] getBytes();
public void getBytes(int srcBegin, int srcEnd, byte dst[], int
   dstBegin);
public byte[] getBytes(String enc) throws
   UnsupportedEncodingException;
public void getChars(int srcBegin, int srcEnd, char dst[], int
   dstBegin);
public int hashCode();
public int indexOf(int ch);
public int indexOf(int ch, int fromIndex);
public int indexOf(String str);
public int indexOf(String str, int fromIndex);
public native String intern();
public int lastIndexOf(int ch);
public int lastIndexOf(int ch, int fromIndex);
public int lastIndexOf(String str);
public int lastIndexOf(String str, int fromIndex);
public int length();
public boolean regionMatches(boolean ignoreCase, int toffset,
   String other, int ooffset, int len);
public boolean regionMatches(int toffset, String other, int
   ooffset, int len);
public String replace(char oldChar, char newChar);
public boolean startsWith(String prefix, int toffset);
public boolean startsWith(String prefix);
public String substring(int beginIndex);
public String substring(int beginIndex, int endIndex);
```

```
public char[] toCharArray();
public String toLowerCase( Locale locale );
public String toLowerCase();
public String toString();
public String toUpperCase( Locale locale );
public String toUpperCase();
public String trim();
```

The *StringBuffer* Class

```
public Class StringBuffer extends Object implements
    java.io.Serializable
```

Constructors
```
public StringBuffer();
public StringBuffer(int length);
public StringBuffer(String str);
```

Methods
```
public StringBuffer append(boolean b);
public synchronized StringBuffer append(char str[]);
public synchronized StringBuffer append(char str[], int
    offset, int len);
public synchronized StringBuffer append(char c);
public StringBuffer append(double d);
public StringBuffer append(float f);
public StringBuffer append(int i);
public StringBuffer append(long l);
public synchronized StringBuffer append(Object obj);
public synchronized StringBuffer append(String str);
public int capacity();
public synchronized char charAt(int index);
public synchronized void ensureCapacity(int minimumCapacity);
public synchronized void getChars(int srcBegin, int srcEnd,
    char dst[], int dstBegin);
public synchronized StringBuffer insert(int offset,
    Object obj);
```

```
public synchronized StringBuffer insert(int offset,
   String str);
public synchronized StringBuffer insert(int offset,
   char str[]);
public StringBuffer insert(int offset, boolean b);
public synchronized StringBuffer insert(int offset, char c);
public StringBuffer insert(int offset, int i);
public StringBuffer insert(int offset, long l);
public StringBuffer insert(int offset, float f);
public StringBuffer insert(int offset, double d);
public int length();
public synchronized StringBuffer reverse();
public synchronized void setCharAt(int index, char ch);
public synchronized void setLength(int newLength);
public String toString();
```

The *StringIndexOutOfBoundsException* Class

```
public Class StringIndexOutOfBoundsException extends
   IndexOutOfBoundsException
```

Constructors

```
public StringIndexOutOfBoundsException();
public StringIndexOutOfBoundsException(String s);
public StringIndexOutOfBoundsException(int index);
```

The *System* Class

```
public Class System extends Object
```

Data

```
public final static PrintStream err = nullPrintStream();
public final static InputStream in = nullInputStream();
public final static PrintStream out = nullPrintStream();
```

Methods

```
public static native void arraycopy(Object src, int
   src_position, Object dst, int dst_position, int length);
```

```
public static native long currentTimeMillis();
public static void exit(int status);
public static void gc();
public static String getenv(String name);
public static Properties getProperties();
public static String getProperty(String key);
public static String getProperty(String key, String def);
public static SecurityManager getSecurityManager();
public static native int identityHashCode(Object x);
private static native Properties initProperties(Properties
    props);
public static void load(String filename);
public static void loadLibrary(String libname);
public static void runFinalization();
public static void runFinalizersOnExit(boolean value);
public static void setErr(PrintStream err);
private static native void setErr0(PrintStream err);
public static void setIn(InputStream in);
private static native void setIn0(InputStream in);
public static void setOut(PrintStream out);
private static native void setOut0(PrintStream out);
public static void setProperties(Properties props);
public static void setSecurityManager(SecurityManager s);
```

The *Thread* Class

```
public Class Thread extends Object implements Runnable
```

Data
```
public final static int MAX_PRIORITY = 10;
public final static int MIN_PRIORITY = 1;
public final static int NORM_PRIORITY = 5;
```

Constructors
```
public Thread();
public Thread(Runnable target);
public Thread(ThreadGroup group, Runnable target);
```

```
public Thread(String name);

public Thread(ThreadGroup group, String name);

public Thread(Runnable target, String name);

public Thread(ThreadGroup group, Runnable target,
    String name);
```

Methods

```
public static int activeCount();

public static native Thread currentThread();

public static void dumpStack();

public static int enumerate(Thread tarray[]);

public static boolean interrupted();

public static native void sleep(long millis) throws
    InterruptedException;

public static void sleep(long millis, int nanos) throws
    InterruptedException;

public static native void yield();

public void checkAccess();

public native int countStackFrames();

public void destroy();

public final String getName();

public final int getPriority();

public final ThreadGroup getThreadGroup();

public void interrupt();

private native void interrupt0();

public final native boolean isAlive();

public final boolean isDaemon();

public boolean isInterrupted();

private native boolean isInterrupted(boolean
    ClearInterrupted);

public final void join() throws InterruptedException;

public final synchronized void join(long millis) throws
    InterruptedException;

public final synchronized void join(long millis, int nanos)
    throws InterruptedException;

public final void resume();

private native void resume0();

public void run();
```

```
public final void setDaemon(boolean on);
public final void setName(String name);
public final void setPriority(int newPriority);
private native void setPriority0(int newPriority);
public synchronized native void start();
public final void stop();
public final synchronized void stop(Throwable o);
private native void stop0(Object o);
public final void suspend();
private native void suspend0();
public String toString();
```

The *ThreadDeath* Class

```
public Class ThreadDeath extends Error
```

The *ThreadGroup* Class

```
public Class ThreadGroup extends Object
```

Constructors
```
public ThreadGroup(String name);
public ThreadGroup(ThreadGroup parent, String name);
```

Methods
```
public int activeCount();
public int activeGroupCount();
public boolean allowThreadSuspension(boolean b);
public final void checkAccess();
public final void destroy();
public int enumerate(Thread list[]);
public int enumerate(Thread list[], boolean recurse);
public int enumerate(ThreadGroup list[]);
public int enumerate(ThreadGroup list[], boolean recurse);
public final int getMaxPriority();
public final String getName();
```

```
public final ThreadGroup getParent();
public final boolean isDaemon();
public synchronized boolean isDestroyed();
public void list();
public final boolean parentOf(ThreadGroup g);
public final void resume();
public final void setDaemon(boolean daemon);
public final void setMaxPriority(int pri);
public final void stop();
public final void suspend();
public String toString();
public void uncaughtException(Thread t, Throwable e);
```

The *Throwable* Class

```
public Class Throwable extends Object implements
   java.io.Serializable
```

Constructors
```
public Throwable();
public Throwable(String message);
public Throwable(String localizationKey, Object[] arguments);
```

Methods
```
public native Throwable fillInStackTrace();
public Object[] getArguments();
public String getLocalizedMessage();
public String getMessage();
public void printStackTrace();
public void printStackTrace(java.io.PrintStream s);
public void printStackTrace(java.io.PrintWriter s);
private native void printStackTrace0(Object s);
public void setArguments(Object[] arguments);
public String toString();
```

The *UnknownError* Class

```
public Class UnknownError extends VirtualMachineError
```

Constructors
```
public UnknownError();
public UnknownError(String s);
```

The *UnsatisfiedLinkError* Class

```
public Class UnsatisfiedLinkError extends LinkageError
```

Constructors
```
public UnsatisfiedLinkError();
public UnsatisfiedLinkError(String s);
```

The *VerifyError* Class

```
public Class VerifyError extends LinkageError
```

Constructors
```
public VerifyError();
public VerifyError(String s);
```

The *VirtualMachineError* Class

```
public abstract Class VirtualMachineError extends Error
```

Constructors
```
public VirtualMachineError();
public VirtualMachineError(String s);
```

The *Void* Class

```
public Class Void extends Object
```

Data
```
public static final Class TYPE =
   Class.getPrimitiveClass("void");
```

The *java.lang.reflect* Package

The *Array* Class

```
public Class Array extends Object
```

Methods

```
public static native Object get(Object array, int index)
   throws IllegalArgumentException,
   ArrayIndexOutOfBoundsException;

public static native boolean getBoolean(Object array, int
   index) throws IllegalArgumentException,
   ArrayIndexOutOfBoundsException;

public static native byte getByte(Object array, int index)
   throws IllegalArgumentException,
   ArrayIndexOutOfBoundsException;

public static native char getChar(Object array, int index)
   throws IllegalArgumentException,
   ArrayIndexOutOfBoundsException;

public static native double getDouble(Object array, int index)
   throws IllegalArgumentException,
   ArrayIndexOutOfBoundsException;

public static native float getFloat(Object array, int index)
   throws IllegalArgumentException,
   ArrayIndexOutOfBoundsException;

public static native int getInt(Object array, int index)
   throws IllegalArgumentException,
   ArrayIndexOutOfBoundsException;

public static native int getLength(Object array) throws
   IllegalArgumentException;

public static native long getLong(Object array, int index)
   throws IllegalArgumentException,
   ArrayIndexOutOfBoundsException;

public static native short getShort(Object array, int index)
   throws IllegalArgumentException,
   ArrayIndexOutOfBoundsException;

private static native Object multiNewArray(Class
   componentType, int[] dimensions) throws
   IllegalArgumentException, NegativeArraySizeException;

private static native Object newArray(Class componentType, int
   length) throws NegativeArraySizeException;

public static Object newInstance(Class componentType, int
   length) throws NegativeArraySizeException;
```

```
public static Object newInstance(Class componentType, int[]
    dimensions) throws IllegalArgumentException,
    NegativeArraySizeException;
public static native void set(Object array, int index, Object
    value) throws IllegalArgumentException,
    ArrayIndexOutOfBoundsException;
public static native void setBoolean(Object array, int index,
    boolean z) throws IllegalArgumentException,
    ArrayIndexOutOfBoundsException;
public static native void setByte(Object array, int index,
    byte b) throws IllegalArgumentException,
    ArrayIndexOutOfBoundsException;
public static native void setChar(Object array, int index,
    char c) throws IllegalArgumentException,
    ArrayIndexOutOfBoundsException;
public static native void setDouble(Object array, int index,
    double d) throws IllegalArgumentException,
    ArrayIndexOutOfBoundsException;
public static native void setFloat(Object array, int index,
    float f) throws IllegalArgumentException,
    ArrayIndexOutOfBoundsException;
public static native void setInt(Object array, int index, int
    i) throws IllegalArgumentException,
    ArrayIndexOutOfBoundsException;
public static native void setLong(Object array, int index,
    long l) throws IllegalArgumentException,
    ArrayIndexOutOfBoundsException;
public static native void setShort(Object array, int index,
    short s) throws IllegalArgumentException,
    ArrayIndexOutOfBoundsException;
```

The *Constructor* Class

```
public Class Constructor extends Object implements Member
```

Methods
```
public boolean equals(Object obj);
public Class getDeclaringClass();
public Class[] getExceptionTypes();
public native int getModifiers();
public String getName();
```

```
public Class[] getParameterTypes();

public int hashCode();

public native Object newInstance(Object[] initargs) throws
  InstantiationException, IllegalAccessException,
  IllegalArgumentException, InvocationTargetException;

public String toString();
```

The *Field* Class

```
public Class Field extends Object implements Member
```

Methods

```
public boolean equals(Object obj);

public native Object get(Object obj) throws
  IllegalArgumentException, IllegalAccessException;

public native boolean getBoolean(Object obj) throws
  IllegalArgumentException, IllegalAccessException;

public native byte getByte(Object obj) throws
  IllegalArgumentException, IllegalAccessException;

public native char getChar(Object obj) throws
  IllegalArgumentException, IllegalAccessException;

public Class getDeclaringClass();

public native double getDouble(Object obj) throws
  IllegalArgumentException, IllegalAccessException;

public native float getFloat(Object obj) throws
  IllegalArgumentException, IllegalAccessException;

public native int getInt(Object obj) throws
  IllegalArgumentException, IllegalAccessException;

public native long getLong(Object obj) throws
  IllegalArgumentException, IllegalAccessException;

public native int getModifiers();

public String getName();

public native short getShort(Object obj) throws
  IllegalArgumentException, IllegalAccessException;

public Class getType();

public int hashCode();

public native void set(Object obj, Object value) throws
  IllegalArgumentException, IllegalAccessException;

public native void setBoolean(Object obj, boolean z) throws
  IllegalArgumentException, IllegalAccessException;
```

```
public native void setByte(Object obj, byte b) throws
    IllegalArgumentException, IllegalAccessException;
public native void setChar(Object obj, char c) throws
    IllegalArgumentException, IllegalAccessException;
public native void setDouble(Object obj, double d) throws
    IllegalArgumentException, IllegalAccessException;
public native void setFloat(Object obj, float f) throws
    IllegalArgumentException, IllegalAccessException;
public native void setInt(Object obj, int i) throws
    IllegalArgumentException, IllegalAccessException;
public native void setLong(Object obj, long 1) throws
    IllegalArgumentException, IllegalAccessException;
public native void setShort(Object obj, short s) throws
    IllegalArgumentException, IllegalAccessException;
public String toString();
```

The *InvocationTargetException* Class

```
public Class InvocationTargetException extends Exception
```

Constructors
```
public InvocationTargetException(Throwable target);
public InvocationTargetException(Throwable target, String s);
```

Methods
```
public Throwable getTargetException();
```

The *Member* Interface

```
public Interface Member
```

Data
```
public static final int DECLARED = 1;
public static final int PUBLIC = 0;
```

Methods
```
public Class getDeclaringClass();
public int getModifiers();
public String getName();
```

The *Method* Class

```
public Class Method extends Object implements Member
```

Methods
```
public boolean equals(Object obj);
public Class getDeclaringClass();
public Class[] getExceptionTypes();
public native int getModifiers();
public String getName();
public Class[] getParameterTypes();
public Class getReturnType();
public int hashCode();
public native Object invoke(Object obj, Object[] args) throws
    IllegalAccessException, IllegalArgumentException,
    InvocationTargetException;
public String toString();
```

The *Modifier* Class

```
public Class Modifier extends Object
```

Data
```
public static final int ABSTRACT = 0x00000400;
public static final int FINAL = 0x00000010;
public static final int INTERFACE = 0x00000200;
public static final int NATIVE = 0x00000100;
public static final int PRIVATE = 0x00000002;
public static final int PROTECTED = 0x00000004;
public static final int PUBLIC = 0x00000001;
public static final int STATIC = 0x00000008;
public static final int SYNCHRONIZED = 0x00000020;
public static final int TRANSIENT = 0x00000080;
public static final int VOLATILE = 0x00000040;
```

Methods
```
public static boolean isAbstract(int mod);
public static boolean isFinal(int mod);
```

```
public static boolean isInterface(int mod);
public static boolean isNative(int mod);
public static boolean isPrivate(int mod);
public static boolean isProtected(int mod);
public static boolean isPublic(int mod);
public static boolean isStatic(int mod);
public static boolean isSynchronized(int mod);
public static boolean isTransient(int mod);
public static boolean isVolatile(int mod);
public static String toString(int mod);
```

The *java.net* Package

The *BindException* Class

```
public Class BindException extends SocketException
```

Constructors
```
public BindException(String msg);
public BindException();
```

The *ConnectException* Class

```
public Class ConnectException extends SocketException
```

Constructors
```
public ConnectException(String msg);
public ConnectException();
```

The *ContentHandler* Class

```
public abstract Class ContentHandler extends Object
```

Methods
```
abstract public Object getContent(URLConnection urlc) throws
    IOException;
```

The *ContentHandlerFactory* Interface

```
public Interface ContentHandlerFactory
```

Methods

```
ContentHandler createContentHandler(String mimetype);
```

The *DatagramPacket* Class

```
public Class DatagramPacket extends Object
```

Constructors

```
public DatagramPacket(byte ibuf[], int ilength);
public DatagramPacket(byte ibuf[], int ilength, InetAddress
    iaddr, int iport);
```

Methods

```
public InetAddress getAddress();
public byte[] getData();
public int getLength();
public int getPort();
```

The *DatagramSocket* Class

```
public Class DatagramSocket extends Object
```

Constructors

```
public DatagramSocket() throws SocketException;
public DatagramSocket(int port) throws SocketException;
public DatagramSocket(int port, InetAddress laddr) throws
    SocketException;
```

Methods

```
public void close();
public InetAddress getLocalAddress();
public int getLocalPort();
public synchronized int getSoTimeout() throws SocketException;
public synchronized void receive(DatagramPacket p) throws
    IOException;
public void send(DatagramPacket p) throws IOException;
```

```
public synchronized void setSoTimeout(int timeout) throws
    SocketException;
```

The *DatagramSocketImpl* Class

```
public abstract Class DatagramSocketImpl extends Object
    implements SocketOptions
```

Methods

```
protected abstract void bind(int lport, InetAddress laddr)
    throws SocketException;
```
```
protected abstract void close();
```
```
protected abstract void create() throws SocketException;
```
```
protected abstract byte getTTL() throws IOException;
```
```
protected abstract void join(InetAddress inetaddr) throws
    IOException;
```
```
protected abstract void leave(InetAddress inetaddr) throws
    IOException;
```
```
protected abstract int peek(InetAddress i) throws IOException;
```
```
protected abstract void receive(DatagramPacket p) throws
    IOException;
```
```
protected abstract void send(DatagramPacket p) throws
    IOException;
```
```
protected abstract void setTTL(byte ttl) throws IOException;
```

The *FileNameMap* Interface

```
public Interface FileNameMap
```

Methods

```
public String getContentTypeFor(String fileName);
```

The *HttpURLConnection* Class

```
public abstract Class HttpURLConnection extends URLConnection
```

Data

```
public static final int HTTP_ACCEPTED = 202;
public static final int HTTP_BAD_GATEWAY = 502;
public static final int HTTP_BAD_METHOD = 405;
public static final int HTTP_BAD_REQUEST = 400;
```

```
public static final int HTTP_CLIENT_TIMEOUT = 408;
public static final int HTTP_CONFLICT = 409;
public static final int HTTP_CREATED = 201;
public static final int HTTP_ENTITY_TOO_LARGE = 413;
public static final int HTTP_FORBIDDEN = 403;
public static final int HTTP_GATEWAY_TIMEOUT = 504;
public static final int HTTP_GONE = 410;
public static final int HTTP_INTERNAL_ERROR = 501;
public static final int HTTP_LENGTH_REQUIRED = 411;
public static final int HTTP_MOVED_PERM = 301;
public static final int HTTP_MOVED_TEMP = 302;
public static final int HTTP_MULT_CHOICE = 300;
public static final int HTTP_NO_CONTENT = 204;
public static final int HTTP_NOT_ACCEPTABLE = 406;
public static final int HTTP_NOT_AUTHORITATIVE = 203;
public static final int HTTP_NOT_FOUND = 404;
public static final int HTTP_NOT_MODIFIED = 304;
public static final int HTTP_OK = 200;
public static final int HTTP_PARTIAL = 206;
public static final int HTTP_PAYMENT_REQUIRED = 402;
public static final int HTTP_PRECON_FAILED = 412;
public static final int HTTP_PROXY_AUTH = 407;
public static final int HTTP_REQ_TOO_LONG = 414;
public static final int HTTP_RESET = 205;
public static final int HTTP_SEE_OTHER = 303;
public static final int HTTP_SERVER_ERROR = 500;
public static final int HTTP_UNAUTHORIZED = 401;
public static final int HTTP_UNAVAILABLE = 503;
public static final int HTTP_UNSUPPORTED_TYPE = 415;
public static final int HTTP_USE_PROXY = 305;
public static final int HTTP_VERSION = 505;
```

Methods

```
public static boolean getFollowRedirects();
public static void setFollowRedirects(boolean set);
public abstract void disconnect();
public abstract boolean usingProxy();
public String getRequestMethod();
```

```
public int getResponseCode() throws IOException;
public String getResponseMessage() throws IOException;
public void setRequestMethod(String method) throws
  ProtocolException;
```

The *InetAddress* Class

```
public Class InetAddress extends Object implements
  java.io.Serializable
```

Methods

```
public static InetAddress getAllByName(String host)[] throws
  UnknownHostException;
public static InetAddress getByName(String host) throws
  UnknownHostException;
public static InetAddress getLocalHost() throws
  UnknownHostException;
public boolean equals(Object obj);
public byte[] getAddress();
public String getHostAddress();
public String getHostName();
public int hashCode();
public boolean isMulticastAddress();
public String toString();
```

The *MalformedURLException* Class

```
public Class MalformedURLException extends IOException
```

Constructors

```
public MalformedURLException();
public MalformedURLException(String msg);
```

The *MulticastSocket* Class

```
public Class MulticastSocket extends DatagramSocket
```

Constructors

```
public MulticastSocket() throws IOException;
public MulticastSocket(int port) throws IOException;
```

Methods

```
public InetAddress getInterface() throws SocketException;

public byte getTTL() throws IOException;

public void joinGroup(InetAddress mcastaddr) throws
  IOException;

public void leaveGroup(InetAddress mcastaddr) throws
  IOException;

public synchronized void send(DatagramPacket p, byte ttl)
  throws IOException;

public void setInterface(InetAddress inf) throws
  SocketException;

public void setTTL(byte ttl) throws IOException;
```

The *NoRouteToHostException* Class

```
public Class NoRouteToHostException extends SocketException
```

Constructors

```
public NoRouteToHostException(String msg);

public NoRouteToHostException();
```

The *ProtocolException* Class

```
public Class ProtocolException extends IOException
```

Constructors

```
public ProtocolException(String host);

public ProtocolException();
```

The *ServerSocket* Class

```
public Class ServerSocket extends Object
```

Constructors

```
public ServerSocket(int port) throws IOException;

public ServerSocket(int port, int backlog) throws IOException;

public ServerSocket(int port, int backlog, InetAddress
  bindAddr) throws IOException;
```

Methods

```
public static synchronized void
   setSocketFactory(SocketImplFactory fac) throws IOException;

public Socket accept() throws IOException;

public void close() throws IOException;

public InetAddress getInetAddress();

public int getLocalPort();

public synchronized int getSoTimeout() throws IOException;

public synchronized void setSoTimeout(int timeout) throws
   SocketException;

public String toString();
```

The *Socket* Class

```
public Class Socket extends Object
```

Constructors

```
public Socket(String host, int port) throws
   UnknownHostException, IOException;

public Socket(InetAddress address, int port) throws
   IOException;

public Socket(String host, int port, InetAddress localAddr,
   int localPort) throws IOException;

public Socket(InetAddress address, int port, InetAddress
   localAddr, int localPort) throws IOException;

public Socket(String host, int port, boolean stream) throws
   IOException;

public Socket(InetAddress host, int port, boolean stream)
   throws IOException;
```

Methods

```
public static synchronized void
   setSocketImplFactory(SocketImplFactory fac) throws
   IOException;

public synchronized void close() throws IOException;

public InetAddress getInetAddress();

public InputStream getInputStream() throws IOException;

public InetAddress getLocalAddress();

public int getLocalPort();

public OutputStream getOutputStream() throws IOException;
```

```
public int getPort();
public int getSoLinger() throws SocketException;
public synchronized int getSoTimeout() throws SocketException;
public boolean getTcpNoDelay() throws SocketException;
public void setSoLinger(boolean on, int val) throws
    SocketException;
public synchronized void setSoTimeout(int timeout) throws
    SocketException;
public void setTcpNoDelay(boolean on) throws SocketException;
public String toString();
```

The *SocketException* Class

```
public Class SocketException extends IOException
```

Constructors

```
public SocketException(String msg);
public SocketException();
```

The *SocketImpl* Class

```
public abstract Class SocketImpl extends Object implements
    SocketOptions
```

Methods

```
protected abstract void accept(SocketImpl s) throws
    IOException;
protected abstract int available() throws IOException;
protected abstract void bind(InetAddress host, int port)
    throws IOException;
protected abstract void close() throws IOException;
protected abstract void connect(InetAddress address, int port)
    throws IOException;
protected abstract void connect(String host, int port) throws
    IOException;
protected abstract void create(boolean stream) throws
    IOException;
protected abstract InputStream getInputStream() throws
    IOException;
protected abstract OutputStream getOutputStream() throws
    IOException;
```

```
protected abstract void listen(int backlog) throws
    IOException;
```
```
public String toString();
```

The *SocketImplFactory* Interface

```
public Interface SocketImplFactory
```

Methods

```
SocketImpl createSocketImpl();
```

The *URL* Class

```
public Class URL extends Object implements
    java.io.Serializable
```

Constructors

```
public URL(String protocol, String host, int port, String
    file) throws MalformedURLException;
```
```
public URL(String protocol, String host, String file) throws
    MalformedURLException;
```
```
public URL(String spec) throws MalformedURLException;
```
```
public URL(URL context, String spec) throws
    MalformedURLException;
```

Methods

```
public static synchronized void
    setURLStreamHandlerFactory(URLStreamHandlerFactory fac);
```
```
public boolean equals(Object obj);
```
```
public final Object getContent() throws java.io.IOException;
```
```
public String getFile();
```
```
public String getHost();
```
```
public int getPort();
```
```
public String getProtocol();
```
```
public String getRef();
```
```
public int hashCode();
```
```
public URLConnection openConnection() throws
    java.io.IOException;
```
```
public final InputStream openStream() throws
    java.io.IOException;
```

```
public boolean sameFile(URL other);
public String toExternalForm();
public String toString();
```

The *URLConnection* Class

```
public abstract Class URLConnection extends Object
```

Data
```
public static FileNameMap fileNameMap;
```

Methods
```
public static boolean getDefaultAllowUserInteraction();
public static String getDefaultRequestProperty(String key);
static public String guessContentTypeFromStream(InputStream
  is) throws IOException;
public static synchronized void
  setContentHandlerFactory(ContentHandlerFactory fac);
public static void setDefaultAllowUserInteraction(boolean
  defaultallowuserinteraction);
public static void setDefaultRequestProperty(String key,
  String value);
abstract public void connect() throws IOException;
public boolean getAllowUserInteraction();
public Object getContent() throws IOException;
public String getContentEncoding();
public int getContentLength();
public String getContentType();
public long getDate();
public boolean getDefaultUseCaches();
public boolean getDoInput();
public boolean getDoOutput();
public long getExpiration();
public String getHeaderField(int n);
public String getHeaderField(String name);
public long getHeaderFieldDate(String name, long Default);
public int getHeaderFieldInt(String name, int Default);
public String getHeaderFieldKey(int n);
```

```
public long getIfModifiedSince();
public InputStream getInputStream() throws IOException;
public long getLastModified();
public OutputStream getOutputStream() throws IOException;
public String getRequestProperty(String key);
public URL getURL();
public boolean getUseCaches();
public void setAllowUserInteraction(boolean
    allowuserinteraction);
public void setDefaultUseCaches(boolean defaultusecaches);
public void setDoInput(boolean doinput);
public void setDoOutput(boolean dooutput);
public void setIfModifiedSince(long ifmodifiedsince);
public void setRequestProperty(String key, String value);
public void setUseCaches(boolean usecaches);
public String toString();
```

The *URLEncoder* Class

```
public Class URLEncoder extends Object
```

Methods

```
public static String encode(String s);
```

The *URLStreamHandler* Class

```
public abstract Class URLStreamHandler extends Object
```

Methods

```
abstract protected URLConnection openConnection(URL u) throws
    IOException;
```

The *URLStreamHandlerFactory* Interface

```
public Interface URLStreamHandlerFactory
```

Methods

```
URLStreamHandler createURLStreamHandler(String protocol);
```

The *UnknownHostException* Class

```
public Class UnknownHostException extends IOException
```

Constructors
```
public UnknownHostException(String host);
public UnknownHostException();
```

The *UnknownServiceException* Class

```
public Class UnknownServiceException extends IOException
```

Constructors
```
public UnknownServiceException();
public UnknownServiceException(String msg);
```

The *java.util* Package

The *BitSet* Class

```
public Class BitSet extends Object implements Cloneable,
    java.io.Serializable
```

Constructors
```
public BitSet();
public BitSet(int nbits);
```

Methods
```
public void and(BitSet set);
public void clear(int bit);
public Object clone();
public boolean equals(Object obj);
public boolean get(int bit);
public int hashCode();
public void or(BitSet set);
public void set(int bit);
public int size();
```

```
public String toString();
public void xor(BitSet set);
```

The *Calendar* Class

```
public abstract Class Calendar extends Object implements
    Serializable, Cloneable
```

Data

```
public final static int AM = 0;
public final static byte AMPM = 9;
public final static int APRIL = 3;
public final static int AUGUST = 7;
public final static byte DATE = 5;
public final static byte DAYOFMONTH = 5;
public final static byte DAYOFWEEK = 7;
public final static byte DAYOFWEEKINMONTH = 8;
public final static byte DAYOFYEAR = 6;
public final static int DECEMBER = 11;
public final static byte DSTOFFSET = 16;
public final static byte ERA = 0;
public final static int FEBRUARY = 1;
public final static byte FIELDCOUNT = 17;
public final static int FRIDAY = 6;
public final static byte HOUR = 10;
public final static byte HOUROFDAY = 11;
public final static int JANUARY = 0;
public final static int JULY = 6;
public final static int JUNE = 5;
public final static int MARCH = 2;
public final static int MAY = 4;
public final static byte MILLISECOND = 14;
public final static byte MINUTE = 12;
public final static int MONDAY = 2;
public final static byte MONTH = 2;
public final static int NOVEMBER = 10;
public final static int OCTOBER = 9;
```

```
public final static int PM = 1;
public final static int SATURDAY = 7;
public final static byte SECOND = 13;
public final static int SEPTEMBER = 8;
public final static int SUNDAY = 1;
public final static int THURSDAY = 5;
public final static int TUESDAY = 3;
public final static int UNDECIMBER = 12;
public final static int WEDNESDAY = 4;
public final static byte WEEKOFMONTH = 4;
public final static byte WEEKOFYEAR = 3;
public final static byte YEAR = 1;
public final static byte ZONEOFFSET = 15;
```

Methods

```
public static synchronized Locale[] getAvailableLocales();
public static synchronized Calendar getDefault();
public static synchronized Calendar getDefault(Locale
   aLocale);
public static synchronized Calendar getDefault(TimeZone zone);
public static synchronized Calendar getDefault(TimeZone zone,
   Locale aLocale);
abstract public void add(byte field, int amount) throws
   IllegalArgumentException;
abstract public boolean after(Object when);
abstract public boolean before(Object when);
protected abstract void computeFields();
protected abstract void computeTime();
abstract public boolean equals(Object when);
abstract public int getGreatestMinimum(byte field);
abstract public int getLeastMaximum(byte field);
abstract public int getMaximum(byte field);
abstract public int getMinimum(byte field);
abstract public void roll(byte field, boolean up) throws
   IllegalArgumentException;
public final void clear();
public final void clear(byte field) throws
   IllegalArgumentException;
```

```
public Object clone();
public final int get(byte field) throws
    IllegalArgumentException;
public int getFirstDayOfWeek();
public int getMinimalDaysInFirstWeek();
public final Date getTime();
public TimeZone getTimeZone();
public boolean getValidationMode();
public final boolean isSet(int field) throws
    IllegalArgumentException;
public final void set(byte field, int value) throws
    IllegalArgumentException;
public final void set(int year, int month, int date);
public final void set(int year, int month, int date, int hour,
    int minute);
public final void set(int year, int month, int date, int hour,
    int minute, int second);
public void setFirstDayOfWeek(byte value);
public void setMinimalDaysInFirstWeek(byte value);
public final void setTime(Date date);
public void setTimeZone(TimeZone value);
public void setValidationMode(boolean mode);
```

The *Date* Class

```
public Class Date extends Object implements
    java.io.Serializable, Cloneable
```

Methods

```
public static long parse(String s);
public static long UTC(int year, int month, int date, int hrs,
    int min, int sec);
public Date ();
public Date (int year, int month, int date);
public Date (int year, int month, int date, int hrs, int min);
public Date (int year, int month, int date, int hrs, int min,
    int sec);
public Date (long date);
public Date (String s);
```

```
public boolean after(Date when);
public boolean before(Date when);
public boolean equals(Object obj);
public int getDate();
public int getDay();
public int getHours();
public int getMinutes();
public int getMonth();
public int getSeconds();
public long getTime();
public int getTimezoneOffset();
public int getYear();
public int hashCode();
public void setDate(int date);
public void setHours(int hours);
public void setMinutes(int minutes);
public void setMonth(int month);
public void setSeconds(int seconds);
public void setTime(long time);
public void setYear(int year);
public String toGMTString();
public String toLocaleString();
public String toString();
```

The *Dictionary* Class

```
public abstract Class Dictionary extends Object
```

Methods

```
abstract public Enumeration elements();
abstract public Object get(Object key);
abstract public boolean isEmpty();
abstract public Enumeration keys();
abstract public Object put(Object key, Object value);
abstract public Object remove(Object key);
abstract public int size();
```

The *EmptyStackException* Class

```
public Class EmptyStackException extends RuntimeException
```

Constructors
```
public EmptyStackException();
```

The *Enumeration* Interface

```
public Interface Enumeration
```

Methods
```
boolean hasMoreElements();
Object nextElement();
```

The *EventListener* Interface

```
public Interface EventListener
```

The *EventObject* Class

```
public Class EventObject extends Object implements
    java.io.Serializable
```

Constructors
```
public EventObject(Object source);
```

Methods
```
public Object getSource();
public String toString();
```

The *GregorianCalendar* Class

```
public Class GregorianCalendar extends Calendar
```

Data
```
public static final byte AD = 0;
public static final byte BC = 1;
```

Constructors

```
public GregorianCalendar();

public GregorianCalendar(TimeZone zone);

public GregorianCalendar(Locale aLocale);

public GregorianCalendar(TimeZone zone, Locale aLocale);

public GregorianCalendar(int year, int month, int date);

public GregorianCalendar(int year, int month, int date, int
    hour, int minute);

public GregorianCalendar(int year, int month, int date, int
    hour, int minute, int second);
```

Methods

```
public void add(byte field, int amount) throws
    IllegalArgumentException;

public boolean after(Object when);

public boolean before(Object when);

public Object clone();

public boolean equals(Object obj);

public int getGreatestMinimum(byte field);

public final Date getGregorianChange();

public int getLeastMaximum(byte field);

public int getMaximum(byte field);

public int getMinimum(byte field);

public synchronized int hashCode();

public boolean isLeapYear(int year);

public void roll(byte field, boolean up) throws
    IllegalArgumentException;

public void setGregorianChange(Date date);
```

The *ListResourceBundle* Class

```
public abstract Class ListResourceBundle extends
    ResourceBundle
```

Methods

```
abstract protected Object[][] getContents();

public Enumeration getKeys();

public final Object handleGetObject(String key);
```

The *Locale* Class

```
public Class Locale extends Object implements Cloneable,
  Serializable
```

Data

```
static public final Locale CANADA = new Locale("en","CA","");
static public final Locale CANADA_FRENCH = new
  Locale("fr","CA","");
static public final Locale CHINA = new Locale("zh","CN","");
static public final Locale CHINESE = new Locale("zh","","");
static public final Locale ENGLISH = new Locale("en","","");
static public final Locale FRANCE = new Locale("fr","FR","");
static public final Locale FRENCH = new Locale("fr","","");
static public final Locale GERMAN = new Locale("de","","");
static public final Locale GERMANY = new Locale("de","DE","");
static public final Locale ITALIAN = new Locale("it","","");
static public final Locale ITALY = new Locale("it","IT","");
static public final Locale JAPAN = new Locale("ja","JP","");
static public final Locale JAPANESE = new Locale("ja","","");
static public final Locale KOREA = new Locale("ko","KR","");
static public final Locale KOREAN = new Locale("ko","","");
static public final Locale PRC = new Locale("zh","CN","");
static public final Locale SIMPLIFIED_CHINESE = new
  Locale("zh","CN","");
static public final Locale TAIWAN = new Locale("zh","TW","");
static public final Locale TRADITIONAL_CHINESE = new
  Locale("zh","TW","");
static public final Locale UK = new Locale("en","GB","");
static public final Locale US = new Locale("en","US","");
```

Constructors

```
public Locale(String language, String country, String
  variant);
public Locale(String language, String country);
```

Methods

```
public static synchronized Locale getDefault();
public static synchronized void setDefault(Locale newLocale);
```

```
public Object clone();
public boolean equals(Object obj);
public String getCountry();
public final String getDisplayCountry();
public String getDisplayCountry(Locale inLocale);
public final String getDisplayLanguage();
public String getDisplayLanguage(Locale inLocale);
public final String getDisplayName();
public String getDisplayName(Locale inLocale);
public final String getDisplayVariant();
public String getDisplayVariant(Locale inLocale);
public String getISO3Country() throws
   MissingResourceException;
public String getISO3Language() throws
   MissingResourceException;
public String getLanguage();
public String getVariant();
public synchronized int hashCode();
public final String toString();
```

The *MissingResourceException* Class

```
public Class MissingResourceException extends RuntimeException
```

Constructors
```
public MissingResourceException(String s, String classname,
   String key);
```

Methods
```
public String getClassName();
public String getKey();
```

The *NoSuchElementException* Class

```
public Class NoSuchElementException extends RuntimeException
```

Constructors
```
public NoSuchElementException();
public NoSuchElementException(String s);
```

The *Observable* Class

```
public Class Observable extends Object
```

Constructors
```
public Observable();
```

Methods
```
public synchronized void addObserver(Observer o);
```

public synchronized int countObservers();
```
public synchronized void deleteObserver(Observer o);
public synchronized void deleteObservers();
public synchronized boolean hasChanged();
public void notifyObservers();
public void notifyObservers(Object arg);
```

The *Observer* Interface

```
public Interface Observer
```

Methods
```
void update(Observable o, Object arg);
```

The *Properties* Class

```
public Class Properties extends Hashtable
```

Constructors
```
public Properties();
public Properties(Properties defaults);
```

Methods
```
public String getProperty(String key);
public String getProperty(String key, String defaultValue);
public void list(PrintStream out);
public void list(PrintWriter out);
public synchronized void load(InputStream in) throws
  IOException;
```

```
public Enumeration propertyNames();
public synchronized void save(OutputStream out, String
   header);
```

The *PropertyResourceBundle* Class

```
public Class PropertyResourceBundle extends ResourceBundle
```

Methods

```
public PropertyResourceBundle (InputStream stream) throws
   IOException;
public Enumeration getKeys();
public Object handleGetObject(String key);
```

The *Random* Class

```
public Class Random extends Object implements
   java.io.Serializable
```

Constructors

```
public Random();
public Random(long seed);
```

Methods

```
public void nextBytes(byte[] bytes);
public double nextDouble();
public float nextFloat();
synchronized public double nextGaussian();
public int nextInt();
public long nextLong();
synchronized public void setSeed(long seed);
```

The *ResourceBundle* Class

```
public abstract Class ResourceBundle extends Object
```

Methods

```
public static final ResourceBundle getResourceBundle(String
   baseName) throws MissingResourceException;
public static final ResourceBundle getResourceBundle(String
   baseName, Locale locale);
```

```
public abstract Enumeration getKeys();

protected abstract Object handleGetObject(String key) throws
    MissingResourceException;

public final Menu getMenu(String key) throws
    MissingResourceException;

public final MenuBar getMenuBar(String key) throws
    MissingResourceException;

public final Object getObject(String key) throws
    MissingResourceException;

public final String getString(String key) throws
    MissingResourceException;

public final String[] getStringArray(String key) throws
    MissingResourceException;
```

The *SimpleTimeZone* Class

```
public Class SimpleTimeZone extends TimeZone
```

Constructors
```
public SimpleTimeZone(int rawOffset, String ID);

public SimpleTimeZone(int rawOffset, String ID, int
    startMonth, int startDayOfWeekInMonth, int startDayOfWeek,
    int startTime, int endMonth, int endDayOfWeekInMonth, int
    endDayOfWeek, int endTime);
```

Methods
```
public Object clone();

public boolean equals(Object obj);

public int getOffset(int era, int year, int month, int day,
    int dayOfWeek, int millis);

public int getRawOffset();

public synchronized int hashCode();

public boolean inDaylightTime(Date date);

public void setEndRule(int month, int dayOfWeekInMonth, int
    dayOfWeek, int time);

public void setRawOffset(int offsetMillis);

public void setStartRule(int month, int dayOfWeekInMonth, int
    dayOfWeek, int time);

public void setStartYear(int year);

public boolean useDaylightTime();
```

The *Stack* Class

```
public Class Stack extends Vector
```

Methods
```
public boolean empty();
public synchronized Object peek();
public synchronized Object pop();
public Object push(Object item);
public synchronized int search(Object o);
```

The *StringTokenizer* Class

```
public Class StringTokenizer extends Object implements
    Enumeration
```

Constructors
```
public StringTokenizer(String str, String delim, boolean
    returnTokens);
public StringTokenizer(String str, String delim);
public StringTokenizer(String str);
```

Methods
```
public int countTokens();
public boolean hasMoreElements();
public boolean hasMoreTokens();
public Object nextElement();
public String nextToken();
public String nextToken(String delim);
```

The *TimeZone* Class

```
public abstract Class TimeZone extends Object implements
    Serializable, Cloneable
```

Methods
```
public static synchronized String[] getAvailableIDs();
public static synchronized String[] getAvailableIDs(int
    rawOffset);
```

```
public static synchronized TimeZone getDefault();
public static synchronized TimeZone getTimeZone(String ID);
public static synchronized void setDefault(TimeZone zone);
abstract public int getOffset(int era, int year, int month,
    int day, int dayOfWeek, int milliseconds);
abstract public int getRawOffset();
abstract public boolean inDaylightTime(Date date);
abstract public void setRawOffset(int offsetMillis);
abstract public boolean useDaylightTime();
public Object clone();
public String getID();
public void setID(String ID);
```

The *TooManyListenersException* Class

```
public Class TooManyListenersException extends Exception
```

Constructors

```
public TooManyListenersException();
public TooManyListenersException(String s);
```

The *Vector* Class

```
public Class Vector extends Object implements Cloneable,
    java.io.Serializable
```

Constructors

```
public Vector(int initialCapacity, int capacityIncrement);
public Vector(int initialCapacity);
public Vector();
```

Methods

```
public final synchronized void addElement(Object obj);
public final int capacity();
public synchronized Object clone();
public final boolean contains(Object elem);
public final synchronized void copyInto(Object anArray[]);
public final synchronized Object elementAt(int index);
```

```
public final synchronized Enumeration elements();
public final synchronized void ensureCapacity(int
  minCapacity);
public final synchronized Object firstElement();
public final int indexOf(Object elem);
public final synchronized int indexOf(Object elem, int index);
public final synchronized void insertElementAt(Object obj, int
  index);
public final boolean isEmpty();
public final synchronized Object lastElement();
public final int lastIndexOf(Object elem);
public final synchronized int lastIndexOf(Object elem, int
  index);
public final synchronized void removeAllElements();
public final synchronized boolean removeElement(Object obj);
public final synchronized void removeElementAt(int index);
public final synchronized void setElementAt(Object obj, int
  index);
public final synchronized void setSize(int newSize);
public final int size();
public final synchronized String toString();
public final synchronized void trimToSize();
```

The *java.util.zip* Package

The *Adler32* Class

```
public Class Adler32 extends Object implements Checksum
```

Methods
```
public long getValue();
public void reset();
public native void update(byte[] b, int off, int len);
public void update(int b);
private native void update1(int b);
```

The *CRC32* Class

```
public Class CRC32 extends Object implements Checksum
```

Methods
```
public long getValue();
public void reset();
public native void update(byte[] b, int off, int len);
public void update(int b);
private native void update1(int b);
```

The *CheckedInputStream* Class

```
public Class CheckedInputStream extends FilterInputStream
```

Constructors
```
public CheckedInputStream(InputStream in, Checksum cksum);
```

Methods
```
public Checksum getChecksum();
public int read() throws IOException;
public int read(byte[] buf, int off, int len) throws
   IOException;
public long skip(long n) throws IOException;
```

The *CheckedOutputStream* Class

```
public Class CheckedOutputStream extends FilterOutputStream
```

Constructors
```
public CheckedOutputStream(OutputStream out, Checksum cksum);
```

Methods
```
public Checksum getChecksum();
public void write(byte[] b, int off, int len) throws
   IOException;
public void write(int b) throws IOException;
```

The *Checksum* Interface

```
public Interface Checksum
```

Methods
```
public long getValue();
public void reset();
public void update(byte[] b, int off, int len);
public void update(int b);
```

The *DataFormatException* Class

```
public Class DataFormatException extends Exception
```

Constructors
```
public DataFormatException();
public DataFormatException(String s);
```

The *Deflater* Class

```
public Class Deflater extends Object
```

Data
```
public static final int BEST_COMPRESSION = 9;
public static final int BEST_SPEED = 1;
public static final int DEFAULT_COMPRESSION = -1;
public static final int DEFAULT_STRATEGY = 0;
public static final int DEFLATED = 8;
public static final int FILTERED = 1;
public static final int HUFFMAN_ONLY = 2;
public static final int NO_COMPRESSION = 0;
```

Constructors
```
public Deflater(int level, boolean nowrap);
public Deflater(int level);
public Deflater();
```

Methods

```
public synchronized native int deflate(byte[] buf, int off,
    int len);
public synchronized native void end();
public synchronized void finish();
public synchronized boolean finished();
public synchronized native int getTotalIn();
public synchronized native int getTotalOut();
private native void init(boolean nowrap);
public boolean needsInput();
public synchronized native void reset();
public synchronized native void setDictionary(byte[] buf,
    int off, int len);
public synchronized void setInput(byte[] buf, int off, int
    len);
public synchronized void setLevel(int Level);
public synchronized void setStrategy(int strategy);
```

The *DeflaterOutputStream* Class

```
public Class DeflaterOutputStream extends FilterOutputStream
```

Constructors

```
public DeflaterOutputStream(OutputStream out, Deflater def,
    int size);
public DeflaterOutputStream(OutputStream out, Deflater def);
```

Methods

```
public void close() throws IOException;
public void write(byte[] buf, int off, int len) throws
    IOException;
public void write(int b) throws IOException;
```

The *GZIPInputStream* Class

```
public Class GZIPInputStream extends InflaterInputStream
```

Data

```
public final static int GZIP_MAGIC = 0x8b1f;
```

Constructors

```
public GZIPInputStream(InputStream in, int size) throws
    IOException;
public GZIPInputStream(InputStream in) throws IOException;
```

Methods

```
public synchronized void close() throws IOException;
public synchronized int read(byte[] buf, int off, int len)
    throws IOException;
```

The *GZIPOutputStream* Class

```
public Class GZIPOutputStream extends DeflaterOutputStream
```

Constructors

```
public GZIPOutputStream(OutputStream out, int size) throws
    IOException;
public GZIPOutputStream(OutputStream out) throws IOException;
```

Methods

```
public synchronized void close() throws IOException;
public synchronized void write(byte[] buf, int off, int len)
    throws IOException;
```

The *Inflater* Class

```
public Class Inflater extends Object
```

Constructors

```
public Inflater(boolean nowrap);
public Inflater();
```

Methods

```
public synchronized native void end();
public synchronized boolean finished();
public synchronized native int getAdler();
public synchronized int getRemaining();
public synchronized native int getTotalIn();
public synchronized native int getTotalOut();
```

```
public synchronized native int inflate(byte[] buf, int off,
    int len) throws DataFormatException;
private native void init(boolean nowrap);
public synchronized boolean needsDictionary();
public synchronized boolean needsInput();
public synchronized native void reset();
public synchronized native void setDictionary(byte[] buf, int
    off, int len);
public synchronized void setInput(byte[] buf, int off, int
    len);
```

The *InflaterInputStream* Class

```
public Class InflaterInputStream extends FilterInputStream
```

Constructors
```
public InflaterInputStream(InputStream in, Inflater inf, int
    size);
public InflaterInputStream(InputStream in, Inflater inf);
```

Methods
```
public int read() throws IOException;
public int read(byte[] buf, int off, int len) throws
    IOException;
public long skip(long n) throws IOException;
```

The *ZipEntry* Class

```
public Class ZipEntry extends Object implements ZipConstants
```

Constructors
```
public ZipEntry(String name);
public ZipEntry();
```

Methods
```
public String getComment();
public long getCompressedSize();
public long getCrc();
public byte[] getExtra();
```

```
public String getName();
public long getSize();
public long getTime();
public boolean isDirectory();
public void setComment(String comment);
public void setCrc(long crc);
public void setExtra(byte[] extra);
public void setName(String name);
public void setSize(long size);
public void setTime(long time);
public String toString();
public String toString(boolean detailed);
```

The *ZipException* Class

```
public Class ZipException extends IOException
```

Constructors
```
public ZipException();
public ZipException(String s);
```

The *ZipFile* Class

```
public Class ZipFile extends Object implements ZipConstants
```

Constructors
```
public ZipFile(String name) throws ZipException, IOException;
public ZipFile(File file) throws ZipException, IOException;
```

Methods
```
public void close() throws IOException;
public Enumeration entries();
public ZipEntry getEntry(String name);
public InputStream getInputStream(ZipEntry e) throws
  ZipException, IOException;
public String getName();
```

The *ZipInputStream* Class

```
public Class ZipInputStream extends InflaterInputStream
    implements ZipConstants
```

Constructors
```
public ZipInputStream(InputStream in);
```

Methods
```
public synchronized void closeEntry() throws ZipException,
    IOException;
public synchronized ZipEntry getNextEntry() throws
    ZipException, IOException;
public synchronized int read(byte[] buf, int off, int len)
    throws ZipException, IOException;
public long skip(long n) throws ZipException, IOException;
```

The *ZipOutputStream* Class

```
public Class ZipOutputStream extends DeflaterOutputStream
    implements ZipConstants
```

Data
```
public static final int DEFLATED = 8;
public static final int STORED = 0;
```

Constructors
```
public ZipOutputStream(OutputStream out);
```

Methods
```
public synchronized void close() throws ZipException,
    IOException;
public synchronized void closeEntry() throws ZipException,
    IOException;
public synchronized void putNextEntry(ZipEntry e) throws
    ZipException, IOException;
public void setComment(String comment);
public void setLevel(int level);
public void setMethod(int method);
public synchronized void write(byte[] buf, int off, int len)
    throws ZipException, IOException;
```

The Java Documentation Tool: *javadoc*

Good documentation can significantly raise the long-term value of a piece of code; bad documentation conversely raises the cost. These considerations are amplified with object-oriented software because the capacity for reuse is increased. Such reuse is greatly simplified by appropriate and convenient documentation. The tool javadoc is part of the standard JDK distribution and facilitates producing and maintaining programmer documentation in a pleasing and usable form.

Java specifies a particular type of comment delimiter to allow documentation to be included in source code and subsequently extracted by an automatic tool to produce either HTML or MIF (Maker Interchange Format) documentation files. A javadoc comment can be applied to class, member variable, and member method declarations. This appendix describes the facilities and caveats that are relevant to the effective use of this tool.

TIP

Maker Interchange Format is a text-only markup format used by a professional-quality document-production package called FrameMaker. FrameMaker is available on a variety of platforms, including Unix and Windows systems. You can find more information about FrameMaker at Adobe's Web site at http://www.adobe.com/prodindex/framemaker/main.html.

Format of Comments

The basic format of a javadoc comment is:

```
/**
 * <Single sentence description>. <Fuller description over
 * several sentences if needed>
 * <special tag line>
 * <more special tag lines>
 */
<Java source item to be described>
```

The overall comment delimiter is the pair / ∗ ∗ and ∗ /, which is similar to the C and C++ comment markers except that the opening marker has a double asterisk.

Inside the comment there are three main parts. The first sentence, ended with a period, should be a brief description of the item being documented. This sentence is used by itself in parts of the output documentation. Take care to avoid including accidental periods in this part—such as for decimal points—because these will confuse the javadoc program.

The remaining text should form a fuller description of the target item, but it should follow logically from the first sentence because both parts are treated as a block in the output document.

After the basic textual descriptions, a number of special tags can be used; these are described in detail later. They provide special annotation of common features, such as method arguments and return types, and as such provide a shorthand in useful conditions.

What to Comment

The Java item being commented can be a class, a member variable, or a method. If a javadoc comment is applied to a local variable in a method, it will be ignored by the program, and the comment will not be propagated into the output documentation.

Only public or protected items cause javadoc to generate output. Again, comments applied to default access or private items will not cause any errors, either in the compiler or in javadoc itself. However, the output document will not contain the comments.

> **TIP**
>
> The output from javadoc includes an entry for the default constructor if one exists. That is, if no constructors are defined in a class, then a single one that takes no arguments is generated automatically. This output is also documented automatically, although there cannot be a description for it.

How the Comment Is Formatted

The body of the comment is not copied directly to the output file. Each line is read, and a single leading asterisk, if present, is stripped off in order to allow comments in either of the following formats:

```
/**
 comments
 here
 */
```

or

```
/**
 * comments
 * here
 */
```

Note that a single asterisk is conventional, as a way of visually picking out the boundaries of the comment. In fact, javadoc allows multiple leading asterisks, provided they are not separated by spaces.

After the lines have been stripped of any leading asterisks, lines up to the first that begin with an @ symbol are treated as part of the text of the comment. Lines starting with the @ symbol are tags and are treated specially.

NOTE It is important to group all the text of the comment at the beginning and keep all the tags at the end. If this grouping method is not followed, comment lines that follow tags will become part of the tag.

HTML in Comments

The text parts of `javadoc` comments may include HTML markup tags, which allow a variety of useful effects to be added to the documentation; for example, the `<pre>` tag allows source code to be presented properly formatted.

In general, any HTML tags can be used, but adherence to a few guidelines, as outlined below, will ensure that the best results are achieved.

The documents created by `javadoc` are laid out with a particular style. Therefore, it is recommended that structural tags, such as heading marks `<h1>` or horizontal rules `<hr>`, be avoided. If used, they do work as intended, but they spoil the visual effect of the overall document. This consideration is particularly important if documentation is being prepared for others to use, as they will expect the standard style to be adopted.

References to other HTML documents can be made using the anchor tags `<a href= ...>`, but in most cases these references are best achieved by using the special tags provided, as discussed in *The Tags*, directly following. Where relative anchors are used, be aware that `javadoc` places all its output HTML documents in the same directory. The names of the files that are generated, and expected in the references, by `javadoc` are described in the section *The Documentation File Set*. In-document anchors use the name of the variable or method that is being described. An anchor that locates a variable simply takes the name of that variable, while an anchor locating a method is constructed by concatenating the name of the method, an opening bracket, the fully qualified class names of the arguments, and a closing bracket. The argument class names are separated by the character sequence comma, space—exactly one comma and exactly one space should be used. The following table clarifies these conventions.

Target	Anchor Name
`main()`	`#main`
`method(int, float)`	`#method(int, float)`
`main(String args[])`	`#main(java.lang.String[])`
`int someVariable`	`#someVariable`

The Tags

Six tags are provided; two are specifically for use in class documentation, three are for documenting methods, and the remaining tag may be used for classes, methods, or variables.

Tag Formatting

In all cases, the tags must be used after the textual comments. Failure to do so will result in bits of the text being treated as part of the tags or as part of the parameters to those tags.

The `javadoc` program does not entirely ignore whitespace and formatting in the tags it reads. Each tag must start a line, although it can extend over more than one line if that is appropriate. To count as being at the start of a line, one of two formats must be used: either the @ symbol must be flush at the left margin, with no characters preceding it, or it may be preceded by *comment continuation*. Comment continuation consists of an arbitrary number of spaces, then an arbitrary number of asterisks, followed by a single optional space. The following table exemplifies the permitted options. The left margin is indicated with the pipe symbol (|), spaces are represented by the bullet symbol (•).

`	@tag`	acceptable
`	•@tag`	unacceptable
`	•*•@tag`	acceptable
`	•••*•@tag`	acceptable
`	•*•••@tag`	unacceptable
`	@•tag`	unacceptable

The Cross-Reference Tag

Cross-references can be made using the `see` tag. This tag can be applied to classes, methods, and member variables and takes the form:

```
@see <target>
```

The `<target>` part can refer to either a class as a whole or an element of a class. The following forms are allowed for `<target>`:

Form of `<target>`	Purpose
`String`	Refers to a class. The short form name must be in scope in this source file.
`java.lang.String`	Refers to a class that may not be in scope in this source file. Note that this form is usually unnecessary. If the source file refers to this target, then it must be imported, otherwise a compiler error would result. If the compiler can find the class, then so can `javadoc`.

Form of `<target>`	Purpose
`#main`	Refers to a member variable or to a method without specifying arguments. Where a method is referred to, the target of the reference will be the first method that has this name.
`#main(java.lang.String[])`	Refers to a member method in this class with a specific argument list.
`String#toString()`	Refers to a member method or variable in another class that is in scope in this source file.
`java.lang.String#toString()`	Refers to a member method or variable in another explicit class. That class need not be in scope in this source file.
`<a href="xxx.html">Text</a>`	Refers to an external html file.

TIP Notice that no text is permitted after the target tag. If any text is present, it will be treated as part of the target tag; not only will it result in warnings when `javadoc` is run, it will also prevent the link from working properly.

The *deprecated* Tag

The introduction of Java 1.1 brought with it a substantial set of new APIs. In addition, the existing ones were rationalized. Some parts of the public interfaces of classes in 1.0 packages were either improved or renamed; but to ensure that existing code continues to work properly, the old functionality has not been removed. Instead a special documentation tag—`deprecated`—has been applied. This tag can be applied to classes, member variables, or methods. When `javadoc` finds this tag, it makes a note in the output files to indicate that this method should be avoided.

Usually, when a feature becomes deprecated, some new feature has been added to provide the same functionality in a more efficient or consistent form. To assist the programmer, cross-reference tags should be placed on the lines immediately following the deprecated tag. These will cause the `javadoc` output file to guide the programmer easily to the proper new methods.

A unique effect of the deprecated tag is that it is noticed by the compiler. When a deprecated item is found by the compiler it makes a note in the resulting classfile to indicate the deprecation. Later, if the feature is used by another class, a warning message is issued to prompt the programmer that the code using this feature should be rewritten. Future versions of the Java compiler might support a `-strict` option, which would convert this warning into a fatal compilation error.

Tags for Classes Only

Two tags are provided for documenting the class as a whole. By default `javadoc` ignores these, but command-line switches modify this behavior so that the information they contain is output. The tags are intended for keeping track of the author(s) of a class and the version from which the documentation was produced. The form of the tags is:

```
@author <Author name or description>
@version <Version description>
```

Notice that in both cases, the descriptive part is free format. Hence, the author can use any form of description that is desired, and the format of the version information can similarly be anything that suits local conventions.

TIP

The author tag can be used as many times as required to identify multiple authors. Where this is done, the author information provided will be separated by commas. If you need to have authors listed on separate lines, you can put the `<br>` HTML tag at the start of the second and subsequent author descriptions.

If multiple version tags are used, only the first one will be effective. It could be used to allow historical information to be retained in the source file, as is done automatically by some version-control programs.

TIP

You can enable the output of author and version information using `javadoc` with the command-line parameters `-author` and `-version` respectively.

Tags for Methods Only

Three tags are provided especially for documenting methods. These allow description of the arguments of a method, the returned value, and of any exceptions that might be thrown by the method. The tags have the following formats:

```
@param <param-name> <description>
@return <description>
@exception <Exception-class-name> <description>
```

A `param` tag should be included for each of the arguments to the method. The tag should be followed by the name of the parameter and then the description of the parameter. The description is a good place to define any boundary conditions that limit the acceptable range of a parameter.

> **WARNING** The name of the parameter is not checked against the actual method. Therefore, you must take care to correctly match the param list with the entries in the formal parameter list of the method. Clearly it would be very confusing to describe parameters called x, y, and z if the actual entries in the method argument list are called p, q, and r. It is also possible to accidentally define more param tags than the number of actual parameters. Again, care should be taken to avoid this error.

The return tag is used to describe the meaning of the value returned from the method. Only one return tag should be used, but if multiple ones are present in the documenting comment, javadoc will issue warnings as it runs, and only the first tag will have any effect on the output documentation.

Any exceptions that might be thrown by the method should be described using the exception tag. Multiple exception tags are permitted, and each should be followed by the classname of the exception being described. The description should indicate the reasons why the exception might be thrown. It is permitted to document an exception that is not listed in the throws part of the method declaration. Not only is this documentation permitted, but it would actually be correct if the exception being documented were a runtime exception, because it is not necessary to declare the possibility of exceptions of this class, or its subclasses, being thrown from a method.

> **TIP** The output from javadoc includes the full method prototypes for all methods. Each classname that describes arguments or return types for a method will be expanded to the fully qualified classname to give the proper cross-reference, provided the source file has the requisite imports to allow it to compile successfully.

The Documentation File Set

Javadoc can be asked to document individual classes, lists of classes, individual packages, or lists of packages, but it generally works best when documenting whole sets of packages. It generates a separate file for each class and each package. Three additional files are created for navigational support.

For each class, a file is produced with a name constructed from the fully qualified package name of that class plus the .html suffix. For every package, a file is created with a name constructed from the package name, prefixed with Package- and including the .html suffix. Hence, if a package called com.friendly.mypackage contains two classes, called ClassA and ClassB, then the output files would include: Package-com.friendly.mypackage.html, com.friendly.mypackage.ClassA.html, and com.friendly.mypackage.ClassB.html.

Support Files

Each of the package- and class-description files can be browsed independently if desired, but they are usually linked together by supporting files acting as a "home" document, an index, and a cross-reference. These are called packages.html, AllNames.html, and tree.html, respectively.

Merging Document Sets

If additional library sets are added to an existing Java installation, it might be desirable to merge the documentation files from different runs of javadoc.

The names of the files that document the classes and packages should be unique. Because documentation files use the fully qualified names of the classes and packages they relate to, there will be naming conflicts for the compiler if the filenames are not unique.

Unfortunately, because the three supporting files have names that are fixed, it is difficult to amalgamate these parts of different documentation sets. In fact, the contents of the `packages.html` are fairly limited and have a simple format. Each package is listed in the form shown below:

```
<h2> Other Packages </h2>
<menu>
<li> package <a href="Package-mystuff.html">mystuff</a>
<li> package <a href="Package-mystuff.morestuff.html">
mystuff.morestuff</a>
</menu>
```

Each line starting `<li> package <`... forms the entry for a single package. Because the packages are all listed together, and there are probably not more than six to a dozen in a distribution, it is practical to copy these lines from one document set to another by hand, using the cut and paste facilities of a text editor.

The format of the `AllNames.html` file is also manageable, but much more tedious. Twenty-six separate cut-and-paste operations would be a minimum required for this file because entries within it are grouped alphabetically. More would be required if you wish each category in the result to be alphabetized.

The format of the file `tree.html` is sufficiently complex that it is unreasonable to consider fixing it up manually. The entire class hierarchy of all classes found in, or referred to by, the packages on which `javadoc` operated are listed within it. Therefore, in two different runs on different packages, some output information will be duplicated and some not. Many hundreds of lines of output are involved, so if it is important to have a single unified documentation set, then two options are possible. If you have all the sources for all the classes, including the public parts of the Java APIs, then you can run `javadoc` once more on all classes. This is time consuming but works well enough. Otherwise, you could write a program that reads the contents of two `tree.html` files and produces a correctly merged output version.

Graphics Files

The output files that `javadoc` produces expect to be located in a directory that contains a subdirectory called `images`, which includes some supporting graphics. These are used for the section headings, such as `Package-Index`, and also for the colored bullets that indicate the nature of each element documented. If a new document set is placed in the same directory as existing `javadoc` documentation, then these files will already be present. However, if the files are to be located in a separate directory, perhaps to allow the `tree.html` files to be kept separate, then the images must be copied over.

The Command-Line Format
for *javadoc*

The `javadoc` program should be invoked with a list of source files and/or package names.

For each listed source file, a documenting HTML file will be generated, but no `Package-xxx` file will be output. For each package name given, sources for that package will be searched for in a directory tree that reflects the package name, and the resulting output will include a documenting HTML file for each class found as well as for the package itself.

A number of command-line options can be specified. These are described in the table below.

`-d <path>`	Put the output files in to this, rather than the current, directory.
`-classpath <path>`	Look for sources relative to entries on this path list, rather than relative to the value defined in the environment variable `CLASSPATH`.
`-sourcepath <path>`	Synonym for `-classpath <path>`.

`-verbose`	Output additional information indicating what files are being read and giving the number of milliseconds taken to parse each file.
`-version`	Include the details specified in the first version tags in output documents.
`-author`	Include details specified in author tags in the output documents.
`-notree`	Do not create the file `tree.html`.
`-noindex`	Do not create the file `AllNames.html`.
`-doctype <type>`	If `<type>` is `mif`, then `javadoc` outputs MIF (Maker Interchange Format) files rather than HTML. MIF files can be useful for printing if you have FrameMaker or some other word processor that can handle MIF format.
`-nodeprecated`	Omit deprecation information.
`-J<flag>`	Pass `<flag>` into the java runtime system. This can be useful if a very large document set causes the runtime to run out of memory, allowing control of the garbage collector and/or heap sizes. However, this option will not generally be required.

APPENDIX

C

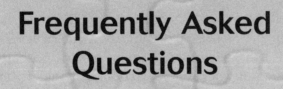

Frequently Asked
Questions

This appendix presents some of the more frequently asked questions that arise when programmers get past the basics of Java and start tackling some real programming tasks. It also contains answers to questions that programmers might not realize they need to ask.

The questions laid out are under the general headings:

- Language and compiler questions
- AWT questions
- Security questions

Language and Compiler Questions

Why Doesn't Java Have a Preprocessor?

Because Java borrows so much from C and C++, it might seem surprising that there is no preprocessor. The *preprocessor* is a feature of C and C++ that allows you to create macros, or shorthands, for use in the program. The preprocessor is commonly used to define literal constants so that, for example, a program can refer to MAX_ARGS instead of 1024. The preprocessor is also used to provide conditional compilation such as would be required to code platform-specific variations in traditional programming languages. Both of these effects can be achieved in other ways; other questions in this FAQ describe how.

The most important reason the preprocessor was left out is that it is so easy to misuse. The preprocessor allows arbitrarily complex macros to be created, and these macros can be used to change the nature of the language; for example, by defining the words BEGIN and END to be used in place of curly braces to indicate blocks. Often, reading a piece of C code involves substantial effort to work out what special macros are in effect in a particular source file and, consequently, what the code really means. On balance, the residual advantages a preprocessor would have offered were greatly outweighed by the disadvantages, and so it was left out.

How Can I Declare a Constant?

Constants of primitive types are simply defined by creating variables with the modifiers static and final applied to them. Therefore, the declaration

```
public static final boolean DEBUG = true;
```

would cause DEBUG to be a constant of type boolean, accessible from any other class as Xxxx.DEBUG, where Xxxx is the enclosing classname and there is no need for an instance of its enclosing variable.

This approach actually has a significant advantage over the preprocessor approach. Because the constant declaration is strongly typed, its use can be checked properly by the compiler. As an aside, programmers who like to use the enum mechanism of C++ also have the advantage that, unlike enum, constants can also be String objects.

I've Tried to Declare a Constant, but I Can Still Change the Value: What's Wrong?

The Java language specification allows the modifiers static and final to be on the declaration of a class instance, like this:

```
public static final StringBuffer sb = new
StringBuffer("Fickle");
```

However, this declaration does not actually define a constant `StringBuffer` object. The `static` modifier affects the declaration and works as expected in this case. Unfortunately, the `final` modifier affects the *value* of the variable, and the problem lies in the meaning of value as applied to variables of nonprimitive types.

For variables that refer to class instances, the value is actually the reference value (typically a memory pointer), so the `final` modifier prevents the reference from being changed. In other words, the variable can never refer to any other object, but the object itself can still be changed.

I Thought Method Arguments Were Passed by Value; Why Is My Method Changing the Value in the Caller?

Method arguments are passed by value in Java, but as outlined in the previous question, the value of a variable of any `Object` type is actually a reference. Consider a method call like this:

```
Date d = new Date();
     :
nextMonth(d);
System.out.println("The date now reads " + d);
     :
public void nextMonth(Date locald)
  locald.setMonth(locald.getMonth() + 1);
}
```

The usual semantics of pass by value would mean that the modifications to `locald` made in the `nextMonth()` method would be lost when the method returns, and the printed message would show today's date. However, although in the `nextMonth()` method `locald` is a private copy of the value of d, the value of d is a *reference* and not the object to which d refers. Hence, the call to `locald.setMonth()` actually modifies the same object as is referred to by d in the caller.

I Thought Objects Were Passed by Reference into Methods; Why Can't I Change the Value?

Consider this example code fragment:

```
Date d = new Date();
     :
nextMonth(d);
System.out.println("The date now reads " + d);
     :
public void nextMonth(Date locald)
  locald = new Date(locald.getYear(),
                    locald.getMonth(),
                    locald.getDate());
}
```

You might mistakenly expect this code to behave the same as the example in the previous question. In this example, at the entry to the nextMonth() method locald refers to the same Date object as in the caller. However, this is not the same as pass by reference. Java always passes method arguments by value, so locald is not the same variable as d; it is a copy of its value. Changing the object to which locald refers does not affect either the value of d nor the object to which d refers.

This arrangement of memory is shown in Figure C.1.

FIGURE C.1

Values and references in a method call

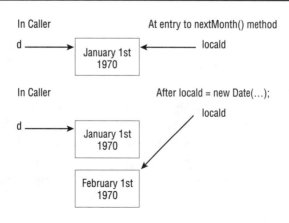

Another possibility to consider is that a number of classes in Java describe *immutable* objects; objects that, once created, have a constant value. These include the String class and the wrappers for the primitive data types, such as the Boolean, Integer, and Double classes.

How Can I Achieve Conditional Compilation?

Conditional compilation provides a way of writing a single source file with parts that are compiled or not compiled under the influence of constants. For example, consider this block of C code, which uses the C preprocessor to achieve conditional compilation:

```
#if defined(DEBUG)
  printf("Value so far is %d", value);
#endif
```

If the DEBUG constant is defined, but without regard to its value, this code would be compiled as a single printf() function call. On the other hand, if no definition has been made of DEBUG, then no code is output for the printf() call.

It turns out that Java can in fact provide conditional compilation as a result of compiler optimizations and the final mechanism for constants. Consider these fragments of code, taken from the Suite .java example described in Chapter 5, *Portability Issues*:

```
public static final TRACE = true;
        :
    if (TRACE) {
      System.out.println("checking " + s);
    }
```

In this example, if the definition of TRACE is changed to false the compiler will not generate any code for the conditional block because it is impossible for the conditional block ever to be executed. So although this appears to be a runtime condition, it is in fact optimized into conditional compilation.

Why Do I Have to Handle Some Exceptions but the Compiler Overlooks Others?

The Java compiler is rather fussy about exception handling. In general, if an exception can occur in a region of code, it is either handled by the `try/catch` mechanism, or the method as a whole is declared with a throws clause to advise the caller that the exception might be passed up.

In fact this rule applies to exceptions that are subclasses of the `Exception` class but is waived for exceptions that are subclasses of either the `RuntimeException` class or the `Error` class.

Why Is There a Distinction among *Exception*, *Error*, and *RuntimeException* Classes?

The `Error` class is used for significant system difficulties, such as running out of memory. There are two general features common to the causes of errors. First, the causes of errors are severe, making it difficult to recover from such problems. For example, writing a handler to recover from running out of memory can be very tiresome. Unless such a handler is carefully designed, the first thing it needs to do is allocate some memory to work with. Given the nature of the original problem such an attempt at memory allocation will fail. The second feature of the causes of errors is that they are not program errors—bugs—but rather are environmental difficulties, such as insufficient memory or missing library components, at execution time.

Runtime exceptions, of which the `NullPointerException` is a well-known example, arise specifically from programming problems. One type of programming problem might be a design error, such that a particular condition was not anticipated and handled, or it might be an implementation bug. The essence of the `RuntimeException` is that a *correct* program never generates one and therefore the source should not be cluttered with handler code for this exception.

All other exceptions can legitimately occur under potentially recoverable conditions in a correct program. Typical examples of these sorts of conditions are disks missing from drives or the disconnection of network cables. Because these exceptions occur under legitimate working conditions, the Java compiler insists that any code that might throw such an exception must either handle it or explicitly declare that the exception is to be passed to the caller of this method.

What Are Runtime Exceptions Really About?

Because runtime exceptions represent programming errors, they are ideal for expressing preconditions and postconditions. A *precondition* is a testable condition that must hold immediately before the invocation of a method, such as limiting the range of valid arguments. A *postcondition* is guaranteed to be true at the method's exit. A method that calculates the square root of a number might have a precondition that the number is not negative. Its postcondition is that the returned value, when multiplied by itself, gives—within the accuracy limits of the calculation system—the original number. By programming checks for these conditions, and throwing a runtime exception where the tests fail, it is possible to significantly improve the reliability of the resulting code. This improvement occurs because bugs are brought out into the open sooner and hence fixed earlier.

Not all methods have readily expressed postconditions, but a great many are written with either implied or explicit preconditions. These might be obvious consequences of the method semantics, such as the square root example; or might be more arbitrary, implementation-specific ones, such as "the total number of characters in all the argument strings must not exceed 128." In either case, testing the precondition at the method entry, and throwing a RuntimeException if the condition is not met, will ensure that misuse of the method either by accidental bug or failure to read (or write) the documentation will be caught immediately when the program is run, not months later when the customer is making mission-critical use of your software.

What Is an Inner Class and How Can I Use One?

Inner classes are a new language feature added with the transition to JDK 1.1. The idea is to allow the definition of a class to be contained within another class. Before this addition, classes could only be defined as members of a package, and their visibility was defined either as public or default access.

An inner class can now be defined like this:

```
class BigAndComplicated {
  class SmallSupport {
    // variables
    // and methods as usual
  };
  // variables, including instances of SmallSupport
  // and methods..
}
```

Although C and C++ do not allow constructions of this sort, the idea is not new; it has been available and shown to be useful in a variety of other languages.

The visibility of the SmallSupport class is restricted to the BigAndComplicated class. This does not mean, however, that SmallSupport objects cannot exist, or cannot be used, outside of a BigAndComplicated object; it is only the visibility of the definition that is restricted. A class can return an instance of an inner class, which is an important use for an inner class. If an inner class implements some public interface, such as the Enumeration interface, it can be much tidier than having the whole outer class implement that interface.

In fact, the inner class can be anonymous. Consider this example:

Inner.java

```
import java.util.*;

public class Inner {
  String s = "Hello";
```

```
public Enumeration listem() {
  return new Enumeration () {
    int x;
    public boolean hasMoreElements() {
      return x < s.length();
    }
    public Object nextElement() {
      return new Character(s.charAt(x++));
    }
  };
}
public static void main(String args[]) {
  Inner that = new Inner();
  Enumeration e = that.listem();
  while (e.hasMoreElements()) {
    System.out.print(
      (Character)(e.nextElement())).charValue());
  }
  System.out.println("\nDone");
}
}
```

Here, the `listem()` method returns an `Enumeration` object. The object it actually returns is an instance of an unnamed inner class (remember that `Enumeration` is an interface, not a class name). The syntax used implies that an unnamed class that implements the `Enumeration` interface has been defined. A particularly useful feature of the inner class is that it has access to the variables of the enclosing class. In fact, it has access to the enclosing instance variables, in effect (and in implementation, too) the instance of the inner class is given a copy of the `this` reference of the object that created it. These mechanisms allow the inner class defined here to access the `String` variable `s`.

Inside the inner class, additional methods and instance variables may be declared. In this example, a variable `x` is used as a counter to track the next character from the string that should be returned when the `nextElement()` method is invoked.

You could reasonably ask why this strategy is better than having the outer class declare that it implements the Enumeration interface. The main reason is that in using the inner class approach, it is possible to define another method in the BigAndComplicated class, which returns another, different, Enumeration object. Additionally, this type of approach can simplify maintenance by improving the clarity of the code.

> **NOTE**
>
> If an inner class is defined inside a method, it will have access to the local variables, including the argument list, of that method. Providing this access requires the lifetime of those variables to be increased, because the inner class instance will usually continue to exist after the method has returned. The language handles this for you with reasonable efficiency, only increasing the lifetime of data items that actually need this treatment.

What Is Reflection and How Can I Use It?

The java.lang.reflect package allows you to examine the class definition of an object at runtime. It allows you to extract a full definition of the accessible API for the object's class, listing the constructors, methods, and variables. Reflection also allows you to access the variables and invoke the methods. This example allows you either to load and run a class, or to examine the constructors, fields, and methods that make it up. The source for this example is located on the CD-ROM in the directory javadevhdbk/appc. The source is in the file Reflector.java, and the corresponding bytecode is in the file Reflector.class.

Reflector.java

```
import java.io.*;
import java.util.*;
import java.lang.reflect.*;
import java.awt.*;
import java.applet.*;
```

```
public class Reflector extends Applet {
  private static final String runText = "Run";
  private static final String examineText = "Examine";

  private Panel topRow = new Panel();
  private Button run = new Button(runText);
  private Button examine = new Button(examineText);
  private TextField classname = new TextField(40);
  private TextArea response = new TextArea(30, 60);

  public Reflector() {
    setLayout(new BorderLayout());

    topRow.add(classname);
    topRow.add(run);
    topRow.add(examine);
    add("North", topRow);

    response.setEditable(false);
    add("Center", response);
  }

  public static void main(String args[]) {
    Reflector that = new Reflector();
    MortalFrame f = new MortalFrame("Reflector");
    f.add("Center", that);
    f.pack();
    f.show();
  }

  public boolean action(Event ev, Object o) {
    try {
      if (runText.equals(o) || (ev.target == classname)) {
        execute(classname.getText());
      }
      else if (examineText.equals(o)) {
        examine(classname.getText());
      }
      else {
        return false;
      }
    }
```

```
    catch (Exception e) {
      response.setText("" + e);
    }
    return true;
}

public void execute(String cmdline) throws Exception {
  String command = null;
  StringTokenizer tok = new StringTokenizer(cmdline, " \t");
  if (tok.hasMoreTokens()) {
    command = tok.nextToken();
  }
  else {
    return;
  }
  // collect arguments
  Vector v = new Vector();
  while (tok.hasMoreElements()) {
    v.addElement(tok.nextElement());
  }
  String [] invokeArgs = new String[v.size()];
  for (int i = 0; i < v.size(); i++) {
    invokeArgs[i] = (String)(v.elementAt(i));
  }

  Class toRun = null;
  Object objectToRun = null;
  toRun = Class.forName(command);
  objectToRun = toRun.newInstance();

  if (objectToRun instanceof Applet) {
    MortalFrame f = new MortalFrame("Applet " + command);
    Applet a = (Applet)objectToRun;
    f.show();
    f.add("Center", a);
    a.init();
    a.start();
    f.resize(200, 200);
  }
  else {
    Class [] mainParamTypes = new Class[1];
```

```
      mainParamTypes[0] = invokeArgs.getClass();
      boolean success = false;
      Object [] invokeParam = new Object[1];
      invokeParam[0] = invokeArgs;
      Method mainMethod = toRun.getMethod("main", mainParamTypes);
      try {
        mainMethod.invoke(null, invokeParam);
      }
      catch (InvocationTargetException e) {
        response.setText("Exception in application:\n" +
                    e.getTargetException());
      }
    }
  }
}

public void examine(String command) throws Exception {
  Class toSnoop = null;
  int i = command.indexOf(' ');
  if (i != -1) {
    command = command.substring(0, i);
  }
  toSnoop = Class.forName(command);
  Constructor [] constructors = null;
  Field [] fields = null;
  Method [] methods = null;
  constructors = toSnoop.getConstructors();
  fields = toSnoop.getDeclaredFields();
  methods = toSnoop.getDeclaredMethods();

  response.setText("Constructors:\n");
  for (i = 0; i < constructors.length; i++) {
    response.append(constructors[i] + "\n");
  }

  response.append("\nFields:\n");
  for (i = 0; i < fields.length; i++) {
    response.append(fields[i] + "\n");
  }

  response.append("\nMethods:\n");
  for (i = 0; i < methods.length; i++) {
```

```
        response.append(methods[i] + "\n");
      }
    }
  }
}

class MortalFrame extends Frame {
  private static int count;

  public MortalFrame(String title) {
    super(title);
    count++;
  }

  public boolean handleEvent(Event e) {
    if (e.id == Event.WINDOW_DESTROY) {
      hide();
      dispose();
      count--;
      if (count == 0) {
        System.exit(0);
      }
    }
    return false;
  }
}
```

Running the Code   The example runs as an application. Start it by selecting the directory and issuing the command

```
java Reflector
```

The program launches a window like the one in Figure C.2.

Enter the name of a class into the text field and press the Examine button. A list of the constructors, fields, and methods of the class is placed in the text area. The fully qualified name of any class on the CLASSPATH is acceptable, so you can enter java.lang.String or any class in the local directory.

FIGURE C.2

The Reflector class running

To run a Java application from the Reflector class, type the name of the class into the text field, followed by any arguments it requires. Then press the Run button. If the class specified is an Applet class, it is invoked as such. To support the applet, a separate window is launched, and the applet is started within that window. If the class is not an Applet class but has a main() method, then that method will be invoked and the arguments provided will be passed to it.

When a classname has been entered in text field, you can press the Examine button, which does not try to run the class, but instead lists the constructors, fields, and methods of the class in the text area.

What It Does   When either of the buttons is pressed, the action() method is called. This method determines which button was pressed and calls either the execute() or examine() method as appropriate.

Both the `execute()` and `examine()` methods start by obtaining the defining `Class` object for the specified class by using the `Class.forName()` static method.

The `execute()` method then creates an instance of the class by invoking the `newInstance()` method on the defining `Class` object. The `instanceof` operator is used to test the object that is returned from the `newInstance()` method to determine it is an applet. If it is an applet, then a frame is created, the applet is added to the frame, and the `init()` and `start()` methods of the applet are called. This same behavior is used in the `MinAppletViewer` example in Chapter 10, *Networking*.

If the newly created object is not an applet, then the `Reflect` package is used to check for, and invoke, the `main()` method.

The `Reflect` package defines a number of classes, including the `Method`, `Field`, and `Constructor` classes. Instances of these classes describe methods, fields, and constructors of a class, respectively. Using instances of these classes, along with instances of the classes they represent, methods and constructors can be invoked and field values can be manipulated. To invoke a method, the following steps are necessary:

1. Obtain a reference to the object for which the method is to be invoked. In other words, to use reflection to invoke `x.method()`, you first must have the reference `x`. This reference is unnecessary if you want to invoke a constructor or static method.

2. Obtain the `Class` object that defines this class by applying the `getClass()` method to an instance or, as is the case in this example, by applying the `Class.forName()` static method, which loads a class when given its name.

3. Once a `Class` object has been obtained, four methods allow you to obtain `Method` objects from that class. The `getMethods()` method returns an array of `Method` objects that define all public methods available in this class, including inherited ones. The

`getMethod()` method takes arguments that specify a particular name and argument list. It then returns a `Method` object describing the single specified method, if it exists. Two similar methods— `getDeclaredMethods()` and `getDeclaredMethod()`— extract methods of any accessibility but do not return inherited methods, only those declared at this class level.

4. Given an instance of the `Method` class, the method that that instance describes can be invoked using the `invoke()` method. The `invoke()` method takes two arguments. The first is a reference to the object that provides the context for the method call. Inside the method, this first reference will become the `this` object. The second argument is an array of `Object` objects that define the parameters to be passed into the invoked method. If the method to be invoked is static, then the first argument may be `null`.

5. When the method returns, its return value is passed back as the return value from the `invoke()` method. If a primitive type is returned, it is wrapped up in an appropriate object. For example, an int is wrapped in an `Integer` object, and a `short` in a `Short` object. If an exception is thrown, then an `Invocation-TargetException` is created with the original exception wrapped up inside. The `InvocationTargetException` is then thrown from the `invoke()` method.

> **TIP**　In this case, `main()` is static, so no object is needed to invoke the method. In fact, one was obtained previously anyway to allow the `instanceof` operator to be used to see if the method was an applet. The class could have been so checked using the `get-Classes()` method of the `Class` class, which would have avoided the need to create an instance that would be redundant if the class turned out not to be an applet.

In the `Reflector` example the `Method` object that defines the `main()` method is obtained from the defining class using the `get-Method()` method. Strictly, the program should verify that the method found is declared as `public static void`, but for the sake of simplicity, this is overlooked.

The method is invoked using an array of `String` objects as its argument. Notice that the definition of the `invoke()` method requires that it takes an array of `Object` objects, and the elements of this array are intended to represent the elements of the argument list. The `main()` method requires one argument, and so the `Object` array should have one element. The single argument to the `main()` method is an array of `String` that has been constructed using the contents of the text field and that is placed as the first and only item in the `invokeargs` array.

The `examine()` method first extracts the classname from the start of the text field, which simply involves checking for any spaces that separate a classname from arguments intended for a `main()` method. Once the class name has been established, the `Class.forName()` static method is used to obtain a `Class` object describing the requested class. The `getConstructors()`, `getDeclaredMethods()`, and `getDeclaredFields()` methods are called on the resulting `Class` object. These methods return arrays of objects that describe constructors, methods, and fields respectively. The `examine()` method proceeds by iterating these arrays in turn, extracting the textual representation of each element of the array and appending it to the text area. The textual representations returned by the implied `toString()` method call (which results from the application of the + operator) return strings that represent the original declarations.

A variety of facilities can be used on a `Constructor`, `Method`, or `Field` object once it has been obtained in the above manner. For methods, the modifiers, parameter types, return type, and exceptions can all be extracted; for constructors, the modifiers, parameter types, and exception types can be extracted; while for fields, the modifiers and type of the field may be extracted.

Methods can be invoked using the `invoke()` method with two arguments. The first argument is the object that is to be `this` in the method call. The second argument is an array of `Object` instances. The elements of the array form the parameters of the method call. Dynamic method lookup is performed to determine the correct overriding version of the method to use.

Constructors can be invoked using the `newInstance()` method with one argument. The `Class` class has provided a `newInstance()` method with zero arguments, but the `Constructor` class allows any constructor to be invoked with whatever arguments are appropriate.

The value of a field can be read and modified as required. A number of methods allow access to fields of primitive types. For fields of object type, it will normally be necessary to make further use of the reflection facilities in order to manipulate the data.

NOTE The facilities of the `java.lang.reflect` package are tightly controlled by the security manager. Applets cannot generally use the introspection facilities just described, and even applications are subject to the language rules governing field access. It is not, for example, possible to use reflection to read private fields.

What Does *Deprecated* Mean in Documentation?

Deprecated is a `javadoc` comment that a class author can add to the source code. `Javadoc` then advertises this comment in the resulting HTML documentation. It indicates that a particular class, method, or field should not be used for new developments. It is usually accompanied by additional information that details the new mechanism for obtaining the functionality using nondeprecated features.

Deprecated features might be removed altogether from future releases of a package, so the warnings issued by the compiler should not be taken lightly.

Further details may be found in Appendix B, *The Java Documentation Tool: Javadoc.*

What Does *clone()* Do?

The clone() method is declared in the Object class and is therefore inherited into every subclass. It creates a duplicate of an object using a shallow copy. *Shallow copy* means that the bit patterns of your original object are duplicated, so if any of the member variables of your object are themselves references, then the objects that are referred to do *not* get duplicated. The alternative form of behavior is called a deep copy. A *deep copy* copies only the primitive variables of an object and actually calls itself recursively to replicate any object instances that are part of the object. A deep copy is more difficult because the programmer needs to ensure that the recursion stops eventually. This problem is most noticeable in self-referential data structures, such as a circular linked list.

Because the clone() method is defined in the Object class, it is available in all other classes. Also, because it is a member of the Object class, you will not normally find it listed in the documentation because the javadoc tool only makes entries for methods actually defined in a particular class.

In some circumstances, the shallow copy behavior of the clone() method might be inappropriate. Consider a class that defines a member variable serialNumber. Cloning such an object should really give it a new serial number value; if it hasn't, the semantics of the object will have been damaged. In such a circumstance, overriding the clone() method will allow you to control the behavior so that it is suitable to your class.

Despite `clone()` being defined in the `Object` class, you cannot call it for every object. There are two reasons for this limitation. First, the `Object clone()` method is declared as protected, so it is inaccessible from some objects. If you define your own `clone()` method for a class, you can make it public. You will find an example of this in Chapter 3, *Creating Custom Components*. Second, the `clone()` method requires that the object it copies implements the `Cloneable` interface, which means that unless the writer of a class intended that you should be able to clone an instance, the attempt will fail, throwing a `CloneNotSupportedException`.

> **NOTE**
>
> You might wonder why `clone()` is defined in the `Object` class if the designers did not intend it to be freely useable in all subclasses. The reason is that `clone()` gets inside your object and copies memory directly with native code that does a block copy of memory. Of course, you can't do that in normal Java code because it requires arbitrary pointer manipulation, so the designers had to provide the mechanism at a central point and allow you to decide whether you wanted it to be enabled for your particular class.

The following example demonstrates the salient points.

Cloner.java

```java
public class Cloner implements Cloneable{
  private int serial;
  private boolean isValid;
  private StringBuffer name;
  private static int lastSerial = 0;

  public Cloner(String name) {
    synchronized(this.getClass()) {
      serial = lastSerial++;
    }
    this.name = new StringBuffer(name);
    isValid = true;
  }
```

```
protected Object oldClone() {
  Cloner newOne = null;
  try {
    newOne = (Cloner)(super.clone());
  }
  catch (CloneNotSupportedException e) {
    e.printStackTrace();
  }
  return newOne;
}

protected Object clone() {
  Cloner newOne = null;
  try {
    newOne = (Cloner)(super.clone());
    synchronized (this.getClass()) {
      newOne.serial = lastSerial++;
    }
  }
  catch (CloneNotSupportedException e) {
    e.printStackTrace();
  }
  return newOne;
}

protected Object newClone() {
  Cloner newOne = null;
  try {
    newOne = (Cloner)(super.clone());
    synchronized (this.getClass()) {
      newOne.serial = lastSerial++;
    }
    newOne.name = new StringBuffer(newOne.name.toString());
  }
  catch (CloneNotSupportedException e) {
    e.printStackTrace();
  }
  return newOne;
}

public String toString() {
  return "[" + getClass().getName() +
```

```
            ",serial=" + serial +
            "," + (isValid ? "" : "in") + "valid" +
            "," + name + "]";
  }

  public static void main(String args[]) {
    Cloner a = new Cloner("fred");
    Cloner b = new Cloner("jim");
    Cloner c = (Cloner)(a.clone());
    Cloner d = (Cloner)(b.oldClone());
    Cloner e = (Cloner)(a.newClone());
    System.out.println("Cloner a is " + a);
    System.out.println("Cloner b is " + b);
    System.out.println("Cloner c is " + c);
    System.out.println("Cloner d is " + d);
    System.out.println("Cloner e is " + e);

    a.name.append("erick");
    System.out.println("Cloner a is " + a);
    System.out.println("Cloner c is " + c);
    System.out.println("Cloner e is " + e);
  }
}
```

Running the Code To run the `Cloner.java` example, select the directory `javadevhdbk\appc\Cloner.java` on the CD-ROM, issue the command

```
java Cloner
```

and you will see this output:

```
Cloner a is [Cloner,serial=0,valid,fred]
Cloner b is [Cloner,serial=1,valid,jim]
Cloner c is [Cloner,serial=2,valid,fred]
Cloner d is [Cloner,serial=1,valid,jim]
Cloner e is [Cloner,serial=3,valid,fred]
Cloner a is [Cloner,serial=0,valid,frederick]
Cloner c is [Cloner,serial=2,valid,frederick]
Cloner e is [Cloner,serial=3,valid,fred]
```

What It Does   Each `Cloner` instance has the three variables `serial`, `isValid`, and `name`. The `main()` method creates two of these objects with the arguments `fred` and `jim`. The program then copies these two objects using the methods `clone()`, `oldClone()`, and `newClone()`.

The `oldClone()` method simply invokes `super.clone()`, which results in the duplicated serial number that you see between the objects `b` and `d`, both of which report serial number 1 in the output.

The `clone()` method corrects this error by reassigning the value of `serial` immediately after the copy. Therefore, the values of `serial` between objects `a`, `c`, and `e` are distinct and correctly allocated.

Next, the `main()` method appends the string `erick` to the string buffer `name` of the object `a` and prints out the values of `a`, `c`, and `e`. The name strings of these are reported as `frederick`, `frederick`, and `fred`, respectively, which indicates that the `clone()` method was a shallow copy because the name object was not duplicated but is shared. By contrast, the `newClone()` method created a new `name` object that is unaffected by modifications to the old object.

What Does *equals()* Do?

It is important to understand that there is nothing special about `equals()`. The intention behind this method is to provide a "deep comparison," as opposed to the "shallow comparison" of the `==` operator. When `==` is applied to two objects, it compares two object references (essentially pointers) and determines whether they refer to the same piece of memory. The idea of the `equals()` method is that it should inspect the instance variables of the two objects and determine whether the instance variables are equal. It could be argued that *equals* is not the best possible name; *matches* or *sameAs* might convey the idea a bit better.

There is an unfortunate misconception among some Java programmers that `equals()` works on the same level as `clone()`; that is, it makes a mysterious system-level call to do a bit-by-bit comparison of the two objects. This is not the case. The `equals()` method is inherited by all classes from `Object`, and each class is responsible for its own implementation.

There is no guarantee that `equals()` will be implemented for all JDK classes. If a class does not explicitly state in its API that it implements an `equals()`, then it will use whatever version it inherits from its superclass. This version will accurately compare the superclass portions of its two objects but will ignore the subclass portions. A return value of `false` can be trusted in this case, but a return value of `true` only means that the objects match each other to a certain extent.

Programmers who are designing utility classes that will be used by other developers should generally provide an `equals()` method for each class. Doing so could greatly ease the debugging cycle in the same way that providing a useful `toString()` method simplifies life.

If a class contains a reference to an object of another class, it must be decided whether `equals()` should do a shallow or a deep comparison on the reference. If the class contains an object-type instance variable called `ref`, should the implementation of `equals(Object that)` check `this.ref == that.ref` (shallow comparison), or should it call `this.ref.equals(that.ref)`? The correct decision depends entirely on the nature of the class, and the only guideline is that the implementation should be clearly documented.

Any implementation of `equals()` should begin by calling the inherited version to check the superclass portions of the two objects being compared. The code fragment below shows how to do so:

```
public boolean equals(Object that)
{
    if (super.equals(that) == false)
        return false;
        ...
}
```

> **WARNING** It is important to realize that the implementation of `equals()` in the `Object` class simply uses pointer comparison; that is, its effect is identical to `==`. Because of this, you should avoid calling `super.equals()` if the resulting method would be the `Object.equals()` method.

The argument to `equals()` is declared to be of type `Object`; in other words, it can be any nonprimitive. For the `equals()` methods in other classes to be overriding—rather than overloading—methods, it is essential that the argument must always be declared as `Object`. Further, the language specification requires that `equals()` should return `false` if called on to compare two objects that are not of the same class. An implementation of `equals()` should therefore start by checking the class of the argument before checking any variables. For example, the `SomeClass` class might do the following:

```
public boolean equals(Object that)
{
    if (!(that instanceof SomeClass))
        return false;
    if (super.equals(that) == false)
        return false;
        ...
}
```

This precaution also ensures that the `equals()` method is commutative; that is, it ensures that the result of

```
a.equals(b)
```

will always be the same as the result of

```
b.equals(a)
```

regardless of the classes of `a` and `b`.

Is There Anything Special about *toString()*?

This method is slightly special; `toString()` is used in Java's overload of the + operator for string concatenation.

When the Java compiler detects that either operand of the + operator is a string, it converts the other operand to a string, uses a string buffer to concatenate the strings, and converts the final string buffer back to a string. A primitive operand is converted to a string by calling the static `String` method `valueOf()` on the primitive. An object is converted to a string by calling the object's `toString()` method.

Consider the following line of code, which assumes that `i` is an int and `thing` is an object:

```
String s = "abc" + i + thing;
```

The Java compiler would treat this line as an abbreviation for:

```
String s = ((new StringBuffer("abc"))
            .append(String.valueOf(i))
            .append(thing.toString())).toString();
```

This simple example shows why it is a very good thing that the designers of Java permitted a single instance of operator overloading to creep into the language.

WARNING   Be cautious when using the + operator to convert operands to strings simply for convenience. Consider the expressions: `"hello "` `+ 1 + 2 + 3` and `1 + 2 + 3 + " hello"` In the first case, the left-to-right associativity of the + operator means that the value of the whole expression is the string `"hello 123"`, but for the second case the result is `"6 hello"`.

Why Can't I Override a Method to Make It Less Accessible?

In Java's view of objected-oriented programming, you are allowed to keep a reference to an object in a variable, provided the type of the variable is appropriate for the object. Suppose you have an `Employee` class and a `Manager` class that extends `Employee`. You can refer to an object of the `Manager` class using either a variable of the `Manager` type or of the `Employee` type because a `Manager` *is an* `Employee` but has extra or modified features. So any operation that can properly be applied to an `Employee` can be applied to a `Manager`, too.

The premise that any operation that applies to an `Employee` must, by virtue of the fact that `Manager` extends `Employee`, allows you to use an `Employee` variable to refer to a `Manager` object. For instance:

```
Employee [] staff = new Employee[10];
staff[0] = new Manager();
```

Now any operations on `staff[0]` are actually working on a `Manager` object.

Imagine then what would happen if a method, say, `getJob-Description()`, was defined public for an `Employee`, but private for a `Manager`. The compiler could not reject the construction `staff[0].getJobDescription()`, nor could the bytecode verifier, but the access would be theoretically illegal. This difficulty precludes you from making methods of a derived class more private when overriding the parent class definition.

> **NOTE** Variables *can* be declared with the same name in both a parent and derived class, and with less accessibility in the derived class. However, in this case the new variable does not override the old one it; rather, it shadows it. *Shadowing* is distinct from overriding and means that dynamic binding does not occur with variables, and the compiler makes a decision about which of the two variables you are referring to at compilation time based on the type of the reference.

What Does *import* Really Do?

The `import` statement sometimes causes a bit of confusion. In fact, it simply provides a context for shortened class names. For example, the classname `java.awt.Button` is commonly referred to simply as `Button`, which is permitted if the statement `import java.awt.*;` has been issued. The import statement does not change a classname, nor does it change the contents or size of the `.class` output file.

So why might you use an explicit import rather than the wildcard form? If you are a Java instructor, you might get into this habit as a deliberate way to learn the detailed contents of each package. If you need to import classes from multiple packages, but some of the classes in those packages have common names, then you might simply import the ones you actually need.

AWT Questions

How Can I Use Unicode Characters?

Although Java uses Unicode internally to represent characters, its keyboard and screen capabilities are constrained by the host platform. At the time of this book's writing, at least, Java does not come with a set of special fonts and a fancy input tool to allow the entry of characters not normally supported by the platform.

What Java does give you, along with the platform-independent internal representation, is the ability to perform appropriate conversions between the internal Unicode and external local format. For example, if your computer is a PC that is set up to run with the code page 863 character set, supporting French Canadian, then characters that are typed at the keyboard will be translated into Unicode as they are read by Java. Similarly, on output, the Unicode characters will be translated back to local form.

Sometimes you will need to read or write characters using a character encoding that is not that of your own machine. This situation could arise if you are making a network connection or using a file prepared on some other machine. Under these conditions, you can explicitly control the translation that is used by creating `InputStreamReader` and `OutputStreamWriter` objects and explicitly specifying an encoding standard rather than accepting the default.

A command-line tool, called `native2ascii`, is provided with the JDK. This tool uses the Unicode escape conventions of Java to convert files between a local character representation and plain ASCII. The documentation for this tool also lists the various encoding formats that can be used.

More details of these mechanisms may be found in Chapter 5, *Portability Issues*, and Chapter 9, *File I/O and Streams*.

Why Does My Component Ignore the Size I Specify?

Setting a size for an AWT component—using either constructor arguments or the `setSize()` or `setBounds()` method—is ineffective if the component is subject to the control of a layout manager. Most layout managers expect to control the position and size of the components in their domain. If you do not want a component size changed by the layout manager, you can either avoid using a layout manager or you can use a layout manager that does not concern itself with size but only with position. In either case, you probably want to avoid losing the facilities of the layout manager with respect to other components in the layout. To ensure that these facilities are preserved, place the component in question in a panel of its own and set the layout manager of that panel to be a `FlowLayout` object.

It is possible to set a container to use no layout manager, but if more than one component is involved, it is generally unwise because you will have to position them all with explicit code and the result is likely to be platform dependent. A better approach is to write a `LayoutManager` class of your own that imposes the layout policy you require. Examples of this approach are given in Chapter 4, *Layout Managers*.

Why Does My Text Component Ignore the Width I Specify?

The width argument to the `TextField` and `TextArea` class constructors specify a preferred size in terms of the average character width. Assuming you are sure the component is not being controlled by a layout manager (see the previous question), the problem probably relates to the font used in your text component.

Most fonts are proportionally spaced or of variable widths, which means that it is not possible to have one width that displays a precise number of characters without considering what the characters are. Lowercase characters are generally narrower than their uppercase equivalents. The preferred width of the component is taken in terms of the average width specified as part of the font definition.

If you really need to display a precise number of characters across a text component, then you will have to use a monospaced font; this will usually be Courier.

Security Questions

I Run a Corporate Intranet and My Applets Need File System Access: How Can I Retain Protection Against Outside Applets?

Sign them!

In JDK 1.0.x, a Java class—whether an applet, application, or supporting class—was granted privileges based on the classloader that had obtained that bytecode for the class. The *primordial* classloader is the built-in classloader that only loads classes from the CLASSPATH value, and only from the local file system. If a class had been loaded by the primordial classloader, then it was granted full privilege on that basis. Alternatively, if a class was not loaded by the primordial classloader, it was considered to be foreign. By default, the security manager prevented foreign code from doing anything that was considered sensitive, such as reading or writing files. It was possible to turn off this protection, but the situation was all or nothing; so if you trusted any foreign code at all, you had to trust all foreign code entirely. Clearly, this is not an acceptable situation in an intranet environment, even if it is not connected to the Internet, because it allows imported applets unrestrained access to important corporate data and facilities.

In an intranet, you will generally have a library of corporate-standard utility programs located on central servers. These will appear to be foreign code to Java, but you probably do want to grant them trusted privileges, such as access to file systems.

Using digital signatures and the `javakey` tool, which are part of Java 1.1, you can mark selected classes as trusted regardless of their origin or the classloader that fetched them. This procedure is called *signing* the class. Typically you might sign classes you have written, and you might sign code supplied to you from a source you trust. However, you almost certainly should not sign anything imported from other sources unless you have the source code, you have checked the source, you compiled the sources yourself, and there is a clearly stated reason why the class requires privilege to achieve its proper job.

How Do I Use *Javakey* to Sign Classes and Files?

`Javakey` uses a local database to keep track of the entities that are trusted and the certificates that allow them to be reliably identified. To create an authorized signer, issue a command of this form:

```
javakey -cs Fred true
```

Substitute some appropriate name in place of `Fred`. This line of code puts an entry into the local database that says `Fred` is a trusted signer. Next, associate a public/private key pair with `Fred`. Issue this command:

```
javakey -gk Fred DSA 512
```

This command creates a new key pair for `Fred` by using the DSA algorithm and a 512-bit key. 1024-bit keys are supported, but the first releases of JDK 1.1 only allow the 512-bit DSA algorithm. The `javakey` tool allows the keys to be written to or imported from files, if you wish. You might write a public key to a file so you could send it via e-mail to someone else. Similarly, if you receive a key this way, you will need to read it from a file. Do not write your private key to a file without a good reason; if it goes astray, your entire identity—at least your electronic identity—can be usurped.

Before you can sign a file, you need to create a certificate. This certificate records your public key so the signature can be checked against it. Creating a certificate requires a directive file like this:

```
issuer.name=Fred
issuer.real.name=Fred Bloggs
issuer.org.unit=FAQ List
issuer.org=Java Developer's Handbook
issuer.country=UK

subject.name=Fred
subject.real.name=Fred Bloggs
subject.org.unit=FAQ List
subject.org=Java Developer's Handbook
subject.country=UK

start.date=1 Jan 1997
end.date=31 Dec 1997
serial.number=1

out.file=cert.cer
```

Most of the elements of this file are fairly self-explanatory and are of a clerical rather than functional nature. The `issuer.name` and `subject.name` parts must refer to identities known in the database and are case sensitive. In this case, you are signing your own certificate, so you are both the issuer and the subject, and most of the file contents are duplicated.

Notice that the certificate is date stamped, so that it is valid only over a fixed period of time.

> **TIP**
>
> The documentation supplied with early releases of JDK 1.1 gave the wrong names for each of the elements of the directive file. The names shown in the sample above work correctly with JDK 1.1 beta releases. Even if the names change again, it is not difficult to determine the correct names because the `javakey` command issues messages like `start.date must be specified in the directive file` if, for example, `start.date` is missing. These messages allows you to determine empirically what the expected names are.

The certificate is output into a file, in this case `cert.cer`, when you issue the command

```
javakey -gc cert.directive
```

where `cert.directive` is taken to be the name of the directive file.

When you have a certificate for yourself, you can sign a jar archive. To sign a jar, `javakey` needs another directive file. If you have an archive called `scratch.jar`, your directive file might look like this:

```
signer=Fred
cert=1
chain=0
signature.file=SIGN
```

The `signer` directive must match the name of a certificate holder, known on this machine. The `cert` directive can indicate a particular certificate to be used for this signing. Because we have only discussed creating a single certificate, the number 1 is appropriate. At some stage

Java will allow chains of trust to be established, and the `chain` directive will be used to control the maximum length of such a chain. In the early releases, however, this strategy was not supported, and the value should be zero.

Given these directives, in a file called `jarsign.directive`, you can issue the command

```
javakey -gs jarsign.directive scratch.jar
```

which will create a signature and add it to the jar file.

Once the jar file has been signed, it will be treated as trusted code by any system that has an entry for `Fred` in its local database, provided that the entry indicates `Fred` is trusted and that a copy of `Fred`'s certificate is also located on the local machine in the `javakey` database. The certificate must of course be in date, and the DSA algorithms must be able to verify that the signature on the certificate matches the signature on the jar.

Once you have a JAR file containing an applet—and perhaps that applet's supporting files—you can arrange to have the JAR file loaded into a browser by modifying the normal applet tag like this:

```
<applet code=myApplet.class archives="mystuff.jar"
width=100 height=100>
</applet>
```

Future versions of Java will allow some degree of granularity in the trust that a signature bestows. At the time of writing, classes signed by someone registered as trusted in the local database are trusted entirely, while unsigned remote classes are not trusted. Clearly some ability to grant partial privileges, perhaps to a limited area of a file system, will be a valuable addition to the security mechanisms.

INDEX

Note to the Reader: Throughout this index page numbers in **bold** indicate primary discussions of a topic. Page numbers in *italic* indicate illustrations.

SYMBOLS

A

B

(

D

E

F

G

H

I

J

K

M

N

O

P

S

U

V

W

Java™ Development Kit Version 1.1
Binary Code License

This binary code license ("License") contains rights and restrictions associated with use of the accompanying software and documentation ("Software"). Read the License carefully before installing the Software. By installing the Software you agree to the terms and conditions of this License.

1. **Limited License Grant.** Sun grants to you ("Licensee") a non-exclusive, non-transferable limited license to use the Software without fee for evaluation of the Software and for development of Java™ compatible applets and applications. Licensee may make one archival copy of the Software. Licensee may not re-distribute the Software in whole or in part, either separately or included with a product. Refer to the Java Runtime Environment Version 1.1 binary code license (http://www.javasoft .com/products/JDK/1.1/index.html) for the availability of runtime code which may be distributed with Java compatible applets and applications.

2. **Java Platform Interface.** Licensee may not modify the Java Platform Interface ("JPI", identified as classes contained within the "java" package or any subpackages of the "java" package), by creating additional classes within the JPI or otherwise causing the addition to or modification of the classes in the JPI. In the event that Licensee creates any Java-related API and distributes such API to others for applet or application development, Licensee must promptly publish an accurate specification for such API for free use by all developers of Java-based software.

3. **Restrictions.** Software is confidential copyrighted information of Sun and title to all copies is retained by Sun and/or its licensors. Licensee shall not modify, decompile, disassemble, decrypt, extract, or otherwise reverse engineer Software. Software may not be leased, assigned, or sublicensed, in whole or in part. **Software is not designed or intended for use in on-line control of aircraft, air traffic, aircraft navigation or aircraft communications; or in the design, construction, operation or maintenance of any nuclear facility. Licensee warrants that it will not use or redistribute the Software for such purposes.**

4. **Trademarks and Logos.** This License does not authorize Licensee to use any Sun name, trademark or logo. Licensee acknowledges that Sun owns the Java trademark and all Java-related trademarks, logos and icons including the Coffee Cup and Duke ("Java Marks") and agrees to: (i) to comply with the Java Trademark Guidelines at http://java.com/trademarks.html; (ii) not do anything harmful to or inconsistent with Sun's rights in the Java Marks; and (iii) assist Sun in protecting those rights, including assigning to Sun any rights acquired by Licensee in any Java Mark.

5. **Disclaimer of Warranty.** Software is provided "AS IS," without a warranty of any kind. ALL EXPRESS OR IMPLIED REPRESENTATIONS AND WARRANTIES, INCLUDING ANY IMPLIED WARRANTY OF MERCHANTABILITY, FITNESS FOR A PARTICULAR PURPOSE OR NON-INFRINGEMENT, ARE HEREBY EXCLUDED.

6. **Limitation of Liability.** SUN AND ITS LICENSORS SHALL NOT BE LIABLE FOR ANY DAMAGES SUFFERED BY LICENSEE OR ANY THIRD PARTY AS A RESULT OF USING OR DISTRIBUTING SOFTWARE. IN NO EVENT WILL SUN OR ITS LICENSORS BE LIABLE FOR ANY LOST REVENUE, PROFIT OR DATA, OR FOR DIRECT, INDIRECT, SPECIAL, CONSEQUENTIAL, INCIDENTAL OR PUNITIVE DAMAGES, HOWEVER CAUSED AND REGARDLESS OF THE THEORY OF LIABILITY, ARISING OUT OF THE USE OF OR INABILITY TO USE SOFTWARE, EVEN IF SUN HAS BEEN ADVISED OF THE POSSIBILITY OF SUCH DAMAGES.

7. **Termination.** Licensee may terminate this License at any time by destroying all copies of Software. This License will terminate immediately without notice from Sun if Licensee fails to comply with any provision of this License. Upon such termination, Licensee must destroy all copies of Software.

8. **Export Regulations.** Software, including technical data, is subject to U.S. export control laws, including the U.S. Export Administration Act and its associated regulations, and may be subject to export or import regulations in other countries. Licensee agrees to comply strictly with all such regulations and acknowledges that it has the responsibility to obtain licenses to export, re-export, or import Software. Software may not be downloaded, or otherwise exported or re-exported (i) into, or to a national or resident of, Cuba, Iraq, Iran, North Korea, Libya, Sudan, Syria or any country to which the U.S. has embargoed goods; or (ii) to anyone on the U.S. Treasury Department's list of Specially Designated Nations or the U.S. Commerce Department's Table of Denial Orders.

9. **Restricted Rights.** Use, duplication or disclosure by the United States government is subject to the restrictions as set forth in the Rights in Technical Data and Computer Software Clauses in DFARS 252.227-7013(c) (1) (ii) and FAR 52.227-19(c) as applicable.

10. **Governing Law.** Any action related to this License will be governed by California law and controlling U.S. federal law. No choice of law rules of any jurisdiction will apply.

11. **Severability.** If any of the above provisions are held to be in violation of applicable law, void, or unenforceable in any jurisdiction, then such provisions are herewith waived to the extent necessary for the License to be otherwise enforceable in such jurisdiction. However, if in Sun's opinion deletion of any provisions of the License by operation of this paragraph unreasonably compromises the rights or increase the liabilities of Sun or its licensors, Sun reserves the right to terminate the License and refund the fee paid by Licensee, if any, as Licensee's sole and exclusive remedy.

JDK1.1 BCL 2-9-97#

WHAT'S ON THE CD-ROM

This companion CD-ROM contains all the source code, executable files, and labs from the book, plus relevant RFCs. You will also find cutting-edge Java Integrated Development Environments (IDEs) and third-party tools to use with Java 1.1.

Products you will find on this CD include:

- **ED for Windows**, from Soft As It Gets, is a complete Java development environment that offers powerful editing capabilities and code navigation features. Trial version 3.71.

- **Jamba**, an authoring tool from Aimtech, enables Internet developers and Web-masters to create interactive, media-rich Java applets and applications without programming or scripting. Trial version 1.1.

- **JDK Version 1.1**, the full development package from Sun Microsystems, Inc. for creating Java applications and applets. Use of this software is subject to the Binary Code License terms and conditions on page 1173. Read the license carefully. By opening this package, you are agreeing to be bound by the terms and conditions of this license from Sun Microsystems, Inc.

- **JetEffects**, from Peak Technologies, is an easy-to-use Java animation tool for home and small-office Web page authors. JetEffects can be used sucessfully by novices and experts. Trial version 2.5.

- **Mojo**, from Penumbra Software, is a complete development environment for creating networking applets. Mojo consists of a GUI Designer and a Coder. Trial version 2.0.

- **nmake**, from Microsoft, is a program that helps generate programs from a set of rules about file interdependencies. Version 15(1).

- **Widgets**™, from Connect! Quick, is a library of sophisticated, prebuilt components for assembling commercial-quality Java applications. Demo version.

- **Vibe**, from Visix Software, is an intuitive integrated development and deployment environment for building Java applications. Vibe comprises a visual Java-specific integrated development environment (IDE), which includes a compiler and debugger, an extensive set of class libraries and ActiveX support. It also contains an enriched virtual machine (VM) for production application deployment across intranets. Evaluation version DE 1.0.

Note to Windows NT 3.51 users: If you are using Windows NT 3.51 (or earlier), you will not be able to read this CD format successfully. However, you *can* use the CD's contents if you obtain them via the Web instead of from the CD—just use your browser to access the Sybex home page (at *http://www.sybex.com*), then click on *Downloads* and follow the links to *Java 1.1 Developer's Handbook*. The files available for downloading include all the source code, executable files, and labs from the book, plus relevant RFCs. Links to the other contents of the CD are also displayed.

Updates and additional information will be available on the Sybex Website:
`http://www.Sybex.com/Update.html`.